THE PROFESSIONAL PRACTICE OF ARCHITECTURAL WORKING DRAWINGS

SECOND EDITION

STUDENT EDITION

THE PROFESSIONAL PRACTICE OF ARCHITECTURAL WORKING DRAWINGS

SECOND EDITION   STUDENT EDITION

Osamu A. Wakita

Professor of Architecture, Los Angeles Harbor College

Richard M. Linde, A.I.A. Architect

Richard M. Linde & Associates, Inc.

JOHN WILEY & SONS, Inc.   New York   Chichester   Brisbane   Toronto   Singapore

To the Student

A *Study Guide* for this textbook is available through your college bookstore under the title *Study Guide for the Professional Practice of Architectural Working Drawings,* second edition, Student Edition, by Osamu A. Wakita and Richard Linde. The *Study Guide* includes review questions, drafting exercises and problems, and case study material to help you master the skills and information you will need as a professional draftsperson. If the *Study Guide* is not in stock, ask the bookstore manager to order a copy for you.

Library of Congress Cataloging-in-Publication Data:
Wakita, Osamu A.
    The professional practice of architectural working drawings/ Osamu A. Wakita, Richard M. Linde.—2nd ed., Student ed.
        p.   cm.
        Includes index.
        ISBN 0-471-59663-9.—ISBN 0-471-04068-1 (study guide)
        1. Architecture—Working drawings.   2. Architectural drawing—Study and teaching—United States.   I. Linde, Richard M.
    II. Title
    NA2713.W34   1994
    720'.28'4—dc20   94-25870

Printed in the United States of America

10 9 8 7 6 5 4 3 2 1

Chapter 2 photo: Courtesy of Hewlett Packard; *Chapter 3 photo:* © Scott Frances/Esto; *Chapter 7 photo:* © Francis X. Craine/Peter Gisolfi Associates; *Chapter 8 photo:* © Peter Aaron/Esto; *Chapter 9 photo:* © Peter Mauss/Esto; *Chapter 10 photo:* © Karin Meyers/Peter Gisolfi Associates; *Chapter 11 photo:* © Peter Mauss/Esto; *Chapter 13 photo:* Courtesy of Studio Becker Zeycko (Robert and Jacque Fontaine).

Figures 3.1, 3.2, 3.3, 3.4, 3.5, 3.8, 3.11, 3.12, 3.13, 3.14 reproduced from the 1991 edition of the *Uniform Building Code*™ copyright © 1991, with the permission of the publisher, the International Conference of Building Officials.

This book is dedicated to the students of architecture and to our families.

PREFACE

This book is designed to teach attitudes, basic drafting skills, and fundamental concepts of architectural drafting to persons who will benefit from this information in their professional lives. Beyond this, the authors hope to communicate to readers an understanding of architectural drafting as a means of graphic communication, that is, a language. The professional architect or draftsperson needs a clear and fluent command of the language of architectural drafting.

The *Professional Practice of Architectural Working Drawings,* second edition, Student Edition, is divided into three parts. Part I, "Professional Foundations," consists of Chapters 1–5 and is designed to provide basic information about drafting equipment, office practice and procedures, fundamental skills, and an understanding of the evolution of construction. We have also added to this edition a chapter on building codes, building accessibility (ADA), and other agencies. Part II, "Document Evolution," includes Chapters 6–14 and bridges the gap between theory and practice. These chapters teach the student to prepare site plans, foundation plans, floor plans, exterior elevations, building sections, and other vital drawings. Throughout this part, the ability to communicate general design ideas and concepts through specific working drawings is emphasized and reinforced through practice.

A hypothetical set of working drawings will be evolved, sheet by sheet, at the end of each of Chapters 6 through 14 and becomes the glue that "bonds" these chapters to one another. This set of drawings is completely evolved in Chapter 15 and becomes the transition between Part II and Part III, "Case Studies," Chapters 15–19. Case studies of real projects, which can be found in Chapters 15–18, will demonstrate the evolution of working drawings from the design concept through the finished construction documents of four different buildings: (1) a hypothetical one-story, three-bedroom residence, (2) a two-story beach house, (3) a heavy-timber mountain cabin, and (4) a fourplex movie theatre. These four buildings make use of different build-

ing materials—wood, masonry, and steel—systems, and environmental considerations. The context for these buildings ranges from an urban to a mountain setting (with heavy snow loads) to a coastal setting, where salt air and earthquakes need to be addressed. Chapter 19 addresses tenant improvement, a subject not covered in any other book of this type but which plays an important role in architectural practice.

This book has been designed to be an effective teaching tool. Each chapter in Parts I and II begins with a Preview that presents an overview of the chapter's contents and a set of Objectives that make clear the concepts or skills that the student is intended to master. At the end of each chapter, a list of Important Terms and Concepts and a set of Review Questions are provided as an opportunity for the student to test his or her mastery of the concepts; Laboratory Problems offer an opportunity to practice those skills that were learned in the chapter. An extensive Glossary is included at the end of the book.

Because regional differences affect construction methods, it is one of the most difficult subjects to address. A national survey was conducted by the authors to illustrate the diverse problems faced by different regions in the country. The results of this survey are carefully summarized and included in Appendix A at the back of this book. Case studies also have been selected to show extreme conditions, such as wind, rain, earthquake, and snow.

Appropriately, the illustration program in this book is its outstanding feature. An additional 300 drawings and photographs have been added to the existing 650 plus illustrations. We believe that, by offering students the opportunity to watch the actual evolution of a building from the earliest sketches through the finished floor plans and elevations, we will make the language of drafting comprehensible and exciting.

The authors have written a *Study Guide,* which provides students with further questions and problems in order to reinforce what they have learned from the text.

ACKNOWLEDGMENTS

We would like to acknowledge the contributions of several people to this book—two in particular. Marilyn Smith, coordinator and administrative assistant, was responsible for all phases, including manuscript preparation, correspondence, and reproduction, to mention just a few. Her participation was invaluable. Louis Toledo was coordinator of all the drafting phases of the book, including most of the freehand lettering and the establishment of the various stages of drawings as developed in the case studies. His supervision proved to be a major asset.

We would also like to thank the following people: Vince Toyama, for his participation in the drafting of the condominium project, and all freehand details and freehand sketches; Gregory Haddon, for developing all of the drawings in Chapter 19, on tenant improvements, and the hardline drawings in Chapter 3. Nancy Wakita, who was responsible for some of the detailed and tedious checking, indexing, and typing; Mark Wakita, whose major responsibility was organizing the research questionnaire, but who also organized the reproduction drawings; Andrea Wakita, who assisted in developing the initial proposal and was a resource person for research and permissions; William Boggs, who was responsible for scheduling and the aerial photography of the major structures in the book; Judy Joseph, whose professional attitudes and approach helped bring the first edition of the book from proposal to reality; Jill Mellick, for her excellent editing of the original and final manuscripts; Georgia Linde, for her preliminary manuscript editing and typing of Chapters 3 and 19; Art Galvan, for his coordination and drafting of the main-revision drawings for this book and for his drafting of the entire Ryan Residence drawings; Huey Lim, who as our project manager was responsible for typing, word processing, layout of preliminary drawings, coordination of artwork, and collation of the manuscript; Koya Kameshima, who was responsible for most of the photography and inking of the specialty/pictorial drawings and coordination of the artwork; Masaya Okada, who was responsible for translating design drawings and preliminary drawings, as well as providing all of the three-dimensional drawings that illustrate space requirements for persons with disabilities; John Kanounji, who coordinated the artwork between the revision of the *Study Guide* and the main body of this book, which included drawing, drafting, and formatting; Edith Martinez, the preliminary layout drafter for many of the details and charts, who aided in collating and final assembly; Amanda Miller, our editor, who made the second edition manuscript a reality.

We are sincerely grateful to the academic reviewers who commented on our manuscript during the course of its development.

Reviewers

J. Sam Arnett, *Pitt Community College*
George T. Balich, *Wentworth Institute of Technology*
Robert J. Berry, *Wentworth Institute of Technology*
James Cates, *Brevard Community College*
Paul J. Chase, *Chicago, Illinois*
A. W. Claussen, Jr., *New River Community College*
Frank Corso, Jr., *Illinois Central College*
George E. Coughenoyr, *Erie Community College*
Charles W. Dennis, *Diablo Valley College*
Rushia Fellows, *Arizona State University*
L. J. Franceschina, *City College of San Francisco*
Leonard G. Haeger, *Santa Barbara, California*
Fred Hassaouna, F.I.A.L., A.I.A., A.I.P., *Saddleback Community College District*
Judith B. Hawk, *Northern Virginia Community College*
Donald A. Hinshaw, *Arizona State University*
Dan Houghtaling, *Delaware Technical and Community College*
William A. Kelly, *Los Angeles Trade-Technical College*

Robert S. Lahtam, *Chemeketa Community College*
Oscar Larrauri, *Miami Dade Community College*
Edward D. Levinson, *Miami Dade Community College*
William D. Lloyd, *Mt. Hood Community College*
James Merrigan, *Brookdale Community College*
Susan M. Messersmith, *Sinclair Community College*
Arnold C. Morgensen, *West Hartford, Connecticut*
Hugh Phares, *American River College*
Kevin Rush, A.I.A., *South Central Technical College*

Dennis M. Sayers, *New River Community College*
Lawrence Seiberlich, *St. Paul, Minnesota*
Douglas Ray Sire, *Des Moines Area Community College*
Kenneth Y. Smith, *Greenville Technical College*
Charles Strieby, *Michigan State University*
T. G. Underwood, *Morse High School, Bath, Maine*
Therese Weedon, *Cuyamaca College*
George R. William, *Los Angeles, California*
Stephen Zdepski, *New Jersey School of Architecture*

Osamu A. Wakita
Richard M. Linde

CONTENTS

PART II   DOCUMENT EVOLUTION   129

THE PROFESSIONAL PRACTICE OF ARCHITECTURAL WORKING DRAWINGS

SECOND EDITION   **STUDENT EDITION**

PROFESSIONAL
FOUNDATIONS

BASIC DRAFTING
REQUIREMENTS

PREVIEW

Starting with the basic equipment necessary for drafting, this chapter explores the vocabulary of the architectural technician and translates this vocabulary into familiar terms. The chapter also covers lettering, the use of scales, and the multiview projection, which are the basis of drafting principles.

OBJECTIVES

1. Know what basic equipment is used in architectural drafting.
2. Understand how to use drafting instruments alone and in combination.
3. Know the various grades of drafting leads.
4. Be able to use and apply architectural terms and lines.
5. Be able to letter legibly.
6. Understand dimensions and their applications.
7. Know how to care for original drawings.
8. Know how to divide a line into equal parts for use in drafting stairs, floor and wall patterns, and other repetitive elements in architectural drawings.
9. Understand how the concept of orthographic projection applies to architectural drafting.

Kinds of Drafting Equipment

Basic Equipment

The drafting tools needed by a beginning draftsperson and the basic uses of those tools are shown in Figure 1.1 and are as follows:

1. **T-square.** A straight edge used to draft horizontal lines and a base for the use of triangles.
2. **Triangle.** A three-sided guide used to draft vertical lines and angular lines in conjunction with a T-square. The 30°/60° and 45° triangles are basic equipment.
3. **Erasing shield.** A metal or plastic card with pre-punched slots and holes used to protect some portions of a drawing while erasing others.
4. **Eraser.** A rubber or synthetic material used to erase errors and correct drawings.
5. **Scale.** A measuring device calibrated in a variety of scales for ease of translating large objects into a small proportional drawing.
6. **Drafting tape.** Tape used to hold paper while drafting.
7. **Drafting pencil and lead holders.** Housing for drafting leads.
8. **Lead pointer.** A device used to sharpen the lead in a lead holder.
9. **Divider.** A device resembling a compass, used mainly for transferring measurements from one location to another.
10. **Compass.** A V-shaped device for drafting arcs and circles.
11. **French curve.** A pattern used to draft irregular arcs.
12. **Circle template.** A prepunched sheet of plastic punched in various sizes, for use as a pattern for circles without using a compass.
13. **Plan template.** Prepunched patterns for shapes commonly found in architectural plans.
14. **Dusting brush.** A brush used to keep drafting surfaces clean and free of debris.

Additional Equipment

In addition to the tools listed above, a number of others aid and simplify the drafting process. They are shown in Figure 1.2.

1. **Track drafter.** A device that allows the drafting pencil to rest against the blade of the scale, and be held stationary while the whole track drafter is moved to draw (track) a line. Look at the track on the left side of the drafting table in Figure 1.2.
2. **Adjustable triangle.** A triangle used to draft odd angles such as those found in the pitch (slope) of a roof.
3. **Triangles of various sizes.** Triangles range in size from extremely small ones, used for detailing or lettering, to very large ones, used for dimension lines, perspectives, and so on.
4. **Lettering guide.** A device used for drafting guidelines of varying heights.
5. **Flat scales.** The scales shown in Figure 1.2 are smaller than those shown in Figure 1.1 and are flat. They provide greater ease of handling, but they do not have as many different scales.
6. **Specialty templates.** Specialty templates include furniture, trees, electrical and mechanical equipment, geometric shapes, and standard symbols.

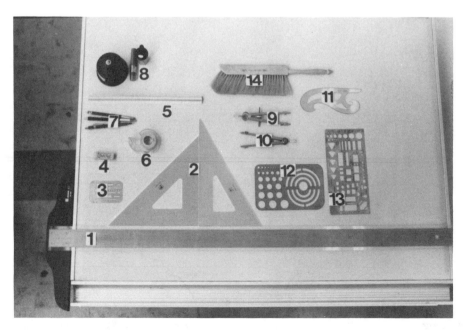

Figure 1.1 Basic drafting equipment.

7. **Proportional dividers.** Dividers used to enlarge or reduce a drawing to any proportion.
8. **Electric eraser.** Particularly useful when you are working with erasable sepias or ink.
9. **Parallel straightedge.** Shown in Figure 1.3, this device is often preferred over a T-square, because it always remains horizontal without the user's constantly checking for alignment. This straightedge runs along cords on both sides, which are mounted on the top or the underside of the drafting board. Parallel straightedges are available in lengths up to 72 inches.

10. **Drafting machine.** Shown in Figure 1.4, this machine uses a pair of scales attached on an arm. These scales move in a parallel fashion so parallel, horizontal, and vertical lines can be drawn. A protractor mechanism allows the drafter to rapidly move the scales to any desired angle. The drafting machine can be mounted onto a drafting board as shown in the illustration or on a drafting desk.

This list is by no means complete. Your selection of tools will be dictated by office standards and the requirements of particular projects.

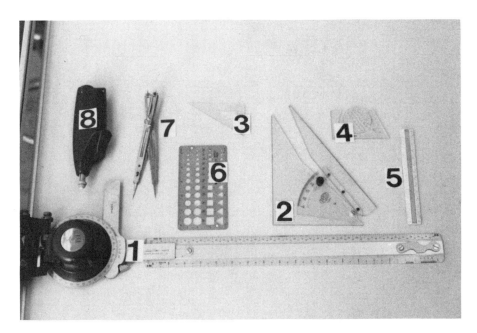

Figure 1.2 Additional drafting equipment.

Figure 1.3 Parallel straightedge. (Courtesy of Kratos/Keuffel & Esser.)

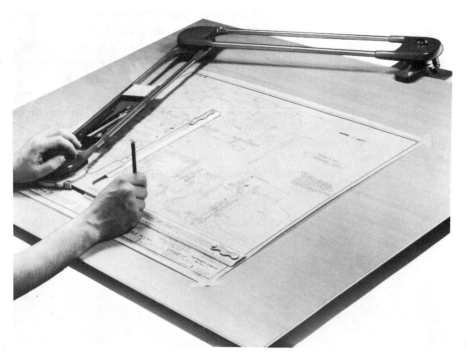

Figure 1.4 Drafting machine. (Courtesy of Kratos/Keuffel & Esser.)

Using Drafting Equipment

Using the T-square

To use a T-square properly, you must have a true straightedge along which to guide the T-square head. As you guide the head against the edge, keep pressure between the edge and the head of the T-square. See Figure 1.5. Notice that the right-handed person keeps pressure against the blade portion while drawing horizontal lines. See Figure 1.6. Never use the T-square on a drafting board in a vertical direction because the board may not be absolutely square or the head of the T-square may not be at a 90° angle with the blade portion; in these instances you will create a line that is not perpendicular with the horizontal line. Even if the T-square is off, say 2 degrees, it will still produce parallel horizontal lines.

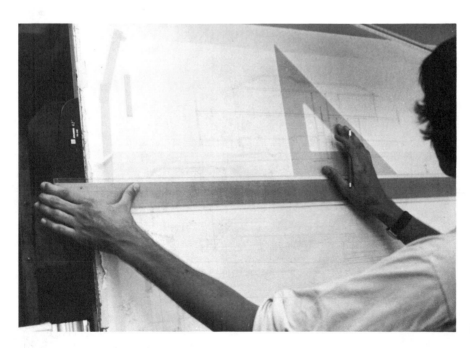

Figure 1.5 T-square and triangle.

Figure 1.6 Drawing with a T-square.

Using the Triangle

The triangle is used in conjunction with the T-square to draft vertical lines and angular lines. See Figures 1.7 and 1.8. In both photographs, note how the draftsperson holds down the T-square firmly with the left palm, and holds the triangles tight against the T-square with the fingers of the left hand, allowing freedom to draw the line with the right hand. You can use the 45° and the 30°/60° triangles in tandem with each other to obtain additional angles as shown in Figures 1.9 and 1.10. Used correctly, triangles enable you to draw lines every 15°. Figure 1.9 shows how a 45° triangle is placed on a 30° triangle to achieve a 75° angle. A 30° triangle can also be placed on a 45° triangle to achieve the same result.

In Figure 1.10, a 45° triangle is used as a base, and correct placement of a 30°/60° triangle gives a 15° angle. To draw these angles in the opposite direction, simply flip both triangles over together.

Drawing Parallel Lines. To draw parallel lines, look at Figure 1.11 and follow these directions:

1. Place one of the triangles on top of a T-square (30° works well).

Figure 1.7 Correct use of a triangle for drawing 90° angles.

Figure 1.8 Using a triangle to draw an angle.

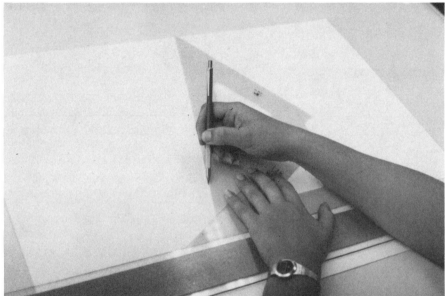

Figure 1.9 Combining triangles to produce a 75° angle.

Figure 1.10 Combining triangles to produce a 15° angle.

Figure 1.11 Drawing parallel lines on an angle.

2. Move the triangle and the T-square together until they line up with the existing line.
3. Holding the T-square with one hand, slide the triangle away from the existing line.
4. As the triangle is moved, draw the parallel lines.
5. The procedure can also be done with two triangles.

Drawing Perpendicular Lines. The procedure for drawing perpendicular lines is illustrated in Figure 1.12 and is similar to the procedure for drawing parallel lines. However, after the triangle surface is aligned with the line, the triangle must be rotated clockwise, so that the 60° surface is against the T-square.

Using Erasing Shields and Erasers

Drawing Dotted Lines. Dotted lines, which are usually called **hidden lines** in drafting, can be drawn rapidly by using an erasing shield and an eraser. An electric eraser is more effective than a regular eraser.

First, draw the line as if it were a solid line, using the correct pressure to produce the desired darkness. Second, lay the erasing shield over the line so that the row of uniformly drilled holes on the shield aligns with the solid line. Next, erase through the small holes. The results will be a uniform and rapidly produced hidden (dotted) line.

This technique is particularly effective for foundation plans, which use many hidden lines. See Figure 1.13.

Using the Scale

The Triangle Scale. The most convenient scale to purchase is a triangular scale because it gives the greatest variety in one single instrument. There are usually 11 scales on a triangle scale, one of which is an ordinary 12-inch ruler. See Figure 1.14.

Reading the Scale. Since structures cannot be drawn full scale, the 12-inch ruler which is full scale is seldom used. Reading a scale is much the same as reading a regular ruler. Translating a full-size object into a reduced scale—1½ scale for example—is more a matter of your visual attitude than of translating from one scale to another. For example, you can simply imagine a 12-inch ruler reduced to 1½ inches in size and used to measure at this reduced scale. The scale is written on a drawing as 1½″ = 1′–0″. See Figure 1.15.

On an architectural scale, inches are measured to the left of the zero. Numbers are often printed here to indicate the inches to be measured. Note the 1½ standing by itself on the extreme left. The number explains the scale.

All 3 sides of the triangle scale (except the side with the 12-inch scale) have 2 scales on each usable surface. Each of these 2 scales uses the full length of the instrument, but one is read from left to right and the other from right to left. Typically, a scale is either one half or double the scale it is paired with. For example, if one end is a ¼-inch scale, the opposite end is a ⅛-inch scale; if one end is a ⅜-inch scale, the opposite end is a ¾-inch scale. The opposite end of the 3-inch scale would be the 1½-inch scale.

Confusion is often caused by the numbers between the two scales. Look carefully at these numbers and notice two sets. One set is closer to the groove that runs the length of the scale and the other is closer to the outside edge. The numbers near the edge will be the feet increments for the smaller scale, and the other numbers will be the feet increments for the larger scale. In Figure 1.15A, notice a lower and a higher 2. The upper, right-

Figure 1.12 Drawing perpendicular lines.

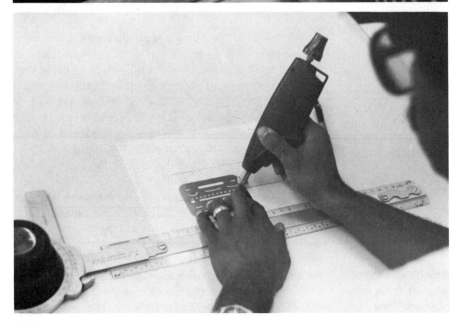

Figure 1.13 Drawing a dotted (hidden) line.

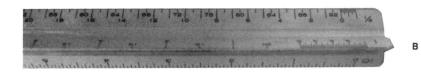

Figure 1.14 The triangle scale.

A

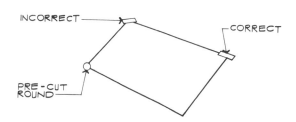

B

Figure 1.15 Reading the scale.

hand 2 is 2 feet on the 1½-inch scale, and the lower, left-hand 2 is the number of feet from 0 on the opposite side, which is the 3-inch scale and not seen in the photograph. Since the lower 2 falls halfway between the 0 and the upper 2, in this example, it is read as 1 on the 1½-inch scale. Starting from the opposite direction, the upper 2 is read as 1½ feet since it is found halfway between the 1 and 2, of the 3-inch scale.

Figure 1.15B shows a ¼-inch scale. Notice, again, the two sets of numbers. Since the opposite end (not shown) contains the ⅛-inch scale, the lower numbers belong to the ¼-inch side. Notice that they are read 0, 2, 4, 6, 8, etc. In between are numbers that read (from right to left) 92, 88, 84, 80, etc. These numbers belong to the ⅛-inch scale on the opposite side.

An easy error to make is to read the wrong number because the "32" on the ⅛-inch scale is so close to the "32" on the ¼-inch scale. Similar pitfalls occur in other pairs of scales on the triangle scale.

Most engineering scales use the same principles as architectural scales, except that measurements are divided into tenths, twentieths, and so on, rather than halves, quarters, and eighths. The section on metrics explains these metric scales further.

Using Drafting Tape

A simple but effective method of taping original drawings is to keep the edges of the tape parallel with the edges of the vellum (a translucent high quality tracing paper), as shown in Figure 1.16. This prevents the T-square or whatever type of straightedge is used from catching the corner of the tape and rolling if off. Vellum taped at an angle creates unnecessary frustrations for the beginning draftsperson. Drafting supply stores sell tape in a round shape (large dot), which is even better.

Figure 1.16 Correct placement of drafting tape.

Rolling Original Drawings

Most beginners begin rolling drawings in the wrong direction. In their attempt to protect the drawings, they often roll the print or the original so that the printed side is on the *inside,* as shown in Figure 1.17A. However, the correct way is to roll the sheet so that the artwork is on the *outside,* as shown in Figure 1.17B.

When a set of prints is unrolled and read, the drawings should roll toward the table and should not interfere

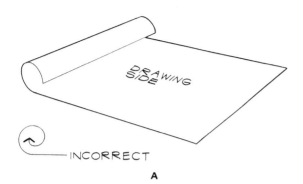

Figure 1.17A Incorrect way to roll a drawing.

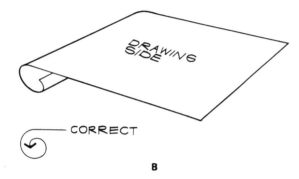

Figure 1.17B Correct way to roll a drawing.

with easy reading by curling up. If originals are rolled correctly, the vellum curls toward the drafting table or blueprint machine, preventing it from being torn when drafting equipment slides across it or when it is being reproduced.

Selecting and Using Drafting Pencils

Types of Leads

Seventeen grades of leads are available, but only a few of these are appropriate for drafting. Harder leads are given an **"H"** designation, while soft leads are given a designation of **"B".** Between the "H" and "B" range are **"HB"** and **"F"** leads. The softest "B" lead is 6B (number 6) while the hardest "H" head is 9H (number 9). See Figure 1.18.

Selection Factors.   Only the central range of leads is used for drafting. 2H, 3H, and 4H are good for light layout, while H is good for a medium weight line. F leads are excellent for dark object lines.

However, many other factors also determine the choice of pencil. Temperature and humidity may dictate

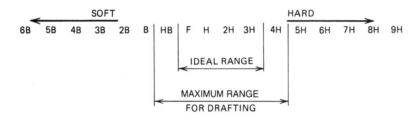

Figure 1.18 Lead hardnesses.

WOOD PENCILS

MECHANICAL LEAD HOLDERS

SUPERTHIN (FINE LINE) LEAD HOLDERS

Figure 1.19 Types of lead holders and pencils.

that certain leads be used. Manufacturers vary in what they designate as a particular grade. And the natural pressure that the drafter places on the pencil varies from individual to individual. The reproduction method to be used also determines the grade of lead chosen.

For photography, a crisp line is better than a dark one because a dark, broad line may end up as a blur on the negative. Diazo prints (blue or black lines on a white background) need to block out light, and so a dense line is more important.

Pencils Versus Lead Holders

Wood pencils are fine for the beginner, but serious drafting requires mechanical lead holders. See Figure 1.19. Wood pencils require sharpening of both the wood and the lead, which is time-consuming. More

important, a lead holder allows you the full use of the lead, whereas a wood pencil cannot.

Lead Pointers

A lead pointer, a tool used to sharpen drafting leads, is a must. Sandpaper can be used for both wood pencils and lead holders, but it is not nearly as convenient, consistent, or rapid as a lead pointer. A good practice after using a lead pointer is as follows: take the sharpened lead and hold the pointer perpendicular to a hard surface such as a triangle; crush the tip of the lead slightly; then hone the tip by drawing a series of circular lines on a piece of scratch paper. You can also use this process with a wood pencil. This stops the lead from breaking on the first stroke. Roll the pencil as you draw to keep a consistent tip on the lead. See Figure 1.20. Draw either

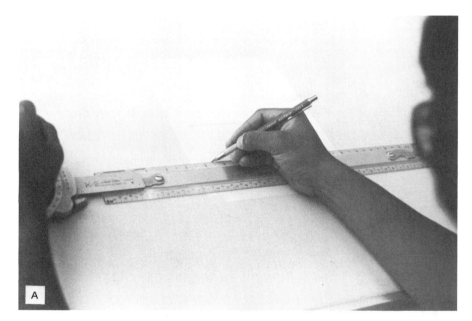

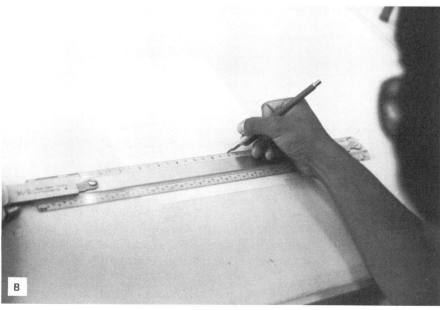

Figure 1.20 Rotating the pencil to keep a rounded point.

clockwise or counterclockwise, depending on whichever produces the best line and is the most comfortable for you. Note the position of the fingers and thumb at the beginning and end of the line.

Superthin Lead Holders

The last type of drafting lead holders, also called fine line lead holders, produces consistent, superthin lines. The diameters of the leads are 0.3 mm, 0.5 mm, 0.7 mm, and 0.9 mm, and the leads come in almost the full range of grades. The most popular of these holders is the 0.5 mm size, because it gives the best thickness of lines. There is no sharpening necessary, so drawing time is maximized. Some drafters still roll this holder as they draw to keep the rounded point, thus avoiding an easily broken chisel point. However, a chisel point is often desirable for lettering. For example, except for the freehand sketches, all of the lettering in this book is done with a chisel end on a superthin holder.

Lines and Line Quality

Basically, lines can be broken down into three types: light, medium, and dark. Each of these types can be broken down further by variation of pressure and lead.

Light Lines. The lightest lines used are usually the guidelines drawn to help with lettering height. These lines should be only barely visible and should completely disappear when a diazo print is made. Darker than guidelines but still relatively light are the lines used in dimension and extension lines, leaders, and break lines.

Medium Lines. Medium weight lines are used in object and center lines, and in the dashed type of line used for hidden or dotted lines.

Dark Lines. The darkest lines are used for border lines and cutting plane lines, major sections, and details. See Figure 1.21.

Choosing Line Quality. Line quality depends on the use of that particular line. An intense line is used to profile and emphasize; an intermediate line is used to show elements such as walls and structural members; and a light line is used for elements such as dimensioning and door swings.

Another way to vary line quality is to increase the width of the line. A thicker line can represent the walls on a floor plan, the outline of a building on a site plan, or the outline of a roof on a roof plan. See Figure 1.21

for line quality examples and uses and Figure 1.22 for an example of the types of lines used to indicate property lines and easements.

Hidden or Dotted Lines. Hidden or dotted lines are used to indicate objects hidden from view. See Figure 1.13. Solid objects covered by earth, such as foundations, can be indicated with hidden lines. This type of line can also depict future structures, items that are not in the contract, public utilities locations, easements, a wheelchair turning radius, or the direction of sliding doors and windows.

A floor plan will often show the roof outline, or a balcony above, or a change in ceiling height with a dotted line. On a site plan, dotted lines indicate the existing grades on the site (see Chapter 6).

Arrowheads. Different types of arrowheads are used in dimensioning. These are shown in Figure 1.23.

Material Designation Lines. Material designation lines are used to indicate the building material used. See Figure 1.24 for a sample of tapered or light-dark lines. (This device saves time; complete lines take longer to draw.) Also note the cross-hatched lines between the parallel lines that represent the wall thickness on Figure 1.25. These diagonal lines represent masonry.

Profiling

Architectural profiling is the process of taking the most important features of a drawing and outlining them. Figure 1.26 shows four applications of this concept.

Example A illustrates the darkening of the lines that represent the walls of a floor plan. The dimension lines or extension lines are drawn as medium weight lines not only to contrast with the walls but to allow the walls of the particular floor plan to stand out. In example B, a footing detail is profiled. Because the concrete work is important here, its outline is drawn darker than any other part of the detail.

Example C shows the top portion (head) of a window. The light lines at the bottom of the detail represent the side of the window. Note how the head section is outlined and the interior parts plus the sides of the walls are drawn lightly.

Example D represents another form of profiling, called "pouché," which enhances the profile technique by using shading. This shading can be done by pencil shading or by lines. Example B also uses this principle: in this instance, the dots and triangles which represent concrete in section are placed along the perimeter (near the profiled line) in greater quantity than toward the center.

In a section drawing, items most often profiled are cut by the cutting plane line. A footing detail, for example, is nothing more than a theoretical knife (a cutting plane) cutting through the wall of the structure. The portion most often cut is the concrete, so it is profiled.

On an elevation, the main outline of the structure should be darkened. See Figure 1.27. This type of profiling is used to simplify the illusion of the elevation to show that the structure is basically an L-shape structure and that one portion does actually project forward.

In the plan view, often the outline of the main structure is heavily outlined (profiled) in order to make the main area stand out more than any other feature of the property. See Figure 1.28 for a finished plan and elevation which have been properly profiled.

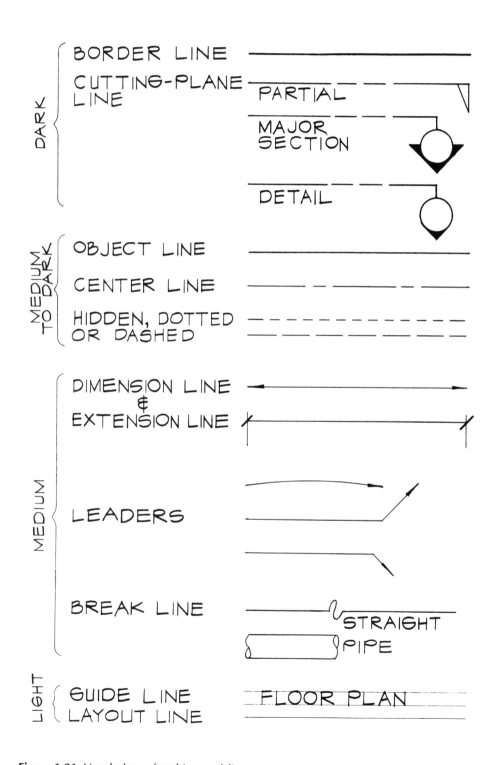

Figure 1.21 Vocabulary of architectural lines.

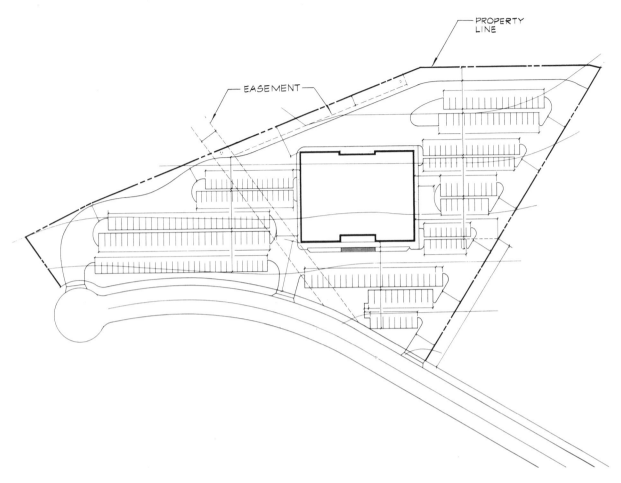

Figure 1.22 Types of lines used for property lines and easements.

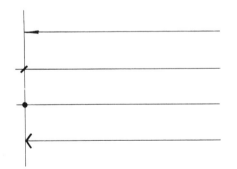

Figure 1.23 Types of arrowheads used in dimensioning.

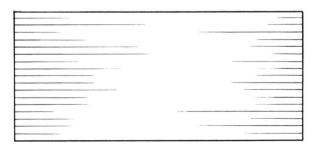

Figure 1.24 Tapered lines.

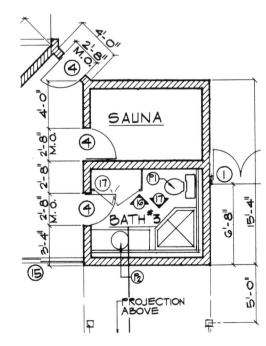

Figure 1.25 Lines representing masonry.

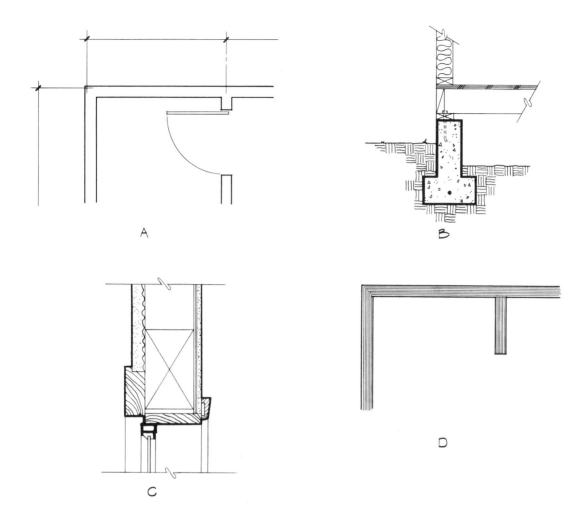

A

B

C

D

Figure 1.26 Profiling.

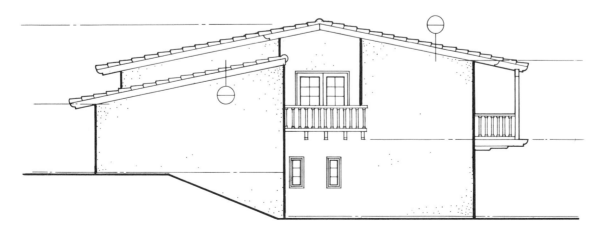

Figure 1.27 Elevation.

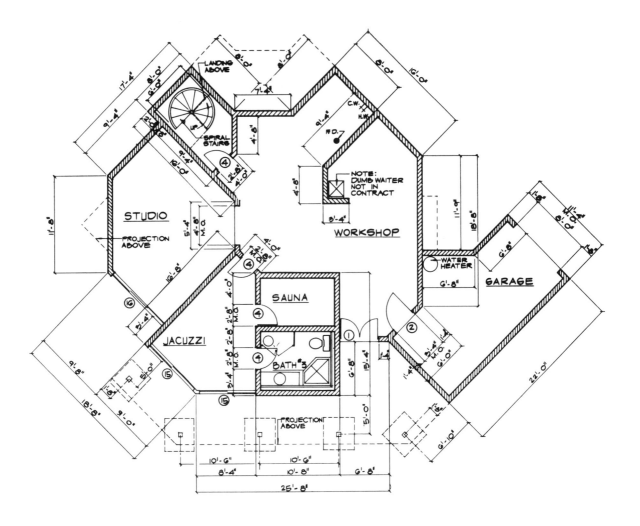

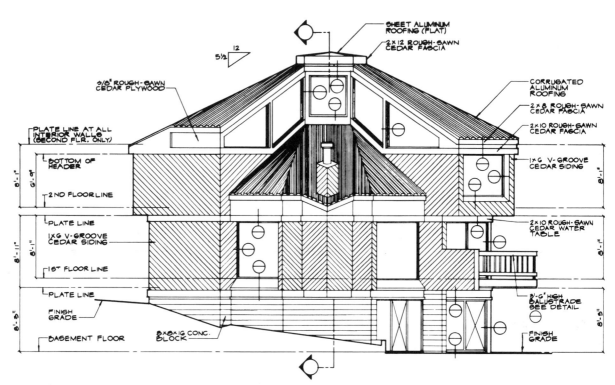

Figure 1.28 Correctly profiled plan and elevation.

Lettering

In architectural drafting, as in mechanical drafting, working drawings are not always hand lettered. A variety of different mechanical devices have come on the market in recent years, and large engineering and aircraft firms have been proving their effectiveness.

The architectural industry, however, is and may continue to be a small office industry. A recent survey by the American Institute of Architects (AIA) found that architectural firms usually contain three to six employees and may not use computerized drafting and lettering machines. For this reason, it is important that architecture students become proficient in lettering. In fact, it is good lettering and good line quality that help a student obtain the first job.

Architectural lettering differs somewhat from the Gothic type letters developed by C. W. Reinhardt about fifty years ago and now called "mechanical lettering." Architectural lettering has evolved from a series of influences, including the demand for speed. We must not, however, interpret speed to mean sloppiness.

Another influence on architectural lettering was style. The architecturally drafted plan was in essence an idea or concept on paper, a creative endeavor. So the lines and the lettering took on a characteristic style of their own. In many firms, stylized lettering serves to identify the individual draftsperson. However, most firms attempt to create a uniform style of lettering for their entire staff. Stylizing must not be confused with overdecoration. Lettering that looks like a new alphabet should not be justified in the name of stylization.

Basic Rules for Lettering and Numbering

Following are a few simple rules for lettering and numbering:

1. Master mechanical lettering before attempting architectural lettering or any type of stylization. A student who cannot letter well in mechanical drafting has less chance of developing good architectural letters.
2. Learn to letter with vertical strokes first. Sloping letters may be easier to master, but most architectural offices prefer vertical lettering. It is easier to change from vertical to sloping letters than the reverse. See Figure 1.29.
3. Practice words, phrases, and numbers—not just individual letters. Copy a phrase from this book for example.
4. The shape of a letter should not be changed. The proportion of the letter may be slightly altered but one should never destroy the letter's original image. While the middle example "W" in Figure 1.30 is in a style used for speed, it can be misconstrued as an "I" and a "V".

5. Changing the proportions of letters changes their visual effect. See Figure 1.31.
6. Certain strokes can be emphasized so that one letter is not mistaken for another. This also forces the draftsperson to be more definitive in the formation of individual strokes. The strokes emphasized should be those most important to that letter; for example, a "B" differs from an "R" by the rounded lower right stroke, and an "L" from an "I" by the horizontal bottom stroke extending to the right only. The beginning or end of these strokes can be emphasized by bearing down on the pencil to insure a good reprint of that portion. See Figure 1.32.
7. Many draftspersons have picked up the bad habit of mixing upper and lower case letters. This is not good lettering.
8. Some draftspersons also have developed a style of leaving space within the letter that is not there. This too is to be discouraged. See Figure 1.33.
9. Consistency produces good lettering. If vertical lines are used, they must all be parallel. A slight variation produces poor lettering. Even round letters such as "O" have a center through which imaginary vertical strokes will go. See Figure 1.34.

ANCHOR BOLT   *ANCHOR BOLT*
VERTICAL LETTERS   SLOPING LETTERS

Figure 1.29 Comparison between vertical and sloping lettering.

MECHANICAL   ARCHITECTURAL
M W   /\ \/ /\/\ ←(Poor)

Figure 1.30 Overworking architectural letters.

MECHANICAL   ARCHITECTURAL
STUD   STUD STUD

Figure 1.31 Changing proportions to produce architectural effect.

EXAMPLE:
B L I T R K

Figure 1.32 Emphasis on certain strokes.

EXAMPLE:
B O Q D P

Figure 1.33 Spaces incorrectly left within letters.

EXAMPLE:
PLYWOOD   PLYWOOD
(Poor)   (Good)

Figure 1.34 Producing consistency.

10. Second only to the letter itself is spacing. Good spacing protects good letter formation. Poor spacing destroys even the best lettering. See Figure 1.35.

11. Always use guidelines and use them to the fullest. See Figure 1.36.

EXAMPLE:

PLYWOOD   P LY WO OD

    (Good)   (Poor)

Figure 1.35 Importance of good spacing.

PLYWOOD   PLYWOOD

    (Poor)   (Good)

Figure 1.36 Full use of guidelines.

Using Guidelines

While a purist might frown on the practice, a guideline or straightedge can be used in lettering to speed up the learning process. Horizontal lines are easier for a beginner than vertical lines and shapes appear better formed when all of the vertical strokes are perfectly perpendicular and parallel to each other. Curved and round strokes are done without the aid of an instrument.

After drawing the guidelines, place a T-square or parallel about 2 or 3 inches below the lines. Locate the triangle to the left of the area to be lettered with the vertical portion of the triangle on the right side. See Figure 1.37. "Eyeball" the spacing of the letters. Position your pencil as if you are ready to make the vertical line without the triangle. Before you make the vertical stroke, slide the triangle over against the pencil and

Figure 1.37 Pencil placement for vertical lettering.

Figure 1.38 Placing the triangle against the pencil.

make the stroke. See Figures 1.38 and 1.39. Draw non-vertical lines freehand. See Figure 1.40.

Using a straightedge helps build up skills. Eventually you should discontinue its use as practice improves your lettering skills.

Drafting Conventions and Dimensions

Using Net and Nominal Sizing. Many architectural offices have adopted the practice of separating the **net size** and the **nominal size** of lumber in their notations. The nominal size (call out size) is used to describe or order a piece of lumber. The net size is the size of the actual piece of wood drawn and used. For example, the nominal size of a "two by four" is 2 × 4 but the net or actual size is 1½″ × 3½″. The distinction between the two sizes is accomplished by the use of inch (″) marks. Figure 1.41A would be very confusing because the nominal size is listed but inch marks are used. Compare this notation with that of Figure 1.41B. The 16″ o.c. (on center) is to be translated as precisely 16 inches while the 2 × 4 is used to indicate nominal size.

Dimensions. Dimensions in feet are normally expressed by a small mark to the upper right of a number (′), and inches by two small marks (″) in the same location. To separate feet from inches, a dash is used. See Figure 1.42. The dash in this type of dimension becomes very important because it avoids dimensions being misread and adds to clarity. If space for dimensions is restricted, an acceptable abbreviated form can be used. This is illustrated in Figure 1.43. The inches are raised and underlined to separate them from the feet notation.

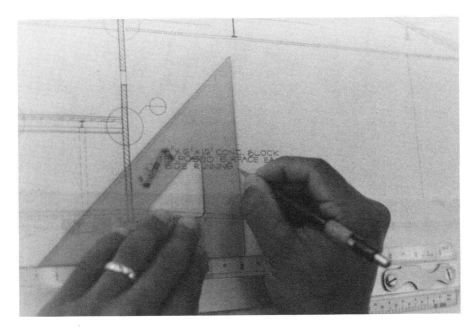

Figure 1.39 Drawing the vertical stroke.

Figure 1.40 Completing the letter.

Placement of Dimensions. Dimension lines can be broken to show the numerical value, but it is faster simply to put numerical values above the lines. See Figure 1.44. When dimension lines run vertically, place the numbers above the dimension line as viewed from the right. See Figure 1.45.

Not all dimension lines, however, are horizontal or vertical. Often dimension lines are angled, and this can cause problems when you position the numerical value. Figure 1.46 suggests a possible location for such values.

Dividing a Line into Equal Parts. Dividing a line or plane into an equal number of parts has many useful applications. There are two main ways of doing this.

The first way is illustrated in Figure 1.47, Method A. Line XY is to be divided into 6 equal divisions. The initial step is to draw two lines perpendicular to XY, one through point X and one through point Y. Next, lay a scale across these newly drawn parallel lines so that 0 is on one of the lines, and a point divisible by six, such as 6 inches, is on the other line. If the line XY had been 7 inches long, 12 inches could have been used, or 9

inches, or any number larger than 7 inches that is divisible by 6.

A small tick mark is drawn above the desired division and parallel lines drawn until they touch line XY, dividing it into 6 equal divisions. The angle of the scale should not be of any concern.

Figure 1.44 Placement of dimensions above or between dimension line.

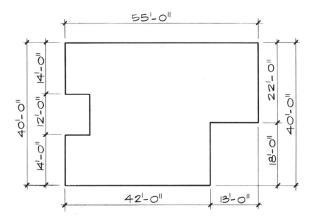

Figure 1.45 Dimensions read from bottom and from the right.

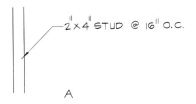

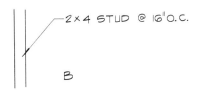

Figure 1.41 Net and nominal notation.

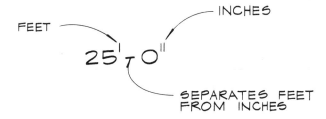

Figure 1.42 Expressing feet and inches.

Figure 1.43 Dimensions in a restricted area.

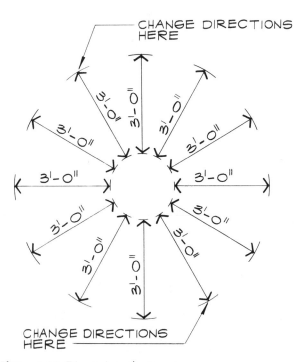

Figure 1.46 Dimension placement.

Method B uses a slightly different approach. See Figure 1.47, Method B. To start with, a line is drawn intersecting line XY at any angle; the new line can be any length. The angle should be larger than 20° to 30°. Next, place a scale on this newly drawn line so that 0 on the scale touches the intersection of line XY and the new line. Find a value divisible by the division desired. For example, if the desired division is 5, find a value on the scale divisible by 5. Draw a line connecting this end point with point Y to form a triangle. Then draw a series of lines parallel to this line toward line XY. See Step 2. These intersections produce the desired division.

Using Terminology: Mechanical Versus Architectural

Mechanical Drafting

While mechanical drafting resembles architectural drafting, the terms used vary greatly. The basis for mechanical drafting is a method of multi-view drawing known as orthographic projection. This method uses a concept in which an object is first housed in a theoretical glass box, as shown in Figure 1.48; second, unfolded as shown in Figure 1.49; and third, viewed in this unfolded form as a flat form. Portions of this six-sided form are given names

such as top view, front view, and right side view. The back, left side, and bottom are eliminated, as Figure 1.50 shows.

Architectural Drafting

The architectural version of orthographic projection is shown in Figure 1.51. The top view (as viewed from a helicopter) is now called the **plan,** and the views all the way around from all four sides are referred to as **elevations.** Each of these elevations has a special name and will be discussed in the chapter on exterior elevations (Chapter 11).

In brief, a top view of the total property is called the site or plot plan. A horizontal section (drawn as if the structure were cut horizontally, the top portion removed, and the exposed interior viewed from above) is simply called a plan. There are many types of plans: floor plans, electrical plans (showing electrical features), framing plans (showing how a floor, ceiling, or roof is assembled), and foundation plans, to mention just a few.

A vertical cut through a structure is called a cross-section or a longitudinal section, depending on the direction of the cut. The cross-section is a cut taken through the short end of a structure.

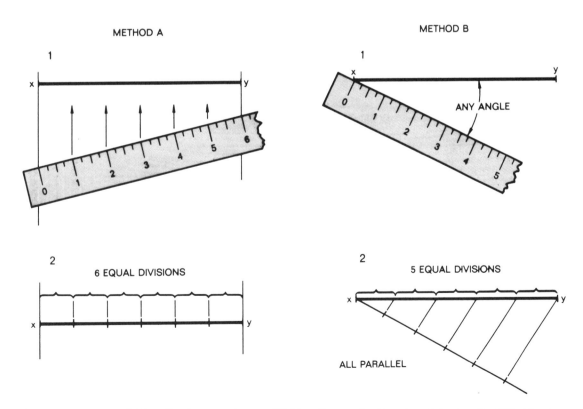

Figure 1.47 How to divide a line into equal parts. (Wakita, *Perspective Drawing: A Student Text/Workbook,* Kendall/Hunt Publishing Co., 1978. Reprinted with permission.)

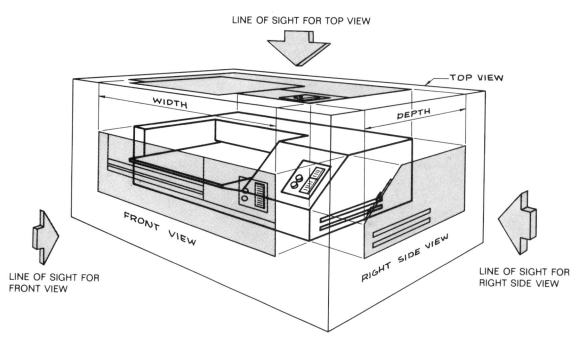

LINE OF SIGHT FOR TOP VIEW

TOP VIEW

WIDTH

DEPTH

FRONT VIEW

RIGHT SIDE VIEW

LINE OF SIGHT FOR
FRONT VIEW

LINE OF SIGHT FOR
RIGHT SIDE VIEW

Figure 1.48 The glass box. (Wakita, *Perspective Drawing: A Student Text/Workbook,* Kendall/Hunt Publishing Co.,
1978. Reprinted with permission.)

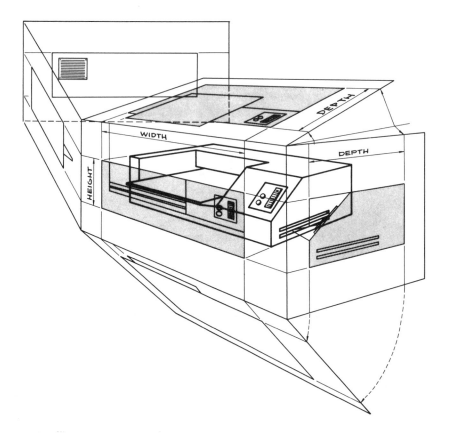

DEPTH

WIDTH

DEPTH

HEIGHT

Figure 1.49 Unfolding the glass box. (Wakita, *Perspective Drawing: A Student Text/
Workbook,* Kendall/Hunt Publishing Co., 1978. Reprinted with permission.)

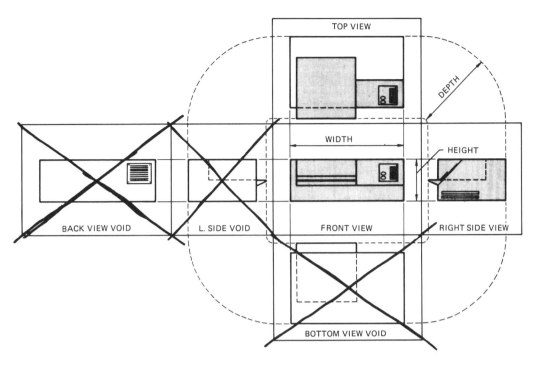

Figure 1.50 Primary and voided views. (Wakita, *Perspective Drawing: A Student Text/Workbook*, Kendall/Hunt Publishing Co., 1978. Reprinted with permission.)

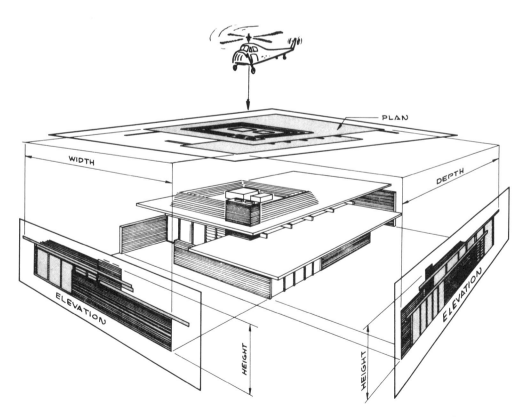

Figure 1.51 Multiview drawing of a structure. (Wakita, *Perspective Drawing: A Student Text/Workbook*, Kendall/Hunt Publishing Co., 1978. Reprinted with permission.)

SUMMARY

Mastery of drafting instruments is absolutely essential for the prospective drafter. Using these instruments—the straightedge, the triangle, and the pencil—should become quite natural, and once you are accomplished, you can then concentrate on lettering and line quality. Mastery of these three instruments, combined with competence in lettering and line quality, produces the first in a series of skills firms look for in an employee. So you acquire a definitely salable skill when you accomplish this first task with proficiency.

Special terms, procedures, and communicative methods are used in architecture, and you should, while learning the skills and methods, try to understand why and how these are used rather than simply memorizing terms and lines.

IMPORTANT TERMS AND CONCEPTS

T-square
Triangle
Erasing shield
Eraser
Scale
Drafting tape
Drafting pencil
Lead holders
Lead pointer
Compass
Divider
French curve
Circle template
Plan template
Dusting brush
Track drafter
Adjustable triangle
Lettering guide
Flat scales
Specialty templates
Proportional dividers

Electric eraser
Parallel straightedge
Drafting machine
Drafting parallel lines
Drafting perpendicular lines
Hidden lines
Triangle scale
Grades of lead: B, HB, F, H
Line quality
Arrowheads
Material designation lines
Profiling
Guidelines
Net size
Nominal size
Dimensions
Dividing a line
Mechanical drafting
Architectural drafting
Plan
Elevation

REVIEW QUESTIONS

1. List all of the angles available to the draftsperson using only a T-square, a 45° triangle, and a 30°/60° triangle.
2. What grades of leads are most practical for drafting?
3. Why are wood pencils seldom used in professional drafting?
4. What kind of line is often used to describe the property line?
5. Explain a simple way of drafting hidden lines without drafting each individual dash line.
6. What is the purpose of profiling, and why is it important?
7. Why is a dash used between feet and inches when dimensions are put on a drawing?
8. Explain the difference between the terms "front view" and "elevation."
9. Explain the difference between net and nominal sizes.

LABORATORY PROBLEMS

1. Construct a 3"-diameter circle. Draft a series of lines through the center of the circle similar to the spokes of a bicycle wheel. When finished, the lines should be 15° apart.
2. Construct a 3"-diameter circle. Using triangles, construct a hexagon.
3. Find literature dealing with an architectural product, such as a door, floor material, or bathroom fixtures, and letter the technical description using ⅛"-high letters; letter a title for this description using ¼"-high letters.

4. Obtain a floor pattern that uses geometric designs and reproduce it at a scale different from the sample.

5. Draft a top, front, and right side view of a book case. Do the same for a picnic bench or a simplified couch.

6. Draft a 12' × 14' bedroom using ¼" = 1'–0" scale. Show 6"-thick walls (in scale). Measure some of your own pieces of furniture and arrange them in the 12' × 14' room.

7. Draft a 6" line. Divide this line into 5 equal parts.

2

REPRODUCTION, STANDARDS, AND DRAWING GUIDELINES

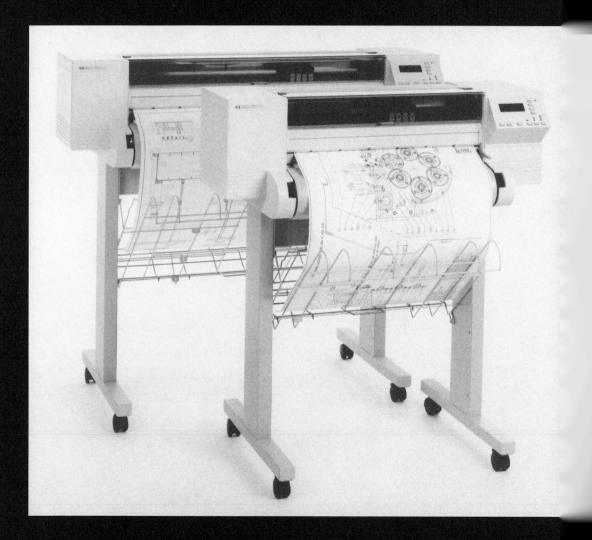

2

PREVIEW

This chapter introduces three topics: reproduction methods, also referred to as application; standards used in practice; and guidelines. Application covers production methods, such as the diazo process and other copiers, and shortcut methods that are rapidly finding their way into offices.

The first two sections cover basic standards used in offices, including sheet size, material designation, and referencing, as well as available information sources, references, and the Dimensional Reference System. Then we examine metric conversion and its implications.

The third section, on working guidelines, covers the preparation of working drawings, emphasizing the importance of attitude rather than skill.

OBJECTIVES

1. Understand reproduction methods used in architectural offices.
2. Be familiar with new and unique shortcuts in reproduction.
3. Understand how photography and computers are used by architects for basic drafting.
4. Know the reasons for and use of basic office standards.
5. Know the proper use of reference materials and available resources.
6. Be familiar with the Dimensional Reference System.
7. Know what part metrics will play in architecture and how to use the system.
8. Appreciate the importance of developing professional attitudes as well as skills.

Reproduction Methods

The Blueprint Process

Decades ago, the prevalent method of reproduction was the "blueprint." **Blueprints** have a blue background and white lines. Bond paper was coated with light-sensitive chemicals much like photographic film. The original, drawn on a translucent medium such as vellum, was placed over the paper and exposed to light. The light bleached out the chemicals except where they were screened off by lines. The paper was then dipped in a developing solution which would react to those sections not exposed to the light. The print was then washed and dried. As you can imagine, this process was time-consuming.

The Diazo Process

Today, blueprints are seldom used in architecture. The **diazo** has replaced it and is now used almost exclusively. Much as in the blueprint process, an original translucent medium (usually **vellum**) is placed over a bond paper which has a coating of light-sensitive chemicals. As the sheets are exposed to the light, the chemicals are bleached out, leaving only those areas that are screened by lines. The print is then exposed to ammonia or another chemical, which develops the unexposed chemicals. The result is a white background and dark lines. Color lines are also available, including brown and green. This diazo process usually only takes from fifteen seconds to one minute.

The Sepia Process

When diazo chemicals are placed onto vellum instead of bond paper, the resulting print is called a sepia print, or simply a **sepia.** This sepia copy becomes a second master. Sepia displays as reddish-brown lines on a white vellum background. The sepia print can be drawn on or, depending on the type, erased with an electric or chemical eraser called an eradicator. Some sepia papers "ghost" back unwanted lines when the effect of the eradicator wears off.

The advantages of a sepia are twofold: first, as another master; and, second, as a time saving device. As a second master, it is often used to make diazo copies so that normal wear and tear takes place on the sepia rather than on the original. If a structure is being built in a different city from the office, sepia prints can be sent from which necessary sets of diazo prints can be made for permits, bids, and contractors.

Sepias have unlimited use as a time-saving device. For example, a floor is initially drawn; before the drawing becomes too complicated, a number of sepia prints are made. Sepias are more effective if they are made in reverse so the drafter can draw on the sheet and make corrections without erasing the original print. These sepia copies can be used for electrical plans, structural drawings, and heating and air-conditioning plans. If a consulting engineer provides information, it, too, can be placed on the sepia sheet. Information such as dimensions and equipment locations is thus accurate; the architect and consultant are both using the same original drawings. The structural consultant may even be given a slightly lighter sepia so that the structural work stands out on the sheet when regular diazo copies are made.

Transparent and Translucent Films. Diazo chemicals are also used with transparent or translucent film materials; the result is simply called "film." This **transparent** or **translucent** material can also be purchased with an adhesive on one side and is called applique film. After you expose this applique film to the image, you can mount it directly onto a vellum original or sepia. Most types of applique film are erasable.

Plain Paper Copiers

Types and Sizes. A variety of plain paper copiers are now on the open market for sale or lease. Some require special paper; others can copy on almost any paper surface. Some machines can enlarge as well as reduce, but presently only in certain proportions. Some copiers do not copy the original to its exact size; they change the size slightly and often in only one direction. Plain paper copiers usually use the standard paper formats of 8½" × 11" and 8½" × 14". The larger copiers can take copy widths up to 36" and unlimited length since the machine accepts roll stock. But on most copiers the maximum reproducible size is presently about 24"; a 36" master must be reduced to a 24" size for reproduction. A 24" master can be reproduced full size. Paper copiers can reproduce on bond paper, vellum, or acetate. Therefore, a 24" × 36" drawing can be reduced onto vellum and used as a master to produce diazo copies.

Reproducing on acetate is advantageous because prints on acetate can be used with an overhead projector for enlarging sketches or for presentations. Acetate film is also available with an adhesive backing for applique uses.

Appliques. Most adhesive films for plain paper copiers have two sheets: one sheet of adhesive film and a backing sheet or carrier. Since the adhesive film has a sticky substance on one side, the carrier is a nonstick material. This material is either a plastic film or a wax impregnated paper similar to wax paper.

When you use adhesive film on a plain paper copier of the heat developing variety, do not choose a wax carrier type; the heat from the developer portion of the copier melts the wax and jams the copier.

Standard decals can be made with adhesive film for symbols, title block information, and even construction notes.

Computer

The new CAD systems are often combined with a printer or a plotter. The plotters can be used to reproduce a drawing and/or re-create a secondary original that can use the previously mentioned reproduction methods. The advantage is that you can change the size and scale of the reproduction instantly.

Shortcut Procedures

Freehand Drawing. One of the best shortcuts you can learn is drawing freehand. Most of the preliminary design procedures and conceptual design details in this book were done freehand. You still should use a scale to maintain accuracy, and adhere to the drafting vocabulary of lines and techniques. Freehand skill is useful in field situations, for informal office communications, and for communications with contractors, building department officials, and clients. Examples of freehand details can be found in the chapter on architectural details (Chapter 14).

Typewritten Notes. Because of the applique film technique and the ease of reproducing spliced drawings, typing is being used more frequently for working drawings. For example, lengthy construction notes may be typed on applique film. However, hand lettering is *still* encouraged at the beginning.

Computer-Aided Drafting (CAD). The recent surge of interest in computers has found its way into the architectural office. Both the large and minicomputers (home variety) are now being used to draft. The size and scope of the drafting to be done is only limited by the equipment used.

Experience has shown, however, that the computer drafter must have a minimum of three years and sometimes as many as fifteen years of on-the-board drafting experience to be effective as a computer-aided drafter. This individual must know such things as the symbology used in architecture and the logic of dimensioning, as well as comprehend materials and other aspects of architecture.

The information, approach, and logic are the same for computer drafting as for conventional drafting; only the tools of the drafter change.

Word Processing. The growing popularity of word processing in architectural offices is due mainly to its competitive price and its easy application to architectural uses. Also, the advent of minicomputers has made word processing accessible to even small firms.

The basic equipment used in word processing is as follows:

1. Hardware
   - A monitor (almost any television can be adapted)
   - A minicomputer
   - A disk drive (similar to a record player but smaller in size)
   - A printer (similar to a typewriter without a keyboard)
2. Software
   - A program (contains the instructions that make the processor work)

These instructions are stored on a disk (like a small record) and loaded into the computer memory by way of the disk drive. The desired text is then typed into the computer on the keyboard, which is usually mounted on the computer, and the text is saved (memorized) on the disk. This information can be retrieved at any time and can be changed, corrected, or updated through the program.

The program allows you to change the margin, remove undesirable items, and select the type of printing and medium desired. The medium can be a sheet of typing paper, vellum, or even adhesive film. Specifications can be typed and stored for future use; engineering calculations can be stored; reports, letters—even employee records—can be stored and easily retrieved.

Drafting Appliques and Manufacturers' Literature. Architectural offices often use manufacturers' literature and their details. More recently, offices have been using manufacturers' literature and drawings together with applique film. Erasable applique film is used, and the desired drawing supplied by the manufacturer is first printed by a plain paper copier or with the diazo process; second, changed or corrected to meet specific needs; and last, applied to the original vellum sheet. This saves time and the cost of developing the detail from scratch.

Recognizing the practicality of this method, many manufacturers now provide appliques upon request as part of product promotion.

Screen Drafting. This method adds a screen to the printing of the original drawing. The screen is film made up of microscopic dots which produce a partial light barrier. Screens are available in a variety of percentages: some block 20% of the light, others 80%, and so on. When used with an original drawing, the screen produces a gray copy instead of black.

Diazo (Screen) Drafting. For diazo (screen) drafting, a sepia print is made first. The diazo machine is reduced in speed in order to produce a light but readable and reproducible sepia print. This sepia print can now serve as the background for a structural or electrical plan, or a heating and air-conditioning layout, for example. When reprinted on the diazo machine, the reproduction emphasizes the material that has been drafted on and deemphasizes (or "screens") the original drawing, while still showing the relationship between them.

Photography and Drafting.   Photography plays a large part in architectural drafting. "Blueprint service" companies have rapidly begun to employ methods of reproduction other than diazo. Many use plain paper copiers and many companies have also added photography. The older photographic method used produced a "photostat." This is rapidly being replaced by the "photo mechanical transfer" (PMT) system. In this process, there is no real negative. Rather, there is an intermediate paper negative that takes about 30 seconds to make; then the image is transferred from this throwaway master to a positive.

Still the best process and the most versatile is regular camera photography. The only limit to the size of print is the equipment itself, and 36" × 42" negatives are now available. Since negatives can be spliced together, the final limit is only restricted by the size of the positive paper available. Uses of photography are described later.

Some stationery suppliers and reproduction centers can take 35 mm slides and produce transparent 8½" × 11" copies by using a 35 mm projector, a plain paper copier, and acetate film.

Reprodrafting

"Reprodrafting" is a term used to describe a number of approaches to improving or revising drafted material in a way that takes advantage of photographic or photocopying processes. These approaches have spawned a number of new terms, including eraser drafting, paste-up drafting, photo-drafting, overlay drafting, pen drafting, and scissors drafting. Reprodrafting, then, actually consists of many processes.

Restoration.   Restoration refers to the process of taking a photograph of an old original or an old print and, by repairing the negative, producing a new master.

Composite Drafting.   Composite drafting is the photographic process of making a single drawing from many, or of taking parts of other drawings to make a new drawing. You will often hear the terms "paste-up," "scissors," "eraser," and "photo-drafting" being used in connection with this process.

Paste-up drafting simply refers to the process of pasting pieces onto a single master sheet, and then photographing and reproducing them. The lines on the negative made by edges of the pieces can be eliminated by the photo retoucher.

Scissors drafting takes an existing drawing and eliminates undesirable or corrected portions by cutting them out before the paste-up process. **Eraser drafting** is similar, but the unwanted portions are simply erased. In both cases, the original is never touched. A good copy on good quality paper is produced first. The copy must be printed in a way that allows easy erasure.

Photo-drafting, as the name indicates, uses drafting and photography. It begins with a photograph of any drawing, such as a plan, elevation, or detail. The drawing is printed on a matte-surfaced film and additional information drafted onto it.

Photo-drafting is an ideal method for dealing with historical restoration drawings. The building to be restored is photographed and printed (to scale) on a matte-surfaced film. Required information, such as dimensions, and methods of restoration are added to this photographic reprint.

All of these methods can be intermixed. For example, a floor plan for an apartment can be drawn once, printed onto an applique film, and then cut and joined on the master sheet to produce a composite of the apartment units. A print of this drawing on a new master allows for the addition of notes and dimensions.

Photo-drafting can be used in conjunction with appliques to show surrounding areas, structural location of various parts of a building, and proposed structural additions or relocations. Applique film is either opaque or transparent. Opaque applique is used in a part of scissors drafting and requires photography, while the transparency applique becomes part of the original and can use the diazo process.

Erasable copies of details can be made, updated, and changed to meet the needs of the specific job, and can be applied right onto a portion of an existing drawing. This allows more than one person to work on a given sheet at the same time.

As with diazo drafting, a screen can also be used photographically to produce a gray image for printing on vellum. This allows any added materials to stand out against the gray. This process enables the same master to be reproduced over and over again for the various plans, such as the electrical and framing plans, thus avoiding errors.

Another advantage of photography is the ease with which it allows the scale of a drawing to be changed accurately. If a floor plan drafted at ¼" = 1'–0" scale is to be used for another drawing, such as a roof framing plan at ⅛" or ¹⁄₁₆" scale, it can be reduced photographically, thus saving many hours of work.

One of the best uses for photography is in preparing plans for highly repetitive structures such as apartments, hospitals, schools, and industrial buildings.

Overlay Drafting.   One of the most significant changes in the production of architectural working drawings is the introduction of overlay drafting or registration drafting. It is a systems approach that works mainly for plans and can be incorporated into CAD. While this is a difficult procedure to learn, with practice and organization, the time savings can be great. Some governmental agencies require this procedure.

The concept of overlay drafting has been used in the printing industry for many years and more recently in the aircraft industry. Overlay drafting combines a base drawing and a series of overlays, ending up with a single drawing. To keep the base sheet aligned with the overlays, a registration bar with pins is used. For this reason, overlay drafting is often called **pin registration.** See Figure 2.1. On a computer, registration can be done automatically, because you can draw one layer over the other while it is being displayed.

Another way to keep the base sheet aligned with the overlay sheets is to use registration marks similar to those in Figure 2.2. Note the two strips of metal shown in Figure 2.1; one is 26½" long with seven ¼"-round registration buttons, and the other much shorter with three buttons. The longer strip is for drawings and the smaller for photographic negatives. The negatives of all the drawings are made at a reduced scale for storage and cost purposes.

A floor plan can be drawn on a prepunched base sheet. See Figure 2.3. Using a pin registration strip, a second prepunched sheet is layed over the base sheet, and the notes and dimensions are placed on the overlay sheet. A title block and border line can be drawn on the third sheet. If the plan follows a specific module, a grid might be drawn on a fourth sheet.

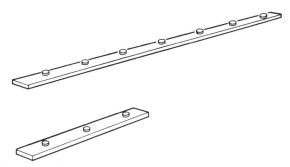

Figure 2.1 Pin registration strips.

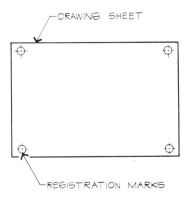

Figure 2.2 Registration marks.

A reduced negative of each sheet is then made, and the four negatives are exposed onto a single print at the original size. This print is called a **blow back.** The result is a composite of the original floor plan with notes and dimensions, title block, and a grid forming the finished product.

Copies are made of the original floor plan and sent to the consultants. Each of the consultants then overlays the original copy of the floor plan and places particular information on the overlay. Reduced negatives are again made of each of the overlays completed by the consultants. These negatives are combined with the original negative of the original floor plan and grid, and printed on a blow back form.

At this point, a dot screen can be introduced to reduce the darkness of the lines. The screen can be placed so that the floor plan and the grid are gray while the consultant's information is dark, thus providing sharp contrast. See Figure 2.4. This procedure is most effective in preparing plans for a multistory building where the greater the combination of overlays, the less the drafting, and thus the greater effectiveness of the whole system.

If the overlay system is used in conjunction with another system, the possibilities are endless. For example, in a structure where there is a repetition of a basic plan, the floor plan can be drafted at ¼" scale, photographically reduced in quantity at ⅛" scale, assembled by scissors drafting, and used as a base sheet for subsequent drawings. Applications for planning and urban design are shown in Figure 2.5.

Other Shortcut Methods

Anytime you combine lines and words in chart form, you can take a number of approaches. Drawing lines in pencil and then lettering directly on the chart is not always the best approach.

Drawing on the Reverse Side.   You can draw lines on the reverse side of the drawing surface and letter on the opposite side. This allows easy correction. You can then erase lettering without disturbing the lines.

Combining Ink and Pencil.   You can use ink for the lines and pencil for the lettering. The ink lines can be drawn on either side of the vellum.

Saving the Original Drawing.   A sepia print can be made from the original, whether it is in pencil or ink. The lettering is then done on the sepia, saving the original.

Using Standardized Sheets.   If an office uses a standardized sheet for all jobs or specializes in a particular building type which calls for the same information each time, a more permanent procedure can be followed.

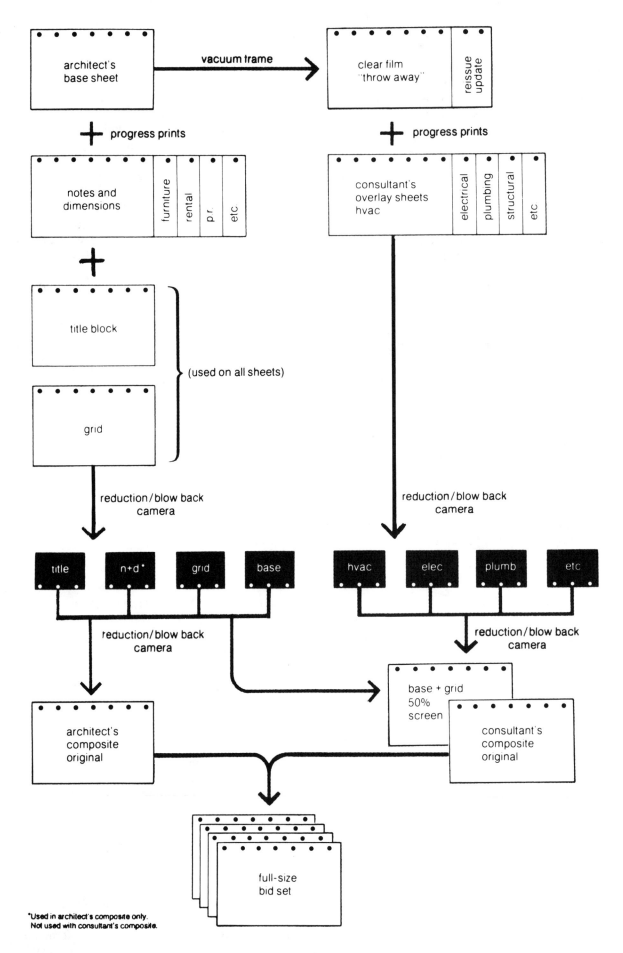

Figure 2.3 Multidwelling residential. (Courtesy of Keuffel & Esser Co., Morristown, N.J.)

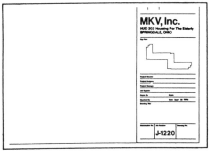
Title Block

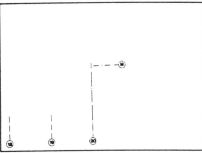
Grid

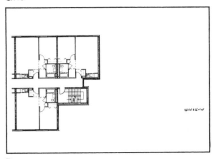
Base

Title block

The Title Block, which is often one separate sheet, can be printed onto punched mylar for all sheets except the Grid and Architectural Base. This allows each consultant to fill out the specific information as to drawings number, name, etc. more readily. This also applies to the Architectural Notes and Dimension sheets, and reduces cost of printing progress prints. Printed and punched sheets are useful for quickly putting down detail sheets on drafting table's pin bar.

Grid

Grid is best kept as separate sheet since for many plan drawings it is not wanted, for some drawings it is screened, for others it is kept solid.

Composite

Composite sheet can be developed in a number of ways for different purposes. Offset colored prints can be issued as half size as an information set for the bidding contractors. It can be used in-house as check sets for the architect and his consultants for final coordination prior to bidding. Notes and dimensions that interfere from one trade to the next can be blocked out on the negative to allow clearer reading. Such a composite sheet is also a valuable guide for preparation of coordinated ceiling shop drawings.

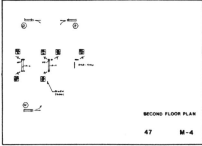
Air Conditioning

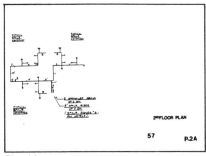
Plumbing

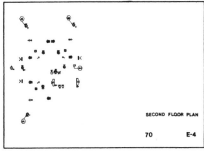
Electrical

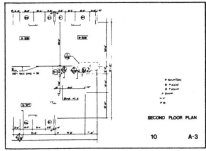
Notes & Dimensions

Courtesy of
**Maple Knoll Village, Inc.
Springdale, Ohio**
Gruzen & Partners, Architects

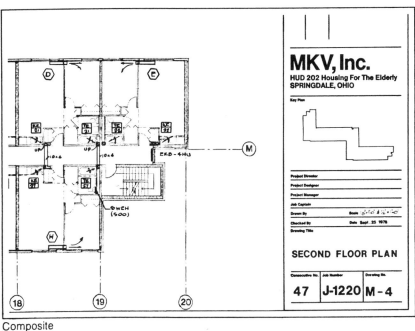
Composite

Figure 2.4 Composite drafting. (Courtesy of Keuffel & Esser Co., Morristown, N.J.)

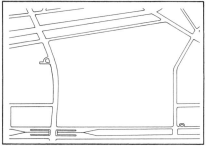

Curbs

Bldgs.

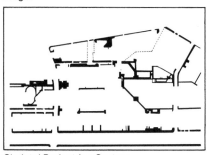

Skeletal Pedestrian System

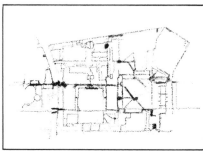

Winter Pedestrian System

Notes

Living Documents

In general, planning studies become frozen in time in the form of an immutable printed report. Since these documents serve little purpose other than for historical reference, there is a way through the pin register system to make them useful *living documents.* As projects become actual structures or forms, they can be photographically incorporated as background information, with future plans retained as overlays. As new data is collected, it can also be produced in the form of an overlay. Therefore, such information as traffic densities, neighborhood character, urban demolition, environmental influences, etc., can be incorporated with the original report to form a complete and living document.

Planning and Urban Design

Master Planning, Regional Planning, Urban Design, Feasibility Studies and all other planning efforts are made easier and more effective with the use of overlay drafting. The illustration on this page is a good example of a living document. It shows the overlays used in the 1978 planning study of Massachusetts Institute of Technology. The development of this 20 year plan for the Institute's East Campus is the work of Mitchel-Giurgola/Gruzen & Partners.

"As-Builts"

As a result of the pin register system, M.I.T. will easily be able to keep vital data of campus information current and incorporate as-built data at large scale. Through the use of reduction/blow back camera, ⅛" or 1/16" = 1'-0" can be turned into more useful campus plans at smaller engineering scales of 1" = 50', 100', and 200'.

By overlays, information can be stored and updated separately such as: campus steam, chilled water, water supply, standpipe and sprinkler systems, storm and sanitary, natural gas, electric service, lighting, signal, computer cable systems, roads, pedestrian walks, fire fighting access, security, building delivery, landscaping, planting maintenance and watering systems.

Overlays shown are skeletal pedestrian system, winter pedestrian system, and annotations of titles. Large composite drawing illustrates winter pedestrian system.

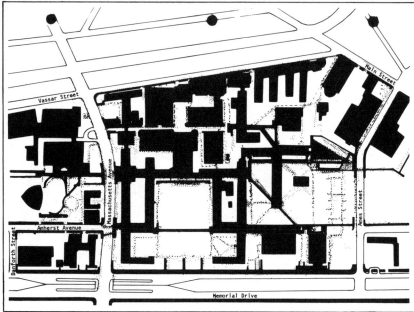

Composite

Figure 2.5 Planning and urban design. (Courtesy of Keuffel & Esser Co., Morristown, N.J.)

The standardized form can be xeroxed onto vellum or reproduced photographically in one of two ways. First obtain a negative to make a print plate and print the image on vellum. This can usually be done through a blueprint reproduction service that also provides photographic services. This negative can then be used to expose a sensitized vellum and make a photographic reproduction on vellum.

Using Standard Titles. Using any number of the procedures previously described, you can produce standard titles such as those found under a drawing or title block, to keep the lettering of titles uniform. Lettering machines which produce letters on a sticky-backed tape are now available with interchangeable type styles and sizes. The final product resembles rub-on letters on adhesive tape.

For example, you can produce the term "floor plan" with rub-on letters or a lettering machine and then reproduce the term in quantity. You can cut out the multiple copies, position them on a sheet, which you can then use as a master to produce appliques with a plain paper copier and adhesive transparent film. In this way, you can cut titles from the adhesive and apply them to the various sheets as needed.

Office Standards

Sheet Size

The drawing sheet size varies from office to office depending on the type of work performed, the method of reproduction used, and the system of drafting used in the office. The most common sheet sizes are 24″ × 36″, 28″ × 42″, and 30″ × 42″.

When sheets are used horizontally, they are usually bound on the left side. Because of this, the border is larger on the left side. A typical border line is 3/8″ to 1/2″ around three sides and 1″ to 1 1/2″ on the left side.

Title blocks can run the full height of the right side rather than simply filling a square in the bottom right corner, as in mechanical drafting. The long title band contains such information as sheet number, client's name or project title, name of firm, name or title of the drawing, person drafting, scale, date, and revision dates. The title block sheets are usually preprinted or can be applied to sheets in the form of decals or appliques.

This location of the title block allows you to leave a rectangular area for drawing purposes, whereas a title block in the lower right corner produces an L-shaped drawing area. (Even when drawing on a large sheet, take care to draft so that you use the sheet to its fullest.)

Many offices establish a sheet module. Here is an example of this method with a 24″ × 36″ sheet:

Binding side	1 1/2″ border
Other 3 sides	1/2″ border
Title block	1 1/2″

This leaves a drawing area of 23″ × 32 1/2″. The vertical 23″ distance can be divided into four equal parts, while the horizontal 32 1/2″ can be divided into 8 equal parts. This provides 32 spaces 4 1/16″ wide by 5 3/4″ high. This office procedure may be followed so that each sheet has a consistent appearance. Whether the sheet is full of details or a combination of a plan and details and/or notes, the module gives you parameters within which to work. You should draft from the right side of the sheet so that any blank spaces remaining are toward the inside (on the binding side).

Lettering Height

The height of lettering depends on the type of reproduction used. If you use normal diazo methods, use the following standards as a rule of thumb:

Main titles under drawings	1/4″ maximum
Subtitles	3/16″
Normal lettering	3/32″–1/8″
Sheet number in title block	1/2″

Increase these sizes when you are reducing drawings. For example, increase normal lettering from 3/32″ to 1/8″ or 3/16″, depending on the reduction ratio.

Scale of Drawings

The scale selected should be the largest practical scale based on the size of the structure and the drawing space available. Listed below are the most common sizes used by offices, with the most desirable size being underlined where there is a choice.

Site Plan: 1/8″ = 1′–0″ for small sites. Drawings are provided by a civil engineer and scales are expressed in engineering terms such as 1″ = 30′, 1″ = 50′, etc.

Floor Plan: 1/4″ = 1′–0″, 1/8″ or 1/16″ = 1′–0″ for larger structures.

Exterior Elevations: Same as the floor plan.

Building Sections: 1/2″ = 1′–0″ if possible or the same as exterior elevations.

Interior Elevations: 1/4″ = 1′–0″, 3/8″ = 1′–0″, 1/2″ = 1′–0″.

Architectural Details: 1/2″ = 1′–0″ to 3″ = 1′–0″, depending on the size of the object being drawn or the amount of information that must be shown. Footing detail: 3/4″ = 1′–0″ or 1″ = 1′–0″. Eave details: 1 1/2″ = 1′–0″. Wall sections: typically, 3/4″ = 1′–0″.

Framing (Roof, Floor, Ceiling): Either the same size as the floor plan, so that it can be superimposed on the floor plan, or smaller.

Materials in Section

Figures 2.6, 2.7, 2.8, and 2.9 show the various methods used throughout the United States to represent different materials in section.

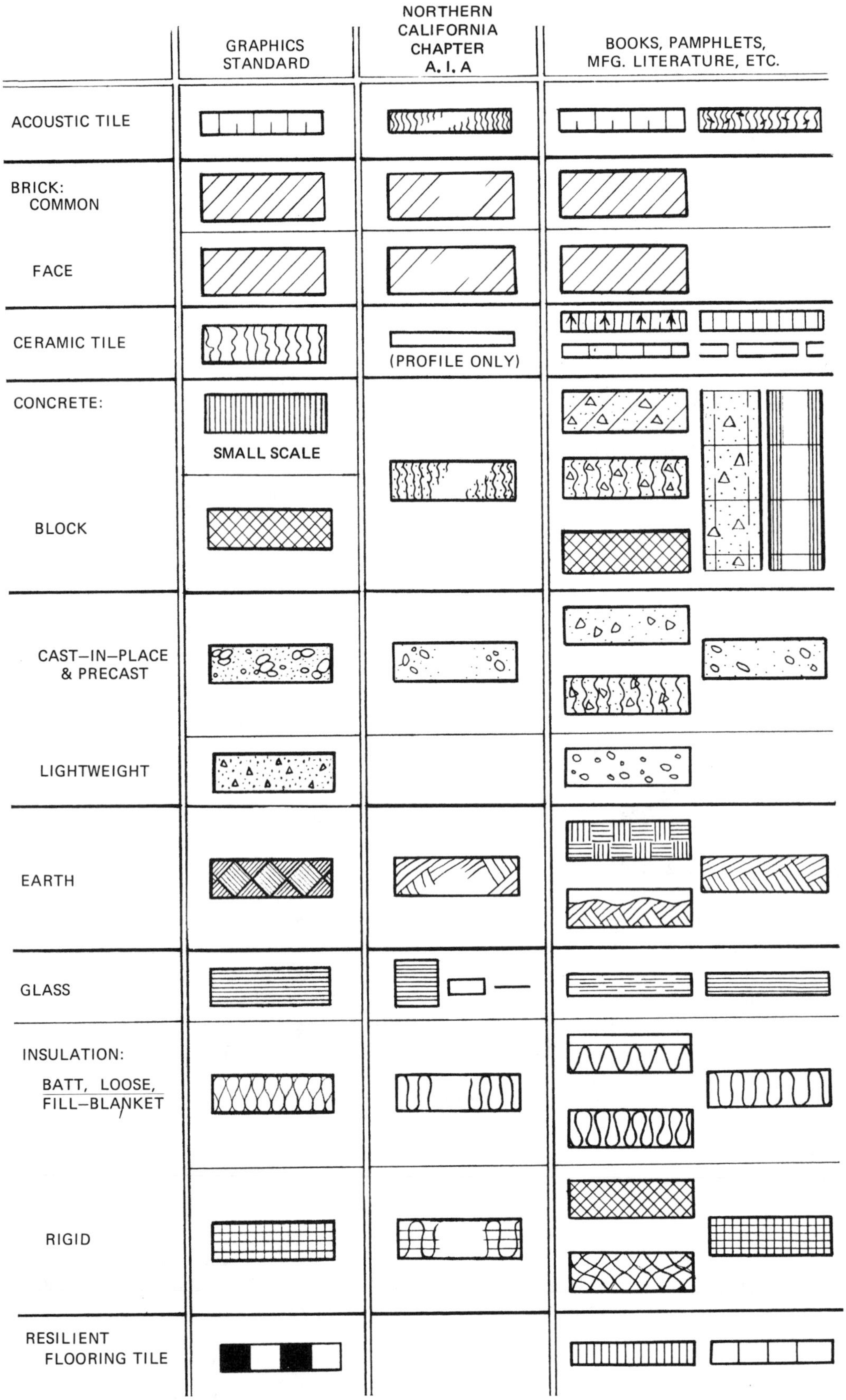

	GRAPHICS STANDARD	NORTHERN CALIFORNIA CHAPTER A.I.A	BOOKS, PAMPHLETS, MFG. LITERATURE, ETC.
ACOUSTIC TILE			
BRICK: COMMON			
FACE			
CERAMIC TILE		(PROFILE ONLY)	
CONCRETE:	SMALL SCALE		
BLOCK			
CAST−IN−PLACE & PRECAST			
LIGHTWEIGHT			
EARTH			
GLASS			
INSULATION: BATT, LOOSE, FILL−BLANKET			
RIGID			
RESILIENT FLOORING TILE			

Figure 2.6 Materials in section.

	GRAPHICS STANDARD	NORTHERN CALIFORNIA CHAPTER A. I. A.	BOOKS, PAMPHLETS, MFG. LITERATURE, ETC.
METAL: ALUMINUM			
BRASS—BRONZE			
STEEL			
METAL: LARGE SCALE		(NO INDICATION IN THIN MATERIAL)	
SMALL SCALE (STRUCT. & SHEET)			
PLASTER: SAND, CEMENT, GROUT			
GYPSUM WALL BOARD			
ROCK & STONE: ROCK			
STONE, GRAVEL, POROUS FILL			(SMALL SCALE)
SLATE, FLAGGING, SOAPSTONE, BLUESTONE			
MARBLE			
ROUGH—CUT			
RUBBLE			
TERRAZZO		(PROFILE ONLY)	

Figure 2.7 Materials in section.

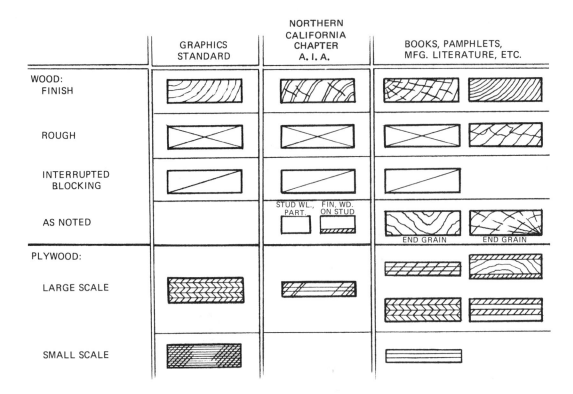

* TO SAVE VALUABLE DRAFTING TIME, THE NORTHERN CALIFORNIA
CHAPTER RECOMMENDS THAT THE TOTAL DETAIL IN SECTION
NOT BE FILLED IN COMPLETELY BUT JUST ENOUGH TO INDICATE
THE MATERIAL IN QUESTION.

Figure 2.8 Materials in section.

In the first column are material designations assembled by the Committee on Office Practice, American Institute of Architects (National) and published in *Architectural Graphic Standards*. The second column designations are prepared by the Task Force on Production Office Procedures of the Northern California Chapter of the American Institute of Architects. The final column lists items from other sources such as pamphlets, manufacturers' literature, textbooks, governmental agencies, and trade and technical organizations or associations.

Clearly, there is standardization and there are variations. For example, all groups agree on the method of representing brick in section, yet there is a great variation in the way concrete block is represented in section.

The last figure shows specialty items from a variety of sources.

Graphic Symbols

The symbols in Figure 2.10 are the most common and acceptable, to judge by the frequency of use by the architectural offices surveyed. This list can be and should be expanded by each office to include those symbols generally used in its practice and not indicated here. Again, each professional is urged to accept the

task force recommendation by adopting the use of these symbols.

Abbreviations

Suggested abbreviations compiled by Task Force #1, National Committee on Office Practice, American Institute of Architects, and published in the AIA *Journal* can be found in the Appendix at the end of this book.

Dimensioning

Dimensioning is the act of incorporating numerical values into drawing as a means of sizing various components and also locating parts of a building. This is accomplished on dimension lines, in notes, and by referral to other drawings or details.

Grouping Dimensions. Group dimensions whenever possible to provide continuity. This takes planning. Try running a diazo print of the drawing in question and dimension it on this check print first. This will allow you to identify dimensions and decide how they can be effectively grouped.

Maintaining a Dimension Standard. The most important dimensions dictate subsequent dimensions. For ex-

ADDITIONAL MATERIALS IN SECTION

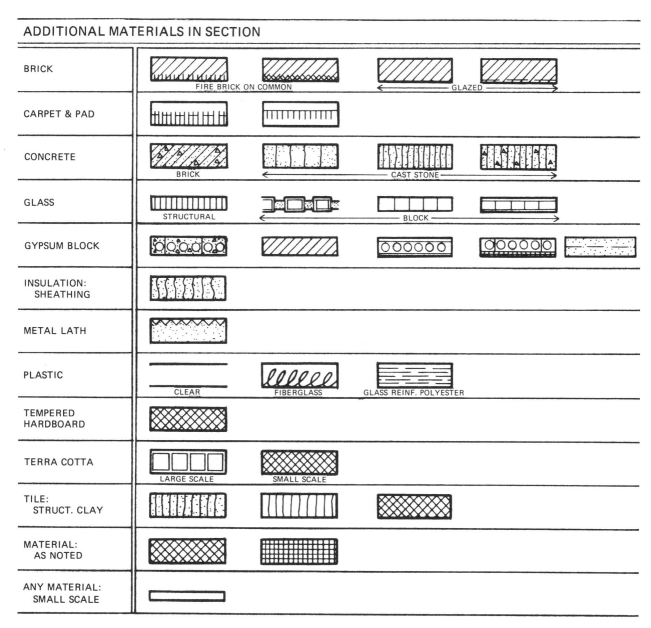

Figure 2.9 Additional materials in section.

ample, if a wall is dimensioned to the center of the wall first, all subsequent dimensions using this wall as a reference point should be dimensioned at its center.

Size Dimensions and Location Dimensions. The two basic kinds of **dimensions** are size and location. See Figure 2.11. Size dimensions indicate overall size. Location dimensions deal with the actual placement of an object or structure, such as a wall, a window, a concrete patio slab, a barbecue grill, or a planter.

The Dimensional Reference System. The dimensional reference system is based on a three-dimensional axis. See Figure 2.12. Critical planes are located by a series of reference bubbles and used as **planes of reference.** Fig-

ure 2.13 shows a box; reference bubbles describe the three planes of height, width, and depth. Now examine this box sliced in two directions as shown in Figures 2.14 and 2.15. The first slice produces a **horizontal control plane,** and the second a **vertical control plane.**

The shaded area in Figure 2.16 represents a horizontal plane at a critical point on the structure, such as the floor line. The shaded area on Figure 2.17 represents a vertical plane at a critical point of the structure, such as the location of a series of columns or beams. There is a definite relationship between the vertical control plane and the horizontal control plane. Compare the **plan** and the **section** shown in Figure 2.18. The section is a vertical cut as in Figure 2.17 and the plan is a horizontal cut as in Figure 2.16. The two vertical and one horizontal

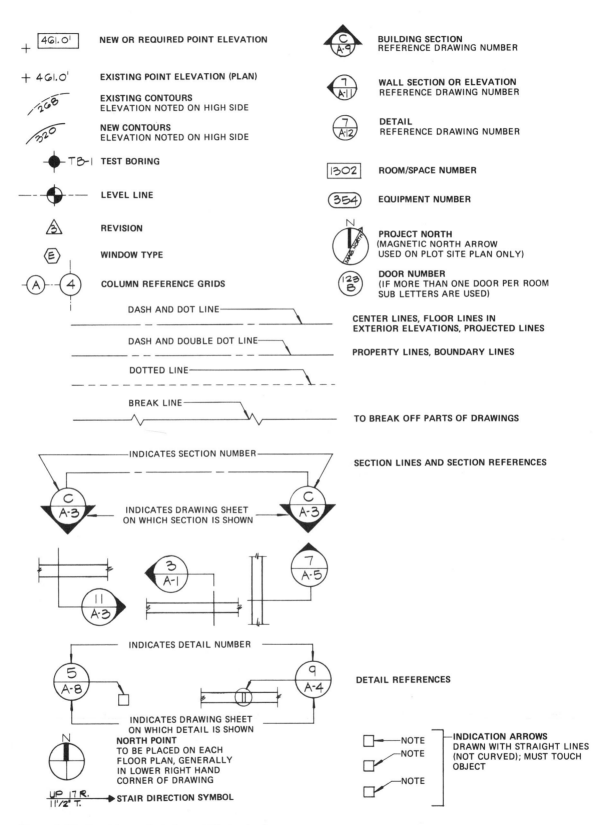

Figure 2.10 Graphic symbols from AIA standards.

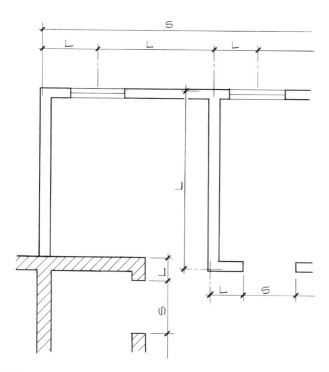

Figure 2.11 Size and location dimensions.

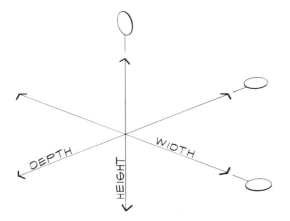

Figure 2.12 Dimensional reference system.

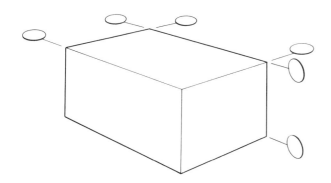

Figure 2.13 Three principle planes using dimensional reference system.

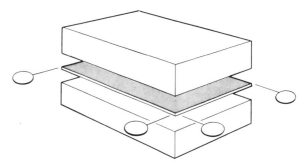

Figure 2.14 Horizontal control plane.

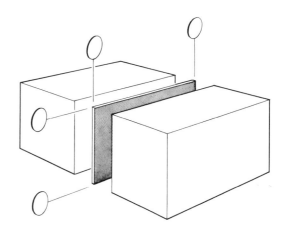

Figure 2.15 Vertical control plane.

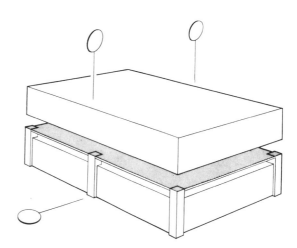

Figure 2.16 Horizontal plane.

reference bubbles on Figure 2.16 are an attempt to show this relationship.

Types of Planes.   There are two types of planes. The first is the **axial plane,** which goes through the center of critical structural items as shown in Figure 2.19. Note how the columns are dimensioned to the center. When pilasters (widening of a masonry wall for support) are used, they become a good location for control dimensions, as they support the structural members above.

The second type of plane is called a **boundary control plane.** See Figure 2.20. In this case, columns and walls are not dimensioned to the center; instead, their

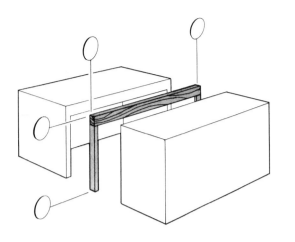

Figure 2.17 Vertical plane.

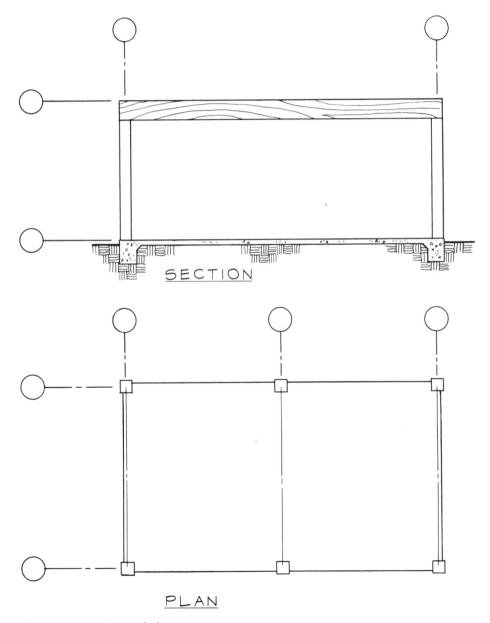

SECTION

PLAN

Figure 2.22 Section and plan.

Figure 2.18 Section and plan.

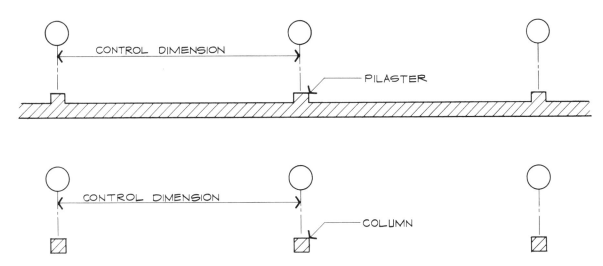

Figure 2.19 Axial control planes.

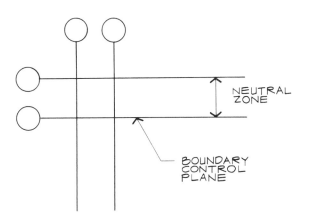

Figure 2.20 Boundary control planes.

boundaries are dimensioned. Figure 2.21 shows examples of columns and walls located in the **neutral zone.** These neutral zones are especially valuable in dealing with the vertical dimensions of a section and with elevations. See Figure 2.22. A neutral zone is established between the ceiling and the floor above. The floor-to-ceiling heights can be established to allow the structural, mechanical, and electrical consultants to perform their work. Once that dimension is established, the neutral zone and floor-to-floor dimensions follow. See Figure 2.23 for a practical application of the **vertical control dimension** and control zone (another term for neutral zone).

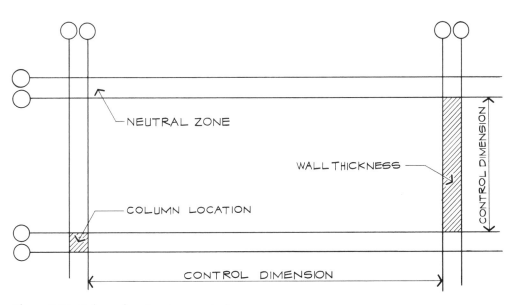

Figure 2.21 Column location in a neutral zone.

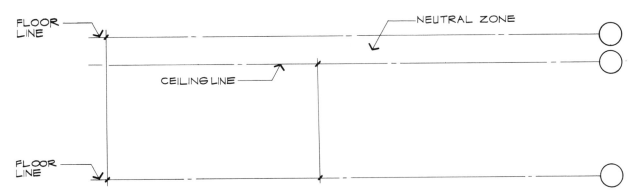

Figure 2.22 Neutral zone in a vertical dimension.

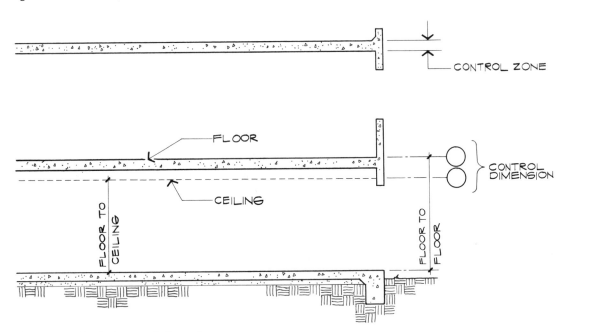

Figure 2.23 Vertical control dimension.

Metrics

Conversion to metric numbers is a change in total concept and attitude that must be incorporated at the basic design stage. Never design in feet and inches and then convert to metric; it creates undesirable metric measurements. Unfortunately, manufacturers of building materials have not been converting consistently to the metric system. Lumber, steel, and masonry units will soon have standards established, but until they are in effect, there is an interim period which involves simple conversion of numbers.

The English system uses different basic units. Liquid is measured differently from linear measurements and weight; for example, 4 quarts = 1 gallon, 12 inches = 1 foot, and 16 ounces = 1 pound.

In the metric system, while the names for liquid, weight, and linear measurements are different, their units are based on tenths, which avoids so much memorizing.

Nomenclature

Since the architectural field deals predominantly with linear measurements, this discussion emphasizes the conversion of feet and inches to metric equivalents.

The largest metric unit of measurement for use in the construction industry is the meter. The most recent standard measurement of a meter is the measurement of the swing of a pendulum during a one-second period. This swinging pendulum is made of platinum and is located at 45° latitude in France. Because of the nature of the way the standard meter is measured and the location of this standard, the length of a meter varies slightly throughout the world. It is hoped that attempts at standardization by the International Standards Organization (ISO) will prove successful, because if different lengths are used for the standard meter, building products made in one country might not correspond to the needs of another.

A meter comprises ten decimeters which, in turn, each comprise ten centimeters. The smallest unit of conversion is the millimeter. Ten meters make a deca-meter; ten times that is a hectometer; and ten times that is a kilometer. Here is a chart showing these values.

kilometer	= 1,000 meters	km
*hectometer	= 100 meters	hm
*decameter	= 10 meters	dam
meter		m
*decimeter	= ¹/₁₀ meter	dm
centimeter	= ¹/₁₀₀ meter	cm
millimeter	= ¹/₁₀₀₀ meter	mm

*Seldom used in modern drawings.

For architectural drafting, the millimeter and the meter are the most desirable units to use.

Notation Method

Locate the decimal point in the center of the line of numerical value rather than close to the bottom of the line. For example, 304.65 is best written 304·65. However, the original notation is acceptable.

Commas are not used. Rather, spaces are left to de-note where commas would have been. For example 10·34674 meters would be written 10·346 74 meters, and 506,473·21 meters would be written as 506 473·21 meters.

Abbreviations of metric units do not have special plural forms. For example, fifty centimeters is written 50 cm, *not* 50 cms. Note, also, the space between the number and the letters. It should read 50, space, centimeters: 50 cm.

Once a standard, such as "all measurements shall be in meters," is established for a set of drawings, it need not be noted on each drawing. A 4 by 8 sheet of ply-wood should be called out not as 121 9·2 m × 243 8·4 m plywood but rather as 121 9·2 × 243 8·4 plywood. However, if a size is in a measure other than meters, this should be noted.

English Equivalents

Here is a quick reference chart for converting linear measurements into metrics:

Length: inches × 2·54	= centimeters (cm)
feet × 0·304 8	= meters (m)
yards × 0·914 4	= meters (m)
miles × 1·609 34	= kilometers (km)
Mass: pounds × 0·453 592	= kilograms (kg)
ounces × 28·35	= grams (g)

General Conversion Rules

Using the equivalent values just given, you can convert by multiplication. For example, 16 inches is:

inches × 2·54 = cm
16 in. × 2·54 = 40·64 cm

To convert 25 feet into metric measurements:

feet × 0·304 8 = m
25 ft. × 0·304 8 = 7·62 m

To convert 75 yards into meters:

yards × 0·914 4 = m
75 yd.× 0·914 4 = 68·58 m

Unit Change

To convert 17 feet 8 inches, follow this procedure:

17 ft. × 0·304 8 = 5·181 6 cm
8 in. × 2·54 = 20·32 cm

In this example, conversion of feet results in meters, and conversion of inches results in centimeters. You cannot add these quantities unless you convert them to the same unit of measurement. Do this simply by mov-ing the decimal point. In this example, if meters are desired, simply move the decimal point of the centi-meter unit two units to the left: 20·32 cm are equal to .203 2 m. Thus,

17 ft. = 5·181 6 m
8 in. = ·203 2 m
5·384 8 m

Actual Versus Nominal

Presently, lumber uses an odd system of notation. When a piece of lumber is drawn, it is drafted to its actual size (net size). In the notes describing this particular piece of wood, it is called out in its nominal size (call out size). For example, a 2 × 4 piece of wood is drawn at 1½" × 3½", but on the note pointing to this piece, it is still called a 2 × 4.

Therefore, when converting to metric, the 1½" × 3½" size must be converted and drawn to the actual size. There is no set procedure for the call out. Some draw-ings convert the 2 × 4 size metrically and note this piece of wood with the 1½" × 3½" size converted. A sample note might read as follows:

·0381 × ·0889 (net) STUD

It is hoped that when metric lumber size is established, the net and nominal sizes will be identical.

Using Double Standards

Due to the newness of using metrics in the American architectural profession, we are not yet geared to note things metrically. Lumber, reinforcing, glass, and other materials are still ordered in the English system. Their sizes, weights, and shapes are also still described in the English system.

There are three approaches to this situation. First, we can note only those things we have control over in metrics, such as the size of a room, the width of a footing, and so on, while noting 2 × 4 studs, #4 reinforcing rods, ½″ anchor bolts, and the like, according to the manufacturer until they change to the metric system.

A second method is dual notation. This system requires dimensions, notes, and all call outs to be recorded twice. For example, a 35′–6″ dimension has a metric value of 10·820 4 written directly below it. If most workers are operating under the old system, they can ignore the metric value and refer to the English system. If, however, the majority of the workers use the metric figure, you have prepared a value that cannot be measured accurately because the decimal is carried out too far. This problem is dealt with later.

The third and final method is to approach everything metrically. This may not be the best way in an office going through a transition, but it is the best student method because you will eventually be asked to work totally in metrics.

Conversion of Drafting

If we are to convert everything to metrics, there are three procedures to consider. First is that of "holding" certain dimension notes and call outs. If, for example, we are dealing with a #4 rebar (which is a steel reinforcing bar ½″ in size) and the manufacturer has not changed to metrics, we must convert the ½″ by multiplying ½″ × 2·54 and note the rebar as:

1·27 cm rebar
or
0·0127 rebar

The second procedure requires "rounding off." See Figure 2.24. In this figure, the scale on the top is an enlarged one that you are accustomed to seeing. The scale directly below is in the same enlarged proportion but in metric units. The numbers in this scale are in centimeters. Notice that 2·54 centimeters equal an inch. Notice also that one centimeter is less than ½ inch. Initially, this is a hard proportion to relate to for anyone making the transition. Also note that half a centimeter (0·5 cm) is smaller than ¼ inch and that one millimeter (one tenth of a centimeter) is less than 1/16 of an inch.

Now compare this knowledge with an actual number. Assume that you wish to dig a trench 12 inches wide for a footing.

12 inches = (12 × 2·54) = 30·48 cm

Hence, there are 30+ units less than ½ inch in size that we can measure. The .4 is less than 3/16″, which is very difficult to measure and impossible to deal with on the

job for a worker. This is the point when we should begin to round off.

The final number (0·08) is even worse. It amounts to just a little more than 1/32 of an inch—a measurement that a draftsperson would have difficulty even reading on the scale, and that the person digging the trench would have to ignore. The final rounded off value should be 31·0 cm or 0·31. This trench is about 3/16 inches wider than the desired 12 inches but is something the people out in the field can measure with their metric scales.

The third conversion procedure requires judgement about whether to increase or decrease. Certain measurements must be increased in the rounding off process—the trench discussed previously is a good example. If we round this number off to 30·0 cm or 0·30, the measurement is less than 2 inches. If the 12 inch requirement had been imposed by the local code, you would have thus broken the code. Had it been set at 12 inches for structural reasons, the building could be deemed unsafe. Another example is a planned opening for a piece of equipment. To round off to the smaller number might result in the equipment's not fitting.

You must be aware of situations that are dictated by health and safety. The minimum depth of a step might be 10½″ or 26·67 cm. If we rounded this off to 26·0 cm, it would not meet the minimum standards for a stair. Another kind of danger lies in exceeding a required maximum. For example, the note for an anchor bolt reads:

½″ × 10″; to anchor bolt embedded 7″ into concrete 6′–0″ o.c. and 12″ from corners.

The spacing of 6′–0″ on center is used to maintain a minimum number of anchor bolts per unit of length. If we increase the distance between bolts, we exceed the required spacing, and as stated in the note reduce the number of bolts per unit of length below the minimum required.

The 12-inch measurement has the same effect. The intent is to have an anchor bolt 12 inches or less from

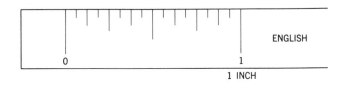

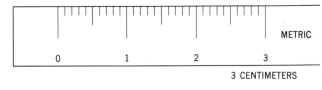

Figure 2.24 Comparison of english and metric scales.

each of the corners. We must, therefore, decrease the measurement when we round off after converting to metric, to insure that there is an anchor bolt closer than 12 inches from every corner. The ½" × 10" ⏀ (⏀ is a symbol for round) becomes what is called a "holding" measurement since it comes from the manufacturer that way. The final numerical value that reads "embedded 7 inches into concrete" must be thought out wisely. The bolt must be embedded enough for strength, yet left exposed adequately to penetrate a sill (the first piece of wood to come into contact with concrete) and still leave enough space for a washer and a nut.

The second and third processes are called soft conversion; that is, an English measurement is converted directly into a metric equivalent and then rounded off into a workable metric value. A hard conversion is the name given to changing the total approach. It is not just a numerical conversion but a change of media as well. If bricks are the medium for example, the procedure would be to subscribe to a brick that was sized metrically and dimension accordingly.

Listed below are some of the recommended rounding off sizes:

⅛"	=	3·2 mm	1¾"	=	44.0 mm
¼"	=	6·4 mm	2"	=	50·0 mm
⅜"	=	9·5 mm	2½"	=	63·0 mm
½"	=	12·7 mm	3"	=	75·0 mm
⅝"	=	16·0 mm	4"	=	100·0 mm
¾"	=	19·0 mm	6"	=	150·0 mm
⅞"	=	22·0 mm	8"	=	200·0 mm
1"	=	25·0 mm	10"	=	250·0 mm
1¼"	=	32·0 mm	12"	=	300·0 mm
1½"	=	38·0 mm			

Zero is used to avoid error in metrics. For example, .8 is written 0.8 or 0·8.

When other conversions are needed, round off fractions to the nearest 5 mm, inches to the nearest 25 mm, and feet to the nearest 0·1 meter.

Metric Scale

The metric scale is used in the same way as the architectural scales. It reduces a drawing to a selected proportion. You can purchase scales with the following metric scales.

1:5	1:50
1:10	1:75
1:20	1:100
1:25	1:125
1:33⅓	1:200
1:40	

While these proportions may not mean anything initially, let us take one example and see what it means. The 1:10 scale indicates that we are taking a known

measurement (a meter) and making it ten times smaller. See Figure 2.25. In other words, if you visualize a meter (39·37 inches) and squeeze it until it is only one-tenth of its original size, you have a 1:10 ratio scale. Everything you draw is then one-tenth of its original size.

This also applies to any other scale. A 1:50 scale means that the original meter has been reduced to one-fiftieth of its original length. Figures 2.26 and 2.27 show the visual appearance of a 1:50, 1:10, 1:20, and 1:100 as they might be seen on an actual scale. Notice how the meter is to be located so you can translate decimeters and centimeters. To measure 12 inches or 30·48 cm (0·30 48 m) on a 1:10 scale, see Figure 2.28.

If you find it difficult to transfer a drawing scaled in inches and feet to a metric drawing, the chart below should help.

1:10 is approximately 1" = 1'–0" (1:12)
1:20 is approximately ½" = 1'–0" (1:24)
1:50 is approximately ¼" = 1'–0" (1:48)
1:100 is approximately ⅛" = 1'–0" (1:96)

Of the four scales in this chart, the 1:50 and 1:100 come closest to being exact conversions.

The conversion charts for feet to meters, and meters to feet, in Appendix B, Tables B.2 and B.3 greatly reduce the need for arithmetical calculations in converting actual dimensions.

Drawing Sheet Size

When the total conversion to metrics takes place, the change will not only affect the drawing but the sheet size of the drawing paper as well. Listed below are some of the typical sizes used internationally. They are expressed in millimeters (mm).

841 × 1189	105 × 148
594 × 841	74 × 105
420 × 594	52 × 74
297 × 420	37 × 52
210 × 297	26 × 37
148 × 210	

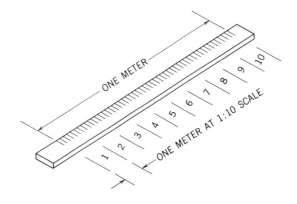

Figure 2.25 Pictorial of reduced metric scale.

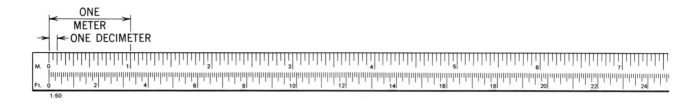

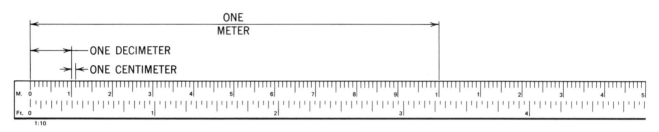

Figure 2.26 How to read an actual scale—1 : 50 and 1 : 10.

Figure 2.27 How to read an actual scale—1 : 20 and 1 : 100.

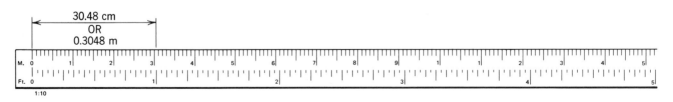

Figure 2.28 One foot equivalent in metric.

A spot check of the various paper companies which sell reproduction paper as well as drawing paper shows that metrically sized paper is already being used for overseas work.

Possible Sizes

Because the various manufacturers have not converted to a uniform size, it is difficult to predict the final evolution of the various building materials. Suggested sizes and those used by other countries are listed below.

Wood (in mm)

38 × 75	44 × 75	50 × 75	63 × 150
38 × 100	44 × 100	50 × 100	63 × 175
38 × 150	44 × 150	50 × 125	63 × 200
38 × 175	44 × 175	50 × 150	63 × 225
38 × 200	44 × 200	50 × 175	
38 × 225	44 × 225	50 × 200	75 × 200
		50 × 300	75 × 300

Brick (in mm)

300 × 100 × 100	200 × 100 × 100
200 × 100 × 75	200 × 200 × 100

Gypsum Lath (in mm)
    9·5   12·7 or 12·00

Miscellaneous
    12 mm diameter for rebar   3 mm for sheet glass
    25 mm for sheathing

Modules

As indicated in Figure 2.29, the standard **module** in metrics is 100 mm. Groups of this standard 100 mm module are called a multi-module. When you select the multi-module, you should consider quantities such as 600 mm, 800 mm, 1200 mm, 1800 mm, and 2400 mm. All of these numbers are divisible in a way that allows you flexibility. For example, the 600 mm multi-module is divisible by 2, 3, 4, and 5. The result of this division gives numbers such as 200, 300, 120, and 150. All of these are numbers for which building materials may be available. This is especially true in masonry units. Most of the sizes listed under "Possible Sizes" work into a 600 mm module. See Figure 2.30.

Sweet's Catalog[1]

Sweet's Catalog File is a retrieval system for the most up-to-date product information. It is a set of volumes that helps people in the construction industry obtain literature and information from the thousands of man-

[1]"Sweet's" is a trademark of McGraw-Hill Inc. Sweet's Catalog Files are copyrighted by McGraw-Hill Inc.

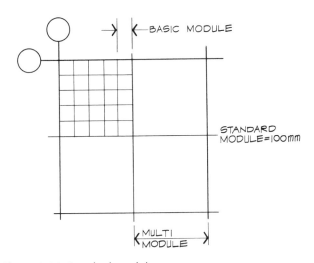

Figure 2.29 Standard module.

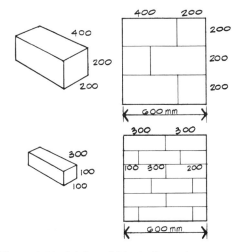

Figure 2.30 Brick and block dimensions.

ufacturers of materials. The beginning of each volume has a complete description of its use. The six basic types of *Sweet's Catalog File* are:

A. Products for General Building and Renovation
    1. Selection Data
    2. Electronic Sweet's
B. Products for Industrial Construction and Renovation
C. Products for Home Building and Remodeling
D. Products for Contract Interiors
E. Products for Engineering and Retrofit
    1. Industrywide Directory
    2. Electronic Sweet's
       a. Mechanical and Related Industrywide Directory
       b. Electrical and Related Industrywide Directory
       c. Civil/Structural and Related
F. Building Products for Export
G. Products for Canadian Construction

Sweet's Catalog Files are a distribution system for catalogs of building product manufacturers who pay to insert their literature. Construction professionals are qualified to receive Sweet's Catalog Files according to the volume and type of projects they carry out.

Architectural offices use mostly the volumes covering "Products for Light Residential Construction" and "Products for General Building."

All sets are based on the "Uniform Construction Index," one of the three major numbering systems used widely in the construction industry. This particular system uses sixteen major divisions:

1. General data
2. Site work
3. Concrete
4. Masonry
5. Metals
6. Wood and plastics
7. Thermal and moisture protection
8. Doors and windows
9. Finishes
10. Specialties
11. Equipment
12. Furnishings
13. Special construction
14. Conveying systems
15. Mechanical
16. Electrical

Each of these major divisions is subsequently subdivided into smaller sections. For example, in Division 8, Doors and Windows, Section 8.1 deals with entrances and storefronts, Section 8.2 with metal doors and frames, and Section 8.32 with exit devices.

An alpha (lower case) numerical system is used when further breakdown is necessary. For example, in Division 11, Equipment, 11.45b deals with incinerators, 11.45c with chutes and collectors. After the number, there is a diagonal slash followed by letters indicating the manufacturer's name. The number 9.13/Du, for example, deals with Division 9, Finishes, and the subsection Wall Coverings; the "Du" stands for DuPont, the manufacturer.

Every volume has the topic and subtopic listed on the spine, on the cover, and on each division sheet. In addition, the front of each volume contains a classification guide listing all of the volumes and subheadings, and a cross reference to other index systems. There is also an index in the front of each book which lists firm name, product name, and trade name. This system is especially helpful if only the trade name or the manufacturer or a broad general classification is known.

In 1982, the Sweet's Catalog set became one volume larger. A new volume called *Selection Data* has now become Volume I. The primary purpose of this volume

is to provide generic information that will help drafters, designers, and architects in the design and development of ideas, and aid them in the selection of the proper product for a specific design problem.

Twenty major categories were selected for this volume:

Cement and Concrete	Floors and Roofs
Stone and Masonry	Roofing
Metals	Insulation
Wood and Wood Products	Sealants and Waterproofing
Glass and Glazine	Facings
Windows and Skylights	Coatings
Entrances and Doors	Partitions and Doors
Curtain Walls	Flooring
Bearing Walls	Ceilings
Enclosures	Solar Control

Each of the major categories contains six topics:

A. Introduction to the material
B. Evaluation charts
C. Selection checklist
D. Firm and product checklist
E. Information sources
F. Energy notes

This gives the reader the proper information to analyze, compare, and select the proper product and manufacturer for a specific design or structural problem.

"Entrances and Doors," alone, contains almost fifty pages, starting with a basic historical background to door definitions and a description of types. This introduction is followed by a visual description of the various types of shapes. Next comes a checklist to aid in selection. An evaluation chart comparing such items as operation, material selection, hinges, locks, weatherstripping, and so on, also will aid in the proper selection of a door.

Availability, by manufacturer, is the next major topic. This is followed by a list of information sources: industry associations, government agencies dealing with doors, professional institutes and agencies, and various regulatory agencies. This list is similar to the Trade, Technical, and Standard organization list found at the end of the book, but deals solely with doors.

Next is the related literature, standard specifications, and testing methods section. The last section has energy notes on the product.

Each category is treated in the same fashion as described for doors, making Volume I a comprehensive tool for anyone involved in architectural decisions.

As a further service "Sweet's Buyline" provides a toll-free telephone number you can call for information on local product distributors or for further manufacturer information.

Manufacturers' Literature

A wealth of product information is available directly from manufacturers in the form of brochures, pamphlets, catalogs, manuals, and even hardbound books. This information may include:

1. Advantages of this product over others
2. Quantitative comparison with others in the trade
3. How the system works or is assembled
4. Necessary engineering
5. Detailed drawings—sometimes on vellum sheets for ease or reproduction
6. Pictorial explanation of the parts and how they are put together
7. Special design features
8. Colors, textures, and patterns available
9. Safety tests that have been performed
10. Dimensions
11. Variations of the products available
12. Ordering instructions
13. Charts and graphs showing advantages and/or comparisons
14. Guarantees
15. Installation procedures
16. Information particular to this specific product

The material is usually available upon request. Sales representatives may also call to explain the product. These sales representatives can also obtain samples for color, texture, or other finish selection.

Other Reference Sources

Retail Sources

Many major book publishers produce architectural reference books, and most major bookstores carry some of them. Many art supply and drafting supply stores also have reference materials.

Public Libraries

Public libraries contain a variety of professional reference materials—books, journals, and magazines. Colleges and universities offering architecture courses also carry architectural resource materials. These fall into one of two categories: broad, general coverage of an area such as architectural drafting, graphics, engineering, or design; or the narrow, specific coverage found in highly technical publications dealing, for example, with acoustics or masonry. An example of a highly technical resource is the AIA *Architectural Graphic Standards,* published by John Wiley & Sons. This book carries the maximum, minimum, and average sizes of a variety of items, and contains such diverse information as the size of a baseball diamond or a bowling alley and the various dimensions of most musical instruments, as well as the standard sizes of most major kitchen utensils and appliances.

Guides and Indexes

Two invaluable general book indexes are the *Subject Guide to Books in Print* and *Books in Print* (author and title volumes). All major bookstores carry these annual reference books. They can also be found in the reference department of many libraries. The *Reader's Guide to Periodical Literature,* which can be found in most libraries, is excellent for locating magazine articles on specific building types, new procedures and methods used in architecture, or specific architects. Four additional sources of architectural information are the *Art Index, Applied Science and Technology, The Humanities Index,* and the *Social Science Index.* These are available in most college and university libraries and in large public libraries.

Trade, Technical, and Standard Organizations

The *Encyclopedia of Associations* found in most local libraries lists many of the larger organizations that deal with the field of architecture. They represent various associations, societies, and institutes that deal with a building product or industry. Many of these provide a great service to the professional by acting as consulting organizations, and most offer informative literature.

Working Guidelines for Preparing Construction Documents

In this time of technological advance and specialization, you might easily assume that working guidelines would be precise and mathematically logical. This is not the case. Guidelines are too important to reduce to a series of steps and formulas to memorize. In fact, working guidelines for drafting are actually attitudes and ideals that are fundamental to good communication. It is this ingredient that makes a success or failure out of a basically skilled draftsperson.

You may well think that much of this material is obvious, common knowledge, or common sense. Yet if these guidelines are assumed but *not acted upon,* mass confusion and anguish result! They have been arrived at through research in supervision, communication, human relationships, and field experiences, particularly with prospective employers. This material is, therefore, not original, but its application often is.

The Rules in Summary

1. Plan every step of your drawing.
2. Establish some manner in which you can check your work.
3. Understand the decisions you will be asked to make.
4. Find out the standards under which you will function.
5. Draft from the other person's point of view.
6. Cooperate, communicate, and work with others.
7. Find out your primary and secondary responsibilities. Don't assume.
8. Think for yourself.
9. Concentrate on improving one aspect of your skills with each task.

The Rules in Detail

1. *Plan every step of your drawing.* Do not get a piece of vellum and start immediately on the top left corner. Each drawing has a distinct procedure and an order. Use your mind's eye to completely draw the object first. Picture yourself at the drafting desk. Watch yourself perform the task. Make mental and/or written notes about the sequence and anticipated problems. Every sheet of a set of architectural plans subscribes to a basic system. The system may be based on the materials used, methods of erection, limits of the technology at the present time, or even the limits of the person, to mention just a few. Whatever the control factors, be aware of them, understand them, digest them intellectually, and put them into effect.

2. *Establish some manner in which you can check your work.* Every office has some method of checking. The method may be a check sheet developed by the principal draftsperson or a person whose primary function is that of checking others. Whatever the system, establish a method to check yourself before you submit a drawing to a senior in the firm. This does two things. First, it builds trust, trust between you and your employer. If your employer thinks that you not only perform the task asked of you but are conscientious enough to double-check your work, the rapport built between you and your employer will be enhanced. Second, it builds the employer's confidence that you have done your best to perform your duty.

   This checking method differs with each person and each drawing. However, remember that the checking method is also based on the construction system used. If you understand the system, you will usually discover the method needed to check it.

   Accuracy transcends all systems—accuracy of representation as well as of arithmetic, grammar, and spelling. Nothing causes as many problems in the field as an "L" that looks like an "I," and an "E" that looks like an "F," or arithmetical totals that are not equal to their parts, or dimensions that do not reflect an established module.

3. *Understand the decisions you will be asked to make.* Know your job. Know what decisions you will be allowed to make, and know when to ask a superior.

   If, every time you are confronted with a decision, you ask a superior for help, you are taking that person's valuable time and reducing the superior's effectiveness. On the other hand, making decisions that are not part of your job will also create problems. For example, if a production draftsperson (a person drafting working drawings) were to change a design decision, the draftsperson might not be aware of all of the factors that led to that decision and might make the wrong decision. It might seem obvious to the draftsperson that a particular change would produce a better effect, but the original may have been based on a code requirement, a client's request, cost of production, or any one of hundreds of reasons of which the draftsperson may not be aware.

   Make sure your duties, responsibilities, and, above all, the decisions you are allowed to make are clearly defined by your superior.

4. *Find out the standards under which you will function.* There are many standards you will encounter. Just as there are office dress and behavior standards, so there are drawing standards.

   Each sheet you draw will have a set-up standard. Certain sheet sizes are used by certain offices. Title blocks, border lines, and sheet space allocation are usually set up in advance. Certain drawing conventions are used by each office. Certain symbols and abbreviations are acceptable. In fact, some offices produce what is called a manual of "office standards." The standard may call for something as simple as all vertical lettering, or as professional as a standard based on building erection procedures followed by a particular contractor. Again, whether it be a building code or state regulated requirement, or a personal whim of an employer, you must immediately incorporate this standard into your assignments.

5. *Draft from the other person's point of view.* Your work involves three people: the person in the field, the person who assigns you your duties, and the client. All of these people influence your attitudes. For example, when you draft for the person in the field, your work becomes a medium of communication between the client's needs and the people who execute those needs, but it must also express an understanding of the limits and capabilities of the workers themselves. Prior to drafting, for example, a detail, plan, or section, you must sufficiently understand the trade involved so that you do not ask a person or machine to perform an unreasonable task.

As for drafting from your employer's point of view, first and foremost understand what your task is. It is better to spend a few minutes with your supervisor at the beginning of a drawing, outlining your duties, and his objectives and needs, than to spend countless hours on a drawing only to find that much of the time you have spent is wasted. We are often so eager to "get on" with a job that we have not spent the proper amount of time understanding what is expected of us. As the ironic saying goes, "There is never enough time to do a job but always enough time to do it over, CORRECTLY."

Finally, look at things from the client's standpoint. The client and the designer have made a number of design and construction decisions. No matter what the reasons are for these decisions, the office and the client have an understanding, which must be respected by you. In other words, you, as a technician, must abide by and subscribe to these decisions and do everything you can to support them. This is not to say you cannot question a decision, but do not make changes without approval. If you know of a better solution or method, verify its appropriateness with a superior before you employ it.

6. *Cooperate, communicate, and work with others.* One of the main criticisms that comes from employers is that employees do not know how to work as members of a team. While education requires you to perform as an individual, each person in an office is a member of a team and has certain responsibilities, duties, and functions on which others rely. There may be many people working on a single project, and you must understand your part and participate with others towards achieving a common goal.

The method of communication is as important as the need for it. Be clear about the way you communicate your ideas. Sketch ideas when possible so others can visualize them. If the office is large, write memos and notes; write formal letters to other companies. Keep in mind that you are a representative of your firm and that proper presentation, grammar, spelling, and punctuation reflect the abilities in the firm.

Communication helps you know what the other people in the firm are doing. The more you understand the overall picture, the more you can participate. Communication also helps you to develop an appreciation of attitudes, goals, and aims of others with whom you will be working. Know what is going on in the office.

7. *Find out your primary and secondary responsibilities. Don't assume.* Nothing gets an office or an employee in as much trouble as making assumptions. Phrases such as "I thought John was going to do it" or "I didn't think, Kay; I assumed you would do it" not only break down the communication process in an office but can create discord and disturb the office harmony. Many bad feelings emerge and ultimately break down office morale.

Known your responsibilities and how and whom to ask for guidance in case of a change in your responsibilities.

A classic example of this was a large office that had two divisions: an architectural division and a structural engineering division. Each prepared a set of drawings: the architectural drawings and the structural drawings. Each division assumed the other would develop a set of details for the project. Thus on the architectural drawings there were notations that read, "See structural drawings for details." The structural group did the same but made the detail reference to the architectural set. Needless to say, the details were never drawn, and when the total set was assembled and the lack of details discovered, a great delay followed and caused much embarrassment to the firm. The client was obviously unhappy.

The size of the firm is not always to blame. Any time there is more than one person working on a project, you need to understand not only your primary responsibilities, but your not-so-obvious secondary responsibilities as well.

8. *Think for yourself.* There is a natural tendency for a draftsperson to feel that all decisions should be made by a superior. However, your supervisor will tell you that certain decisions have been delegated to you. The process of thinking for yourself also involves fully understanding your primary and secondary responsibilities.

If, each time a problem arises, you ask Bob for help, Bob will not be able to do his job effectively. There is also a cost factor involved. Your immediate supervisor or head draftsperson is earning two to five times as much as you are because of additional responsibilities. Therefore, each time you ask a question and stop production, the cost is that of your salary plus that of your supervisor.

The solution to this dilemma is a simple one. Research the solution before you approach your seniors, look through reference and manufacturers' literature, construction manuals, *Sweet's Catalog File,* reference books, and so on. Make a list of problems and questions and work around them until your superior is free and available to deal with them. Arrange your time to suit your supervisor's convenience. THINK and be able to propose solutions or suggestions yourself. In this way, you will be prepared to understand the answers you are given, and a potential frustration will have become a learning situation.

Above all, don't stop production and wait around for superiors to be free; don't follow them around. Employers react very negatively to this.

9. *Concentrate on improving one aspect of your skills with each task.* Maybe a special effort with each new assignment to improve some part of your skills. Constantly improve your lettering, your line quality, your accuracy. As athletes work to perfect some part of their ability, so should you. Work on your weakness first. Because it is your weakness, you may want to shy away from it. For example, if spelling is your problem, carry a dictionary around with you. If sketching is your weakness, practice and use it as a communication method whenever possible. The most valuable athlete is often the most versatile one—the person who can throw and catch and play defense as well as offense. A draftsperson who can draft, sketch, do simple engineering, and do research is a valuable commodity in an office and will always be employed, because an office cannot afford to lose such a versatile person.

An employer wants an employee who is punctual, dependable, and accurate, has a high degree of integrity, and is able to work with a minimum amount of supervision.

We have said many of the principles listed here are obvious. Yet if they are so obvious, why do teachers, employers, and supervisors lament the absence of these principles when desirable employee traits are discussed? To admit to your shortcomings is to confront and deal with them. To ignore them and act as if they don't exist is to run away from them.

SUMMARY

There are various reproduction methods and shortcut methods. Among these methods are reproduction techniques such as reprodrafting, which includes overlay drafting and scissors drafting.

Office standards are of various types, including sheet size, methods of representing materials on a drawing, standard abbreviations, and graphic symbols.

Resources for information such as *Sweet's Catalog,* manufacturers' literature, technical reference books, and publications of trade and professional organizations are some typical resources.

The most important guidelines for developing clear and thorough construction documents have to do with attitudes rather than specific drafting skills.

IMPORTANT TERMS AND CONCEPTS

Blueprint process
Diazo process
Sepia process
Transparent and translucent films
Plain paper copiers
Appliques
Freehand drawing
Word processing
Diazo drafting
Reprodrafting
Composite drafting
Paste-up drafting
Scissors drafting
Eraser drafting
Photo-drafting
Overlay drafting
Pin registration
Blow back
Office standards

Scale of drawings
Materials in section
Graphic symbols
Dimensioning
Dimensional reference system
Planes of reference
Horizontal control plane
Vertical control plane
Plan
Section
Axial plane
Boundary control plane
Neutral zone
Vertical control dimension
Planes
Metrics
Sweet's Catalog File
Working guidelines

REVIEW QUESTIONS

1. Why is it necessary in architecture to draft on a transparent or translucent paper?
2. How does a sepia differ from a regular diazo print?
3. What is the main advantage of transparent or translucent applique film?
4. List three uses of a plain paper copier in the development of a set of construction documents.

5. Explain the term "word processing." How can word processing be used in the preparation of construction documents?
6. What is "restoration?"
7. Outline the steps used in scissors drafting.
8. How and why are pin registration strips or bars used?
9. How can a set of construction documents using a dimensional reference system be most easily identified as compared with those using another system?
10. What is a "neutral zone?"
11. Convert the following dimensions to meters and round off to the nearest centimeter.
    A. 3'–6"
    B. 6'–8"
    C. 11 inches
    D. 58'–2"
12. What are three of the important working guidelines necessary for a skilled technician to follow? Why?

LABORATORY PROBLEMS

1. Using a slide projector in a dark room, project a slide of a building on a piece of undeveloped diazo paper. Begin with a time of 15 minutes. At the end of the time, develop the print in the ammonia portion of the print machine. Based on these results, try the experiment again until a good quality print is obtained.
2. Using the *Sweet's Catalog,* locate a manufacturer of a set-in oven. From the manufacturer's literature, obtain the necessary information to draft a plan view (top view) and an elevation (front view) of a set-in oven. Draft as if the oven were located in a counter with drawers on one side and a cabinet on the other.
3. Draft the following materials in section.
   a. Brick   **c.** Earth
   b. Concrete block **d.** Plywood
4. Visit the reference section of a library. Become familiar with the *Reader's Guide* and the various indexes available.
   a. List all indexes dealing with architecture.
   b. What are three of the most-mentioned architectural magazines in the different guides and indexes?
5. Find an architectural detail in *Sweet's Catalog* and draft it using metrics.

3

CODES AND AGENCIES

3

PREVIEW
This chapter provides examples of how building codes influence the design of modern buildings and includes the primary divisions that are found in most building codes.

Also discussed and illustrated are examples of building requirements derived from energy codes and accessibility requirements for persons with disabilities.

OBJECTIVES
1. Understand the basic format of a building code and the procedures for establishing requirements for a specific type of building.
2. Be familiar with the basic design requirements for the building envelope in regard to energy conservation as required by energy codes.
3. Be able to plan and provide the accommodations in a public building that are necessary for ensuring accessibility to persons with disabilities.

The requirements of various agencies and codes are of paramount influence in the design and detailing of today's structures. There are a great number of codes that govern and regulate the many elements that are integrated into the construction of a building. The major codes that are used in the design and detailing of buildings are the building code, mechanical code, electrical code, fire code, energy code, and accessibility design criteria for persons with disabilities.

Building Codes

The purpose of building codes is to safeguard life, health, and the public welfare. Building codes are continually being revised and incorporating additional regulations based on tests or conditions caused by catastrophic events, such as hurricanes, earthquakes, and fires. In most cases, the governing building codes are similar in organization and context. The following building code examples and portions are derived from the 1991 edition of the *Uniform Building Code.*

Building Code Divisions

Primarily, the *Uniform Building Code* is divided into eleven parts with specific chapters and sections incorporated into the various parts. The various parts are as follows:

Part I	Administration
Part II	Definitions and Abbreviations
Part III	Requirements Based on Occupancy
Part IV	Requirements Based on Types of Construction
Part V	Engineering Regulations—Quality and Design of the Materials of Construction
Part VI	Detailed Regulations
Part VII	Fire-Resistive Standards for Fire Protection
Part VIII	Regulations for Use of Public Streets and Projections over Public Property
Part IX	Wall and Ceiling Coverings
Part X	Special Subjects
Part XI	Uniform Building Code Standards

Design Influenced by Codes

There are a number of procedures that dictate architectural design that you, as architect or designer, will incorporate in developing a design program for a specific structure. You will first review the code in order to establish the group designation of the structure, based on its use and type of occupancy. Once the group designation is established, it will dictate and govern such features as the building site setbacks, maximum floor areas, size of building, materials, construction

assemblies, number of exits, building height, and many other items required by the building code.

For example, to establish the design program for a proposed two-story office building having a floor area of 10,000 square feet per floor, it will first be necessary to review the building code table to determine the occupancy group predicted for the use of this building. In Chapter 5 of *Uniform Building Code,* Table No. 5-A illustrates the types of occupancies and the various groups to which specific uses are assigned.

This table is illustrated in Figure 3.1, which shows, under "Description of Occupancy," that office buildings are within Group B, Division 2. Figure 3.1 also illustrates the fire resistance of exterior walls as they relate to the building setbacks from the property line. Also shown are the various setbacks permitted for openings in exterior walls. These items will be considered in the site plan design phase for the two-story office building design program.

Type of Construction.   The next step in the architectural design program for this building, is to determine the type of construction that is dictated by the governing building code. Figure 3.2 illustrates Table No. 5-C of the *Uniform Building Code,* which will determine the type of construction based on the occupancy and floor area. The proposed two-story office building with 10,000 square feet per floor has a Group B-2 occupancy, in which case Figure 3.2 establishes a Type V, one-hour fire-resistive type of construction. The Type V, one-hour type of construction is defined as follows: A Type V building may be of any material allowed by this code, in which case wood construction will be selected for this office building, and "one-hour" means that the office building will be of one-hour fire-resistive construction throughout.

Another table that determines the various building elements that will be affected by the type of construction is shown in Figure 3.3. This table illustrates that under the Type V, one-hour designation, the various building elements, such as exterior bearing walls, partitions, ceilings, floors, and others, will be one-hour fire-resistive assemblies.

Fire-Rated Wall Assemblies.   As indicated in Figure 3.3, all the walls of the proposed office building will have to be constructed so as to meet the requirements of one-hour fire-rated assemblies acceptable by the governing code. Most codes provide a chapter on acceptable fire-resistive standards as assemblies, so that the architect or designer is able to select an assembly that satisfies his or her specific condition. An example of the assembly of a one-hour fire-rated 2″ × 4″ wood stud partition is given in Figure 3.4, item 16-1.4. This wall assembly will now be part of the building design program.

TABLE NO. 5-A—WALL AND OPENING PROTECTION OF OCCUPANCIES BASED ON LOCATION ON PROPERTY
TYPES II ONE-HOUR, II-N AND V CONSTRUCTION: For exterior wall and opening protection of Types II One-hour, II-N and V buildings, see table below and Sections 504, 709, 1903 and 2203.
This table does not apply to Types I, II-F.R., III and IV construction, see Sections 1803, 1903, 2003 and 2103.

GROUP	DESCRIPTION OF OCCUPANCY	FIRE RESISTANCE OF EXTERIOR WALLS	OPENINGS IN EXTERIOR WALLS[1]
A See also Section 602	1—Any assembly building or portion of a building with a legitimate stage and an occupant load of 1,000 or more	Not applicable (See Sections 602 and 603)	
	2—Any building or portion of a building having an assembly room with an occupant load of less than 1,000 and a legitimate stage 2.1—Any building or portion of a building having an assembly room with an occupant load of 300 or more without a legitimate stage, including such buildings used for educational purposes and not classed as a Group E or Group B, Division 2 Occupancy	2 hours less than 10 feet, 1 hour less than 40 feet	Not permitted less than 5 feet Protected less than 10 feet
	3—Any building or portion of a building having an assembly room with an occupant load of less than 300 without a legitimate stage, including such buildings used for educational purposes and not classed as a Group E or Group B, Division 2 Occupancy	2 hours less than 5 feet, 1 hour less than 20 feet	Not permitted less than 5 feet Protected less than 10 feet
	4—Stadiums, reviewing stands and amusement park structures not included within other Group A Occupancies	1 hour less than 10 feet	Protected less than 10 feet
B See also Section 702	1—Repair garages where work is limited to exchange of parts and maintenance requiring no open flame, welding, or use of Class I, II or III-A liquids, motor vehicle fuel-dispensing stations and parking garages not classified as Group B, Division 3 open parking garages or Group M, Division I private garages	1 hour less than 20 feet	Not permitted less than 5 feet Protected less than 10 feet
	2—Drinking and dining establishments having an occupant load of less than 50, wholesale and retail stores, office buildings, printing plants, police and fire stations, factories and workshops using material not highly flammable or combustible, storage and sales rooms for combustible goods, paint stores without bulk handling Buildings or portions of buildings having rooms used for educational purposes, beyond the 12th grade, with less than 50 occupants in any room		

TABLE NO. 5-A—Continued
TYPES II ONE-HOUR, II-N AND V ONLY

GROUP	DESCRIPTION OF OCCUPANCY	FIRE RESISTANCE OF EXTERIOR WALLS	OPENINGS IN EXTERIOR WALLS
B (Cont.)	3—Aircraft hangars where no repair work is done except exchange of parts and maintenance requiring no open flame, welding, or the use of Class I or II liquids Open parking garages (For requirements, see Section 709) Helistops	1 hour less than 20 feet	Not permitted less than 5 feet Protected less than 20 feet
	4—Ice plants, power plants, pumping plants, cold storage and creameries Factories and workshops using noncombustible and nonexplosive material Storage and sales rooms of noncombustible and nonexplosive materials that are not packaged or crated in or supported by combustible material	1 hour less than 5 feet	Not permitted less than 5 feet
E See also Section 802	1—Any building used for educational purposes through the 12th grade by 50 or more persons for more than 12 hours per week or four hours in any one day	2 hours less than 5 feet, 1 hour less than 10 feet[2]	Not permitted less than 5 feet Protected less than 10 feet[2]
	2—Any building used for educational purposes through the 12th grade by less than 50 persons for more than 12 hours per week or four hours in any one day		
	3—Any building or portion thereof used for day-care purposes for more than six persons		
H	See Table No. 9-C		
I See also Section 1002	1.1—Nurseries for the full-time care of children under the age of six (each accommodating more than five persons) Hospitals, sanitariums, nursing homes with nonambulatory patients and similar buildings (each accommodating more than five persons)	2 hours less than 5 feet, 1 hour elsewhere	Not permitted less than 5 feet Protected less than 10 feet
	1.2—Health-care centers for ambulatory patients receiving outpatient medical care which may render the patient incapable of unassisted self-preservation (each tenant space accommodating more than five such patients)		

Figure 3.1 Occupancy description.

	2—Nursing homes for ambulatory patients, homes for children six years of age or over (each accommodating more than five persons)	1 hour	Not permitted less than 5 feet
	3—Mental hospitals, mental sanitariums, jails, prisons, reformatories and buildings where personal liberties of inmates are similarly restrained	2 hours less than 5 feet, 1 hour elsewhere	Protected less than 10 feet
M[3] See also Section 1102	1—Private garages, carports, sheds and agricultural buildings	1 hour less than 3 feet (or may be protected on the exterior with materials approved for 1-hour fire-resistive construction)	Not permitted less than 3 feet
	2—Fences over 6 feet high, tanks and towers	Not regulated for fire resistance	
R See also Section 1202	1—Hotels and apartment houses Congregate residences (each accommodating more than 10 persons)	1 hour less than 5 feet	Not permitted less than 5 feet
	3—Dwellings and lodging houses, congregate residences (each accommodating 10 persons or less)	1 hour less than 3 feet	Not permitted less than 3 feet

[1]Openings shall be protected by a fire assembly having at least a three-fourths-hour fire-protection rating.

[2]Group E, Divisions 2 and 3 Occupancies having an occupant load of not more than 20 may have exterior wall and opening protection as required for Group R, Division 3 Occupancies.

[3]For agricultural buildings, see Appendix Chapter 11.

NOTES: (1) See Section 504 for types of walls affected and requirements covering percentage of openings permitted in exterior walls.

(2) For additional restrictions, see chapters under Occupancy and Types of Construction

(3) For walls facing yards and public ways, see Part IV.

Figure 3.1 Occupancy description (continued).

TABLE NO. 5-C—BASIC ALLOWABLE FLOOR AREA FOR BUILDINGS ONE STORY IN HEIGHT[1]
(In Square Feet)

	TYPES OF CONSTRUCTION								
	I	II			III		IV	V	
OCCUPANCY	F.R.	F.R.	ONE-HOUR	N	ONE-HOUR	N	H.T.	ONE-HOUR	N
A-1	Unlimited	29,900	Not Permitted						
A-2-2.1[2]	Unlimited	29,900	13,500	Not Permitted	13,500	Not Permitted	13,500	10,500	Not Permitted
A-3-4[2]	Unlimited	29,900	13,500	9,100	13,500	9,100	13,500	10,500	6,000
B-1-2-3[3]	Unlimited	39,900	18,000	12,000	18,000	12,000	18,000	14,000	8,000[3]
B-4	Unlimited	59,900	27,000	18,000	27,000	18,000	27,000	21,000	12,000
E-1-2-3	Unlimited	45,200	20,200	13,500	20,200	13,500	20,200	15,700	9,100
H-1	15,000	12,400	5,600	3,700	Not Permitted				
H-2[4]	15,000	12,400	5,600	3,700	5,600	3,700	5,600	4,400	2,500
H-3-4-5[4]	Unlimited	24,800	11,200	7,500	11,200	7,500	11,200	8,800	5,100
H-6-7	Unlimited	39,900	18,000	12,000	18,000	12,000	18,000	14,000	8,000
I-1.1-1.2-2	Unlimited	15,100	6,800	Not Permitted[8]	6,800	Not Permitted	6,800	5,200	Not Permitted
I-3	Unlimited	15,100	Not Permitted[5]						
M[6]	See Chapter 11								
R-1	Unlimited	29,900	13,500	9,100[7]	13,500	9,100[7]	13,500	10,500	6,000[7]
R-3	Unlimited								

[1]For multistory buildings, see Section 505 (b).

[2]For limitations and exceptions, see Section 602.

[3]For open parking garages, see Section 709.

[4]See Section 903.

[5]See Section 1002 (b).

[6]For agricultural buildings, see also Appendix Chapter 11.

[7]For limitations and exceptions, see Section 1202 (b).

[8]In hospitals and nursing homes, see Section 1002 (a) for exception.

N—No requirements for fire resistance   **F.R.**—Fire resistive   **H.T.**—Heavy timber

Figure 3.2 Allowable types of construction.

TABLE NO. 17-A—TYPES OF CONSTRUCTION—FIRE-RESISTIVE REQUIREMENTS (In Hours)
For details see chapters under Occupancy and Types of Construction and for exceptions see Section 1705.

BUILDING ELEMENT	TYPE I	TYPE II			TYPE III		TYPE IV	TYPE V	
	NONCOMBUSTIBLE				COMBUSTIBLE				
	Fire-resistive	Fire-resistive	1-Hr.	N	1-Hr.	N	H.T.	1-Hr.	N
1. Exterior Bearing Walls	4 Sec. 1803 (a)	4 1903 (a)	1	N	4 2003 (a)	4 2003 (a)	4 2103 (a)	1	N
2. Interior Bearing Walls	3	2	1	N	1	N	1	1	N
3. Exterior Nonbearing Walls	4 Sec. 1803 (a)	4 1903 (a)	1 1903 (a)	N	4 2003 (a)	4 2003 (a)	4 2103 (a)	1	N
4. Structural Frame[1]	3	2	1	N	1	N	1 or H.T.	1	N
5. Partitions—Permanent	1[2]	1[2]	1[2]	N	1	N	1 or H.T.	1	N
6. Shaft Enclosures[3]	2	2	1	1	1	1	1	1	1
7. Floors-Ceilings/Floors	2	2	1	N	1	N	H.T.	1	N
8. Roofs-Ceilings/Roofs	2 Sec. 1806	1 1906	1 1906	N	1	N	H.T.	1	N
9. Exterior Doors and Windows	Sec. 1803 (b)	1903 (b)	1903 (b)	1903 (b)	2003 (b)	2003 (b)	2103 (b)	2203	2203
10. Stairway Construction	Sec. 1805	1905	1905	1905	2004	2004	2104	2204	2204

N—No general requirements for fire resistance.   H.T.—Heavy Timber.

[1]Structural frame elements in an exterior wall that is located where openings are not permitted or where protection of openings is required, shall be protected against external fire exposure as required for exterior bearing walls or the structural frame, whichever is greater.

[2]Fire-retardant-treated wood (see Section 407) may he used in the assembly, provided fire-resistance requirements are maintained. See Sections 1801 and 1901, respectively.

[3]For special provisions, see Sections 1706, 706 and 906.

Figure 3.3 Fire-resistive requirements.

TABLE NO. 43-B—RATED FIRE-RESISTIVE PERIODS FOR VARIOUS WALLS AND PARTITIONS[a][1]—

MATERIAL	ITEM NUMBER	CONSTRUCTION	MINIMUM FINISHED THICKNESS FACE-TO-FACE[2] (In Inches)			
			4 Hr.	3 Hr.	2 Hr.	1 Hr.
15. Noncombustible Studs—Interior Partition with Gypsum Wallboard Each Side	15-1.3	No. 16 gauge approved nailable metal studs[10] 24″ on center with full-length ⅝″ Type X gypsum wallboard[7] applied vertically and nailed 7″ on center with 6d cement-coated common nails. Approved metal fastener grips used with nails at vertical butt joints along studs.				4⅞
16. Wood Studs—Interior Partition with Gypsum Wallboard Each Side	16-1.1[11][16]	2″ x 4″ wood studs 16″ on center with two layers of ⅜″ regular gypsum wallboard[7] each side, 4d cooler[12] or wallboard[12] nails at 8″ on center first layer, 5d cooler[12] or wallboard[12] nails at 8″ on center second layer with laminating compound between layers. Joints staggered. First layer applied full length vertically, second layer applied horizontally or vertically.				5
	16-1.2[11][16]	2″ x 4″ wood studs 16″ on center with two layers ½″ regular gypsum wallboard[7] applied vertically or horizontally each side, joints staggered. Nail base layer with 5d cooler[12] or wallboard[12] nails at 8″ on center, face layer with 8d cooler[12] or wallboard[12] nails at 8″ on center.				5½
	16-1.3[11][16]	2″ x 4″ wood studs 24″ on center with ⅝″ Type X gypsum wallboard[7] applied vertically or horizontally nailed with 6d cooler[12] or wallboard[12] nails at 7″ on center with end joints on nailing members. Stagger joints each side.				4¾
	16-1.4[11]	2″ x 4″ fire-retardant-treated wood studs spaced 24″ on center with one layer of ⅝″ thick Type X gypsum wallboard[7] applied with face paper grain (long dimension) parallel to studs. Wallboard attached with 6d cooler[12] or wallboard[12] nails at 7″ on center.				4¾[4]

Figure 3.4 Fire-resistive wall assemblies.

TABLE NO. 43-B—RATED FIRE-RESISTIVE PERIODS FOR VARIOUS WALLS AND PARTITIONS[a] [1]—

MATERIAL	ITEM NUMBER	CONSTRUCTION	MINIMUM FINISHED THICKNESS FACE-TO-FACE[2] (In Inches)			
			4 Hr.	3 Hr.	2 Hr.	1 Hr.
17. Exterior or Interior Walls	17-1.3[11] [16]	2″ x 4″ wood studs 16″ on center with 7/8″ exterior cement plaster (measured from the face of studs) on the exterior surface with interior surface treatment as required for interior wood stud partitions in this table. Plaster mix 1:4 for scratch coat and 1:5 for brown coat, by volume, cement to sand.				Varies
	17-1.4	3 5/8″ No. 16 gauge noncombustible studs 16″ on center with 7/8″ exterior cement plaster (measured from the face of the studs) on the exterior surface with interior surface treatment as required for interior, nonbearing, noncombustible stud partitions in this table. Plaster mix 1:4 for scratch coat and 1:5 for brown coat, by volume, cement to sand.				Varies[4]
	17-1.5[16]	2 1/4″ x 3 3/4″ clay face brick with cored holes over 1/2″ gypsum sheathing on exterior surface of 2″ x 4″ wood studs at 16″ on center and two layers 5/8″ Type X gypsum wallboard[7] on interior surface. Sheathing placed horizontally or vertically with vertical joints over studs nailed 6″ on center with 1 3/4″ by No. 11 gauge by 7/16″ head galvanized nails. Inner layer of wallboard placed horizontally or vertically and nailed 8″ on center with 6d cooler[12] or wallboard[12] nails. Outer layer of wallboard placed horizontally or vertically and nailed 8″ on center with 8d cooler[12] or wallboard[12] nails. All joints staggered with vertical joints over studs. Outer layer joints taped and finished with compound. Nailheads covered with joint compound. No. 20 gauge corrugated galvanized steel wall ties 3/4″ by 6 5/8″ attached to each stud with two 8d cooler[12] or wallboard[12] nails every sixth course of bricks.			10	

Figure 3.4 Fire-resistive wall assemblies (continued).

Maximum Height of Buildings. The building heights and numbers of stories for specific occupancies and types of construction are also regulated by building codes. Table No. 5-D of the *Uniform Building Code*, gives the maximum height in feet and the maximum number of stories that are allowed for various types of occupancies and types of construction. Figure 3.5 illustrates this table, in which case the Group B, Division 2 occupancy, incorporating a Type V, one-hour fire resistive construction, allows a maximum height of 50 feet and a maximum of 3 stories. These factors will also be inserted into the building design program.

Code Influence on Building Design

An example of code-related design requirements is provided by the site plan for the proposed two-story office building. The architect desires that all four sides of the building have windows. To satisfy this design factor, the minimum building setback from the property line will be ten feet, as indicated in Figure 3.1, under openings in exterior walls. Figure 3.6 depicts the proposed site plan for the two-story office building, showing property line setbacks satisfying one design requirement.

As the design program is developed, it is helpful to provide code-required assemblies in graphic form as a visual means for reviewing what is required for the various elements of the office building. An example of such a graphic aid is illustrated in Figure 3.7. As previously illustrated, Figures 3.2 and 3.3 determine the fire-resistive requirements for the various elements of the

building, and Figure 3.4 is a partial example of some of the many acceptable construction assemblies that may be selected for the use of wall assemblies that are found in building codes.

Exit Requirements. Another very important part of a building code is the chapter dealing with egress requirements. This chapter sets forth the number of required exits for a specific occupancy use, based on an occupant load factor. The occupant load will depend on the use of the building. In the case of a two-story building that is designed for office use, the occupant load factor, as illustrated in Figure 3.8, will be 100 square feet. To determine the number of exits required, the 100 square-foot occupant load factor is divided into the office floor area of 10,000 square feet. The resultant occupant factor of 100 exceeds the factor of 30, therefore requiring a minimum of two exits.

The next step in the design program is to plan the location of the required exits, required stairs, and an acceptable egress travel. Egress travel is the path to a required exit. The codes will regulate the maximum distances between required exits, the minimum width of exit corridors, and the entire design of required exit stairways. Figure 3.9 depicts the second level floor plan of the proposed office building, illustrating an acceptable method for the planning of required exits and stair locations. An acceptable egress travel will terminate at the first-floor level, exiting outside the structure to a public right-of-way. A public right-of-way may be a sidewalk, street, alley, or other passage. On the first

TABLE NO. 5-D—MAXIMUM HEIGHT OF BUILDINGS

OCCUPANCY	I	II			III		IV	V	
	F.R.	F.R.	ONE-HOUR	N	ONE-HOUR	N	H.T.	ONE-HOUR	N
TYPES OF CONSTRUCTION									
MAXIMUM HEIGHT IN FEET									
	Unlimited	160	65	55	65	55	65	50	40
MAXIMUM HEIGHT IN STORIES									
A-1	Unlimited	4	Not Permitted						
A-2-2.1	Unlimited	4	2	Not Permitted	2	Not Permitted	2	2	Not Permitted
A-3-4[1]	Unlimited	12	2	1	2	1	2	2	1
B-1–2-3[2]	Unlimited	12	4	2	4	2	4	3	2
B-4	Unlimited	12	4	2	4	2	4	3	2
E[3]	Unlimited	4	2	1	2	1	2	2	1
H-1[4]	1	1	1	1	Not Permitted				
H-2[4]	Unlimited	2	1	1	1	1	1	1	1
H-3-4-5[4]	Unlimited	5	2	1	2	1	2	2	1
H-6-7	3	3	3	2	3	2	3	3	1
I-1.1[5]-1.2	Unlimited	3	1	Not Permitted	1	Not Permitted	1	1	Not Permitted
I-2	Unlimited	3	2	Not Permitted	2	Not Permitted	2	2	Not Permitted
I-3	Unlimited	2	Not Permitted[6]						
M[7]	See Chapter 11								
R-1	Unlimited	12	4	2[8]	4	2[8]	4	3	2[8]
R-3	Unlimited	3	3	3	3	3	3	3	3

Figure 3.5 Maximum building heights.

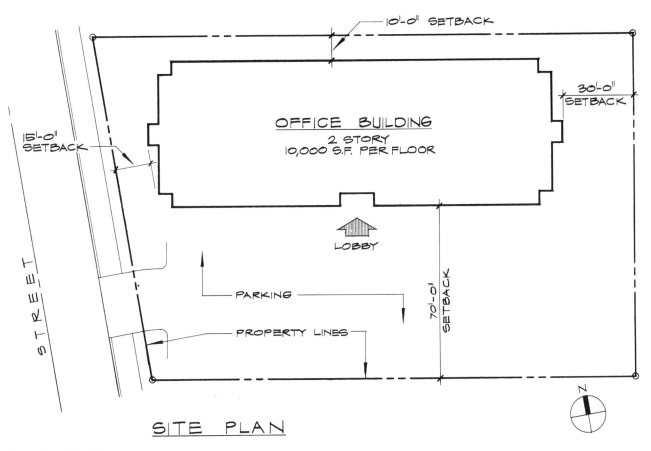

Figure 3.6 Site plan.

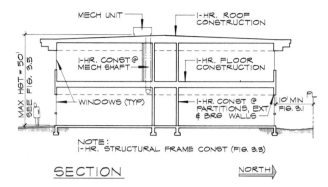

Figure 3.7 Graphic building section.

level floor plan, illustrated in Figure 3.10, the egress travel path terminates outside the building through an exit corridor at the east and west walls of the building.

This particular chapter in the *Uniform Building Code* entitled "Exits," provides a great amount of information to which the architect or designer will continually refer in order to satisfy the many code regulations that will

influence the planning and detailing of his or her specific building.

Code Nailing Schedule. In most cases, building code regulations determine minimum standards for the many considerations associated with the construction of a building in order to safeguard public health and welfare. However, this does not mean that the architect or the various engineers cannot increase the quality of these standards to satisfy their design solutions and opinions. An example of a minimum nailing schedule for Type V (wood) construction is illustrated in Figure 3.11. For structures subjected to wind or seismic forces, the engineered design may require more nails and a larger size of nails in order to satisfy the engineered design criteria.

Standards for Wood. The use of wood is prominent in the construction of many types of buildings currently being designed. The building codes have an extensively developed chapter for the various standards required for wood design. This chapter provides an array of tables

TABLE NO. 33-A—MINIMUM EGRESS REQUIREMENTS[1]

USE[2]	MINIMUM OF TWO EXITS OTHER THAN ELEVATORS ARE REQUIRED WHERE NUMBER OF OCCUPANTS IS AT LEAST	OCCUPANT LOAD FACTOR[3] (sq. ft.)
1. Aircraft hangars (no repair)	10	500
2. Auction rooms	30	7
3. Assembly areas, concentrated use (without fixed seats) Auditoriums Churches and chapels Dance floors Lobby accessory to assembly occupancy Lodge rooms Reviewing stands Stadiums	50	7
Waiting Area	50	3
4. Assembly areas, less-concentrated use Conference rooms Dining rooms Drinking establishments Exhibit rooms Gymnasiums Lounges Stages	50	15
5. Bowling alley (assume no occupant load for bowling lanes)	50	4
6. Children's homes and homes for the aged	6	80
7. Classrooms	50	20
8. Congregate residences (accommodating 10 or less persons and having an area of 3,000 square feet or less) Congregate residences (accommodating more than 10 persons or having an area of more than 3,000 square feet)	10 / 10	300 / 200
9. Courtrooms	50	40
10. Dormitories	10	50
11. Dwellings	10	300
12. Exercising rooms	50	50

Figure 3.8 Egress requirements.

TABLE NO. 33-A—MINIMUM EGRESS REQUIREMENTS[1]—(Continued)

USE[2]	MINIMUM OF TWO EXITS OTHER THAN ELEVATORS ARE REQUIRED WHERE NUMBER OF OCCUPANTS IS AT LEAST	OCCUPANT LOAD FACTOR[3] (sq. ft.)
13. Garage, parking	30	200
14. Hospitals and sanitariums— Nursing homes Sleeping rooms Treatment rooms Health-care center	6 / 10 / 10	80 / 80 / 80
15. Hotels and apartments	10	200
16. Kitchen—commercial	30	200
17. Library reading room	50	50
18. Locker rooms	30	50
19. Malls (see Chapter 56)	—	—
20. Manufacturing areas	30	200
21. Mechanical equipment room	30	300
22. Nurseries for children (day care)	7	35
23. Offices	30	100
24. School shops and vocational rooms	50	50
25. Skating rinks	50	50 on the skating area; 15 on the deck
26. Storage and stock rooms	30	300
27. Stores—retail sales rooms	50	30
28. Swimming pools	50	50 for the pool area; 15 on the deck
29. Warehouses	30	500
30. All others	50	100

[1]Access to, and egress from, buildings for persons with disabilities shall be provided as specified in Chapter 31.
[2]For additional provisions on number of exits from Groups H and I Occupancies and from rooms containing fuel-fired equipment or cellulose nitrate, see Sections 3319, 3320 and 3321, respectively.
[3]This table shall not be used to determine working space requirements per person.
[4]Occupant load based on five persons for each alley, including 15 feet of runway.

Figure 3.8 Egress requirements (continued).

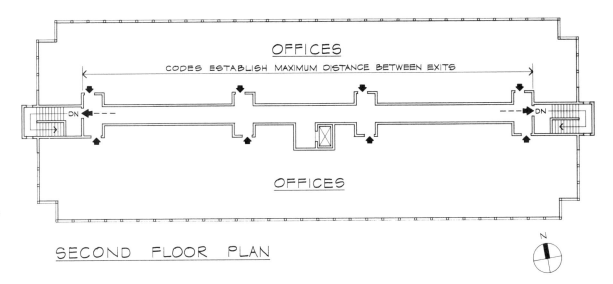

Figure 3.9 Second level floor plan.

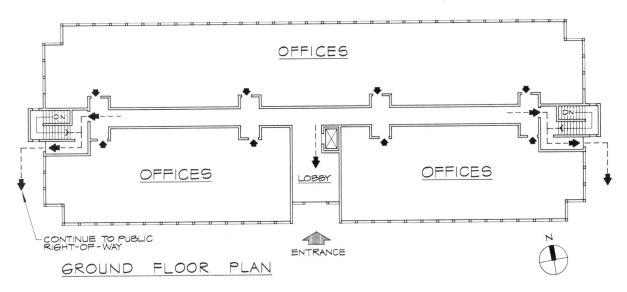

Figure 3.10 First level floor plan.

dealing with examples, such as allowable unit stresses for various types of wood species and their grades, the structural capabilities of plywood relative to its thickness and properties, the numerous species combinations for glued-laminate timber design, and allowable spans for roof rafters, ceiling joists, and floor joists. An example of one of the many tables to be found in the chapter on wood is given in Figure 3.12. This table includes the allowable spans for various sizes and spacing of floor joists, based on a specific weight per square foot and on deflection design criteria.

Bolts in Concrete. For the structural design engineer or architect the building codes offer a vast number of working values for wood, concrete, masonry, and structural steel. These values provide a basis for the selection of the various components that are part of many construc-

tion assemblies found in a specific structure. Figure 3.13 illustrates a value table for various sized anchor bolts embedded in concrete. These design loads would be the maximum allowable pounds per bolt, with a minimum embedded factor.

Minimum Foundation Requirements

As previously mentioned, many code requirements stipulate minimum standards for a specific phase of the construction process. An example is the minimum standards for foundations for wood stud-bearing walls. Figure 3.14 illustrates a table for foundations where there are no frost conditions or unfavorable soils and geology reports and no excessive weights acting on the roof and floor systems.

TABLE NO. 25-Q—NAILING SCHEDULE

CONNECTION	NAILING[1]
1. Joist to sill or girder, toenail	3-8d
2. Bridging to joist, toenail each end	2-8d
3. 1″ x 6″ subfloor or less to each joist, face nail	2-8d
4. Wider than 1″ x 6″ subfloor to each joist, face nail	3-8d
5. 2″ subfloor to joist or girder, blind and face nail	2-16d
6. Sole plate to joist or blocking, face nail	16d at 16″ o.c.
7. Top plate to stud, end nail	2-16d
8. Stud to sole plate	4-8d, toenail or 2-16d, end nail
9. Double studs, face nail	16d at 24″ o.c.
10. Doubled top plates, face nail	16d at 16″ o.c.
11. Top plates, laps and intersections, face nail	2-16d
12. Continuous header, two pieces	16d at 16″ o.c. along each edge
13. Ceiling joists to plate, toenail	3-8d
14. Continuous header to stud, toenail	4-8d
15. Ceiling joists, laps over partitions, face nail	3-16d
16. Ceiling joists to parallel rafters, face nail	3-16d
17. Rafter to plate, toenail	3-8d
18. 1″ brace to each stud and plate, face nail	2-8d
19. 1″ x 8″ sheathing or less to each bearing, face nail	2-8d
20. Wider than 1″ x 8″ sheathing to each bearing, face nail	3-8d
21. Built-up corner studs	16d at 24″ o.c.
22. Built-up girder and beams	20d at 32″ o.c. at top and bottom and staggered 2-20d at ends and at each splice

Figure 3.11 Nailing schedule.

The student or technician should constantly review the many aspects of the governing building code as it relates to the specific region and building techniques.

Energy Codes

The Council of American Building Officials has published a model energy code that is used by the various building code enforcement agencies throughout the country. The purpose of this code is to regulate the design of various types of new building construction, so that various methods of design can provide high efficiency in the use of energy. The basic energy design criteria for new construction deals with the building envelope, which is defined as all the elements of a building encompassing spaces that are conditioned by various sources of energy. These sources of energy are those that are required to heat, cool, and provide illumination.

Design Methods

The energy code provides methods and techniques and encourages innovative design systems to achieve an effective use of energy. There are three methods of design that are accepted as a means of compliance with the intent of the code:

TABLE NO. 25-U-J-1—ALLOWABLE SPANS FOR FLOOR JOISTS—40 LBS. PER SQ. FT. LIVE LOAD

DESIGN CRITERIA: Deflection—For 40 lbs. per sq. ft. live load. Limited to span in inches divided by 360. Strength—Live load of 40 lbs. per sq. ft. plus dead load of 10 lbs. per sq. ft. determines the required fiber stress value.

JOIST SIZE (IN)	SPACING (IN)	Modulus of Elasticity, E, in 1,000,000 psi													
		0.8	0.9	1.0	1.1	1.2	1.3	1.4	1.5	1.6	1.7	1.8	1.9	2.0	2.2
2x6	12.0	8-6 / 720	8-10 / 780	9-2 / 830	9-6 / 890	9-9 / 940	10-0 / 990	10-3 / 1040	10-6 / 1090	10-9 / 1140	10-11 / 1190	11-2 / 1220	11-4 / 1280	11-7 / 1320	11-11 / 1410
2x6	16.0	7-9 / 790	8-0 / 860	8-4 / 920	8-7 / 980	8-10 / 1040	9-1 / 1090	9-4 / 1150	9-6 / 1200	9-9 / 1250	9-11 / 1310	10-2 / 1360	10-4 / 1410	10-6 / 1460	10-10 / 1550
2x6	24.0	6-9 / 900	7-0 / 980	7-3 / 1050	7-6 / 1120	7-9 / 1190	7-11 / 1250	8-2 / 1310	8-4 / 1380	8-6 / 1440	8-8 / 1500	8-10 / 1550	9-0 / 1610	9-2 / 1670	9-6 / 1780
2x8	12.0	11-3 / 720	11-8 / 780	12-1 / 830	12-6 / 890	12-10 / 940	13-2 / 990	13-6 / 1040	13-10 / 1090	14-2 / 1140	14-5 / 1190	14-8 / 1230	15-0 / 1280	15-3 / 1320	15-9 / 1410
2x8	16.0	10-2 / 790	10-7 / 850	11-0 / 920	11-4 / 980	11-8 / 1040	12-0 / 1090	12-3 / 1150	12-7 / 1200	12-10 / 1250	13-1 / 1310	13-4 / 1360	13-7 / 1410	13-10 / 1460	14-3 / 1550
2x8	24.0	8-11 / 900	9-3 / 980	9-7 / 1050	9-11 / 1120	10-2 / 1190	10-6 / 1250	10-9 / 1310	11-0 / 1380	11-3 / 1440	11-5 / 1500	11-8 / 1550	11-11 / 1610	12-1 / 1670	12-6 / 1780
2x10	12.0	14-4 / 720	14-11 / 780	15-5 / 830	15-11 / 890	16-5 / 940	16-10 / 990	17-3 / 1040	17-8 / 1090	18-0 / 1140	18-5 / 1190	18-9 / 1230	19-1 / 1280	19-5 / 1320	20-1 / 1410
2x10	16.0	13-0 / 790	13-6 / 850	14-0 / 920	14-6 / 980	14-11 / 1040	15-3 / 1090	15-8 / 1150	16-0 / 1200	16-5 / 1250	16-9 / 1310	17-0 / 1360	17-4 / 1410	17-8 / 1460	18-3 / 1550
2x10	24.0	11-4 / 900	11-10 / 980	12-3 / 1050	12-8 / 1120	13-0 / 1190	13-4 / 1250	13-8 / 1310	14-0 / 1380	14-4 / 1440	14-7 / 1500	14-11 / 1550	15-2 / 1610	15-5 / 1670	15-11 / 1780
2x12	12.0	17-5 / 720	18-1 / 780	18-9 / 830	19-4 / 890	19-11 / 940	20-6 / 990	21-0 / 1040	21-6 / 1090	21-11 / 1140	22-5 / 1190	22-10 / 1230	23-3 / 1280	23-7 / 1320	24-5 / 1410
2x12	16.0	15-10 / 790	16-5 / 860	17-0 / 920	17-7 / 980	18-1 / 1040	18-7 / 1090	19-1 / 1150	19-6 / 1200	19-11 / 1250	20-4 / 1310	20-9 / 1360	21-1 / 1410	21-6 / 1460	22-2 / 1550
2x12	24.0	13-10 / 900	14-4 / 980	14-11 / 1050	15-4 / 1120	15-10 / 1190	16-3 / 1250	16-8 / 1310	17-0 / 1380	17-5 / 1440	17-9 / 1500	18-1 / 1550	18-5 / 1610	18-9 / 1670	19-4 / 1780

NOTES:

(1) The required extreme fiber stress in bending (F_b) in pounds per square inch is shown below each span.

(2) Use single or repetitive member bending stress values (F_b) and modulus of elasticity values (E) from Tables Nos. 25-A-1 and 25-A-2.

(3) For more comprehensive tables covering a broader range of bending stress values (F_b) and modulus of elasticity values (E), other spacing of members and other conditions of loading, see U.B.C. Standard No. 25-21.

(4) The spans in these tables are intended for use in covered structures or where moisture content in use does not exceed 19 percent.

Figure 3.12 Floor joist span table.

TABLE NO. 26-H—SHEAR ON ANCHOR BOLTS AND DOWELS—REINFORCED GYPSUM CONCRETE[1]

BOLT OR DOWEL SIZE (Inches)	EMBEDMENT (Inches)	SHEAR[2] (Pounds)
³/₈ Bolt	4	325
¹/₂ Bolt	5	450
⁵/₈ Bolt	5	650
³/₈ Deformed Dowel	6	325
¹/₂ Deformed Dowel	6	450

[1]The bolts or dowels shall be spaced not closer than 6 inches on center.
[2]The tabulated values may be increased one third for bolts or dowels resisting wind or seismic forces.

Figure 3.13 Bolt value table.

TABLE NO. 29-A—FOUNDATIONS FOR STUD BEARING WALLS—MINIMUM REQUIREMENTS[1] [2]

NUMBER OF FLOORS SUPPORTED BY THE FOUNDATION[3]	THICKNESS OF FOUNDATION WALL (Inches)		WIDTH OF FOOTING (Inches)	THICKNESS OF FOOTING (Inches)	DEPTH BELOW UNDISTURBED GROUND SURFACE (Inches)
	CONCRETE	UNIT MASONRY			
1	6	6	12	6	12
2	8	8	15	7	18
3	10	10	18	8	24

[1]Where unusual conditions or frost conditions are found, footings and foundations shall be as required in Section 2907 (a).
[2]The ground under the floor may be excavated to the elevation of the top of the footing.
[3]Foundations may support a roof in addition to the stipulated number of floors. Foundations supporting roofs only shall be as required for supporting one floor.

Figure 3.14 Foundation table.

I. A systems approach for the entire building and its energy-using subsystems that may use nondepletable sources. This method establishes design criteria in terms of total energy use by a building, including all of its systems.

II. A component performance approach for the various building elements and mechanical systems and components. This method provides for buildings that are heated or mechanically cooled. These are constructed so as to provide the required thermal performance of the various components.

III. Specified acceptable practice. The requirements for this method are applicable only to buildings of less than 5,000 square feet in gross floor area and three stories or less in height. This method is also limited to residential buildings that are heated or mechanically cooled and to other buildings that are heated only.

Design Influences

If your project falls into the category of Method III, you will be faced with many design decisions as to the construction of the various assemblies within the building envelope, as well as in the selection of mechanical and electrical equipment. Examples of building assemblies include the design and detailing of elements such as the roof, floors, and walls. For these detailed

assemblies, it will be necessary to provide the required amount of insulation and to use the method that satisfies the design and energy code criteria.

For the energy design program, it is recommended that the architect or designer develop a typical building section in order to visualize the various building elements that will be affected by the energy design requirements. Figure 3.15 illustrates a building section showing elements of the building envelope that will have to be insulated. In some cases the size of some of the members of the envelope may need to be increased to accommodate the required depth of insulation, such as the depth of wood studs and roof joist. Items such as windows and skylights (in Figure 3.15) will be of major concern in the design of the building envelope. The area of glass and type of glass and the number of skylights will be determined by the energy design computations. These computations may indicate that the windows and skylights will have to be dual-glazed glass rather than single-glazed.

Building Insulation. Insulation requirements for the roof, wall, and floor assemblies will be determined by the required "U factor" for that particular element. The **U factor** is defined as the time rate of heat flow per unit area and unit temperature difference between the warm side and cold side air films. The U factor applies to combination of all the materials that constitute a specific

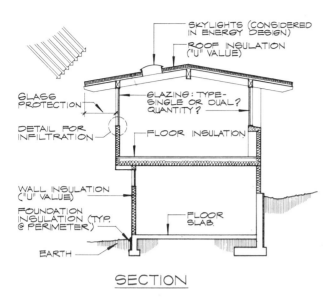

Figure 3.15 Envelope insulation.

assembly used along the heat-flow path, single materials used for a building assembly, cavity air spaces, and surface air films on both sides of a building assembly. Figure 3.16 depicts an example of an exterior wall assembly with a combination of various materials that establish a U factor.

Mechanical Equipment. Other influences that will be integrated into the design program are items such as mechanical and electrical equipment. The heating and cooling systems equipment will be sized according to the required efficiency factor. This factor may be expressed in the maximum allowable Btu (British thermal unit) rating of the equipment, as well as satisfying a prescribed efficiency rating of the equipment. The efficiency rating of the equipment is established by the equipment manufacturer. In Method III, which deals mainly with residential construction, it is required that all heating and cooling equipment be equipped with one thermostat for regulating the space temperature, as

well as a readily accessible manual or automatic means to partially restrict or shut off the heating or cooling input to each zone. In general, various control methods may be implemented to reduce the consumption of energy in heating and cooling systems.

Air Leakage in the Building Envelope. For energy design in the working drawing process, you will be required to provide solutions and details for all exterior joints that are sources for air leakage through the building envelope. These exterior joints are such assemblies as windows, doors, wall cavities, spaces between walls and foundations, spaces between walls and roof/ceiling members, and openings for the penetration of various utility services through the roof, walls, and floors. All these openings and any others must be sealed by means of caulking, gaskets, weatherstripping, or other acceptable methods.

Service Water Heating. Water heating storage tanks and supply piping will have to be installed in accordance with the energy code. The energy code ordinance will require that specific water heaters be labeled as meeting the established efficiency requirements, as well as being equipped with automatic controls for acceptable temperature settings and a separate switch for shutdown when the use of the system is not required for a specific period of time. It should be noted that an analysis of energy expenditure for electrical power distribution and lighting systems is exempt for detached dwellings and dwelling portions of multifamily complexes and is regulated by Method III.

The foregoing discussion and illustrations have given a few examples of the influencing factors that will have to be resolved in the design and working drawing program. In most cases, because of the complexity of the energy design process, the energy design calculations, the specifications for equipment, insulation, glass, and construction assemblies will be provided by an energy consultant or mechanical engineer. It is recommended that the student or technician obtain a copy of the energy code for reference in conjunction with the building code.

Public Building Accessibility

The Americans with Disabilities Act (ADA) is a result of legislation for the protection of persons with disabilities. The ADA is a civil rights law—not a building code. This law is divided into four major titles that prohibit discrimination against those who are disabled: Title I, Employment; Title II, Public Services and Transportation; Title III, Public Accommodations; and Title IV, Telecommunications. For the purpose of building design and

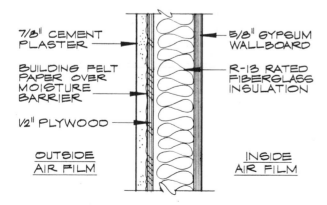

Figure 3.16 Wall assembly combination.

construction detailing, this chapter discusses Title III, Public Accommodations, and provides graphic illustrations depicting required methods to accommodate the necessary tasks of persons who are disabled in public buildings.

To offer greater accessibility and better accommodations in public buildings for those with disabilities, various representatives of organizations for disabled persons have worked with federal agency officials to establish recommended requirements. These requirements have been compiled in a list of elements that will be of concern to you as you prepare drawings and details to satisfy the various recommended design criteria:

1. Path of travel—exterior accessibility route to the facility
2. Accessible parking
3. Curb ramps
4. Entrances
5. Interior access route
6. Ramps
7. Stairs
8. Elevators
9. Platform lifts
10. Doors
11. Drinking fountains
12. Toilet rooms and bathrooms
13. Water closets
14. Urinals
15. Lavatories and mirrors
16. Sinks
17. Bathtubs
18. Shower stalls
19. Grab bars
20. Tub/shower seats
21. Assembly areas
22. Storage
23. Alarms
24. Signage
25. Public telephones
26. Seating and tables
27. Automatic teller machines
28. Dressing and fitting rooms

There are also recommendations for special applications that apply to the following buildings:

A. Restaurants and cafeterias
B. Medical care facilities
C. Business and mercantile facilities
D. Libraries
E. Transient lodging facilities

Design Elements

The following paragraphs discuss several examples that are applicable to elements derived from the building

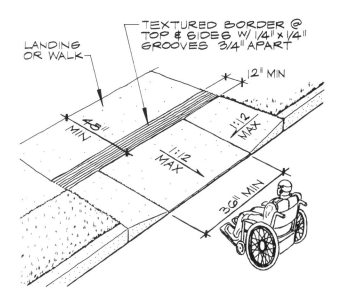

Figure 3.17 Curb ramp.

codes and from representatives and officials of various agencies. The accompanying figures graphically depict the necessary dimensional spaces and other requirements that you will need to plan for in order to accommodate those with disabilities.

Curb Ramps and Parking Stalls. Figure 3.17 illustrates a curb ramp detail, one example of providing an accessible exterior route of travel to a specific facility. For specific buildings, the required number of parking spaces for those with disabilities is determined by the total number of spaces provided for that facility. This determination is based on ratios of the cars required. An example of ratios for handicapped parking may be 2 handicap spaces for 80 required spaces. The planning of a parking space for those with disabilities is illustrated in Figure 3.18. Note that there are provisions for a marked access aisle, a curb ramp, a handicapped parking sign, and a parking surface handicapped symbol. Figure 3.19 depicts separately the freestanding handicapped sign and the parking surface handicapped symbol. In most municipalities a severe fine is imposed on nondisabled persons who use these parking facilities.

Ramps. Another way of providing exterior accessibility to a facility is through the use of ramps. Ramps have proven to be a desirable method to ensure accessibility when there are grade changes in a path of travel to a building. Figure 3.20 illustrates an example of an acceptable ramp with various changes in levels. Handrails are required on both sides of a ramp if the rise exceeds 6 inches or the horizontal projection exceeds 72 inches. If handrails are required, they will have to be drawn and detailed in accordance with the recommended requirements. Figure 3.21 depicts handrail requirements for the ramp shown in Figure 3.20.

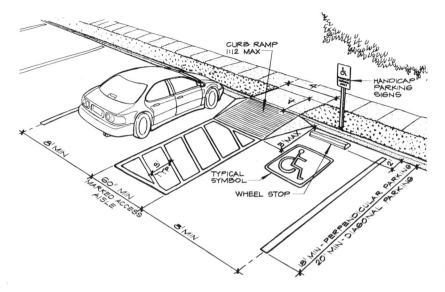

Figure 3.18 Parking spaces.

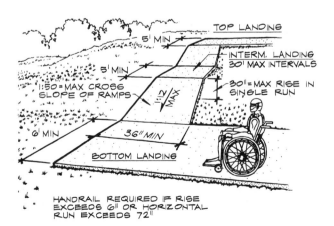

Figure 3.19 Parking sign and symbol.

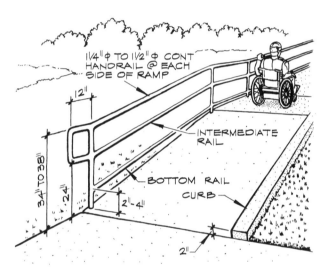

Figure 3.21 Ramp handrail.

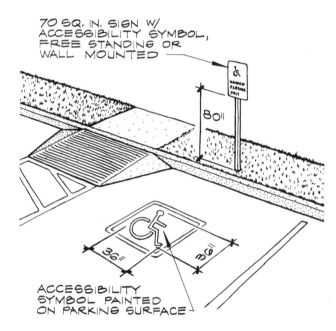

Figure 3.20 Ramp.

Wheelchair Space Requirements

In cases where there are no specific rules for a particular planning situation, it is prudent for the architect or designer to be aware of the space requirements needed for the maneuverability of someone using a wheelchair. Figures 3.22A through 3.22E illustrate some examples of floor space areas and reaching dimensions that are desirable for those who function from a wheelchair.

Locations for Controls and Shelving. As shown in Figures 3.22A through 3.22E, there are dimensional limitations in various directions for a person using a wheelchair. Therefore, controls such as thermostats, window controls, electric switches, pullcords, convenience outlets, and so forth, will have to be located within the required reach limitations. Figure 3.23 illustrates such

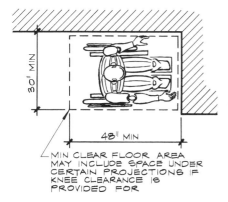

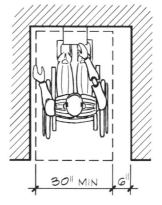

Figure 3.22A Wheelchair space requirements.

Figure 3.22D Wheelchair space requirements.

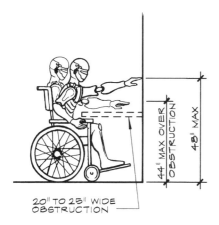

Figure 3.22B Wheelchair space requirements.

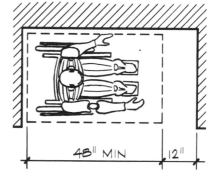

Figure 3.22E Wheelchair space requirements.

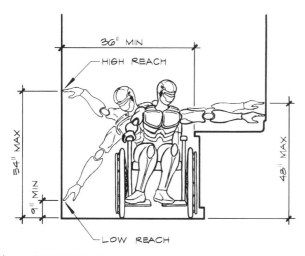

Figure 3.22C Wheelchair space requirements.

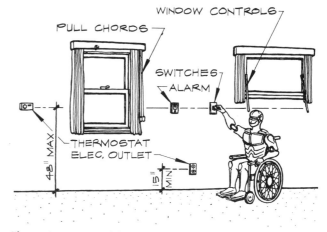

Figure 3.23 Control heights.

controls. Another concern in regard to reach limitations is accessibility to bookshelves that are found in educational and library facilities. Figure 3.24 illustrates maximum shelf heights and passage dimensions for various types of aisles.

Doors and Doorways. The maneuvering capabilities of a person in a wheelchair when dealing with accessibility in regard to doors and doorways will be determined by minimum required floor plan dimensions. An example of a floor plan configuration involving a door and doorway access is depicted in Figure 3.25. Note that the door clearance does not include the door thickness nor any hardware. Door-swing direction in access corridors will be dictated by required minimum clearances for maneuvering a wheelchair to access doors. If building code requirements specify that certain

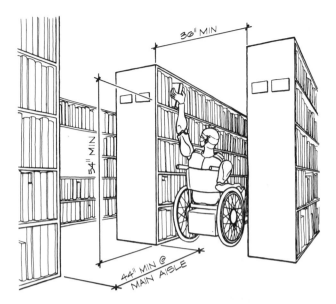

Figure 3.24 Shelf heights.

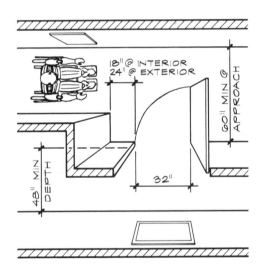

Figure 3.25 Doorway maneuvering clearances.

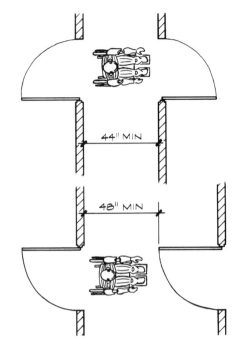

Figure 3.26 Doorway maneuvering clearances.

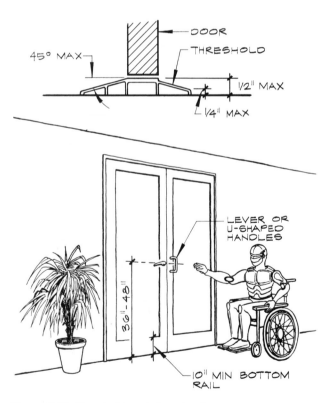

Figure 3.27 Threshold and door hardware.

doors have to swing into corridors, then corridor dimensions may have to be adjusted to satisfy wheelchair clearances. Figure 3.26 illustrates two examples of door-swing directions that affect the dimensional width of a corridor.

Access doors and the various hardware assemblies required for their functioning must meet certain requirements. For example, the selection of door handle hardware will be regulated to a lever-type U-shaped handle with a minimum and maximum dimensional location above the floor. The slopes and heights of door thresholds will have to satisfy accessibility requirements. An illustration of hardware for door handles and an example of an acceptable threshold is shown in Figure 3.27.

Drinking Fountains. When planning drinking fountain locations, the architect or designer will have to be aware of minimum required dimensions for recessed or projected installation of drinking fountains. Figure 3.28

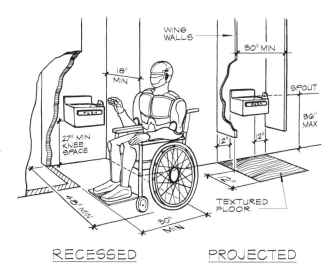

Figure 3.28 Drinking fountains.

provides a view of these two types of installation, illustrating dimensional clearances as well as the maximum height to the spout and clearance for knee space.

Plumbing Facility Requirements. An important facet of the building design process is the provision of accessible plumbing facilities in order to accommodate people with disabilities. These facilities, which include such fixtures as water closets, lavatories, and urinals, are planned to ensure accessibility for those who have disabilities. First of all, a floor plan is designed, providing the minimum required space clearances and accessibility to specific plumbing fixtures. Figure 3.29 illustrates an overall pictorial view of a proposed restroom facility incorporating minimum access clearances for the various plumbing fixtures. Note the required grab bar sizes and locations relative to the water closet. The installation of the various plumbing fixtures is regulated with reference to their dimensional height above the floor, side wall clearances, and knee and toe spaces for the use of lavatories. Figure 3.30 provides pictorial views of a lavatory, water closet, and urinal, illustrating fixture heights and clearances. Note that hot water and drain pipes are required to be insulated in order to protect against contact. Lavatory clearances are most important, because the knee will project under the lavatory fixture and will therefore require additional clearance. To provide a clearer illustration of the required clearances beneath the lavatory, see Figure 3.31. In planning for accessibility to the toilet compartments, the location of the door to the compartment will dictate the required fixture layout. Figure 3.32 shows an example of a toilet compartment plan, illustrating optional door locations.

These illustrations are examples of the elements within a public building that the architect or designer must plan for in order to accommodate people with disabilities.

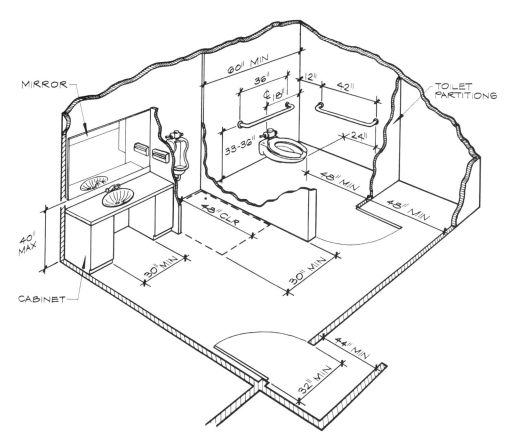

Figure 3.29
Restroom facilities.

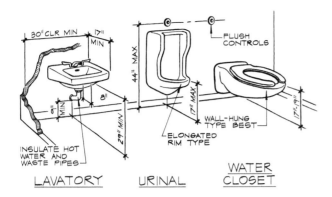

Figure 3.30 Plumbing fixtures.

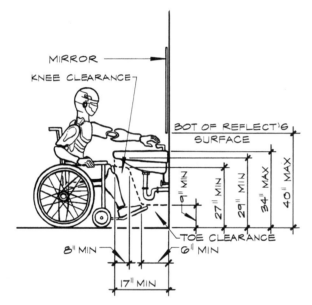

Figure 3.31 Lavatory access.

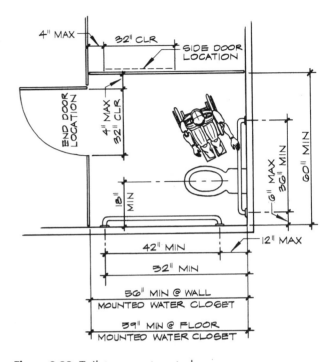

Figure 3.32 Toilet compartment plan.

SUMMARY

This chapter provided the initial direction regarding code requirements for a specific building and occupancy use. It illustrates some specific items that are found in building codes and how they perfect the design of a structure.

The influence of other agencies, such as those governing energy requirements and providing building accessibility to persons with disabilities, have been discussed, and various illustrations depicting solutions for their recommended requirements have been provided.

IMPORTANT TERMS AND CONCEPTS

Building group occupancy
Fire-rated wall assemblies
Exit requirements
Nailing schedule
Building code tables
Energy code
Building envelope

"U" factor
Building insulation
Air leakage
Americans with Disability Act (ADA)
Public accommodations
Wheelchair space requirements

REVIEW QUESTIONS

1. The use of a specific building establishes what segment of a building code?
2. Name three types of building construction.
3. What is the occupancy load factor for classrooms?
4. Name three functions in a building that would require sources of energy.
5. For wood structures, what is most commonly done to conserve energy?
6. Name one type of building that provides building accessibility for persons with disabilities.
7. What is the maximum ramp slope ratio for wheelchair use?

LABORATORY PROBLEMS

1. Provide an interior 2″ × 4″ stud wall detail that satisfies code requirements for a one-hour fire resistive assembly. The scale is to be determined by your instructor.
2. Draft an exterior foundation detail for a wood stud-bearing wall that illustrates minimum code requirements. Foundation detail will support two floors. The scale should be ¾″ = 1′–0″.
3. Provide a restroom floor plan with one lavatory and one water closet that illustrates dimensionally space requirements for wheelchair use. Toilet partitions are not to be used. The scale of drawing should be ¼″ = 1′–0″.

4

CONSTRUCTION
PRINCIPLES
AND METHODS

4

PREVIEW

This chapter examines the various light construction principles and methods used in modern construction and prepares you for comparing and selecting systems. The three major parts of a structure are examined. The first section of the chapter examines conventional foundation systems, using wood and concrete floors. The second examines wall systems, including principles, methods, and applications. Wall systems use wood, masonry, and steel. The last section explains and illustrates roof systems.

OBJECTIVES

1. Be familiar with types and selection of floor systems, including detailing and construction principles for wood and concrete floors.
2. Be familiar with types and selection of wall systems.
3. Be familiar with types and selection of roof systems and the application of roofing to wood, masonry, and steel walls.

Today's buildings use various construction principles, methods, and building systems. These principles, methods, and systems are generally selected according to the type and use of the structure, code requirements, logical and simple structural solutions, economic considerations, and satisfactory planning and design elements. So when you are asked to provide solutions for a specific building, you should investigate these various construction principles and methods.

The *primary components* of a structure include *the foundation system, the wall system,* and *the roof system.*

Foundation and Floor Systems

Foundation systems are usually designed to use either wood structural members or a concrete slab as the floor support. When you select a foundation system for a structure, consider the following criteria:

1. Structural considerations
2. Type of structure and its use
3. Desirability of wood or concrete to support the finish floor
4. Finish floor material
5. Topography of the site
6. Soil conditions
7. Client preference

If a foundation for a wood floor has been selected, you should also select a wood floor system.

Wood Floor: Joist System

The most conventional wood floor system uses **floor joists** as structural members and plywood as a subfloor for supporting the finish floor material. Floor joists are generally spaced at 16″ on centers (o/c) and may vary in size from 2 × 6 to 2 × 12, depending on their spans. These members are supported on the exterior perimeter of the structure by a concrete foundation and, in the interior, by a concrete foundation and/or wood girders and concrete piers.

Advantages. Major advantages of this method of floor construction include (1) being able to produce greater spans length if needed, by using recommended joist sizes and developing a beam in the floor system by nailing or bolting joists together; (2) being able to use fewer internal supporting foundation walls, girders, and piers; and (3) being able to cantilever the floor joists if this is called for by the design. A **cantilever** is a projecting structural member supported at only one end.

Disadvantages. This system should not be selected in regions where buildings are susceptible to termite infestation and/or dry rot; the wood deteriorates and reduces the structural integrity of the wood members. And, in buildings where noise transmission through the floor system needs to be minimized, other floor systems such as concrete are more desirable. Figure 4.1 shows a foundation plan using floor joists, concrete piers, wood girders, and concrete foundation walls. Symbols for construction assemblies are shown for further explanations and reference.

Construction Principles. There are some primary construction principles for this system:

1. Ensure floor members are not in direct contact with concrete.

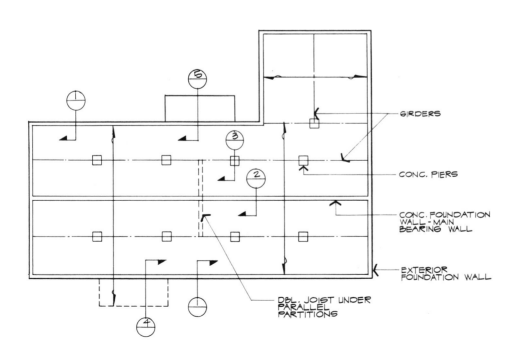

Figure 4.1 Foundation plan— floor joist and pier and girder.

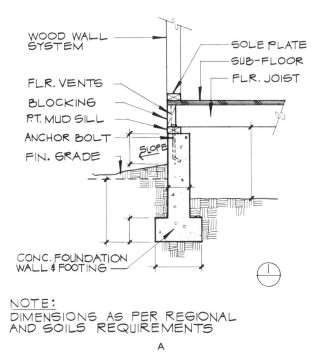

Figure 4.2A Exterior foundation wall—wood floor joist.

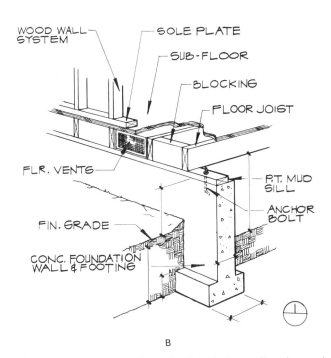

Figure 4.2B Isometric of exterior foundation wall with wood floor joist.

2. Provide recommended underfloor clearance from soil.
3. Provide proper flashing to protect wood from possible moisture problems. (Flashing is a general term for any sheet metal barrier at a joint, etc., to prevent water infiltration.)
4. Provide more than minimum-size joists, blocking and supporting members to avoid deflection or floor movement.
5. Provide adequate ventilation.

Example of Floor Joists. In Figure 4.1 an exterior foundation wall, footing, and floor assembly using wood floor joists is referenced as ⊖. It is illustrated in detail in Figure 4.2A and three dimensionally in Figure 4.2B. The depth of the foundation wall and footing will vary depending on soils and geological conditions, frost line depth, vertical loads acting along the foundation wall, and local code requirements.

Load Bearing Foundations

Supporting Internal Walls. Before you position and dimension internal foundation walls and piers, pay attention to the interior walls. These walls are subjected to heavy loads from the roof, ceiling, and other structures. When heavy loads accumulate on a particular wall, position a concrete foundation wall directly below that wall. Figure 4.3 shows a floor and foundation assembly for a load-bearing interior wall. Solid blocking is pro-

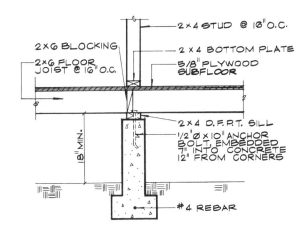

Figure 4.3 Drafted detail of interior bearing footing with wood floor.

vided between the floor joists directly beneath the wall for stability.

Intermediate Supports. For intermediate supports of wood floor joists, use wood **girders** and concrete **piers** (column footings). Positioning of these members depends on the size of the floor joists and their allowable spans. It is good practice to add an additional row of

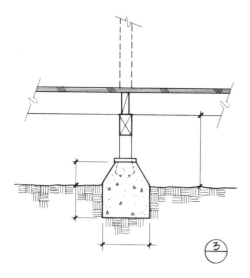

Figure 4.4A Interior pier.

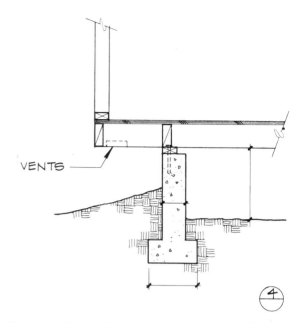

Figure 4.5 Exterior foundation—floor joist cantilever.

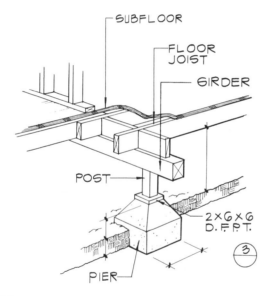

NOTE:
DIMENSIONS AS PER REGIONAL
AND SOILS REQUIREMENTS

Figure 4.4B Isometric of interior pier.

piers and girders where the joists have been extended to their maximum span. This decreases the amount of deflection in the floor system and therefore provides a stiffer floor at minimum construction cost. Whenever possible, locate wood girders directly beneath partition walls. Figure 4.4A shows a pier and girder assembly where solid blocking between the wood joists is provided directly above the wood girder. Figure 4.4B is an isometric drawing of Figure 4.4A.

Using floor joists in a wood floor system allows the designer to cantilever the floor joists, thereby solving certain design problems. The length of the cantilever

depends on the size and spacing of the floor joists as well as on structural loads from above. Figure 4.5 shows a detail of floor joists cantilevered beyond the exterior foundation wall. The underfloor vents may be located underneath the cantilevered joist rather than in the blocking area. Visually, this is a more desirable location than the face of the exterior wall.

Flashing. Moisture in the floor system can cause dry rot and swelling or buckling of wood floor members. Wood floor systems, therefore, always require adequate **flashing** (sheet metal protection of wood) as a deterrent to moisture infiltration. Figure 4.6A shows an exterior foundation wall adjacent to a concrete porch or patio. The metal flashing is positioned to shield against water seepage into the wood floor. Always provide flashing when you are dealing with conditions like these. An isometric view of Figure 4.6A is shown in Figure 4.6B.

Joining Floor Joists. Using wood floor joists allows you to develop floor beams under load-bearing walls and columns. This is a great asset. In many cases, two or three joists may be joined together to form a beam for a structural support. These members may be joined by nails or bolts.

Figure 4.7 shows floor joists joined to develop a beam for the support of a load-bearing wall.

Wood Floor: Tongue-and-Groove System

Frequently, 2-inch thick (2") **tongue-and-groove planking** is used to span over wood girders and concrete foundation walls. Figure 4.8 shows a foundation plan with 2" tongue-and-groove planking for a floor system.

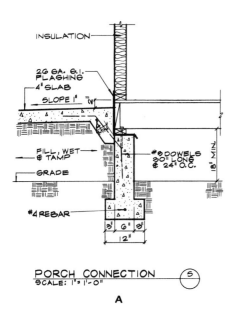

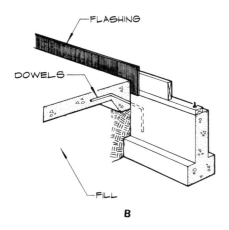

Figure 4.6A Porch slab to wood floor system.

Figure 4.6B Isometric of porch slab to wood floor system.

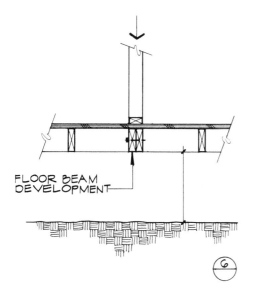

Figure 4.7 Floor beam.

Additional rows or piers and girders are necessary because of the short spans. Symbols for details of construction assemblies are shown for reference and further explanation.

Figure 4.9A shows an exterior foundation wall of a wood floor system using 2″ tongue-and-groove planking (referenced as ⊕ on Figure 4.8). Here you can immediately see two major differences between this and the floor joist system: first, the height is less from finish grade to the subfloor; second, a block-out is required in the foundation wall forming (molding) for installing the under-floor vents. As mentioned earlier, the width and depth of the foundation wall and footing depend on numerous factors. Figure 4.9B shows the tongue-and-groove planking in section.

If an interior wall must support a large tributary area of roof and ceiling loads, a concrete foundation wall should be positioned directly beneath the wall, instead of a girder-and-pier support. This is shown in Figure 4.10.

Remember, this floor system needs additional rows of piers and girders because of the span limitations of the 2″ tongue-and-groove planking. The pier-and-girder detail resembles the floor joist system, as you can see in Figure 4.11. This system, too, requires metal flashing to protect wood floor members against moisture infiltration, as you can see in detail in Figure 4.12.

Because this floor system, unlike the floor joist system, does not permit floor beams, additional girders must be positioned directly below load-bearing walls. Another method for positioning a beam for the support of a load-bearing wall is to locate the beam at the base of the wall and span between the girders. This is shown in Figure 4.13.

Advantages.   There are some major advantages to using this system:

1. Tongue-and-groove provides a stiff floor.
2. The system has a lower noise factor than that of a wood joist floor system.
3. It has a lower exterior height silhouette because the depth of the floor joists has been eliminated.
4. It provides a more rigid subfloor when concrete or a grouted tile floor is to be applied directly above.

Disadvantages.   There are also disadvantages in using this system:

1. Some regions are subjected to excessive termite infestation and dry rot.
2. Short spans require additional girders and foundation walls.
3. The system does not allow joining joists together to make beams.
4. The system does not permit floor cantilevers.

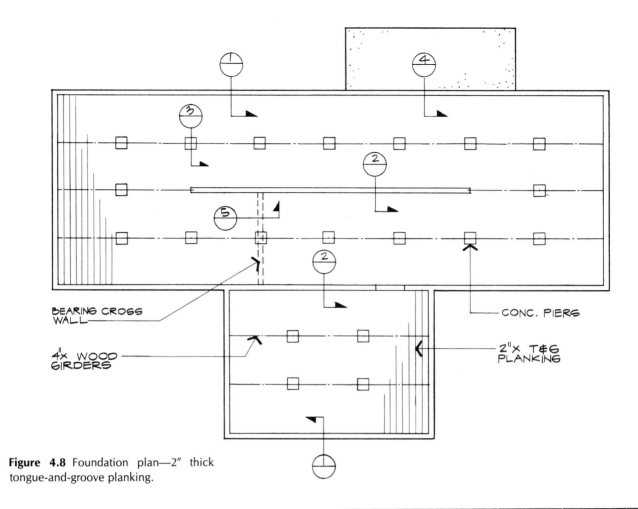

Figure 4.8 Foundation plan—2″ thick tongue-and-groove planking.

BEARING CROSS WALL

4″x WOOD GIRDERS

CONC. PIERS

2″x T&G PLANKING

2×6 T&G SUBFLOOR
SCALE: 3″=1′-0″

(1A)

B

Figure 4.9B Tongue-and-groove subfloor in section.

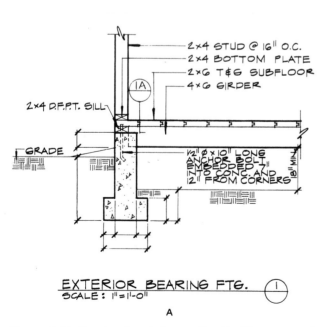

2×4 STUD @ 16″ O.C.
2×4 BOTTOM PLATE
2×6 T&G SUBFLOOR
4×6 GIRDER

(1A)

2×4 D.F.P.T. SILL

GRADE

½″∅ × 10″ LONG ANCHOR BOLT EMBEDDED 7″ INTO CONC. AND 12″ FROM CORNERS

8″ MIN.

EXTERIOR BEARING FTG. (1)
SCALE: 1″=1′-0″

A

Figure 4.9A Exterior foundation wall with 2″ tongue-and-groove planking.

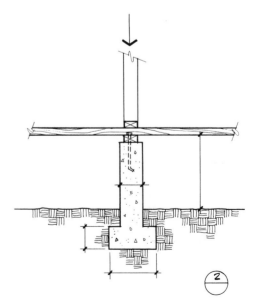

(2)

Figure 4.10 Interior bearing concrete foundation—2″ tongue-and-groove planking.

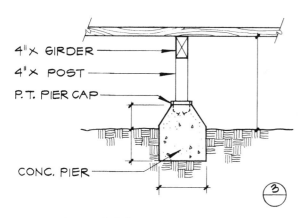

4"X GIRDER
4"X POST
P.T. PIER CAP
CONC. PIER

③

Figure 4.11 Pier and girder.

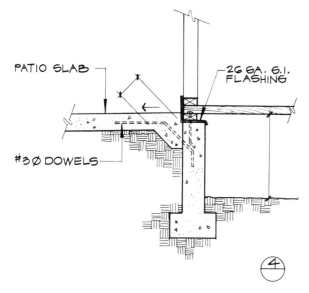

PATIO SLAB
26 GA. G.I. FLASHING
#3 Ø DOWELS

④

Figure 4.12 Exterior foundation and patio slab—2" tongue-and-groove floor.

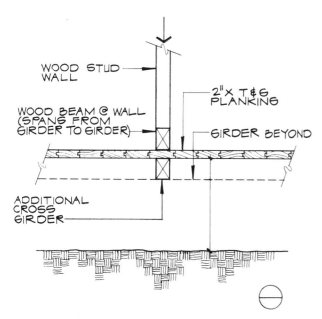

WOOD STUD WALL
WOOD BEAM @ WALL (SPANS FROM GIRDER TO GIRDER)
2"X T&G PLANKING
GIRDER BEYOND
ADDITIONAL CROSS GIRDER

Figure 4.13 Wall support beam.

This system, too, requires metal flashing to protect wood floor members against moisture infiltration, as you can see in detail in Figure 4.12.

Concrete Floor

When concrete has been selected as the supporting material, the factors influencing the choice of construction methods resemble those influencing wood floor construction: soils and geological conditions, waterproofing and insulation requirements, varying temperature conditions, reinforcing requirements, and finished flooring.

Suppose, for example, that the **soils report** indicates that the proposed site has expansive soil, as shown in Figure 4.14; expansive soil generates upward and downward forces that can fracture or crack concrete members. Given this condition, the following construction methods should be considered:

1. Deeper footings
2. Reinforcing at top and bottom of foundation wall
3. Sand bed at base of footing
4. Crushed rock or sand below concrete floor slab
5. Concrete slab reinforcing
6. Water saturation of soil prior to pouring of concrete

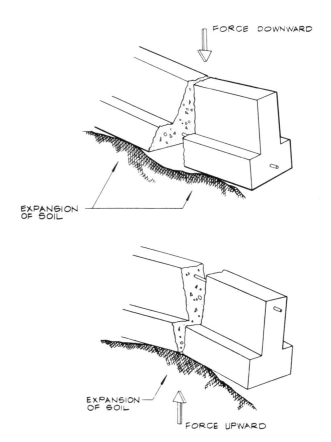

FORCE DOWNWARD
EXPANSION OF SOIL

EXPANSION OF SOIL
FORCE UPWARD

Figure 4.14 Forces on concrete in expansive soil.

Figure 4.15 shows a concrete foundation and floor section on grade, detailed for expansive soil conditions.

Concrete Floor Reinforcing. In much the same way that the foundation needs reinforcing, the concrete floor also needs reinforcing to prevent cracking. Current methods include using either deformed reinforcing bars running in each direction or welded wire mesh.

The welded wire mesh is usually made of number 10 wire spaced 6 inches apart in each direction. The size and spacing of reinforcing bars is based on the soil report recommendations and determined by the engineer. Figure 4.16 shows on-grade concrete floor reinforcing.

Types of Concrete Floor Foundations. There are two main types of concrete floor foundations or footings: the monolithic **one-pour system,** where the concrete floor

and foundation are poured in one operation, and the **two-pour system,** where the foundation and concrete floor are poured independently.

These two differ in construction: in the monolithic footing, the trenches themselves become the forms, as shown in Figure 4.17; in the two-pour method, formwork is provided, as shown in Figure 4.18. More concrete is used in the monolithic footing.

One way to hold two different pours of concrete together is to use steel **dowels.** These dowels resemble reinforcing bars but work differently. An application of steel dowels holding a porch slab to the foundation of a structure is shown in Figure 4.19.

An interior two-pour bearing (supporting) footing resembles the exterior footing and carries the vertical loads from the structure above. Figure 4.20 shows a drafted detail for a two-pour bearing footing. Nonbearing footings support the wall weight only. Bearing footings support heavy loads from the roof, ceiling, or floor above.

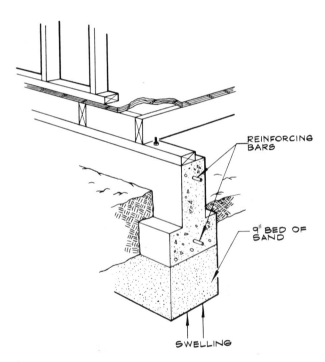

Figure 4.15 Reinforcing for expansive soil conditions.

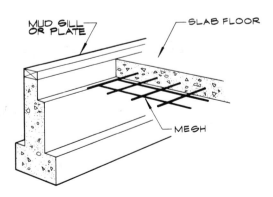

Figure 4.16 Use of mesh in slab.

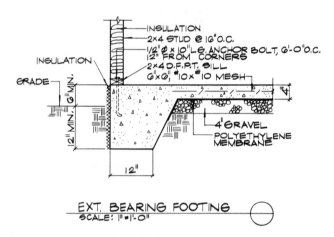

Figure 4.17 Drafted detail of a monolithic footing.

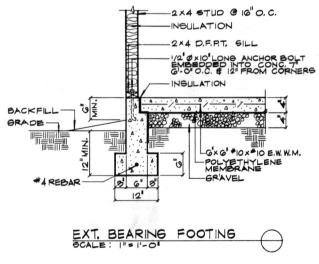

Figure 4.18 Drafted detail of a two-pour structure.

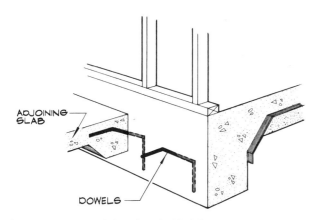

Figure 4.19 Use of dowel to hold slab to structure.

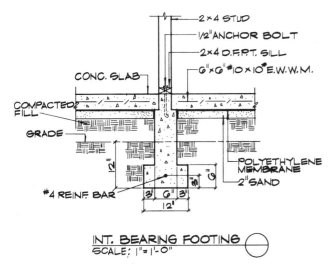

Figure 4.20 Drafted detail of a two-pour interior bearing footing.

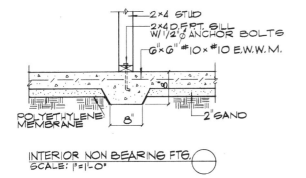

Figure 4.21 Drafted detail of an interior nonbearing footing.

The purpose of the interior nonbearing footing, however, is to give support for the wall load above and to provide only sufficient thickness to accommodate the anchor bolts that secure the sill, as you can see in Figure 4.21.

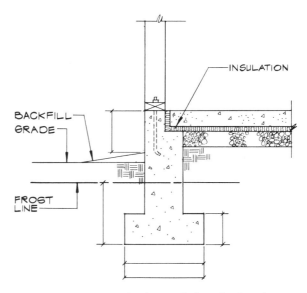

Figure 4.22 Measuring the footing below the frost line.

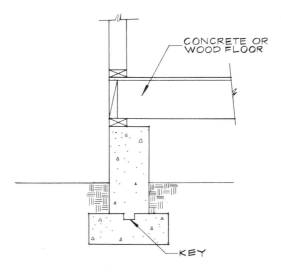

Figure 4.23 Use of a key in a two-pour system.

Where temperatures are very cold, wider footings are needed to accommodate heavy snow loads, and the footing must be placed far below the frost line. Colder climates also require **insulation** under the concrete floor and around the perimeter of the foundation. Figure 4.22 shows foundation detail and concrete floor detail for colder temperatures.

When the footing is poured separately from the foundation wall, a key should be provided in the footing to give lateral stability. This is shown in Figure 4.23.

You must also be aware of areas that are potentially weak and may produce cracks in the concrete, such as the connection between a concrete floor slab and the foundation in a monolithic pour operation. This area must be "beefed up," or strengthened, as you can see in Figure 4.24.

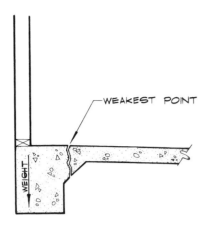

Figure 4.24 Weak points.

Wall Systems

Two main types of wood wall-framing methods are used in construction: the **balloon frame** and the **Western or platform-framing** method. The main differences between these systems lie in the construction methods for the walls and floor assembly.

Balloon Frame

In two-story construction, the balloon frame system uses continuous wall studs from the first floor level up to the roof assembly. The second floor supporting members are then framed to the continuous studs. Stud sizes are 2 × 4 or 2 × 6 at 16 center to center and 2″ thick blockings to be fitted to fill all openings in order to provide firestops and prevent drafts from one space to another.

Wood or metal members at a 45° angle, attached securely at the top and bottom of the studs, provide horizontal bracing for walls. Where exterior walls are solid sheathed, additional bracing may not be required. However, this may be determined by the governing building code or structural engineering requirements.

This system has minimum vertical shrinkage or vertical movement and may be used with brick veneer or stucco exteriors. Figure 4.25 gives an isometric (three dimensional) view and shows an exterior wall section. It also shows solid sheathing on the exterior walls. Use of sheathing such as this depends on the region and on the exterior materials selected.

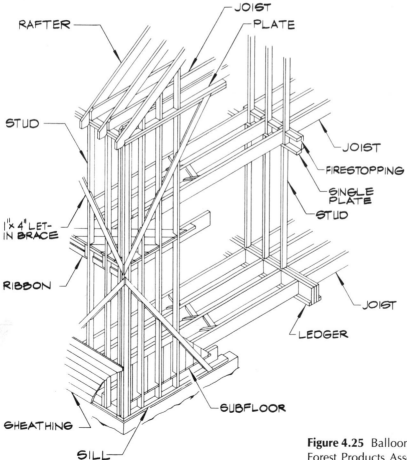

Figure 4.25 Balloon frame construction. (Courtesy of National Forest Products Association.)

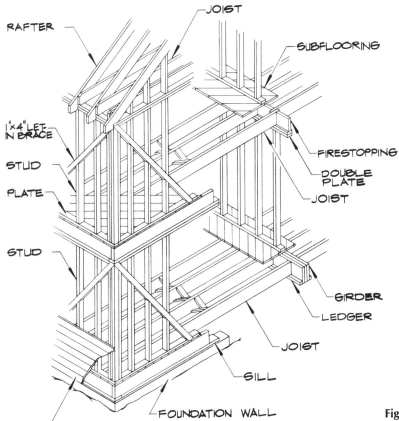

RAFTER

JOIST

SUBFLOORING

1"x4" LET-IN BRACE

STUD

PLATE

STUD

FIRESTOPPING

DOUBLE PLATE

JOIST

GIRDER

LEDGER

JOIST

SILL

FOUNDATION WALL

SHEATHING

Figure 4.26 Western or platform framing.
(Courtesy of National Forest Products Association.)

Western or Platform Framing

Western or platform framing uses a different procedure. First, the lower floor walls are assembled. Then the supporting floor members and subfloor for the upper floor are framed. The upper subfloor then provides a platform for assembling the upper floor walls. The walls are framed with 2 × 4 or 2 × 6 studs at 16″ center to center. Required blocking is 2″ thick and fitted to prevent drafts between spaces.

Solid sheathing or diagonal braces may provide bracing for walls, regional differences determining which is used. Figure 4.26 shows an isometric and wall section using Western framing.

Post and Beam Frame

A third method for framing wood structures is the **post and beam** system. Less common than platform or balloon framing, this method uses a beam-to-post spacing that allows the builder to use 2″ roof or floor planking. Figure 4.27 compares the system with conventional framing. For best use of this system you should provide a specific module of plank-and-beam spacing for planning. Supplementary framing is put on the exterior walls so that exterior and interior finishes can be attached.

The term **planking** is used to refer to members that have a minimum depth of 2″ and a width from 6 to 8. The edges of these members are normally tongue-and-grooved. Using such edges enables a continuous joining of members so that a concentrated load is distributed onto adjacent members. Figure 4.28 illustrates a commonly used planking with tongue-and-grooved edges.

You must provide a positive connection between the post and beam and secure the post to the floor. You can use different types of metal framing connectors. However, if these connectors are visually undesirable, you may use dowels. Examples of doweled post-to-beam and post-to-floor connections are shown in Figures 4.29 and 4.30.

When you are asked to provide architectural details for this framing method, detail members that are properly fastened together. Because fewer pieces are used with this method, pay special attention to connections where beams abut (touch) each other and where beams join posts. When connections are securely fastened together, the building acts as a unit in resisting external forces.

Types of Walls

Masonry. Masonry for exterior structural walls is widely used in commercial, industrial, and residential con-

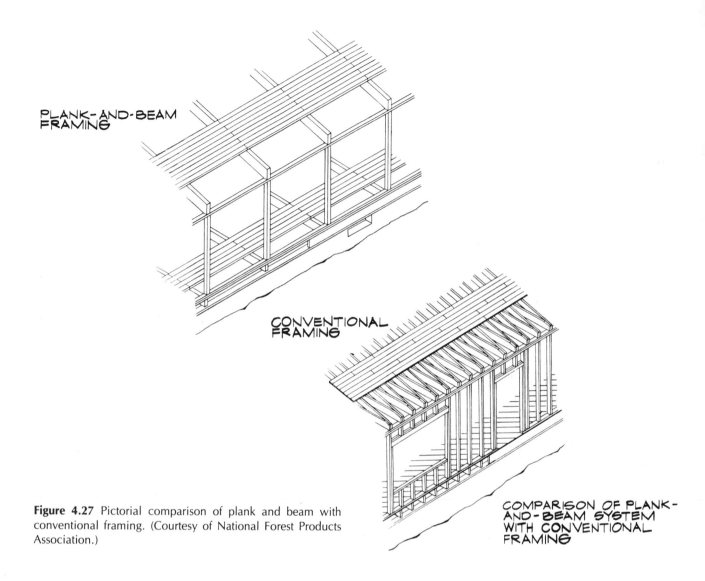

PLANK-AND-BEAM FRAMING

CONVENTIONAL FRAMING

COMPARISON OF PLANK-AND-BEAM SYSTEM WITH CONVENTIONAL FRAMING

Figure 4.27 Pictorial comparison of plank and beam with conventional framing. (Courtesy of National Forest Products Association.)

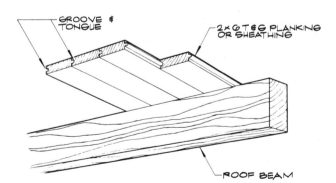

GROOVE & TONGUE

2×6 T&G PLANKING OR SHEATHING

ROOF BEAM

Figure 4.28 Pictorial of roof planking.

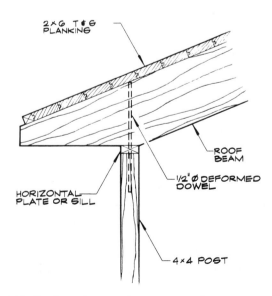

2×6 T&G PLANKING

ROOF BEAM

1/2" Ø DEFORMED DOWEL

HORIZONTAL PLATE OR SILL

4×4 POST

Figure 4.29 Section of post-to-beam connection.

struction. The main masonry units used are brick and concrete block. These are available in many sizes, shapes, textures, and colors.

Masonry is fire resistant, providing excellent fire ratings ranging from 2 to 4 hours or more (the time it takes a fire-testing flame temperature to penetrate a specific

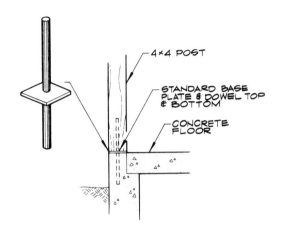

Figure 4.30 Section of post base dowel.

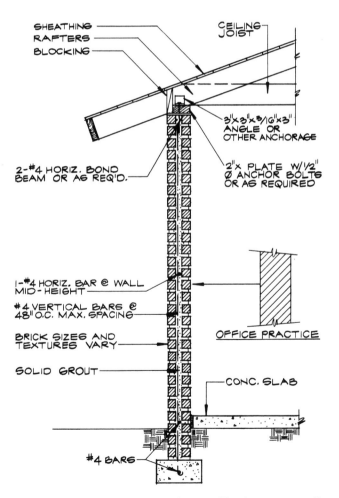

Figure 4.31 Section of reinforced grouted brick masonry wall.

wall assembly). It also acts as an excellent sound barrier. When solid brick units are used for an exterior structural wall, the primary assembly is determined by geophysical conditions. For example, steel reinforcing bars and solid grout may be needed to resist earthquake forces. Figure 4.31 shows a reinforced grouted brick masonry wall. The size and placement of horizontal and vertical reinforcing steel is determined by local codes and regional requirements.

In regions without high wind conditions or earthquakes, reinforcing steel and grout are not needed. The unreinforced masonry wall or brick cavity wall is excellent for insulating exterior walls. Two 3" or 4" walls of brick are separated by a 2" airspace or cavity. This cavity provides a suitable space for insulating materials and the two masonry walls are bonded together with metal ties set in mortar joints. A wall section illustrating the cavity wall is shown in Figure 4.32.

Concrete block units for structural walls are generally 6" to 8" in thickness, depending on the height of the wall. The hollow sections of these units are called **cells.** These vertical cells may be left clear or filled solid with grout and reinforcing steel. This depends on regional and code requirements. In regions where reinforcing steel and solid grout are not required, the open cells may

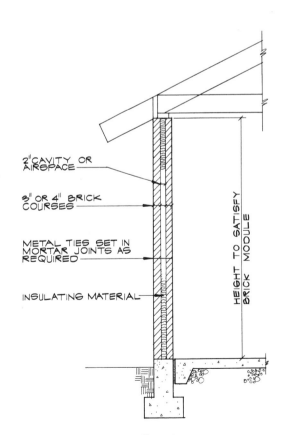

Figure 4.32 Brick cavity wall section.

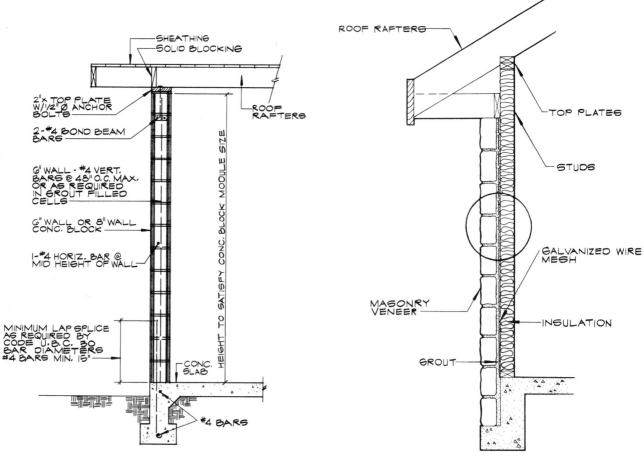

Figure 4.33 Reinforced concrete block wall section.

Labels for Figure 4.33:
- SHEATHING
- SOLID BLOCKING
- 2" x TOP PLATE W/1/2" Ø ANCHOR BOLTS
- 2-#4 BOND BEAM BARS
- 6" WALL - #4 VERT. BARS @ 48" O.C. MAX. OR AS REQUIRED IN GROUT FILLED CELLS
- 6" WALL OR 8" WALL CONC. BLOCK
- 1-#4 HORIZ. BAR @ MID HEIGHT OF WALL
- MINIMUM LAP SPLICE AS REQUIRED BY CODE U.B.C. 30 BAR DIAMETERS #4 BARS MIN. 15"
- ROOF RAFTERS
- HEIGHT TO SATISFY CONC. BLOCK MODULE SIZE
- CONC. SLAB
- #4 BARS

Figure 4.34 Wall section, masonry veneer.

Labels for Figure 4.34:
- ROOF RAFTERS
- TOP PLATES
- STUDS
- GALVANIZED WIRE MESH
- MASONRY VENEER
- INSULATION
- GROUT

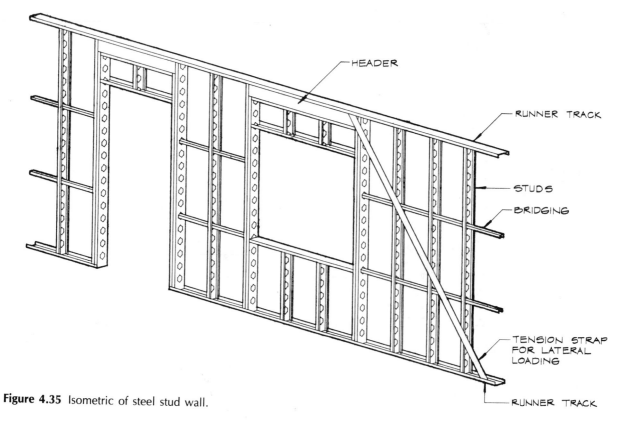

Figure 4.35 Isometric of steel stud wall.

Labels for Figure 4.35:
- HEADER
- RUNNER TRACK
- STUDS
- BRIDGING
- TENSION STRAP FOR LATERAL LOADING
- RUNNER TRACK

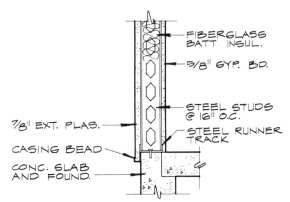

Figure 4.36 Partial steel stud wall section.

be filled with a suitable insulating material. When you detail concrete block wall, dimension the height of the wall to satisfy the modular heights of the masonry units selected. Figure 4.33 shows a reinforced concrete block wall.

Masonry Veneer Wall. Masonry veneer includes the use of brick, concrete block units, or stone. The maximum thickness of masonry veneer is regulated by most building codes and generally recognized as 5″. The term **masonry veneer** may be defined as a strictly masonry finish that is nonstructural and generally used for appearance.

Code requirements for the attachment of masonry or stone veneer may vary, depending on regional differences. In areas with seismic disturbances, a positive bond between the veneer and a stud wall is needed. A wall section using masonry veneer as an exterior wall finish is illustrated in Figure 4.34.

Steel Stud Walls. Using lightweight, cold-formed, steel members provides a solid wall-framing system for load-bearing walls. These walls provide an incombustible support for fire-rated construction and are well suited for preassembling. Moreover, shrinkage is of no concern with steel stud walls. The material of the studs varies from 14-gauge to 20-gauge galvanized steel with sizes from 3⅝″ to 10″.

These walls are constructed with a channel track at the bottom and top of the wall with the steel studs attached to the channels. Horizontal bridging is achieved with the use of a steel channel positioned through the stud punch-outs and secured by welding.

An isometric (a type of three-dimensional drawing) of a steel stud wall assembly is shown in Figure 4.35. The attachment of wood sheathing to steel framing members can be achieved with the use of self-tapping screws. A partial section of a steel stud wall using exterior stucco is shown in Figure 4.36.

Roof Systems

The principles underlying roof systems and the methods of developing these systems depends on the finish roof material. While roofing applications may vary, roofing manufacturers' literature should be consulted for installation recommendations. The four roofing materials generally used in construction are:

1. Wood shingle and shake
2. Asphaltic composition
3. Clay or concrete tile
4. Aluminum

Wood Shingles and Shakes

Each of these materials has its own set of requirements and construction methods for installation. For example, if you select wood shingles as the roof material, consider the following:

1. 4-in-12 minimum **roof pitch** (degree of inclination)
2. Spaced sheathing or stripping for air space requirements
3. Shingle exposure relative to roof pitch
4. Ventilation
5. Attachment technique
6. Flashing assemblies
7. Weathering qualities
8. Fire resistance
9. Cost

Figure 4.37 shows a drafted eave detail using wood shingles as the roofing material. This detail is shown in pictorial form in Figure 4.38.

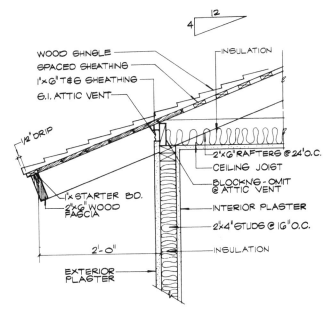

Figure 4.37 Eave detail.

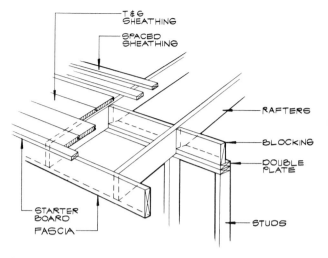

Figure 4.38 Pictorial, eave detail.

If a boxed-in eave is selected for architectural reasons, allow for ventilation. Provide a continuous vent or spaced vents in the soffit (overhead) area. Figure 4.39 shows a drafted detail of this condition. In this case, spaced sheathing is used at the overhand since the plaster soffit becomes the finish of the underside of the eave.

Roof construction methods vary depending on the building's architectural design. If the exterior design calls for exposed tail rafters, this requires a different construction method for the roof system. An example of this is shown in drafted form in Figure 4.40 and in pictorial form in Figure 4.41.

Build-up Asphaltic Composition Roof

Using a built-up asphaltic composition roof requires methods and principles contrary to those of a wood roof.

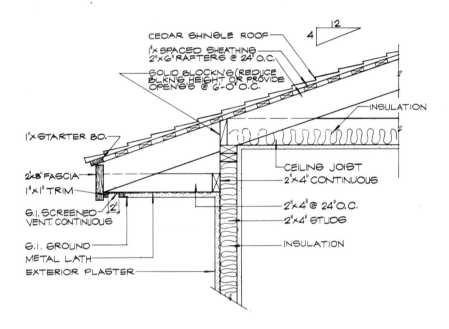

Figure 4.39 Boxed-in eave.

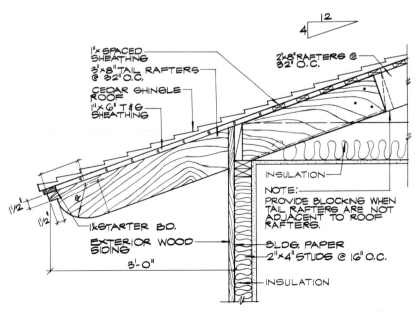

Figure 4.40 Eave detail.

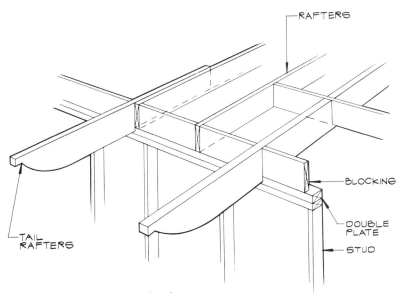

Figure 4.41 Pictorial, eave detail.

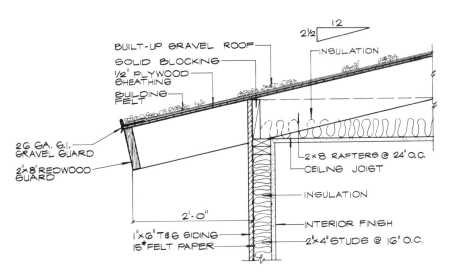

Figure 4.42 Eave detail.

The recommended pitch for wood shingles is a minimum of 4 in 12, while the recommended maximum pitch for a built-up roof is 3 in 12. Also, using spaced sheating is unsatisfactory for a built-up roofing system.

The quality of this type of roofing depends on the number and weight of the layers of asphaltic paper and hot tar mopping applications. The roof paper and hot mopping application are the primary deterrents against roof leaks, while the finish material is selected for beauty and architectural style. Two examples of built-up asphaltic composition roofs are shown in Figures 4.42 and 4.43.

Clay or Concrete Roof Tile

Clay or concrete roof tiles are one of the heaviest finish materials used and require large framing members such

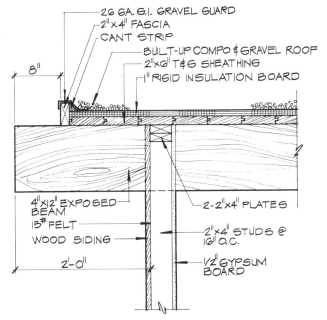

Figure 4.43 Eave detail.

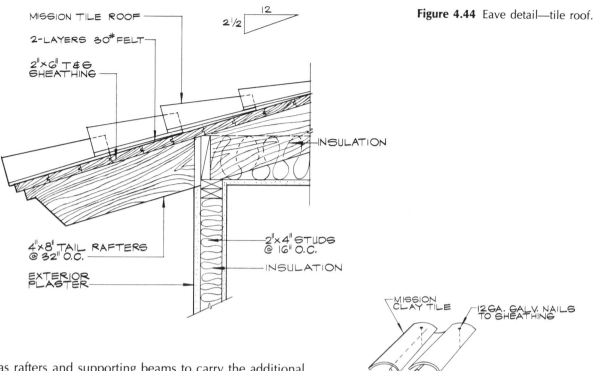

Figure 4.44 Eave detail—tile roof.

as rafters and supporting beams to carry the additional weight. Figure 4.44 shows a drafted eave detail using mission clay as a finish roof material.

Two acceptable methods for securing the tile to the framing members are, first, using 12-gauge galvanized nails secured to sheathing and, second, using wires spaced along the roof plane with wire ties attached to each individual tile. The wire ties are made from either 12-gauge galvanized wire, 10-gauge copper wire, or .084 diameter stainless steel wire. Figure 4.45 gives a pictorial representation of the use of nails for attaching tiles. Figure 4.46 shows wire ties used in tile attachment. Using wire ties reduces the risk of potential roof leaks because wires are secured only at the ridge and eave.

Aluminum Roofing

Aluminum roofing is available in various shapes, gauges, and colors. Panel thickness may range from 0.032″ to 0.040″ with baked-on enamel colors. The versatility of the aluminum roof permits application directly to steel girders or **purlins** (horizontal roof supports), or to plywood or solid sheathing roof decks, with insulation installed directly under the aluminum sheets.

Attachment of the aluminum sheet depends on the structure supporting the finish roofing. Generally, anchor clips or metal fasteners are used for attachment. The configuration of the aluminum varies in design. An example of an aluminum roof is shown in Figure 4.47. The shingle principle of lapping applies also to aluminum roofs. A drafted section for the assembly of an aluminum roof is illustrated in Figure 4.48.

Figure 4.45 Pictorial, tile roof fastening—nailing.

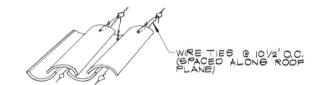

Figure 4.46 Pictorial, tile roof fastening—wire ties.

Figure 4.47 Aluminum roofing.

Figure 4.48 Aluminum roofing section.

SUMMARY

This chapter provided a basic understanding of construction principles, dealing with foundation, wall, and roof systems. These principles were illustrated and discussed, giving reasons for selection of one method or system over another.

Various details of foundation, wall, and roof assemblies were provided in order to point out different elements you must consider when detailing these assemblies.

IMPORTANT TERMS AND CONCEPTS

Foundation and floor systems
Floor joists
Cantilever Load-bearing foundations
Piers and girders
Flashing
Tongue-and-groove planking
Soils report
One-pour and two-pour systems
Dowels and reinforcing
Insulation
Wall systems
Balloon framing
Western or platform framing

Post and beam framing
Planking
Reinforced masonry wall
Brick cavity wall
Concrete block cells
Masonry veneer
Steel studs
Roof systems
Wood shingles and shakes
Roof pitch
Asphaltic composition roof
Clay or concrete roof tile
Aluminum roofing

REVIEW QUESTIONS

1. Give two reasons that a wood floor system might *not* be selected.
2. Name two conventional wood floor systems.
3. Given expansive soil conditions, provide three considerations for foundation design.
4. What is the main difference between Western and balloon wood framing?
5. Name four factors that should be considered when detailing a wood shingle roof assembly.
6. Name two methods for securing tiles to a roof assembly.

LABORATORY PROBLEMS

1. Using a scale of 1/8″ = 1′–0″, draw a foundation plan of 60′ × 30′ and provide a layout for two different wood floor systems.
2. Provide an exterior two-story wall section, using the Western framing method. The first floor is to be a concrete slab, and the second floor is to be a 2 × 10 joist at 16″ o.c., and exterior walls are to be 2 × 4 studs at 16″ o.c. The roof assembly will consist of 2 × 6 rafters at 24″ o.c. and ½″ exterior grade plywood sheathing. The finish roof material is to be built-up composition and gravel with a roof pitch of 2:12. Provide a 3′–0″ overhang. The scale will be assigned by your instructor.

5

PRELIMINARY STEPS IN PREPARING CONSTRUCTION DOCUMENTS

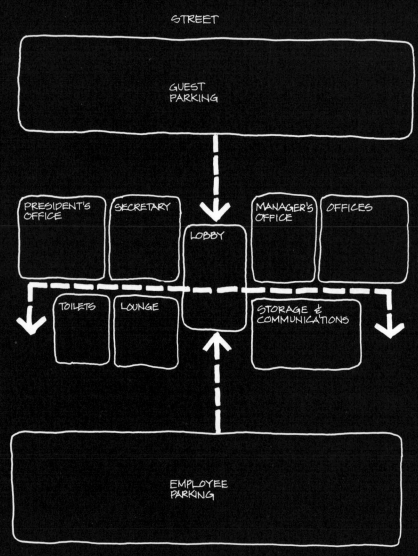

5

PREVIEW
This chapter examines the procedures and requirements that need to be considered before producing construction documents. These factors include building code requirements, regional differences and project programming. Discussions of each of these steps are illustrated and various conditions are considered and resolved.

OBJECTIVES
1. Be familiar with requirements necessary for the transition from preliminary drawings to construction documents.
2. Realize the importance of communication with consulting engineers before developing construction documents.
3. Be familiar with construction assemblies influenced by regional differences.
4. Understand the need for drawings to be constantly cross-checked during the preparation of construction documents.
5. Be aware of methods and requirements for project programming.

Making the Transition from Preliminary Drawings to Construction Documents

Making the transition from approved preliminary drawings to construction documents is important because it completes the process of making decisions about the physical characteristics of the building. Once this transition is made, the production of construction documents can proceed.

Accomplishing this transition—the design development phase—requires that the following basic requirements be satisfied and thoroughly investigated:

1. Building code and other requirements, such as those set by the zoning department, fire department, health department, planning department, and architectural committees
2. Primary materials analysis
3. Selection of the primary structural system
4. Requirements of consultants, such as mechanical and electrical engineers
5. Regional considerations
6. Energy conservation considerations and requirements
7. Interrelationship of drawings
8. Project programming

Building Code Requirements

Building code requirements are extremely important to research. Figure 5.1, for example, shows a small office building with a code requirement of a minimum dimension between required exit stairs. The correct placement of these stairs is important because the whole structural concept, the office layouts, and many other factors will be affected by their location.

Many people frequently overlook the building code requirements for correct stair dimensions. Often they give a little attention to the width of stairs and landings or to the provisions for the necessary number of risers (stair height) and treads (step width) to satisfy the vertical dimensions between floors. See Figure 5.2.

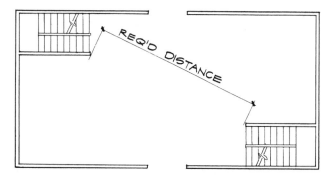

Figure 5.1 Stair separation (commercial).

Two further examples of satisfying the physical requirements dictated by the code are illustrated in Figure

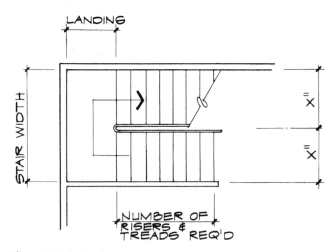

Figure 5.2 Stair dimensions (commercial).

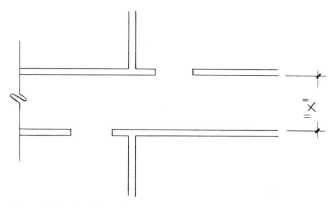

Figure 5.3 Corridor dimension (commercial).

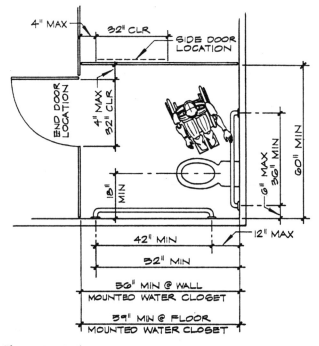

Figure 5.4 Toilet compartment for wheelchair use.

5.3, which shows corridor dimensions, and Figure 5.4, which shows handicapped toilet access.

In multiple housing projects as well as in residential projects, building codes establish minimum physical requirements for various rooms. Figure 5.5 shows the minimum floor areas and dimensions required for the bedroom and kitchen.

Primary Materials Analysis

The most important building materials to be selected are for foundations and floors, exterior and interior walls, and ceiling and roof structures. There are several factors that influence selection, and many of these require considerable investigation and research:

A. Architectural design
B. Building codes
C. Economics
D. Structural concept
E. Region
F. Ecology
G. Energy conservation

An example of the importance of selection is given in Figure 5.6. Concrete block units have been selected as the material for the exterior walls of a structure. Using this material affects the exterior and interior dimensions because concrete blocks have fixed dimensions. Establishing the exterior and interior dimensions *before* the production of construction documents is most important because other phases, such as the structural engineering, are based on these dimensions.

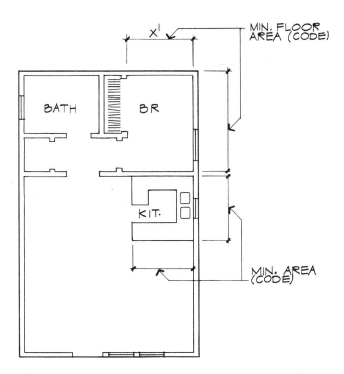

Figure 5.5 Apartment unit.

Modular and Nonmodular Units

The term "module" refers to a predetermined dimension from which structures are designed. "Block module" is usually used in conjunction with masonry units, such as bricks, concrete blocks, or structural clay tiles.

Masonry units can be broadly classified as either modular or nonmodular. The mortar joint between two units is usually either $3/8''$, $7/16''$, or $1/2''$ thick. Modular sizes are designed to ensure that final measurements including mortar joints are in whole numbers. Nonmodular units result in fractional measurements.

As an example, an 8 × 8 × 16 modular concrete block unit measures $7 5/8'' × 7 5/8'' × 15 5/8''$, so that a $3/8$-inch mortar joint produces a final 8 × 8 × 16 measurement to work with. There are also half sizes available, so that when the units are stacked on top of each other, lapping each other by one half the length of the block, the end of the structure comes out even. See Figure 5.7.

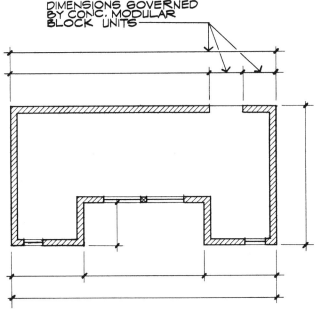

Figure 5.6 Exterior concrete block walls.

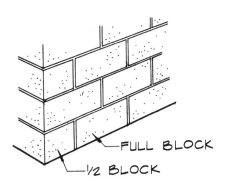

Figure 5.7 Use of half block.

Certain lengths are commonly available. See Appendix B, Table B.6, left column. These measurements follow three rules: first, all even numbers of feet are available (2'–0", 8'–0", 24'–0", etc.); second, all odd-numbered feet have four inches added to them (for example, the length closest to 3 feet is 3'–4", the length closest to 9 feet is 9'–4", etc.); third, all even-numbered feet are also available in 8" increments, such as 4'–8", 8'–8", and 32'–8".

Using the preceding rules or Appendix B, Table B.6, left column, Table A, check to see if the following measurements are good for lengths of a concrete block structure using an 8 × 8 × 16 modular construction.

A. 28'–8"
B. 42'–9"
C. 101'–4"
D. 89'–4"
E. 93'–8"

All but B and E are correct. B should be 42'–8" and E should be 93'–4".

The height on left column Table B.6 is calculated in the same way and presented in two columns—one for 4"-high blocks and one for 8"-high blocks. The 4"-high blocks do not completely follow the rules mentioned earlier. A careful examination of the chart will reveal a single rule: all modular dimensions will be 4", 8", or 0" (for example, 3'–4", 6'–8", or 10'–0").

Tables B and C are for a nonmodular system. The same size concrete block is used here but with a different mortar joint. Odd fractions begin to appear. Only heights are shown. The mortar joints—both ⁷⁄₁₆" and ½"—affect window and door sizes and heights.

Brick also comes in modular and nonmodular sizes. Examples of sizes for a modular unit are 5⅝" × 2¼" × 7⅝" for a ⅜" joint and 3½" × 2³⁄₁₆" × 7½" for a ½" joint. 2½" × 3⅞" × 8¼" is a nonmodular size. See Appendix B, Table B.7 for an interpretation of nonmodular height and length applications.

Here are some of the things you should consider when deciding whether or not to use the block module system:

1. Heights of the structure
2. Ceiling heights
3. Size of foundation if walls are masonry units
4. Size of floor plan if foundation wall is made of masonry units
5. Window and door openings
6. Window and door heights

If you have a choice of modular or nonmodular materials, use modular. The dimensions are easier to figure out, and, as contractors report, the structure is faster, easier, and cheaper to build.

Why, then, would you choose nonmodular? You may be forced into nonmodular sizes. For example, building function might dictate overall size, as in an assembly

plant. The client may require that a building occupy the full width or depth of a piece of property to maximize the site use. An auditorium size is often dictated by seating arrangement or acoustics. A fire department regulation may determine certain size corridors for schools. These are only a few of the reasons for using a nonmodular system. If all these kinds of restraints can be satisfied by using modular units, use modular units.

Because of the state of the technology, the cost of cutting masonry units is rapidly decreasing, thus giving greater selection for almost any size structure. Cutting reduces the visual unity of the building and should be used with discretion.

The importance of selecting primary building materials is further shown in Figure 5.8. The roofing material selected here actually governs the roof pitch. This in turn establishes the physical height of the building and also dictates the size of the supporting members relative to the weight of the finished roof material.

Selecting the Primary Structural System

The selection of a structural system and its members is influenced by the following: meeting building code requirements, satisfying design elements, and using the most logical system based on sound engineering principles, economic considerations, and simplicity.

For most projects, the architect consults with the structural engineer about systems or methods that will meet these various considerations. Figures 5.9 and 5.10 illustrate the importance of establishing a structural concept before producing construction documents. Figure 5.9 shows a residential floor plan in which an exposed wood post and beam structure system has been selected. Here, the walls should fall directly beneath the beam

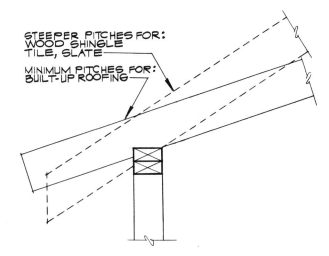

Figure 5.8 Roof material and roof pitches.

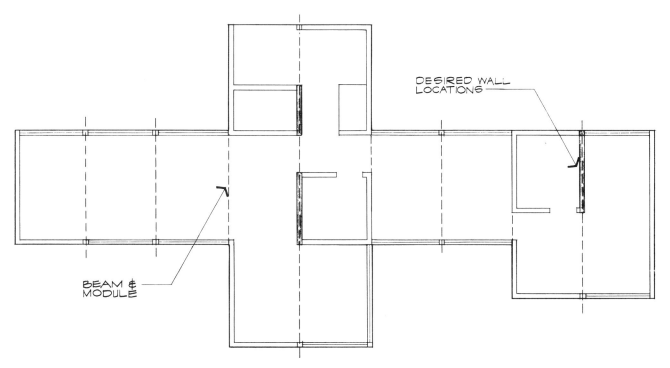

Figure 5.9 Wood post and beam structural system.

module. To achieve these desired wall locations and to accommodate the modular structural system, you may need to adjust the floor plan.

Another example of structural factors is the need, at times, for shear (earthquake resistant) walls to resist lateral forces. Figure 5.10 shows a retail store floor plan which has an extensive amount of glass. However, preliminary structural engineering calculations also require the use of shear walls at various locations in order to resist earthquake (seismic) or wind forces. To satisfy these requirements, you would need to make a physical adjustment to the floor plan.

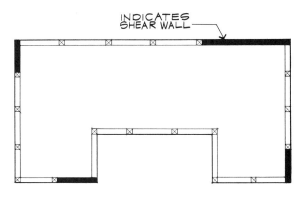

Figure 5.10 Plan view—shear wall locations.

Requirements of Consultants

Early involvement of structural, electrical, mechanical, and civil engineering consultants is highly recommended. Their early involvement generally results in physical adjustments to the finalized preliminary drawings in order to meet their design requirements. For example, the mechanical engineer's design may require a given area on the roof to provide space for various sizes of roof-mounted mechanical equipment. See Figure 5.11. For projects that require mechanical ducts to be located in floor and ceiling areas, necessary space and clearances for ducts must be provided. Figure 5.12 shows a floor and ceiling section with provisions for mechanical duct space.

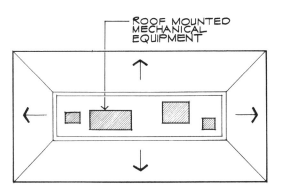

Figure 5.11 Roof plan—mechanical equipment area.

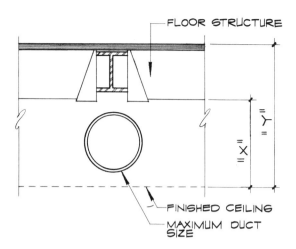

Figure 5.12 Mechanical duct space equipment.

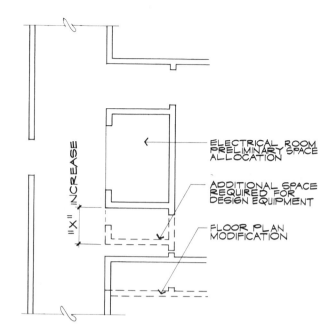

Figure 5.13 Electrical equipment room modification.

The electrical engineer should also be consulted about any physical modifications to the building that may be required to provide space for electrical equipment. In most cases, the architect or project manager provides for an electrical equipment room or cabinet in the plans. However, with the increasing sophistication and size of equipment, additional space may be required. This increase in the electrical room dimension may require a floor plan adjustment, which can even result in a major or minor plan modification. Figure 5.13 illustrates a floor plan modification to satisfy space requirements for electrical equipment.

Regional Considerations

Regional differences in construction techniques are mainly controlled or influenced by climatic conditions, soil conditions, and natural events such as very high winds and earthquakes. These are considered in greater detail later.

In brief, regional differences influence:

1. Foundation design
2. Exterior wall design
3. Framing system
4. Roof design
5. Structural considerations
6. Insulation

Figure 5.14 illustrates a type of foundation used in regions with cold climatic conditions: an exterior foundation wall and footing with a concrete floor. The depth of the foundation is established from the frost line, and insulation is required under the concrete floor.

Where temperatures are mild and warm, the foundation design and construction techniques are primarily governed by soils investigations and local building

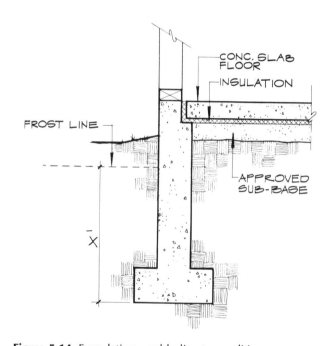

Figure 5.14 Foundation—cold climate conditions.

codes. Figure 5.15 illustrates an exterior foundation detail where the depth of the footing is established to a recommended depth below the natural grade.

Another example of regional influence is the change in exterior wall design. Figure 5.16 shows a section of an exterior wall with wood frame construction. This open frame construction is suitable for mild climates. A wood frame exterior wall recommended for Eastern regions is shown in Figure 5.17. Here, solid sheathing is used, and this in turn requires the wood studs to be set in

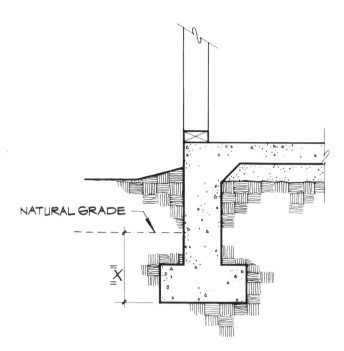

Figure 5.15 Foundation—recommended depth in warm climate.

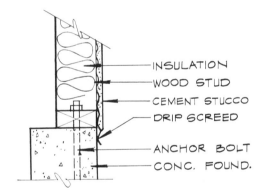

Figure 5.16 Exterior wall—open frame construction.

from the face of the foundation wall. This one regional difference can affect many procedures and detailing throughout the construction documents such as wall dimensioning, window details, and door details.

Energy Conservation

To determine what you must do to satisfy local and federal energy conservation requirements, you must complete preliminary research. These requirements can affect exterior wall material and thickness, amount and type of glazing, areas of infiltration (leakage of air), amount of artificial lighting to be used, thickness and type of insulation, mechanical engineering design, and

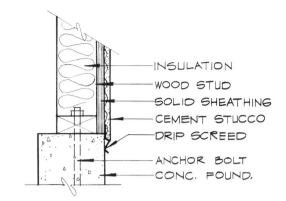

Figure 5.17 Exterior wall—sheathed frame construction.

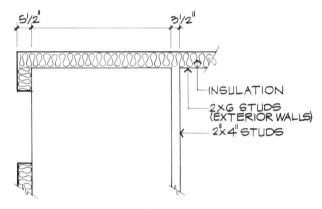

Figure 5.18 Floor plan wall thickness.

so forth. For example, a wood building requires exterior walls to be 2 × 6 studs intead of 2 × 4 to allow for the thickness of the building insulation. This particular requirement dictates procedures in the construction document process, such as floor plan wall thickness and dimensioning, window and exterior door details, and other related exterior wall details. Figure 5.18 shows a segment of a floor plan and indicates the thickness of walls and the locations of required insulation.

Interrelationship of Drawings

When you develop construction documents, you must have consistent relationships between the drawings for continuity and clarity. These relationships vary in their degree of importance.

For example, the relationship between the foundation plan and the floor plan is most important because continuity of dimensioning and correlation of structural components are both required. See Figure 5.19. The dimensioning of the floor plan and the foundation plan are identical and this provides continuity for dimensional accuracy.

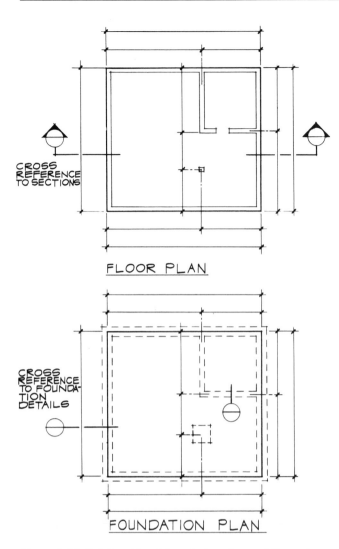

Figure 5.19 Relationship of foundation plan and floor plan.

The relationship between drawings for the electrical plan and the mechanical plan is also important. This relationship is critical because the positioning of electrical fixtures must not conflict with the location of mechanical components, such as air supply grilles or fire sprinkler heads.

Cross-reference drawings with important relationships such as these and constantly review them throughout the preparation of the construction documents. Only in this way will you avoid conflicts.

This cross-referencing and review is not as critical with drawings that are not so closely related, such as the electrical plan and the civil engineering plans, or the interior elevations and the foundation.

Project Programming

For many construction projects, a construction firm uses a time schedule process to coordinate all trades and services necessary to finish the project on the scheduled completion date. Architects also use a time schedule for programming phases of a project.

The primary phases of a project are preliminary design, client review, preliminary budget, agency review (when required), construction documents, final construction bids, and building department approvals and permits.

Office Procedure and Planning Strategy

Most offices have a set procedure for planning the transition from preliminary drawings to the development and execution of working drawings. In a small office it may be a simple matter of the principal giving verbal commands to employees until a specific system is understood. In a large office the system may be an intricate network of planned procedures.

There are two items in any office with which the beginner will be confronted. These are described herein as **standards**, standard graphic and written patterns to which the office subscribes, and **procedures**, the methods that are instituted during this transition.

Standards

Many offices have a booklet called *Office Standards* or *The Drafting Room Manual*. It contains such items as the following:

A. A Uniform List of Abbreviations for working drawings
B. Material designations in plan, section, and elevation
C. Graphic symbols
D. Methods of representing doors and windows in both plan and elevation
E. Electrical and plumbing symbols
F. Graphic representations of appliances and fixtures
G. Sheet standards and drawing modules

These standards might be presented in an informal packet, photocopied and stapled or housed in a binder with divisions for specific standards to be followed. There is such a collection of standards printed at the end of the Student Manual and in the specific chapters within this text. For example, the graphic symbols and methods of representing doors and windows in a plan are included in Chapter 8 of this book as well as in the Student Manual.

Procedures

For a beginner, the transition process of changing design proposals to working drawings appears to be a complex one, because there are so many pieces to the puzzle. If you understand the system, then not only will you understand the steps to follow but you will begin to comprehend how you fit into this system.

As in sports, there is a game plan (the procedure) with specific plays (standards) for the individual player (drafter). One must know how the game is to be played, the specific play being incorporated, and each player's individual responsibility within each specific plan. Standardization is critical, because if an injury occurs (illness), another player must be able to take over without missing a beat.

Think of the process, as described here, as parallel to a basketball, football, or even a baseball game. It is important to understand the role of the owner of the team, the manager, the offense and defense coaches, and the team members, including the team captain. In this comparison the owner might be viewed as the principal, the manager as the person in charge of the specific job, the offense and defense coaches as professional associates such as the electrical engineer and structural engineer, and, finally, the players as the drafters. The more seasoned the player (drafter) the more responsibility he or she takes on. These players often become the spirit, the determination, and the core around whom new players rally.

To take the analogy a step further, the spectators are the clients with certain expectations and the umpires and referees can be compared with the building inspectors who check for violation of the rules of the game.

There are however, large differences: the duration of the project, the cost/investment, and the life span of the project being executed. Moreover, our profession also addresses the health and safety, as well as the creative needs, of generations of clients.

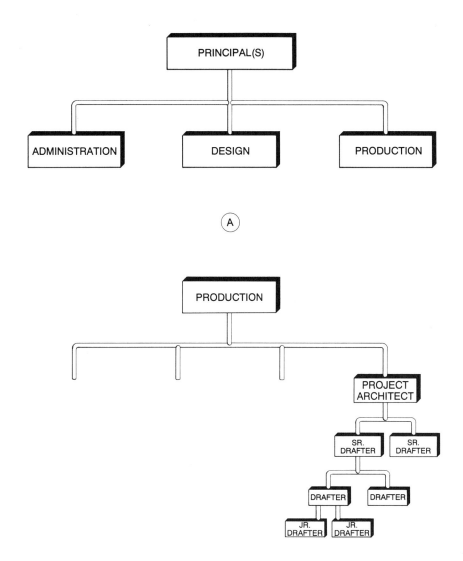

Figure 5.20 Vertical office structure.

Office Structure

An architectural office may be set up in what can be described as a horizontal or a vertical configuration. Figure 5.20(A) shows individual departments in a vertical office structure. In this example, the principal(s) are positioned at the top of the structure, much like a president of a college. Directly below this level are the main departments: the Administration Department, the Design Department, and the Production Department.

Because we are dealing with working drawings in this example, see Figure 5.20(B) for a further breakdown of the Production Department. The project architect or manager, as they are often called, becomes the key figure in the designation of responsibility, selection of standards, and, usually, establishing and planning the man-hours. There is a distinct hierarchy, with certain responsibilities and salaries inherently built into this system.

In contrast to the vertical structure is the horizontal office structure. See Figure 5.21. At the top of the structure are the principal(s), as in the vertical structure. Yet this is where the similarity ends. The rest of the staff is now broken down into teams, studios, or groups—the name of a grouping is not as important as its physical makeup. All teams large or small take on a total project from initial concept to finished product. Therefore, all components of a project are found within a single group: the administration, the designers, and, certainly, the production people.

In this scheme, there may be distinct separation of the three basic components within the team or, as has been experimented with, all members of a team may make their contributions to the specific functions, namely, administration, design, and production. Each individual becomes a teacher and a student, depending on his or her expertise and the component within which he or she is working.

Because much learning takes place within this type of structure, the teams have a tendency to grow in proficiency and speed. There is also a sense of pride inherently built into a system that allows each person on a team to participate in all facets of a project. Auxiliary services, such as model making, billing, reproduction, coordination with associates, CAD, and so on, may be interwoven in the fiber of either structure or may be jobbed out to an outside firm.

In this day of specialization, we can also find firms that predominately perform one of the main functions, such as design, while using another firm to translate design ideas into production drawings, or even to supervise. This is most often the case when an architect is hired outside a particular region, state, or country. For instance, suppose a European-based firm is awarded a commission to design a structure in the United States. In this case, the design is often translated into production drawings via a local or regional firm familiar with the ecological problems of the particular U.S. region, the building code restrictions, and the symbols and conventions (the architectural language of the region) of the particular city or county.

Project Architect

Let us look now at the possible responsibility of the project architect or project manager, as this person is known in some offices. In tandem with the principal (in a small office) or an immediate senior, the project architect sets out to form a project notebook. This notebook will contain everything known about a specific project. It is like a project diary. Among the items that the project notebook might contain are the following:

A. Design and schematic sketches
B. Cartoon of the project
C. Listing of the structural considerations
D. List of the finishes
   1. Exterior
   2. Interior
E. List of equipment, appliances, and fixtures
F. Drawing sequences to be followed
G. Job number, legal description, and task numbers
H. Planned man-hours
I. Record of telephone conversations pertaining to the job correspondence
J. Manufacturers' literature
K. Code requirements, restrictions, plan check forms, permits
L. Standards

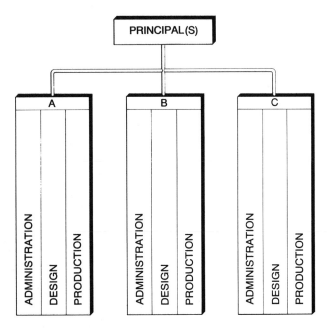

Figure 5.21 Horizontal office structure.

Using the example of the Ryan Residence, which is found in the Student Manual, we will trace through the process described here and show how a complete set of working drawings is developed. As a basis, we will use the main headings of the project notebook.

The development of each drawing will be presented at the end of the chapter dealing with that particular topic. For example, to see the evolution of the Floor Plan of the Ryan Residence, refer to Chapter 8, or to Chapter 10 for the various stages needed in the development of Ryan Residence building sections. Accordingly, the following aspects and drawings of the Ryan Residence are found at the end of the corresponding chapters:

6. Site Plan
7. Foundation Plan
8. Floor Plan
9. Schedules
10. Building Section
11. Exterior Elevations
12. Roof and Ceiling Framing
13. Interior Elevations
14. Architectural and Structural Details
15. Completed Stages of the Residence

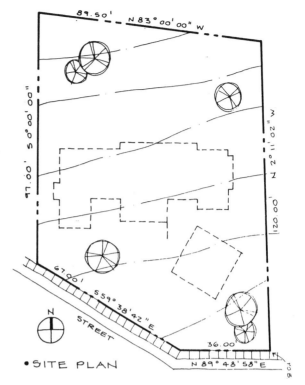

Figure 5.22 Preliminary site plan.

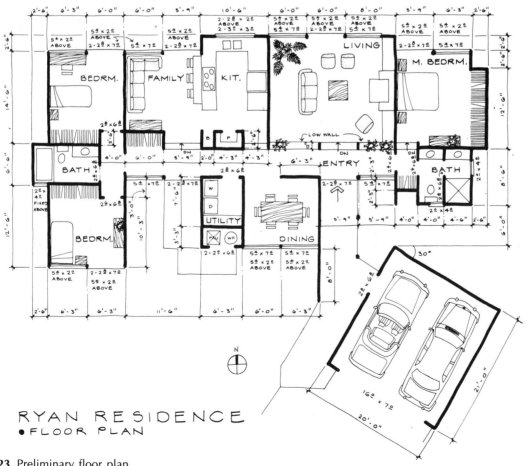

Figure 5.23 Preliminary floor plan.

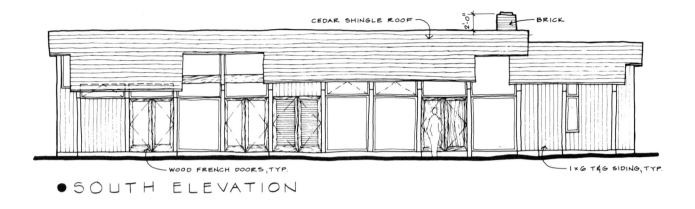

CEDAR SHINGLE ROOF — | 2'-0" | — BRICK

WOOD FRENCH DOORS, TYP.

1 × 6 T&G SIDING, TYP.

● SOUTH ELEVATION

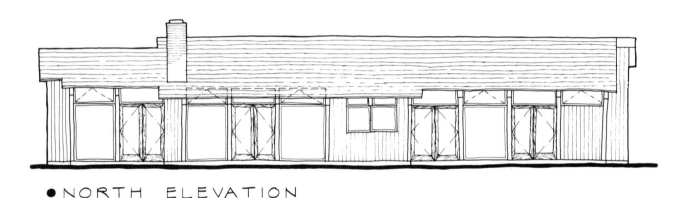

● NORTH ELEVATION

Figure 5.24 Preliminary elevations.

Design and Schematic Drawings

The design sketches and schematic drawings represent the culmination of many hours of designer-client decisions. Some sets may even include the evolution of a design as a final presentation to the client, and the final changes incorporated by the client based on such things as financing or the scaling-down of the structure because of the projected number of users. At some point a final decision is made, signed, and becomes the final design proposal used by the project manager to evolve as a set of drawings.

There are two kinds of design and schematic drawings to be considered. The first group is the first set of preliminary drawings developed by the designer in response to the client's needs. These provide the basis for the formulation and incorporation of changes and new ideas. Included are a site plan (Figure 5.22), floor plan (Figure 5.23), and a couple of elevations (Figure 5.24).

If this set of drawings is approved, additional preliminary structural drawings are conceived, which may include a foundation plan (Figure 5.25), a building section (Figure 5.26), and possibly a framing plan. A complete set of these preliminary design and structure drawings can be seen in the Student Manual.

However, changes will more than likely be requested by the client based on his or her additional thoughts after viewing the preliminaries or on the available finances or on any number of unanticipated factors, such as acquiring a mobile home or a boat.

These changes lead to another set of preliminary drawings. Changes are shown in Figure 5.27 and reflected in Figure 5.28 (site plan), Figure 5.29 (floor plan) and Figure 5.30 (elevation). Once these are approved, the preliminary foundation plan, building sections, and framing plans (Figures 5.31, 5.32, and 5.33 respectively) are developed. Of course, different roof systems, floor systems, exterior wall coverings, and so on are discussed with the client during consideration of the changes.

The project manager then sets the production-drawing wheels in motion by developing a cartoon of the project.

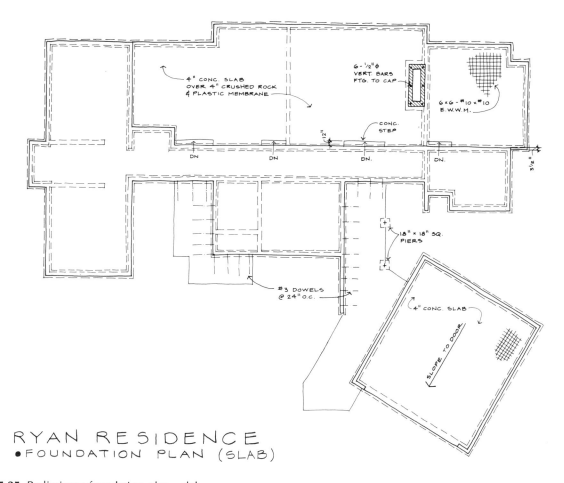

RYAN RESIDENCE
•FOUNDATION PLAN (SLAB)

Figure 5.25 Preliminary foundation plan—slab.

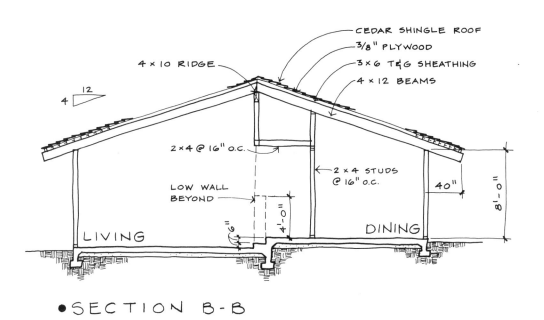

•SECTION B-B

Figure 5.26 Preliminary building section.

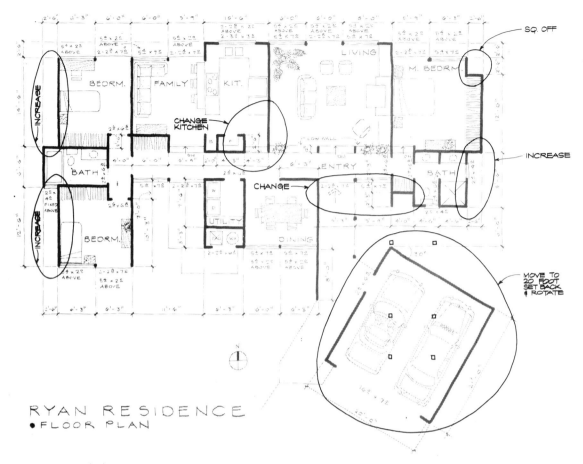

Figure 5.27 Requested changes.

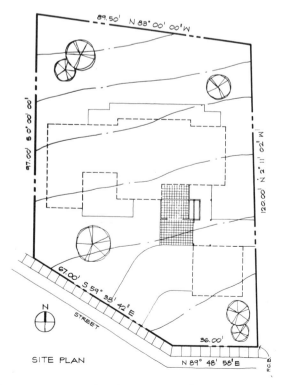

Figure 5.28 Revised preliminary site plan.

Examples of this type of cartoon are shown in Figure 5.37 and 5.38.

A complete cartoon set for the Ryan Residence (both types) can be seen on Sheets A-1 through A-6 in Chapter 15.

Sheet Layout

Every office uses a particular sheet size and format. Sheet sizes range from 24 × 36 and larger—for example, 28 × 42 or 36 × 42.

A typical sheet might look like that shown in Figure 5.39. In this example, there is a ½-inch border on the top, bottom, and right side of the sheet, whereas the left side has a 1½-inch border to accommodate for binding the set of drawings.

Years ago, the architectural industry borrowed from the mechanical and aircraft industries and had a square title block mounted on the bottom-right corner of the sheet. This left an unfriendly L-shaped space in which to draw. For the past few decades, we have used a strip title block on the right side of the sheet, as shown in the example. These can be preprinted or make use of title blocks printed onto a translucent sheet with a glue backing, which is called a sticky back.

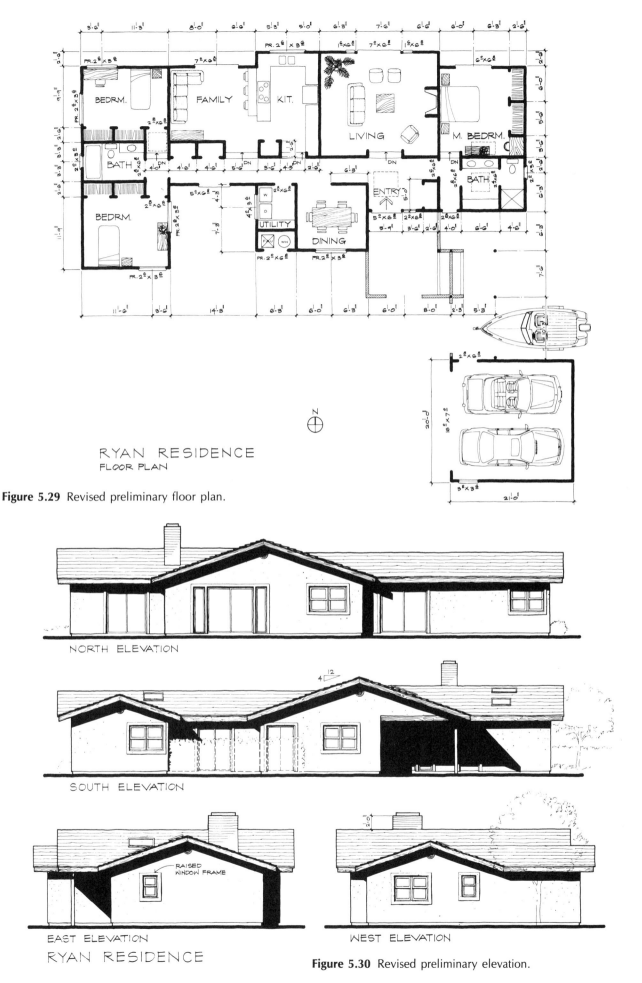

RYAN RESIDENCE
FLOOR PLAN

Figure 5.29 Revised preliminary floor plan.

NORTH ELEVATION

SOUTH ELEVATION

EAST ELEVATION

WEST ELEVATION

RYAN RESIDENCE

Figure 5.30 Revised preliminary elevation.

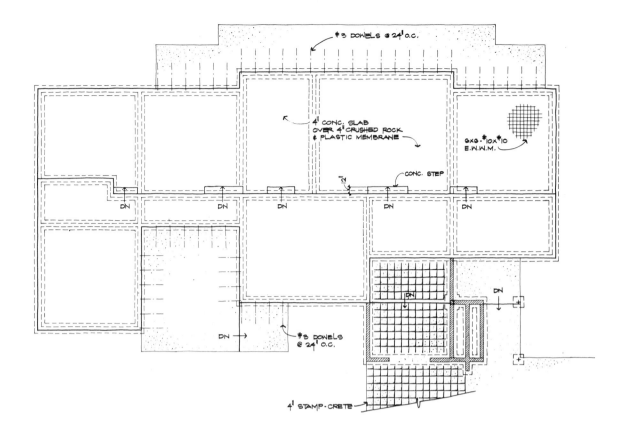

#3 DOWELS @ 24" O.C.

4" CONC. SLAB
OVER 4" CRUSHED ROCK
& PLASTIC MEMBRANE

6x6 - #10 x #10
E.W.W.M.

CONC. STEP

DN

#3 DOWELS
@ 24" O.C.

4" STAMP-CRETE

RYAN RESIDENCE
FOUNDATION PLAN (SLAB)

Figure 5.31 Revised preliminary foundation plan.

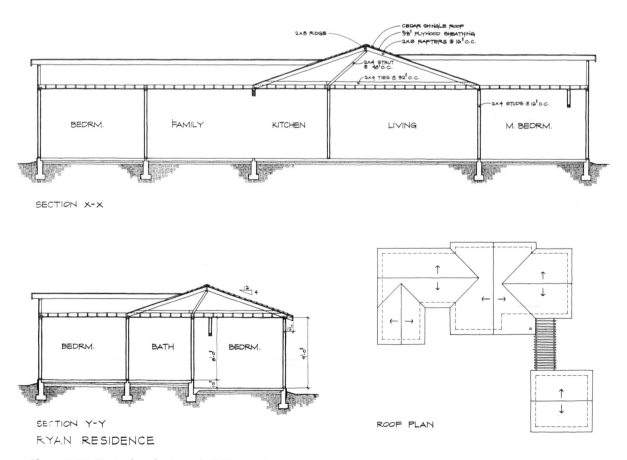

CEDAR SHINGLE ROOF
3/8" PLYWOOD SHEATHING
2x8 RAFTERS @ 16" O.C.

2x8 RIDGE

2x4 STRUT
@ 48" O.C.

2x4 TIES @ 32" O.C.

2x4 STUDS @ 16" O.C.

BEDRM.   FAMILY   KITCHEN   LIVING   M. BEDRM.

SECTION X-X

BEDRM.   BATH   BEDRM.

SECTION Y-Y
RYAN RESIDENCE

ROOF PLAN

Figure 5.32 Revised preliminary building sections.

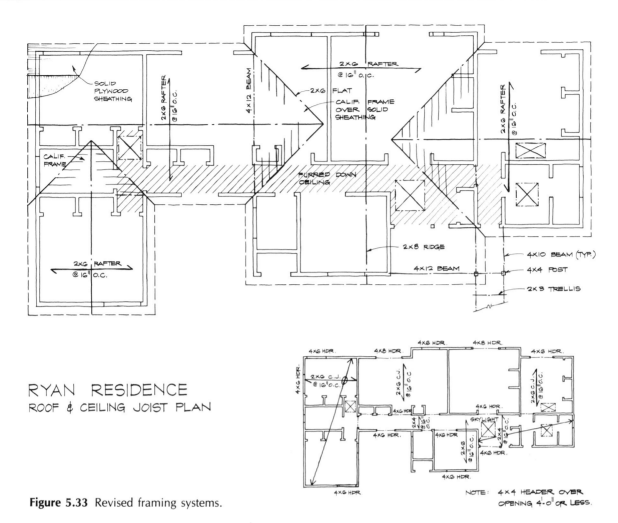

RYAN RESIDENCE
ROOF & CEILING JOIST PLAN

Figure 5.33 Revised framing systems.

Cartoon of the Project

A cartoon, or mock set as it is called in some regions, is a reduced replica of the distribution of the drawings on each of the working drawing sheets drawn on an 8½" × 11" sheet of paper. They can be accomplished by substituting rectangles in place of the actual drawings, as shown in Figures 5.34 and 5.35, or the preliminary design studies can be reduced on a plain paper copier to the proper scale and pasted into place as shown in Figure 5.36. The second procedure is much faster, and the final image is a close replication of the final drawing.

Note the tick marks on the sheet around the borderline. If these are extended horizontally and vertically, they will form a matrix. The project manager will try to use this matrix to establish the drawing size limits and distribute the drawings in such a manner as to stay within these limits. In this way, general notes, details, schedules, and so forth can be drawn on separate sheets, reproduced onto sticky backs, and positioned onto the large sheets without encroaching onto other drawing on the sheet.

Throughout the development of the Ryan Residence, you will note the adherence to this matrix. There will be times that, owing to the scale or size of a detail, or the length of a note, we will not be able to adhere to this module. The fireplace detail is a good example of such nonadherence. The footing details adjacent to the foundation plan provide a good example of the use of the matrix.

At some point during this development, structural considerations will be discussed with the structural engineer, architect, or someone in the office in charge of structure. These are listed in a format similar that found in Figure 5.40. Although this list addresses only the overall structural approach to the structure, the drafter must understand the specifics in regard to sizes of the members, materials used to create an energy-efficient building, and, of course, the overall structural concept.

For example, in dealing with the Ryan Residence, if you wish to find out how the roof is configured, read the section at the end of Chapter 12. Similarly, if you wish to understand the specific architectural features around the window or the type and shape of the fireplace, see the last part of Chapter 14.

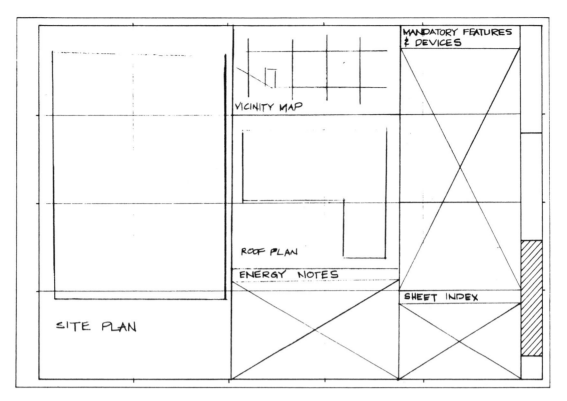

Figure 5.34 Cartoon showing distribution of drawing and notes.

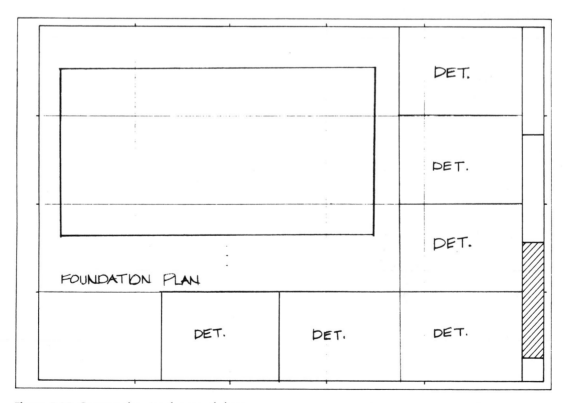

Figure 5.35 Cartoon showing format of sheet.

Figure 5.36 Cartoon preparation.

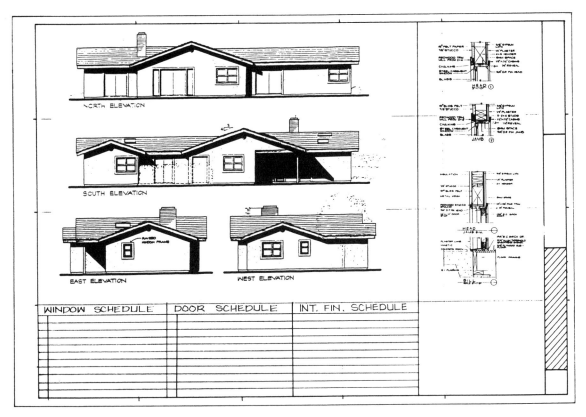

Figure 5.37 Cartoon of Ryan Residence exterior elevation.

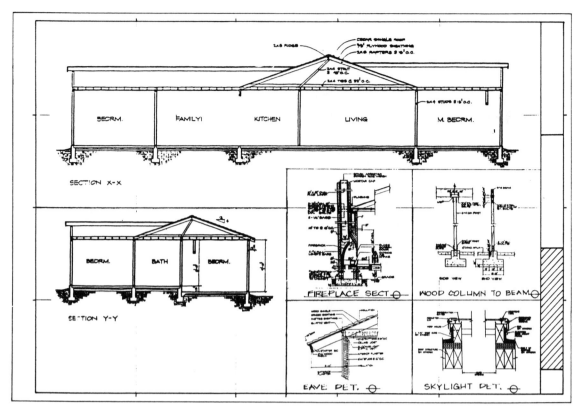

Figure 5.38 Cartoon of Ryan Residence building section.

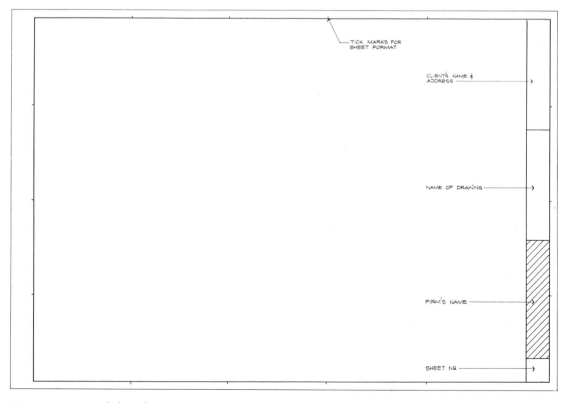

Figure 5.39 Typical sheet layout.

I. Structural

    A. Foundation

        1. Conventional slab-on-grade

        2. Post-tensioned slab

        3. Wood floor

        4. Other _____

    B. Typical Wall Framing

        1. 2 × __ wood studs

        2. 2 × wood studs per structural consultant

        3. Other _____

    C. Typical Floor Framing

        1. 2 × __ wood floor joists

        2. 2 × wood floor joists per structural consultant

        3. TJI

        4. 1½″ lightweight concrete

           over _____

        5. Other _____

        Note: Specify any minimum sizes.

    D. Typical Roof Framing

        1. Conventional (wood rafters and beams)

        2. TJI

        3. Trusses

        4. Trusses and conventional framing

        Note: Specify any minimum sizes.

Figure 5.40 Listing of structural considerations.

Exterior Finishes

In the development of the exterior elevation, the drafter must be able to identify the various materials used on the exterior surface, as well as the type of fenestration via windows and doors. As with structural considerations, a chart is again the instrument used to convey the information to the drafter. See Figure 5.41.

Interior Finishes

To allow an accurate drawing of the floor plan, interior elevation, and finish schedule, interior finishes are selected by the client in conjunction with the designer. The drafter can find this information in the project book on a chart similar to the one found in Figure 5.42. Although this list is called "Interior Finishes," it often includes appliances and other amenities such as fireplaces, a security system, a safe, and so on.

II. Exterior Finishes

    A. Walls

        1. Stucco (specify texture)

           a. Sand texture

           b. Other _____

        2. Cedar Siding

           a. Lap with mitered corners

           b. Lap with corner boards

        3. Masonite Siding

           (specify other manufacturers)

           _____

           a. Lap with metal corners

           b. Lap with corner boards

           c. V-groove with corners boards

           d. Other _____

        4. Masonry Veneer

           a. Thin set brick

              (manufacturer _____)

           b. Full brick

              (manufacturer _____)

           c. Stone

           d. Stucco stone

           e. Other _____

    B. Trims, Barges, and Fascia

        1. Size:

           a. × __ Trim at windows and doors

              __ Whole house

              __ Front elevation only

           b. × __ Barge and fascia with

              __ × __ Trim over

        2. Texture

           a. S4S

           b. Resawn

           c. Rough sawn

           d. Other _____

    C. Roofing

        1. Material

           a. Wood shakes

           b. Wood Shingle

           c. Concrete "s" tile

              (manufacturer _____)

           d. Clay "s" tile

              (manufacturer _____)

Figure 5.41 Listing of exterior finishes.

e. Clay 2-piece mission tile

(manufacturer _____)

f. Flat concrete tile

(manufacturer _____)

g. Composition shingle

(manufacturer _____)

h. Built-up

i. Built-up with gravel surface

j. Other _____

2. Gutters

a. At whole house

b. At doors only

Note: Gutters will be assumed at all tight eave conditions.

3. Diverters at doors (composition shingle, wood-shake and shingle, and flat conc. tile only)

D. Decks and Balconies

1. 2 × spaced decking

2. Dex-o-Tex waterproof membrane decking

3. Other _____

E. Stairs

1. Treads

a. Open wood treads

b. Precast concrete treads

c. Concrete-filled metal pan treads

d. Dex-o-Tex waterproof membrane

2. Stringers

a. Steel stringers

b. Wood stringers

F. Doors

1. Entry

a. 3068 1¼" s.c.

(manufacturer _____)

b. 3080 1¼" s.c.

(manufacturer _____)

c. Other _____

2. Patio/Deck

a. Aluminum sliding glass door

b. Aluminum French doors

c. Wood sliding glass door

d. Wood French doors

e. Other _____

3. Garage

a. Overhead

b. Wood roll-up

(manufacturer _____)

c. Metal roll-up

(manufacturer _____)

G. Windows

1. 　　　　　　Aluminum　　Wood

Sliding　　____　　____

Single-hung　　____　　____

Double-hung　　____　　____

Awning　　____　　____

Casement　　____　　____

2. Muntins

a. All windows

b. Front elevation and related rooms

3. Dual-glazed

4. Single and dual glazing per Title 24

5. Other _____

H. Skylights

1. Glass (manufacturer _____)

Color

a. Bronze

b. Gray

c. Clear

d. White

e. Other _____

2. Acrylic (manufacturer _____)

Color

a. Bronze

b. Gray

c. Clear

d. White

e. Other _____

Shape

a. Flat

b. Dome

c. Pyramid

d. Other _____

3. Glazing

a. Single

b. Double

c. Per Title 24 report

d. Other _____

Figure 5.41 Listing of exterior finishes (continued).

III. Interior Finishes

   A. Walls

      1. Drywall—texture _____

      2. Plaster—texture _____

      3. Other _____

      4. Bullnose corners

   B. Floors

	Carpet	Sheet Vinyl	Cer. Tile	Other
Entry	____	____	____	____
Living	____	____	____	____
Dining	____	____	____	____
Family	____	____	____	____
Den	____	____	____	____
Kitchen	____	____	____	____
Nook	____	____	____	____
Hall	____	____	____	____
MBR	____	____	____	____
Sec. BR	____	____	____	____
M. Dress	____	____	____	____
Sec. Bath	____	____	____	____
Powder	____	____	____	____
Service	____	____	____	____

   C. Ceiling

      1. Drywall—texture _____

      2. Plaster—texture _____

      3. All dropped beams shall be drywall wrapped

      4. All dropped beams shall be exposed

      5. Other _____

   D. Cabinet Top and Splash

	Cer. Tile	Corian	Cult. Marb.	Cult. Onyx	Plas. Lam.	Wood	Other	Splash Height
Kitchen	____	____	____	____	____	____	____	____
Service	____	____	____	____	____	____	____	____
Wet bar	____	____	____	____	____	____	____	____
Powder	____	____	____	____	____	____	____	____
Linen	____	____	____	____	____	____	____	____
MBA	____	____	____	____	____	____	____	____
Sec. Bath	____	____	____	____	____	____	____	____

   E. Interior Doors

      1. Passage

        Master bedroom

        a. 3068

        b. 2868

        c. Other _____

        Secondary bedrooms

        a. 2868

        b. 2668

        c. Other _____

      2. Wardrobe

        a. 6'-8" high sliding

        b. 8'-0" high sliding

        c. 6'-8" high bifold

        d. 8'-0" high bifold

        e. Other _____

      3. Mirrored

        a. Master bedroom

        b. Secondary bedroom

        c. Other _____

   F. Bathroom Fixtures

	Master Bath	Secondary Bath
1. Tubs and Tub/Showers		
a. 3'-6" × 5'-0" cast iron oval tub	____	____
b. 3'-6" × 5'-0" porc./ stl. oval tub	____	____
c. 3'-6" × 5'-0" fiberglass oval tub	____	____
d. 3'-6" × 5'-0" 1-piece fiberglass oval tub and surround	____	____
e. 2'-8" × 5'-0" cast iron tub	____	____
f. 2'-8" × 5'-0" porc./ stl. tub	____	____
g. 2'-8" × 5'-0" 1-piece fiberglass oval tub and surround	____	____
h. Other _____	____	____
Note: Specify surround material.	____	____

Figure 5.42 Listing of interior finishes.

	Master Bath	Secondary Bath

2. Showers
   a. Fiberglass pan and
      surround   ___   ___
   b. Hot mopped
      Cer. tile pan with
      cer. tile surround   ___   ___
   c. Precast pan with
      surround   ___   ___
      Specify:
      Type pan   ___   ___
      Type surround   ___   ___
   d. Shatterproof enclosure   ___   ___
   e. Curtain rod   ___   ___
3. Mirrors
   a. 3'-0" high   ___   ___
   b. 3'-6" high   ___   ___
   c. 3'-8" high   ___   ___
   d. 4'-0" high   ___   ___
   e. Full height to ceiling   ___   ___
4. Medicine Cabinets   ___   ___

G. Kitchen Appliances
   1. Sink
      a. Double
      b. Double with garbage disposal
      c. Triple
      d. Triple with garbage disposal
   2. Built-in Oven
      a. Double—gas
      b. Double—electric
      c. Single with microwave
   3. Built-in Cooktop
      a. Gas
         size: _____
      b. Electric
         size: _____
      c. Downdraft—gas
         size: _____
      d. Downdraft—electric
         size: _____
      e. Hood, light, and fan above
      f. Microwave above
   4. Slide-in Range/Oven (30")
      a. Gas
      b. Electric
      c. Downdraft—gas
      d. Downdraft—electric
      e. Hood, light, and fan above
      f. Microwave above

   5. Hi/Low Slide-in Range/Oven (30")
      a. Gas
      b. Electric
      c. Oven below and above
      d. Oven below, microwave above
   6. Dishwasher
      a. Included
   7. Trash Compactor
      a. Included
         size: _____
   8. Refrigerator
      a. 3'-3"-wide space
      b. 3'-0"-wide space
      c. Other _____
      d. Stub-out for ice maker
      e. Recessed stub-out for ice maker
H. Laundry
   1. Dryer
      a. Gas
      b. Electric—220V
      c. Both
I. Mechanical
   1. F.A.U.
      a. Gas
      b. Electric
      c. Zoned—specify number
         of units. _____
   2. Air Conditioner
      a. Included
      b. Optional
J. Plumbing
   1. Water Heater—Gas
      a. Recirculating
      b. Water softener—included
      c. Water softener—loop only
   2. Exterior Hose Bibb
      a. Total required: _____
      b. Locations: _____
   3. Exterior Fuel—Gas Stub-Out
      a. Total required: _____
      b. Locations: _____

Figure 5.42 Listing of interior finishes (continued).

K. Electrical

1.

	Surf. Mtd.	Rec. Can Light	Square Flush Light	Lum. Clg. (Fluor.)	Lum. Soffit (Fluor.)	Lum. Soffit (Incand.)	Wall Mtd.	Pendant	Other
Entry	——	——	——	——	——	——	——	——	——
Living	——	——	——	——	——	——	——	——	——
Dining	——	——	——	——	——	——	——	——	——
Family	——	——	——	——	——	——	——	——	——
Den	——	——	——	——	——	——	——	——	——
Kitchen	——	——	——	——	——	——	——	——	——
Nook	——	——	——	——	——	——	——	——	——
Stair	——	——	——	——	——	——	——	——	——
Hall	——	——	——	——	——	——	——	——	——
MBR	——	——	——	——	——	——	——	——	——
Sec. BR	——	——	——	——	——	——	——	——	——
M. Dress	——	——	——	——	——	——	——	——	——
Sec. Dress	——	——	——	——	——	——	——	——	——
M. Bath	——	——	——	——	——	——	——	——	——
Sec. Bath	——	——	——	——	——	——	——	——	——
Powder	——	——	——	——	——	——	——	——	——
Service	——	——	——	——	——	——	——	——	——

2. Outlet for Garage Door Opener

3. Exterior W.P. Outlets
   a. Total required— _____
   b. Location: _____

4. Phone Outlets—Locations
   _____
   _____

5. TV Outlets—Locations
   _____
   _____

6. Intercom System
   a. Wired
   b. Option

7. Security System
   a. Wired
   b. Option

L. Fireplaces
   1. Prefab Metal _____
      a. Manufacturer _____
      b. Size _____
      c. Gas stub-out _____
   2. Precast Concrete _____
      a. Manufacturer _____
      b. Size _____
      c. Gas stub-out _____
   3. Masonry Sizes _____
      a. Size _____
      b. Gas stub-out _____

M. Miscellaneous Amenities
   1. Safe
      a. Wall—location _____
      b. Floor—location _____
   2. Wet Bar—Plans _____
      Under-counter
      Ice maker _____
      Refrigerator _____
   3. Other (Specify)
      a. _____
      b. _____

Figure 5.42 Listing of interior finishes (continued).

Numbers—Job, Legal, Task

Legal Description

Every project has some type of legal description. A simple description might look like this:

Lot # _____ Block # _____
Tract # _____, as recorded in book _____, page _____,
_____ county recorder's office.

This is a description that must appear on the set of working drawings. It may be on the first sheet or, more appropriately, on the site plan sheet.

The legal description is used when researching the zoning requirements of your client's site, setback requirements, or any other information you might need for a specific design feature of the project.

Job Number

Every office has its own way of identifying a specific project. Generally, each project is assigned a job num-

ber, which might reveal the year of the project, the month a job was started, or even the order in which the project was contracted. For example, Job #9403 might reflect the third project received in an office in the year 1994. By using this system, an office can rapidly identify the precise year a job was constructed and never duplicate a number.

Task Number

In all offices, a time card or some such form is used to keep track of the performance of a drafter. In a small office, a drafter might log the time spent on a project by simply writing the date, the job number, a written description of the task performed, and amount of time, such as:

6–14   Job #9403—Ryan Floor Plan   2 hrs.

If you are working on one or two projects at one time, this method might suffice, but in a large office each task is also numbered. Figure 5.43 displays a chart describing the work to be performed as "work packages," the task number at the left assigned to the specific package,

ADDITIONAL SERVICE CHECK LIST
SINGLE-FAMILY SUMMARY OF PLANNED MANHOURS

PROJECT NAME: _____
PROJECT NO: _____
PROJECT MANAGER: _____
START DATE: _____

	WORK PACKAGE NAMES	PLANNED MANHOURS
110	BUILDING DEPARTMENT PLAN CHECK	
120	BUILDING DEPARTMENT SUBMITTAL	
130	IN-HOUSE PLAN CHECK	
140	SITE VISIT	
150	PRODUCTION ASSISTANT/PRINTING	
160	CONSTRUCTION DOCUMENTS (DIR. & ASSOC. DIR.)	
170	FOUNDATION LAY-OUT (ARCHITECTURAL)	
180	FLOOR PLAN	
190	ARCHITECTURAL BACKGROUND	
200	EXTERIOR ELEVATIONS	
210	BUILDING SECTIONS	
220	DETAILS	
230	INTERIOR ELEVATIONS	
240	ROOF PLAN	
250	STAIR PLANS	
260	NOT USED	
270	NOT USED	
280	FOUNDATION PLAN (STRUCTURAL INFORMATION)	
290	FRAMING PLAN (STRUCTURAL)	
300	TITLE SHEET	
310	SITE PLAN	
320	SCHEDULES	
330	PLAN CHANGE (SINGLE FAMILY)	
340	PROJECT MANAGEMENT (PROJECT MGR./ARCHITECT)	
350	PROJECT MEETINGS (TEAM MEMBERS)	
360	CADD COORDINATION (DIR. OF CADD SERVICES)	
370	CAN BE USED FOR ADDITIONAL WORK	
380	CAN BE USED FOR ADDITIONAL WORK	
390	CAN BE USED FOR ADDITIONAL WORK	
	TOTAL PLANNED MANHOURS	

APPROVED BY: _____

Figure 5.43 Task numbers and summary of planned man-hours.

SUMMARY OF PLANNED MAN-HOURS

Project Name: The Professional Practice of Architectural Drawings
Case Study—Mr. & Mrs. _____   Residence

Task No.	Work Package Names	Planned Man-Hours
310	Site Plan, Roof Plan, and Energy Notes	10
170	Foundation Plan and Details	20
180	Floor Plan and Electrical Plan	20
220/320	Door/Window Details and Schedules	32
200	Exterior Elevations and Details	20
210	Building Sections	10
290	Roof Framing and Details	20
230	Interior Elevations	16
130	Project Coordination and Plan Check	18
	Total Hours	166
	166 Hours $ _____/Hr. =	$ _____

Figure 5.44 Planned man-hours for a project.

and a column at the right indicating the total man-hours planned for the particular work package. The task numbers jump by ten, allowing the flexibility, on a complex project, to have sub-work packages. For example, 140 Site Visit might use 141 as a task number for measuring an existing structure to be altered.

Figure 5.44 is an example of the total man-hours for a particular job, such as the Ryan Residence. Note the task numbers and the computer display of the corresponding work package names.

Each week as the drafters turn in their time cards, the man-hours and tasks performed are loaded into a computer, allowing the project manager to ascertain instantly the progress on a particular job or check to see if the project has been budgeted correctly. Figure 5.45 provides an example of such a spot check.

Document Numbering System

Although this book is mainly concerned with architectural working drawings, it includes other drawings which constitute a complete set of construction documents. To keep all of the drawings in their proper spaces, they are numbered differently. For example, the set of architectural drawings can easily be identified by the letter A: Sheets A-1, A-2, A-3, and so on. In contrast, S can be used for structural drawings (S-1, S-2, S-3), E for electrical, L for landscape, and M for mechanical, to mention but a few categories.

A typical sheet number might look like this:

It is extremely important also to indicate the number of sheets in the set. In this example there are 15. If the total number of sheets is not indicated, the recipient of the set will never know whether there is a sheet missing should Sheet 15 accidentally be excluded.

Drawing Sequence

Now to the actual performance—the development of the drawings themselves. As indicated previously, most offices have a game plan. Although such plans may vary slightly from one office to another, Figure 5.46 displays what we feel is a rather typical sequence. The term *lay out* or *block out* in this list means to draw lightly so that changes and corrections can easily be implemented. Key or special notes (*Keynotes*) refers to the fact that noting is vitally important. The drafter should respond to this or any list just as it's written. Proceed *no* further than

SUMMARY OF MAN-HOURS THROUGH 12-15-93

310	Site Plan	2 hrs. 40 min.
310	Vicinity Map	20 min.
310	Roof Plan	1 hr. 15 min.
170	Foundation Plan	3 hrs. 15 min.
320	Foundation Details	3 hrs. 55 min.
180	Floor Plan	4 hrs. 5 min.
200	Exterior Elevations	3 hrs. 55 min
210	Sections (Garage)	15 min.
290	Roof Framing Plan	40 min.
130	Projection Coordination	2 hrs. 5 min.
	Total	22 hrs. 25 min.

Figure 5.45 Progress for a specific time period.

what is listed and assigned, because at certain intervals a spot check will be made by the project manager. Some of these checks are noted on the "Working Drawing Procedures" list.

Also note that in between numbers 9 and 10 is a "50% Complete" note. This is a point at which the time sheets are checked in the computer to validate that the drawing budget is approximately 50% used.

The Working Drawing Development

The actual development of the working drawing is not addressed in this chapter, but in subsequent chapters, Chapters 6 through 14. For a look at the complete assembly of the various components such as general notes, details, vicinity maps, and so forth, refer to Chapter 15.

WORKING DRAWING PROCEDURES

PROJECT

1. Lay Out Unit Floor Plans—¼"
   ____ Block out walls.
   ____ Doors and windows.
   ____ Cabinets, appliances, and fixtures.
   ____ Dimension overalls.
   ____ Calculate square footages.

2. Lay Out Roof Plan—⅛"
   ____ Indicate exterior line of building.
   ____ Indicate roof lines and pitch.

3. Lay Out Building Sections—¼"
   ____ Indicate type of framing.
   ____ Dimension floor and plate heights.

4. Lay Out Exterior Elevations—¼"
   ____ Indicate doors and windows.
   ____ Indicate exterior materials.
   ____ Dimension floor and plate heights.

5. Lay Out Addenda Plans—¼"
   ____ Partial floor plans.
   ____ Exterior elevations (per step #4).
   ____ Roof plan (per step #2).

6. Project Manager to Select Keynotes
   ____ Floor plans.
   ____ Exterior elevations.
   ____ Interior elevations.
   ____ Sections.

7. Project Manager to Select Details
   ____ Doors and windows.
   ____ Exterior elevations.
   ____ Interior elevations.

8. Project Manager to Lay Out Framing and Mechanical Study
   ____ Overlays.

9. Plot
   ____ Floor plans.
   ____ Addenda plans/exterior elevations/roof plans.
   ____ Sections.
   ____ Submit package to structural, T-24 engineers, and applicable consultants.
   ____ In-house back check of package (designer and project architect).

50% Complete

10. Floor Plans—¼"
    ____ Lay out electrical plan.
    ____ Finish interior/exterior dimensions.
    ____ Note plans.
    ____ Reference details.

11. Lay Out Interior Elevations and Fireplaces—¼"
    ____ Indicate ceiling heights.

____ Dimension cabinet heights.
____ Dimension appliances.
____ Note interiors.
____ Dimension fireplaces.
____ Note fireplaces.

12. Architectural Detail Sheets
    ____ Finish all details.
    Consultant design information due for in-house plan check aand application to drawings.

13. Addenda
a3   13.1 Partial Floor Plans
    ____ Electrical.
    ____ Dimension.
    ____ Note—Plans.
    ____ Reference details.

    13.2 Roof Plans—¼"
    ____ Reference details.
    ____ Reference notes.

    13.3 Exterior Elevations
    ____ Reference details.
    ____ Reference notes.
    ____ Exterior materials finish schedule.

14. Sections
    ____ Reference notes.
    ____ Coordinate consultant design.

15. Title Sheet
    ____ Code tabulation.
    ____ Consultant information.
    ____ Vicinity map.
    ____ Sheet index.

16. Final Coordination
    ____ Building department submittal information.
    ____ Final plotting for building department.
    ____ Submit for plan check.

90% Complete

17. Formal In-House Plan Check
    ____ Plan check.

18. Building Department Plan Check
    ____ Incorporate correction into plans.
    ____ Coordinate client/cyp in-house plan checks and incorporate into plans.
    ____ Final plot for building department submittal.

19. Signatures
    ____ Upon building department approval (permit), route plan set for consultant approval and signatures.

100% Complete

Ready for plotting and submittal

Figure 5.46 Working drawing procedures—the game plan.

SUMMARY

Preliminary design factors such as building code requirements, structural analysis, regional differences, and so forth must be considered and satisfied before producing construction documents. It is important to complete these design requirements and procedures in order to properly finalize the physical characteristics of a structure. Initial communications and programming with consultants is most important.

IMPORTANT TERMS AND CONCEPTS

Building code requirements
Primary materials analysis
Modular units
Primary structural system
Programming and consultant requirements
Regional considerations
Energy conservation

Interrelationship of drawings
Office standards
Project architect
Program
Cartoon
Project book

REVIEW QUESTIONS

1. Name the procedures and requirements that should be considered and satisfied before beginning construction documents.
2. Under the building code requirements, what are three design factors that should be satisfied with respect to dimension?
3. Building material selections are based on various factors. Name five of these factors.
4. Give two examples of consulting engineers' requirements that would dictate physical space provisions.
5. Regional differences influence various parts of a structure. Name four parts of a structure.
6. Name three parts of a structure that are considered in meeting energy conservation requirements.
7. Cross-referencing between mechanical and electrical drawings is important. Give two examples of cross-referencing.

LABORATORY PROBLEMS

1. Using your local building code, draw a straight-run stair plan for an office building and provide the following drawings:
   a. Minimum required clearances
   b. Minimum tread and maximum risers
   c. Dimensions for the space required for this stair, given a 10'–0" floor-to-floor dimension
   d. Scale to be ⅜" = 1'–0"
2. Drawing to a scale of ⅛" = 1'–0", prepare a floor plan approximately 70' × 30' using 16" concrete block wall units. Provide wall dimensions to satisfy block units.
3. Using a ¼" = 1'–0" scale, draw a wall section using 8" high concrete block units with an approximate wall height of 14 feet.
4. Provide a detail through a floor and ceiling section that will satisfy mechanical duct requirements with the following members:
   a. 2" × 14" floor joists
   b. A 12" × 27" W steel beam under the joists
   c. An 18" × 12" rectangular heating and cooling duct
   d. Suspended ceiling below
   e. Scale to be ¾" = 1'–0"
5. Using a scale of ⅜" = 1'–0", draw a section of a roof, wall, and foundation footing and indicate the important features of each that are influenced by conditions in your geographical region.
6. Provide a bar chart for a class project showing time allocation for the following:
   a. Preliminary studies
   b. Instructor's review
   c. Finished drawings
   Instructor to assign project.

DOCUMENT
EVOLUTION

6

DEVELOPING
THE SITE PLANS

6

PREVIEW
This chapter examines the kinds of technical information required in site development. The plat map is used to provide additional information, including the topography map, soils and geological investigation, grading plan, utility plan, landscape plan, and total site development plan.

OBJECTIVES
1. Be able to draw a plat map from a given lot line bearings and dimensions.
2. Be familiar with a topography map as viewed in section form.
3. Be familiar with the findings and presentation of a soils investigation.
4. Understand the basics of grading plans and their drawings.
5. Know what is to be delineated on a landscape plan.

The Plat Map

The Function of a Plat Map

The site plan is developed through stages, each dealing with new technical information and design solutions. The first step in site plan development is the **plat map.** This map, normally furnished by a civil engineer, is a land plan which delineates the property lines with their bearings, dimensions, streets, and existing easements. The plat map forms the basis of all future information and site development. An example of a plat map is shown in Figure 6.1. The property line bearings are described by degrees, minutes, and seconds; the property line dimensions are noted in feet and decimals.

Even when the architect or designer is furnished with only a written description of the metes and bounds of the plat map, a plat map can still be delineated from this information. Lot lines are laid out by polar **coordinates;** that is, each line is described by its length plus the angle relative to the true North or South. This is accomplished by the use of compass direction, degree, minutes, and seconds. A lot line may read N 6° 49′ 29″ W. The compass is divided into four quadrants. See Figure 6.2.

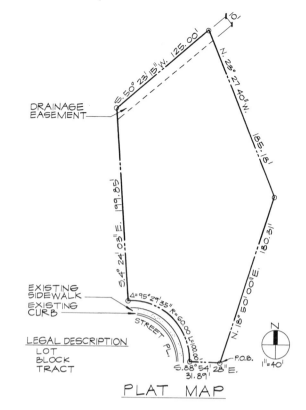

Figure 6.1 Plat map.

Drawing a Plat Map

Figure 6.3A shows a plat map with the given **lot lines, bearings,** and dimensions. To lay out this map graphically, start at the point labeled **P.O.B. (point of beginning).** From the P.O.B., you can delineate the lot line in the North-East quadrant with the given dimension. See Figure 6.3B. The next bearing falls in the North-West quadrant, which is illustrated by superimposing a compass at the lot line intersection. See Figure 6.3C. You can delineate the remaining lot lines with their bearings and dimensions in the same way you have delineated the previous lot lines, closing at the P.O.B. See Figures 6.3D, 6.3E, and 6.3F. For a plat map layout, accuracy within ½° is acceptable.

With the completion of the plat map layout, there is now a specific plot of ground that has been established for locating building **setbacks,** existing setbacks, and other factors that will influence the development of the property. For the purpose of the architectural working drawings, this portion of the drawings will be called the **site plan.** In some offices, "plot plan" is the term used for this part of the working drawings. In Figure 6.3G, the front yard, side yard, and rear yard setbacks are illustrated for the purpose of defining the governing building setback locations. The next step in site plan development is to provide a dimensional layout for a proposed building. One method, as shown on Figure 6.3H, is to provide a dimension along the west and east property lines. Starting from the front property line, a line joining

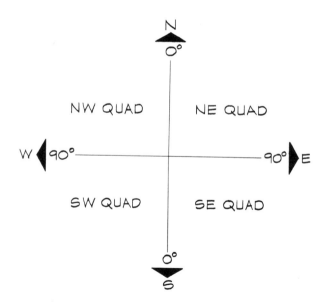

Figure 6.2 Compass quadrants.

these two points will establish a parallel line with the front of the building, thus eliminating the problem of determining the angle of the front of the house to the front property line. In addition, from this parallel line, dimensional **offsets** of the building can be established. Note also in Figure 6.3H that all required yard setbacks will be maintained with no encroachments.

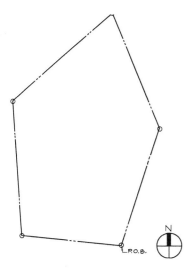

Figure 6.3A Point of beginning.

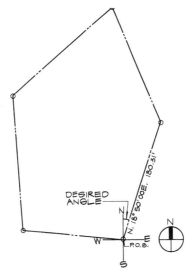

Figure 6.3B Point of beginning and first angle.

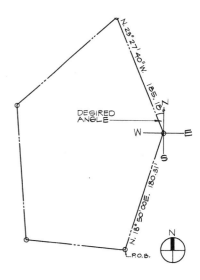

Figure 6.3C P.O.B. and second angle.

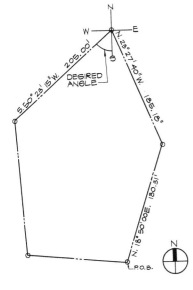

Figure 6.3D P.O.B. and third angle.

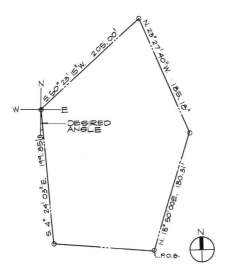

Figure 6.3E P.O.B. and fourth angle.

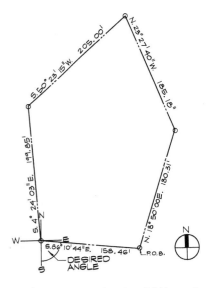

Figure 6.3F P.O.B. and fifth angle.

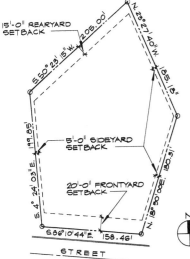

Figure 6.3G Site plan—building setbacks.

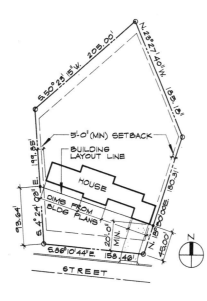

Figure 6.3H Site plan—building layout.

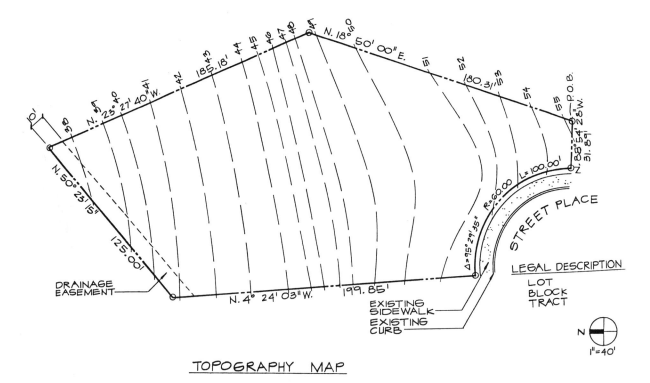

Figure 6.4 Topography map.

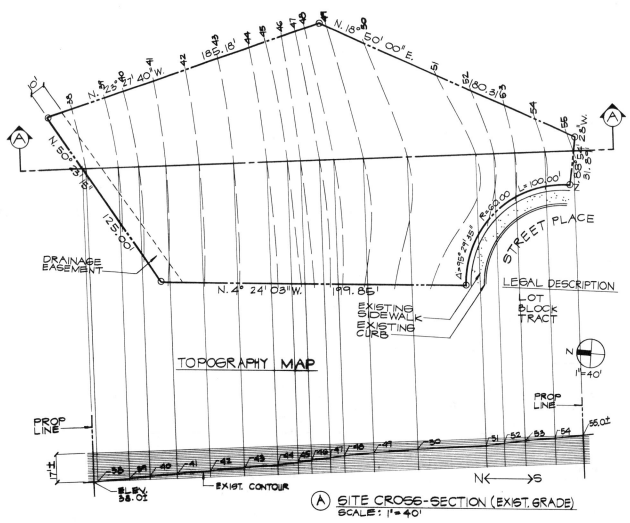

Figure 6.5 Topography map with section lines and cross-section.

The Topography Map

The Function of a Topography Map

For most projects, the architect adjusts the existing contours of the site to satisfy the building construction and site improvement requirements. Because **finish grading**—that is, the adjusting of existing contours—is a stage in the site improvement process, the architect or designer needs a topography map to study the slope conditions which may influence the design process. Usually, a civil engineer prepares this map and shows in drawing form the existing **contour lines** and their accompanying numerical elevations. Commonly, these contour lines are illustrated by a broken line.

The **topography** map is, therefore, actually a plat map, and its broken lines and numbers indicate the grades, elevations, and contours of the site. Figure 6.4 is a topography map showing existing contour lines.

Site Cross-Sections

A topography map can appear complex. However, a cross-section through any portion of the site can make the site conditions clearer and will also be valuable for the finish grading. Figure 6.5 shows a **cross-section** of a portion of a topography map. The fall of the contours from the front of the site to the rear is almost as high as a two-story building. This site slopes to the North at approximately 1' for every 15'.

To make a cross-section, draw a line on the topography map at the desired location. This is called the section line. Next, on tracing paper, draw a series of horizontal lines using the same scale as the topography map and spacing equal to the grade elevation changes on the topography map. Project each point of grade change to the appropriate section line. Now connect the series of grade points to establish an accurate section and profile through that portion of the site.

The Soils and Geology Map

Soils and geology investigations evaluate soil conditions such as type of soil, moisture content, expansion coefficient, and soil bearing pressure. Geological investigations evaluate existing geological conditions as well as potential geological hazards.

Field investigations may include test borings at various locations on the site. These drillings are then plotted on a plat map, with an assigned test boring identification and a written or graphic report. This report provides findings from the laboratory analysis of boring samples under various conditions.

When there are geological concerns and soil instability, the particular problem areas may be plotted on the **soils and geology map** for consideration in the design process. Figure 6.6 shows a plat map with each test boring identified. This map becomes a part of the soils and geological report. Sometimes, the architect or structural engineer requests certain locations for borings according to building location or area of structural concern. Figure 6.7 shows a **boring log** in graphic form. Notice the different types of information presented in the sample boring log. Figure 6.8 shows a geological cross-section.

Normally, architectural technicians are not involved in *preparing* drawings for geology and soils information; however, it is important to have some understanding of their content and presentation.

The Utility Plan

Plotting existing utilities is necessary to the site improvement process. See Figure 6.9. Such a plan should show the location of all existing utilities, including sewer laterals, water and gas lines, and telephone and electrical services. This drawing then provides a basis for new utility connections. It may also influence the locations of electrical rooms and meter rooms in the structure itself.

The Grading Plan

The grading plan shows how the topography of the site will be changed to accommodate the building design. This plan shows the existing grades and new grades or finished grades. It should also indicate the finished grade

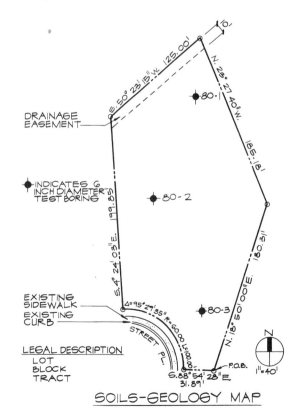

Figure 6.6 Soils-geology map.

BORING: 79-7   ELEVATION: 677'

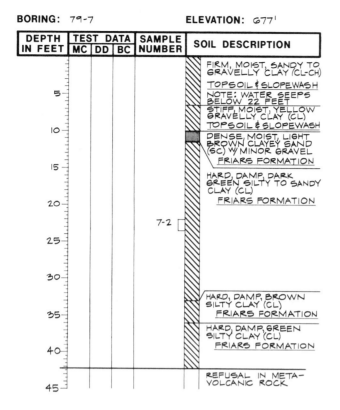

DEPTH IN FEET	TEST DATA			SAMPLE NUMBER	SOIL DESCRIPTION
	MC	DD	BC		
5					FIRM, MOIST, SANDY TO GRAVELLY CLAY (CL-CH)
					TOPSOIL & SLOPEWASH
					NOTE: WATER SEEPS BELOW 22 FEET
					STIFF, MOIST, YELLOW GRAVELLY CLAY (CL)
10					TOPSOIL & SLOPEWASH
					DENSE, MOIST, LIGHT BROWN CLAYEY SAND (SC) W/ MINOR GRAVEL
15					FRIARS FORMATION
					HARD, DAMP, DARK GREEN SILTY TO SANDY CLAY (CL)
20					FRIARS FORMATION
25				7-2	
30					
35					HARD, DAMP, BROWN SILTY CLAY (CL) FRIARS FORMATION
					HARD, DAMP, GREEN SILTY CLAY (CL) FRIARS FORMATION
40					
45					REFUSAL IN META-VOLCANIC ROCK

Figure 6.7 Example of a boring log.

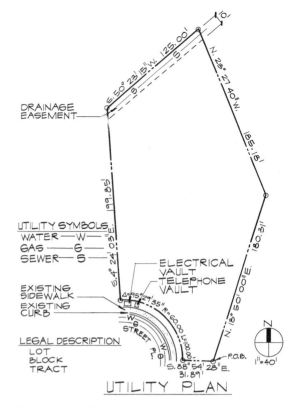

Figure 6.9 Utility plan.

elevations and the elevations of floors, walks, and walls. Existing grade lines are shown with a broken line, and finished grades with a solid line. Finished grading lines show how the site is to be graded. See Figure 6.10.

Floor Elevations

Once the orientation and location of the building has been established, the process of preparing a grading plan may begin. The first step is to designate tentative floor-level elevations, which will be determined by the structure's location in relation to the existing grades. It should be noted that in the process of designing a grading plan, tentative floor elevations may have to be ad-

justed to satisfy the location of the finished contours and their elevations. This particular building has two different floor levels, which provides greater compatibility with the existing sloping grades. The upper floor Level-2 elevation has tentatively been set at 44.5, and the lower floor Level-1 has been set at 42.5, providing a two-foot floor transition. With the establishment of the floor-level elevations it will then be necessary to reshape the existing grade lines to satisfy floor clearances and site drainage control. Figure 6.10A illustrates that the existing grades, at the South side of the building, will need to be cut back, in which case finished grades will need to be lower in elevation than the floor Level—1, which is tentatively set at an elevation of 44.5.

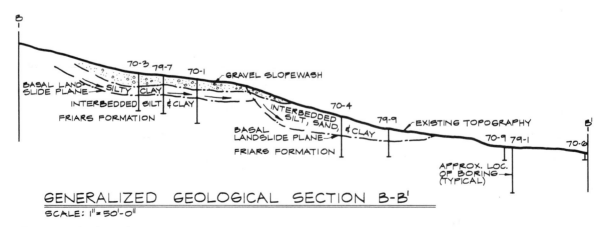

GENERALIZED GEOLOGICAL SECTION B-B'
SCALE: 1"=50'-0"

Figure 6.8 Geological cross section.

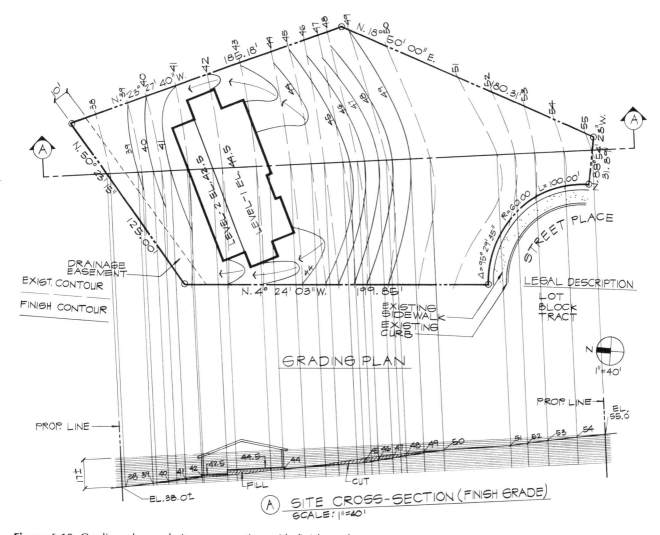

Figure 6.10 Grading plan and site cross section with finish grades.

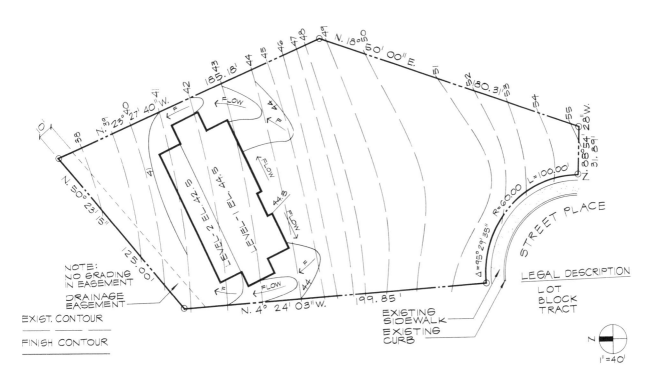

Figure 6.10A Initial grading.

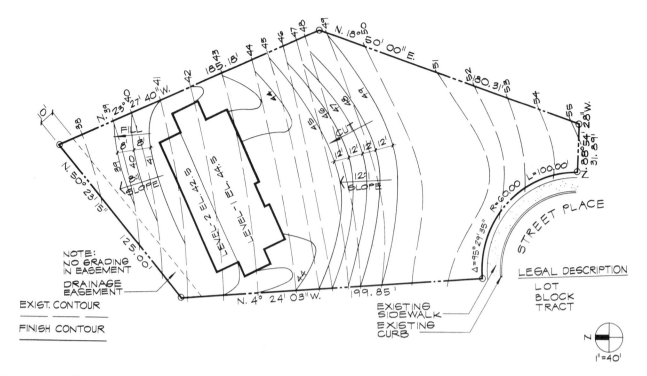

Figure 6.10B Finished slope designs.

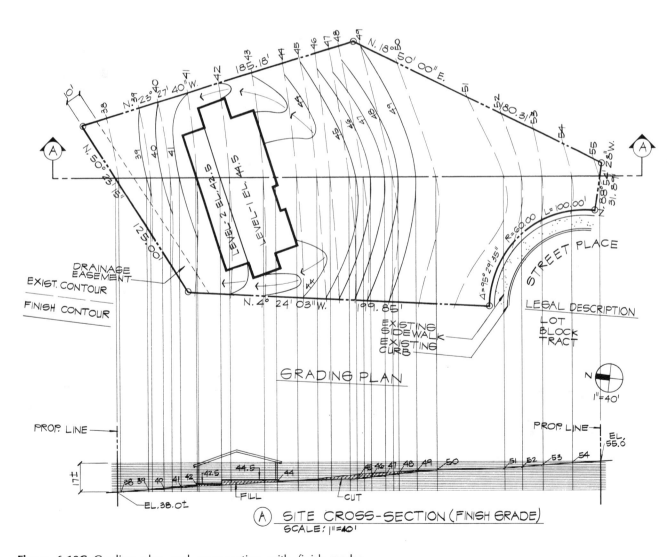

Figure 6.10C Grading plan and cross-section with finish grades.

For the purpose of providing proper drainage around the building, a high-point elevation of 44.3 has been established at the middle portion of the building, as shown in Figure 6.10A. This grade elevation is below the finished floor elevation of Level-1 and higher than the finished grades at the East and West sides of the building, in which case surface drainage will flow to each side of the building, continue around, and follow the natural slope of the site. Finished contour elevations 42.0, 43.0, and 44.0 at the East and West sides have been contoured to provide a gentle slope at the front and sides of the building.

At the rear of the building a floor-level change has been incorporated to accommodate the natural slope of the site. This floor elevation is set at +42.5 feet, which is two feet below Level-1. The adjacent natural grade at this level will be reshaped to provide a more gradual slope and maintain proper drainage and floor clearances. The remaining finished grading will be reshaped, using a 8:1 slope ratio, providing a slope that is consistent with the existing grades and will not cause grading in the drainage casement. The design of slope ratios, like that of floor elevation, may be only tentative as a starting point for the shaping of the finish contours.

A starting point for the design of slope ratios is laid out with horizontal scaled increments for the tentative slope ratio. As depicted in Figure 6.10B, a 12:1 slope ratio is anticipated for the grade cut at the south side of the building. In this case, 12-foot horizontal increments will start from the established grades adjacent to the building. At the front of the building (South side), from an elevation grade of +44.0, twelve horizontal increments will be plotted at three locations. These increments will start at grade elevation +44.0 and stop at grade elevation +49.0, inasmuch as there would be no finish grade intrusion at the existing grade elevation +50.0. Once the various increments have been plotted, these points can be connected with a french curve or other instruments to delineate the finished contour line elevation. A similar procedure will be used for the rear of the building (North side), illustrating finished contours and slope ratios. The cut section of the site will occur at the south portion of the building, whereas the fill portion will be to the north of the building. In most cases, all finished grade elevations will start at an existing or natural grade elevation and terminate at the respective existing grade elevation, as illustrated in Figure 6.10C.

Cut and Fill Procedures

The contour changes previously described require a removal of soil—a "cut" into the existing contours. The opposite of this situation, which requires the addition of soil to the site, is called a "fill." In Figure 6.10C, reshaping contours with cut and fill procedures has provided a relatively level area for construction. Depending on the soils condition and soil preparation, the maximum

allowable ratio for cut and fill slopes may vary from 1½:1 to 2:1. A ratio of 2:1 means that for each foot change in elevation, there is a minimum 2-foot separation of the horizontal. To clarify grading conditions, grading sections should be taken through these areas. See Figure 6.10C.

Developing the Site Plan

Site Grading and Options

As previously mentioned, the grading plan drawing illustrates and defines the various alterations of the land contours in order to satisfy the site development for a specific structure. It is an important and powerful tool that helps the architect or designer understand grading techniques in order to incorporate grading into architectural planning and site development.

The drawings that follow illustrate various examples of grading options for the site development and architectural planning for a specific residential lot. Initially, the architect or designer is furnished with a topography map depicting the existing grade elevations and contours for this residential site.

Figure 6.11 illustrates the topography map and depicts the contours and assigned grade elevations. The grade elevations are in 1-foot intervals representing changes in heights. As in most cases, the slope ratio, which represents the relationship between the horizontal dimension and the vertical dimension, will vary at different locations on the site. For example, area A as shown on the topography map depicts the grade condition and slope ratio in this area, which is adjacent to the access street. Figure 6.12 illustrates a cross-section in this area and also provides the determination of the slope ratio. Since the grade rises 5 feet in 25 feet, this can be interpreted as a 1:5 slope ratio and further defined as a 20% slope. Figure 6.13 depicts a cross-section of grade condition that is found in the site area designated B on the topography map. Note that this area has a slope ratio of 1:8. Figures 6.12 and 6.13 illustrate an example of varying grade conditions that are discovered on this site. Figure 6.14 depicts a overall cross-section of a major portion of this site, providing a clearer picture of the general grade conditions.

Grading Option I

Option I calls for the design and orientation of the residence to be developed on the site with a minimum amount of grading. The existing grades and contour lines will then dictate the building configuration and floor transitions in order to accommodate the changes in grade elevation. The first step is to develop the grading

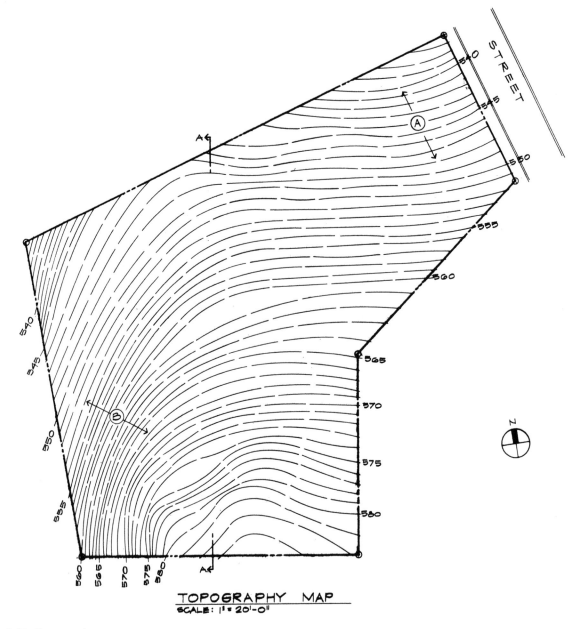

Figure 6.11 Topography map.

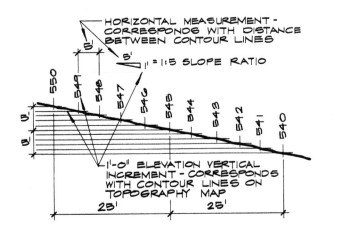

Figure 6.12 Site area A.

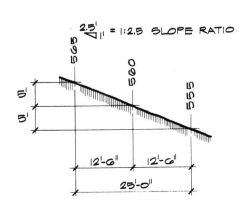

Figure 6.13 Site area B.

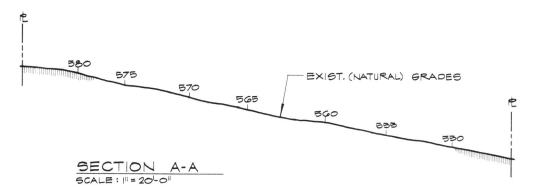

SECTION A-A
SCALE : 1" = 20'-0"

Figure 6.14 Cross-section of existing grades.

for a driveway that will provide acceptable slopes for access to the garage, which will determine the garage location and floor elevation. As a means of reference for an explanation of the finish grading for the driveway design, see Figure 6.15. Starting at the street grade elevation of 542.0', the initial grade transition from the street to the driveway should not be so steep as to scrape the front bumper of a automobile. The initial slope ratio is approximately 1 foot vertically to 10 feet horizontally, or 10% slope. A slope of 20% or a one 1 : 5 ratio would be too steep at this transition. To proceed with the driveway slope design, we have selected an average slope of 9% or a ratio of 1 : 11 for relative ease of access to the garage. The finished driveway grades from 542.0 feet to 549.0 feet are now drawn at approximately 11-foot intervals. Note in Figure 6.15 that there are approximately 20 feet between the finished grade elevation of 548.0 feet and the garage floor elevation of 549.0 feet. This will provide a minimal slope condition in front of the garage for the parking of automobiles.

The finished driveway grades on the south side of the driveway will be joined to their respective existing grade elevations, providing a natural conformity with this area of the site. Along the north side of the driveway, a steep condition exists that will necessitate a 3-to-1 fill condition, as indicated in Figure 6.15. Because of this condition, 1-foot high concrete curb is recommended for directing surface water to the street and to eliminate possible water erosion on the 3 : 1 slope condition. The finished grading on the east side of the garage has been contoured in order to decrease the height of retaining walls that would be necessary at that portion of the garage. The slope ratio at this location is approximately 4 : 1.

For further clarity, a cross-section through the garage and the adjacent existing grades is shown in Figure 6.16. It should be emphasized that it may take numerous attempts to solve all facets of the grading design—somewhat like attempts to solve architectural planning designs.

The next step in Option I is to orientate a predetermined size residence on the site with a minimum amount of finished grading. Since the primary location and floor elevation have been established for the garage, the formation and planning for the residence may now proceed, with the intention of providing compatibility

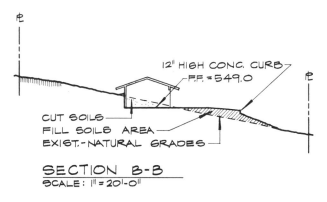

SECTION B-B
SCALE: 1" = 20'-0"

Figure 6.15 Driveway grading and design (1" = 20).

Figure 6.16

with the existing grade elevations and the contour configurations of the existing grades. In view of the fact that a city view exists to the north of the site and that the existing grade contours slope to the north, we decided to develop a rectilinear building configuration that would accommodate minimal finished grading conditions and that would provide a more compatible development with the natural terrain. Figure 6.17 illustrates graphically a rectangular shape that falls within a grade transition area of 5 to 8 feet. This condition is depicted in a cross-section in Figure 6.18. Note on Figure 6.18 that floor elevation changes are utilized to further the compatibility between the structure and the existing grades. As shown on Figure 6.17, the westerly portion of the residence has been pivoted to the south in order to

follow the contours of the existing grade elevations. This is another method of site planning if one wishes to minimize the finished grading in the development of a site. A cross-section through this area is illustrated in Figure 6.19. Note that some excavation will occur below the floor levels in order to provide under-floor clearances that are required by building codes for wood floors.

After completing an analysis of the existing grades and their contours in conjunction with the architectural planning of the residence, a grading plan can be prepared for Option I. It should be mentioned that, if you are working on a topography plan in which the natural grade lines are erasable on the top sides of the drawing, it is advisable to trace the natural grades on the back of

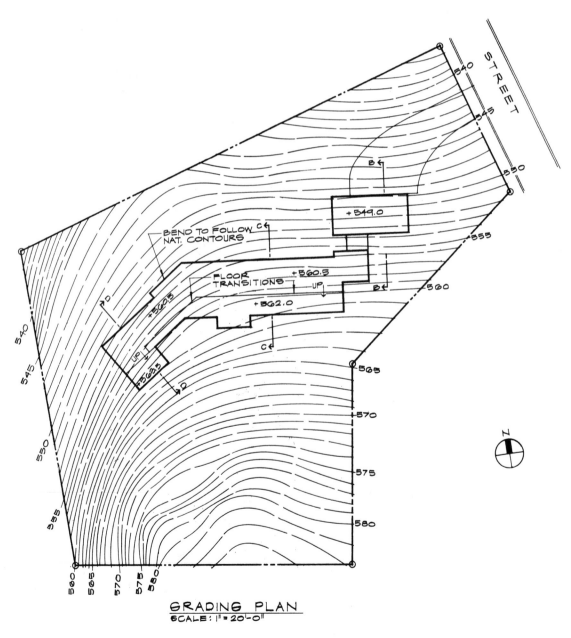

Figure 6.17 Planning house for existing contours.

the drawing, since you will find that the finished grade lines may need adjustment and you would not want to erase the natural grade lines during this process.

Figure 6.20 illustrates a grading plan for Option I that incorporates a minimum amount of finished grading. In order to describe the procedure for reshaping the con-

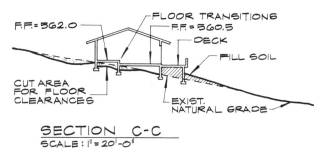

Figure 6.18 Cross-section.

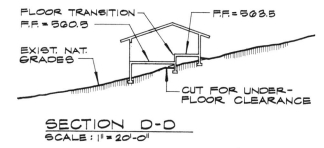

Figure 6.19 Cross-section.

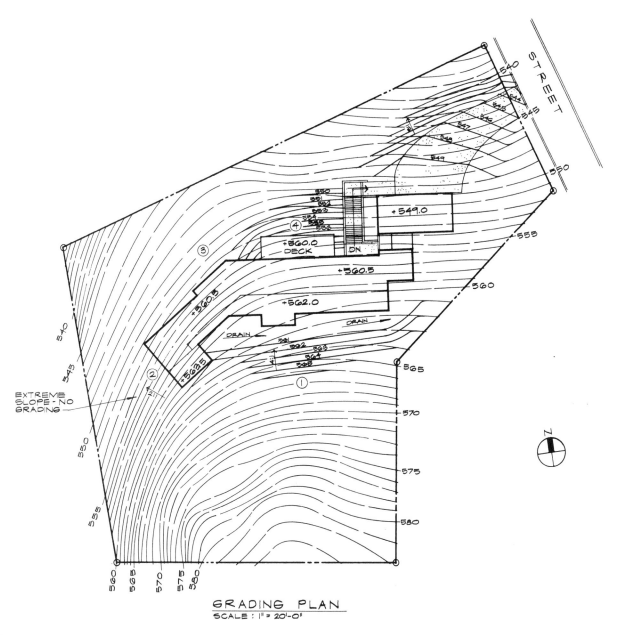

Figure 6.20 Option I—grading plan.

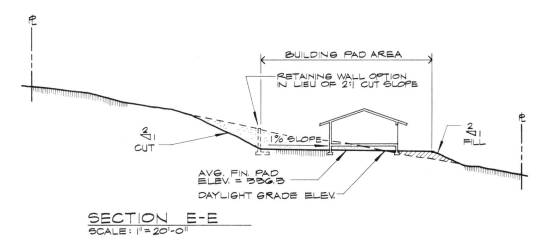

BUILDING PAD AREA

RETAINING WALL OPTION
IN LIEU OF 2:1 CUT SLOPE

1% SLOPE

2
1
CUT

2
1
FILL

AVG. FIN. PAD
ELEV. = 556.5

DAYLIGHT GRADE ELEV.

SECTION E-E
SCALE: 1" = 20'-0"

Figure 6.21 Cross-section building pad-I.

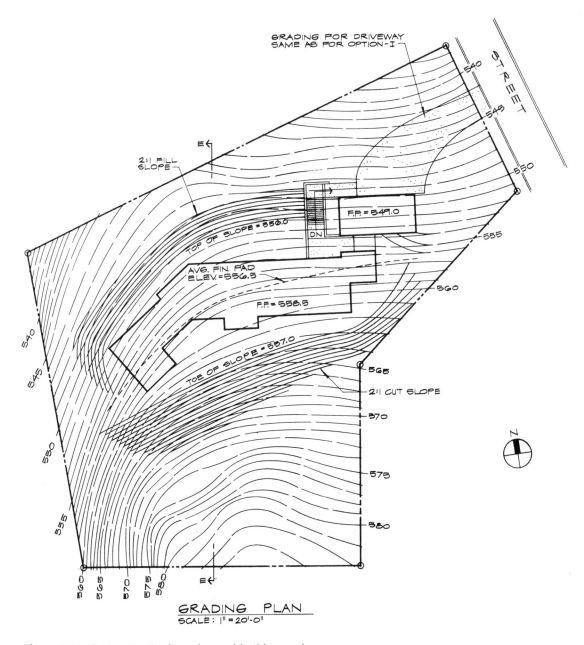

GRADING FOR DRIVEWAY
SAME AS FOR OPTION-I

STREET

2:1 FILL
SLOPE

F.F. = 549.0

DN

TOP OF SLOPE = 556.0

AVG. FIN. PAD
ELEV. = 556.5

F.F. = 558.5

TOE OF SLOPE = 557.0

2:1 CUT SLOPE

N

GRADING PLAN
SCALE: 1" = 20'-0"

Figure 6.22 Option II—Grading plan and building pad.

tours and finished grade elevations, four key areas are shown on the grading plan. Area 1, which is on the south side of the residence, illustrates that a minimum cut will be necessary to accommodate minimum grade clearances below the desired floor elevation of 562.0 feet located at that portion of the residence. This cut condition is depicted by reshaping the existing contours of 561.0 feet through 564.0 feet, resulting in a 4 : 1 slope ratio. Note that the finish grades are again connected to their respective existing grade elevations. Figure 6.18 provides a cross-section that incorporates this area.

Area 2 on the west side of the residence has an existing 2 : 1 slope ratio. It will remain in its natural state, since this is an extreme slope condition and any changes in these grades may result in the use of retaining walls. Refer to Figure 6.19 for a visual inspection of the grade condition in this area.

Another portion of a site where the finish grading is not mandatory is in area 3. The slope ratio in this area is approximately 4 : 1. Area 4 will require some grading in order to ensure that the finished grade elevations will be compatible and will relate to the entry stairs and landing elevations. Since the established garage floor elevation is 549.0 feet and the residence entry is at an elevation of 560.5 feet, this translates into a stair and landing design that will satisfy this 10'-6" height difference between the floor elevations. The method of relating floor elevations to existing and finished grades also pertains to the stair design. The location of the risers, treads, and landings relate to the adjacent grade elevations. In area 4, note that the existing grade elevations 550, 551, 552, 553, and 554 have been contoured to provide finished grades that relate to the stair run and landings. The remaining area to be graded, which is the garage and driveway, is illustrated in Figure 6.15.

Grading Option II

The approach in Option II is to develop a level area on this site for the construction of a residence. The level area is defined as a building pad that will have a minimal slope for drainage. The creation of a building pad will provide the architect or the designer with more flexibility in the design, since he or she will not be dictated by grade elevations, floor transitions, building shapes, or other considerations.

One approach in developing a building pad is to try to create a balanced cut and fill. In this approach, the earth that is cut from the site slope will be dispersed for the use of fill material to increase the building pad site. The fill material must then be compacted to an acceptable soil-bearing capacity if a structure is to be founded in the fill area. To develop the size, shape, and grading for the building pad, it is recommended that an assumed pad elevation be established. This pad elevation may be

determined by what is referred to as a "daylight grade elevation." The term **daylight grade elevation** may be defined as that point or elevation where the cut-and-fill portions of the grading of the site intersect at a given grade elevation. To illustrate this graphically, see Figure 6.21, which is a cross-section of the proposed grading for the building pad.

The grading plan for the building pad development is shown in Figure 6.22. A building pad elevation of 536.5 feet has been established with 1% slope for drainage. Note that pad elevation is at the approximate daylight grade elevation. As mentioned previously, it may take various preliminary design approaches in order to satisfy a cut-and-fill balance. Another option in the cut-and-fill process would be to instigate the use of a retaining wall. Figure 6.21 illustrates in cross-section that the use of a retaining wall at the south portion of the pad would reduce the amount of earth to be cut from the slope. In this case, the grading plan will reflect a 2 : 1 ratio cut slope condition.

The finished slope designs and the grade elevations have been shown at a 2 : 1 slope ratio. To lay out these contour lines, start at the top of the fill slope and scale off 2-foot increments in order to establish the grade elevations for a 2 : 1 fill condition. The identical process will be done at the toe of the slope for the cut portion of the site. Again, note that the finished contours will be drawn and connected to their respective existing grade elevations. The amount of grading for Option II is substantially greater than that for Option I, as depicted on the grading plans.

Grading Option III

The grading approach for Option III is to develop the site that will incorporate two building pads. This approach will necessitate the greatest amount of finished grading in comparison to Options I and II.

The grading design procedure for pad 2 will differ from the initial approach for the grading of pad 1, because the pad elevation will not originate from an approximate daylight elevation. For this situation, the pad 2 elevation will be determined by the top of the slope elevation located at the top of the south slope of pad 1, which is illustrated on the grading plan shown in Figure 6.23. From the top of slope elevation 571.0 feet, a graded pad will be developed to an approximate distance that will be determined by the toe of a 2 : 1 cut slope on the remaining portion of the site. The approximate north-south dimension of pad 2 will be determined by the remaining horizontal dimension of the site that will comfortably provide for a maximum 2 : 1 slope, as is shown on the grading plan. The approach for determining the north-south pad dimension is to start at the rear property line with a gradual slope and then

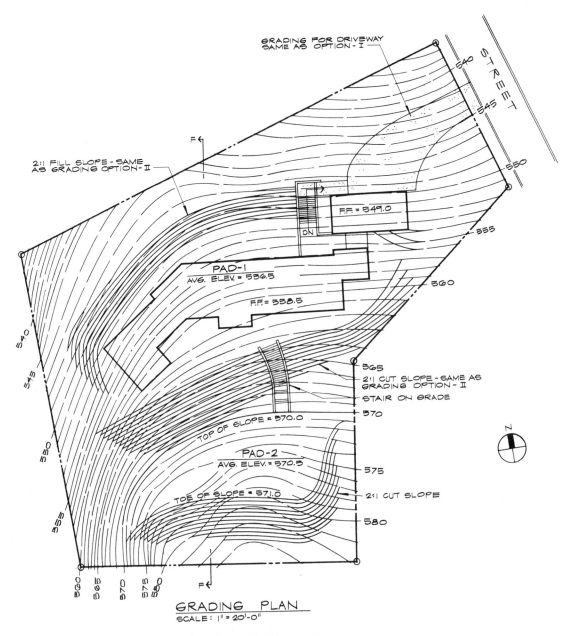

GRADING PLAN
SCALE: 1" = 20'-0"

Figure 6.23 Option III—Grading plan with two building pads.

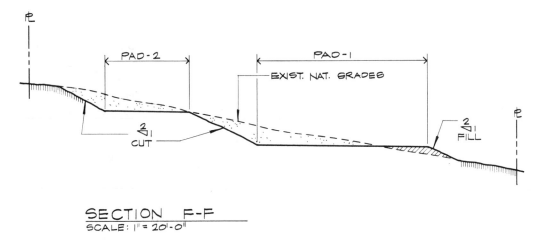

SECTION F-F
SCALE: 1" = 20'-0"

Figure 6.24 Cross-section of building pads I and II.

dimensionally lay out 2-foot horizontal increments for the finished contour lines that will depict a 2:1 slope condition, as shown in Figure 6.23. Again, note that all of the finished contour elevations will be connected to their respective existing grade elevations.

For projects on which there are steep slopes that will necessitate many contours lines, the use of a French curve and other similar graphic tools is recommended for the drawing of contour lines.

To illustrate graphically the cut-and-fill conditions that will occur for the grading of pad 1 and pad 2, a cross-section is shown in Figure 6.24. Note that there is a balanced cut-and-fill condition for the development of pad 1 where the forming of pad 2 is totally reliant on a cut slope condition. This means that the earth from pad 2 will be exported rather than be used for fill conditions on the site. These two conditions illustrate grading options for the development of building pads.

The Landscape Plan and the Irrigation Plan

Landscape Plan and Plant List

The final stage of site development for most projects is landscaping. The landscape drawing shows the location of trees, plants, ground covers, benches, fences, and walks. Accompanying this is a **plant list,** identifying plant species with a symbol or number and indicating the size and number of plants. See Figure 6.25.

Irrigation Plan

An irrigation plan often accompanies the landscape plan. This shows all water lines, control valves, and types of watering fixtures needed for irrigation.

The Site Improvement Plan: An Overview

The basic requirement for all construction documents is clarity. The site improvement plan is no exception. It can incorporate any or all of the plans just discussed, depending on the complexity of the information and on office practice.

The primary information to be found in the site improvement plan is as follows:

1. Site lot lines with accompanying bearings and dimensions
2. Scale of the drawing
3. North arrows
4. Building location with layout dimensions
5. Paving, walks, walls with their accompanying material call-outs, and layout dimensions

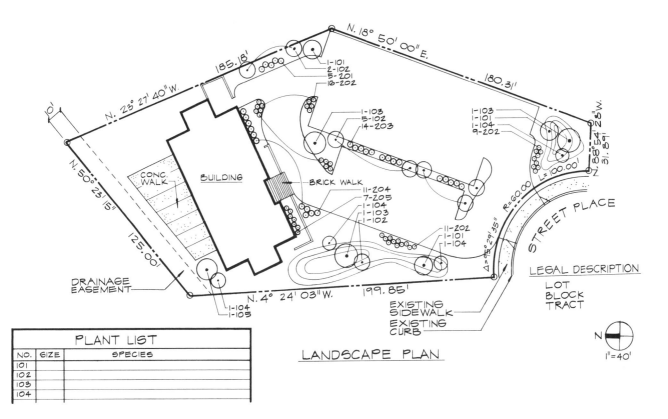

Figure 6.25 Landscape plan and plant list.

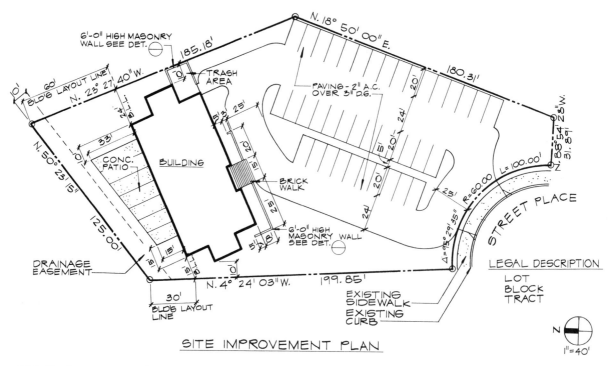

SITE IMPROVEMENT PLAN

Figure 6.26 Site improvement plan.

Figure 6.26 shows the primary information found on a site improvement plan. The building layout dimension lines at the East and West property lines are parallel to their respective property lines, providing two measuring points at the East and West property lines. This, in turn, provides offset dimensions to each corner of the building. This is helpful when the property lines do not parallel the building. This method may apply to patios, walks, paving, and walls, also dimensioned on the site improvement plan.

Site plans for large sites such as multiple-housing projects must show primary information such as utility locations, driveway locations, and building locations. See Figure 6.27. Further examples of site development plans appear in later chapters. See Figure 6.28 for a Site Plan Checklist.

Size and Location

As you position the structure on the site and subsequently position architectural features adjacent to the building, two considerations come to mind: size and location.

Size includes width, length, and thickness (sometimes even height), plus location dimension. See Figure 6.29; in this illustration S refers to the size and L refers to the positioning that we call "location dimension."

Consider the example of the freestanding wall. S (size) refers to the length, the note indication, the height, and

the two "L" dimensions that position the wall with respect to the building. This is a very generic note, which depends on a written description (specifications) about the size of the block unit, how it is stacked, and the size and appearance of the joint. Another type of note might read:

8 × 8 × 16 conc. block freestanding wall, stretcher, running bond, V-jointed, 6'–0" high

The patio slab at the center of the illustration shows one location dimension and three size dimensions. Two are marked with S, and the third comes in the form of a note at the center which describes thickness. The composition and quality of the concrete will be dealt with in the specifications, and the shape of the footing around the perimeter will be dealt with in the footing detail, as will the size and frequency of the dowels that hold the slab to the building.

Driveway and Curb

Often one side of your site is bound with a sidewalk, parkway, and a small curb. In most cities this portion, adjacent to a street, is maintained by the Department of Public Works or some such agency. To break the curb for a driveway, permits are obtained from such an agency or a subdivision, perhaps the Road Department Bureau. Based on the size of the curb, the agency will configure an angle at which you can cut the curb to form the driveway. Figure 6.30 is a before-and-after type drawing showing the appearance of a driveway.

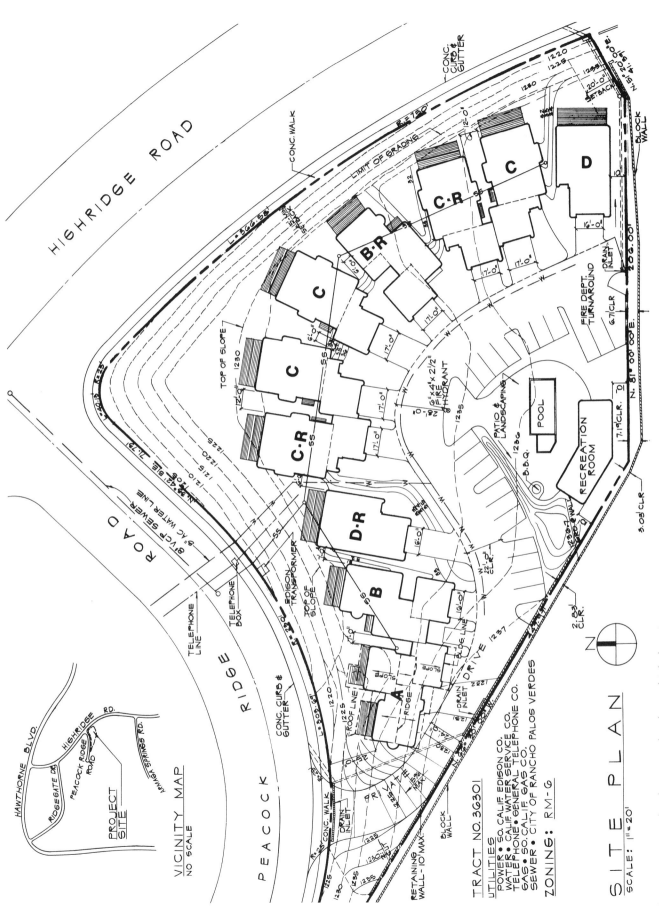

Figure 6.27 Site development plan for multiple housing.

1. Vicinity Map
2. Property lines
   a. lengths—each side
   b. correct angles if not 90°
   c. direction
3. Adjoining streets, sidewalks, parking, curbs, parkways, parking areas, wheel stops, lanes and lighting
4. Existing structures and buildings and alleys
5. Structures and buildings to be removed
   a. Trees
   b. Old foundations
   c. Walks
   d. Miscellanea
6. Public utilities locations
   a. Storm drain
   b. Sewer lines
   c. Gas lines
   d. Gas meter
   e. Water lines
   f. Water meter
   g. Power line
   h. Power pole
   i. Electric meter
   j. Telephone pole
   k. Lamp post
   l. Fire plugs
7. Public utilities easement if on property
8. Contours of grade
   a. Existing grade—dotted line
   b. Finish cut or fill—solid line
   c. Legend
   d. Slopes to street
9. Grade elevations
   a. Finish slab or finish floor
   b. Corners of building (finish)
   c. Top of all walls
   d. Amount of slope for drainage

10. Roof plan—new building
    a. Building—hidden line
    b. Roof overhang—solid line
    c. Garage
    d. Slopes (arrows)
    e. Projecting canopies
    f. Slabs and porches
    g. Projecting beams
    h. Material for roof
    i. North arrow
    j. Title and scale
    k. Show ridges and valleys
    l. Roof drains and downspouts
    m. Parapets
    n. Roof jacks for T.V., telephone, electric service
    o. Note building outline
    p. Dimension overhangs
    q. Note rain diverters
    r. Sky lights
    s. Roof accessways
    t. Flood lite locations
    u. Service pole for electrical
11. New construction
    a. Retaining walls
    b. Driveways and aprons
    c. Sidewalks
    d. Pool location and size
    e. Splash blocks
    f. Catch basins
    g. Curbs
    h. Patios, walls, expansion joints, dividers etc.
12. North arrow (usually towards top of sheet.)
13. Dimensions
    a. Property lines
    b. Side yards
    c. Rear yards
    d. Front yards

    e. Easements
    f. Street center line
    g. Length of fences and walls
    h. Height of fences and walls
    i. Width of sidewalks, driveways, parking
    j. Utilities
    k. Location of existing structures
    l. Note floor elevation
    m. Dimension building to property line
    n. Set backs
14. Notes
    a. Tract no.
    b. Block no.
    c. Lot no.
    d. House no.
    e. Street
    f. City, county, state
    g. Owner's name
    h. Draftsman's name (title block)
    i. Materials for porches, terraces; drives, etc.
    j. Finish grades where necessary
    k. Slope of driveway
    l. Scale (⅛", 1"-30', 1"-20' etc.)
15. Landscape lighting, note switching
16. Area drains, drain lines to street
17. Show hose bibs
18. Note drying yard, clothes line equipment.
19. Complete title block
    a. Sheet no.
    b. Scale
    c. Date
    d. Name drawn by
    e. Project address
    f. Approved by
    g. Sheet title
    h. Revision box
    i. Company name and address (school)

Figure 6.28 Site Plan Checklist.

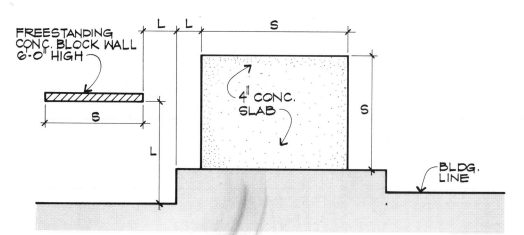

Figure 6.29 Size and location dimension.

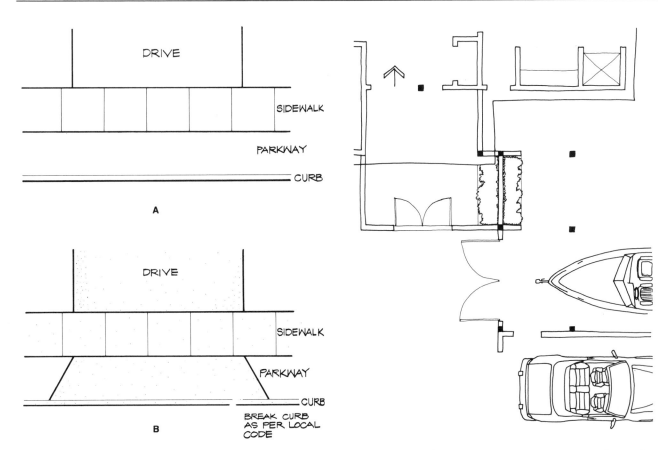

Figure 6.30 How to break a curb for a driveway.

Figure 6.31 Redesigning entry court to accommodate trellis.

Ryan Residence Site Plan

As the site plan for the Ryan Residence was in its final phase, it became apparent that the trellis, which ties the house to the garage, could not be formatted the way originally proposed. A new study was executed, as shown in Figure 6.31. This drawing was sent to the client for approval and included in the Project Book for incorporation into the site plan, floor plan, and all other drawings it affected.

STAGE I   (Figure 6.32). In the preparation of the site plan, its position on the sheet was determined by the cartoon (see Chapter 5). After positioning the outline of the site on the sheet, the setbacks should be drawn. In this instance they were 20′–0″ in the front, 5′–0″ on the side, and the rear has a minimum of 15′–0″ but was not drawn in because the drafter knew in advance that this structure would not be very close to the rear property line. These setback lines should be drawn with nonprinting lead. Such leads are usually blue or blue/purple. They are identified as nonphoto, nonprinting or fade-away lead. Although these setback lines appear black on this drawing, they do not

appear in Stage II, as they had been drawn in fade-away blue. These leads are also ideal for layout work and positioning drawings. Vellum can be purchased with fade-away lines already printed on it. These are helpful as guidelines for lettering, establishing the site and structure margins, or drawing anything of a tabular nature. This is drafted at an ⅛″ scale for the Ryan Residence.

Next, take this ⅛″ drawing of the Floor Plan and place it under the drawing for positioning. See Figure 6.32. The garage was positioned as close as possible to the required setback on the bottom right corner, and the house as close as possible to the left limits. This positioning established the space between the two structures. The security and entry area was the next item to be drafted and positioned to align with the garage, leaving enough space for a gate to be added later for boat storage.

STAGE II   (Figure 6.33). The first step was to dimension the house and garage onto the site. Dimension lines were positioned to locate the structure from all sides of the property line. The sidewalk, parkway, and power pole were then drawn in, the driveway was positioned, and the textured concrete walk between the driveway and house was completed. The walkway will be concrete, stamped with a pattern while still

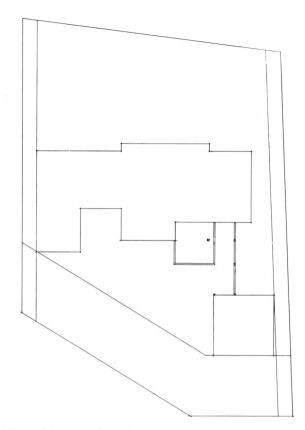

Figure 6.32 Site plan—Stage I.

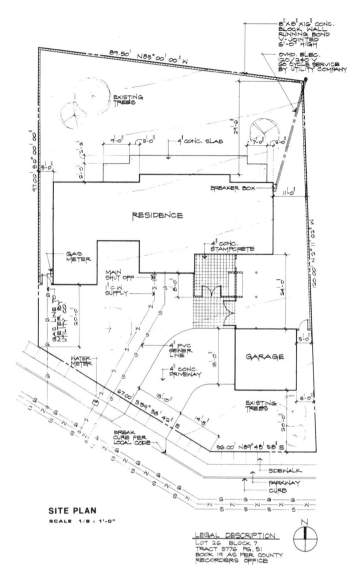

SITE PLAN
SCALE 1/8 : 1'-0"

LEGAL DESCRIPTION
LOT 26 BLOCK 7
TRACT 3776 PG. 51
BOOK 19 AS PER COUNTY
RECORDERS OFFICE

Figure 6.34 Site plan—Stage III.

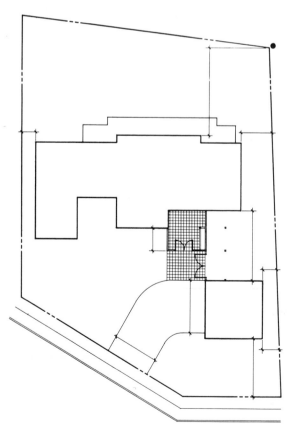

Figure 6.33 Site plan—Stage II.

wet. This material is called stampcrete. Next in the sequence were gates to the entry and to the boat storage area, and these (drive, entry, and walk) were dimensioned. The living room, family room, and master bedroom are connected by a concrete walk as a final step. All lines were hardlined and the stampcrete texture was added, along with the posts that will hold up the trellis and a small planter positioned to the right of the entry court. The planter area will be changed after the trellis is designed and aligned with the roof overhang.

STAGE III (Figure 6.34). Prior to advancing to Stage III of the drawing sequence, the project manager will review the drawing and make some corrections and changes. This is done on a diazo copy, which is often referred to as the "check print." In this case, three-dimensional errors were noted. These were the three-dimensional lines that locate the house and the garage on the right side of the site. The side yard dimension on the left side of the site is proper, because the property line and the building line are parallel to each other. The property line on the garage side is not parallel to the garage or the house. These will be the first to be corrected with extension lines.

Existing trees are positioned, and dimensioning continues with the location dimensions of the drive at the bend in the property line. Numerical values are now lettered. The positioning of the house and the garage onto the lot must be checked with the final overall dimensions of the Floor Plan. This is to ensure that the house *can* in fact fit onto the lot as shown. Remember, the house is dimensioned to the stud line outside of the house (the stucco). The overall dimension of the house (from the Floor Plan) must be added to side yard dimensions, *and* two inches must be added for the thickness of the stucco.

Public utility lines were next in the drawing order and included sizing and noting. Finally, the legal description and a description of the concrete block wall, curb break, and all other notes including the North arrow were given. The title and scale were produced by a lettering machine, a device that makes strips of letters on a sticky-back material. These strips are then placed on the drawing sheet.

SUMMARY

A site development program may contain much technical information and therefore require additional drawings for clarity. Cross-sections illustrate the topography conditions as they relate to natural and finish grades. Other illustrations of one site point out the various plans that may be needed in the site development process.

IMPORTANT TERMS AND CONCEPTS

Plat map
Polar coordinates
Lot lines and bearings
P.O.B. (point of beginning)
Topography map
Finish grading
Contour lines
Setbacks
Site plan
Site cross-section

Soils and geology map
Boring log
Utility plan
Grading plan
Floor elevation
Cut and fill procedures
Landscape plan
Plant list
Irrigation plan
Daylight grade elevation

REVIEW QUESTIONS

1. What is the main drawing that is required for the site development plan?
2. What is the name of the map that shows the natural or existing contours of a site?
3. Name two pieces of information gleaned from the soils investigation.
4. What plan shows the alteration or reshaping of the existing contours of a site?
5. Name five important pieces of information found on a site development plan.

LABORATORY PROBLEMS

1. Lay out a site (scale: 1' = 10') with the following given bearings and dimensions: starting at a point of beginning, N 00° 18' 00" E, Length 172.50', N 82° 18' 14" W, Length 233.78', S 00° 18' 00" W, Length 249.00', N 79° 31' 11" E, Length 235.61'.
2. Construct a site and topography model from Figure 6.4. Material and scale will be determined by your instructor.

7

FOUNDATION PLANS

7

PREVIEW

This chapter examines foundation plans, details for concrete and wood floors, and combinations of both of these. It also examines a foundation design that uses concrete pads as the primary support, and provides photographs of job site foundation conditions.

OBJECTIVES

1. Understand the need to provide foundation detail sketches preliminary to the drawing of a foundation plan.
2. Determine the types of lines used to represent a foundation detail in plan view.
3. Be familiar with the dimensioning process as it relates to the floor plan.
4. Appreciate the use of foundation reference symbols.
5. Appreciate the importance of noting all the concrete accessories and hardware on the foundation plan.

A foundation plan is a drawing that shows the location of all concrete footings, concrete piers, and structural underpinning members required to support a structure. The main purpose of all the foundation footings is to distribute the weight of the structure over the soil.

Types of Foundations

Two types of floor systems are usually used in foundation plans. These floor systems are constructed of concrete or wood or a combination of both. Each floor system requires foundation footings to support the structure and the floor.

Concrete Slab Floor: Foundation Plans

If you have selected concrete as the floor material for a specific project, first investigate the types of **foundation footing details** required to support the structure before drawing the foundation plan. The **footing design** will be influenced by many factors such as the vertical loads or weight it is to support, regional differences, allowable soil bearing values, established frost line location, and recommendations from a soils and geological report which will determine a minimum footing depth as well as reinforcing requirements. Figure 7.1 illustrates a concrete footing and concrete floor with various factors influencing design.

You may sketch the foundation details in freehand form. Figure 7.2A shows a freehand drawing with an exterior bearing wall footing and concrete slab floor. The sketch then becomes the guide for drawing an exterior bearing footing on the foundation plan. See Figure 7.2B. The broken line represents the footing and foundation wall, located under the concrete slab or grade. This broken line, as you will remember, is referred to as a hidden line. The solid line shows the edge of the concrete floor slab as projected above the grade level. Broken lines are mainly used to show footing sizes, configurations, and their locations below grade level or below a concrete floor; solid lines show those above.

The investigation and freehand sketch for a required interior bearing footing might look like Figure 7.3A. If it does, draw the plan view of this detail only with broken lines, because all the configurations are under the concrete slab floor and grade. See Figure 7.3B.

An interior nonbearing footing (a footing that supports a much lighter load than a bearing footing) is drawn in the plan view as the section configuration dictates. Figure 7.4A shows a section through a nonbearing footing.

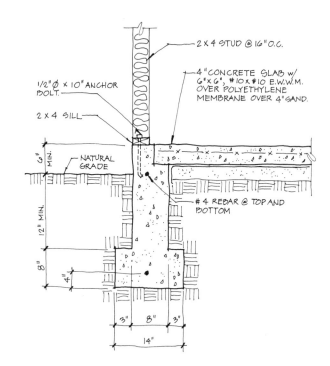

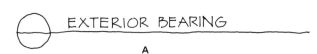

Figure 7.2A Exterior bearing—Beach House.

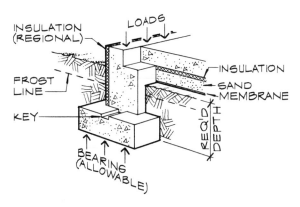

Figure 7.1 Concrete footing and concrete floor with various influencing design factors.

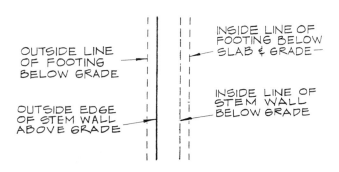

Figure 7.2B Plan view of foundation detail.

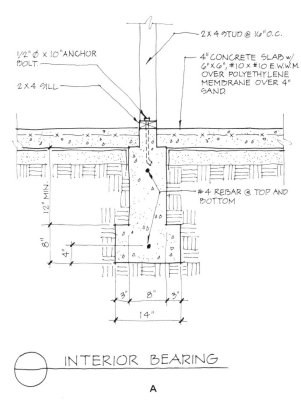

Figure 7.3A Detail of interior bearing footing—Beach House.

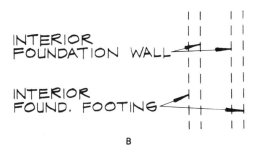

Figure 7.3B Plan view of interior bearing footing.

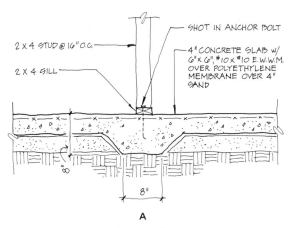

Figure 7.4A Interior nonbearing footing.

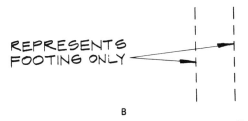

Figure 7.4B Plan view of interior nonbearing footing.

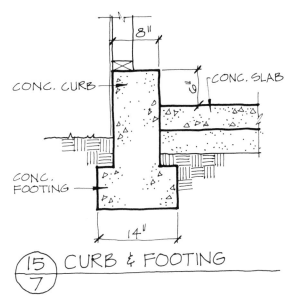

Figure 7.5A Concrete curb and footing.

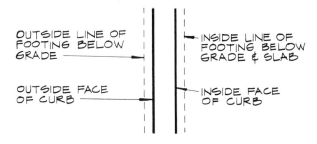

Figure 7.5B Plan view—concrete curb.

Figure 7.4B shows this footing in the plan view. Note here that only the width of the footing is shown since the foundation wall and footing are in this case one and the same.

Often, concrete curbs above the concrete floor levels are used, as, for example, in garage areas where wood studs need to be free from floor moisture. As with the other foundation conditions, draw a freehand sketch of this detail. See Figure 7.5A for an example. The plan view of this detail is shown in Figure 7.5B, and Figures 7.6A and 7.6B show this photographically.

When you are faced with drawing concrete steps and a change of floor level, a freehand sketch of the section clarifies this condition. See Figure 7.7A. A plan view may then be drawn reflecting this section. See Figure 7.7B.

Figure 7.6A Forms for concrete curb.

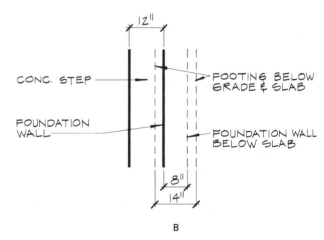

Figure 7.6B Poured concrete curb.

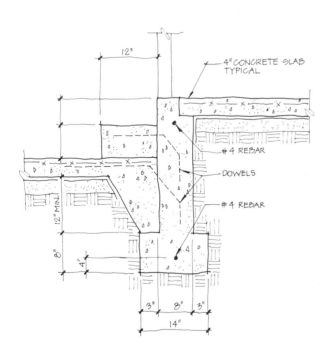

12"

4" CONCRETE SLAB
TYPICAL

#4 REBAR

DOWELS

#4 REBAR

12" MIN.

8"

4"

3"   8"   3"

14"

$\frac{3}{7}$ CHANGE OF LEVEL w/ STEP
(BEARING FOOTING)

A

Figure 7.7A Change of level with step (bearing footing).

12"

CONC. STEP

FOUNDATION
WALL

FOOTING BELOW
GRADE & SLAB

FOUNDATION WALL
BELOW SLAB

8"

14"

B

Figure 7.7B Plan view—steps and level change.

Drawing the Foundation Plan

You are now ready to draw the **foundation plan** for a concrete slab floor. Lay your tracing over a tracing of the floor plan drawing, then lightly draw the configuration of the floor plan, as well as the internal walls, columns, fireplaces, and so on, that require foundation sections. (Do not trace the foundation plan from a reproduction of the floor plan, because reproductions alter the scale of the original drawing.) After this light tracing, you are ready to finalize the drafting.

The final drafting is a graphic culmination in plan view of all the foundation walls and footings. Start with all the interior bearing and nonbearing foundation conditions. Represent these with a dotted line according to the particular sections in plan view. Figure 7.8 shows an example of a foundation plan for a two-story residence, incorporating the plan views in Figures 7.2B, 7.3B, 7.4B, 7.5B, and 7.7B, as previously discussed. Note reference symbols on foundation details and Figure 7.8.

Usually, various notes are required for items to be installed prior to the concrete pouring. An item like a **post hold-down**, (a U-shaped steel strap for bolting to a post and embedded in concrete for the use of resisting lateral forces) should be shown on the foundation plan because its installation is important in this particular construction phase. Note the **call-out** for this item on Figure 7.8. A photograph of this is shown in Figure 7.9.

Drawing Fireplaces. A drawing of a masonry fireplace on the foundation plan should have the supporting walls crosshatched. (To **crosshatch** is to shade with crossed lines, either diagonal or rectangular.) Show its footing with a broken line. When numerous vertical reinforcing bars are required for the fireplace, show their size and location, because they are embedded in the fireplace.

Strengthening Floors. Requirements for strengthening concrete floors with reinforcing vary for specific projects, so it is important to show their size and spacing on the foundation plan. Figure 7.8's foundation plan calls for a 6″ × 6″—#10 × #10 welded wire reinforcing mesh to strengthen the concrete floor. This call-out tells us that the mesh is in 6″ × 6″ squares and made of number 10 gauge wire. Figure 7.10 shows how the reinforcing mesh and a plastic membrane are placed before the concrete is poured. Deformed reinforcing bars are also installed to strengthen concrete slab floors. The size and spacing of these bars are determined by factors such as excessive weights expected to be carried by the floor and unfavorable soils conditions.

Sloping Concrete Areas. When concrete areas have to be sloped for drainage, indicate this, too, on the foundation plan. You can do this with a directional arrow, noting the number of inches the concrete is to be sloped. See Figure 7.8; here a garage slab is sloped to a door.

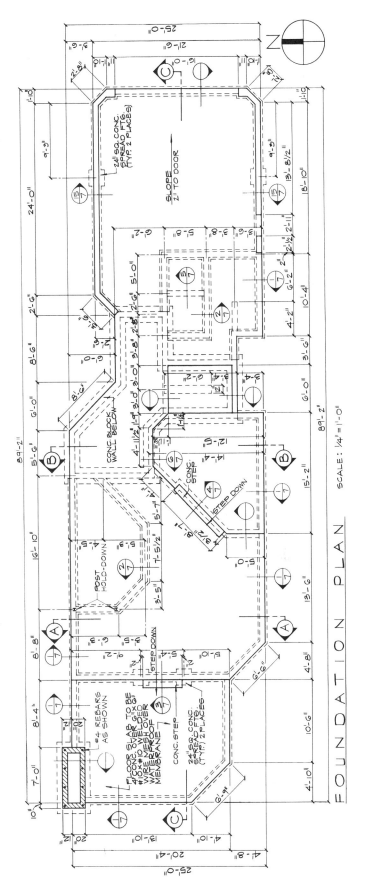

Figure 7.8 Foundation plan—concrete floor. (Residence of Mr. and Mrs. Ted Bear.)

Figure 7.9 Post hold-down.

Figure 7.10 Reinforcing mesh and plastic.

Your foundation plan dimensioning should reflect the identical dimension line locations of the floor plan. For example, center line dimensions for walls above should match center line dimensions for foundation walls below. This makes the floor and foundation plans consistent. When you lay out dimension lines, such as perimeter lines, leave space between the exterior wall and first dimension line for foundation section symbols. As Figure 7.8 shows, you must provide dimensions for every foundation condition and configuration. Observe offset dimensioning where angled walls occur. Remember, people in the field do not have the luxury of protractors or other measuring devices and therefore rely on all the dimensions you have provided on the plan.

In some cases, the foundation dimensioning process may require you to make adjustments for stud wall alignments. For example, if studs and interior finish need to be aligned, be sure to dimension for foundation offset correctly to achieve the stud alignment. See Figure 7.11. In this figure, the 3½″ stud, the foundation wall, and footing of the exterior wall are not aligned with the interior foundation wall and footing.

Provide reference symbols for foundation details for all conditions. Provide as many symbols as you need, even if there is some repetition. Remove any guesswork for the people in the field. As Figure 7.8 shows, the arrowheads on these circular reference symbols face the direction in which the detail is drawn and also have enough space within the circle for letters and/or numbers for detail and sheet referencing.

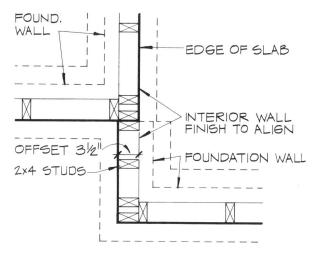

Figure 7.11 Stud wall alignment.

Foundation Details for Concrete Slab Floor. You can now draft finished drawings of the foundation details, using freehand sketches as a reference. For most cases, foundation details are drawn using an architectural scale of ½″ = 1′–0″, ¾″ = 1′–0″ or 1″ = 1′–0″. Scale selection may be dictated by office procedure or the complexity of a specific project.

Different geographical regions vary in depth, sizes, and reinforcing requirements for foundation design. Check the requirements for your region.

Foundation details for the residence shown in Figure 7.12 are drawn to incorporate a **two-pour system;** that is, the foundation wall and footing are poured first and the concrete floor later. Figure 7.12 shows the exterior bearing footing drawn in final form. Notice the joint between the foundation wall and concrete floor is filled with insulation.

The interior bearing footing detail should also be drawn to reflect a two-pour system with call-outs for all the components in the assembly. See Figure 7.13. The nonbearing footing is drafted differently from the exterior and interior bearing footings. This detail, Figure 7.14, is shown as one pour, because it is only deep enough to accommodate the **anchor bolt embedment** and can

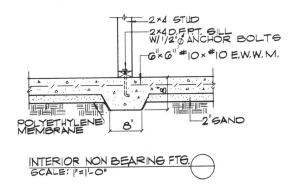

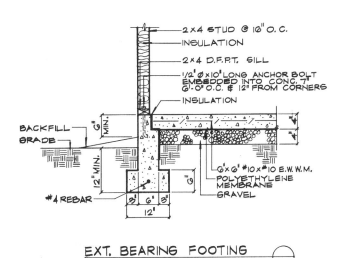

Figure 7.12 Drafted detail of a two-pour footing.

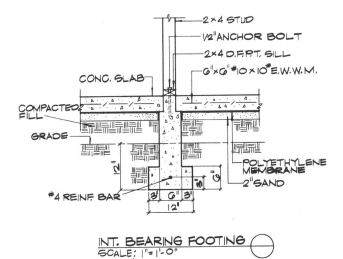

Figure 7.13 Drafted detail of a two-pour interior bearing footing.

Figure 7.14 Drafted detail of an interior nonbearing footing.

therefore be poured at the same time as the floor slab. The remaining foundation details are drafted using the freehand sketches for reference.

Wood Floor: Foundation Plans

Prepare a foundation plan for a wood floor the same way you do for a concrete floor. Sketch the different footings required to support the structure.

Your first sketch should deal with the exterior bearing footing, incorporating the required footing and wall dimensions and depth below grade. Show earth-to-wood clearances, sizes and treatment of wood members, floor sheathing, and the exterior wall and its assembly of components above the sheathing or subfloor level. See Figure 7.15A. Figure 7.15B describes the exterior bear-

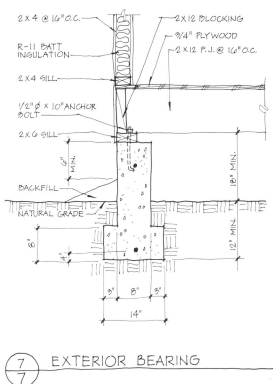

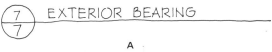

Figure 7.15A Exterior bearing footing detail.

ing footing in plan view. An investigation of the interior bearing footing requirements can be done with a scaled freehand sketch. See Figure 7.16. In the plan view the interior bearing footing looks similar to the exterior bearing footing in Figure 7.15B.

When laying out the foundation plan for a wood floor system, provide intermediate supporting elements located between exterior and interior bearing footings. You can do this with a pier and girder system, which can be spaced well within the allowable spans of the floor joists selected. This layout will be reviewed later in the discussion of the foundation plan. The girder-on-pier

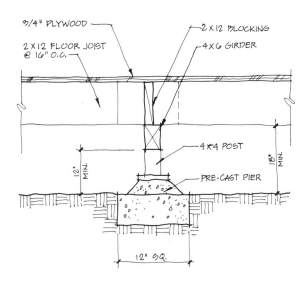

Figure 7.17A Pier and girder detail.

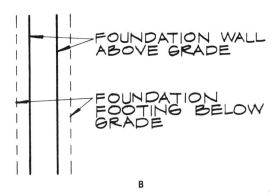

Figure 7.15B Plan view of exterior bearing footing.

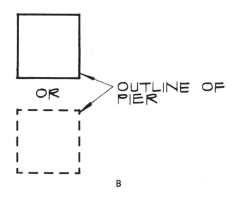

Figure 7.17B Plan view of concrete pier.

detail can be sketched in the same way as the previous details. See Figure 7.17A. Figure 7.17B describes the concrete pier in plan view. The pier spacing depends on the size of floor girder selected. With a 4 × 6 girder, a 5' or 6' spacing is recommended under normal floor loading conditions.

Regional building codes help you to select floor joists and girder sizes relative to allowable spans.

Drawing the Foundation Plan

Begin the foundation plan drawing by laying the tracing directly over the floor plan. Lightly trace the outside line of the exterior walls, the center line of the interior load bearing walls (walls supporting ceiling, floor, and roof), and curb and stud edges that define a transition between the wood floor members and the concrete floor. It is not necessary to trace nonbearing wall conditions for wood

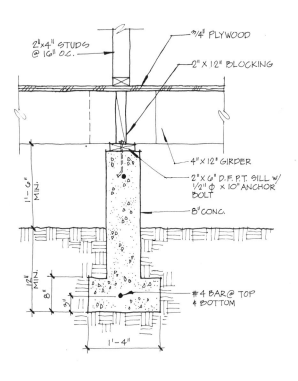

Figure 7.16 Interior bearing footing detail.

floors because floor girders can be used to support the weight of the wall.

Refer to your freehand sketches of the foundation details to help finalize the foundation plan. As a review of this procedure, Figure 7.18 shows a foundation plan with wood floor construction, incorporating the plan views shown in Figures 7.15B and 7.17B. The floor plan is the same one used for the concrete floor foundation plan. The spacing for floor girders and the concrete piers supporting the girders is based on the selected floor joist size and girder sizes. As shown, the floor girders can be drawn with a broken line while the piers, being above grade, can be drawn with a solid line. Dimension the location of all piers and girders. Wherever possible, locate floor girders under walls. Show the direction of the floor joists and their size and spacing directly above the floor girders. The fireplace foundation and reinforcing information can be designated as indicated earlier.

In Figure 7.18 a concrete garage floor is connected to a house floor system with #3 dowels at 24″ on center. This call-out should also be designated for other concrete elements such as porches and patios. On this foundation plan, the basement area has supporting walls built of concrete block. The concrete block walls have been crosshatched on the foundation plan as a reference for the material used and to define the basement area. A sketch of the foundation condition through the basement area is shown in Figure 7.19.

Incorporate dimensioning and foundation detail symbols the same way you did for a concrete foundation. An important note to be located on the foundation plan drawing is the number of foundation vents required, and their sizes, material, and location. This requirement is regulated by governing building codes.

Foundation Details for a Wood Floor Foundation. Finished drawings for the foundation details can be drafted with call-outs and dimensions for each specific detail. As with concrete floor foundation sizes, depths and reinforcing requirements vary regionally. Finished details for exterior and interior bearing footings as well as a typical pier and girder are shown in Figures 7.20, 7.21, and 7.22. Figure 7.23 illustrates the use of concrete block for a foundation wall supporting a wood floor. Figure 7.24 combines Figure 7.20 with a porch and stair connected to the exterior foundation detail. Here dowels have been added to tie the concrete porch to the building and metal flashing has been used to protect against dryrot from water seepage.

A foundation detail through the garage concrete floor and house floor is shown in Figure 7.25. This important detail shows the placement of dowels and provisions for a nailer in which a finished interior material can be secured at the concrete foundation wall. Remaining foundation sections are drafted in the same way using investigative sketches for reference.

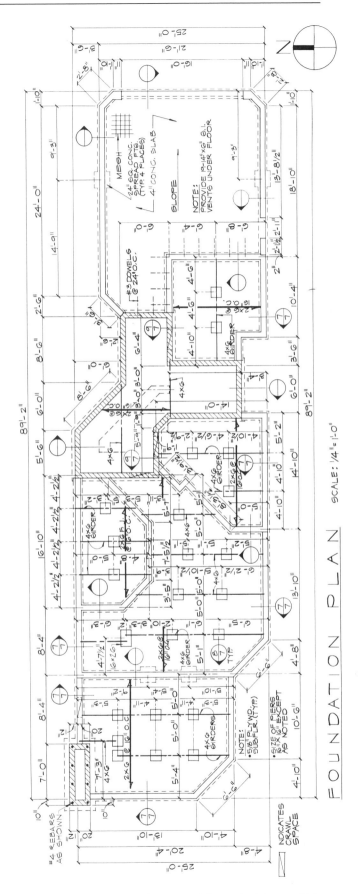

Figure 7.18 Foundation plan—wood floor. (Residence of Mr. and Mrs. Ted Bear.)

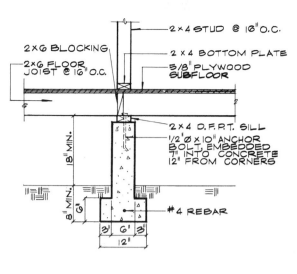

2x6 BLOCKING
2x6 FLOOR JOIST @ 16" O.C.
2x4 STUD @ 16" O.C.
2x4 BOTTOM PLATE
5/8" PLYWOOD SUBFLOOR
2x4 D.F.R.T. SILL
1/2" Ø x 10" ANCHOR BOLT, EMBEDDED 7" INTO CONCRETE 12" FROM CORNERS
18" MIN.
8" MIN.
6"
#4 REBAR
3" 6" 3"
12"

INTERIOR BEARING FOOTING
SCALE: 1" = 1'-0"

Figure 7.21 Drafted detail of interior bearing footing with wood floor.

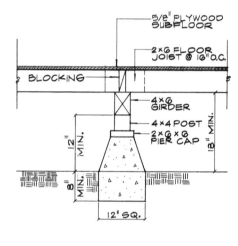

5/8" PLYWOOD SUBFLOOR
2x6 FLOOR JOIST @ 16" O.C.
BLOCKING
4x6 GIRDER
4x4 POST
2x6x6 PIER CAP
12" MIN.
18" MIN.
8" MIN.
12" SQ.

TYPICAL PIER DET.
SCALE: 1" = 1'-0"

Figure 7.22 Pier detail perpendicular to girder.

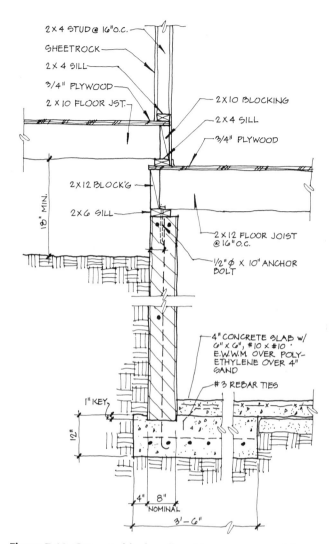

2x4 STUD @ 16" O.C.
SHEETROCK
2x4 SILL
3/4" PLYWOOD
2x10 FLOOR JST.
2x10 BLOCKING
2x4 SILL
3/4" PLYWOOD
2x12 BLOCK'G
2x6 SILL
2x12 FLOOR JOIST @ 16" O.C.
1/2" Ø x 10" ANCHOR BOLT
18" MIN.
4" CONCRETE SLAB w/ 6"x6", #10 x #10 E.W.W.M. OVER POLY-ETHYLENE OVER 4" SAND
#3 REBAR TIES
1" KEY
12"
4" 8"
NOMINAL
3'-6"

Figure 7.19 Concrete block wall and basement—wood floor.

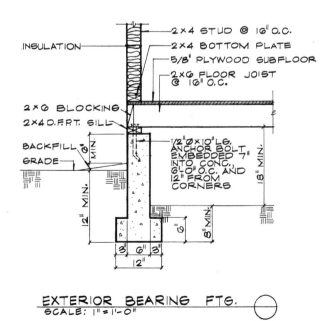

INSULATION
2x4 STUD @ 16" O.C.
2x4 BOTTOM PLATE
5/8" PLYWOOD SUBFLOOR
2x6 FLOOR JOIST @ 16" O.C.
2x6 BLOCKING
2x4 D.F.R.T. SILL
BACKFILL
GRADE
1/2" Ø x 10" LG. ANCHOR BOLT EMBEDDED 7" INTO CONC., 6'-0" O.C. AND 12" FROM CORNERS
6" MIN.
12" MIN.
6"
18" MIN.
8" MIN.
3" 6" 3"
12"

EXTERIOR BEARING FTG.
SCALE: 1" = 1'-0"

Figure 7.20 Drafted detail of typical exterior.

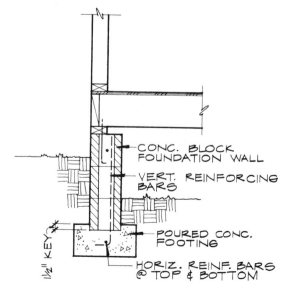

CONC. BLOCK FOUNDATION WALL
VERT. REINFORCING BARS
POURED CONC. FOOTING
HORIZ. REINF. BARS @ TOP & BOTTOM
1/2" KEY

Figure 7.23 Concrete block foundation wall supporting a wood floor.

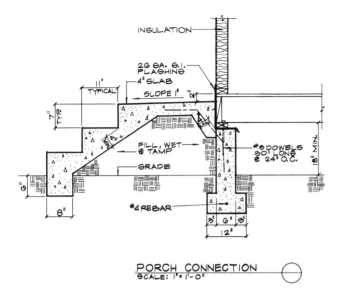

PORCH CONNECTION
SCALE: 1"=1'-0"

Figure 7.24 Drafted detail of a porch connection.

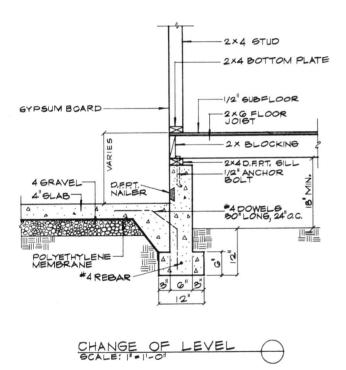

CHANGE OF LEVEL
SCALE: 1"=1'-0"

Figure 7.25 Drafted detail of change of level from a wood floor to a concrete slab.

Examples

Example 1: A Building with Masonry Walls

When projects use concrete or masonry for exterior and interior walls, the walls may continue down the concrete footing. Figure 7.26 shows an exterior masonry wall and concrete footing. If interior walls are constructed of masonry, the foundation section is similar to Figure 7.26. Drawing the foundation plan using masonry as the foundation wall requires delineation of the foundation walls by crosshatching those areas representing the masonry.

The building in this example is a theatre with exterior and interior masonry walls. Its foundation plan, details, and photographs of the construction of the foundation follow.

The foundation plan, shown in Figure 7.27, defines all the masonry wall locations as per Figures 7.26 and 7.28. The footings are drawn with a broken line. For this project **pilasters** are required to support steel roof beams. A pilaster is a masonry or concrete column designed to support heavy axial and/or horizontal loads. See Figure 7.28. The footing width is not called out but refers to the foundation plan for a specific pilaster footing dimension. Many projects do this because the total loads acting on the pilaster vary.

Steel columns are also required to support heavy axial loads and they, in turn, require a foundation. These foundation members are commonly referred to as concrete piers or **concrete pads.** The size of these pads varies with different loading conditions. Because of the various pad sizes, you may need to use a column pad schedule. This schedule should note the column designation, size, depth, and required steel reinforcing.

An example of a pad schedule is shown in Figure 7.27. Locate the pad schedule directly on the foundation plan sheet for ease of reference. It should show dimensions for all footings, walls, and pad locations with reference symbols clearly defined for specific conditions. Similar notes are provided for items such as ramp and floor slopes, pilaster sizes, and required steel reinforcing.

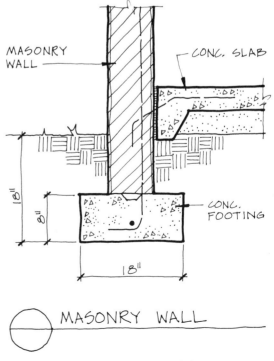

MASONRY WALL

Figure 7.26 Exterior masonry wall and footing.

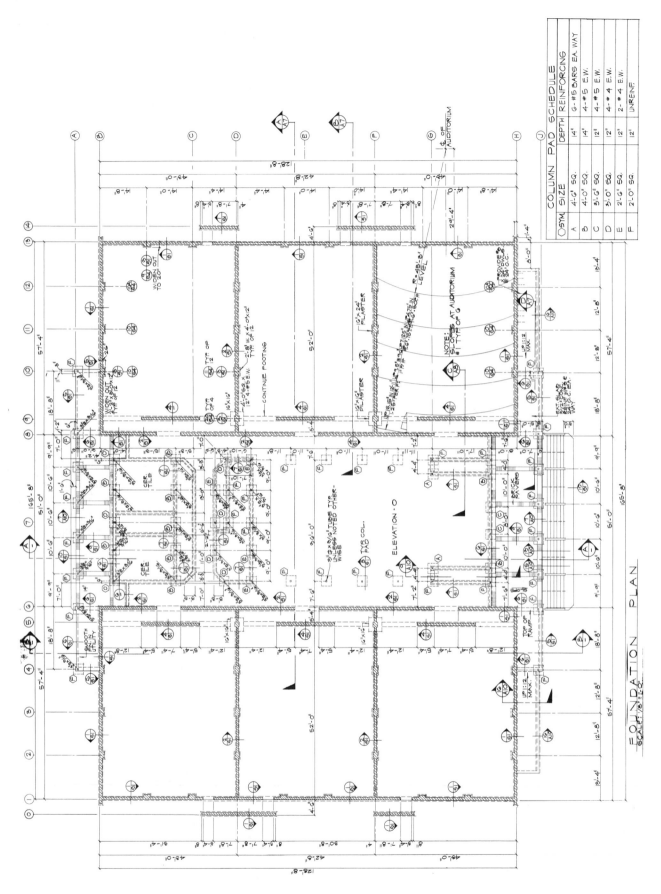

Figure 7.27 Foundation plan—masonry walls. (Courtesy of AVCO Community Developers, Inc. and Mann Theatres Corporation of CA.)

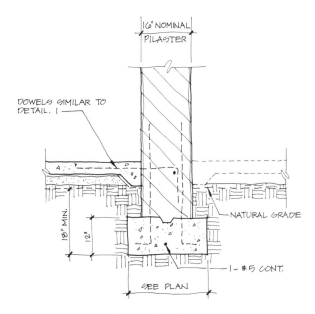

Figure 7.28 Pilaster footing detail.

From the information on the foundation plan, the various foundation conditions are laid out on the site using chalk lines. In Figure 7.29, the footing for the masonry walls and pilasters is clearly visible on the right side of the structure.

When **chalking** has been completed for the footing locations, trenching for these details is dug and made ready for the pouring of the concrete. Once the reinforcing rods and footings are installed, the masonry work can begin. Figure 7.30 shows masonry work in progress. Note the pilasters and chalking for the various concrete pads.

Example 2: A Foundation Using Concrete Pads and Steel Columns

Drawing foundation plans varies depending on the foundation requirements of the method of construction for a specific structure. The example that follows uses a structure requiring concrete pads to support steel col-

Figure 7.29 Chalking for foundation layout. (Courtesy of AVCO Community Developers, Inc. and Mann Theatres Corporation of CA.; William Boggs Aerial Photography. Reprinted with permission.)

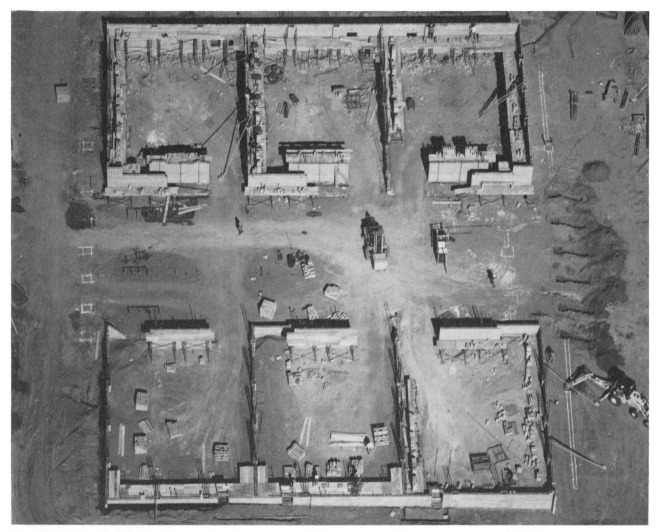

Figure 7.30 Foundation development. (Courtesy of AVCO Community Developers, Inc. and Mann Theatres Corporation of CA.; William Boggs Aerial Photography. Reprinted with permission.)

umns with a continuous footing to support masonry walls.

This foundation plan, as Figure 7.31 shows, is handled differently from the foundation plan in Example 1. As you place the tracing paper directly over the floor plan tracing, first establish the column locations as they relate to the **axial reference locations.** Masonry walls are then drawn and delineated. Concrete pads, located under a concrete floor, are represented with a broken line. See Figure 7.31. Figure 7.32 provides a visual example of this column pad footing detail in section. The column pad sizes may vary due to varying loads, and may be sized using a pad schedule or noted directly on the foundation plan. In this case, sizes are noted on the foundation plan. These pads are drawn to scale, relative to their *required* sizes, rather than their actual sizes. Provide, at the bottom of the foundation plan drawing, a **legend** defining the size and shape of the steel column and the base stem that supports it.

Because of all the critical information required in the field, a schedule for column base plates and their required anchorage may be necessary. Put this at the bottom of the plan. Dimensioning this type of foundation depends on the axial reference locations, which are identical to the floor plan referencing. Other foundation conditions are dimensioned from these axial reference lines. See Figure 7.31.

After you complete all the necessary dimensioning, show section reference symbols and notes. Figure 7.31 has a double broken line representing a continuous footing underneath, which connects to all the concrete pads. The main purpose of this footing is to provide continuity for all the components of the foundation.

The concrete pads are the main supports for this structure. Figure 7.33 shows the trenching and some formwork for a concrete pad. Note particularly the placement of the reinforcing steel and the footing, which is used to tie all the pads together. After the concrete is

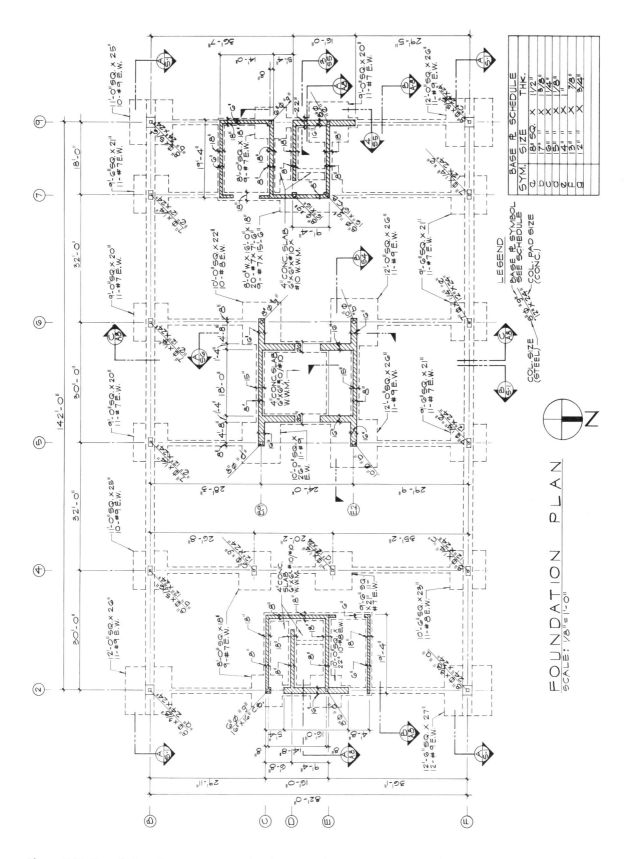

Figure 7.31 Foundation plan—concrete pads. (Courtesy of Westmount, Inc., Real Estate Development, Torrance, CA.)

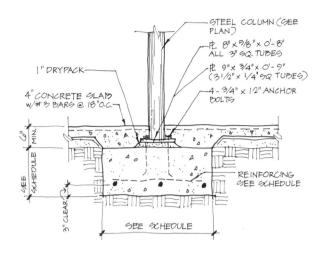

Figure 7.32 Column footing detail.

Figure 7.33 Forming for concrete pad. (William Boggs Aerial Photography. Reprinted with permission.)

Figure 7.34 Steel column on concrete pad.

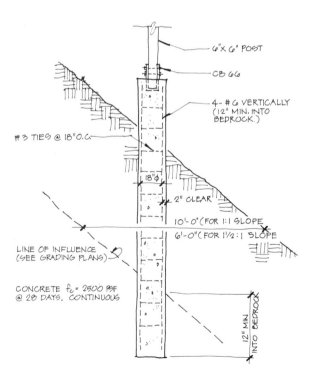

Figure 7.35 Concrete caisson.

poured and anchor bolts embedded, the steel column with the attached base plate is bolted to the concrete pad. See Figure 7.34.

When columns are used for structural support, **concrete caissons** may be needed in unfavorable soil conditions. A concrete caisson is a reinforced column designed specifically for the loads it will support and is located at a depth that provides good soil bearing. The concrete caisson shown in Figure 7.35 is used on a sloping site to provide firm support for a wood column which in turn is part of the structural support for a building. Figure 7.36 shows a job site drilling rig providing holes for concrete caissons.

Figure 7.36 Drilling holes for concrete caissons. (William Boggs Aerial Photography. Reprinted with permission.)

Example 3: A Concrete Floor at Ground-Floor Level

This foundation plan is for a small two-story residence with a concrete floor at the ground-floor level. See Figure 7.37. The plan view drawing of the foundation sections is similar to those in Figures 7.2B, 7.3B, 7.4B, 7.5B, and 7.7B.

Note on the foundation plan everything that is to be installed prior to the pouring of the concrete. If terms are located somewhere else in the drawings, the foundation contractor may miss these items, causing problems after the pouring. Specific locations call for anchor bolt placement, steel column embedment, post holdown hardware, and other symbols, all explained in the legend below. Dimensions for the location of all founda-

tion walls and footings are shown with reference symbols for the various footing conditions.

Figure 7.38 demonstrates the importance of noting all the required hardware or concrete accessories on the foundation plan. You can well imagine the problems that would arise if these items were not installed before the concrete was poured! Trenching and formwork for the foundation (see Figure 7.37) is shown photographically in Figure 7.39. The next step in completing the foundation phase of this residence is the pouring of the concrete and finishing of the concrete floor in preparation for the wood framing. See Figure 7.39. Often, a checklist also is furnished that provides specific information required for a project. See Figure 7.40.

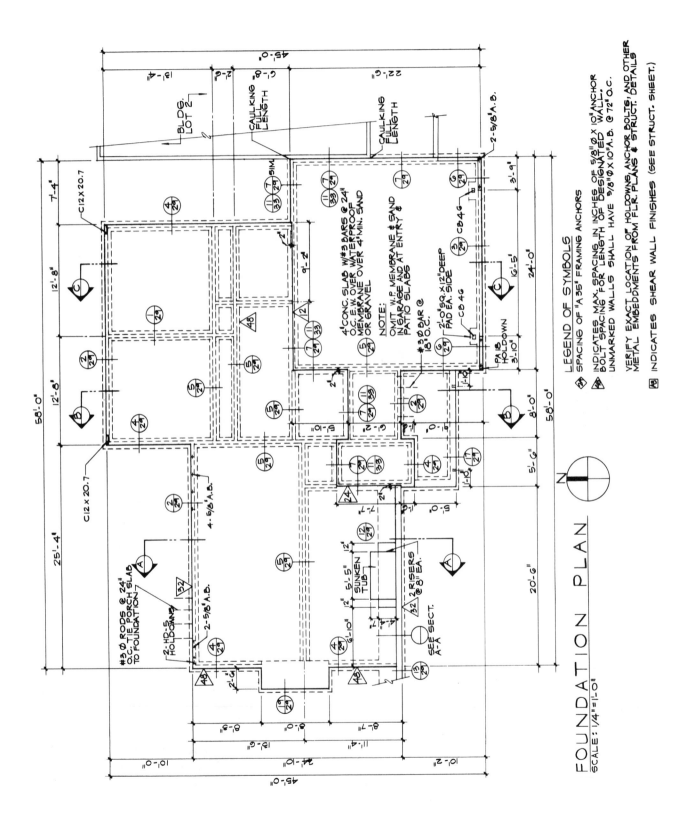

Figure 7.37 Foundation plan with concrete floor. (Courtesy of William F. Smith—Builder.)

Figure 7.38 Embedded hardware (concrete accessories). (Courtesy of William F. Smith—Builder.)

Figure 7.39 Foundation trenching—poured concrete floor and foundation. (Courtesy of William F. Smith—Builder; William Boggs Aerial Photography. Reprinted with permission.)

FOUNDATION PLAN AND DETAIL CHECKLIST

1. North arrow
2. Titles and scale
3. Foundation walls 6″ (solid lines)
   a. Overall dimensions
   b. Offset dimensions (corners)
   c. Interior bearing walls
   d. Special wall thickness
   e. Planter wall thickness
   f. Garage
   g. Retaining wall
4. Footings—12″ (hidden lines)
   a. Width of footing
   b. Stepped footing as per code
   c. Fireplace footing
   d. Belled footing
   e. Grade beams
   f. Planter footing
   g. Garage
   h. Retaining wall
5. Girder (center line)
   a. Size
   b. Direction
   c. Spacing (center to center)
6. Piers
   a. Sizes
   b. Spacing (center to center)
   c. Detail
      (1) 8″ above grade (finish)
      (2) 8″ below grade (natural)
      (3) 2 × 6 × 6 redw'd block secure to pier
      (4) 4 × 4 post
      (5) 4 × 6 girder
      (6) 2 × ? floor joist (o/c)
      (7) Subfloor 1″ diagonal
         (a) T & G
         (b) Plyscord
      (8) Finished floor (usually in finished schedule)
7. Porches
   a. Indicate 2″ lip on foundation (min.)
   b. Indicate steel reinforcing (3/8″-24″ o/c)
   c. Under slab note: Fill, puddle, and tamp
   d. Thickness of slab and steps
8. Sub-floor material and size

9. Footing detail references
10. Cross section reference
11. Column footing location and sizes
12. Concrete floors:
    a. Indicate bearing and nonbearing footings
    b. Concrete slab thickness and mesh size
13. Fireplace foundation
14. Patio and terrace location
    a. Materials
    b. See porches
15. Depressed slabs or recessed area for ceramic tile, etc.
16. Double floor joist under parallel partitions
17. Joist—direction and spacing
18. Areaways (18″ × 24″)
19. Columns (center line dimension and size)
20. Reinforcing—location and size
    a. Rods
    b. Wire mesh
    c. Chimney
    d. Slabs
    e. Retaining walls
21. Apron for garage
22. Expansion joints (20′ o/c in driveways)
23. Crawl holes (interior foundation walls)
24. Heat registers in slab
25. Heating ducts
26. Heat plenum if below floor
27. Stairs (basement)
28. Detail references
    a. "Bubbles"
    b. Section direction
29. Trenches
30. Foundation details
    a. Foundation wall thickness (6″ min.)
    b. Footing width and thickness (12″ min.)
    c. Depth below natural grade (12″ min.)

d. 8″ above finish grade (FHA) (6″—UBC)
e. Redwood sill or as per code (2 × 6)
f. ½″ × 10″ anchor bolts, 6′-0″ o/c, 1′ from corners, imbedded 7″
g. 18″ min. clearance bottom floor joist to grade
h. Floor joist size and spacing
i. Sub-floor (see pier detail)
j. Bottom plate 2 × 4
k. Studs—size and spacing
l. Finish floor (finish schedule)
31. All dimensions—coordinate with floor plan dimensions
32. Veneer detail (check as above)
33. Areaway detail (check as above)
34. Garage footing details
35. Planter details
36. House-garage connection detail
37. Special details
38. Retaining walls over 3′-0″ high (special design)
39. Amount of pitch of garage floor (direction)
40. General concrete notes
    a. Water-cement ratio
    b. Steel reinforcing
    c. Special additives
41. Note treated lumber
42. Special materials
    a. Terrazzo
    b. Stone work
    c. Wood edges
43. Elevations of all finish grades
44. Note: solid block all joists at midspan if span exceeds 8′-0″
45. Specify grade of lumber (construction notes)
46. Poché all details on back of vellum
47. Indicate North arrow near plan
48. Scale used for plan
49. Scale used for details
50. Complete title block
51. Check dimensions with floor plan
52. Border lines heavy and black

Figure 7.40 Foundation plan checklist.

Summary of Typical Conventions—Foundation Plan (Figure 7.41)

A. Plan view of an exterior bearing footing for a slab-on-ground. For a description, see Figures 7.2A and 7.2B.
B. Plan view of a footing with a concrete curb as seen in Figures 7.5A and 7.5B. Also represents bearing footing for a wood floor system original, as seen in Figure 7.15A and 7.15B.

C. Plan view of an interior bearing footing for a slab-on-the-ground system. Originally shown in Figures 7.3A and 7.3B.
D. Convention could represent a pier, as shown in Figures 7.17A and 7.17B, or as a concrete pad for a column.
E. A widening of the footing portion of a foundation for a column, actually a combination of B and D.
F. A plan view of a masonry wall, such as shown in Figure 7.26.
G. A system showing a pier and girder convention, such as seen in Figure 7.18.

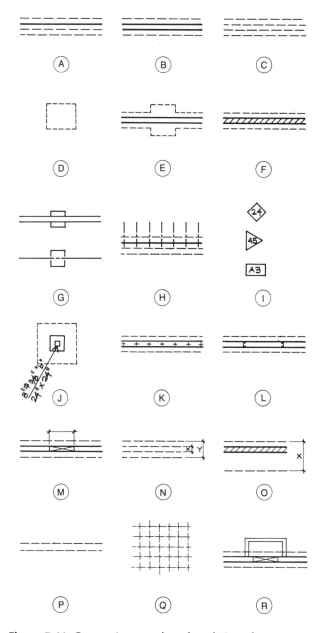

Figure 7.41 Conventions used on foundation plan.

½" dia. A.B. @ 12" o.c. (shear wall)

Note: All hardware in place prior to pouring of concrete.

L. The ([) shapes represent hold-downs at shear walls. It is critical to include a note to the effect of "all hardware in place prior to pouring of concrete."

M. Shows the location of underfloor vents and/or crawl hole from one chamber of underfloor space to another. As shown, the rectangle should be dimensioned.

N. The four hidden lines shown in this convention represent an interior bearing footing for a slab-on-the-ground system. If the stem wall and width of the footing vary from location to location, dimensions for them are indicated right at the location on the foundation plan. This negates the need to draw a separate detail for each condition, but rather a single generic detail with a dimension that includes a note such as "See foundation plan."

O. This convention represents a retaining wall. As in the previous example, the plan view could be dimensioned if they are of varying sizes throughout a structure.

P. A convention for a nonbearing footing for a slab-on-the-ground system.

Q. This matrix is used to represent concrete slab reinforcement. The size of the reinforcing is to be determined by the structural engineer, for example, #4 @18" o.c. ea./way. It is not shown throughout the foundation plan, but on only a portion of it.

R. This convention represents an underfloor access, with the rectangle having an X as the actual opening through the foundation wall. This symbol can also be used for a transom window in a basement area.

Ryan Residence Foundation Plan

Having considered the ingredients of a foundation plan and the graphic (drafted) translation of these forms, we next sequentially draft a foundation plan for the Ryan Residence. It will be developed as a slab-on-the-ground system. Be sure to read Chapters 5 and 12 to understand the structural system by which the building is assembled so that you can better appreciate the location and position of bearing and nonbearing footings, posts and their pads, and the need for and location of shear walls.

The process begins with the positioning of the foundation plan onto the vellum, as per cartoon, and using the floor plan as an underlay. This is done to speed the drawing process, but more important, to ensure that the foundation does, in fact, sit under the floor plan and aligns with it. See Figure 7.42.

Exterior/Interior Walls

As we overlay the vellum over the floor plan for alignment, the walls should be directly translated, except for

H. Short perpendicular center lines as shown here represent dowels. This convention can be seen in Figure 7.18.

I. The diamond shape, triangle, and rectangle are used to identify such things as anchor bolt spacing, shear wall finishes, and spacing of framing anchors. See Figure 7.37 and note how they are positioned.

J. This is a multiple convention, indicating pad, pedestal, steel column, and base plate sizes. The letter refers you to a schedule in which the plate size, pad size, or even the reinforcing are described. See Figures 7.27 and 7.31.

K. The (+) symbols represent anchor bolt locations for shear walls. This symbol should be accompanied with a note similar to the following:

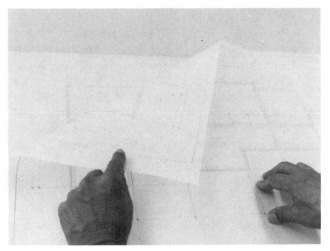

Figure 7.42 Aligning the foundation plan with the floor plan.

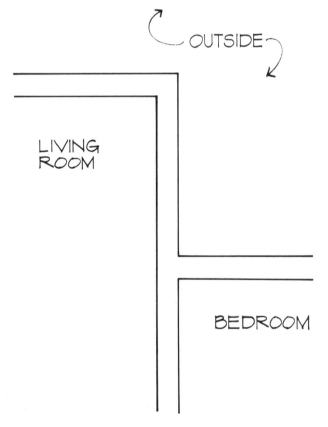

Figure 7.43 Partial floor plan.

Figure 7.44 Exterior/interior framed wall.

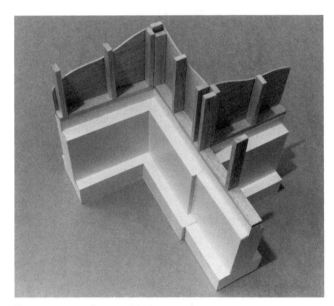

Figure 7.45 Offset in the foundation.

those that start as exterior and continue as interior walls. Figure 7.43 shows a partial floor plan of the living room wall adjacent to the master bedroom that begins as an exterior wall and turns into an interior wall. A model was constructed to show this translation, as seen from above in Figure 7.44. The problem reveals itself when we remove the slab, as seen in Figure 7.45. Note that the stem wall is not aligned, but that the plates are. If we align the foundation as shown in Figure 7.46, the plates (sills) are out of alignment, thus creating a framing prob-

lem. On the surface the solution might appear to be easily resolved by moving the plate and the anchor bolt, but the bearing surface for the plate is the same width as the plate, making this impossible.

For a quick look at the details of this condition, see Figures 7.12 and 7.13 and review the text in reference to Figure 7.11. There are a couple of ways of representing this condition. One, as shown in Figure 7.47(A), is to actually show the offset by jogging the hidden lines. Another method, as shown in Figure 7.47(B), is to show the exterior/interior foundation wall as continuous and identify the jog with a note. A third option (not shown) is to use means—actually show the job and so noting.

The stem wall (vertical portion of the footing for the Ryan Residence) is 8 inches wide with a 2 × 4 (actually

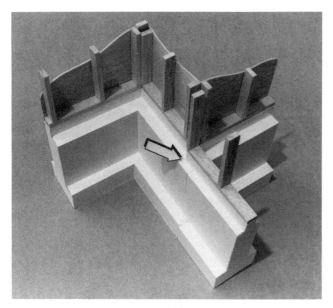

Figure 7.46 Wall plates out of alignment.

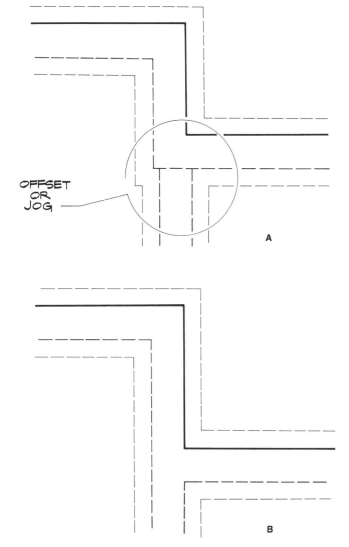

OFFSET
OR
JOG

A

B

Figure 7.47 Partial foundation plan.

3½" wide) plate on top. The exterior bearing wall has the plate along the edge, and the interior bearing footing has the plate located in the center, or, to put it another way, 2¼ inches from the edge. This becomes the amount of the jog—2 inches as we round off the 2¼ inches measurement. On this surface, it appears that the need for a jog can be solved by merely moving the plate. Yet this cannot be done, because the anchor bolt will miss the plate completely.

Remember, this problem does not exist with the interior nonbearing walls, because there will be no footings under them and the plates can be positioned with powder-actuated bolts with case-hardened nails shot through a solid washer and used on interior walls only.

Evolution of the Ryan Residence Foundation Plan

Because of the size of the sheet we are evolving and the way this problem is assigned in the Student Manual, we have decided not to show the garage on the foundation plan or on the floor plan. The garage will be drawn in its entirety (floor plan, elevation, section, etc.) on a sheet of its own.

STAGE I (Figure 7.48). After tracing the wall line onto and in the correct position, a line was added on either side of this pair of lines that represent the width of the footing. Next, the steps were positioned from the floor plan. An erasing shield with sequential holes was used in conjunction with an electric eraser to change these solid lines to dotted or hidden lines. See Figure 7.49.

STAGE II (Figure 7.50). Dimension lines were introduced at this stage, as well as the footing for the entry compound and the pads for the trellis columns. A check print of this sheet will be made, and the sizes and location dimensions placed on the check print. The drafter and/or project manager will check these numerical values against those that are used on the floor plan for alignment of the foundation with the walls above it.

STAGE III (Figure 7.51). A check print is used to perform this final stage of the foundation plan. See Figure 7.52. The diazo check print has blue lines, and the added information is usually of a different color (such as red) so that the information will stand out from the blue background and lines. As each task or series of tasks is performed, the drafter should cross out the information on the check print. A highlighter may be used; be sure that it is of a contrasting color. A highlighter is preferred because it does not cover the information and can again be checked if and when an error is made. Highlighting should always be done after the task has been done. All too often well-

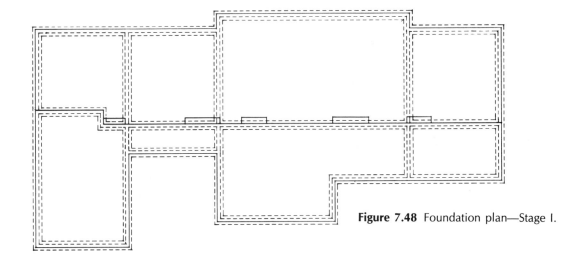

Figure 7.48 Foundation plan—Stage I.

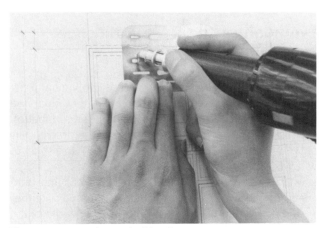

Figure 7.49 Producing hidden lines.

meaning drafters highlight information first, thinking they will get right onto the original, only to be called away from the desk to work on some other task—and the job in question is filed away by another person, thinking it was completed.

Numerical values, noting, and referencing are done in that order. The small, pointed bubbles refer the viewer to the details that will be on this sheet but are drawn on a separate original and combined photographically. Each large bubble with a triangle drawn around half of it refers the viewer to the building section.

If there is only one area to be depressed, a simple notation, "1½ depressed slab" is sufficient. In this resi-

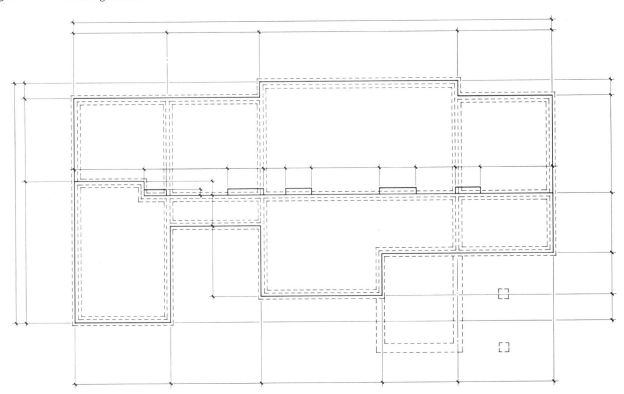

Figure 7.50 Foundation plan—Stage II.

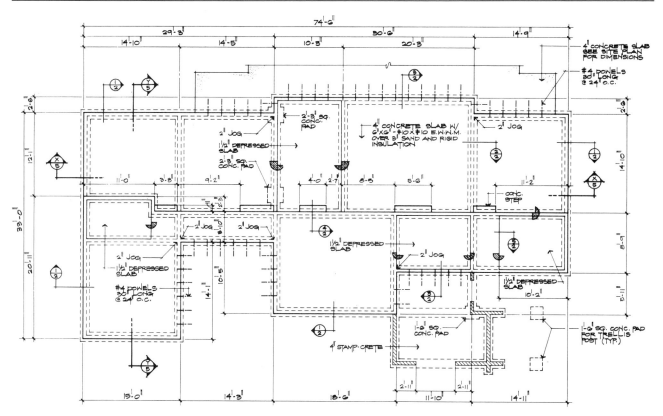

Figure 7.51 Foundation plan—Stage III.

dence, we have four areas with depressed slabs and one major change of level. To ensure that the viewer reads the plans correctly, a half bubble with the horizontal portion showing the high and low side, is employed. It is crosshatched so as to be noticeable.

In some offices all of the symbols—depressed slab, detail reference, North arrow, and so on—are predrawn and placed onto an adhesive back and scissored onto the drawing. On a computer, a library of symbols can be produced in the office, recalled, and positioned.

A final check will be made of the set before it is considered finished. To avoid massive changes at the end, great care must be taken at each stage.

Finally, the titles and scale are positioned, thus concluding the foundation plan.

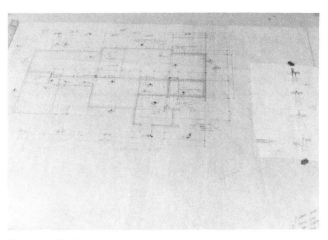

Figure 7.52 Foundation plan check print.

SUMMARY

Foundation sketches and plans for wood and concrete floors and isolated concrete pads are an important part of drafting. Notes and legends should be a part of the foundation plan, and a checklist should be provided as a guide for completion. The dimensional process is a particularly crucial aspect of drawing the foundation plan.

IMPORTANT TERMS AND CONCEPTS

Foundation detail   Two-pour system   Axial references
Footing design   Anchor bolt embedment   Legend
Post hold-down   Pilaster   Concrete caisson
Crosshatch   Concrete pads
Call-out   Chalking

REVIEW QUESTIONS

1. Describe briefly the initial step in drawing a foundation plan.
2. Name three types of footings used to support a structure.
3. Name two important concrete accessories noted on a foundation plan.
4. Explain briefly the purpose of dowels in a foundation system.
5. A footing or pier on a foundation is depicted with what type of line?
6. Dimension lines on the foundation plan relate to another drawing. What is it?
7. What method is used for referencing and dimensioning for projects with isolated columns and concrete pads?
8. What material other than concrete is used for foundation walls?

LABORATORY PROBLEMS

1. Using a scale of ½″ = 1′–0″, freehand sketch each of the following foundation details:
    a. A one-story exterior concrete wall and footing supporting a wood floor
    b. An interior footing supporting an 8″-thick masonry wall
    c. An interior nonbearing footing for a concrete floor
2. Using a scale of ¾″ = 1′–0″, draw a plan view portion of each of the following:
    a. A 6″-thick concrete curb with a 14″-wide footing
    b. An 8″-wide masonry foundation wall and 16″-wide footing
    c. A 30″ × 30″ concrete pad located beneath a concrete floor
3. Provide a girder, post, and pier detail for a wood floor. Scale to be selected by you.
4. Draw a garage foundation plan incorporating the following:
    a. Size 24′ × 24′
    b. Raised 6″-thick concrete curb on three sides
    c. Exterior footing 14″ wide with a foundation wall 6″ thick
    d. Provide detail symbols and freehand sketches of foundation details
    e. Note on the plan the following:
        (1) Floor thickness and material
        (2) Reinforcing
        (3) Subbase
        (4) Slopes
        (5) Any concrete accessories
    f. Scale to be selected by instructor

8

FLOOR PLANS

8

PREVIEW
This chapter is divided into four sections. The first explains how and why floor plans are drawn and then looks at ways of representing different materials in plan and at ways of dimensioning. These differ with each material: wood frame construction, masonry, and finally steel studs and steel frame. The second section introduces the symbols used to represent electrical and plumbing fixtures. The third section looks at ways to show a variety of other conditions. The last section evolves a hypothetical floor plan.

OBJECTIVES
1. Understand how floor plans are drawn.
2. Appreciate the implications of building materials for floor plan drafting.
3. Understand the dimensioning and noting methods used for floor plans.
4. Recognize symbols used to represent fixtures.
5. Be able to check your own work.

Types of Floor Plans

A floor plan is a drawing viewed from above. It is called a plan, but actually it is a horizontal section taken at approximately eye level. See Figure 8.1.

To better understand this, imagine a knife slicing through a structure and removing the upper half (the half with the roof on a single-story structure). The remaining half is then viewed from the air. This becomes the floor plan. See Figure 8.2.

The floor plan for a split-level residence is more complicated. This plan requires a lower, middle, and upper level. In the example, the entry, powder room, and garage are at the mid-level, which is also the level of the street and sidewalk. Use this level as a point of reference.

The stairs at the rear of the entry lead to the upper and lower levels. The lower level contains the master bedroom, master bath, study, bedroom, laundry, and bath-

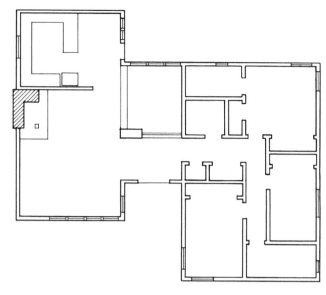

Figure 8.2 Floor plan. (Courtesy of William F. Smith—Builder.)

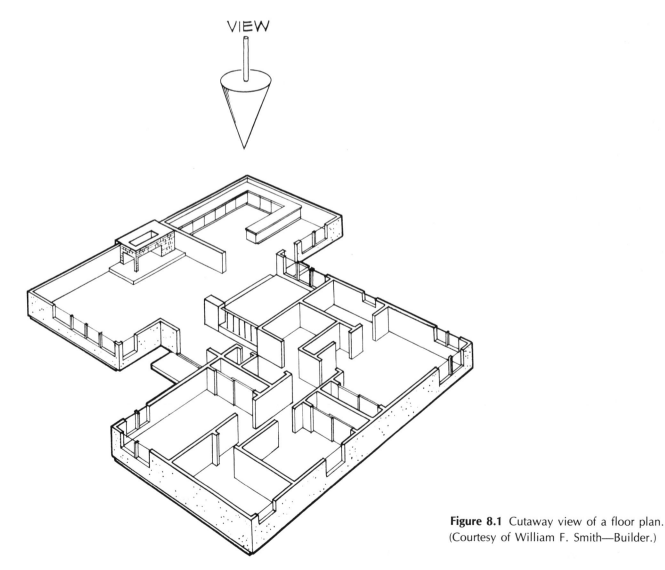

Figure 8.1 Cutaway view of a floor plan. (Courtesy of William F. Smith—Builder.)

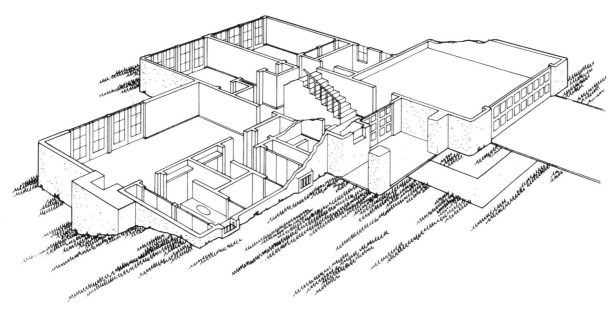

Figure 8.3 Pictorial of lower floor plan. (Courtesy of William F. Smith—Builder.)

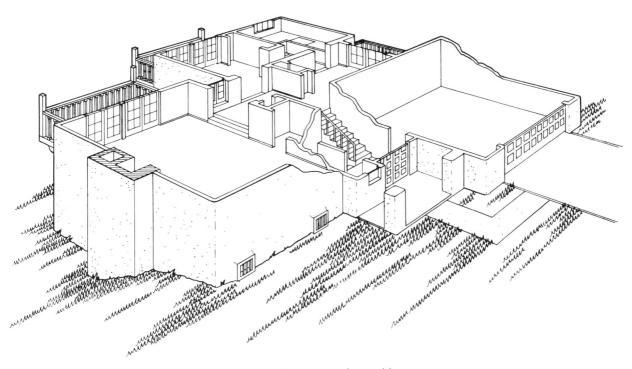

Figure 8.4 Pictorial of upper floor plan. (Courtesy of William F. Smith—Builder.)

room. See Figure 8.3. The upper level contains the living room with a wet bar, and the dining room, kitchen, breakfast room, and foyer. See Figure 8.4. When these are translated into a floor plan, they appear as in Figures 8.5 and 8.6. The mid-level is duplicated and common to both drawings. A second approach is to use a **break line** (a line with a jog in it to indicate that a portion has been deleted), showing only a part of the

garage on one of the plans. Another approach is to use a straight break line, through the garage shown on Figure 8.7A and draft it as showing only part of the garage on one of the plans. (See Figure 8.7B).

In a two-story building, a single room on the first floor is sometimes actually two stories high. If this room were a living room, for example, it would be treated as a normal one-story living room on the first floor plan;

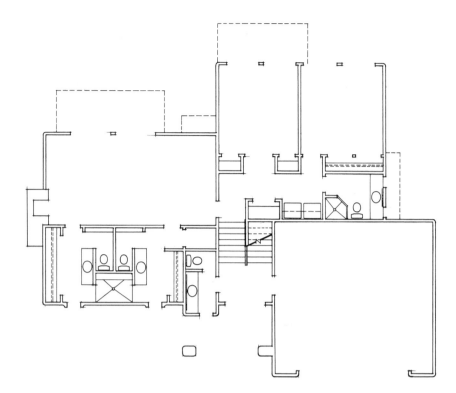

Figure 8.5 Lower floor plan. (Courtesy of William F. Smith—Builder.)

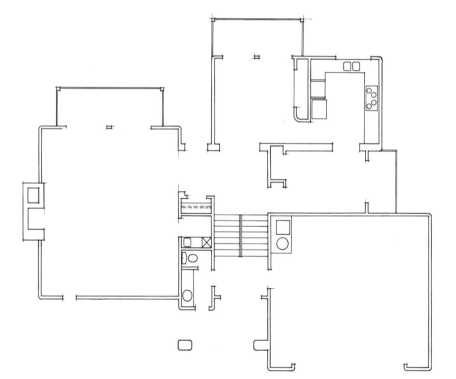

Figure 8.6 Upper floor plan. (Courtesy of William F. Smith— Builder.)

however, the area would be repeated on the second floor plan and labeled as upper living room or just labeled "open."

To simplify the image to be drafted, not every structural member is shown. For example, in a wood framed structure, if every vertical piece of wood were shown, the task would be impossible. Simplifying this image of the wood structure is done with two parallel lines. Sometimes the insulation is shown in symbol form and is not shown through the total wall. See Figure 8.8. The

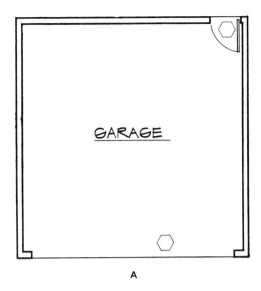

Figure 8.7A Full garage.

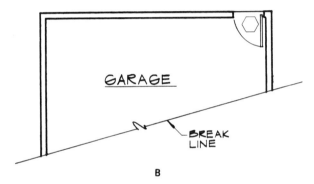

Figure 8.7B Partial garage shown with break lines.

same parallel series of lines can also be used to represent a masonry wall by adding a series of diagonal lines. See Figure 8.9. Steel frame can be represented as shown in Figure 8.10.

Wood Framing

Figures 8.11 and 8.12 show the appearance of a corner of a wood frame structure. Each side of the wall is built separately. An extra stud is usually placed at the end of the wall; it extends to the edge of the building. It therefore acts as a structural support, and gives a greater nailing surface to which wall materials can be anchored. Figure 8.13 shows a plan view of the condition at the corner of the wall.

Figures 8.14 and 8.15 show the intersection of an interior wall and an exterior wall. Figure 8.16 is the plan view of this same intersection.

Walls are not the only important elements in the framing process, of course. You must also consider the

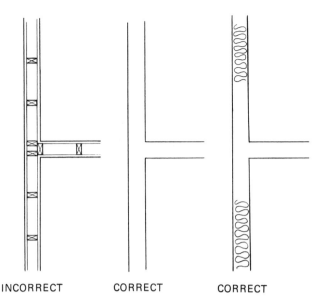

INCORRECT   CORRECT   CORRECT

Figure 8.8 Representation of wood frame.

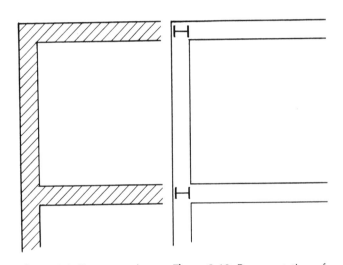

Figure 8.9 Representation of masonry.

Figure 8.10 Representation of steel frame.

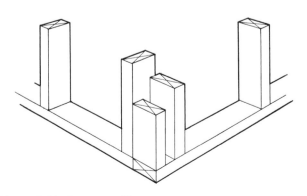

Figure 8.11 Corner at sill.

Figure 8.12 Corner at sill.

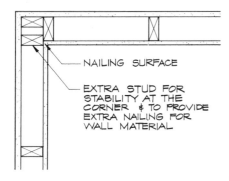

NAILING SURFACE

EXTRA STUD FOR
STABILITY AT THE
CORNER & TO PROVIDE
EXTRA NAILING FOR
WALL MATERIAL

Figure 8.13 Actual appearance of the corner of a wood-framed wall.

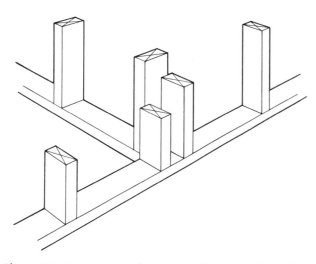

Figure 8.14 Intersection of exterior wall and interior wall.

Figure 8.15 Intersection of exterior wall and interior wall.

locations of doors and windows and the special framing they require. See Figure 8.17.

Various photographic views of intersections are shown in Figures 8.18, 8.19, and 8.20. Figure 8.21

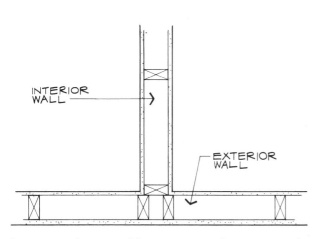

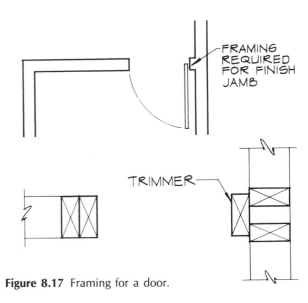

Figure 8.16 Plan view of the intersection of an exterior and an interior wall.

Figure 8.17 Framing for a door.

Figure 8.18 Intersection of interior walls at the sill.

Figure 8.19 Intersection of interior walls at the top plates. (Courtesy of William F. Smith—Builder.)

Figure 8.20 Top plates showing intersections of exterior and interior walls. (Courtesy of William F. Smith—Builder.)

Figure 8.21 Precutting of sills and headers. (Courtesy of William F. Smith—Builder.)

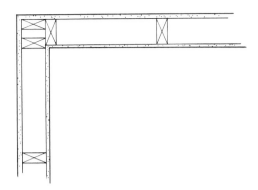

Figure 8.22 Dimensioning a corner of a wood-framed wall.

shows how **sills** and **headers** are precut and aligned with the anchor bolts. (A sill is the bottom portion of a door or window. Headers are the structural members above a door or window.)

Interior Dimensioning. Since a wood-framed wall is a built-up system, that is, a wall frame of wood upon which plaster or another wall covering is added, dimension lines must sometimes be drawn to the edge of studs and sometimes to their center.

Figure 8.22 shows how the corner of a wood-framed wall is dimensioned to the stud line. Figure 8.23 shows how an interior wall intersecting an exterior wall is dimensioned. It is dimensioned to the center so that the two studs which the interior wall will join can be located.

The process of drawing each stud in a wall becomes tiresome. So usually two lines drawn 6″ apart (in scale) are used to represent wood. To make sure that the person reading this set of plans does know that the stud is being dimensioned and not the exterior surface, the extension is often brought inside the 6″-wide wall lines. Another way to make this clear is to take extension lines to the outside surface and write **"F.O.S." (face of stud)** adjacent to the extension lines. See Figure 8.24.

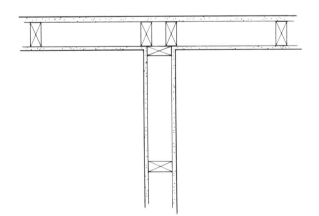

Figure 8.23 Dimensioning an intersection of an interior wall and an exterior wall.

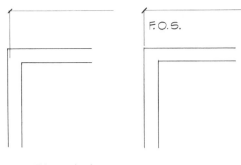

Figure 8.24 Dimensioning corners.

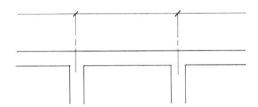

Figure 8.25 Dimensioning interior walls.

Dimensioning interior walls requires a center line or an extension line right into the wall intersection, as shown in Figure 8.25. A center line is more desirable than a solid line.

Windows and doors are located to the center of the object, as shown in Figure 8.26. When a structural column is next to a window or door, the doors and windows are dimensioned as in Figure 8.27. The size of a particular window or door can be obtained from a chart called a schedule. This schedule can be found by locating the sheet number on the bottom half of the **reference bubble** adjacent to the window or door. See Figure 8.28. (A reference bubble is a circle with a line drawn through it horizontally.)

Exterior Dimensioning. There are normally three dimension lines needed on an exterior dimension of a floor plan. The first dimension line away from the object includes the walls, partitions, centers of windows and doors, and so forth. See Figure 8.29. The second dimension line away from the object (floor plan) includes walls and partitions only. See Figure 8.30. If, in establishing the second dimension line, you duplicate a dimension, eliminate the dimension line closest to the object. See Figure 8.31. The third dimension line away from the object is for overall dimensions. See Figure 8.32. The first dimension line away from the structure should be measured ¾″ to 1½″ from the outside lines of the plan to allow for notes, window and door reference bubbles, equipment that may be placed adjacent to the structure, and so on. The second dimension line away from the structure should be approximately ⅜″ to ½″ away from the first dimension line. The distance between all subsequent dimension lines should be the same as the distance between the first and second dimension lines.

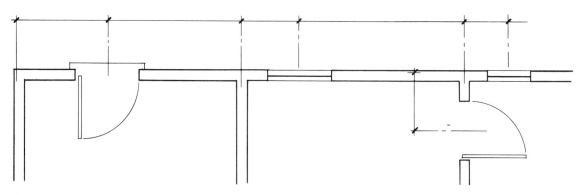

Figure 8.26 Dimensioning doors and windows.

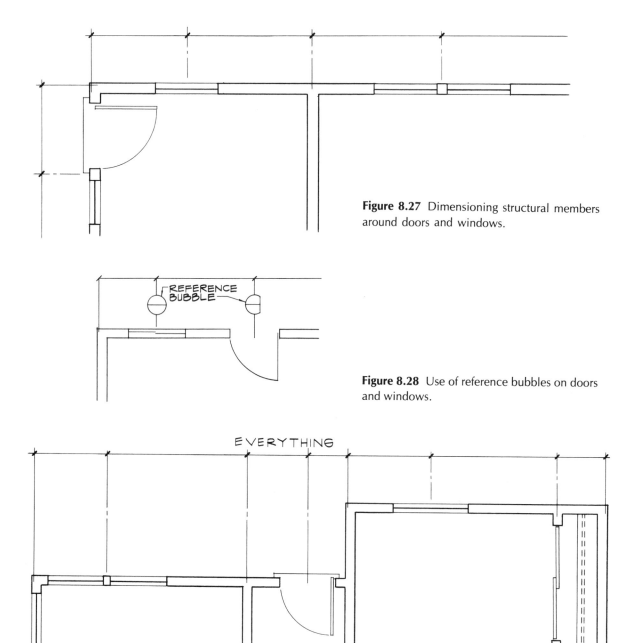

Figure 8.27 Dimensioning structural members around doors and windows.

Figure 8.28 Use of reference bubbles on doors and windows.

EVERYTHING

Figure 8.29 First dimension line away from the object.

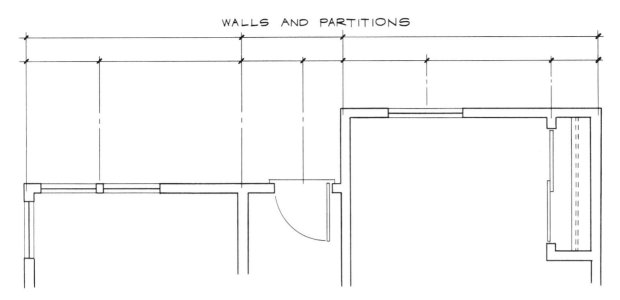

Figure 8.30 Second dimension line away from the object.

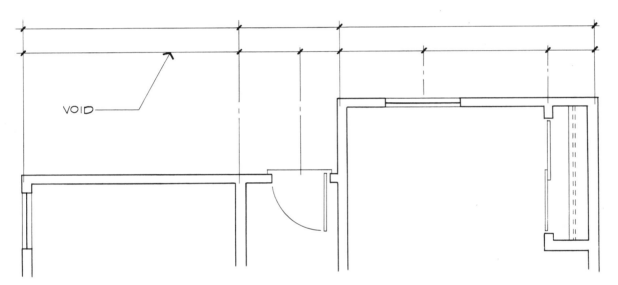

VOID

Figure 8.31 Void duplicating dimension lines.

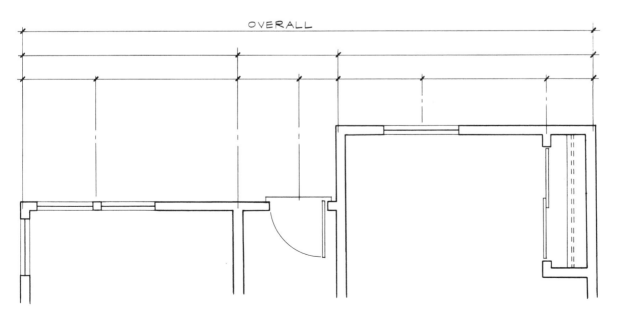

OVERALL

Figure 8.32 Third dimension line away from the object.

A large jog in a wall is called an **offset.** Because the jog is removed from the plane that is being dimensioned, you must decide whether to use long extension lines or whether to dimension the offset at the location of the jog. See Figure 8.33.

Objects located independently or outside of the structure, such as posts (columns), are treated differently. First, the order in which the items are to be built must be established. Will the columns be built before or after the adjacent walls? If the walls or the foundation for the walls are to be erected first, then major walls near the columns are identified and the columns are located from them. Never dimension from an inaccessible location! See Figure 8.34.

Masonry

When walls are built of bricks or concrete block instead of wood frame, the procedure changes. Everything here is based on the size and proportion of the masonry unit used. Represent masonry as a series of diagonal lines. See Figure 8.35. Show door and window openings the same way you did for wood frame structures. You may represent concrete block in the same way as brick for small scale drawings, but be aware that some offices do use different material designations. See Figure 8.36. (These methods of representing concrete blocks were obtained from various sources, including association literature, AIA standards, and other reference sources.) Extension lines for dimensioning are taken to the edge (end) of the exterior surface in both exterior and interior walls. See Figure 8.37. Pilasters, that is, columns built into the wall by widening the walls, are dimensioned to the center. The size of the pilaster itself can be lettered adjacent to one of the pilasters in the drawing. Another method of dealing with the size of these pilasters is to refer the reader of the plan to a detail with a note or reference bubble. See Figure 8.38. All columns consist-

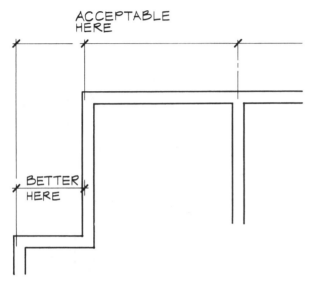

Figure 8.33 Offset dimension locations.

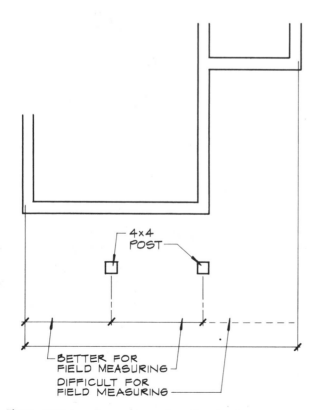

Figure 8.34 Locating columns from the structure.

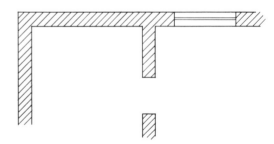

Figure 8.35 Masonry floor plan.

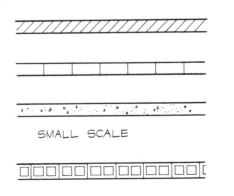

Figure 8.36 Concrete block material designations used on floor plans.

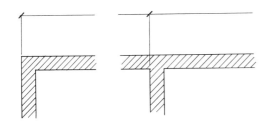

Figure 8.37 Dimensioning masonry walls.

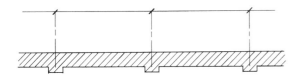

Figure 8.38 Dimensioning pilasters.

Figure 8.39 Rough opening in masonry wall.

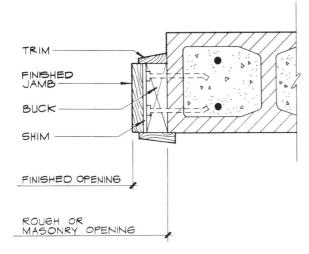

TRIM

FINISHED
JAMB

BUCK

SHIM

FINISHED OPENING

ROUGH OR
MASONRY OPENING

Figure 8.40 Door jamb at masonry opening.

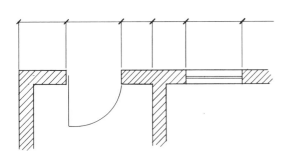

Figure 8.41 Locating doors and windows.

ing of masonry or masonry around steel are also dimensioned to the center.

Windows and Doors. Windows and doors create a unique problem in masonry units. In wood structures, windows and doors are located by dimensioning to the center and allowing the framing carpenter to create the proper opening for the required window or door size. In masonry, the opening is established before the installation of the window or door. This is called the **"rough opening"**; the final opening size is called the **"finished opening."**

The rough opening, which is the one usually dimensioned on the plan, should follow the masonry block module. See Figure 8.39. This block module and the specific type of detail used determine the most economical and practical window and door sizes. See Figure 8.40. Therefore, you should provide dimensions for locating windows, doors, and interior walls or anything of a masonry variety to the rough opening. See Figure 8.41.

Steel

There are two main types of steel systems: **steel stud** and **steel frame**. Steel studs can be treated like wood stud construction. As with wood stud construction, you need to dimension to the stud face rather than to the wall covering (skin).

There are various shapes of steel studs. See Figures 8.42 and 8.43. Drawings A and B in Figure 8.43 show how these shapes appear in the plan view. Drawing each steel stud is time-consuming and so two parallel lines are drawn to indicate the width of the wall. See drawing C in Figure 8.43. Steel studs can be called out by a note.

If only a portion of a structure is steel stud and the remainder is wood or masonry, you can shade (**pouché**)

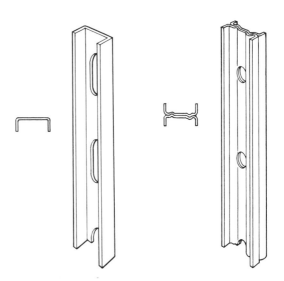

Figure 8.42 Basic steel stud shapes.

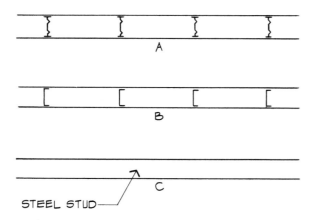

Figure 8.43 Method of representation of steel studs in a floor plan.

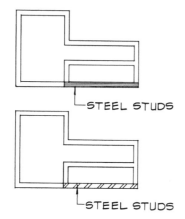

Figure 8.44 Combination of wood and steel.

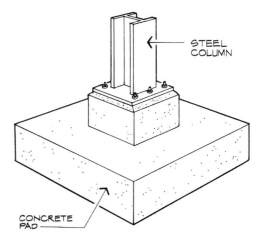

Figure 8.45 Steel column and concrete pad.

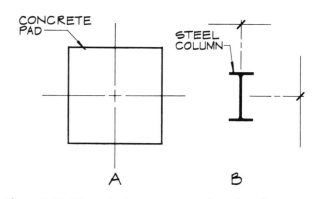

Figure 8.46 Dimensioning concrete pads and steel columns.

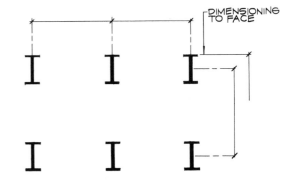

Figure 8.47 Dimensioning a series of columns.

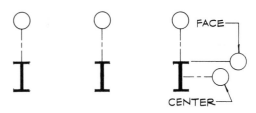

Figure 8.48 Dimensioning a series of columns by way of the axial reference plane.

the area with steel studs or use a steel symbol. See Figure 8.44.

Dimensioning Columns. Steel columns are commonly used to hold up heavy weights. This weight is distributed to the earth by means of a concrete pad. See Figure 8.45. This concrete pad is dimensioned to its center, as Figure 8.46(A) shows. When you dimension the steel columns, which will show in the floor plan, dimension them to their center. See Figure 8.46(B). This relates them to the concrete pads. Dimensioning a series of columns follows the same procedure. See Figure 8.47. The dimensions are taken to the centers of the columns in each direction.

Sometimes, the column must be dimensioned to the face rather than to the center. As Figure 8.47 shows, the extension line is taken to the outside face of the column. Axial reference planes are often used in conjunction with steel columns as shown in Figure 8.48 and the column may be dimensioned to the face. (The dimensional reference system was discussed in Chapter 2.) A sample of a portion of a floor plan dimensioned with and without a series of axial reference planes is

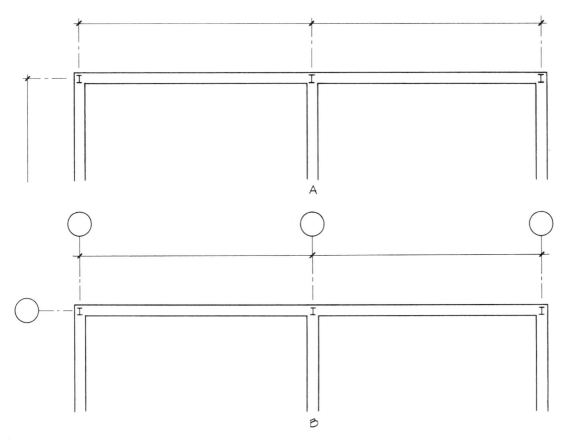

Figure 8.49 Dimensioning a floor plan with steel columns.

shown in Figures 8.49(A) and 8.49(B). Because of the **grid** pattern often formed by the placement of these columns, a center line or a plus (+) type symbol is often used to help the drawing. See Figure 8.50.

Dimensioning Walls. Walls, especially interior walls that do not fall on the established grid, need to be dimensioned—but only to the nearest dimension grid line. Figure 8.51 is a good example of an interior wall dimensioned to the nearest column falling on a grid.

Combinations of Materials

Due to design or code requirements for fire regulations or structural reasons, materials are often combined: concrete columns with wood walls; steel mainframe with wood walls as secondary members; masonry and wood; steel studs and wood; and steel and masonry, for example. Figure 8.52 shows how using two different systems requires overlapping dimension lines with extension lines. Since dimension lines are more critical than extension lines, extension lines are *always* broken in favor of dimension lines. The wood structure is located to the column on the left side once, then dimensioned independently.

Wood and Masonry. Wood and masonry, as shown in Figure 8.53, are dimensioned as their material dictates:

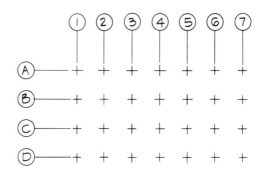

Figure 8.50 Columns forming a grid pattern.

the masonry is dimensioned to the ends of the wall and the rough opening of windows, while the wood portions are dimensioned to the center of interior walls, center of doors, and so forth. The door in the wood portion is dimensioned to the center of the door and to the inside edge of the masonry wall. This assumes the block wall will be built first.

Masonry and Concrete. Masonry walls and concrete columns, in Figure 8.54, are treated in much the same way as wood and concrete columns. In both instances, the building sequence dictates which one becomes the reference point. See Figure 8.55. Here, steel and masonry are used in combination. Using the dimensional refer-

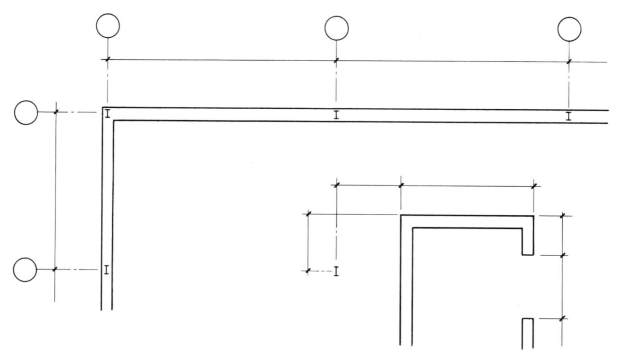

Figure 8.51 Locating interior walls from axial reference bubbles.

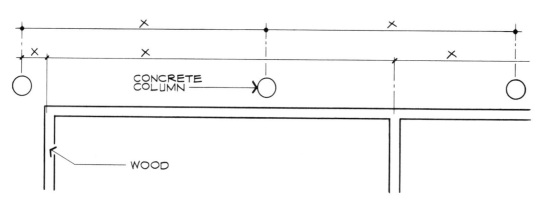

Figure 8.52 Concrete and wood.

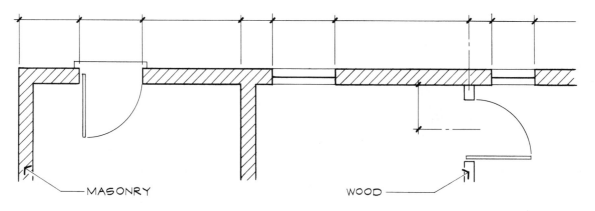

Figure 8.53 Wood and masonry.

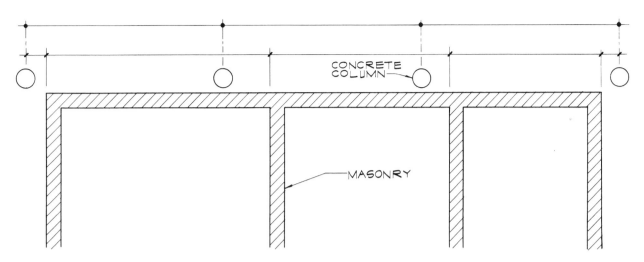

Figure 8.54 Concrete columns and masonry walls.

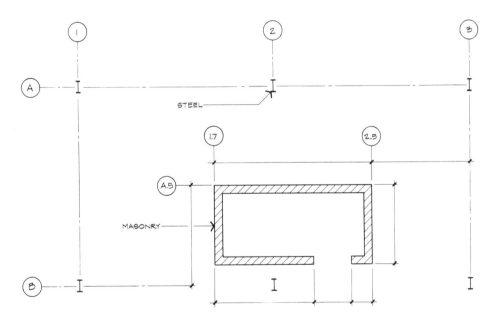

Figure 8.55 Steel and masonry.

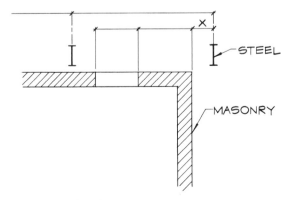

Figure 8.56 Steel and masonry.

ence system, the steel is installed first. The interior masonry wall is then located from the nearest axial reference plane, and dimensioned according to the block module for that kind of masonry. Additional axial reference plane sub-bubbles are provided. Numbers are in decimals. Since one face of the masonry wall is between 1 and 2, $^{7}/_{10}$ of the distance away from axial reference plane 1, the number 1.7 is used in the sub-bubble. And, since the same wall is also halfway between A and B, A.5 is used as a designation. Another example of the process is found in Figure 8.56. The fabricators will locate the steel first, then the masonry wall. Dimension "X" relates one system to another.

Doors in Plan View

The general method of dimensioning a window or a door was discussed earlier. Here, we examine a variety of doors and windows and how to draft them. Figure 8.57 shows a sampling of the most typically drafted doors.

Hinged.   Doors A and B in Figure 8.57 show the main difference in drafting an **exterior and interior hinged door.** A straight line is used to represent the door and a radial line is used to show the direction of swing. Door "I" shows the same kind of door with its thickness represented by a double line. Doors A, B, and I are used in the floor plans to show flush doors, panel doors, and sculptured doors (decorative and carved).

Flush.   Flush doors, as the name indicates, are flush on both sides. They can be solid on the interior (solid slab) or hollow on the inside (hollow core).

Panel.   Panel doors have panels set into the frame. These are usually made of thin panels of wood or glass. A variety of patterns are available. See *Sweet's Catalog File* under Doors for pictures of door patterns. Also see the earlier discussion of elevations for a drafted form of these doors.

Sculptured and Decorative.   Sculptured and decorative doors can be carved forms put into the doors in the form of a panel door or added onto a flush door in the form of what is called a "planted" door. Different types of trim can also be planted onto a slab door.

Double Action.   Door C in Figure 8.57 represents a double action door, a door that swings in both directions. Double action doors can be solid slab, panel, or sculptured.

Sliding.   Two types of sliding doors are shown in Figure 8.57. Door D, when used on the exterior, typically is made of glass framed in wood or metal. Pocketed sliding doors are rarely found on the exterior because the pocket is hard to weatherproof, and rain, termites, and wind are hard to keep out of the pocket.

Folding.   Doors F and G are good doors for storage areas and wardrobe closets.

Revolving.   Where there is a concern about heat loss or heat gain, a revolving door is a good solution. See door H, which shows a cased opening, that is, an opening with trim around the perimeter with no door in it.

Windows in Plan View

Typical ways of showing windows in the plan view are shown in Figure 8.58. When a plan is drawn at a small

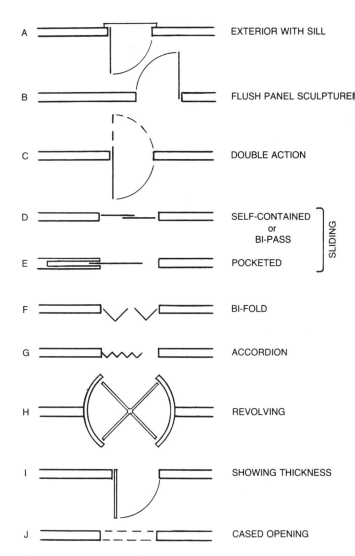

Figure 8.57 Doors in plan view.

scale, each individual window, of whatever type, may simply be drawn as a fixed window (Window A, Figure 8.58), depending for explanation on a pictorial drawing (as shown in Chapter 9). Ideally, casement, hopper, and awning-type windows should be used only on the second floor or above, for the sake of safety. If they are used on the first or ground floor, they should have planters or reflection pools or something else around them to prevent accidents.

Sizes of Doors and Windows

The best way to find specific sizes of windows and doors (especially sliding glass doors) is to check *Sweet's Catalog File.* There you will find interior doors ranging from 1'–6" to 3'–0" and exterior doors from 2'–4" to 3'–6". Sizes of doors and windows also depend on local codes. Local codes require a certain percentage of the square footage to be devoted to windows and doors to provide light and ventilation. These percentages often come in the form of minimum and maximum areas as a measure of energy efficient structures. Still another criteria for door size is consideration of wheel chairs and the size required for building accessibility (ADA compliance).

Symbols

Just as chemistry uses symbols to represent elements, architectural floor plans use symbols to represent electrical and plumbing equipment. Figure 8.59 shows the most typical ones used. These are symbols only. They do not represent the shape or size of the actual item. For example, the symbol for a ceiling outlet indicates the *location* of an outlet, not the shape or size of the fixture. The description of the specific fixture is given in the specifications document.

Electrical and Utility Symbols

Some symbols are more generally used than others in the architectural industry. A floor plan, therefore, usually contains a legend or chart of the symbols being used on that particular floor plan.

Number Symbols

Symbols 1, 2, and 3 in Figure 8.59 show different types of switches. Symbol 2 shows a weatherproof switch, and symbol 3 shows a situation in which there might be a

number of switches used to turn on a single light fixture or a series of light fixtures. See Figure 8.60. A center-line type line is used to show which switch connects with which outlet. This is simply a way of giving this information to the electrical contractor. (However, Figure 8.60 is not a wiring diagram.) If one switch controls one or a series of outlets, it is called a two-way switch. A three-way switch comprises two switches controlling one outlet or a series of outlets. Three switches are called a four-way, and so on. Thus you will name switches by the number of switches plus one. For example, the number 3 is placed next to the switch when there are two switches, the number 4 for three switches, and so on. See Figure 8.60 for examples of switches, outlets, and their numbering system.

Symbol 4 represents a duplex convenience outlet with two places to plug in electrical appliances.

Numbers are used to indicate the number of outlets available other than the duplex, the most typical. For example, if a triplex (3) outlet is required, the number 3 is placed beside the outlet symbol. A number in inches, such as 48″, may be used to indicate the height of the outlet from the floor to the center of the outlet. See Figure 8.59, symbols 6, 7, and 9.

Letter Symbols

A letter used instead of a number represents a special type of switch. For example, "K" is used for key-operated, "D" for dimmer, "WP" for weatherproof, and so forth.

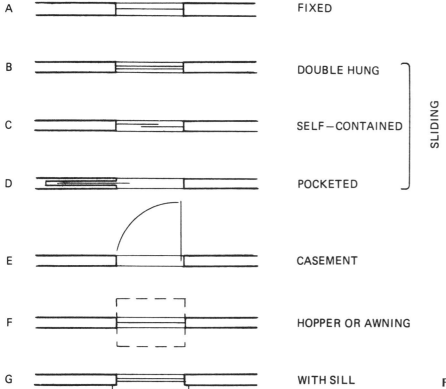

A   FIXED

B   DOUBLE HUNG

C   SELF–CONTAINED   SLIDING

D   POCKETED

E   CASEMENT

F   HOPPER OR AWNING

G   WITH SILL   **Figure 8.58** Windows in plan view.

As with switches, letter designations are used to describe special duplex convenience outlets: "WP" for waterproof, and so on. A duplex convenience outlet is generally referred to by the public as a wall plug.

The call letters "GFI" mean ground fault interrupt. They designate a special outlet used near water (bathrooms, kitchens, etc.) to prevent electric shock. "SP" designates special purpose—perhaps a computer outlet on its own circuit and unaffected by electrical current flowing to any other outlet.

A combination of a switch and a regular outlet is shown in Figure 8.59, 8. This illustration shows a duplex convenience outlet that is half active (hot) at all times. In other words, one outlet is controlled by a switch and the other is a normal outlet. The switch half can be used for a lamp, and the normal outlet for an appliance.

Other Symbols

A round circle with a dot in it represents a floor outlet. See symbol 13, Figure 8.59. The various types of light outlets are shown by symbols 14 through 18.

A flush outlet is one in which the fixture will be installed flush with the ceiling. The electrician and carpenter must address the problem of framing for the fixture in the members above the ceiling surface. See symbol 21.

A selection of miscellaneous equipment is shown in symbols 22 through 36.

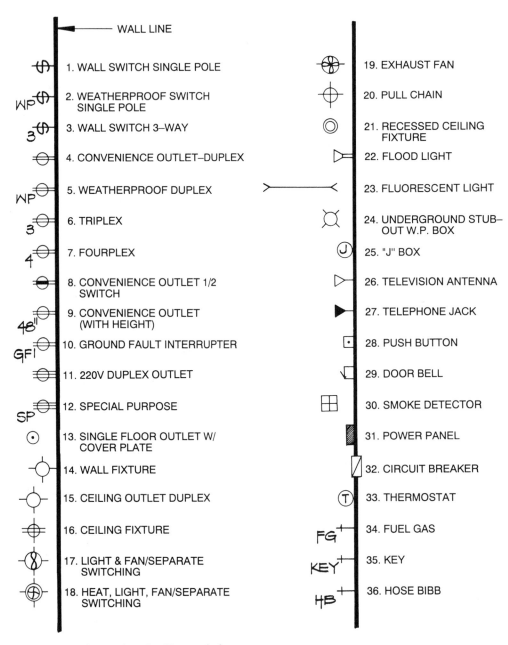

WALL LINE

1. WALL SWITCH SINGLE POLE
2. WEATHERPROOF SWITCH SINGLE POLE
3. WALL SWITCH 3–WAY
4. CONVENIENCE OUTLET–DUPLEX
5. WEATHERPROOF DUPLEX
6. TRIPLEX
7. FOURPLEX
8. CONVENIENCE OUTLET 1/2 SWITCH
9. CONVENIENCE OUTLET (WITH HEIGHT)
10. GROUND FAULT INTERRUPTER
11. 220V DUPLEX OUTLET
12. SPECIAL PURPOSE
13. SINGLE FLOOR OUTLET W/ COVER PLATE
14. WALL FIXTURE
15. CEILING OUTLET DUPLEX
16. CEILING FIXTURE
17. LIGHT & FAN/SEPARATE SWITCHING
18. HEAT, LIGHT, FAN/SEPARATE SWITCHING

19. EXHAUST FAN
20. PULL CHAIN
21. RECESSED CEILING FIXTURE
22. FLOOD LIGHT
23. FLUORESCENT LIGHT
24. UNDERGROUND STUB– OUT W.P. BOX
25. "J" BOX
26. TELEVISION ANTENNA
27. TELEPHONE JACK
28. PUSH BUTTON
29. DOOR BELL
30. SMOKE DETECTOR
31. POWER PANEL
32. CIRCUIT BREAKER
33. THERMOSTAT
34. FUEL GAS
35. KEY
36. HOSE BIBB

Figure 8.59 Electrical and utility symbols.

Special Explanation

Symbols 24, 25, 26, 28, 31, and 32 in Figure 8.59 require special explanation.

Symbol 24—Used for electrical connections (usually on the outside) for such things as outdoor lighting and sprinkler connections.

Symbol 25—A "J" box is an open electrical box allowing the electrician to install later such things as fluorescent light fixtures.

Symbol 26—This is not the TV antenna itself, but the point at which you connect a television antenna line at the wall.

Symbol 28—Location at which you push a button to ring a door bell or chime.

Symbol 31—The connection between the utility company and the structure where the power panel is installed.

Symbol 32—As the structure is zoned for electrical distribution, circuit breaker panels are installed. This allows you to reset a circuit at a so-called

substation without going outside to the main panel or disturbing the rest of the structure.

Symbol 34 represents a gas outlet, and 35 a control for fuel gas. Symbol 34 would be used to indicate a gas jet in a fireplace, and 35 would be used to indicate the control for the gas, probably somewhere near the fireplace. Symbol 36 is a hose bibb, a connection for a water hose.

Appliance and Plumbing Fixture Symbols

Many templates are available for drafting plumbing fixtures and kitchen appliances. A good architectural template contains such items as:

Circles	Various kitchen appliances
Door swings	Various plumbing fixtures
Electrical symbols	Typical heights marked along edges

Figure 8.61 shows some of these fixtures and appliances.

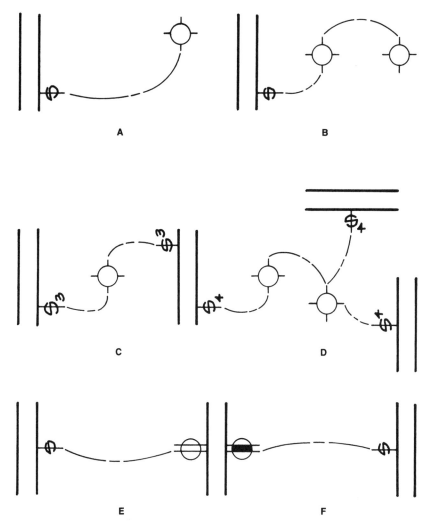

Figure 8.60 Switch to outlet.

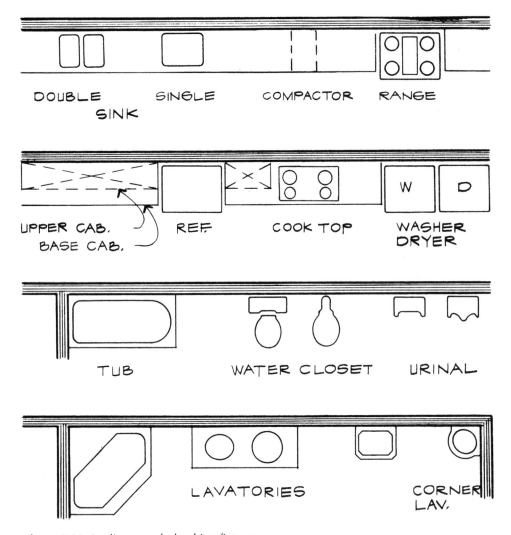

Figure 8.61 Appliance and plumbing fixtures.

Other Floor Plan Considerations

It is often necessary to show more than one or two building materials on a floor plan. Let us take a college music building as an example of a structure that has a multitude of walls of different materials including:

1. Masonry
2. Wood studs
3. Two types of soundproof partitions
4. Low walls
5. Low walls with glass above

We need to establish an acceptable symbol for each material and to produce a legend similar to that in Figure 8.62. A sample of a partial floor plan using some of these materials symbols is shown in Figure 8.63.

Combining Building Materials

Because of ecological requirements (such as insulation); structural reasons; aesthetic concerns; and fire regula-

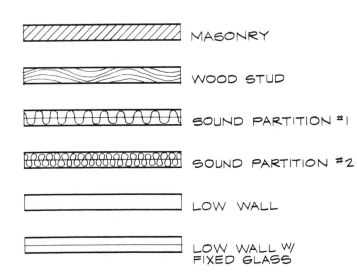

Figure 8.62 Legend for music building floor plan.

tions, materials must often be combined. For example, insulation may be adjacent to a masonry wall, a brick veneer may be on a wood stud wall, and steel studs may

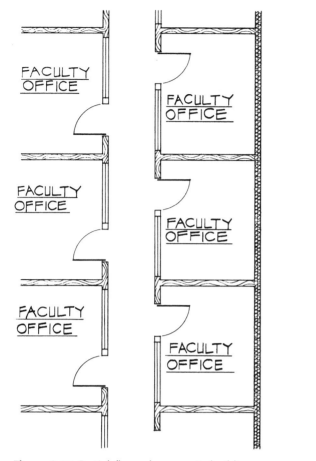

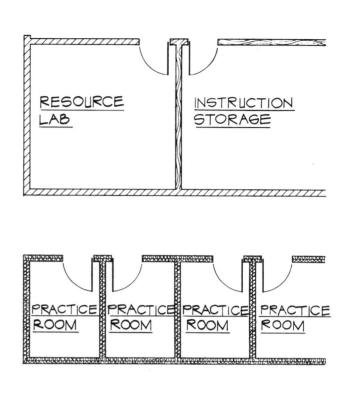

Figure 8.63 Partial floor plan—music building.

be next to a concrete block wall. Figure 8.64 shows examples of what some of the walls will look like on the floor plan.

Repetitive Plans and Symmetrical Items

If a plan or portions of a plan are symmetrical, a center line can be used and half of the object dimensioned. If a plan is repetitive—for example, an office building or an apartment or condominium—each unit is given a letter designation (Unit A, Unit B, etc.). These are then referenced to each other and only one is dimensioned.

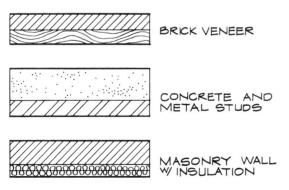

Figure 8.64 Combinations of building materials.

For example, suppose you were drafting a floor plan for an eight-unit apartment structure; these eight units are to be divided into four one-bedroom units and four two-bedroom units, all using the same basic plans. Your approach could be to draft the overall shape of the structure and then to draft the interior walls only on one typical unit and label it completely. The remaining units (three of each) are referenced to the original unit by a note such as, "See Unit A for dimensions and notes."

This type of plan lends itself well to the use of adhesives (see Chapter 2). A typical unit is drawn at the proper scale; then a series of adhesives are made of this plan. The whole plan is made by putting the adhesive plans in the proper position to produce the overall shape.

Dimensional Reference Numbers and Letters

The dimensional reference system has already been discussed earlier. Responsibility for placement of the letters and numbers and often the drafting of the dimensional reference bubbles rests with the structural engineer. Because the structural engineer is responsible for sizing and locating the columns for proper distribution of the building weight, only the structural engineer can make the proper decision. This information can then be taken and put in the reference bubbles on the foundation plan, building section, framing plans, and so forth.

Pouché Walls

The word *pouché* was mentioned earlier. This is the process of darkening the space between the lines which represent wall thickness on a floor plan. Special pouché pencils can be purchased at most drafting supply stores. Graphite pencils, like drafting pencils or colored pencils, can be used to pouché. Do not use red, yellow, or orange; they will block light in the reproduction of the plan and leave the walls black. Do not use wax-based pencils.

Stairs

An arrow is used on the plan of the stair to show the direction in which the stair rises. See the partial floor plan, Figure 8.65. Notice how the arrowheads show direction and how the number and size of the treads and risers are indicated.

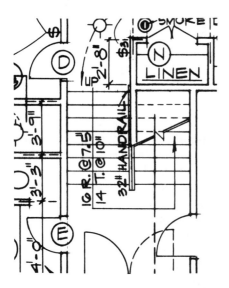

Figure 8.65 Stair direction and number of treads. (Residence of Mr. and Mrs. Ted Bear.)

Noting Logic

The basic approach used here is to show a complete set of working drawings as if a complete set of specifications were included. Specifications are the written documentation of what is drafted; they give information that is not given in the drawings. Brand names, model numbers, installation procedures, and quality of material are just a few of the items discussed in a set of specifications. So the inclusion of the specifications affects the noting of the floor plan.

Because of the precise descriptions contained in the specifications, only general descriptions are necessary on the floor plan. For example, it is sufficient to call out a "cook top" as a generic name and let the specifications take care of the rest of the description. "Tub" and "water closet" are sufficient to describe plumbing fixtures. Further description would only confuse the drawing, and these items should be described in the "specs" (short for specifications).

In other words, specific information should not be duplicated. If it is, changes can present problems. For example, suppose brand "A" is selected for a particular fixture and is called brand "A" on the floor plan rather than by its generic term. Later, it is changed to brand "B." Now both the floor plan and specs need to be changed; if one is missed, confusion results.

Electrical Rating

Many architectural firms that superimpose the electrical plan on top of the floor plan note the **electrical rating** necessary for a particular piece of equipment; for example, range 9KW, oven 5KW, dishwasher 1.5KW, and refrigerator 110V. Electrical ratings can also be included in an electrical appliance schedule if one exists.

Room Sizes

Because sizes of rooms are often found on presentation drawings (scaled drawings), some people think that sizes of rooms (9 × 12, 10 × 14) belong on a floor plan. They do not. These approximate sizes are fine for client consumption but are useless in the construction process.

Providing Satisfactory Dimensions

One of the most common criticisms from the field (workers on the job) is that the floor plans do not contain enough dimensions. Because these people cannot scale the drawings (something we would not want them to do anyway), they are dependent on dimensions, so be sure they are all included. Remember that notes take precedence over the drawing itself. If a member is called 2 × 10 but is drawn as a 2 × 8, the note takes precedence.

Checklist: Checking Your Own Drawing

There are so many minute things to remember in the development of a particular drawing that most offices have worked out some type of checking system. A **checklist** (or check sheet) is one frequently used device. It lists the most commonly missed items in chart form, making it easy for you to precheck your work before a checker is asked to review a particular drawing. See Figure 8.66 for a floor plan checklist.

OTHER FLOOR PLAN CONSIDERATIONS

1. Walls
   a. Accuracy of thickness
   b. Correctness of intersections
   c. Accuracy of location
   d. 8-inch wall
   e. Openings
   f. Pony walls designated
   g. Pouché
2. Doors and windows
   a. Correct use
   b. Location
   c. Correct symbol
   d. Schedule reference
   e. Header size
   f. Sills, if any
   g. Show swing
   h. Direction of slide if needed
   i. Door swing
3. Steps
   a. Riser and treads called out
   b. Concrete steps
   c. Wood steps
4. Dimensioning
   a. Position of lines
   b. All items dimensioned
   c. All dimensions shown
   d. All arrowheads shown
   e. Openings
   f. Structural posts
   g. Slabs and steps
   h. Closet depth
   i. Check addition
   j. Odd angles
5. Lettering
   a. Acceptable height and appearance
   b. Acceptable form
   c. Readable
6. Titles, notes, and call-outs
   a. Spelling, phrasing, and abbreviations
   b. Detail references
   c. Specification references
   d. Window and door references
   e. Appliances
   f. Slabs and steps
   g. Plumbing fixtures
   h. Openings
   i. Room titles
   j. Ceiling joist direction
   k. Floor material
   l. Drawing title and scale
   m. Tile work
      (1) Tub
      (2) Shower
      (3) Counter (kitchen and bath)

   n. Attic opening—scuttle
   o. Cabinet
   p. Wardrobe
      (1) Shelves
      (2) Poles
   q. Built-in cabinets, nooks, tables, etc.
7. Symbols
   a. Electrical
   b. Gas
   c. Water
   d. Heating, ventilating, and air conditioning
8. Closets, wardrobes, and cabinets
   a. Correct representation
   b. Doors
   c. Depths, widths, and heights
   d. Medicine cabinets
   e. Detail references
   f. Shelves and poles
   g. Plywood partitions and posts
   h. Overhead cabinets
   i. Broom closets
9. Equipment (appliances)
   a. Washer and dryer
   b. Range
   c. Refrigerator
   d. Freezer
   e. Oven
   f. Garbage disposal
   g. Dishwasher
   h. Water heater
   i. Forced draft vent
10. Equipment (special)
    a. Hi-fi
    b. TV
    c. Sewing machine
    d. Intercom
    e. Game equipment (built-in)
    f. Others
11. Legend
12. Note exposed beams and columns
13. Special walls
    a. Masonry
    b. Veneers
    c. Partial walls, note height
    d. Furred walls for plumbing vents
14. Note sound and thermal insulation in walls
15. Fireplaces
    a. Dimension depth and width of firepit
    b. Fuel gas and key
    c. Dimension hearth width
16. Mail slot

17. Stairways
    a. Number of risers
    b. Indicate direction
    c. Note railing
18. Medicine cabinet, mirrors at bath
19. Attic and underfloor access ways
20. Floor slopes at wet areas
21. Hose bibbs
22. Main water shut-off valve
23. Fuel gas outlets
    a. Furnace
    b. Range
    c. Oven
    d. Dryer
    e. Water heater
    f. Fireplace
24. Water heater: gas fired
    a. 4″ vent through roof
    b. 100 sq. in. combustion air vent to closet
25. Furnace location: gas fired
    a. Exhaust vent through roof
    b. Combustion air to closet
    c. Return air vent
26. Electric meter location
27. Floodlights, wall lights, note heights
28. Convenience outlets, note if 220V, note horse power if necessary
29. Note electric power outlets
    a. Range 9 KW
    b. Oven 5 KW
    c. Dishwasher 1.5 KW
    d. Refrigerator 110 V
    e. Washer 2 KW
    f. Dryer 5 KW
30. Clock, chime outlets
31. Doorbell
32. Roof downspouts
33. Fire extinguishers, fire hose cabinets
34. Interior bathroom, toiletroom fans
35. Bathroom heaters
36. Kitchen range hood fan and light
37. Telephone, television outlets
38. Exit signs
39. Bathtub inspection plate
40. Thermostat location
41. Door, window, and finish schedules
42. Line quality
43. Basic design
44. Border line
45. Title block
46. Title
47. Scale

Figure 8.66 Floor plan checklist.

Ryan Residence Floor Plan

The Ryan Residence floor plan is evolved over several stages. The floor plan is by far the most important drawing in a set of working drawings, because it sets the stage for all dimensions in terms of width and length.

An intermediate stage is often reproduced several times using either a xerographic process onto vellum or a sepia using a diazo process and given to associates to generate additional masters for framing plans, structural drawings, and/or separate electrical plans, to mention just a few.

It would be most convenient to have a ¼" scale drawing as well as a ⅛" drawing of the floor plan. An ⅛" drawing is easily obtained by reducing the ¼" drawing by mechanical means. Many copiers have enlarging and reducing capabilities. Thus, an ⅛" scale drawing can be produced in a matter of minutes. Many so-called blue-

print shops can also provide you with enlargements or reductions, as well as erasable vellum "second originals."

In addition to the normal information carried on the floor plan, as described in this chapter, we will superimpose an electrical plan and a ceiling framing plan onto this drawing. To understand the ceiling joist framing information, refer to the end of Chapter 12, Figures 12.43 to 12.46.

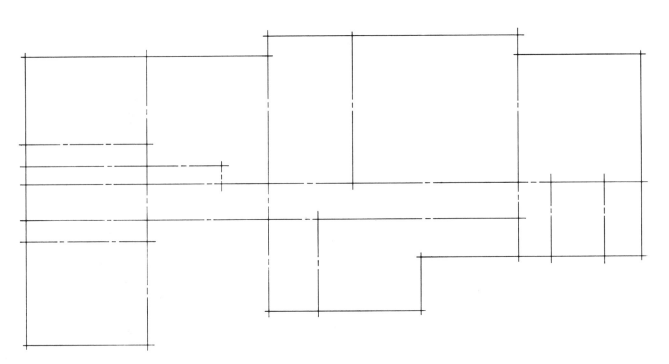

Figure 8.67 Floor plan—Stage I.

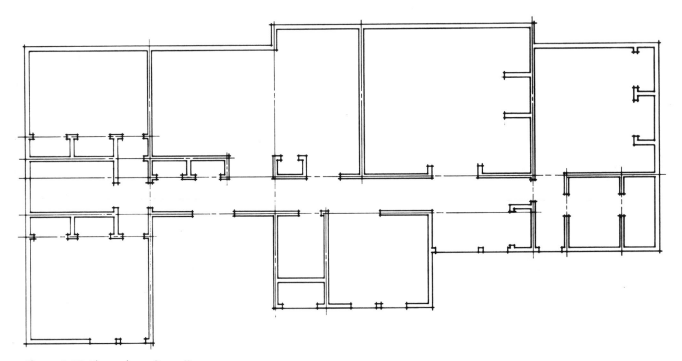

Figure 8.68 Floor plan—Stage II.

Notice that the garage floor plan is not included in this evolution because of the constraints and limits of the vellum. The garage plans, sections, elevations, and so on will be placed on a separate sheet.

STAGE I (Figure 8.67). The general shape of the structure is blocked out, possibly using fade-away (blue) pencil. The block-out is accomplished with a single line. The line that defines the perimeter is drawn with a solid line. This is the outside wall line, which allows the drafter to check outside overall dimensions to ensure proper positioning on the site. The interior walls are positioned with center lines. These will eventually become the extension lines during the dimensioning process.

STAGE II (Figure 8.68). Into this single-lined floor plan wall thickness is incorporated. Start with the outside perimeter. The only wall that does not use the single line as the outer surface is the wall opposite the family room and in between the utility room and the front bedroom. This wall starts at the left as an interior wall, becomes an exterior wall, and then becomes an interior wall again.

Next, a line is drawn on both sides of the center line defining the thickness of the interior walls. Openings in the wall (windows and doors) are located and positioned. As a drafter, be sure to verify the minimum openings for the door and be sure to comply with ADA and the sizes of the windows. Notice that jambs were left on both sides of the windows and doors to house the support for the beam and/or headers that will eventually be used. The next step is to darken the complete floor plan. When printed, the

center lines (drawn in fade-away lead) will disappear and look like the drawing in Figure 8.69.

STAGE III (Figure 8.70). Before commencing Stage III, the drafter should turn to the project book and glean all the specifics in reference to appliances, plumbing fixtures, and fireplaces. This information is then translated into drawings, as shown in Figure 8.70. Windows have also been incorporated into the drawing. Sizes are found in the preliminary schedule based on energy analysis. See the end of Chapter 9 for exact sizes.

STAGE IV (Figure 8.71). This is the next to the last stage and the most critical, because all of the dimensions are established at this time. A check print was made of Stage III, and the dimensions and their numerical values established. This was all done rapidly in freehand, but with great accuracy.

There are in Figure 8.71 a number of exterior walls that become interior walls on this plan. For example, the wall that separates the family room from the bedroom is an interior wall but becomes an exterior wall on the opposite side. The total width is 15'–0" measured face-of-stud to face-of-stud. However, on the opposite side, this same wall becomes an interior wall, and the measurement reads 14'–10", measured face-of-stud to center-of-wall.

The 2 × 4 stud measures 3½", half of which is 1¾". This 1¾" measurement is rounded off to a 2-inch measurement, which accounts for the two-inch difference on either side. Notice how the drafter included what we call a 2" "look-out" dimension along the exten-

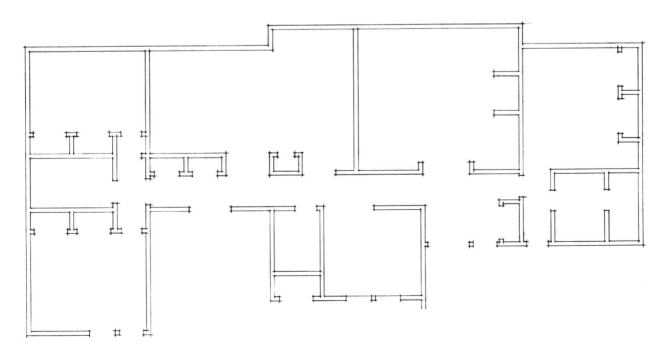

Figure 8.69 Floor plan as it will actually appear.

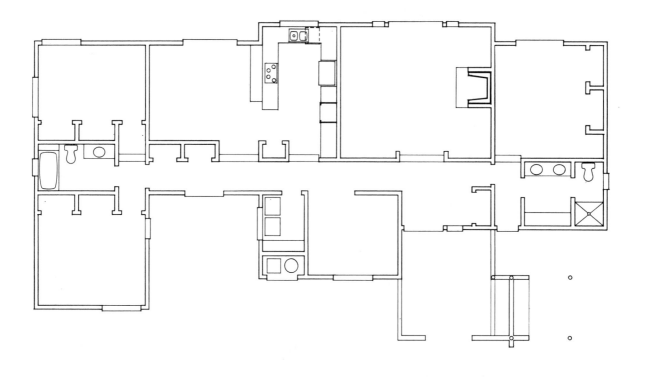

Figure 8.70 Floor plan—Stage III.

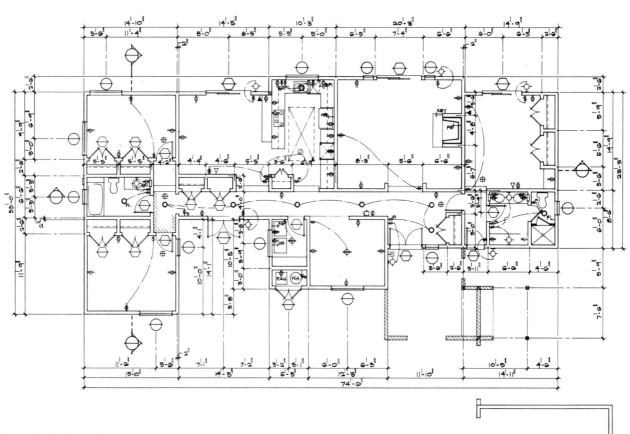

Figure 8.71 Floor plan—Stage IV.

sion line. This is a drafter warning to the rough carpenter to watch out for the discrepancy.

This happens again at the wall between the living room and the master bedroom, and along the interior wall of the dining room and laundry room, which becomes an exterior wall for a short time, and then an interior wall again, as it separates the closet and the bath room.

Notice the string of dimensions on the inside of the house, especially the one that goes through the kitchen. If the wall is dimensioned on the face of the stud on the outside, then the interior dimensions should be dimensioned to this point; and if the wall had been dimensioned on the exterior dimension line to the center, then the interior dimension should use this position as a point of reference. The only exception might be that where 2″ look-out dimensions exist, either position could be used—the center or face-of-stud.

Based on this positioning of extension and dimension lines, totals are carefully checked to ensure that the sum of the parts are equal to the totals.

The electrical plan is next superimposed onto the floor plan and the door and window conventions drafted,

including the reference symbol adjacent to each door and window that connects the plan with schedules.

Cutting plane lines and their respective bubbles are drawn to refer the reader to the building section drawings.

A check print will be made at this stage, and dimensional corrections will be noted as well as any other change or correction to take place. The project manager might even overlay the original over the foundation plan to discover any other errors or omissions.

One such oversight is the floor of the pair of closets in the hall adjacent to the family room. If the change of level occurs at the face of the doors, the depth of these two closets will be at the same level as the family room, creating a 12-inch drop in the closet. A section/elevation shown in Figure 8.72 also reveals this problem. The solution was to build a wood floor even with the hall side and to use this space in one of five ways:

A. Leave the space under the wood floor as dead space.
B. Use this space, with a removable floor, to hide a floor safe.

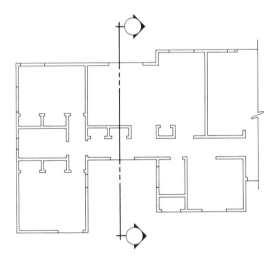

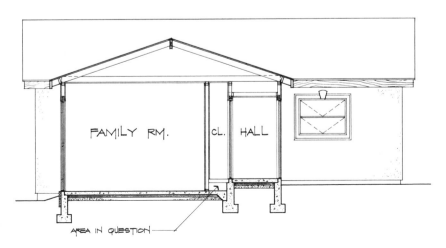

Figure 8.72 Section/elevation revealing unresolved space.

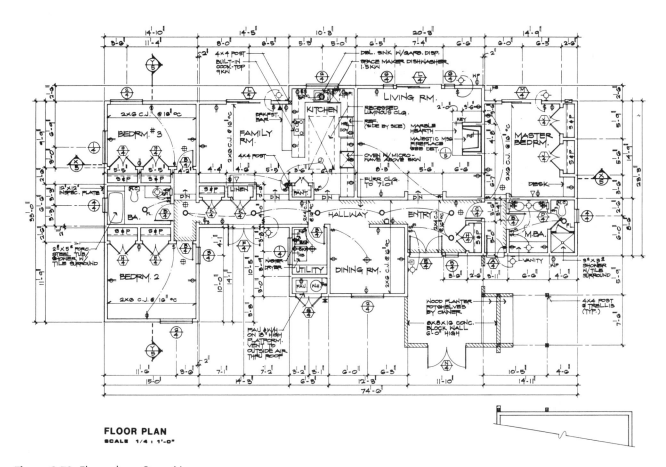

FLOOR PLAN
SCALE 1/4 : 1'-0"

Figure 8.73 Floor plan—Stage V.

C. Build low drawers openable to the family-room side. The top of the drawer space will be the floor of the closet.

D. Face the closet toward the family-room side and use it as a built-in entertainment center.

E. Move the interior bearing footing between the closet and the family room.

STAGE IV (Figure 8.73). After receiving a check print from the project manager, a good procedure would be to follow up on this check print with a procedure sheet of your own. This could be done by using the floor plan checklist found in Figure 8.66 and adding to it with notation from the check print. Because this is a standard office form for all floor plans, not all items will apply. You can make this one a job-specific checklist by highlighting what you feel is critical information and/or have your immediate supervisor check the list for you. Armed with this new tool you can proceed, with confidence, to draft the final stage of this most critical sheet.

Most of the notes can be reduced to five categories:

A. Identification of the rooms, appliances, and equipment

B. Identification of items that are in the contract and those that are to be provided by the owner. The wood planter shelves at the entry compound is a good example of such items.

C. Positioning and locating structural members (some of which are inside a wall). The posts for the trellis and the posts inside the wall between the family room and kitchen are good examples of positioning and locating.

D. Special needs that may be established by codes, such as the inspection plates and notes dealing with the FAU (forced air unit) and W/H (water heater).

E. Finally, the superimposing of the ceiling joist plan over the floor plan. This can be identified by the directional line with half-arrowheads on each side, with a note about sizing and spacing the ceiling joists.

SUMMARY

The floor plan is essential to a set of construction documents. Of particular importance in the preparation of the floor plan are the influence of materials (wood, masonry, steel) on the approach used, the logic of the dimensioning methods used and the thoroughness of the noting procedures.

The floor plan includes many things beyond the simple location of walls and the size of the structure. It locates windows and doors, may indicate electrical and plumbing fixtures, and may even dictate the construction procedure or erection process to be followed.

The drafting of a floor plan can be enhanced by incorporating shortcut methods such as applique drafting. The size and complexity of the project determine the approach.

IMPORTANT TERMS AND CONCEPTS

Break line
Wood framing
Sills
Headers
F.O.S. (face-of-stud)
Reference bubble
Offset
Rough and finished openings
Steel stud and steel frame
Pouché

Grid
Plan views—windows and doors
Exterior and interior hinged doors
Flush, panel, and sculptured doors
Double action, sliding, folding, and revolving doors
Electrical, appliance, and plumbing fixture symbols
Repetitive plans
Electrical rating
Room sizes

REVIEW QUESTIONS

1. If the floor plan is in reality a section, at what level is the cutting plane slicing the structure?
2. Explain what is meant by stud line dimensioning.
3. What does "F.O.S." mean? Where is it used on a floor plan?
4. Explain why interior walls are dimensioned to the center while exterior walls are dimensioned to the face of the stud.
5. Explain how dimensioning a masonry wall differs from dimensioning a wood stud wall.
6. What is a pilaster?
7. Explain why certain dimensions are more available than others for a masonry wall.
8. What is the main difference between steel frame and steel stud construction?
9. Explain why the dimensional reference system works so well on a steel frame structure.
10. Explain A.5 on a dimensional reference system.

LABORATORY PROBLEMS

1. Using a ¼″ = 1′–0″ scale, draft a partial floor plan of the smallest, most efficient bathroom for a residence. Include a tub, a 30″ × 30″ shower, a water closet, and a lavatory.
2. Using ¼″ = 1′–0″ scale, draft a floor plan of a two-car garage. Garage to be 20′ wide by 22′ deep with a 16′–0″ garage door.
3. Draft a floor plan, using a ¼″ = 1′–0″ scale, of a plan provided you by the instructor.
4. Select a simple structure, such as a 3- or 4-room mountain cabin, a beach house, or a lakeside retreat, from an advertisement or magazine. Using a scale, figure out likely sizes for the rooms. Using a scale to measure with, draft (freehand) a floor plan of this structure at ¼″ = 1′–0″. Include dimension lines and electrical symbols as well as plumbing fixtures.

9

SCHEDULES: DOOR, WINDOW, AND FINISH

9

PREVIEW

This chapter reviews various types of schedules that may be incorporated into a set of construction documents and provides illustrations and discussions of tabulated and pictorial door and window schedules. Graphics and shapes for schedule symbols are also illustrated together with recommendations for use.

An interior finish schedule is provided and examined relative to room and space designations. Other types of schedules, such as plumbing fixture and appliance schedules, are also shown, and the chapter examines when these types of schedules would be used.

OBJECTIVES

1. Understand different types of schedules.
2. Understand the reasons for using one type over another because of project requirements.

The Purpose of Schedules

A schedule is a list or catalog of information that defines the doors, windows, or finishes of a room. The main purpose for incorporating schedules into a set of construction documents is to provide clarity, location, sizes, materials, and information for the designation of doors, windows, roof finishes, and plumbing and electrical fixtures.

Tabulated Schedules: Doors and Windows

Schedules may be presented in **tabulated** or **pictorial** form. While tabulated schedules in architectural offices vary in form and layout from office to office, the same primary information is provided.

Figures 9.1 and 9.2 are examples of tabulated **door and window schedules**. The door schedule provides a space for the symbol, the width and height, and the thickness of the door. It also indicates whether the door is to be solid core (SC) or hollow core (HC). The "type"

column may indicate that the door has raised panels, or that it is a slab door or french door, and so forth.

Information

The material space may indicate what kind of wood is to be used for the door, such as birch or beech. Space for remarks is used to provide information such as the closing device or hardware to be used, or the required fire rated door. In some cases, where there is insufficient space for remarks, an asterisk (*) or symboled number may be placed to the left of the schedule or in the designated box and referenced to the bottom of the schedule with the required information. This information must under no circumstances be crowded or left out. For any type of schedule including lettering, provide sufficient space in each frame so that your lettering is not cramped or unclear.

Symbols

Symbol designations for doors and windows vary in architectural offices and are influenced by each office's procedures. For example, a circle, hexagon, or square

DOOR SCHEDULE

SYM.	WIDTH	HEIGHT	THK.	TYPE	MATERIAL	HC/SC	GLAZ. AREA	REMARKS
1	PR.2'-9"	7'-0"	1 3/4"	SLAB	WOOD	SC		
2	PR.2'-10"	"	"	FRENCH	"	"	11.3 ☐	1/4" TEMP. GL./TINTED GL.
3	PR.3'-1"	"	"	"	"	"	"	" "
4	3'-6"	"	"	"	"	"	13.8 ☐	" "
5	3'-0"	"	"	SLAB	"	"		
6	2'-8"	"	"	"	"	"		
7	2'-8"	"	"	"	"	"		1 HOUR SELF-CLOSING
8	2'-6"	"	"	"	"	"		
9	2'-4"	6'-8"	1 3/8"	SLAB	WOOD	HC		
10	2'-0"	"	"	"	"	"		
11	2'-6"	"	"	"	"	"		
12	PR.3'-7"	"	"	BI-FOLD	WOOD	"		
13	PR.3'-8"	"	"	"	"	"		
14	PR.3'-2"	"	"	"	"	"		
15	8'-8"	8'-0"	3"	GARAGE	WOOD	—		2x3 W/1x6 T&G R/S CEDAR
⬡								
⬡								

Figure 9.1 Door schedule.

WINDOW SCHEDULE

SYM.	WIDTH	HEIGHT	TYPE	FRAME	SCR.	GLAZ. AREA	VENT. AREA	REMARKS
A	5'-8"	7'-0"	FIXED/AWNING	WOOD	YES	39.6 ☐	9.9 ☐	PR. 1'-9" HIGH AWNING BELOW
B	4'-6"	"	FIXED	"	NO	31.5 ☐		1/4" TEMP. GLASS
C	5'-6"	"	"	"	"	38.5 ☐		"
D	4'-0"	3'-0"	AWNING	"	YES	12.0 ☐	12.0 ☐	
E •	5'-8"	7'-0"	FIXED	"	NO	39.7 ☐		1/4" TEMP. GLASS
F	4'-0"	3'-6"	GARDEN	WOOD	YES	14.0 ☐	5.0 ☐	OPERABLE SIDE VENTS
G	1'-8"	3'-3"	CASEMENT	"	"	5.4 ☐	5.4 ☐	
H	PR. 2'-0"	4'-0"	"	"	"	16.0 ☐	16.0 ☐	
I	4 @ 1'-4"	5'-8"	FIXED	"	NO	30.2 ☐		
J	3 @ 1'-8"	4'-0"	FIXED/CASEMENT	WOOD	YES	20.0 ☐	6.7 ☐	MIDDLE IS CASEMENT
K	PR. 1'-3"	"	CASEMENT	"	"	10.0 ☐	10.0 ☐	
L •	5'-6"	7'-0"	FIXED	"	NO	38.5 ☐		1/4" TEMP. GLASS

NOTES: ALL WINDOWS DOUBLE GLASS-THERMAL EXCEPT WINDOW (F)
ALL WINDOWS TINTED GLASS, EXCEPT WHERE NOTED BY •

Figure 9.2 Window schedule.

may be used for all or part of the various schedules. Figure 9.3 illustrates symbol shapes and how they may be shown. There are various options, such as using a letter or number or both, and choosing various shapes. Door and window symbol shapes should be different from each other. To clarify reading the floor plan, the letter "D" at the top of the door symbol and the letter "W" at the top of the window symbol are used. The letter "P" is used for plumbing fixtures, "E" for electrical fixtures, and "A" for appliances. Place the letter in the top part of the symbol. Whatever symbol shape you select, be sure to make the symbol large enough to accommodate the lettering that will be inside the symbol.

Whenever possible, the door and window schedules should be on the floor plan sheet. This helps locate the various doors and windows on the floor plan. If you cannot place these schedules on the floor plan sheet, use an adjacent sheet.

Draw the lines for the schedules with ink on the front side of the vellum or with lead on the reverse side of the sheet. In this way, when changes are made in the schedule information, you run no risk of erasing the lines.

When you provide lines for the anticipated number of symbols to be used, allow extra spaces for door and window types that may be added.

Pictorial Schedules: Doors and Windows

Pictorial Representations

In many cases, tabulated schedules cannot clearly define a specific door or window. In this case, you can add to a schedule a call-out with a pictorial drawing of a door or window adjacent to your schedule, as in Figure 9.4; Door 1 is difficult to explain, so a pictorial representation makes it clearer.

Pictorial Schedules

A pictorial schedule, as distinct from a pictorial representation, is totally pictorial. Each item is dimensioned and provided with data such as material, type, and so

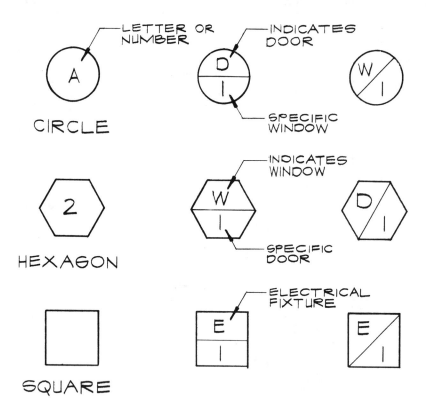

Symbol designations

LETTER OR NUMBER

INDICATES DOOR

SPECIFIC WINDOW

CIRCLE

HEXAGON

INDICATES WINDOW

SPECIFIC DOOR

SQUARE

ELECTRICAL FIXTURE

Figure 9.3 Symbol designations.

SYM.	WIDTH	HEIGHT	THK.	HC/SC	TYPE	MATERIAL	REMARKS
①	PR.3'-2"	7'-0"	13/4"	HC	NL	STEEL	1-HR. SELF CLOSING, PANIC HDW.
②	3'-0"	"	"	"	FLUSH	"	" " " NO GLASS
③	"	"	"	SC	SLAB	WOOD	
④	"	6'-8"	"	"	"	"	1-HR, SELF CLOSING, MTL. JAMBS
⑤	"	"	"	"	"	"	
⑥	"	"	"	"	"	"	SELF CLOSING, PUSH PLATES

DOOR SCHEDULE

6/A9

6/A9

5" 7"

1'-8"

3'-10"

1/4" WIRE GLASS 100 SQ. IN. MAX.

7/A9

8/A9

ELEVATION - DOOR ⬡1

Figure 9.4 Pictorial representation on a tabular schedule.

forth. Figure 9.5 provides a pictorial schedule of a window. A pictorial schedule provides section references for the head, jamb, and sill sections, so you no longer need to reference the exterior elevations. (The head is the top of a window or door, the jamb refers to the sides of a window or door, and the sill is the bottom of the window or door.)

Choosing a Tabulated or Pictorial Schedule

Tabulated

Your choice of a tabulated schedule may involve the following factors:

1. Specific office procedures.
2. Standardization or simplicity of doors and windows selected.
3. Large number of items with different dimensions.
4. Ease of changing sizes.

Pictorial

Choice of a pictorial schedule may involve the following factors:

1. Specific office procedures.
2. Unusual and intricate door or window design requirements.

3. Very few doors and windows in the project or very few types used.
4. Desired clarity for window section referencing.

Interior Finish Schedules

Interior finish schedules provide information such as floor and wall material, trim material, and ceiling finish. Architectural offices vary in their layout of an interior finish schedule because of their office philosophy and specific information they receive for various types of projects.

Figure 9.6A shows an interior finish schedule. The column allocated for room designation may show the room name or an assigned space number or both. This selection may be dictated by the project itself. See Figure 9.6B. Another method of defining finishes combines the room finish schedule with a room finish key, which uses numbers and letters to indicate the various materials to be used for floors, walls, and so forth. An example of this type of schedule is shown in Figure 9.6C. Using space numbers is more logical for a large office building, for example, than for a very small residence. Once again, when extensive information is required in the remarks section of the schedule, use an asterisk (*) or footnote number for reference at the bottom of the schedule.

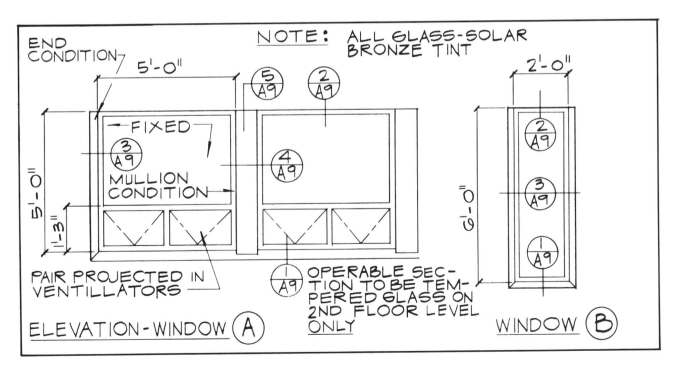

Figure 9.5 Pictorial schedule.

Figure 9.6A Interior finish schedule.

ROOM	FLOOR								BASE					WAINSCOT			WALLS						CEILING HEIGHT	CEILING						REMARKS
	RESILIENT FLR	CARPET	EXP. CONC.	LINOLEUM	VINYL ASBES	HARDWOOD	CER. TILE	TERRAZZO	TOPSET	WOOD	CER. TILE	COVED	PAINT	CER. TILE	TERRAZZO	PAINT	PLASTER	EXP. MASONRY	EXP. WOOD	5/8 DRYWALL	WALLPAPER	PAINT		PLASTER	AC PLASTER	EXP. WOOD	5/8 DRYWALL	ILLUM.	EXP. JST. & SUBFLR	
ENTRY						●				●										●							●			
GALLERY				●						●										●							●			
LIVING ROOM		●								●										●							●			
DINING ROOM				●						●										●							●			
DEN			●							●										●							●			
KITCHEN			●							●										●							●			
PANTRY			●							●										●							●			
POWDER RM.				●						●										●							●			
STORAGE																														
MASTER BEDRM.		●								●										●							●			
WARDROBE		●								●										●							●			
VANITY NO. 1			●							●										●							●			
BATH NO. 1			●							●										●							●			USE WATER PROOF DRYWALL
BEDROOM NO. 2	●									●										●							●			
BEDROOM NO. 3	●									●										●							●			
VANITY NO. 2			●							●										●							●			
BATH NO. 2			●							●										●							●			USE WATER PROOF DRYWALL
STUDIO NO. 1		●									●					●			●							●				
HALL				●						●										●							●			
STUDIO NO. 2				●						●									●							●				
WORKSHOP		●									●								●							●				
SAUNA		●								●									●							●				
JACUZZI					●					●										●							●			
BATH NO. 3							●			●										●							●			USE WATER PROOF DRYWALL
SHOP				●						●										●							●			
STAIR (BASEMENT)																													●	
STAIR (1ST FLR)				●						●										●							●			
STAIR (2ND FLR)				●						●										●							●			

Figure 9.6B Interior finish schedule.

ROOM		FLOOR			BASE			WALLS	CEILING		AREA	REMARKS
		CARPET	LINOLEUM	TILE	WOOD	VINYL TOPSET	COVED	5/8" SHEETROCK	CEILING HEIGHT	5/8" SHEETROCK	SQUARE FEET	
101	ENTRY			●	●			●	7'-6"	●	73	
102	KITCHEN		●			●		●	8'-0"	●	184	
103	LIVING	●			●			●	9'-3"	●	270	CEILING SLOPES
104	DINING	●			●			●	8'-6"	●	284	
105	FAMILY	●			●			●	7'-9"	●	167	
106	BAR		●			●		●	8'-0"	●	26	
107	LAUNDRY		●				●	●	11	●	39	
108	MUD ROOM		●				●	●	11	●	28	
201	MASTER BATH		●			●		●	7'-6"	●	77	
202	DRESSING	●			●			●	11	●	60	
203	MAST. BEDROOM	●			●			●	8'-0"	●	380	
204	BATH		●			●		●	7'-6"	●	55	
205	BEDROOM	●			●			●	8'-0"	●	146	
206	STAIRS	●			●			●	—	●	54	

ROOM FINISH SCHEDULE

NO.	ROOM	FLOOR	BASE	WALLS	CEILING	CEIL. HGT.	ROOM AREA	REMARKS
101	RECEPTION	B	1	A	2	9'-0"	110□'	
102	OFFICE	A		B	2	8'-0"	170□'	
103	OFFICE	A		B	2	"	180□'	
104	OFFICE	A		B	2	"	185□'	
105	WOMENS TOIL.	C	1	A	1	7'-6"	30□'	
106	MENS TOILET	C	1	A	1	7'-6"	25□'	

ROOM FINISH KEY

	FLOORS		BASES		WALLS		CEILINGS
A	CARPET	1	WOOD	A	5/8" SHEETROCK	1	5/8" SHEETROCK
B	OAK PARQUET			B	1x6 T&G CEDAR	2	SUSP. AC. TILE
C	CERAMIC TILE						

Figure 9.6C Room finish schedule—key type.

Additional Schedules

Other types of schedules used depend on office procedure and the type of project. For example, if a project has many types of plumbing and appliance fixtures in various areas, provide additional schedules to clarify and to locate items with their designated symbols.

Figures 9.7 and 9.8 show a **plumbing fixture schedule** and an **appliance schedule.** If these types of schedules are not used in a project, the fixture types, manufacturers, catalog numbers, and other information needed must be included in the project specifications.

For most projects, the specifications will augment information found in the schedules. Examples of information usually found in the specifications include the

PLUMBING FIXTURE SCHEDULE

SYM.	ITEM	MANUFACTURER	CATALOG NO.	REMARKS
1	WHIRLPOOL BATH	FIXTURES INC.	2640.061	FITTING 1108.019
2	LAVATORY	"	0470.039	FAUCET 2248.565
3	BIDET	"	5005.013	FITTING 1852.012
4	TOILET	"	2109.395	

Figure 9.7 Plumbing fixture schedule.

APPLIANCE SCHEDULE

SYM.	ITEM	MANUFACTURER	CATALOG NO.	REMARKS
1	COOKTOP	APPLIANCES INC.	RU38V	WHITE
2	MICROWAVE	"	JKP65G	
3	DISHWASHER	"	GSD2500	WHITE
4	DISPOSER	"	GFC510	

Figure 9.8 Appliance fixture schedule.

window manufacturer, the type and manufacturer of the door hardware, and the type and manufacturer of paint for the trim.

Ryan Residence Schedules

On the surface, the development of schedules appears to be a simple matter of picking sizes, selecting materials, and determining the types. Although this may be part of the process, there are other factors that might not be apparent initially.

In this age of concern for energy conservation and with the advent of the Americans with Disabilities Act (ADA) described earlier in this book, there are many specific reasons for the selection of a particular size of window or width of door. Years ago, there existed only minimum standards in terms of light and ventilation and very few restrictions in regard to maximums. Large picture windows came into vogue in regions of moderate climate. As energy sources, such as fuel for heating, became scarce and costly and our concern for energy conservation increased, we began to treat residences as an envelope of space to be protected from heat loss. We did this by insulating our walls and reducing areas through which heat would be lost, such as windows, doors, and fireplaces.

We turn again to the Ryan Residence and follow the process of selecting windows and doors sizes, using the existing criteria established by the local agencies.

Square Footage

In order to establish maximums and minimums, the square footage of the structure in question must be computed, as well as the square footage of each individual room. The chart to the right gives the square footage of the Ryan Residence.

Minimums

Minimums for light and ventilation are often computed by building departments as a percentage. For example, we would use what is called the superficial floor area, such as 14 × 14 for the master bedroom (Ryan Residence), excluding closets or wardrobes, to find a percentage of the square footage:

$$14 \times 14 = 196 \text{ sq. ft.} \times 10\% = 19.6$$

This means that the minimum (window or sliding glass door) light and ventilation for this room would be 19.6 square feet. A single 4 × 5 window or two 2 × 5 windows would satisfy this minimum requirement. In this particular instance 10% is used, but for other rooms or in other municipalities the percentage may vary—for example, 20% for a bathroom or a minimum 3 square feet, whichever is greater. In most instances this would take care of the light requirement. In addition, to meet the ventilation requirement, 50% of this opening must be openable.

Maximums

Maximums for light and ventilation can be estimated and then documented by an energy specialist licensed to

SQUARE FOOTAGE BY ROOM

Room	Approx. Size	Sq. Ft.	Min. (10%) Lt. & Vent.
Master Bedroom	14 × 14	196	19.6
Master Bath	8 × 10	80	8.0–4.0
Living Room	16 × 20	320	32.0
Dining Room	11.5 × 10	120	12.0
Utility Room	7 × 6	42	4.2
Kitchen	10 × 17	170	17.0
Family Room	14 × 14	196	19.6
Bedroom No. 1	12 × 14	168	16.8
Bathroom	6 × 10	60	6.0–3.0
Bedroom No. 2	13 × 14	182	18.2
		Total Square Footage =	2,080 +

perform such calculations. This specialist, or energy engineer, can compute the heat loss and heat gain in a structure based on type of windows, doors, and walls plus insulation in the ceiling, walls, and floor, to see if a particular structure will comply with a preset standard. An estimated maximum in certain regions can be ascertained, for example, by multiplying the square footage by 16% (a preestablished percentage), thus arriving at an approximate maximum glazing area. In the case of the Ryan Residence, its 2,080 square feet of floor area is multiplied by 16%, giving us 332.80 square feet of glazing possible. Certainly, dual-glazed windows and skylight, as well as better insulation in the walls, ceiling, and floors, can increase the glazing area. Remember, this is an extremely simplified assessment of the estimated maximum.

To verify compliance with established standards, an Energy Compliance Certificate is attached to the set of construction documents. A sample of this type of certificate is shown in Chapter 15 as part of the working drawings as they are assembled for the Ryan Residence (see Figure 15.16). Notice the inclusion of the designer, the owner, the author of the documentation, and the enforcement agency (state or federal) listed.

Selection of Sizes

Once the sizes of openings are established and a particular manufacturer selected, the drafter can view the literature provided by the manufacturer as to available sizes and shapes.

Much as in a game of ticktacktoe, Xs and Os are used by many manufacturers to describe the openable and fixed portions of a sliding window or door. An XOX, for example, is a fixed glass window in the center with one sliding unit on either side. A designation of XO means that the sliding unit is on the left side as seen from outside the structure.

Although many offices use an arrow to indicate a sliding unit, as shown in Figure 9.9(A), others subscribe to the descriptive X and O method, placing an X into the openable portion as shown in Figure 9.9(B).

Atrium windows will be used for the Ryan Residence. Figure 9.10 gives an example of the available stock window sizes. The windows will be vinyl clad on the outside and wood on the inside, which can be painted, stained, or finished in whatever way the client desires. In the sizes listed the first two numbers indicate width and the second two indicate height. For atrium windows, the first letter indicates the type of window and the second refers to the color. For example, CW 2436 simply means a casement window, white, 24 inches wide and 36 inches in height. (By the way, this is rough opening size. The real outside window size is ½" smaller than this call-out size.)

Any set of windows can be mulled (combined) together to form different combinations. Such methods will be used in the Ryan Residence by combining pairs of windows in some of the bedrooms.

All of this information will be organized in a tabular form called a schedule, as described at the beginning of this chapter. Schedules follow a standard format, depending on the practice of the particular architectural office. Two such schedules are shown in Figure 9.11. Figure 9.11(A) may be printed on paper; this sheet is placed under the vellum and traced. A better procedure might be to lightly trace the schedule on the top side of the vellum, reverse the vellum, and darken the tracing on the back side of the vellum. All the information can be lettered on the top side. Anytime an error is made, you can simply erase the information without concerning yourself about erasing the lines of the schedule itself.

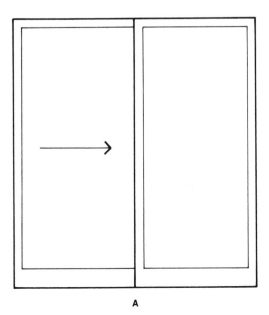

A

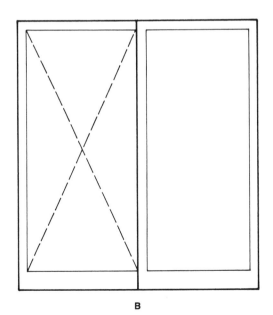

B

Figure 9.9 Identifying the openable portion of a window and a door.

THE ATRIUM WINDOW®
DOUBLE-TILT
Specifications

To simplify ordering windows, we've made our callout size the same as the rough opening size. A 2030 window fits a 2-foot by 3-foot rough opening exactly. Plus, most of our casement, awning and double-tilt windows are designed to fill the same rough opening.

Because our window sizes match aluminum window sizes, they are ideal for both remodeling projects and new construction. Atrium offers the most comprehensive range of standard sizes and configurations available. It's more than a window... it's a system.

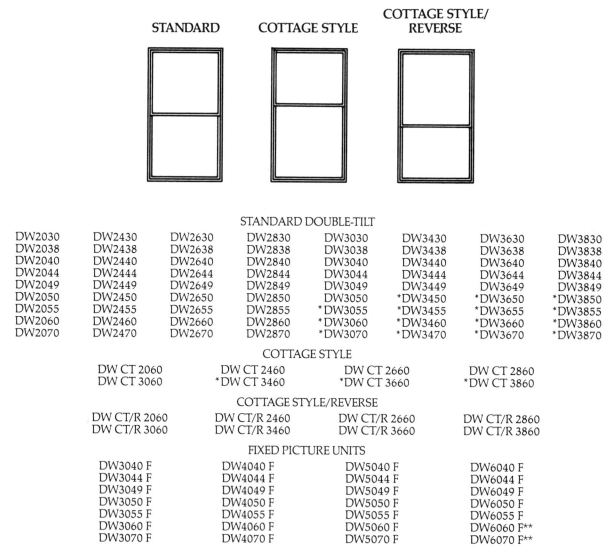

STANDARD   COTTAGE STYLE   COTTAGE STYLE/ REVERSE

STANDARD DOUBLE-TILT

DW2030	DW2430	DW2630	DW2830	DW3030	DW3430	DW3630	DW3830
DW2038	DW2438	DW2638	DW2838	DW3038	DW3438	DW3638	DW3838
DW2040	DW2440	DW2640	DW2840	DW3040	DW3440	DW3640	DW3840
DW2044	DW2444	DW2644	DW2844	DW3044	DW3444	DW3644	DW3844
DW2049	DW2449	DW2649	DW2849	DW3049	DW3449	DW3649	DW3849
DW2050	DW2450	DW2650	DW2850	DW3050	*DW3450	*DW3650	*DW3850
DW2055	DW2455	DW2655	DW2855	*DW3055	*DW3455	*DW3655	*DW3855
DW2060	DW2460	DW2660	DW2860	*DW3060	*DW3460	*DW3660	*DW3860
DW2070	DW2470	DW2670	DW2870	*DW3070	*DW3470	*DW3670	*DW3870

COTTAGE STYLE

DW CT 2060	DW CT 2460	DW CT 2660	DW CT 2860
DW CT 3060	*DW CT 3460	*DW CT 3660	*DW CT 3860

COTTAGE STYLE/REVERSE

DW CT/R 2060	DW CT/R 2460	DW CT/R 2660	DW CT/R 2860
DW CT/R 3060	DW CT/R 3460	DW CT/R 3660	DW CT/R 3860

FIXED PICTURE UNITS

DW3040 F	DW4040 F	DW5040 F	DW6040 F
DW3044 F	DW4044 F	DW5044 F	DW6044 F
DW3049 F	DW4049 F	DW5049 F	DW6049 F
DW3050 F	DW4050 F	DW5050 F	DW6050 F
DW3055 F	DW4055 F	DW5055 F	DW6055 F
DW3060 F	DW4060 F	DW5060 F	DW6060 F**
DW3070 F	DW4070 F	DW5070 F	DW6070 F**

Figure 9.10 Atrium window sizes.

A further refinement might be to make a transparency of the schedule on a plain paper copier. This transparency is turned over and placed back onto a plain paper copier, and a reverse image, similar to Figure 9.11(B), is made and filed. When a schedule is needed, this reverse image is reproduced onto an adhesive sheet and mounted onto the back side of the vellum, as shown in Figure 9.12. You then letter the desired information on the front side. This means that you are lettering on vellum, and not on the slick adhesive material.

The best of all solutions would be to type the information (if known in advance) onto a regular copy of a

WINDOW SCHEDULE

SYM.	WIDTH	HEIGHT	TYPE	FRAME	SCR.	GLAZ. AREA	VENT. AREA	REMARKS
◯								
◯								
◯								
◯								
◯								
◯								
◯								
◯								
◯								
◯								
◯								
◯								
◯								
◯								

A

WINDOW SCHEDULE

(table shown mirror-reversed)

SYM.	WIDTH	HEIGHT	TYPE	FRAME	SCR.	GLAZ. AREA	VENT. AREA	REMARKS
◯								
◯								
◯								
◯								
◯								
◯								
◯								
◯								
◯								
◯								
◯								
◯								
◯								
◯								
◯								

B

Figure 9.11 Predrawn schedules.

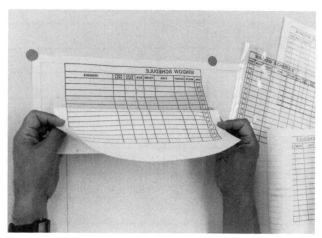

Figure 9.12 Using an adhesive to generate the schedule.

schedule, transfer onto an adhesive, and place this on your drawing. The main drawback to this method is that the finished product is *so* final. It is difficult to add or delete information and nearly impossible to remove the adhesive. However, there is solution: if a change, addition, or deletion is necessary, a xerographic copy can be made of the whole sheet onto erasable vellum and this product can be altered.

Preprinted Sheets

Many offices prepare preprinted sheets that contain many of the standards established by them, along with schedules, abbreviations, standard symbols, and so on. A simple way of preparing one of these sheets is to ink a schedule onto a sheet of vellum. Lettering can be done with a mechanical lettering machine that produces words and phrases on a transparent adhesive material. Standard symbols can also be drafted on a separate (possibly 8½ × 11) sheet, the written portion typed, and attached to the original sheet to produce a composite drawing. Much of the work described in Chapter 15 uses this method.

The final assembled sheet is sent to a reproduction company that can produce a vellum copy the same size as the original.

Thus the original can be filed and the new information, such as the schedule, is performed on the xerographic vellum copy and becomes an original for that specific set.

Computer

When done by CAD, the schedules, symbols, abbreviations, and so on can be drawn and merged by the computer and plotted on a sheet of vellum. The information to appear on the schedules can even be placed on

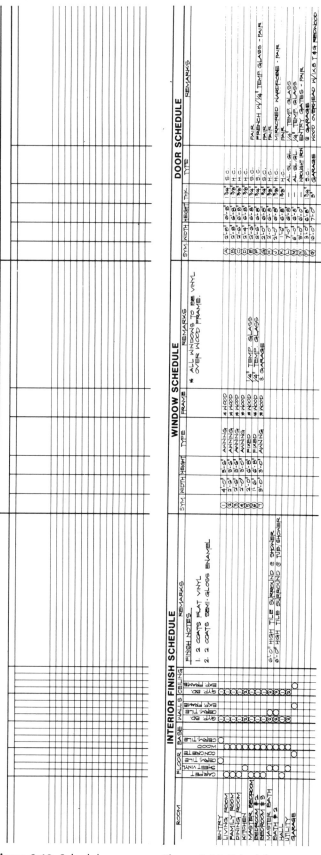

Figure 9.13 Schedules—Stage I.

Figure 9.14 Schedules—Stage II.

the schedules in the computer, and the result is a finished sheet when plotted.

Procedure for Ryan Residence—Schedules

The Window, Door, and Interior Finish Schedules will be completed in two short stages: the layout of the schedule and the addition of the desired information. See Figures 9.13 and 9.14 for examples of these two stages.

The schedules for the Ryan Residence will be drawn on a separate sheet and merged with the exterior elevations. See Chapter 15.

SUMMARY

Tabulated or pictorial schedules may be used to provide information about doors and windows. Choice of one or the other type of schedule, or both, depends on a number of factors. Schedules employ graphics for the delineation of door and window symbols. Interior finish schedules use space numbers or names of rooms. Other schedules, such as plumbing and appliance schedules, may or may not be incorporated into the construction documents.

IMPORTANT TERMS AND CONCEPTS

Schedules: Tabulated, pictorial
Door and window schedules
Symbol designations

Interior finish schedules
Plumbing fixture schedules
Appliance schedules

REVIEW QUESTIONS

1. Name two types of door and window schedules.
2. When a door or window is too intricate to describe in a schedule, what should you do?
3. Name two results of providing insufficient space in a schedule.
4. Name two methods of laying out schedule lines on tracing paper (vellum).
5. On what sheet is it most desirable to incorporate the door and window schedule?
6. Give two reasons for selecting a pictorial door and window schedule.
7. A plumbing fixture schedule might be employed for what reasons?
8. What other document may add to the information given in schedules?

LABORATORY PROBLEMS

1. Illustrate, graphically, recommended shapes for door and window symbols with letter and number designations.
2. Using a recommended method, lay out on tracing paper a tabulated window schedule incorporating at least eight windows. Your instructor will provide window information.
3. Illustrate, graphically, an intricate door or window as it might be depicted for a pictorial schedule. Your instructor will select the scale, type of drawing, and design of the item.
4. Prepare an interior finish schedule incorporating the following:

Space—6 rooms   Walls
Floor   Ceiling
Base   Remarks
Trim

10

BUILDING SECTIONS

10

PREVIEW
Structural sections are an important tool for investigating structural conditions.

OBJECTIVES
1. Be familiar with types of structural sections using wood frame, masonry, and steel construction.
2. Understand how to provide as many sections as needed to clearly illustrate the structural conditions.
3. Be able to draw a structural section and its related components.

Building Sections

A building section cuts a vertical slice through a structure or a part of a structure. Figure 10.1 shows a vertical slice cut through a wood-framed, two-story residence. To further examine the various roof, floor, and wall conditions found at that particular slice location, we can separate the two elements as viewed in Figure 10.2.

Drawing a Building Section

Drawing a building section is done by making a cross-section giving relevant architectural and structural information. When given the task of drawing a building section, you first need to gather basic information including:

1. Type of foundation
2. Floor system
3. Exterior and interior wall construction
4. Beam and column sizes and their material
5. Plate and/or wall heights
6. Floor elevations
7. Floor members (size and spacing)
8. Floor sheathing, material and size
9. Ceiling members (size and spacing)
10. Roof pitch
11. Roof sheathing, material and size
12. Insulation requirements
13. Finished roof material

When you have gathered this information, select a suitable architectural scale. Usually, the scale ranges from $\frac{1}{8}'' = 1'-0''$ to $\frac{3}{4}'' = 1'-0''$. The scale depends on

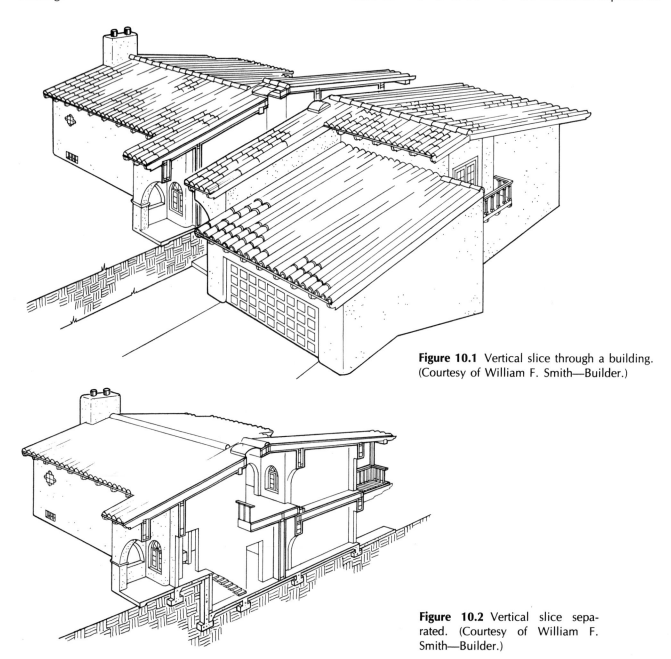

Figure 10.1 Vertical slice through a building. (Courtesy of William F. Smith—Builder.)

Figure 10.2 Vertical slice separated. (Courtesy of William F. Smith—Builder.)

the size and complexity of a project and should also be chosen for clarity.

As you draw the building section, visualize the erection sequence for the structure and the construction techniques of the material being used. Figure 10.3 shows a building section derived from Figures 10.1 and 10.2.

The first step is to show the concrete floor and foundation members at that particular location. While foundation details should be drawn accurately, they do not need to be dimensioned or elaborated upon; all the necessary information will be called out in the larger scale drawings of the individual foundation details.

Next, establish a **plate height.** (A plate is a horizontal timber that joins the tops of studs.) Here the plate height is 8'–0", measuring from the top of the concrete floor to the top of the two plates (2—2 × 4 continuous) of the wood stud wall. This height also establishes the height to the bottom of the floor joist for the second floor level. Once the floor joists are drawn in at the proper scale, repeat the same procedure to establish the wall height that will support the ceiling and roof framing members.

As indicated, the roof pitch for this particular project is a ratio of 3 in 12; for each foot of horizontal measurement, the roof rises 3 inches (for every 12 feet, the roof rises 3 feet). You can draw this slope or angle with an architectural scale or you can convert the ratio to an angle degree and draw it with a protractor or adjustable triangle. Draw the roof at the other side of the building in the same way, with the intersection of the two roof planes establishing the ridge location. Mission clay tile

was chosen for the finished roof member for this project and is drawn as shown.

When you have drawn in all the remaining components, such as stairs and floor framing elevation changes, note all the members, roof pitch, material information, and dimensions.

Figure 10.3 shows various reference symbols. These symbols refer to an enlarged drawing of those particular assemblies. To demonstrate the importance of providing enlarged details, Figure 10.4 shows a building section of a wood-framed structure with critical bolted connections. A reference symbol (the number 1 over the number 8, in a reference bubble) is located at the roof framing and wall connection. This connection is made clear with an enlarged detail showing the exact location and size of bolts needed to satisfy the engineering requirements for that assembly. See Figure 10.5.

Number and Place of Sections

Draw as many building sections as you need to convey the greatest amount of information and clarity for those building the structure.

Usually, building sections are used to investigate various conditions that prevail in a structure. These sections can point out flaws in the building's structural integrity, and this information can lead to modifications in the initial design.

The number of building sections required varies according to the structural complexity of the particular building. Figures 10.6 and 10.7 illustrate two buildings

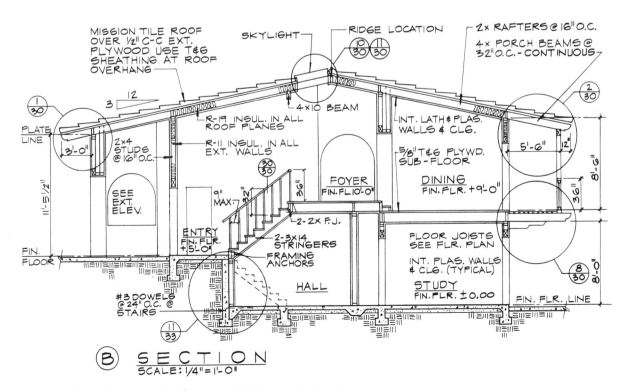

Figure 10.3 Building section. (Courtesy of William F. Smith—Builder.)

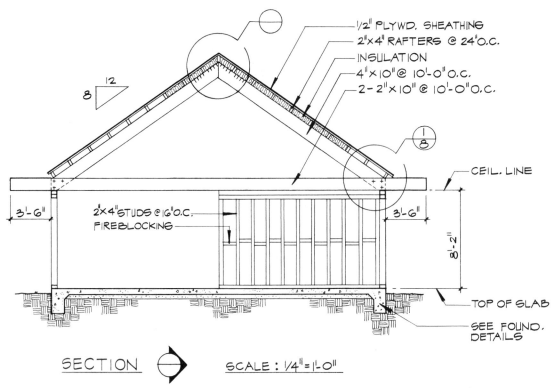

1/2" PLYWD. SHEATHING
2"×4" RAFTERS @ 24" O.C.
INSULATION
4"×10" @ 10'-0" O.C.
2-2"×10" @ 10'-0" O.C.

8 ⟋ 12

CEIL. LINE

3'-6"

2"×4" STUDS @ 16" O.C.
FIREBLOCKING

3'-6"

8'-2"

TOP OF SLAB

SEE FOUND.
DETAILS

SECTION   SCALE : 1/4"=1'-0"

Figure 10.4 Structural section.

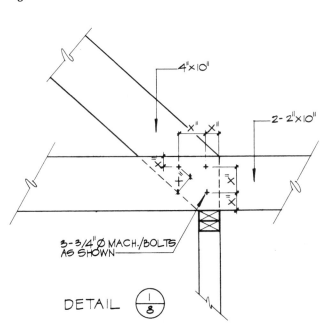

4"×10"

2- 2"×10"

3-3/4" Ø MACH./BOLTS
AS SHOWN

DETAIL 1/8

Figure 10.5 Bolted connection.

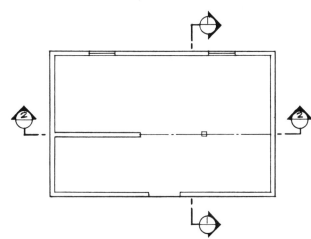

Figure 10.6 Two structural sections.

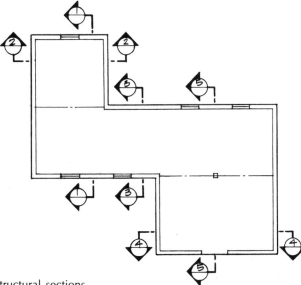

Figure 10.7 Five structural sections.

varying in complexity. Figure 10.6 shows a rectangular building, which probably needs only two building sections to clearly provide all the information required. However, the building in Figure 10.7 requires at least five sections to provide all the structural information.

Types of Sections

Because the design and complexity of buildings vary, types of sections also vary.

Wall Sections

Simple structural conditions may only require wall sections to convey the necessary building information. Structural sections for a small industrial building, for example, might use wall sections.

In most cases, wall sections can be drawn at larger scales such as ½″ = 1′–0″. These larger scale drawings allow you to clearly elaborate building connections and call-outs without having to draw separate enlarged details.

Figures 10.8, 10.9, 10.10, and 10.11 show an industrial building and also show how wall sections are incorporated into a set of construction documents. Figure 10.8 shows the floor plan with two main exterior and one interior bearing wall conditions. These wall conditions are referenced to wall sections and are shown in Figures 10.9, 10.10, and 10.11.

To draw a wall section, first select a scale that clearly shows the wall and foundation assembly details as well

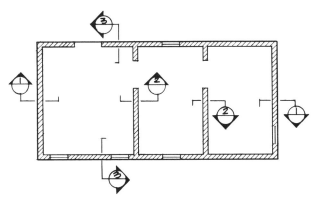

Figure 10.8 Floor plan—industrial building.

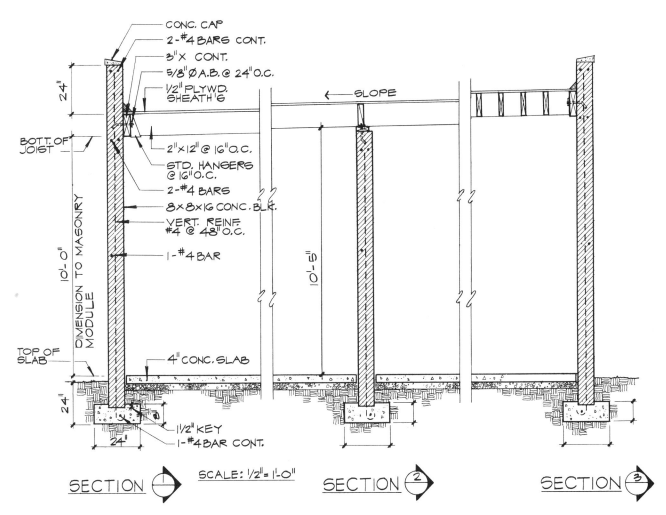

Figure 10.9 Exterior wall section. **Figure 10.10** Interior wall section. **Figure 10.11** Exterior wall section.

as the adjacent structural members and components. Then, using wall section 1, Figure 10.9, as an example, draw and dimension the footing for the masonry wall. Because you are drawing at a large scale, you can note all the footing information directly on the wall section, thereby making separate foundation details unnecessary. Next draw the masonry wall using 8 × 8 × 16 concrete block as the wall material. Because a modular unit is being used for the wall construction, a wall height is established that satisfies the 8″ concrete block increments. Draw the roof-to-wall assembly at the desired height above the concrete floor, with the various framing connections and members needed to satisfy the structural requirements. After you finish the drawing, add notes for all members, steel reinforcing, bolts, and so forth. Other wall sections, as shown in Figures 10.10 and 10.11, are drawn and noted similarly. Note that while Figure 10.11 is similar to Figure 10.9, different roof framing conditions exist.

In short, large-scale wall sections allow the structural components and call-outs to be clearly drawn and usually make larger-scale details such as framing connections and foundation details unnecessary.

Full Sections

For projects with complex structural conditions you should draw an entire section. This gives a better idea of the structural conditions in that portion of the building, which can then be analyzed, engineered, and clearly detailed.

Figure 10.12 shows a building section through a residence that has many framing complexities. Here you can clearly understand the need for a full section to see the existing conditions. To show the full section, you should draw this type of section in a smaller architectural scale, ¼″ = 1′–0″. Again, when you use a smaller scale for drawing sections, you must provide enlarged details of all relevant connections. The circled and referenced conditions in Figure 10.12, for example, will be detailed at a larger scale.

Partial Sections

Many projects have only isolated areas of structural complexities. These areas are drawn in the same way as a cross-section, but they stop when the area of concern has been clearly drawn. This results in a partial section of a structural portion.

Figure 10.13 shows a partial section that illustrates the structural complexities existing in that portion. Additional detailing is required to make other assemblies clear.

One of these assemblies, for example, may require a partial framing elevation to show a specific roof framing condition. This condition may be referenced by the use of two circles—each with direction arrows, reference letters, and numbers—attached to a broken line. Figure 10.14 shows this partial framing elevation as referenced on Figure 10.13.

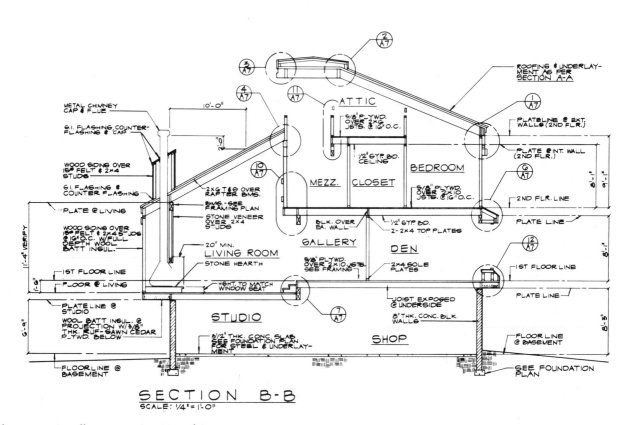

Figure 10.12 Full section. (Courtesy of Steve L. Martin.)

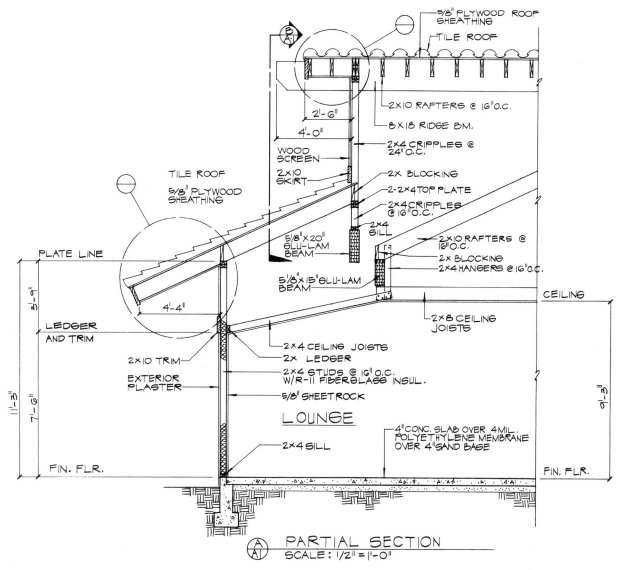

Figure 10.13 Partial section.

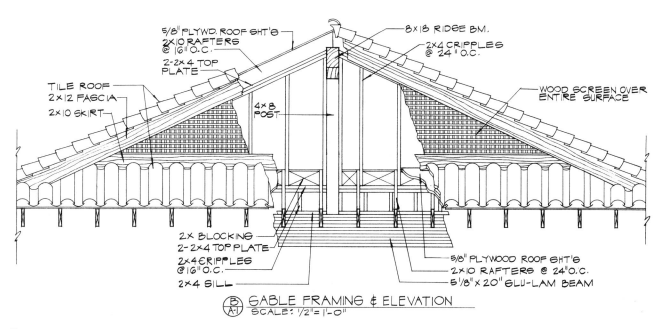

Figure 10.14 Framing elevation.

Steel Sections

For buildings built mainly with steel members, use elevations to establish column and beam heights. This approach coincides with the procedures and methods for the shop drawings provided by the steel fabricator.

Figure 10.15 shows a structural section through a steel-frame building. In contrast to sections for wood-frame buildings, where vertical dimensions are used to establish plate heights, this type of section may establish column and beam heights using the top of the concrete slab as a beginning point. Each steel column in this section has an assigned number because the columns are identified by the use of an axial reference matrix on the framing plan, shown in Figure 10.16.

Examples

These two examples of buildings show how their unique structural systems dictate different ways of showing a building section.

Example 1: A Theatre

The first building, constructed of masonry and steel, has a mainly symmetrical floor plan. Therefore, the structural design is similar for both sides, if not identical. As Figure 10.17 shows, the symmetry of this theatre may mean that only two major building sections are required. The first section has been taken through the

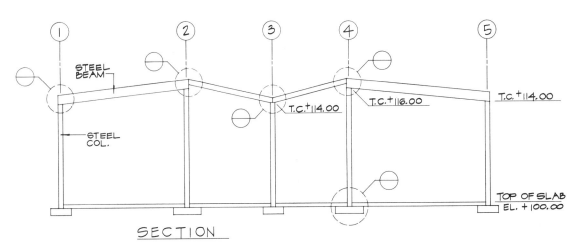

Figure 10.15 Steel-frame section.

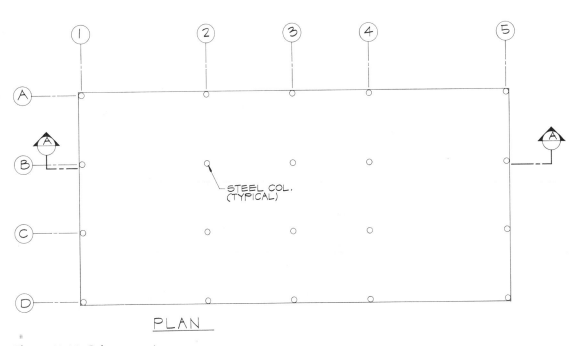

Figure 10.16 Column matrix.

lobby in the East-West direction. The other has been taken through one side of the lobby in the North-South direction.

Draw the first building section, Figure 10.18 shows, by first lightly laying out the dimensional reference planes to accurately locate beams, columns, and walls relative to those shown on the floor plan in the East-West direction.

For this type of structure and its overall dimensions, a scale of ¼" = 1'–0" gives enough clarity for the mem-

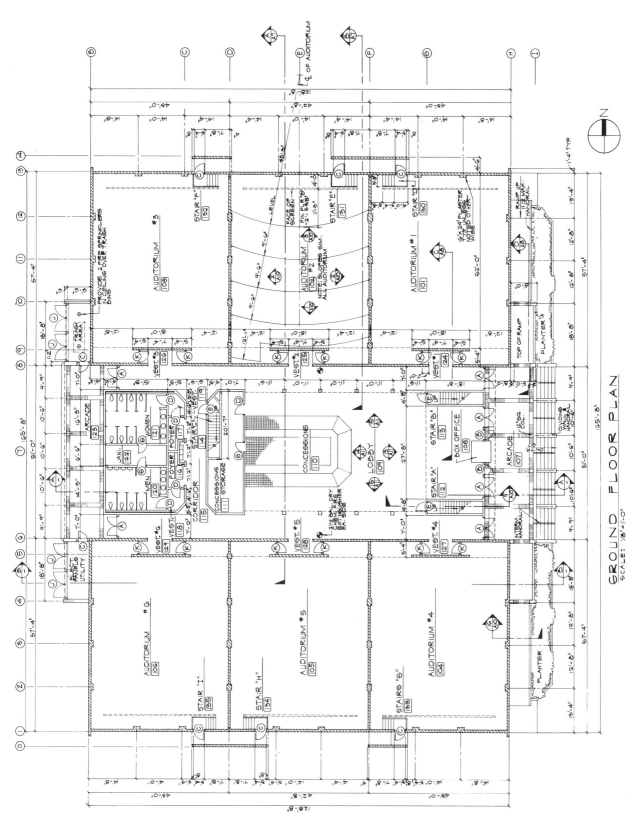

Figure 10.17 Theatre floor plan. (Courtesy of AVCO Community Developers, Inc.)

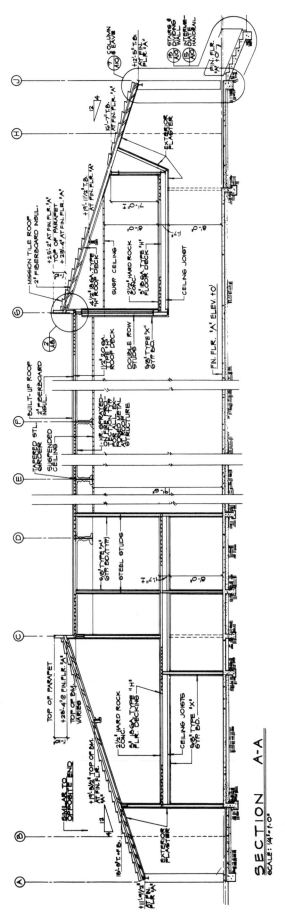

Figure 10.18 Building section, East-West direction.

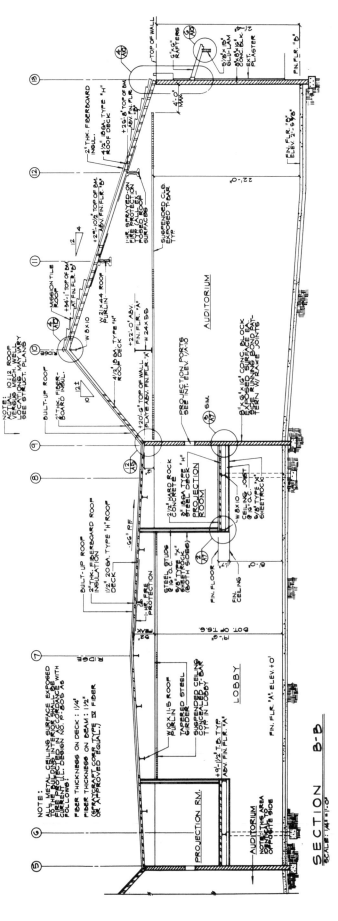

Figure 10.19 Building section, North-South direction.

bers and required assemblies. Because the overall dimensions of the building are large and the area through the lobby is mainly open space, you may simply provide break lines between supporting members, as indicated between dimensional reference planes Ⓓ and Ⓔ, Ⓔ and Ⓕ, Ⓕ and Ⓖ. This helps when the size of the vellum is restricted.

When you have drawn the foundation members and concrete floor, then draft wall locations and their respective heights in place. In this way, the second floor members are shown in their respective locations. The finished ceiling is attached directly to the bottom of the steel joist. Steel decking with a 2½"-thick concrete topping is drawn in as shown. From the second floor level, plate heights are set and then minimum roof pitches are drawn, establishing the roof height at reference planes Ⓓ and Ⓖ. You can now draw all the remaining structural members, at their respective locations and heights.

Because the North and South auditoriums are identical in size and structural design, you may simply provide a section through one auditorium and the lobby. See Figure 10.19. This partial building section is delineated in the same way as Figure 10.18; first, the reference planes are laid out, and then the foundation sections and the concrete floor are drawn relative to the foundation plan. The concrete floor slopes in the auditorium area. This slope ratio is determined by recommended seating and viewing standards for cinema theatres. Next, draw in the various walls and their heights.

The exterior masonry wall height at reference ⑬, established by the recommended interior ceiling height of 22'–0", satisfies the required height for the viewing screen. From the top of this wall, you can draw in the steel decking and roof assembly at a roof pitch of 4 in 12. The ridge location is established by the reference number ⑩. From this point, a roof pitch of 10 in 12 is drawn to where it intersects the lobby roof along the dimensional reference line ⑨. All the structural members for the roof and walls within the lobby area are now drawn in and noted.

For reference, show a portion of the opposite identical side for this type of partial section. In Figure 10.19 this is indicated at reference line ⑤, the back wall of the opposite auditorium. Use the correct material designation for the wall, floor, and roof materials.

Example 2: A Three-Story Office Building

This three-story office building has structural steel beams and columns as the main supporting members. Spanning the steel beams, open web **trusses** are used for the floor joists. Plywood and lightweight concrete are installed directly above the joists. Supporting members, at the ground floor level, are composed of steel columns

encased in concrete, and masonry walls located at the lobby and stairway areas.

Figure 10.20 shows the ground floor plan for this structure and the dimensional axial reference planes for column and wall locations. Building section cuts have been referenced in the North-South and East-West directions. The floor plan for the second and third levels, which are similar, is provided so that the building sections can be drawn. See Figure 10.21.

The first section to draw is Section Ⓐ. This is taken between reference planes Ⓓ and Ⓔ in the East-West direction. Begin the drawing by lightly laying out the reference planes and incorporating section break lines between the reference planes as indicated between beam lines ④ and ⑤ as well as between ⑥ and ⑦. See Figure 10.22A, building section Ⓐ.

Starting from the lobby's finished floor elevation of 100.0, we establish a clearance height of approximately 8'–0" in the parking area, in which the **soffit** (finished underside of spanning members) framing elevation is designated at 108.00. Now, consult with the structural and mechanical engineers about what space is required for structural members and plumbing lines. In this case, a height of 4'–10" satisfies their requirements, thus establishing a second floor elevation of 112.8. From the second to the third floor level, a height of 14'–0" is required to satisfy the space requirements for structural and mechanical members, as well as for the desired suspended ceiling height. The space required for mechanical and electrical components is called the **plenum area**. An example of this is shown on Figure 10.22B.

A top plate height of 12'–0" or an elevation of 139.33 establishes the exterior wall height, from which point the roof pitch will be drawn. Roof rafters are drawn in with a roof pitch of 4 in 12, extending 2 feet beyond the exterior walls to provide support for the soffit framing. The steel roof beams at the various reference numbers are drawn in at various elevations to provide adequate roof drainage for the various drains located in the roof well area.

These elevations are shown at the various beam locations. From these locations, wood members are framed between the main steel beams which provide the required roof pitches. When all the required members have been drafted in, the various notes and dimensions can be lettered accordingly. When you provide notes, organize lettering as shown on reference lines ⑤, ⑦, and ⑩ in Figure 10.22A.

Building section Ⓒ, cut in the North-South direction, is shown in Figure 10.23. This section is drawn in the same way as building section Ⓐ. However, many of the notes have not been shown because they are identical to those noted in section Ⓐ. This is acceptable practice as long as you make clear they are identical, as is done in

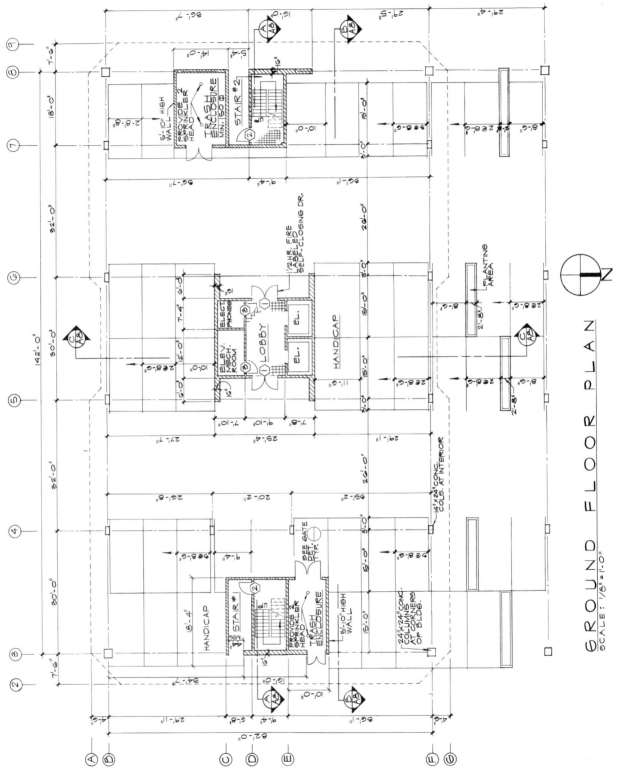

Figure 10.20 Ground floor plan—office building. (Courtesy of Westmount, Inc., Real Estate Development, Torrance, CA.)

240

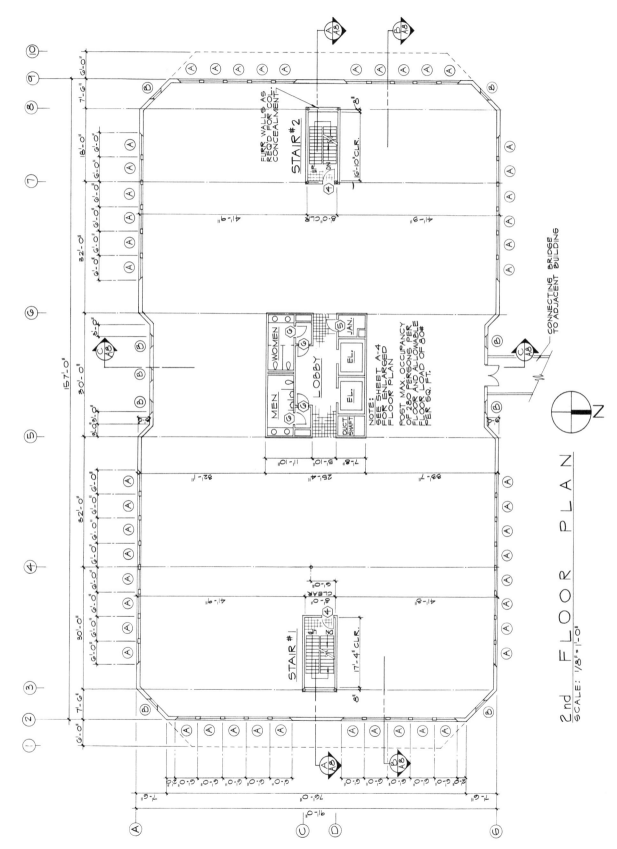

Figure 10.21 Floor plan—2nd level of office building. (Courtesy of Westmount, Inc., Real Estate Development, Torrance, CA.)

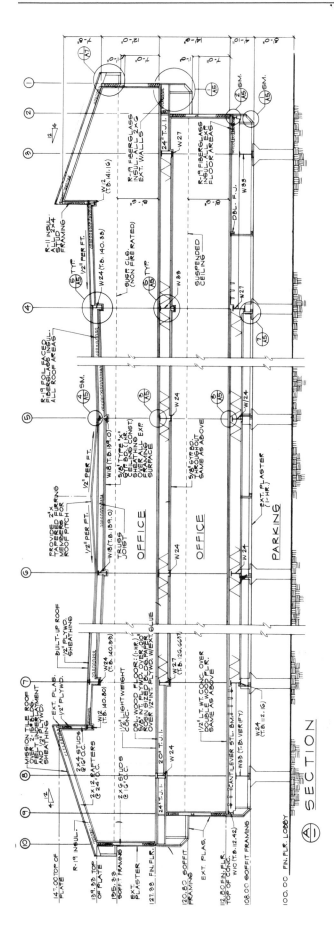

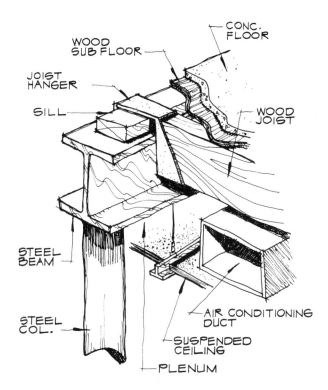

Figure 10.22A Office building section—East-West direction. (Courtesy of Westmount, Inc., Real Estate Development, Torrance, CA.)

Figure 10.22B Plenum area.

this case at the bottom of reference ⒡. In this way, changes can be made on one drawing and also corrected elsewhere. The section shown in Figure 10.23 was taken through an area with many elements relevant to the construction process.

The checklist (opposite, top) covers the basic information that should be found on building sections as well as characteristics of a well-thought-out set of sections.

Drafting a Building Section

After deciding where a section is to be taken that reveals the greatest amount of the structure, a grid pattern is drafted. The horizontal lines of the grid represent the floor line and the plate line (at the top of the two top plates). All of the vertical lines represent the walls of the structure. See Figure 10.24.

The section should be drawn at as large a scale as the drawing sheet allows. A scale of ½″ = 1′–0″ is ideal, but because of the size of the structure or the limits of the

BUILDING SECTIONS CHECKLIST

1. Sections that clearly depict the structural conditions existing in the building
2. Sections referenced on plans and elevations.
3. Dimensioning for the following (where applicable):
   a. Floor to top plate
   b. Floor to floor
   c. Floor to ceiling
   d. Floor to top of wall
   e. Floor to top of column or beam
   f. Cantilevers, overhangs, offsets, etc.
   g. Foundation details
4. Elevations for top of floor, top of columns and beams.
5. Call-out information for all members, such as:
   a. Size, material, and shape of member
   b. Spacing of members
6. Call-out information for all assemblies if enlarged details are not provided
7. Column and beam matrix identification if incorporated in the structural plan
8. Call-out for sub-floor and sheathing assembly
9. Roof pitches and indication of all slopes
10. Reference symbols for all details and assemblies that are enlarged for clarity
11. Designation of material for protection of finish for roof, ceiling, wall, and structural members
12. Structural notes applicable to each particular section, such as:
    a. Nailing schedules
    b. Splice dimensions
13. Structural sections corresponding accurately to foundation, floor, and framing plans
14. Scale of drawing provided

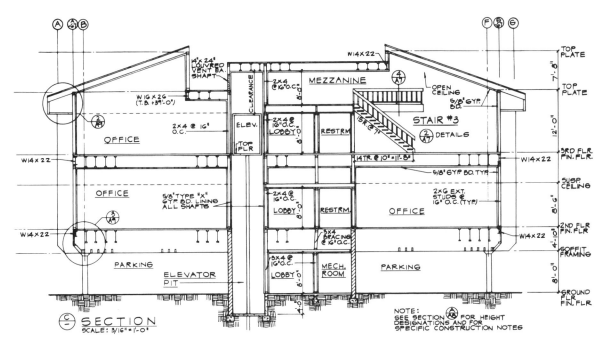

Figure 10.23. Office building section—North-South direction. (Courtesy of Westmount, Inc., Real Estate Development, Torrance, CA.)

sheet a scale of ⅜" = 1'–0" or even ¼" = 1'–0" might be used.

Before you decide on a smaller scale, explore the possibility of removing portions of the building that are redundant by virtue of break lines. See Figures 10.9, 10.18, and 10.22A. If the building is symmetrical, a partial section, as shown in Figure 10.13, may suffice.

Looking at the cartoons, the project manager may have already made this decision.

From Floor Plan to Building Section

If the building section is to be drawn at the same scale as the floor plan, the drafter need only transfer measure-

ments by scaling, or, better yet, by using a pair of dividers. If the building section is drafted at twice the size of the floor plan, one can simply transfer the measurements by reading the ½" scale or, as mentioned earlier, by using a divider and pace the distance off twice with the divider.

Let's say that the floor plan was drawn at ¼" scale and the building section is to be drawn at ⅜" scale. A proportional divider is used. See Figure 10.25. There is a set of numbers on this particular instrument, which are proportions; ¼ is two-thirds of ⅜, the proportional divider is set at the ⅔ setting. If 6'–0" is measured on the top (the smaller side) at ¼" scale, the instrument will translate the 6'–0" distance on the bottom side, but at a

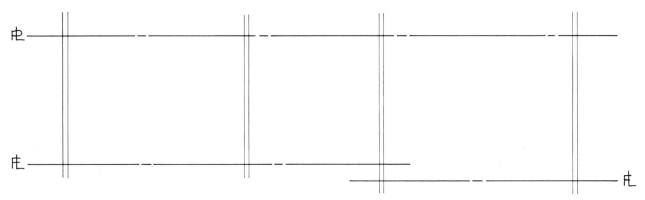

Figure 10.24 A grid pattern for the Ryan Residence.

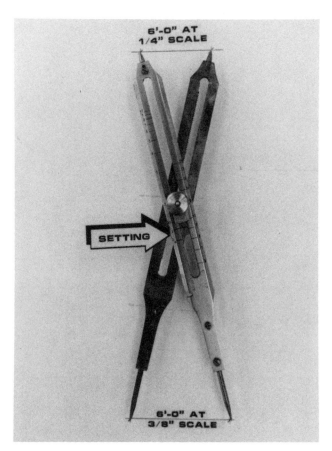

Figure 10.25 Proportional divider for scale change.

⅜" scale. Thus, by using the proportional divider, one can easily transfer measurements from one drawing to another even if the scale is different.

Pitch

If there is a pitch (an angle) involved and it is constant, an adjustable triangle is handy. If the building section is drafted at the top of the sheet, the adjustable triangle can be positioned with ease. Had the building section been drafted at the bottom of the sheet, using the adjustable triangle can be cumbersome. See Figure 10.26. This is

because of the distance between the base of the triangle and the desired angle. In this instance it would be easier to actually measure the pitch. If you have a template, look for a pitch scale printed on its side. If you are in the market for a plan template, check the various brands carefully, because there are templates that will measure pitch, have markings for typical heights of equipment from the floor, and even plot spacing, such as for 4" and 6" tile, 16" spacing for stud and joist position, and door swings, among other items.

Another alternative is to make your own pitch template using an ink marking on your triangle. This ink tick mark can be saved by covering it with clear fingernail polish. See Figure 10.27(A). Still better would be to start with an index away from the end or point of the triangle, which might be slightly rounded, and because of the rounded form it might be difficult to find the beginning point of the pitch. See Figure 10.27(B).

If you understand the process of drafting a building section, you might develop a shortcut method. For example, if you have access to a plain paper copier that enlarges and reduces, it would be a simple matter of reproducing, to the proper scale, an eave detail with the same pitch on an acetate sheet, place it under the building section, and trace. It is reproduced onto an acetate sheet so that it can be flipped over and used on the opposite side of the building section as the shape and pitch reverse direction. See a sample being used in Figure 10.28.

Ryan Residence Building Section

Before a building section of any building is undertaken, it is essential to understand and comprehend the structural system at work and how the building will be assembled using this system. Be sure to read "Framing the Ryan Residence" in Chapter 12 before you proceed. The walls, bearing footings, their locations, and how the weight of the structure, starting at the roof, is distributed downward is explained in Chapter 12.

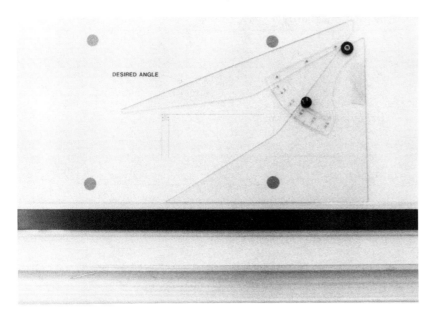

Figure 10.26 Use of adjustable triangle at the bottom of the drawing.

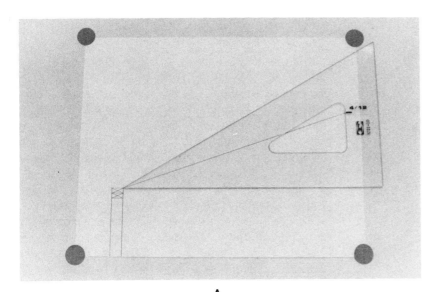

A

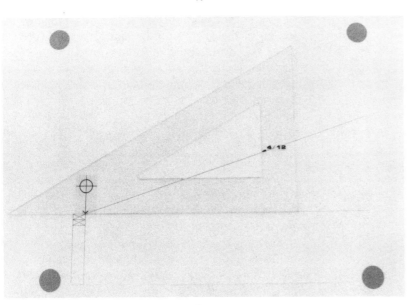

B

Figure 10.27 Triangle formatted for pitch.

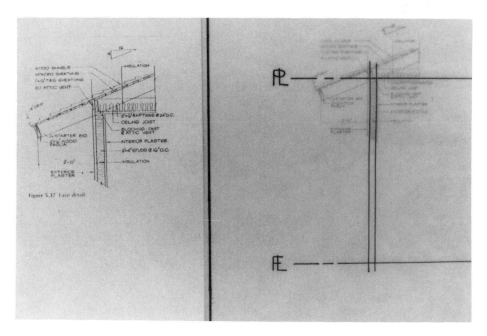

Figure 10.28 Acetate template.

STAGE I (Figure 10.29). Although we call this Stage I, it is really a combination of two steps. The first step looks like that expressed in Figure 10.24: Plate line, floor line, and the position of the walls. Add to this the concrete slab, the shape of the footings, and an outline of the roof, and you have the two steps in one as performed by the drafter.

Although the lines appear dark on this figure, they are in reality done very lightly as a block-out and may even be done in blue fade-away pencil.

STAGE II (Figure 10.30). As seen in the drawing, the building section is receiving detail at the various intersections and hard-lining is commencing. The top and bottom plates, as well as the seat in the stem wall for the slab, are drafted. Notice in particular the way the chapter illustrates the backfill at the end walls.

STAGE III (Figure 10.31). This is a very critical stage, because it establishes all of the structural components, their position and direction, and even the direction in which the section was taken.

Note the inclusion of the material designation and the makeup of the foundation with its insulation and sand. Walls show drywall, and the ceiling reveals the direction of the ceiling joist.

At this point a check print is made, and the project manager can freehand the errors, position dimensions, and notes for a beginning drafter right onto this check print.

Correction of Drawing Errors

As in all drawings, errors are made. It is no different with a building section. Some errors are simple to correct, whereas others are a bit more complex. Both types of errors are addressed here, and possible solutions are suggested.

Because a building section is the result of the foundation plan, roof plan, and roof framing systems used, the framing is checked and corrections clearly noted on the check print. Compare the ceiling joist direction with Figure 12.46. It changes direction in the bedroom wing (left side), but this change of direction is not incorporated in either of the two building sections. This will most certainly be corrected in the final stage.

An even greater error is revealed if you compare this drawing with the various plans (floor plan, foundation plan, etc.) and the original cartoon. The building sections are drawn in the same way as the cartoon, yet the cut for the section is taken in the opposite direction that the arrows indicate in the various plans.

A quick fix of this problem would be to change the direction of the arrows on the cutting plane line, thus making the drawing technically correct. The arrows would be changed in the roof plan, foundation plan, floor plan, and roof framing plan.

Another and more complex approach would be to turn the bottom building section around to produce a mirror image. This would align the image with all of the cutting plane lines and produce a more comfortable look at the structure for the carpenters (framers) in the field. The mirror image would be a better look at the structure, because you are cutting away the smaller piece of the building and looking in the direction of the larger portion of the building.

If this drawing had been done on a computer, the solution would be simple. Most computers can isolate a drawing and produce a mirror image of it with a set of simple commands. However, if the drawing was hand drawn, the solution is a bit more complex.

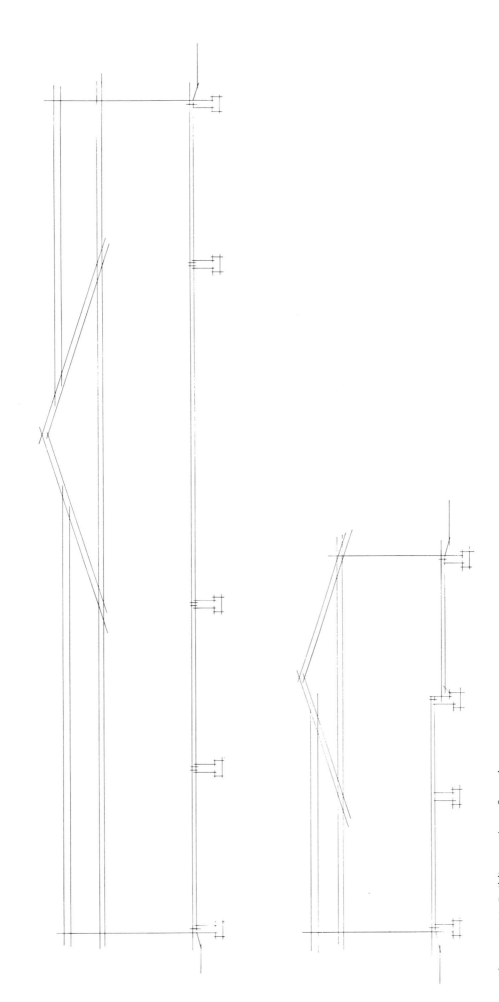

Figure 10.29 Building section—Stage I.

247

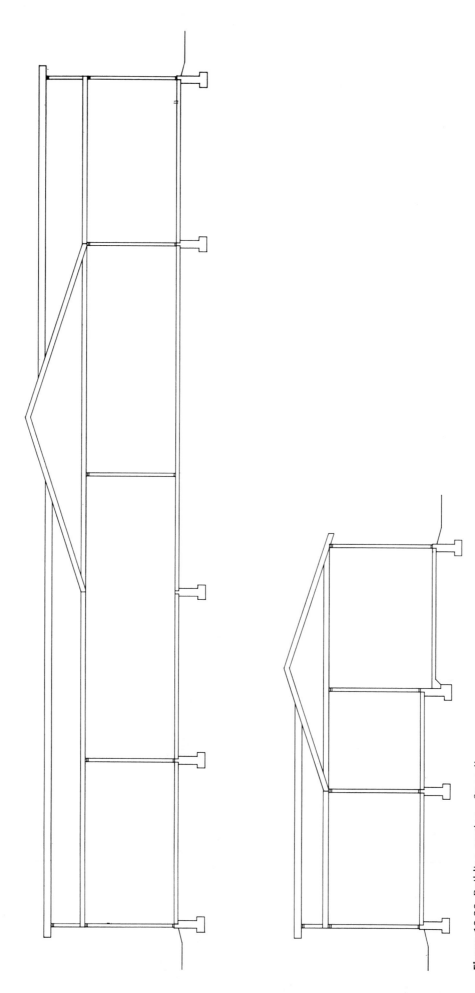

Figure 10.30 Building section—Stage II.

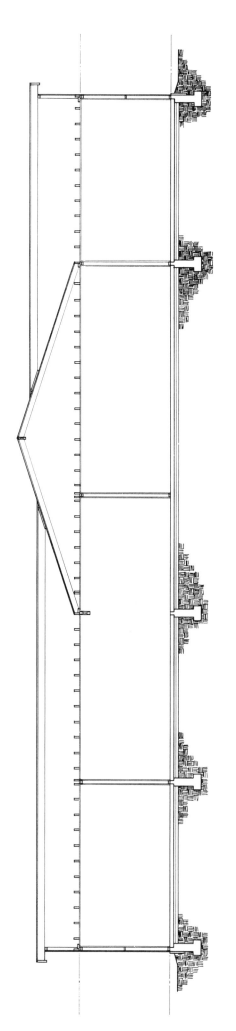
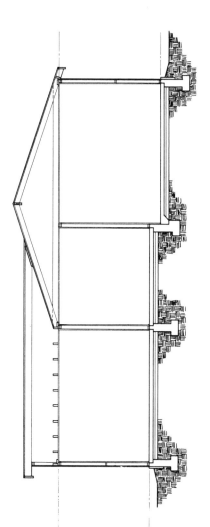

Figure 10.31 Building section—Stage III.

249

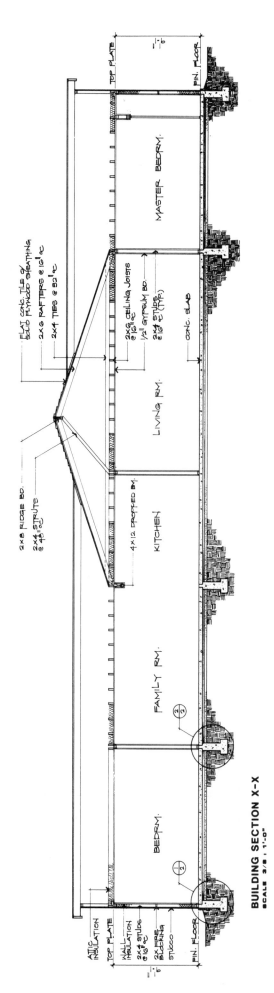

Because a diazo copy will eventually be made of this drawing, a satisfactory solution is feasible. Make the ceiling joist corrections, cut the lower building section out, scissor it back into the original vellum with the image on the back side (which will mirror-image the drawing) and continue to draft on the correct side of the vellum. In this way, the original is saved and the new information will be on the opposite side of the drawing. As a diazo copy is made, no one will ever know you have drawn on both sides of the vellum.

STAGE IV (Figure 10.32). Having made all the necessary corrections at the previous stage, this stage becomes very straightforward. Noting of the component parts and dimensioning become the utmost important tasks. All the parts should be identified as if you were labeling a drawing showing how to assemble a bicycle. Material designations for insulation, roof material, and concrete are done at this stage, as well as referencing to reveal footing details and eave details.

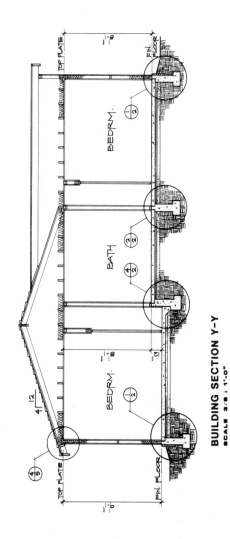

Figure 10.32 Building section—Stage IV.

SUMMARY

Building sections are required in every set of construction documents and vary according to whether the structure is wood, masonry, or steel, or a combination of all three materials. Sections should be taken at recommended places and drawn according to established procedures.

IMPORTANT TERMS AND CONCEPTS

Building sections: wall, full, partial, and steel
Floor elevation
Floor trusses
Column
Plate height

Ceiling joist
Ridge
Soffit
Plenum area

REVIEW QUESTIONS

1. Name two kinds of building sections.
2. Briefly describe the purpose of building sections.
3. What scale is recommended for wall sections?
4. On large projects, what is an appropriate scale for drawing a full section?
5. What term is used for locating columns and walls?
6. What kind of section illustrates clearly the foundation, wall assembly, and structural connections?
7. Name two consultants who will dictate space requirements for the drawing of building sections.
8. Give two methods of designating floor heights.
9. What information is found at the top of columns and beams on a section of a building contructed in steel?
10. At what point on a wall is the plate height found?
11. What type of lines are used to make a section more compact by eliminating repetitive portions?

LABORATORY PROBLEMS

1. Using the floor plan of Figure 10.7, draw a full building section 5, based on the following information:
   a. Width of building: 40'–0"
   b. Concrete floor
   c. Top of wall: 9'–0"
   d. Exterior walls: 2 × 4 studs @ 16" o/c
   e. 2 × 8 ceiling joist @ 16" o/c
   f. Roof pitch: 3 in 12
   g. Roof material: composition and gravel
   h. Beam at mid-span: 6 × 14
   Student to select scale.
2. Draw a wall section incorporating the following:
   a. Concrete footing width: 16"
   b. Foundation wall thickness: 8"
   c. Exterior wall: 2 × 6 studs @ 16" o/c
   d. First floor: 2 × 6 floor joists @ 16" o/c
   e. Floor sheathing: ¾" plywood
   f. Plate height—first floor: 9'–2"
   g. Floor joists—second floor: 2 × 12 @ 16" o/c
   h. Sheathing same as first floor
   i. Plate height—second floor: 9'–2"
   j. Roof rafters: 2 × 8 @ 24" o/c
   k. Roof sheathing: ½" plywood
   l. Roof pitch: ½ in 12
   m. Full insulation at exterior walls.
   n. Composition and gravel roofing material
   Student to select scale.
3. Draw examples of material designations for steel, concrete, and masonry, as they are shown on a building section.

11

EXTERIOR ELEVATIONS

11

PREVIEW

Exterior elevations give information about the exterior materials of a structure. Elevations depend on the floor plan for horizontal measurements, the sections for vertical dimensions, the assembly method for the structure, and the roof plan and/or roof framing plan for the roof configuration. This chapter outlines two basic procedures that generally apply for preparing exterior elevations in wood frame, masonry, and steel-with-wood construction.

OBJECTIVES

1. Understand the systematic approach to drafting exterior elevations.
2. Understand the relationships between exterior elevations and other drawings.
3. Be familiar with the necessary object lines and hidden lines.
4. Be able to decide which dimensions and notes are necessary and unnecessary.
5. Know how the choice of material can affect planning.

Introduction to Exterior Elevations

Purpose

Exterior elevations are an important part of a set of construction documents because they can show information not found anywhere else in the set.

The exterior elevations will:

1. Describe exterior materials found on the structure.
2. Provide a location for horizontal and vertical dimensions not found elsewhere.
3. Show, by using hidden lines, structural members that are found inside the walls. (Diagonal bracing is a good example of such hidden members.)
4. Show the relationship of two elements such as the height of the chimney in relationship to the roof of the structure.

5. Incorporate reference bubbles for building, window, and door sections.
6. Show any exterior design elements that cannot be shown elsewhere.

Basic Approach

In mechanical or engineering drafting, the elevations are described as the front, side, and rear. In architecture, exterior elevations are called North, South, East, and West. See Figure 11.1. Figure 11.2 shows how we arrive at the names for exterior elevations.

Orientation

The North, South, East, and West elevations may not be true North or true East. They might have been taken from an "orientation North," or as it has been called in other

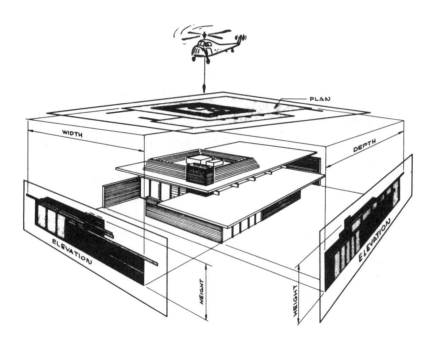

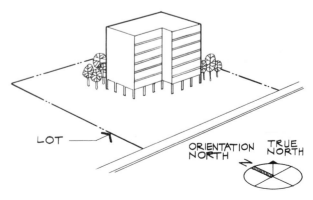

Figure 11.1 Multiview drawing of a structure. (Wakita, *Perspective Drawing: A Student Text/Workbook,* Kendall / Hunt Publishing Co., 1978. Reprinted with permission.)

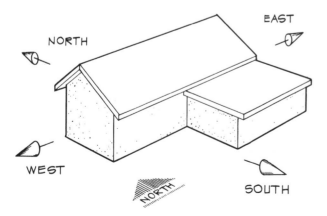

Figure 11.2 Names of elevations.

Figure 11.3 Use of orientation North.

regions, "Plan North," which may not be parallel to true North. For example, if a structure's boundaries are not parallel with true North, an orientation North is established, and used from then on to describe the various elevations. See Figure 11.3.

These terms, then, refer to the direction the structure is facing. In other words, if an elevation is drawn of the face of a structure that is facing south, the elevation is called the South elevation; the face of the structure that is facing west is called the West elevation, and so on. Remember, the title refers to the direction the structure is facing, *not* to the direction in which you are looking at it.

Finally, because of the size of the exterior elevations, they are rarely drawn next to the plan view as in mechanical drafting. See Figure 11.4.

Method 1: Direct Projection

Exterior elevations can be drafted by directly projecting sizes from the plan views or sections. Figure 11.5 shows how elevations can be directly projected from a plan view (a roof plan in this case). Figure 11.6 shows how the heights are obtained. Locations of doors, windows, and other details are taken from the floor plan. Figure 11.7 shows a slightly more complex roof being used to form the roof shape on an elevation.

Method 2: Dimensional Layout

Exterior elevations can also be drafted by taking the dimensions from the plans and sections and drafting the elevation from scratch. First, lightly lay out the critical vertical measurements. In the example shown in Figure 11.8, these measurements are the subfloor line and the plate line, (top of the two top plates above the studs).

See Figure 11.9A. This measurement is taken directly from the building section.

The second step establishes the location of the walls and offsets in the structure from the floor plan. Draw these lines lightly because changes in line length may be required later. See Figure 11.9B.

Third, establish the grade line (earth) in relationship to the floor line. See Figure 11.9C. This dimension is from the building sections or footing sections.

Next, as Figure 11.9D shows, the roof configuration is added. To better understand the relationship between the roof and structure, draw the **eave** in a simple form as shown in Figure 11.9E. These dimensions are found on the building section. The finished roof shape depends on the roof framing plan or the roof plan for dimensions. See Figure 11.9F.

Finally, windows and doors are located. Sizes are found on the window and door schedule, and locations on the floor plan. Material designations, dimensions, notes, and structural descriptions complete the elevation. See Figure 11.9G.

To help you visualize the transition from a drafted elevation to the actual building, see Figures 11.10 and 11.11. Compare the drafted elevation with the photograph.

Choice of Scale

Selection of the scale for elevations is based on the size and complexity of the project and the available drawing space. For small structures, ¼" = 1'–0" is a common scale. For a larger project, a smaller scale can be used. The exterior elevation is usually drawn at the same scale as the floor plan. For medium and large elevations, you may have to decrease the scale in relationship to the floor plans.

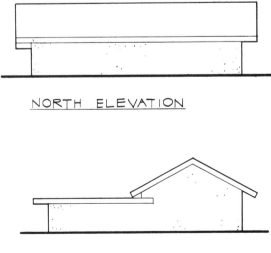

SOUTH ELEVATION

NORTH ELEVATION

WEST ELEVATION

EAST ELEVATION

Figure 11.4 Elevation arrangement.

Because we are dealing with small structures, two to four stories in height, we are using the largest scale allowed by the available drawing space not exceeding ¼″ = 1′–0″.

Odd-Shaped Plans

Not all plans are rectangular; some have irregular shapes and angles. Figure 11.12 shows several building shapes and the North designation. For these kinds of conditions, all elevations are drawn.

Shape A. Figure 11.13 shows the exterior elevations for a relatively simple L-shaped building and how these elevations were obtained using the projection method.

Shape B. The elevations for Shape B in Figure 11.14 present a unique problem on the East and particularly

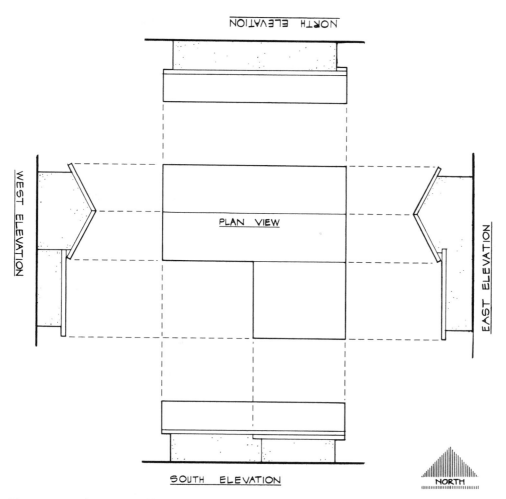

Figure 11.5 Obtaining width and depth dimensions.

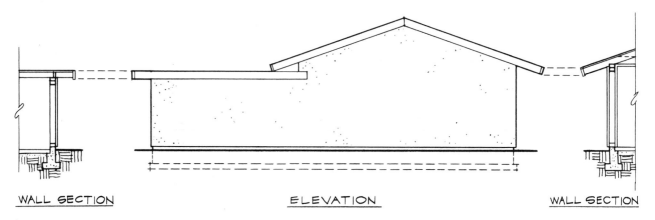

Figure 11.6 Heights from wall sections.

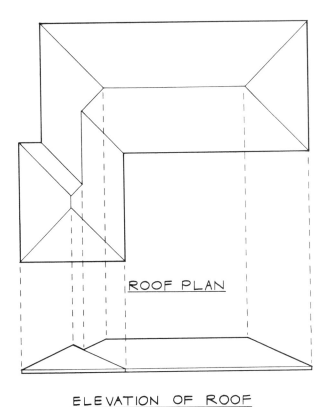

ROOF PLAN

ELEVATION OF ROOF

Figure 11.7 Roof elevation from roof plan.

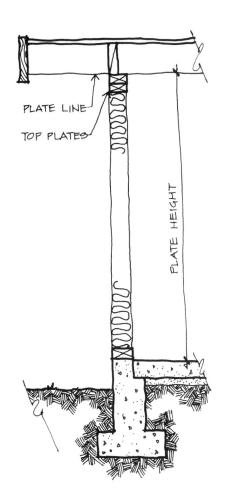

PLATE LINE

TOP PLATES

PLATE HEIGHT

Figure 11.8 Subfloor to plate line.

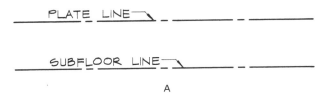

PLATE LINE

SUBFLOOR LINE

A

Figure 11.9A Establishing floor and plate lines.

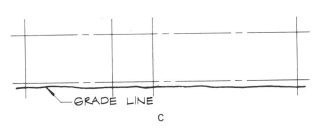

OUTLINE OF BLD'G

B

Figure 11.9B Drafting exterior outline.

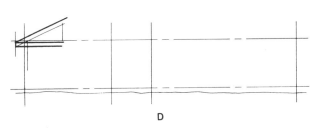

GRADE LINE

C

Figure 11.9C Establishing the grade line.

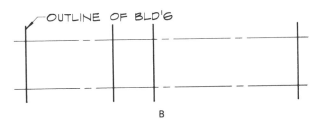

D

Figure 11.9D Incorporating the roof structure into the exterior elevation.

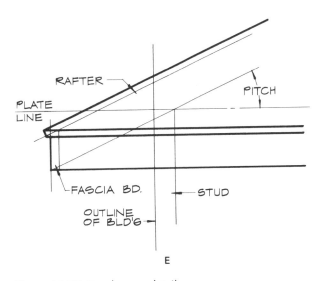

RAFTER

PITCH

PLATE LINE

FASCIA BD.

STUD

OUTLINE OF BLD'G

E

Figure 11.9E Rough eave detail.

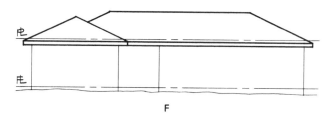

F

Figure 11.9F Finishing the roof shape.

G

Figure 11.9G Locating doors and windows.

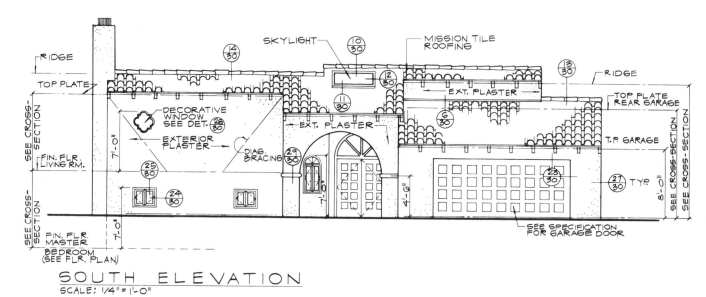

SOUTH ELEVATION
SCALE: 1/4" = 1'-0"

Figure 11.10 Drafted South elevation of a condominium. (Courtesy of William F. Smith—Builder.)

Figure 11.11 Pictorial view of South elevation of a condominium. (Courtesy of William F. Smith—Builder; Aerial Photography by William Boggs. Reprinted with permission.)

258

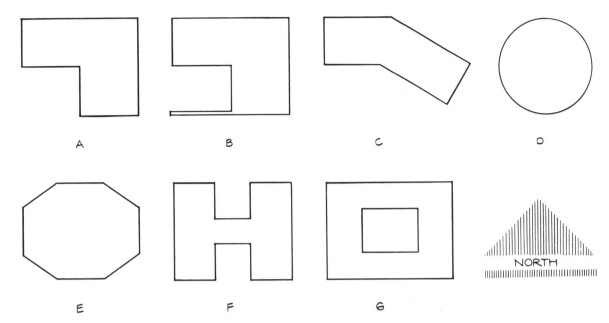

Figure 11.12 Irregularly shaped plans.

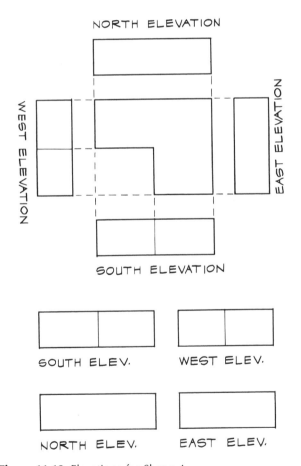

Figure 11.13 Elevations for Shape A.

the South elevation. Because the fence is in the same plane as the south side of the structure, include it in the South elevation. Had the fence been in front of the structure, you could either delete it or include it in order to show its relationship to the structure itself.

The inclusion of the fence may pose additional problems such as preventing a view of portions of the structure behind. You can overcome this difficulty in one of two ways: either eliminate the fence altogether (not show it) or use a break line, as shown in Figure 11.14. This allows any item behind it, such as the window, to be exposed, referenced, and dimensioned. Break lines still allow dimensioning and descriptions of the fence.

Shape C. The two portions on the right of the South elevation and all of the East elevation are *not* true shapes and sizes because they are drawn as direct 90° projections from the *left* portion of the plan view. This is sometimes a problem. See Figure 11.15. The West and North elevations will also have distortions. See Figure 11.12.

To solve this problem, we use an auxiliary view: a view that is 90° to the line of sight. The elevations are projected 90° to the sight lines and a break line is used to stop that portion which is not true. Notice on Figure 11.16 how the break line splits the South elevation into two parts. Each part is projected independently of the other, and its continuation, which is not a true shape, is voided.

The South elevation in Figure 11.15 appears to have three parts rather than two, as in Figure 11.16. In the latter case, the third part will be left to the East elevation. With a more complex shape, a break line beyond the true surface being projected can be confusing. See Figure 11.17. To avoid confusion, introduce a pivot point (P.P.) and show it as a dotted (hidden) line or a centerline type line (dots and dashes). See Figure 11.18. Use a **pivot point.** (A pivot point is the point at which the end of one elevation becomes the beginning of another elevation.)

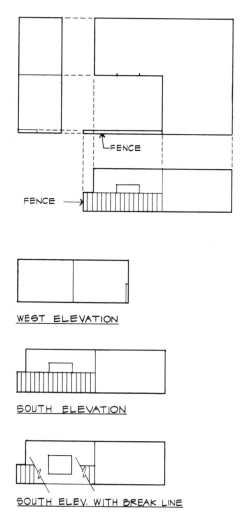

WEST ELEVATION

SOUTH ELEVATION

SOUTH ELEV. WITH BREAK LINE

Figure 11.14 Elevations for Shape B.

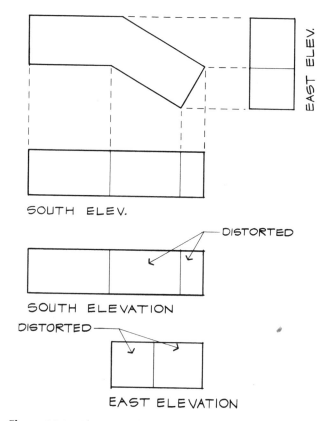

Figure 11.15 Elevations for Shape C.

Pivot points can cause a problem in selecting a title for a particular elevation. To avoid confusion, introduce a **key plan.** The key plan is usually drawn on the bottom right corner of the drawing sheet. See Figure 11.19. Draw and label a reference bubble for every necessary elevation. These reference bubbles will become the title for the elevation. If the surface contains important information about the structure or surface materials, it deserves a reference bubble. Figure 11.20 shows how these elevations are represented with titles and pivot point notations.

Shape D. With Shape D, in Figure 11.12, nothing is true shape and size, regardless of the direction of the elevation. See Figure 11.21. Figure 11.22 shows a pivot point together with a fold-out (called a "development drawing" in mechanical drawing).

Shape E. Shape E in Figure 11.12 can be drawn in one of three ways: first, drawing it as a direct projection so that one of the three exposed faces will be in true shape and size; second, using a key plan and drawing each

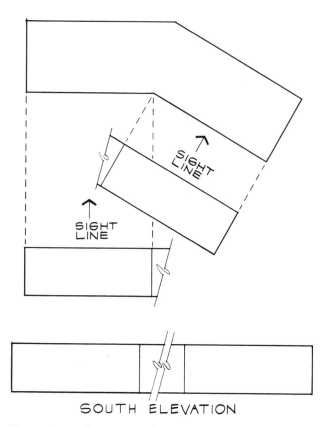

Figure 11.16 Elevations with new sight line. (William Boggs Aerial Photography. Printed with permission).

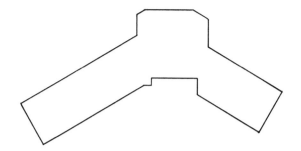

Figure 11.17 Complicated shape.

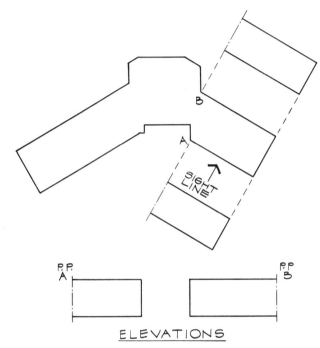

Figure 11.18 Use of pivot point in exterior elevations.

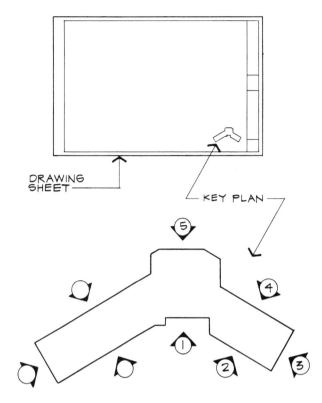

Figure 11.19 Using a key plan.

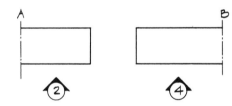

Figure 11.20 Elevations using key plan.

surface individually; and third, drawing it as a fold-out similar to Figure 11.22. Choose the method that will explain the elevations best. For example, if all other sides are the same, the direct projection method may be the best. If every wall surface is different, then the key plan or fold-out method is best.

Shape F. Surfaces that will be hidden in a direct projection, such as some of the surfaces of Shape F in Figure 11.12, can effectively be dealt with in one of two ways. The first uses a key plan and the second uses a combination of an elevation and a section. Both methods are shown in Figure 11.23. The combination of the section and the elevation shows the structure and its relationship to the elevation more clearly.

Shape G. Shape G in Figure 11.12 can be drawn simply as the South elevation, North elevation, East elevation, and West elevation using a direct projection method. The interior space (atrium) can also be drawn

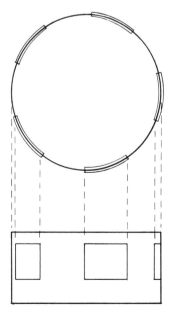

Figure 11.21 Elevations of a cylinder.

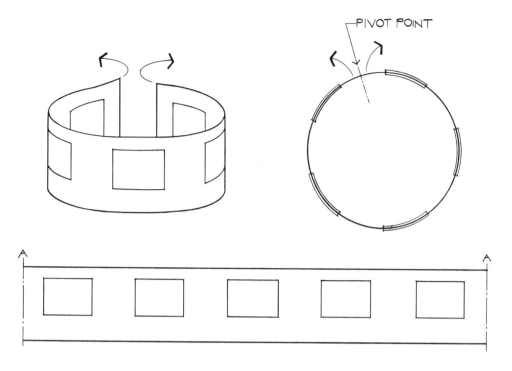

Figure 11.22 Elevation of cylinder using pivot point.

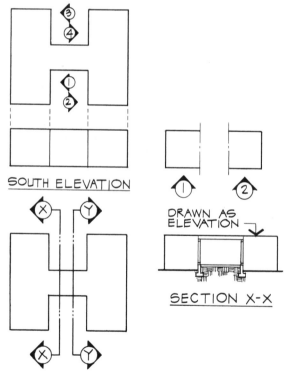

Figure 11.23 Elevations for Shape F.

as a direct projection with titles "Atrium North Elevation," "Atrium South Elevation," "Atrium East Elevation," and "Atrium West Elevation." A way to simplify this is shown in Figure 11.24.

Drawing Doors and Windows

Draw doors and windows on elevations as closely as possible to the actual configuration. Horizontal location dimensions need not be included because they are on the floor plan; and door and window sizes are contained in the door and window schedule. However, vertical location dimensions are shown with indications of how the doors and windows open.

Doors

Doors and their surface materials can be delineated in various ways. Illustrations A and B in Figure 11.25 show the basic appearance of a door with and without surface materials—wood grain in this instance. Illustration C shows the final configuration of a dimensioned door. Note that the 6'–8" dimension is measured from the

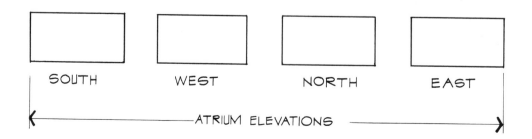

Figure 11.24 Simplified elevation titles.

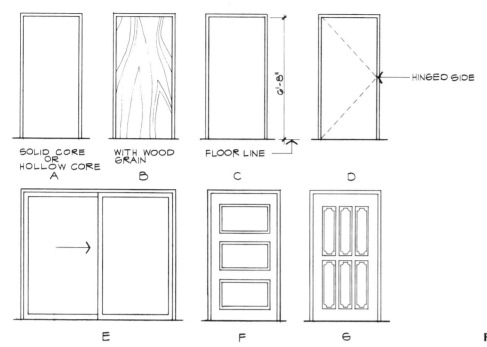

Figure 11.25 Doors in elevation.

floor line to the top of the door. The other line around the door represents the trim. For precise dimensions for the trim, consult the door details. Illustrations D and E of Figure 11.25 show how a door opens or slides. Panel doors are shown in illustration F, while plant-on doors (doors with decorative pieces attached) are shown in illustration G.

Windows

Windows are drafted much like doors. Their shape, their operation, and the direction in which they open are represented. Double-hung windows and louver windows are obvious exceptions because of their operation. See Figure 11.26.

On the double-hung and the sliding windows, one portion of the window is shown in its entirety while the moving section shows only three sides of the window. Using the sliding window as an example, the right side of the window shows all four sides because it is on the outside. The left section shows only three sides because the fourth is behind the right section.

Fixed Windows. If the window is fixed (non-opening), as shown in Figure 11.27, you must know if the window is to be shop made (manufactured ahead of time) or

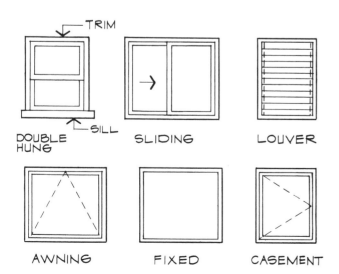

Figure 11.26 Windows in elevation.

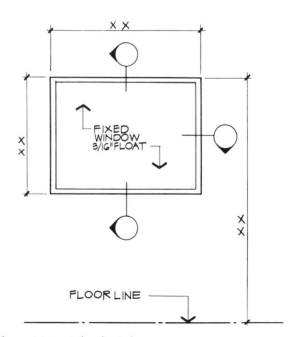

Figure 11.27 A fixed window.

constructed on the job. If the frame can be ordered—in aluminum, for example—treat it like other manufactured windows and include it in the window schedule. If the window is to be job made (made on the site), provide all the necessary information about the window on the window schedule or exterior elevations as shown in Figure 11.28. However, keep all this information in one place for consistency and uniformity.

Referencing Doors and Windows

Reference doors and windows with bubbles. Bubbles can refer to details or to a schedule for size. See Figure 11.28. If, for some reason, there are no schedules or details for a set of drawings, all information pertaining to the windows or doors will be on the exterior elevations near or on the windows and doors. See Figure 11.27.

Material Designations

Describing the Materials

The exterior elevations also describe the exterior wall surface material. For a wood structure, describe both the surface covering and any backing material. **Wood siding,** for example, is described with the backing behind it. See Figure 11.29.

In some cases, one word, such as "stucco," describes the surface adequately unless a special pattern is to be applied. Here, the draftsperson assumes that the contractor understands that the word "stucco" implies building paper (black waterproof paper) mesh (hexagonal woven wire), and three coats of exterior plaster. Often a more detailed description of the material is found in the specifications.

Even if the complete wall is made up of one material such as concrete block (as opposed to a built-up system

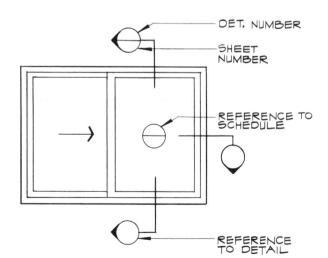

Figure 11.28 Referencing doors and windows.

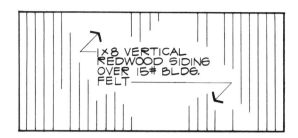

Figure 11.29 Wood siding in elevation.

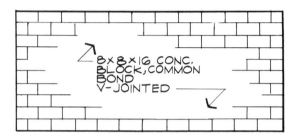

Figure 11.30 Concrete block in elevation.

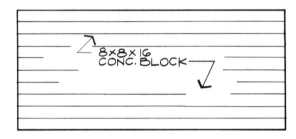

Figure 11.31 Abbreviated concrete block pattern.

as in wood construction) describe the surface. See Figure 11.30.

Drawing the Materials

In both Figures 11.29 and 11.30 a facsimile of the material is shown. The material represented does not fill the complete area but is shown in detail around the perimeter only, which saves production time. Figure 11.31 shows more of the area covered with the surface material but in a slightly more abstract manner. Another method is to draft the surface accurately and erase areas for notes.

Figure 11.32 shows other materials as they might appear in an exterior elevation. These are only suggestions. Scale and office practice dictate the final technique. See Figure 11.33.

Eliminating Unnecessary Information

Because exterior elevations are vital in the construction document process, unnecessary information should be eliminated. Shades and shadows, cars, bushes and trees, people and flowers add to the looks of the drawings *but* serve no purpose here.

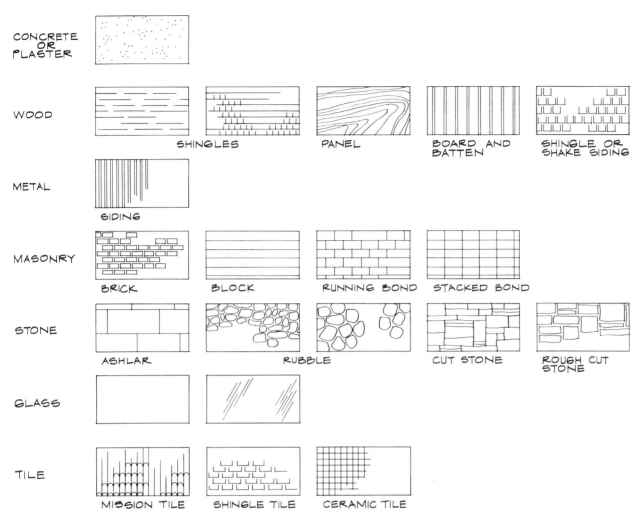

Figure 11.32 Material designations.

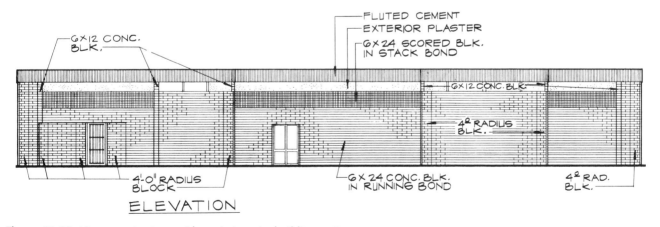

Figure 11.33 Masonry structure with variations in building patterns.

Notes

Order of Notes

Notes on elevations follow the same rules as notes on other drawings. The size of the object is first, then the name of the material, and then any additional information about spacing, quantity, or methods of installation. For example,

1″ × 8″ redwood siding over 15# (15 lb) building felt

OR

Cement plaster over concrete block

OR

Built-up composition gravel roof

OR

1″ × 6″ let-in bracing

In the second example, there are no specific sizes needed, so the generic name comes first in the note.

Noting Practices

Noting practices vary from job to job. A set of written specifications is often provided with the construction documents. Wall material on a set of elevations may be described in broad, generic terms such as "concrete block" when the specific size, finish, stacking procedure, and type of joint are covered in the specifications.

If there are differences between the construction documents and the specifications, the specifications have priority. In the construction documents, often the same material note can be found more than once. If an error is made or a change is desired, many notes must be revised. In the specifications, where it is mentioned once, only a single change has to be made.

There are exceptions. When there are complicated changes and variations of material and patterns on an elevation, it is difficult to describe them in the specifications. In this case, the information should be located on the exterior elevations. See Figure 11.33.

Dotted Lines

Doors and Windows

Dotted lines are used on doors and windows to show how they operate. See illustration D of Figure 11.25 and the awning and casement windows in Figure 11.26. These dotted lines show which part of the door or window is hinged. See Figure 11.34. Not all offices like to show this on an elevation. One reason is that the direction the door swings is shown on the floor plan and therefore does not need to be indicated on the elevations.

Foundations

At times you may have to delineate the foundation on the elevations in order to explain the foundation better. Dotted lines are used in various ways relating to the foundation. Dotted lines (center-line type lines are also used) show the top of a slab as in Figure 11.35. They are used to show the elevation of the footings. See Figure

11.36 for elevations of a two-pour footing and a one-pour footing.

Dotted lines are also used to describe a **stepped footing.** When the property slopes, the minimum depth of the footing can be maintained by stepping the footing down the slope. See Figure 11.37.

Structural Features

Structural features below the grade can be shown by dotted lines if this helps to explain the structure. See Figure 11.38. Dotted lines can also be used to help show structural elements of the building. In Figure 11.10, center-line type lines (which can also be used) show **let-in braces** (structural angular braces in a wall). (The plate line is the top of the two horizontal members at the top of the wall, called **top plates.**) In Figure 11.35, dotted lines show the top of the roof, which slopes for drainage, and a pilaster (a widening of the wall for a beam) and beam (here, a laminated beam called a Glulam).

As with doors and windows, the footing on an elevation can be referenced to the foundation plan, details, and cross sections. The system is the same. Reference bubbles are used. See Figure 11.39.

Whatever the feature, the dotted line is used for clarity and communication. How can you keep the message clear for construction purposes? How can you communicate this best on the drawings?

Controlling Factors

Each type of construction has unique restrictive features that you need to know about to effectively interpret the transition from design elevations to production of exterior elevations in the construction documents.

Wood Frame Structures

With wood frame structures, elevations are usually dictated by plate line heights. The **plate height** is measured from the floor to the top of the two top plates. See Figure 11.8. Efficient use of material is dictated by this dimension because studs are available in certain lengths and sheathing usually comes in 4′ × 8′ sheets.

Floor, Plate, and Grade Lines. When the floor elevations and plate heights are established, the first thing to draw is the floor line and its relationship to the grade. Next, draw the plate line. If the structure is of post and beam construction, measure from the floor line to the bottom of the beam. Some offices prefer these dimensions on the building sections.

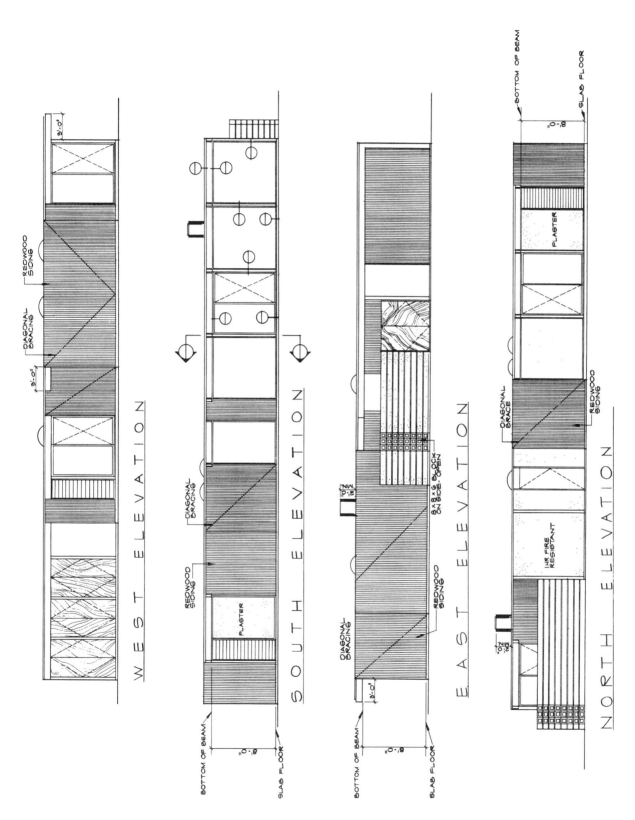

Figure 11.34 Elevation in wood.

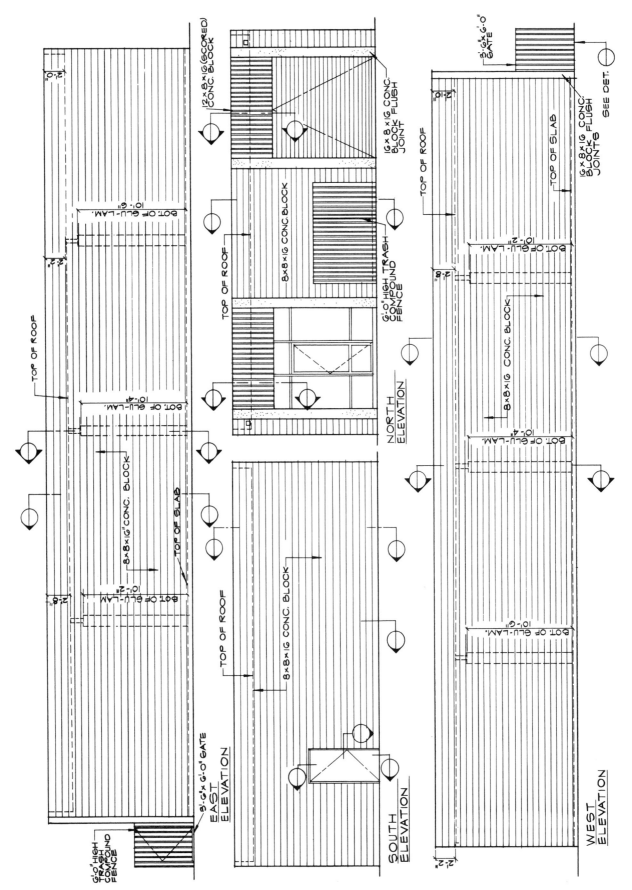

Figure 11.35 Elevation in masonry.

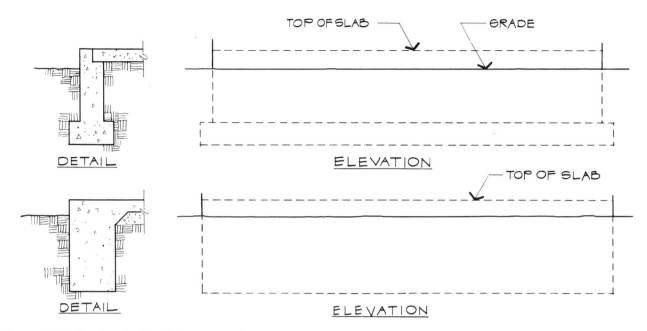

Figure 11.36 Showing the foundation on an elevation.

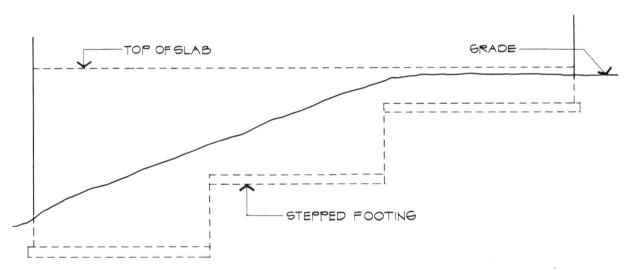

Figure 11.37 Stepped footings in elevation.

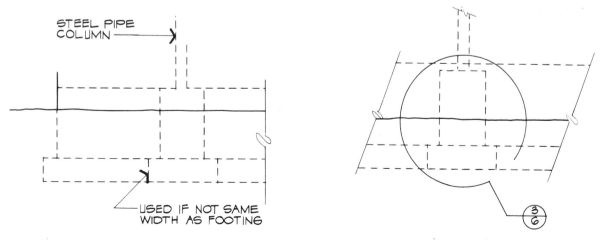

Figure 11.38 Structural features below grade.

Figure 11.39 Referencing hidden lines.

Find the distance between the floor line and the grade line from the grading plan, foundation plan, footing details, and building sections. If the lot is relatively flat, just draw a grade line with the floor line measured above it and the plate line height above the floor as a start. If the site is not flat, carefully plot the grade line from the grading plan, foundation plan, and details or the site plan.

Some site plans, grading plans, and foundation plans indicate the grade height, marked F.G. (finished grade), in relation to the structure at various points around the structure. In Figure 11.40, the grade line is figured by making a grid where the horizontal lines show grade heights and vertical lines are projected down from the structure. Once this grade line is established, the top of the slab—that is, the floor line—is drawn. The plate line is then measured from the floor line. There is no need to measure the distance between the grade and the floor line. See Figure 11.41.

Masonry Structures

Masonry structures such as brick or concrete block must be approached differently. The deciding factor here is

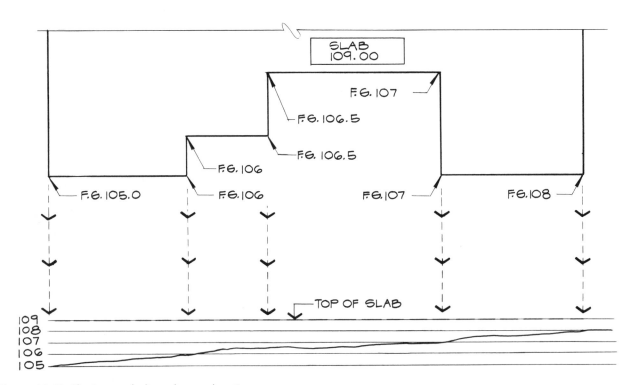

Figure 11.40 Plotting grade lines for an elevation.

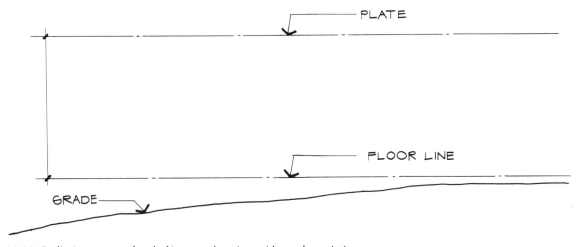

Figure 11.41 Preliminary steps for drafting an elevation with grade variation.

the size of the concrete block or brick, the pattern, the thickness of the joint, and the placement of the first row in relationship to the floor. Unlike wood, which can be cut in varying heights, masonry units are difficult to cut, so cutting is minimized. As Figure 11.33 shows, dimensions of the masonry areas are kept to a minimum. Refer to the discussion of noting, earlier in this chapter, for suggested practices and sample illustrations.

Steel Structures

Structures where the main members are steel and the secondary members are, for example, wood, are treated differently from wood structures or masonry. The configuration is arrived at in the same way and representation of material is the same, but dimensioning is completely different.

In a wood frame structure, the lumber can be cut to size on the job. In masonry, the size of the masonry units often dictates such things as the location of windows and doors, the modular height, and so on. Some of the controlling factors in steel construction are: the size of the structural members; the required ceiling heights; and the **plenum** area (the space necessary to accommodate the mechanical equipment and duct work). See Figure 11.42.

Drawing an exterior elevation for a steel structure is a relatively simple task. Usually, the floor elevations on a multistory structure of steel are established by the designer. The building section usually provides the necessary height requirements. See Figure 11.42. Figure 11.43 is a checklist for exterior elevations.

Drafting an Exterior Elevation

The drafting of an exterior elevation is a straightforward procedure, because most of the structural and shape descriptions have been completed by the time it is drafted: the shape of the roof, the size of the site component parts, the shape and size of the foundation, and all of its vertical heights were determined when drafting the building section. For a small structure, such as those contained in this book, we believe it is the easiest drawing to accomplish.

The drafter can use any or all of the shortcuts described in Chapter 10, on building sections, namely, the use of acetate templates or, in this case, a reduction of the building section (or a portion thereof) itself as an underlay drawing.

Because exterior elevations are drafted at the same scale as the floor plan, a diazo copy of the floor plan can be positioned under the plate line and floor line to position the walls. See Figure 11.44.

Guide to Dimensioning

Do not dimension anything on the exterior elevation that has been dimensioned elsewhere. For example, the distance between the floor line and the plate line is dimensioned on the building section and should not be repeated on the exterior elevation. In contrast, windows have been described (width and height) on the schedule,

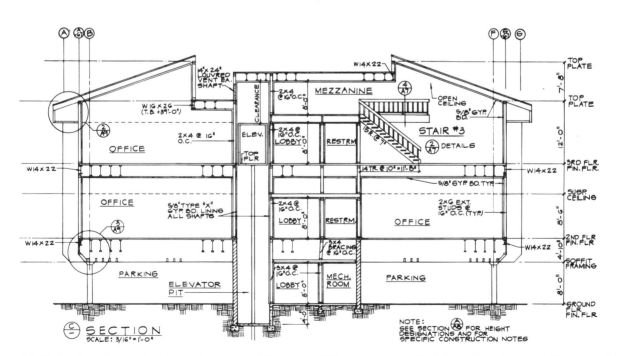

Figure 11.42 Section of a steel and wood structure. (Courtesy of Westmount, Inc., Real Estate Development, Torrance, CA.)

EXTERIOR ELEVATIONS

1. Natural grade
2. Finish grade
3. Floor elevations
4. Foundation (hidden lines)
   a. Bottom of footing
   b. Top of foundation (stepped footing)
   c. Detail reference
5. Walls
   a. Material
      (1) Wood
      (2) Stucco
      (3) Aluminum
      (4) Other
   b. Solid sheathing
      (1) Plywood
      (2) 1 × 6 diagonal
      (3) Other
   c. Diagonal bracing (hidden lines)
      (1) Cut-in
      (2) Let-in
6. Openings
   a. Heights
      (1) Door and window min. 6' -8"
      (2) Post and beam special
   b. Doors
      (1) Type
      (2) Material
      (3) Glass
      (4) Detail reference
      (5) Key to schedule
   c. Windows
      (1) Type

      (2) Material
      (3) Glass—obscure for baths
      (4) Detail reference
      (5) Key to schedule
   d. Moulding, casing and sill
   e. Flashing (gauge used)
7. Roof
   a. Materials
      (1) Built-up composition, gravel
      (2) Asphalt shingles
      (3) Wood shingles or shake
      (4) Metal-terne-aluminum
      (5) Clay and ceramic tile
      (6) Concrete
   b. Other
8. Ground slopage
9. Attic and sub floor vents
10 Vertical dimensions from floor to plate
11. Window, door fascia, etc. detail references
12. Roof slope ratio
13. Railings, note height
14. Stairs
15. Note all wall materials
16. Types of fixed glass and thicknesses
17. Window and door swing indications
18. Window and door heights from floor
19. Gutters and downspouts
20. Overflow scuppers at parapets
21. Mail slot
22. Stepped foundation footings—if occur
23. Dimension chimney above roof

Figure 11.43 Exterior Elevations Checklist

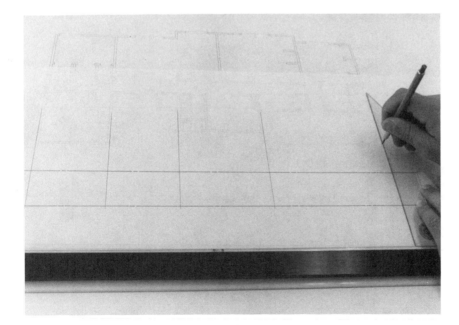

Figure 11.44 Using the floor plan as a base for the exterior elevation.

yet their positions in relation to the floor line have not. This makes the exterior elevation an ideal place to dimension these positions, as well as architectural features such as signage on a commercial building.

Descriptions

Anything that can be described better by drawing should be drawn, and anything that would be better as a written

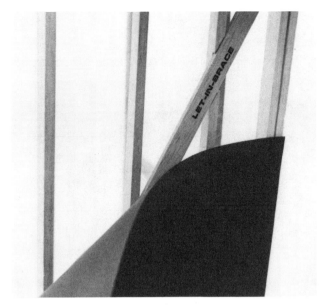

Figure 11.45 Revealing let-in brace.

description should be included in the specifications. Noting should use generic terms. It would be sufficient to label the exterior covering (called skin) "redwood siding" or "stucco" (exterior plaster), rather than describing the quality of the siding or the number of coats and quality of the stucco.

Concerns

Compare the exterior elevation to the human body. In both instances the outside cover is called the skin. Directly below the skin is the muscle. The muscle might be comparable to the substructure that strengthens a structure, such as metal straps, let-in braces, and shear panels. See Figure 11.45. The purpose of these members is to resist outside forces such as wind, hurricane, and earthquake. Our skeleton might parallel the "bone structure" of a building, which is in the form of a network of wood pieces called studs.

The exterior elevation addresses the "skin and muscle," and the building section emphasizes the skeletal form.

Use of Hidden Lines

Hidden lines are used on an exterior elevation to reveal structural members behind the surface. See Figure 11.35. Notice, in this figure, the used of hidden lines to show the slope of the roof, the pilaster, the hinged side of doors and windows, and, in Figure 11.34 to show diagonal bracing.

Now look at Figure 11.46. The outline of a gable roof (roof plan) is translated into elevations. Notice that in the front view the small bend in the roof at the top-right corner does not show, whereas in the rear view the

entire shape is shown and the right side view shows only a single roof but nothing behind it. All hidden roof lines are not shown.

Pictorial vs. Written Description

It often takes a combination of a drawing and a generic description to describe a material used for covering the outer surface of a structure. For example, a series of horizontal lines are used to describe siding, a row of masonry units, or possibly a texture pattern on exterior plaster.

The preliminary East elevation of the Ryan Residence shown in Figure 5.13 has been redrawn in Figure 11.47, showing an example of horizontal siding as a finish. Wood siding as shown here can be applied in two ways: first, with individual pieces of (possibly) redwood over solid sheathing and a waterproof membrane, or second, in sheet form. Sheets of simulated horizontal siding may be purchased in 16'–0" lengths that are preprimed with paint. See Figure 11.48.

Material Designation

The designation of material on the surface of the elevation will be done with a template called Burnish-On, distributed by the Alvin Company. These high-impact templates are available in a variety of scales and textures, among which are stone, cedar shake, brick, and river rock. The material designations are shown in the plan as well as in the elevational view.

As shown in Figure 11.49(A), the template is placed under the vellum and burnished with a sharp pencil, as

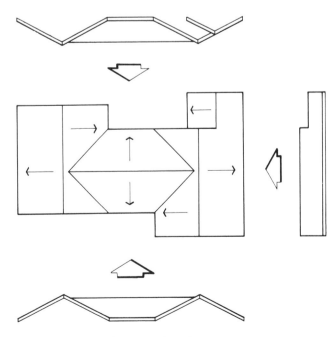

Figure 11.46 Visualizing roof in elevation.

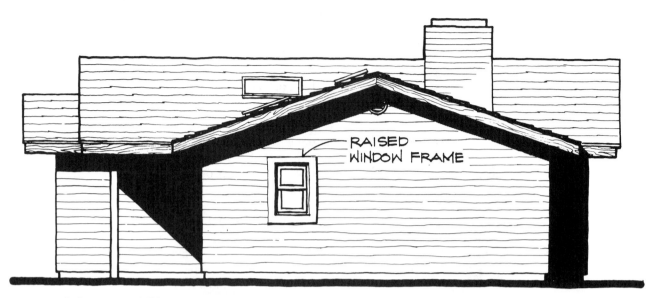

RAISED
WINDOW FRAME

EAST ELEVATION

RYAN RESIDENCE

Figure 11.47 Preliminary exterior elevation.

A

Figure 11.48 Hardboard siding.

you would do to tracing paper over a coin to reveal the pattern beneath. Even if the texture goes beyond the limit of the border, it can easily be removed with an eraser and the border of the material redrawn when profiling, as was done in Figure 11.49(B). The patterns are better placed on the back side of the vellum if a diazo print is to be used, and on the top side if photographic or plain paper copies are made.

If CAD drafting is used, you will find that most of these patterns already exist in the library of many of the programs. These can be rapidly employed by setting borders, selecting patterns, and allowing the computer to do the rest.

B

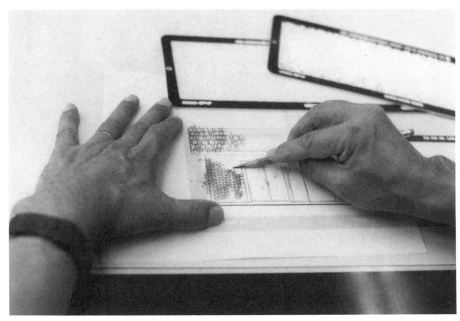

A   ADDING TEXTURE

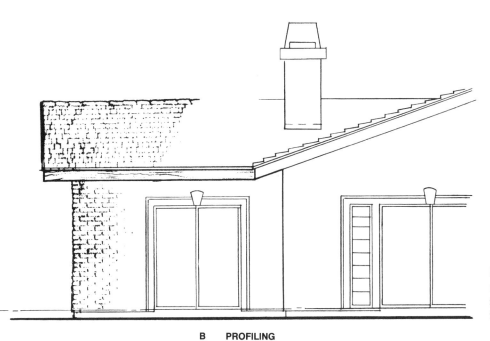

B   PROFILING

Figure 11.49 Using template for material designation. (With permission from Alvin Company, distributor of Burnish-On templates.)

Weatherproofing

Weatherproofing a structure basically means keeping out wind, rain, and ultraviolet rays (UVR) of the sun. UVR reduction is necessary because these rays are harmful to our skin and will fade the color from drapery, furniture, and carpets. The solution is rather simple in a residence. Large overhangs on roofs can eliminate these harmful rays, as can the newly developed high-performance glass used in windows.

Windows and doors are now made, or can be retrofitted, with weatherstripping. This keeps the structure energy efficient and prevents dust from entering the structure as a result of driving winds. The selection of the type of window or door for wind control is addressed in Chapter 14 in the section on window detailing. The present discussion focuses mainly on wind and rain, with an emphasis on water control.

As you may have learned in a science course, the structure of water is different in its various phases: solid, liquid, and vapor. Therefore, a variety of materials are used to combat the migration of moisture from the outside to the inside of structures.

Generally, a cover is placed over the structure (especially the walls) much like a raincoat on a human.

Yet, depending on the material of the raincoat, the wearer's body heat, the temperature of the air, and especially the humidity (moisture in the air), the inside surface of the raincoat will react differently. So it is with buildings. Building do perspire. Consider the following scenario: Driven by wind, moisture migrates from the outside to the inside of a structure in the form of vapor. This moisture changes its state through condensation because of temperature change and is unable to leave the inside of the wall. As night approaches the temperature drops drastically, and the moisture now expands as it becomes a solid (ice). If moisture happens to be inside the wood or insulation within the wall, it can cause terrible deterioration and damage. Had a vapor barrier been used, moisture might come from the inside of the structure and condense along this membrane as it tried to escape.

Solution to Condensation

A solution to condensation in the attic and underfloor space in a wood floor system can easily be achieved by proper ventilation and recirculation of the air. This is done with small openings through which venting can take place, using the wind as an ally, or the air can be recirculated mechanically, as is often done for bathroom ventilation.

Figure 11.50 is a map of the United States. Notice how it is divided into three major zones. Zone A experiences severe damage to structures as a result of condensation. Zone B experiences moderate damage, whereas the damage in Zone C is slight to almost none. This does not mean that there will never be moderate-to-

severe damage in mountainous areas in Zone C; rather, this is a more generalized look at large geographic areas. Therefore, the drafter must be aware that a building in Southern California will *not* be dealt with in the same way as a building in the Dakotas, nor can a building in southern Texas be treated the same as one in Colorado.

Waterproofing

Waterproofing can be achieved in four ways:

1. The use of admixtures that render concrete impermeable.
2. Hydrolithically: this is done by applying a coat of asphalt or plastic to a surface, making it waterproof.
3. Chemically: a specially formulated paint is applied to a basically porous surface such as concrete. Upon contact with water this chemical explodes into crystals, sealing the pores. Such products are used more often for a retro-fix.
4. The use of a membrane. Older houses used bituminous-saturated felts (called building felts), which have recently been replaced with asphalt-saturated kraft paper.

For a structure in Zone A, you may wish to select a material that will keep the colder side of the wall wind resistant and airtight and require that the material be a vapor retarder. On the warm side of the wall, you might wish to stop the migration of moisture into the wall by using a foil-backed lath product. There are a number of products on the market today which can be specified by the project architect, including a vapor-proof mem-

ZONE A—Severe

Zone B—Moderate

Zone C—None to Slight

Figure 11.50 U.S. condensation hazard zones.

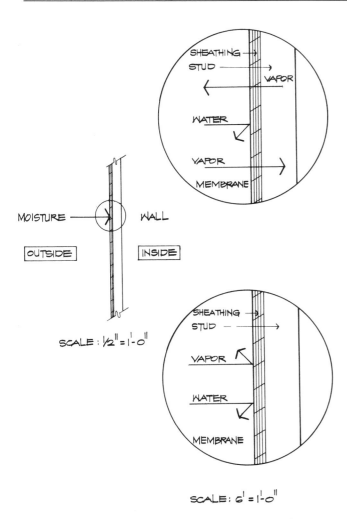

Figure 11.51 Breathing membranes and vapor membranes.

brane, a membrane that can breathe, and a self-sealing membrane for ice and water, as shown in Figure 11.51.

A drafter must know what is being used to properly ensure that he or she uses the correct convention and notation for drawings and details.

Counterflashing

Anytime you break the surface of a waterproof membrane, whether it is plastic or paper, a second sheet (usually of heavier weight) is used. This sheet, called counterflashing, is found around openings and at the ends of the membrane, inasmuch as these are the places most likely to leak. In Zone C, for example, where asphalt-saturated (grade D) kraft paper is often used, a heavier-grade band of kraft paper, called sisal-kraft, is used. In other instances, a strip of self-sealing vapor membrane may be used around the opening. In either case it should be done carefully so as to shed water; lapping and overlapping so as to let gravity take its natural course and help us eliminate moisture. See the section on window detailing in Chapter 14 for a discus-

sion on how the overlapping and installation sequence is performed and shown in detail by the drafter.

Evolution of Ryan Elevations

The Ryan Residence exterior skin will be stucco. A three-coat system will be used, which includes an initial coat called "scratch," a second coat called "brown," and a thin final coat called a finished "color coat." If raised portions made of wood are to be used, they will be installed prior to the three coats of exterior plaster (stucco). If Styrofoam is used to raise portions of the wall surface, two coats of plaster are placed first; then the foam and the final coat (color coat) is placed over the entire ensemble. See Chapter 14 for the method of installing these raised window and door frames in relation to the building paper and the placement of the stucco. The roof is gabled with vents in the gable end, which is called the rake.

STAGE I (Figure 11.52). The procedure outlined at the beginning of this chapter in Figures 11.9A through 11.9E should be followed to establish the basic shape of the Ryan Residence. As seen in the drawing (Figure 11.52), Stage I, two horizontal centerlines were established first. These represent the plate line and the floor line, around which the basic shape is drawn. The beginning and end points of the wall are constructed, and the pitch is measured from the intersection of these wall lines and the plate line. Once the pitch has been established, the drafter gives the roof thickness. The drafter obtains the roof thickness via the rafter size and the outline of the roof's shape from the roof plan.

STAGE II (Figure 11.53). The drawing that was initially laid out lightly or drawn with a fade-away blue pencil is now hard-lined. It will go through one more stage of hard-lining during the profiling stage. Window and door locations are obtained from the floor plan, and the openings are defined.

STAGE III (Figure 11.54). At this stage, many things have transpired. The material designation for the roof has been drawn. Notice how the drafter indicated the roof material on the outside edge of the roof. This serves two purposes: to save time and to profile the roof. Next, the outline of the chimney has been located, the chimney extending 2'–0" above the highest point within a 10'–0" radius, with the dotted lines representing flashing. Finally, the material designation for wood has been placed on the fascia and the beam that supports the roof at the entry.

The finished configuration for the windows and doors have also been drawn at this stage. This includes any changes requested by the client or the firm's design

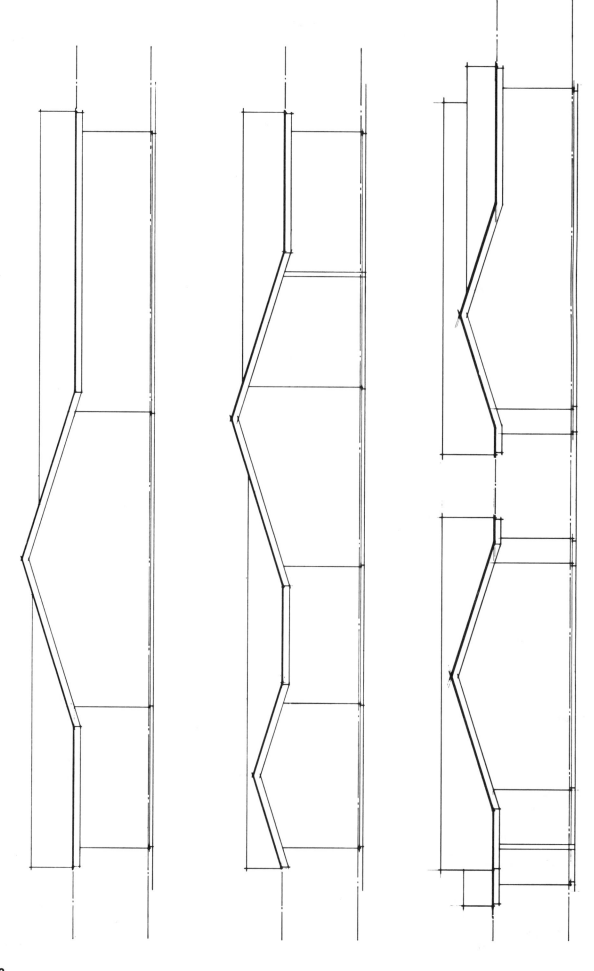

Figure 11.52 Exterior elevations—Stage I.

278

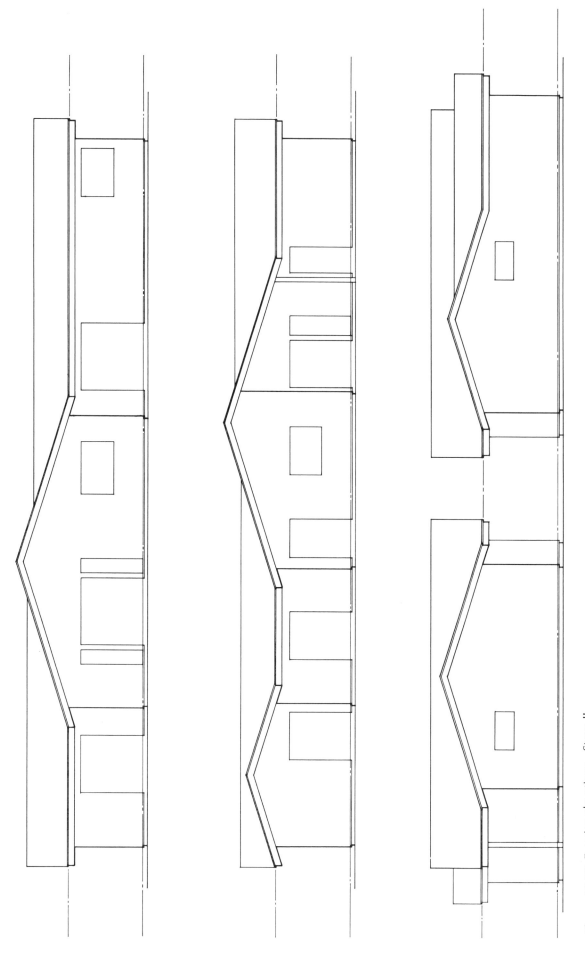

Figure 11.53 Exterior elevations—Stage II.

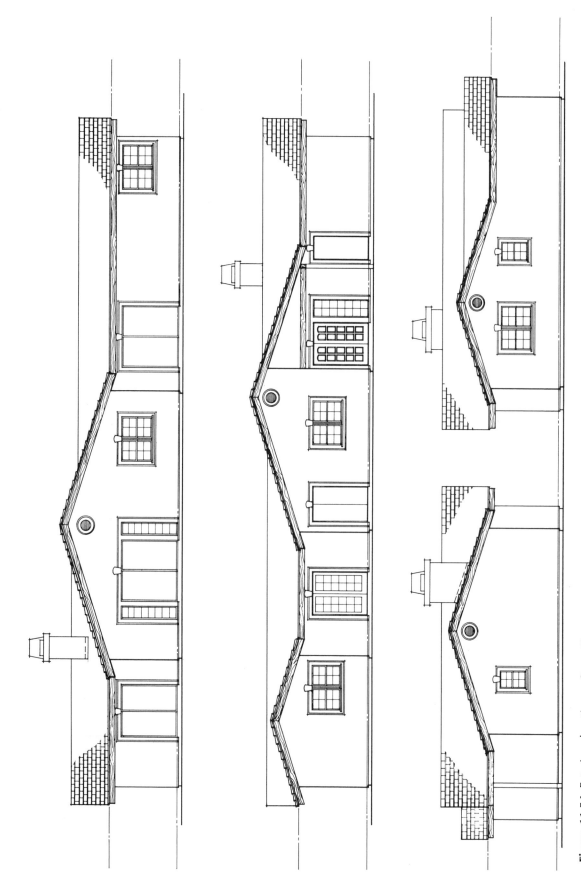

Figure 11.54 Exterior elevations—Stage III.

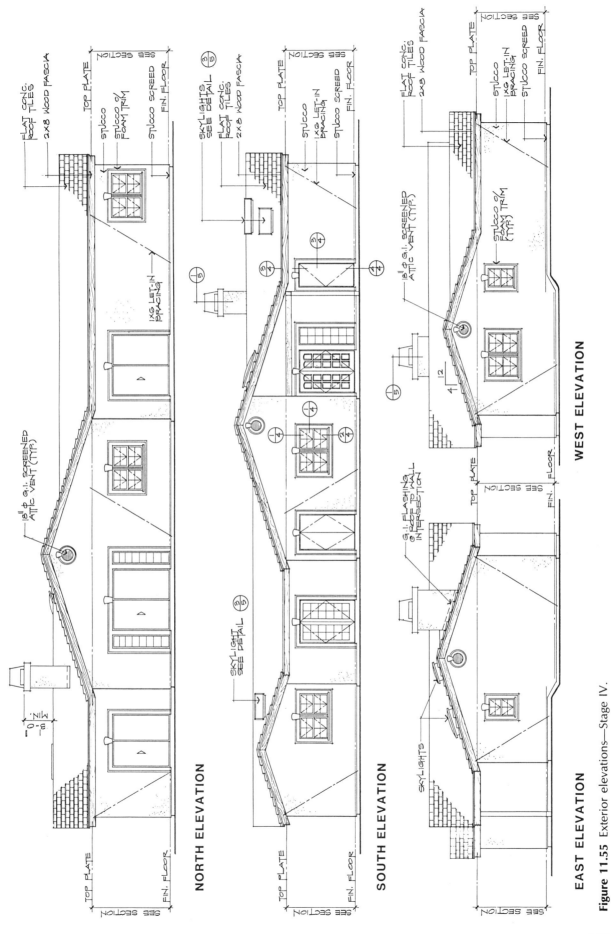

Figure 11.55 Exterior elevations—Stage IV.

division. In this case the raised wood frames around the windows and doors have been reduced in width, and a keystone form placed on the tops. A keystone form may be included on the vent, which will be dealt with at the next stage. A remark to this effect might be placed in the left margin of the drawing sheet as a reminder for the drafter to check on its inclusion.

If the project manager fails to inform the drafter about the final disposition of the vent keystone, the drafter can take the initiative and follow through. Through such action, a drafter can stay on top of the project and become a dependable and valuable asset to the firm.

In comparing this stage with the previous stage you will notice that additional hard-lining has taken place.

STAGE IV (Figure 11.55). This is the dimensioning, noting, and referencing stage. It is also the stage at which some items, required but held up for owner approval, were drawn. A keystone form for the vent is a carry-over from the previous stage, as is the location and positioning of the skylights. These are now included. Notice the dimensioning procedure used on the exterior elevation. The floor-to-plate lines refer to the building section and roof pitch expressed as a ratio; the chimney as minimum clearances.

Referencing

Referencing is the process of referring a specific area to an enlarged detail. Thus, the top half of the reference bubble indicates the name of the detail, and the bottom number indicates the sheet on which the particular detail can be found. Had this been a complete set with details of all conditions, you would see detail reference bubbles around all windows, doors, beam connections, and so on.

Noting

Whenever possible, noting was done outside the elevation within the right margin. You cannot fit all of the notes in one place without having to use long leaders pointing to the subject. Therefore, certain notes were made inside the elevation to reduce the length of the leaders. A good rule of thumb in regard to leaders is not to allow them to cross more than one object line, never cross a dimension line, and keep the leader length to a minimum.

Keynoting is used by many offices. This is a procedure of numbering and placement of all of the notes on one side (usually the right). You then place a leader in the desired location and, rather than placing the note at the end of the leader, you use a reference bubble that refers to the correct note. A detail used to show the keynoting procedure can be seen in Figure 14.34.

Keynoting can be done with either hand-drafted or CAD-drafted elevations. If computers are not available in an office, keynoting can still be done by word processing and positioned on the sheet with adhesives.

The advantage of keynoting is the standardization of the notes. Keynoting also allows the drafter to make direct references to the specification numbers right on the notes. Numbering systems recommended by the American Institute of Architects are similar to the numbering system used by our libraries and can be incorporated here.

SUMMARY

Exterior elevations cannot be drawn independently of other drawings. They depend on the cross-sections for height, the floor plan for widths, the roof or roof framing plan for the configuration of the roof, and the foundation plan and its details for shapes under the grade. The scale and position of the exterior elevations on the drawing surface are mainly decided by the size of the structure and the size needed to convey important features. The shape of the plan and the basic materials used determine your final approach, and the purpose determines the type of information needed. With wood, floor lines and plate lines are critical for dimensioning. With masonry, the size of the masonry units dictates the possible dimensions. With steel, exterior elevations have the floor heights established by the architect or structural engineer.

IMPORTANT TERMS AND CONCEPTS

Exterior elevations
Direct projection
Dimensional layout
Eave
Pivot point
Key plan

Wood siding
Stepped footing
Let-in braces
Top plate
Plate height
Plenum

REVIEW QUESTIONS

1. How is the floor plan used in drafting exterior elevations?
2. Why is the building section so important in drafting exterior elevations?
3. What determines the correct scale for a set of exterior elevations?
4. What is a key plan? How is it used?
5. What is the purpose of dotted lines on windows and doors?
6. Apart from windows and doors, how and why are dotted lines used?
7. What is the plate line? Where is it measured?

LABORATORY PROBLEMS

1. Find any photographs or drawings of an exterior of a structure and sketch (freehand) a preliminary exterior elevation.
2. From a preliminary exterior elevation (the one described in Problem 1 can be used), construct a finished drafted exterior elevation. Include dimensions and notes.
3. Select a drafted exterior elevation of a wood structure and convert the system to a masonry wall with a wood roof system. Draft a new set of elevations for masonry.
4. Select an irregularly shaped structure from a magazine and sketch a set of exterior elevations for it.
5. Draw a wall section of a corner of a structure. Overlay a piece of tracing paper and convert the wall section into a partial elevation.

12

ROOF PLAN AND FRAMING SYSTEMS

12

PREVIEW

Two different methods are used to illustrate ceiling, floor, and roof framing members. One method shows all the ceiling, floor, and roof framing members directly on the finished floor plan. Another provides separate floor and roof framing plans, which differ for wood, steel, and materials in combination. Roof plans are sequentially developed, giving the reader a full understanding of the procedures.

OBJECTIVES

1. Understand which of the two methods is more logical for a given project.
2. Know how each method is shown in a drawing.
3. Understand the necessity of developing a geometrically correct roof plan.
4. Understand different framing systems and approaches.

Methods of Representation

There are two main ways to represent floor, ceiling, and roof framing members as part of construction documents: drawing framing members on the floor plan and drawing them separately.

Drawing Framing Members on the Floor Plan

This first method illustrates and notes ceiling and/or floor framing members directly onto the finished floor plan. It is a good method to use when the framing conditions are simple and do not require many notes and reference

symbols that might be confused with the other finished floor plan information.

Figure 12.1 shows the lower floor plan of a two-story residence. This plan contains all the information and symbols needed; no separate drawing of the ceiling framing members is required. Note how the ceiling joist size, spacing, and direction are illustrated in bedroom #1 and the study. Note also the use of broken lines to represent exposed ceiling beams in the master bedroom. As you can see, if a great deal more framing information were required, the drawing would lose its clarity.

The upper floor plan of this residence designates ceiling joist sizes, spacing, and direction, as well as roof

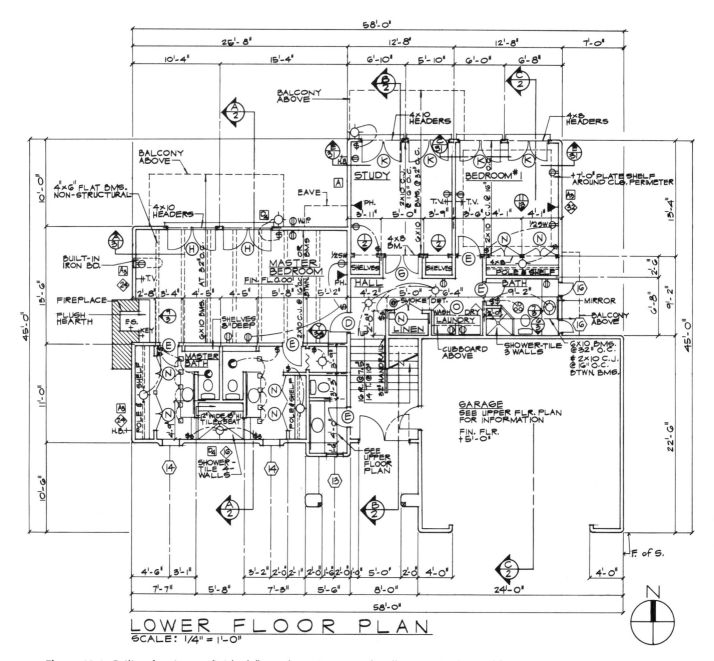

Figure 12.1 Ceiling framing on finished floor plan. (Courtesy of William F. Smith—Builder.)

framing information such as rafter sizes, spacing, and direction; ridge beam size; and the size and spacing of exposed rafter beams in the living room. See Figure 12.2A. **Headers** and beams for framing support over openings are also shown in this figure. If you are using this method to show framing members, you can delineate beams with two broken lines at the approximate scale of the beam or with a heavy broken line.

The structural design of beams and footings is calculated by finding the total loads that are distributed to any specific member. This total load is found by computing the tributary area affecting that member. Figure 12.2B illustrates a cross-section showing the various tributary areas which accumulate loads to the ridgebeam, floor beam, and foundation pier.

Drawing Framing Members Separately

The second way to show ceiling, floor, and roof framing members is to provide a separate drawing that may be titled "ceiling framing," "floor framing," or "roof framing." You might choose this method because the framing is complex or because construction document procedures require it.

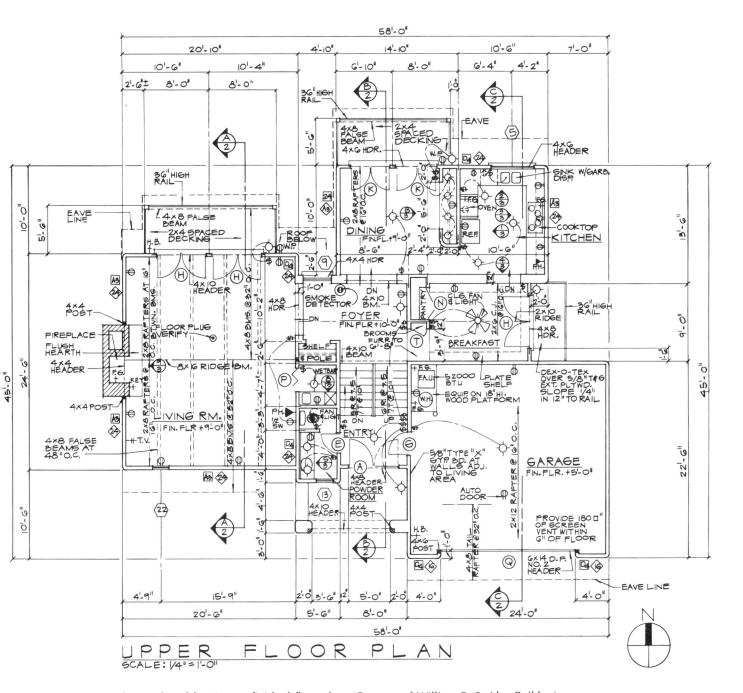

Figure 12.2A Ceiling and roof framing on finished floor plan. (Courtesy of William F. Smith—Builder.)

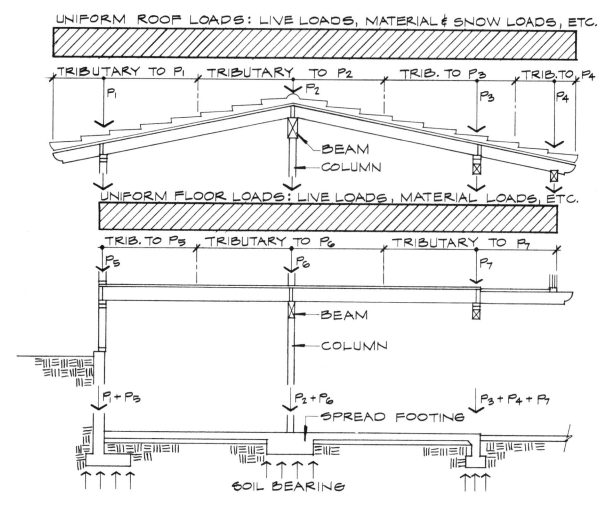

Figure 12.2B Tributary loading section.

The first step is the same as that of the foundation plan's. Lay a piece of tracing paper directly over the floor plan tracing. Trace all the walls, windows, and door openings. The line quality of your tracing should be only dark enough to make these lines distinguishable after you have reproduced the tracing. In this way, the final drawing, showing all the framing members, can be drawn with darker lines like a finished drawing. This provides the viewer with clear framing members, while the walls are just lightly drawn for reference.

Another way to provide a basis for a framing plan is to reproduce the floor plan from the initial line drawing with a mylar or sepia print. By doing this, you can print the floor plan drawing when only the walls and openings have been established. Later, when you are prepared for framing plans, you can go back to these prints and incorporate all the required information to complete the framing plan.

Figure 12.3 shows the floor plan of the first floor of a two-story, wood-framed residence with all the framing members required to support the second floor and ceiling directly above this level. Because the second floor

framing and ceiling for the first floor are the same, this drawing is titled "Upper Floor Framing Plan."

First draft in all the floor beams, columns, and headers for all the various openings. Then incorporate the location and span direction of all the floor joists into the drawing. In Figure 12.3, the floor joist locations and span directions are shown with a single line and arrowhead at each end of the line. This is one way to designate these members. Another method is shown later when the roof framing plan is discussed.

Dimensioning for framing plans mainly applies to beam and column locations. Provide dimensioning for all floor beams and columns located directly under load-bearing members. These members, such as walls and columns, are located on the second floor. Dimensioning for these members is similar to that on a floor plan. When you have finished the drawing, provide the required notes for all the members included in the drawing.

Drawing the ceiling plan for the second floor level involves only the immediate ceiling framing members. See Figure 12.4. This drawing deals only with headers

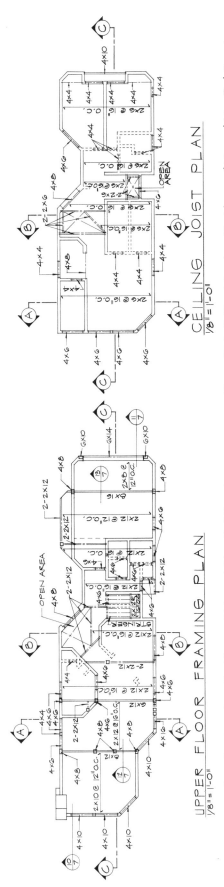

Figure 12.3 Upper floor framing plan. (Residence of Mr. and Mrs. Ted Bear.)

Figure 12.4 Ceiling joist plan. (Residence of Mr. and Mrs. Ted Bear.)

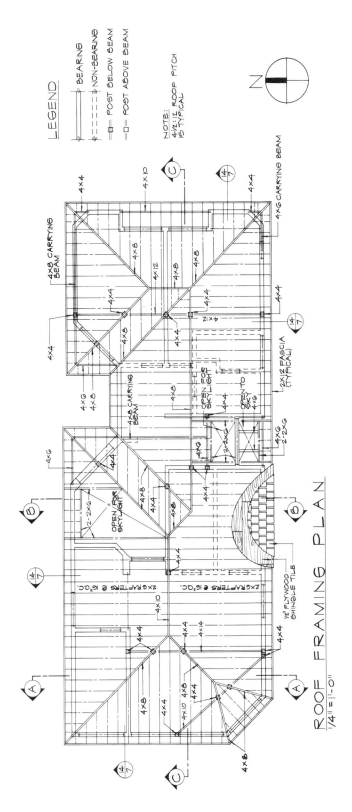

Figure 12.5 Roof framing plan. (Residence of Mr. and Mrs. Ted Bear.)

over openings and with ceiling joist location, span, direction, size, and spacing for a specific ceiling area. Where applicable, notes and dimensioning are shown as in Figure 12.3.

The final framing plan for this project is the roof framing plan. See Figure 12.5. As mentioned previously, another way to show framing members is to draw in all the members that apply to that particular drawing. This obviously takes more time to draw but is clearer for the viewer.

Framing with Different Materials

Framing Plan: Wood Members

When wood structures have members spaced anywhere from 16" to 48" on centers, show them with a single line broken at intervals. Figure 12.5 shows the roof framing plan for this residence incorporating all the individual rafters, ridges, **hip rafters** (the members that bisect the angle of two intersecting walls), and supporting columns

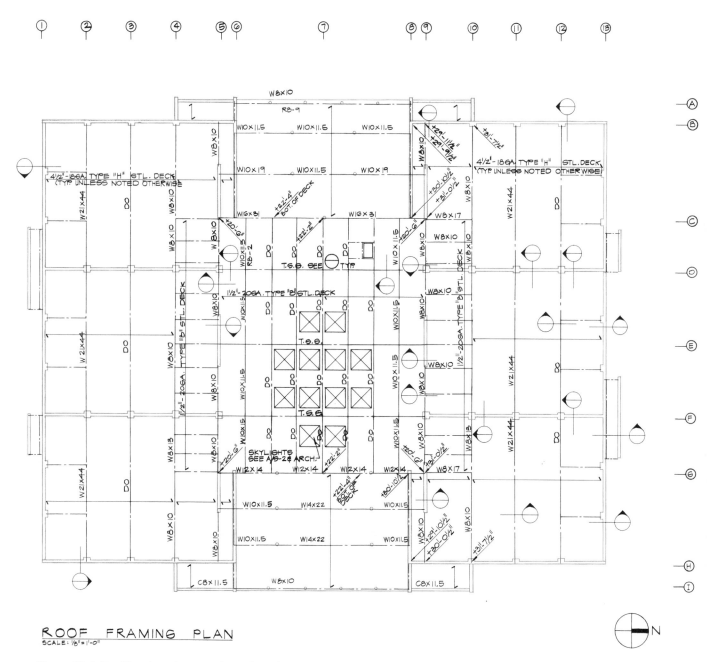

ROOF FRAMING PLAN
SCALE: 1/8" = 1'-0"

Figure 12.6 Roof framing plan—steel members. (Courtesy of AVCO Community Developers, Inc. and Mann Theatres Corporation of California.)

and beams under the rafters. Show the rafters, which are closely spaced, with a single line. Lightly draft the walls so that the members directly above are clear. Provide dimensioning for members with critical locations as well as call-outs for the sizes, lumber grade, and spacing of all members.

Framing Plan: Steel Members

When you are using steel members to support ceilings, floors, and roof, show all the members on the framing plans. The method of drawing the framing plan is similar to the method for drawing wood framing plans.

After you have selected a method, show steel members with a heavy single line. See Figure 12.6, which is a roof framing plan for a theatre using various size steel members and steel decking. The interior walls have been drawn with a broken line, which distinguishes the

heavy solid beam line and the walls below. As you can see, all the various beam sizes are noted directly on the steel members. Some members have an abbreviated "DO" as their call-out; this tells the viewer that this member is identical to the one noted in the same framing bay.

In some cases, a beam may also be given a roof beam number, noted as "RB–1", "RB–2", etc. The structural engineer uses this beam reference in the engineering calculations. It can also be incorporated into a roof beam schedule, if one is needed. Any elements that require openings through a roof or floor should be drawn directly on the plan. On Figure 12.6, an open area for skylights and a roof access hatch are shown with a heavy solid line.

A framing plan can also be useful to show detail reference symbols for **connections** of various members that cannot otherwise be shown on the building sec-

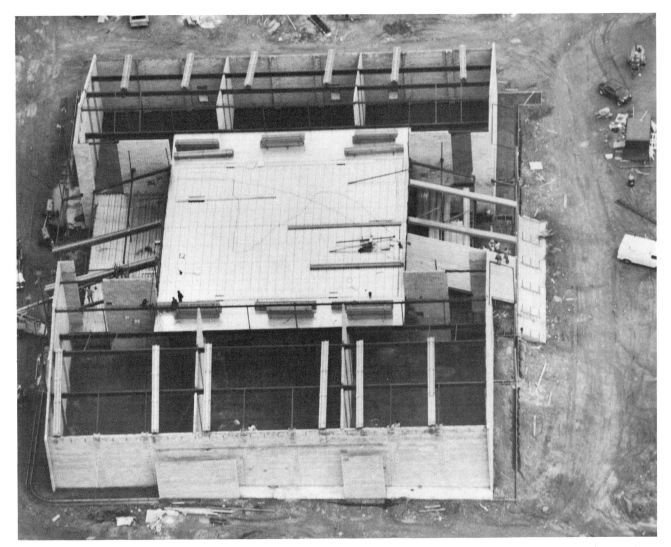

Figure 12.7 Roof framing. (Courtesy of AVCO Community Developers, Inc. and Mann Theatres Corporation of California; William Boggs Aerial Photography. Reprinted with permission.)

tions. Figure 12.6 shows several detail symbols for various connecting conditions. Show building section reference symbols at their specific locations.

Axial reference lines form the basis for dimensioning steel framing members. These lines provide a reference point for all other dimensioning. In Figure 12.6, axial reference symbols are shown on all the major beam and wall lines. From these, subsequent dimension lines to other members are provided. These same reference lines are used on the foundation plan.

Beam and column elevation heights are often shown on the framing plan. See the axial reference point H–10 in Figure 12.6. The diagonal line pointing to this particular beam has an elevation height of 31'–7½" noted on the top of the diagonal line. This indicates that this is the height to the top of the beam. If the height at the bottom of that beam were required, you would note it un-

derneath the diagonal line. Columns usually only require the elevations to the top of the column.

An aerial photograph showing a stage of the roof framing is shown in Figure 12.7. You can clearly see the main supporting steel members, as per axial reference line ②, ③, ④, ⑩, ⑪, and ⑫, and some placement of the steel decking on top of these members.

Framing Plan: Wood and Steel Members

Framing plans using wood and steel members to support ceilings, floors, and roof are drawn in a similar fashion to framing plans using steel alone. Steel members are drawn with a heavy solid line and the wood members with a lighter line broken at intervals. You can also show wood members with a solid line and directional arrow.

Figure 12.8 shows a floor framing plan using steel and wood members to support the floor. This particular

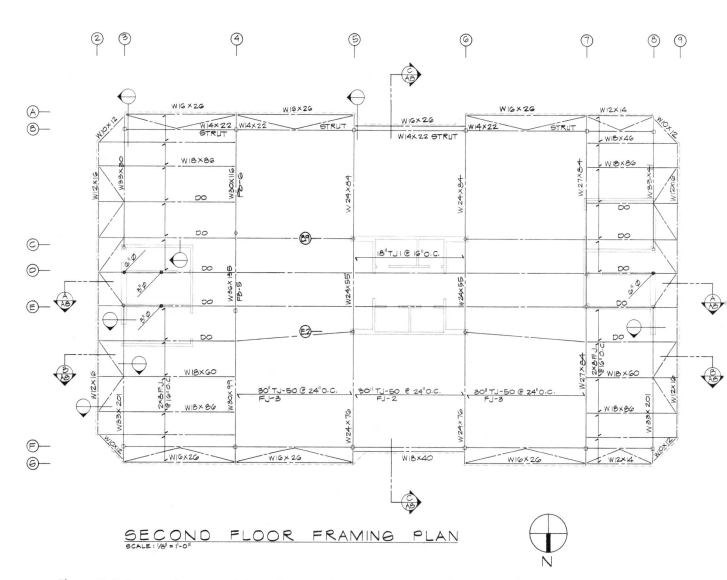

Figure 12.8 Framing plan—second floor. (Courtesy of Westmount, Inc., Real Estate Development, Torrance, CA.)

Figure 12.9 Steel beams for floor framing. (Courtesy of Westmount, Inc., Real Estate Development, Torrance, CA; William Boggs Aerial Photography. Reprinted with permission.)

Figure 12.10 Main steel floor beam and column with joist hangers. (Courtesy of Westmount, Inc., Real Estate Development, Torrance, CA; William Boggs Aerial Photography. Reprinted with permission.)

building is supported mainly on round steel columns, with the wall only being used to enclose a lobby and stairwells. For clarity, draw these columns in solid, and be careful to align them with each other. After you have laid out the required columns and walls below, draw in the main steel members with a solid heavy line. The designation of floor trusses spaced at 24" on centers is shown between these steel members.

Because these members are closely spaced, a solid line is used with directional arrows at the end and the size and spacing of trusses noted directly above the solid line. The bottom of the line shows a notation, "FJ–3." This is the abbreviation for floor joist number 3, which is referenced in the structural engineer's calculations and may be used in a floor joist schedule. When you are asked to draw a similar framing plan, be sure to show the joist for all bay conditions. As we saw earlier, "DO" is shown between axial reference lines ⑦ and ⑧. When you use this abbreviation, be sure it is clear. Detail reference symbols are shown for the connections of

various members. Sizes and shapes for all the steel columns have been designated as well as the elevation height to the top of each column. Building section reference symbols and locations are shown. Whenever possible, take these sections directly through an axial reference plan.

Dimensioning for this type of project relies totally on axial reference planes as they relate to the column locations. Usually, you should locate notes satisfying various requirements on this same drawing. For example, these notes might designate the thickness, type, and nailing schedule for the plywood subfloor or the location of the fire draft stops within the floor framing.

To understand this structure better, look at the series of framing photographs. Figure 12.9 gives a general view of the overall steel and wood skeleton used in the erection of this building. The floor joist truss member seen in the foreground will eventually be attached between the main steel beams. Figure 12.10 is a close-up view of a main steel floor beam and column with joist

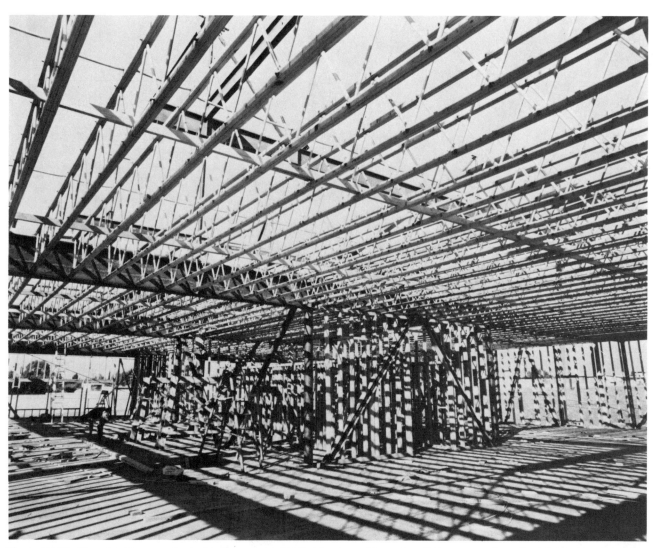

Figure 12.11 Floor joist trusses attached to hangers and nailed in place. (Courtesy of Westmount, Inc., Real Estate Development, Torrance, CA; William Boggs Aerial Photography. Reprinted with permission.)

hangers located at the top of the beam in preparation for the attachment of the floor truss members.

In Figure 12.11, floor joist trusses have now been attached to the hangers and nailed in place. Reference symbols for connection details should be located throughout the framing plan drawing. Figures 12.12 and 12.13 give examples of what these details may look like in their construction phase.

FRAMING PLAN CHECKLIST

1. Titles and scales.
2. Indicate bearing and non-bearing walls.
    a. Coordinate with foundation plan.
    b. Show all openings in walls.
3. Show all beams, headers, girders, purlins, etc.
    a. Note sizes.
4. Show all columns, note sizes and materials.
5. Note accessway to attic—if occurs.
6. Note ceiling joist sizes, direction, spacing.
7. Draw all rafters, note sizes and spacing.
8. Draw overhangs.
    a. Indicate framing for holding overhangs up.
    b. Dimension width.
9. Note shear walls.
10. Note roof sheathing type and thickness.
11. Indicate all ridges, valley. Note sizes.
12. Note all differences in roof levels.

Roof Plan Framing Systems

As you look at the various framing plans, there may be many conventions that require clarification. For this reason we have included a chart of typical conventions in Figure 12.14. You may find it helpful to flag this chart as you look at the various framing plans and use it as you would a dictionary; that is, a reference table that defines the conventions used. The explanations to these conventions are listed below (letters correspond to the chart).

A. A beam, header or lintel over an opening, door, or window within a wall.

B. Used to show the direction of a framing member or a system of framing members, such as floor joist, rafters, or ceiling joist. Lettering occurs right along the line indicating size, name, and spacing, for example, "2 × 6 ceiling joist at 16″ o.c." Note that a half arrowhead is on one side and another half on the opposite side.

C. The line with the half arrowheads is the same as described in definition B. The diagonal line with a full arrowhead on both ends indicates the duration of the system, for example, where a particular system of ceiling joists begins and ends. When sizes of

Figure 12.12 Beam and column connection. (Courtesy of Westmount, Inc., Real Estate Development, Torrance, CA.)

Figure 12.13 Floor beam to main beam assembly. (Courtesy of Westmount, Inc., Real Estate Development, Torrance, CA.)

the ceiling joists vary on the structure, for example, this symbol is used to convey to the contractor where one size ends and another begins.

D. A beam, girder, or joist over a post.

E. A beam, girder, or joist under and supporting a post.

F. The employment of a framing anchor or joist hanger at the intersection of two members.

G. A structural post within a wall.

H. Two framing systems on the drawing. For example, one might represent ceiling joists, and the other roof rafters.

I. "W12 × 44" is a call-out for a steel beam or girder. When these members are sequentially repeated the center lines are still drawn to represent them, but the description (call-out) is abbreviated with the letters DO, which is short for "ditto."

J. In using conventional wood framing, which is subject to lateral forces such as wind and earthquake, a plywood membrane is often placed on a portion or on the complete wall surface. The adjacent hexagon symbol refers you to a nailing schedule to ensure minimums for nails to secure the plywood to the studs. These are call shear walls or shear panels, a drawing of which can be found in a companion to this book, *The Professional Practice of Architectural Detailing.*

K. Still another way to show a shear wall. The space within the wall that is designated as a shear wall is pouchéd in pencil.

L. The rectilinear box that contains the 8'–2" dimension is a convention used to indicate height of an object in plan view. In this example, the two dotted

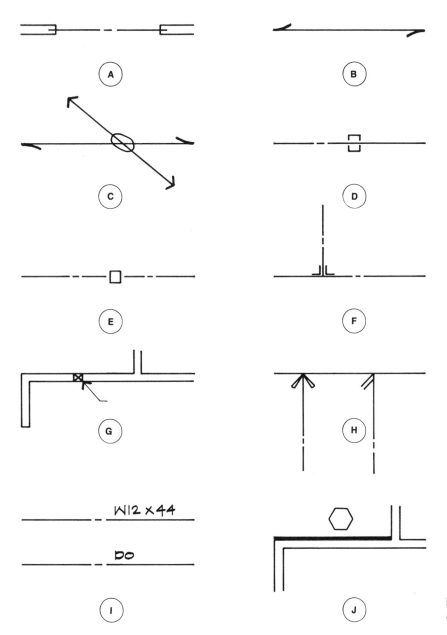

Figure 12.14 Summary of typical framing conventions.

lines might represent the top of a beam or the plate line at a wall, while the numbers indicate height.

M. The use of three lines instead of two to represent a partition designates a double joist at the partition.

N. Shows a post on top of a beam similar to E with a post size notation.

O. This is the method architects use to represent an opening in a floor, ceiling, or roof system. The three lines surrounding the opening represent the doubling of the joists, and the dark L-shape indicates the use of framing anchors. The large X is the area of the opening. This convention is used for skylights and openings in the ceiling or roof for chimneys, a hatch, or attic access.

Roof Plan

A roof plan is a simple look at the top of a structure, as if you were aboard a helicopter. Unless you are looking at a flat roof, the view is usually a distorted one. The reason is that a roof plan cannot reveal the entire surface of the roof in its true shape and size if there are slopes involved.

There are a multitude of roof forms. Among the most commonly known are domes, gable, hip, Dutch gable, and shed roofs.

Most small structures, especially residential structures, use a flat, gable, or hip roof. See Figure 12.15. Throughout this section we will devote most of our attention to the hip roof. If you can configure a hip roof, a gable or Dutch gable becomes a simple task.

Our approach will be to create a roof system that is geometrically correct and consistent in pitch, and avoiding flat areas that can entrap rain, thus causing leaks through the roof structure. Note the roof structure in Figure 12.16(A). Between the two roof systems, you will notice a flat (parallel to the ground) line. This space can entrap water, causing deterioration of the roof material and, eventually, leaks. A short-term solution is to place a triangular metal form to induce the water to travel outward. Figure 12.16(B) shows a standard solution to a roof that was configured incorrectly to begin with. See

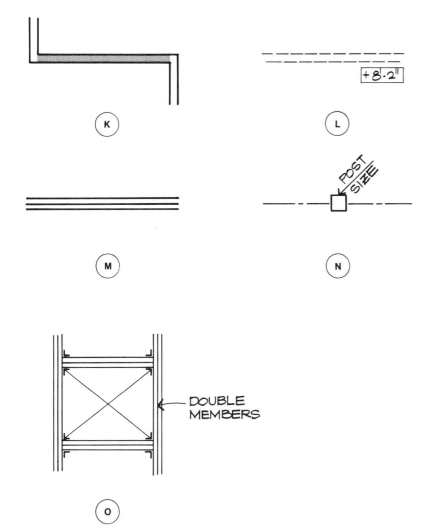

Figure 12.14 Summary of typical framing conventions (continued).

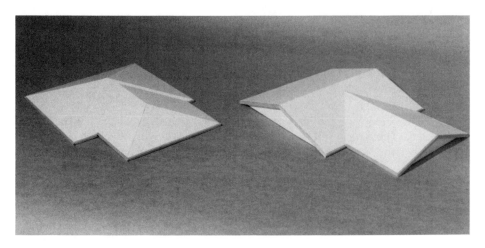

Figure 12.15 Hip and gable roof systems.

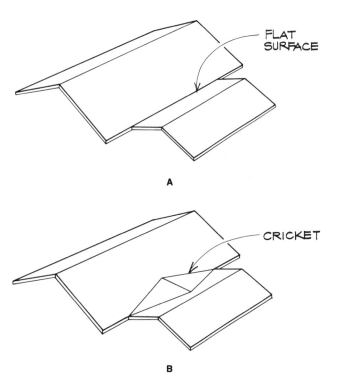

Figure 12.16 Incorrectly configured roof.

Figure 12.17 for the geometrically correct way to solve the problem in this roof outline.

So that you might configure the most complex of roof systems, we describe here the procedure you should follow in even the simplest of roof outlines. With this knowledge, you will be able to create the most complex outline. Once you know the system, you might even alter the building configuration slightly to avoid tricky problems in your plan. See the main roof structure of the Ryan Residence in this chapter, Figure 12.34.

The approach we use always solves the roof as a hip roof. Even if the desired roof was a gable or Dutch gable, in its initial form it will be a hip roof. Once having configured the roof as a hip roof, the conversion to a gable or Dutch gable is a simple one, as you will discover later.

SOLUTION TO PROBLEM 1

STEP I. Identify the perimeter of the roof as shown in the plan view in Figure 12.18. Be sure to indicate the overhang.

STEP II. Reduce the shape into rectilinear zones. This is done by finding the largest rectilinear shape that will

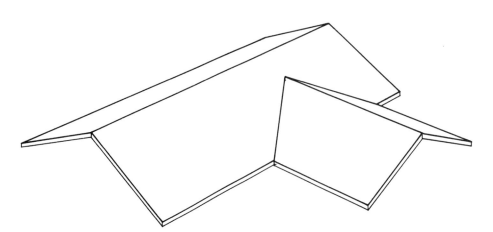

Figure 12.17 Ideal solution to avoid water problem.

fit into the space. Figure 12.19(A) shows an outline of a roof, and Figure 12.19(B) shows the selection of the major area, as designated by the number 1. The major area is not selected according to square footage, but by greatest width. Look at another shape, similar to the preceding outline, on Figure 12.20(A). Had the dimension of the base, designated by the letter B, been larger than A, the major zone would be zone 1, as shown on Figure 12.20(B).

STEP III. At this stage, you will locate both the hip rafter and the ridge. See Figure 12.21(A). A 45° triangle is used to ensure the same pitch (angle of roof) on both sides of the roof, as shown in Figure 12.21(B). This is possible when the corners are at 90° to each other.

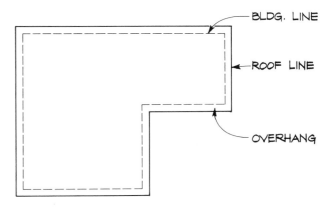

Figure 12.18 Draft the perimeter of the roof to be configured.

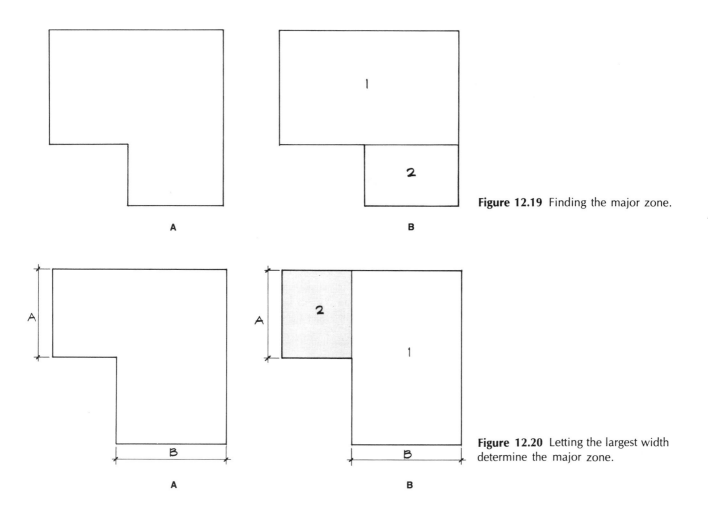

Figure 12.19 Finding the major zone.

Figure 12.20 Letting the largest width determine the major zone.

Note, in Figure 12.22, that the outline has been organized into three zones: the main zone (1) in the center, with zones 2 and 3 above and below. These angles have been identified by the letters A, B, and C. For the sake of this solution, any angle such as A, which is 90°, will be called an "inside" corner. The other two corners (nos. 2 and 3) have angles greater than 90° and will be referred to as "outside" corners.

STEP IV. Configure the roof. Let us take this configuration and develop it into a hip roof with the information already learned.

● Figure 12.23(A): Taking the major zone identified as zone 1, we strike 45° hip lines from each of the floor's inside corners to form the main structure around which the other two zones will appear.

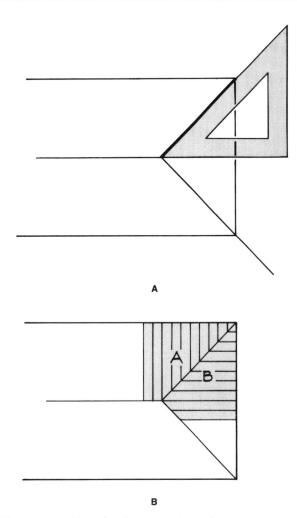

A

B

Figure 12.21 Use of 45° to maintain pitch.

- Figure 12.23(B): We now approach zone 2 with an eye out for inside and outside corners. There are two of each. The inside corners at the top are drawn toward the center of the rectangle. The outside corners have their 45° lines going away from the zone 2 rectangle, thus forming the valleys of the roof.

- Figure 12.23(C): The same approach is used for zone 3 as was used for zone 2. In the process of drawing the outside corners, you will notice that the one on the right overlaps an existing line. When this happens, the lines cancel each other, creating a continuous plane. See Figure 12.23D, which displays the final roof shape.

As you look at the final roof form, it may appear foolish to have gone through such an elaborate system, because you may have been able to visualize the finished roof from the beginning. Let's reinforce and validate the procedure by attempting roofs of varying complexities.

SOLUTION TO PROBLEM 2

STEP I, Figure 12.24(A). The figure displays an area in the center that appears to be the major zone. By square footage, it might be but remember, it is the zone with the greatest width.

STEP II, Figure 12.24(B). Notice the relocation of the major zone by greatest width. Compare zone 1 with zone 2. The one with the greatest width will produce the highest ridge because it takes longer rafters in the framing of this roof. Knowledge of the highest point is often helpful in staying within code limits or blocking someone's view.

STEP III, Figure 12.24(C). This shows all of the zones with roofs outlined. Remember the outside/inside corner rule.

STEP IV, Figure 12.24(D). As can be seen in the previous step, many of the lines overlap. We show them side by side for ease of understanding, but in reality they are on top of each other. This means they cancel each other and are erased.

To continue this exploration of problems, we have selected an outline whose major roof configuration will all but disappear as we develop the roof.

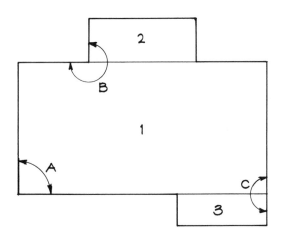

A - INSIDE (ANGLE) CORNER
B - OUTSIDE (ANGLE) CORNER
C - OUTSIDE (ANGLE) CORNER

Figure 12.22 Defining inside and outside corners.

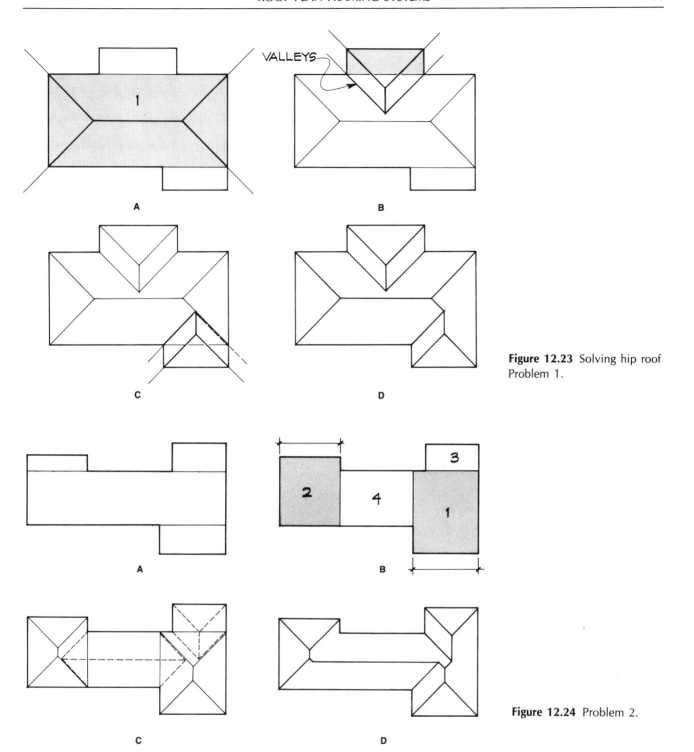

Figure 12.23 Solving hip roof Problem 1.

Figure 12.24 Problem 2.

SOLUTION TO PROBLEM 3

STEP I, Figure 12.25(A). The main zone is situated vertically through the center of the total form. Check this area, in width, with a horizontal rectangle drawn through the top.

STEP II, Figure 12.25(B). Draw the hip and ridge lines. Identify inside and outside corners, and proceed with drawing the hip lines as well as the valley lines.

STEP III, Figure 12.25(C). As the lines overlap each other, happen in three locations, these locations are identified with dotted lines. Notice that three of the four hip lines of the major zone are eliminated in the process.

There are configurations in which the major zones are well hidden. There are also shapes that have overlapping zones. These are far by the most difficult challenges. The following five-step example demonstrates.

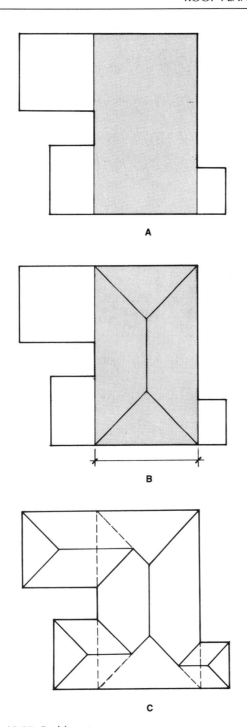

A

B

C

Figure 12.25 Problem 3.

SOLUTION TO PROBLEM 4

STEP I, Figure 12.26(A). Covering all but the top illustration, see if you can identify the major zone on this outline of the structure.

STEP II, Figure 12.26(B). Validate your initial selection with this figure. Next, identify the second largest zone which has been "X"ed out. Notice the overlap of zones 1 and 2.

STEP III, Figure 12.26(C). Solve zones 3 and 4 next. Two lines will overlap, causing their removal.

STEP IV, Figure 12.26(D). Zone 2 has inside corners only. Solve zone 2 as you did zone 1. The points that overlap have been identified with the letters W and X. These are outside corners, which become valleys. Extend point X toward zone 1, and W toward zone 2. These lines will intersect a hip line, identified by the letters Y and Z, respectively.

STEP V, Figure 12.26(E). Y and Z are connected to form a ridge. This ridge is slightly lower than the ridge of zones 1 and 2. The hip lines below points Y and Z are also eliminated to form the final roof configuration.

Saving the most challenging for last, we encounter a shape that includes an angle other than 90° around the perimeter. At first glance the task of roofing this outline seems difficult, but if you apply the principles learned in this chapter, the solution is easier than it may first appear.

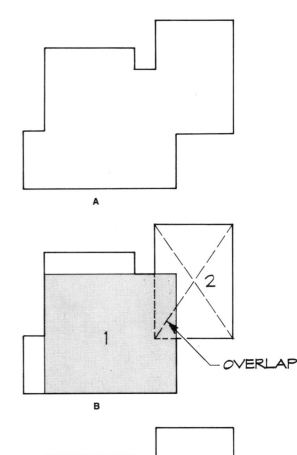

A

B

OVERLAP

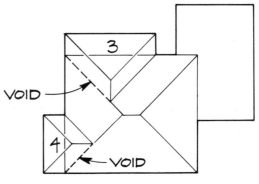

VOID

VOID

C

Figure 12.26 Problem 4.

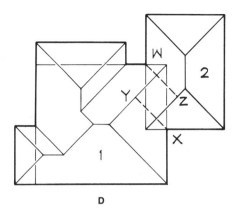

D

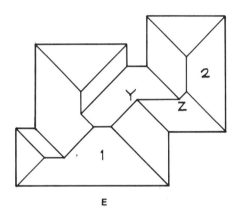

E

Figure 12.26 Problem 4 (continued).

SOLUTION TO PROBLEM 5

STEP I, Figure 12.27(A). Extending the center portion toward the left does not produce the rectangle with the largest width, so change your approach and solve the major zoning as explained in the next step.

STEP II, Figure 12.27(B). After checking the various possible zones, we hope you have selected zone 1 and zone 2 as shown in this figure.

STEP III, Figure 12.27(C). With all inside corners in zones 1 and 2, the solution is simple. Zone 3 should also be easy, with two inside and two outside corners, and thus will be shown as a finished section in the next step.

STEP IV, Figure 12.27(D). Zone 4 has four outside corners, two of which overlap zone 1. To find the ridge, use the upper two outside corners and extend the ridge well into zone 1, as shown in this figure. The valleys will start at points X and Y.

Because points X and Y are not the normal outside angles (180° or 270°), they must be bisected. It is easier to bisect the outside rather than the inside angle around points X and Y because these angles are less than 180°. This can be accomplished by measuring the angle with a protractor and mathematically dividing the angle, or by using a method, which you may have learned in a basic drafting class or in a geometry class, that requires use of a compass.

The compass is set at any radius, and an arc is struck, using X and Y as the center of the arc. See Figure 12.28(A). Next, open the compass wider than the original settings and strike two more arcs, starting where the original arc struck the angular lines. See Figure 12.28(B). Let's call this new intersection Z. When a line is drawn through Z and X (or Z and Y, depending on which angle you are bisecting), you have bisected the angle.

STEP V, Figure 12.27(E). Extend the bisecting lines from X and Y to the inside until they hit the ridge. We have identified these points as M and N.

STEP VI, Figure 12.27(F). Next, connect M and N. This line represents another valley at a different angle and defines the true geometric shape of zones 1 and 4 as they collide into each other. The dotted line, which is the underside of the hip of zone 1, is eliminated in a roof plan but might be shown on a subsequent roof framing plan.

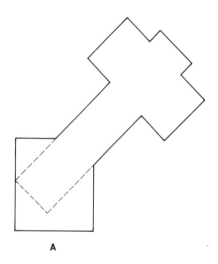

A

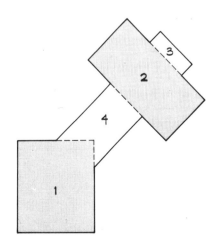

B

Figure 12.27 Problem 5.

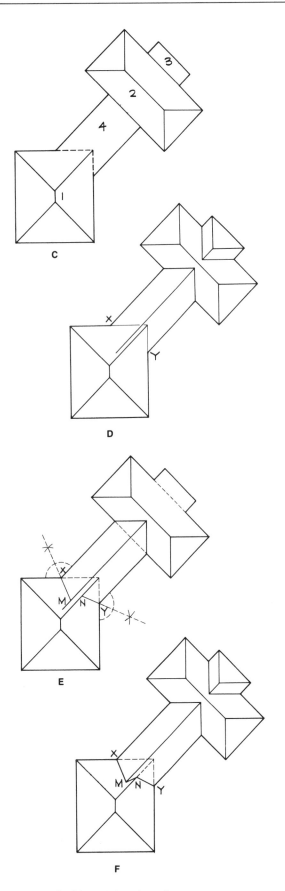

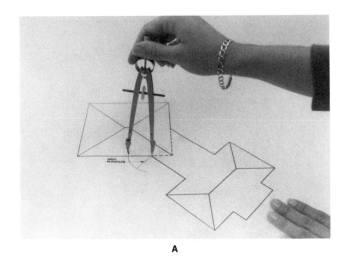

Figure 12.28 Bisecting an angle.

Figure 12.27 Problem 5 (continued).

Changing Configuration

After having configured an outline of a roof to its correct geometric shape, you can readily convert it to other than a hip roof. For example, consider the roof shown in Figure 12.29(A).

Gable Roof. To change this roof to a gable roof is accomplished by simply extending the ridges to the edge of the roof, as shown by the arrows. The final gable roof is displayed in Figure 12.29(B). Notice the return of the valley lines (marked X).

In the next example, found in Figure 12.30, a slight bit of interpretation is needed for the top right corner of the structure. An elevation of this particular roof can be found at the end of the Chapter 11 in Figure 11.46.

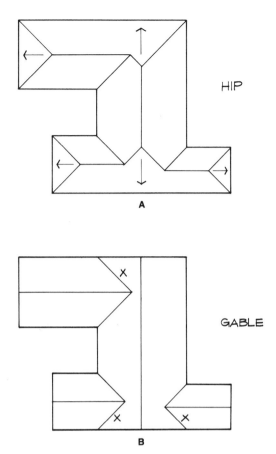

Figure 12.29 Changing configuration.

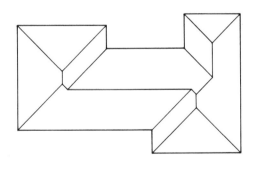

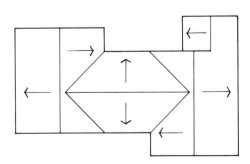

Figure 12.30 Hip to gable conversion.

Dutch Gable Roof. The procedure for converting a hip roof to a Dutch gable is almost the same as for gable conversion, except that the ridge stops short of the perimeters of the building. The extension of ridge can stop anywhere. The limiting factor might be the designer's desire to produce a particular proportion for the gable portion of this roof. See dimensions X and Y on Figure 12.31.

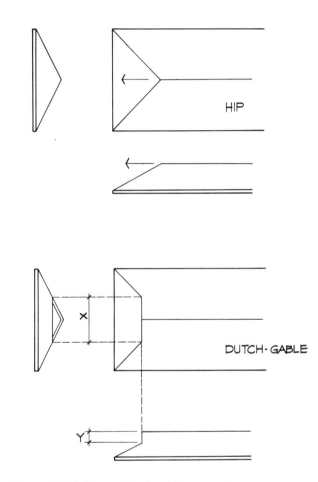

Figure 12.31 Hip to Dutch-gable conversion.

Skylight Attic Location—Ventilation

A roof plan in conjunction with an exterior elevation gives the designer a perfect opportunity to position and check the appearance of such things as an attic ventilating system that must comply with energy standards. Standards have been instituted by local, state, and even federal commissions for energy conservation. An effective system might simply be a screened opening or a screened opening enhanced with a mechanical device.

Because heat rises, it is best to place ventilating systems as high as possible, at the ends of a roof, for thorough ventilation—also taking into consideration the

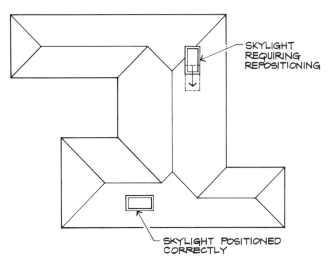

Figure 12.32 Verifying skylight location.

prevailing winds and any other environmental factors that might dictate their position.

Traditionally, ventilation systems were placed on the ends of gable roofs, on the gable portion of a Dutch gable roof, or at the eaves of a hip roof. There are presently available roof-surface-mounted units and ridge ventilating systems, as well as numerous mechanical systems for industrial, commercial, and residential structures. As a drafter, you should be aware of the ventilating system used by your particular place of employment.

The position of skylights must always be verified on the roof plan. This will ensure that you are not cutting through a strategic area, such as a hip or valley of the roof. For example, the skylight shown at the bottom of Figure 12.32 does not bridge any structural roof member, so it can be placed in the desired location directly above the room below. However, this is not the case with the skylight at the top of this figure. Because it crosses a hip member (a pleated plane), it must be moved to another area, which is shown as a dotted line. The opening below may be in the original position, but with the skylight shifted, the light shaft will be bent. See Figure 12.33.

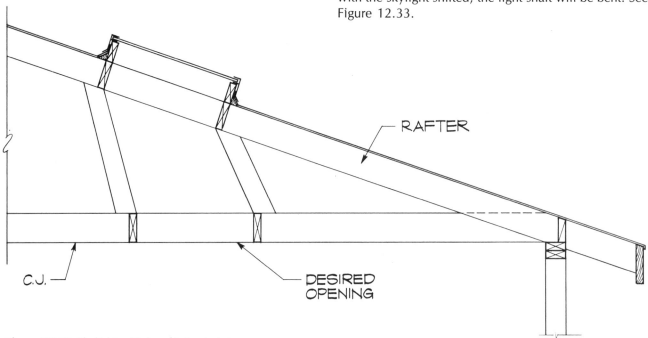

Figure 12.33 Skylight with bent light shaft.

A Newly Built Major Roof Zone

Rather than restricting yourself to a particular outline, you can alter the configuration with porches, balconies, colonnades, and so on. Note the example of the Ryan Residence described in Chapter 5, Figure 5.29. To simply follow the outline of the structure would produce an unusual roof, one that is difficult to frame. The simple addition of a roof over the entry can protect the entry,

create the basis for a better structural form, and even simplify the roof form. A simpler roof allows ease of construction, a system that is structurally stable, and, if it answers a functional need (covered entry), the best of all solutions. See Figure 12.34 for the transition from a simple outline to an extension of the roof over the entry and the beginning of a structural system that improves the strength of the total structure.

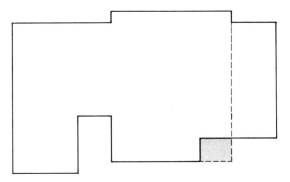 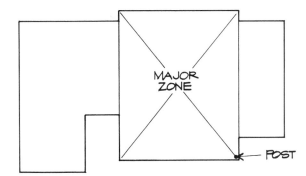

Figure 12.34 Changing the outline.

Framing a Residence

In considering the Ryan Residence, let's examine the specific detail as well as the overall look. A model of the Ryan Residence was constructed to illustrate the framing approach (see Figure 12.35(A) and (B)). This is not usually done in an office for such a simple structure.

As in all structural analysis, we first describe the over-all structure, starting with the top of the building and working downward.

The roof, as you have seen, is a gable roof, built of rafters to form a triangle. The sides of the base of the triangle accept the weight of the roof (called the dead load) and the weight of movable objects (called the live load). Movable objects might be architectural decor, roofers walking about, and so on. Thus, in the photo-

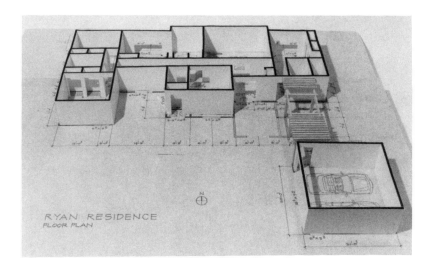

A

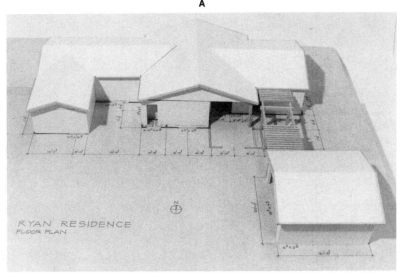

B

Figure 12.35 Floor plan model and roof system for the Ryan Residence.

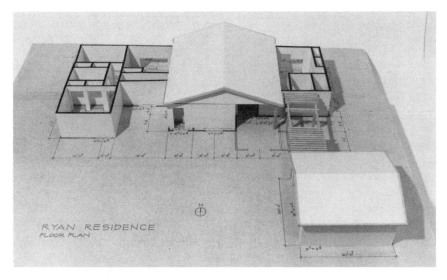

Figure 12.36 Main roof system.

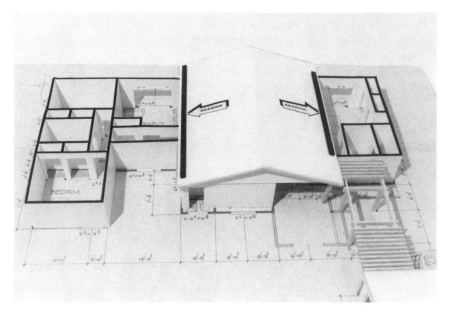

Figure 12.37 Distributing main roof load.

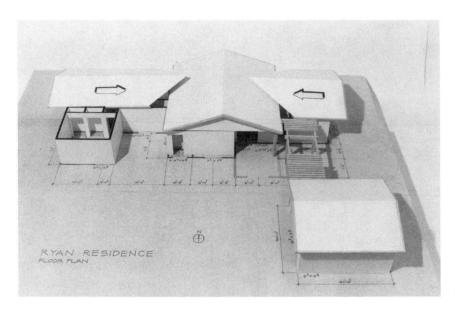

Figure 12.38 Interlocking roof system.

graph seen in Figure 12.36, notice how the main form of the roof places its weight on the wall between the master bedroom and the living room and necessitates a beam to bridge the opening between the kitchen and the family room. This structural consideration is demonstrated in Figure 12.37. The walls in the two areas become load-bearing walls and must, in turn, have bearing footings beneath them.

The main roof is completely sheathed, and the two adjacent roofs are locked into the main roof by means of a framing system called a California frame. In this system, complete roofs are interlocked. See Figure 12.38. In reality, a 2x_member is laid flatwise onto the sheathed roof, as shown in Figure 12.39, the new ridge is attached, and the jack rafters (shaft rafters) and the common rafters (full-length rafters) are installed.

Now look at Figure 12.40. Because of the positioning of the new roof to the left of the main roof, there is a need for a new bearing wall between the bathroom and the front bedroom.

When the final segment of the roof is installed via a California frame, the total roof system is complete. See Figure 12.35(B). In every instance, the previous roof is totally sheathed before the California frame roof is installed. The sheathing in turn acts as a diaphragm to resist earthquakes, wind, or any other force acting upon this structure. In addition, the total wall surface will also be sheathed with plywood to resist any lateral forces acting upon the structure. This plywood wall membrane will also, along with other material, work to prevent heat loss on cold days and heat gain on hot days.

A second way of holding up the roof by changing the direction of the ceiling joist is to turn the ridge into a beam. This beam is subsequently supported by a post and by a concrete pad to distribute this concentrated load over the ground. Figure 12.41 shows a model

Figure 12.39 California frame method.

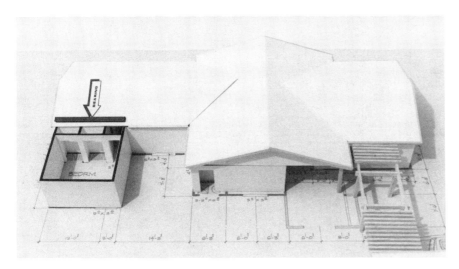

Figure 12.40 Additional bearing walls identified.

Figure 12.41 Ridge beam and its support.

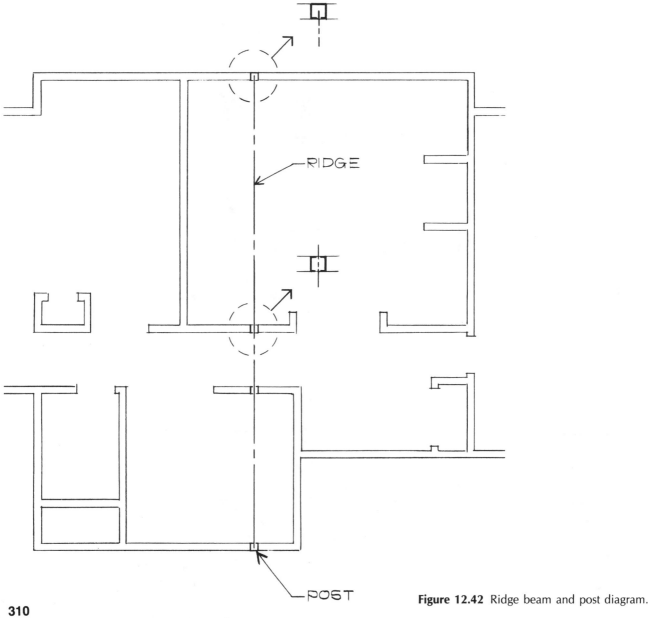

RIDGE

POST

Figure 12.42 Ridge beam and post diagram.

illustrating this method, and Figure 12.42 shows a diagram for positioning the posts.

Next, consider the ceiling system. The ideal procedure is to install the ceiling joist in the same direction as the rafters, to complete the desired triangle. See Figure 12.43. The beginning, the end points, and the lap of other ceiling joists are well secured to form a solidly built triangle. In this system, the ceiling joist also rests on the wall between the kitchen and the living room, making this a bearing wall (structural wall) and requiring a bearing footing. Another solution is to use a wood truss system, as opposed to the conventional rafter/ceiling joist system.

In a wood truss, the rafter as seen in Figure 12.41 and ceiling joist are integrated as a total unit. Because of the way they are configured, the forces on trusses are distributed to the ends of the trusses and thus can span greater distances. They are prebuilt in the shop and delivered ready for erection. Light roof trusses (built of 2 × 4 and 2 × 6 members) are light enough that two framers can lift the units in place. Spaced at 16 to 24 inches on center, these trusses can easily span between 20 and 30 feet, depending on exterior forces such as snow loads, wind, earthquake, and so forth. Heavy

timber trusses can span upward of 100 feet. Look at Figure 12.44 and compare the appearance of the structure with the previous illustration. The metal plates used to connect the various components are toothed plates. (A piece of metal is punched to form a nail like a tooth, which is pressed into position by the manufacturer of the truss.)

Perpendicular to the trusses and on the top side are members called purlins. Purlins keep the trusses from toppling over like dominos.

The negative aspect to the use of trusses, if you can call it a negative, is the reduction of attic space.

To show alternative solutions and their implications, we run the ceiling joist parallel to the ridge and perpendicular to the rafters. This shortens the span of the ceiling joist and runs them in the same direction as required by the two roofs adjacent to the main roof. However, this causes two additional problems. We have not created a triangle, and we must find a way to hold up the ridge.

We will hold up the ridge by the introduction of a member called a strut, placed at 4'–0" o.c. and resting on the kitchen/living room wall, as shown in Figure 12.45. We will produce the desired triangle by placing a

Figure 12.43 Creating a structural triangle.

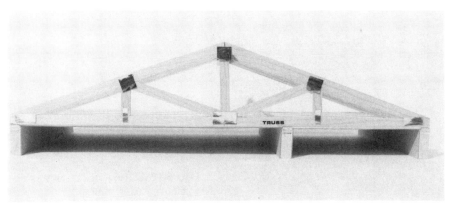

Figure 12.44 Truss system.

Figure 12.45 Configuration for ceiling joist perpendicular to rafters.

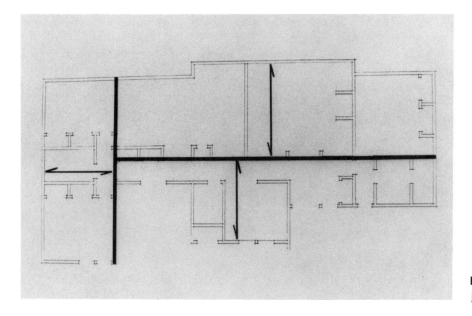

Figure 12.46 Bearing wall for ceiling joist.

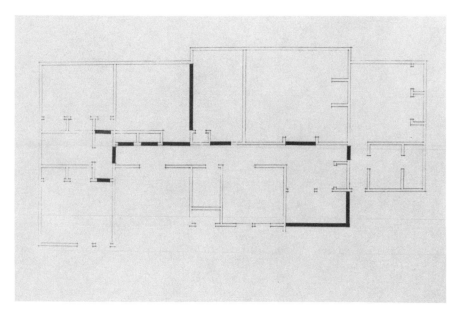

Figure 12.47 Required beams as result of roof and ceiling.

series of members (32" o.c.) parallel to the rafter. The members positioned above the ceiling joist are called ties. This is the way we will configure the ceiling joist during the evolution of the Ryan Residence.

The direction of the ceiling joist of the two-bedroom wing at the left will be changed, producing the necessity for still another bearing wall and, subsequently, a bearing footing. Figure 12.46 is a simple diagram for interior walls that become bearing walls for the ceiling joist. These bearing walls are added to those produced by the rafters and will determine the configuration for the foundation plan.

Within these bearing walls are openings. A header or lintel is used to distribute the weight of the ceiling and roof around the openings. These beams, headers, and lintels are marked on Figure 12.47.

Evolution of Ryan Roof Plan

Ryan Residence Roof Plan

The roof plan is often superimposed on the site plan. In the evolution of the Ryan Residence these plans will be kept separate, which makes them easier to understand and is much better practice. When a roof plan is superimposed on a site plan, the building line and the roof outline are reversed, with the building line solid and the roof line dotted. On a true roof plan the outline of a roof is a solid line.

STAGE I (Figure 12.48). The scale selected for the Ryan Residence roof plan is 1/8" = 1'–0". The outline of the building can be drawn by taking the first stage of the floor plan and making a 1/2 reduction and tracing. The garage plan is positioned adjacent to the main structure.

STAGE II (Figure 12.49). The roof and building lines are darkened at this stage. Arrows are drawn to indicate the direction of the slope of the trellis that connects the residence to the garage via the master bedroom. The patio is drawn.

Next, an erasing shield with a uniform series of circular openings is used in conjunction with an electric eraser to produce near-perfect hidden lines, which represents the building line.

STAGE III (Figure 12.50). Skylight and chimney locations are the first to be located at this stage. Some architectural offices show plumbing vents that come

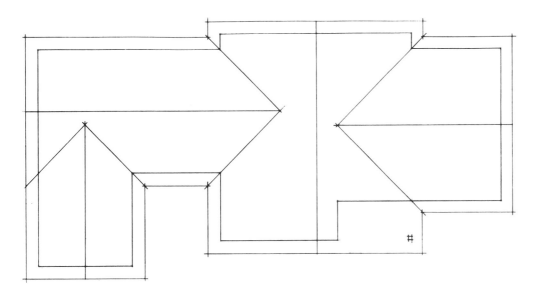

Figure 12.48 Roof plan—Stage I.

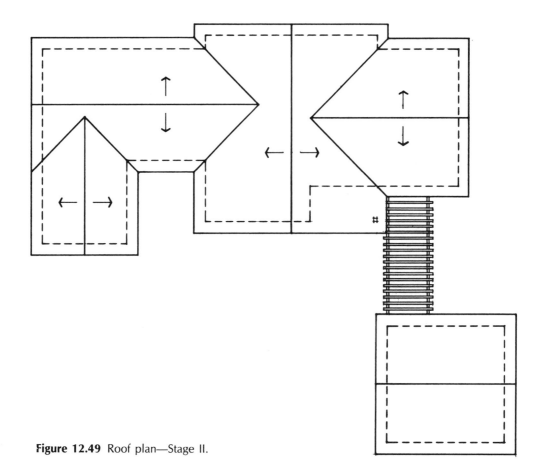

Figure 12.49 Roof plan—Stage II.

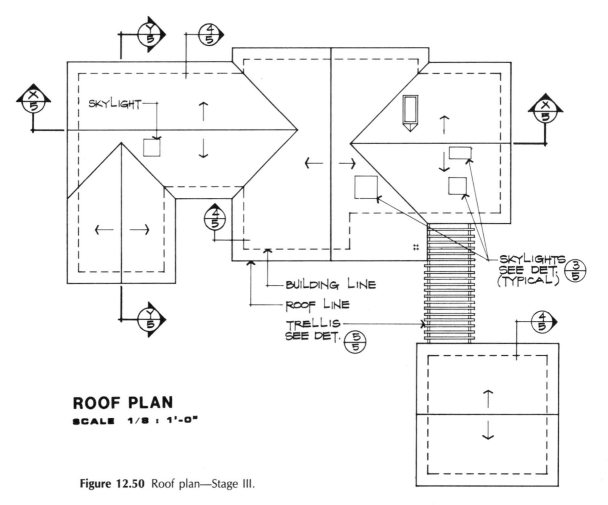

SKYLIGHT

SKYLIGHTS
SEE DET.
(TYPICAL)

BUILDING LINE

ROOF LINE

TRELLIS
SEE DET.

ROOF PLAN
SCALE 1/8 : 1'-0"

Figure 12.50 Roof plan—Stage III.

through the roof, as a confirmation of their positions. Detail and section reference bubbles are next and, finally, noting is completed.

Evolution of Ryan Roof Framing Plan

Ryan Residence Roof Framing

As described at the beginning of this chapter, there are two ways of developing framing plans; superimposition and separate development. For the Ryan Residence, the ceiling joist plan will be superimposed on the floor plan, making this plan a three-in-one plan; a floor plan, an electrical plan, and a ceiling framing plan.

For the roof framing plan, the initial procedure is as follows:

A xerographic copy of the floor plan, prior to the dimensioning stage, is printed onto vellum. If your office does not have a plain paper copier capable of producing the necessary reproduction size, local blueprint shops often do and can make a copy for

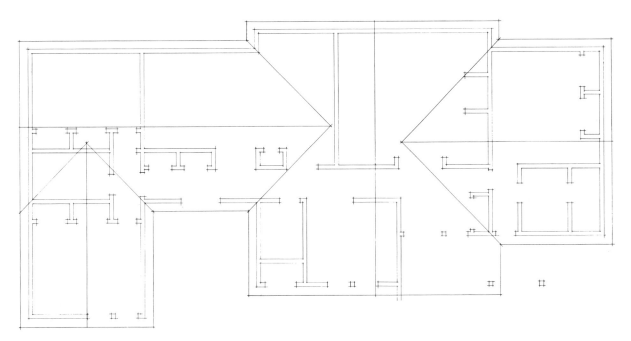

Figure 12.51 Roof framing plan—Stage I.

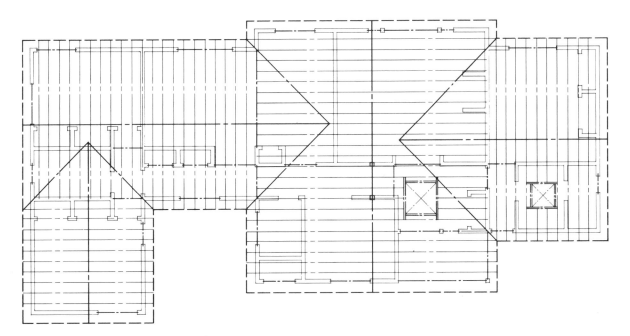

Figure 12.52 Roof framing plan—Stage II.

you, or a diazo process can be used. When a diazo copy is printed onto vellum, it is called a sepia copy. It is onto this copy that the roof framing plan is drawn.

STAGE I (Figure 12.51). The roof plan is constructed on a xerographic vellum copy. Be sure that the angles are 45° to ensure consistent pitch.

STAGE II (Figure 12.52). Skylights and beams over critical openings (in load-bearing walls) are placed. At this

stage, two skylights are missing. This is an oversight on the part of the drafter. They are the skylight in the master bedroom and another at the end of the hall (near the rear bedroom). The second skylight conflicts with the beam placed to accept the weight of the struts, and should be discussed with the project manager and/or the structural engineer. The framing around the two existing skylights is indicated, which can be

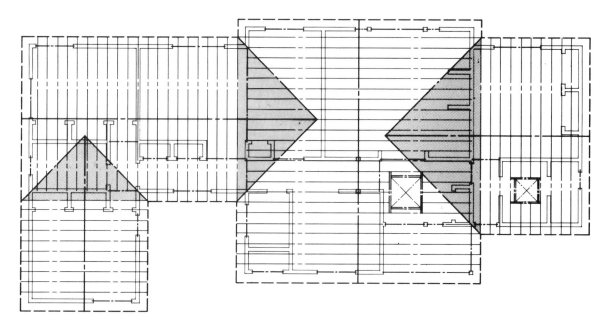

Figure 12.53 Roof framing plan—Stage III (alternate).

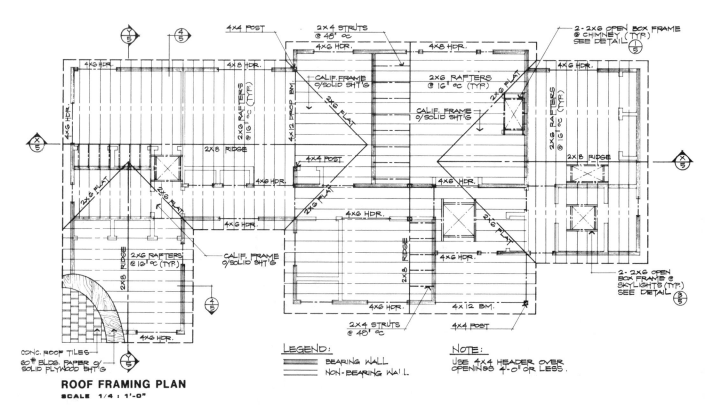

Figure 12.54 Roof framing plan—Stage III.

viewed from a different perspective as you look at the detail. All of the rafters are positioned, except for the California framed areas.

STAGE III (alternate) (Figure 12.53). Normally, it is sufficient to pouché (shade) the California framed area and call out the critical members in notes.

STAGE IV (Figure 12.54). The final stage of the roof framing plan is drawn in diagrammatic fashion and includes notations for the struts, California frame, ties, and so on.

All headers and beams are also positioned and labeled. To eliminate the redundant task of labeling every beam or header, a special note can be included to identify all 4 × 4 or less. A legend identifying bearing and nonbearing walls is also included.

Finally, locate a portion of the roof that is somewhat typical, that is, without beams or windows beneath it, and display the roof material plus the sheathing in this area.

SUMMARY

There are two main methods of incorporating framing information into a set of construction documents: drawing framing members on the floor plan and drawing them separately. These methods vary slightly with wood, steel, and combinations of wood, steel, and masonry.

IMPORTANT TERMS AND CONCEPTS

Framing members
Drawing framing members on the floor plan
Ceiling, floor, or roof framing
Framing plan: wood and/or steel

Header
Hip rafters
Framing connections
Column and beam elevations

REVIEW QUESTIONS

1. Separate framing plans for ceilings, floor, and roof are recommended for certain projects. Which are these?
2. Describe and illustrate a way to show beams and joists directly on the finished floor plan.
3. Give two ways of providing a plan drawing in preparation for a framing drawing.
4. What dimensions are critical on the framing plan?
5. What type of line should you use when you draw closely spaced wood members?
6. Describe two methods of designating specific beams.
7. A framing plan provides a tool for showing certain conditions in the framing. What are these?
8. What type of dimensioning procedure should be used for structures mainly supported on columns?
9. How do you show steel beams on a framing plan?

LABORATORY PROBLEMS

1. Using a scale of ¼" = 1'-0", draw a ceiling framing plan for Figure 12.1.
2. Draw and correctly locate the beam elevations for the following case: top of beam to be 20'-1½" and bottom of beam to be 19'-2".
3. Draw a floor framing plan and call-outs with complete dimensions for the following figure. Instructor to assign scale of drawing and sizes of members.

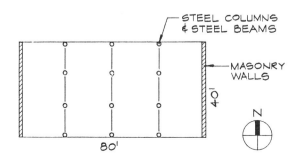

13

INTERIOR ELEVATIONS

13

PREVIEW
Special drafting techniques are used to represent materials on the surface of a wall, and hidden lines are used to indicate various features of the interior elevations. There are established symbols and references used for these elevations as well as special generic terms for call-outs. The chapter provides many examples of interior elevations and their origin.

OBJECTIVES
1. Understand the reasons for drafting interior elevations.
2. Understand how floor plans are referenced to interior elevations.
3. Understand the use of hidden lines in interior elevations.
4. Be familiar with cabinet door configurations.
5. Be aware of the need to outline and profile.
6. Know how to deal with the intersection of wall to floor.
7. Be able to develop an approach to dimensioning and noting.
8. Satisfy building accessibility for persons with disabilities (ADA compliance).

Purpose and Content of Interior Elevations

The drawing process for **interior elevations** resembles the drafting procedure for exterior elevations. You should be familiar with the chapter on exterior elevations before proceeding with this chapter.

Sources of Measurements

Use the floor plan and building sections for accurate measurements of the width and height of an interior elevation wall. When you use these plans, remember that these dimensions are usually to the stud line or center line of the wall. Interior elevations are drafted to the plaster line.

Interior elevations may not always be drafted at the same scale as the floor plans or sections. Since this requires a scale transition, use caution to avoid errors. In this chapter, if the same scale is used and the drawings are directly projected from the plan and section, it is done only to show the theory of where to obtain shapes and configurations.

Information Shown on Interior Elevations

Some architectural offices draft interior elevations for every wall of every room. While this can guard against errors, many wall surfaces are so simple that they do not need a formal drafted interior elevation. These simple walls depend primarily on the interior finish schedule for their proper description.

Use interior elevations when you need to convey an idea, dimension, construction method, or unique feature that you can better describe by drafting than by a written description in the specification. For example, in a residence, the kitchen, bathrooms, special closets, and wet bars have walls that are usually drafted. On a commercial structure, you might select typical office units showing bookcases, cabinets, display cases, and so on. In an industrial structure you might draw the locations of equipment, conveyor belts, and special heights for bulletin boards or tool racks.

In other words, interior elevations are the means of controlling the interior walls of a structure in terms of construction, surface finishes, and the providing of information to subcontractors.

Naming Interior Elevations

In exterior elevations, the titles assigned—North, South, East, and West—are based on the direction the structure faces. In interior elevations this is reversed: the title is based on the direction in which the viewer is looking. For example, if you are standing in a theatre lobby facing north, the interior wall you are looking at has the title "North Lobby Elevation." See Figure 13.1. To avoid

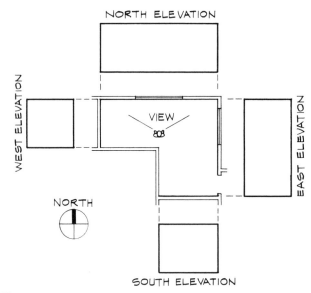

Figure 13.1 Naming interior elevations.

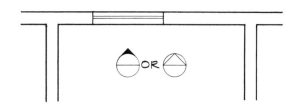

Figure 13.2 Interior elevation reference bubbles.

confusion when you are naming an interior elevation, you should use reference bubbles like those in Figure 13.2.

The reference symbol shown on the left is the same as the one used in the foundation plans and framing plans when you need to refer to details. Remember that the reference bubble is a circle with a darkened point on one side which points to the elevation being viewed and drawn.

The reference symbol shown on the right in Figure 13.2 shows a circle with a triangle inside it. The point of the triangle tells the viewer which elevation is being viewed, and the placement of the triangle automatically divides the circle in half. The top half contains a letter or number which becomes the name of that interior elevation. The lower half contains the sheet number on which the interior elevation can be found.

Figure 13.3 shows a floor plan and a symbol used to show multiple elevations. Letter "A" is for the North elevation, "C" is for the South elevation, "B" for the West elevation, and "D" for the East elevation. Figure 13.4 shows two types of **title references.**

Choosing a Scale

The most desirable scale to use on an interior elevation is ½" = 1'–0". Most floor plans are drafted at ¼" = 1'–0", so using this scale makes the translation from

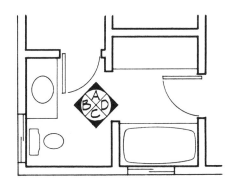

Figure 13.3 Symbol used to show multiple interior elevations.

Figure 13.4 Interior elevation titles.

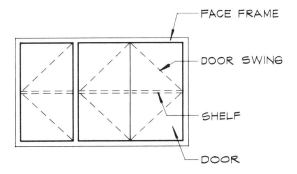

Figure 13.5 Typical elevation of cabinet.

floor plan to interior elevation easy because you only need to use a pair of dividers and double every measurement. Interior elevations are seldom drawn larger than this.

If the drawing space does not permit you to use a ½″ = 1′–0″ scale, or if the scale of the drawing calls for a smaller interior elevation, you may use a ⅜″ = 1′–0″ or ¼″ = 1′–0″ scale. The scale could also depend on the complexity of the wall to be shown.

Using Dotted Lines

Dotted lines are used extensively on interior elevations. As in the drafting of exterior elevations, the dotted line is used to show door-swing direction—for example, for cabinets or for bi-fold doors on a wardrobe closet. See Figure 13.5. Dotted lines are also used to represent items hidden from view, for example, the outline of a kitchen sink, shelves in a cabinet, or the vent above a hood vent, range, or cook top.

Dotted lines are also used to show the outline of objects to be added later or those **not in the contract** (designated as **"N.I.C."**). For example, the outline of a washer and dryer or refrigerator is shown. Even though the appliances themselves are not in the contract, space must be allowed for them. The wall behind the appliance is shown, including duplex convenience outlets, and moulding or trim at the base of the wall.

Other Drafting Considerations

To draft interior elevations of cabinets, you must know the type, counter top material, heights, general design, and number of cabinet doors.

Types of Cabinet Doors.   There are three main types of cabinet doors: **flush, flush overlay,** and **lip.** As Figure 13.6 shows, flush overlay doors cover the total face of the cabinet. The front surface, called the **face frame** of the cabinet, does not show. The flush door is shown in Figure 13.7 and the lip door in Figure 13.8. Because the face frame of the cabinet shows in both the lip and flush cabinet doors, they appear the same in the interior elevation.

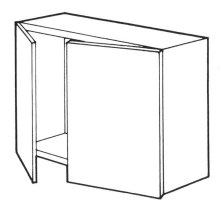

Figure 13.6 Flush overlay doors.

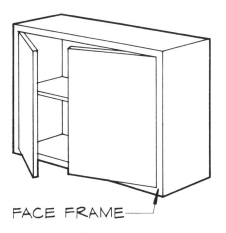

Figure 13.7 Flush doors.

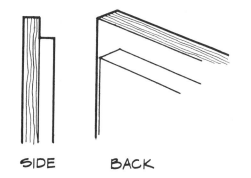

SIDE   BACK

Figure 13.8 Lip door.

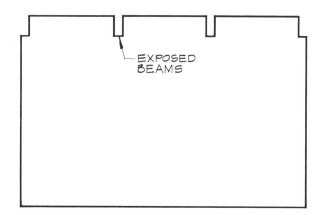

Figure 13.9 Exposed beams.

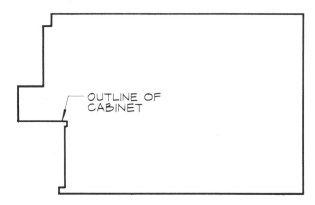

Figure 13.10 Outline of cabinet.

Material Designation and Noting

Materials for interior elevations are represented like the materials for exterior elevations. Refer to Chapter 11, on exterior elevations, for samples.

Noting is kept simple and generic terms are often used. Specific information, brand names, workmanship notes, procedures, applications and finishes are placed in the specifications. Later in this chapter, you will see examples of generic noting for such items as ceramic tile counter tops, an exhaust hood (with a note to "See specs."), and metal partitions.

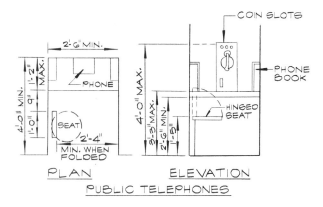

PLAN   ELEVATION
PUBLIC TELEPHONES

Figure 13.11 Public telephone for disabled persons. (Courtesy of AVCO Community Developers, Inc. and Mann Corporation of California.)

Outline of Interior Elevations

The outline of an interior elevation represents the outermost measurement of a room. Objects that project toward the viewer, such as cabinets, beams, or air-conditioning ducts, are drawn. Some architectural offices deal with these as if they were in section but most prefer to treat them as shown in Figures 13.9 and 13.10. Note in Figure 13.10 that the tops of the cabinets have been eliminated in drafting the outline of the cabinet.

Planning for Children and Persons with Disabilities

Always have information available on standards affecting facilities that should be usable by children and persons with disabilities. Here are some of the standards established by several states for disabled persons:

1. Door opening: minimum size 2'–8" clear
2. Restroom grab bars: 33–36" above the floor
3. Towel bars: 3'–4" maximum above floor
4. Top of lavatory: 34" maximum above floor
5. Drinking fountains: 3'–0" maximum

Many standards can be obtained by writing to the proper authority, such as the State Architect's office. Most standards are presented in the form of a drawing; see Figure 13.11 for an example.

Dimensions and Intersections

Dimensions

When you draft a set of interior elevations, do not repeat dimensions that appear elsewhere. For example, you do not need to indicate the width of rooms on the interior elevation. In fact, avoid repeating dimensions at all costs. In this way, if you need to make changes on one plan—such as the floor plan—you do not risk forgetting to change the interior elevations.

In a similar way, you do not need to dimension the interior elevation of the counter of Figure 13.12, because it will occupy the total width of the room. The boundaries, which are the walls, are already dimensioned on the floor plan.

The interior elevations for Figure 13.12 will show a counter, walls, a window, and an opening. The portion of the counter that returns toward the opening should be dimensioned either on the floor plan or on the interior elevations, but not on both. See Figure 13.13.

Notice how the base cabinet is dimensioned; in fact, the space between the door and the cabinet could have been dimensioned instead. Deciding whether to dimension the space or the cabinet is based on which is more important. If the space is left for an appliance or some other piece of equipment, then the space should be dimensioned.

The interior elevation is also the place to provide such information as the location of medicine cabinets, the heights of built-in drawers, the locations of mirrors, the required clearance for a hood above a range, and the heights of partitions.

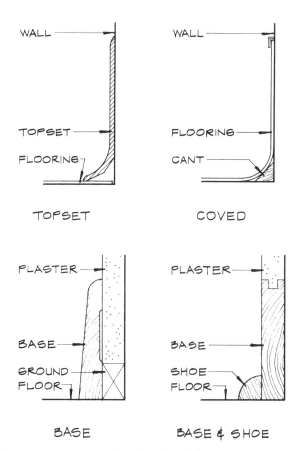

Figure 13.14 Intersection of wall and floor.

Intersection of Wall and Floor

Interior elevations can also show, in a simple way, the wall and floor intersection. This can be achieved by applying a topset, coving the floor, or using a base or a base and a shoe. This creates a transition between the floor and wall planes. **Topset** is made of flexible material such as rubber and placed on the wall where it touches the floor. **Coving** is a method whereby the floor material is curved upward against the wall. A **base** is used to cover or as a guide to control the thickness of the plaster on the wall, while the **shoe** covers the intersection between the wall and floor. See Figure 13.14.

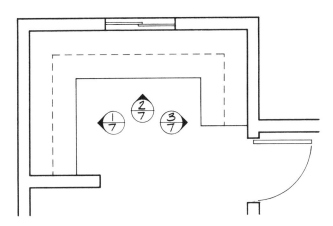

Figure 13.12 Partial plan of food preparation area.

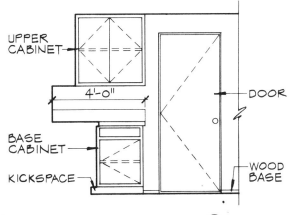

Figure 13.13 Partial interior elevation of ⟨3/7⟩.

Drafting an Interior Elevation: Examples

A Kitchen

Figure 13.15 shows a perspective view of a kitchen. The main portion has lip doors on the cabinets, and the extreme left side (not shown in the perspective) has flush overlay doors. Different types of cabinet doors are not usually mixed on a single project; here the intention is simply to show the different methods used to represent them on an interior elevation. Figure 13.16 shows a floor plan of the perspective drawing in Figure 13.15. Note the flush overlay cabinet on the left and the lip or flush cabinets on the right. The upper and base cabinets, slightly left of center, project forward.

Figure 13.17 shows the drafted interior elevation of one side of floor plan of the kitchen. You should take careful note of these points:

1. The difference in the method of representing a flush overlay and a lip door on the cabinets.
2. The outlining of the cabinet on the extreme right side of the drawing.

3. The use of dotted lines to show door swing, shelves, and the outline of the sink.
4. The handling of the forward projection of the upper and base cabinets slightly to the left of center.
5. Dimensions and, eventually, the location of notes.

A Condominium

Figures 13.18, 13.19, and 13.20 are partial floor plans of a two-story condominium project. The corresponding interior elevations can be found in Figures 13.21 through 13.28. Different ways of showing door open-

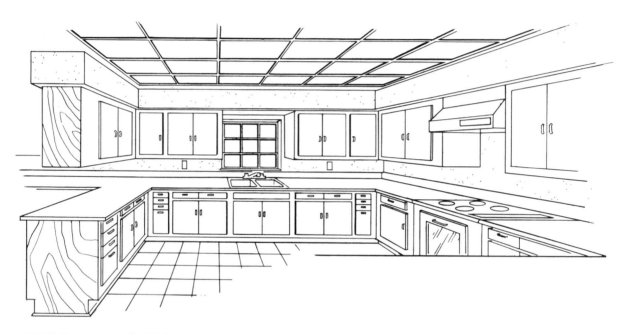

Figure 13.15 Perspective of a kitchen.

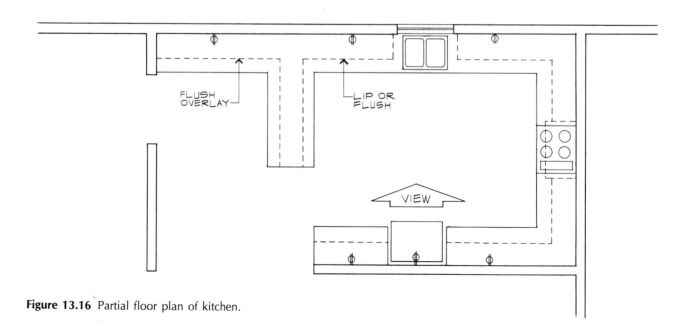

Figure 13.16 Partial floor plan of kitchen.

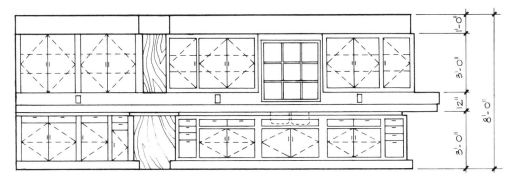

Figure 13.17 Interior elevation of Figure 13.16.

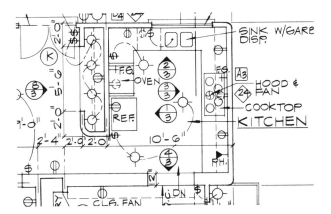

Figure 13.18 Partial floor plan of kitchen. (Courtesy of William F. Smith—Builder.)

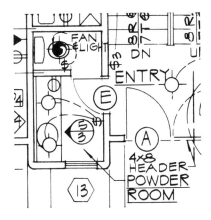

Figure 13.19 Partial floor plan of powder room. (Courtesy of William F. Smith—Builder.)

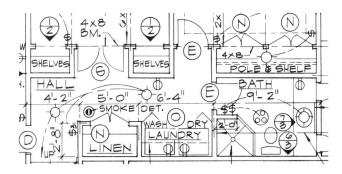

Figure 13.20 Partial lower floor plan. (Courtesy of William F. Smith—Builder.)

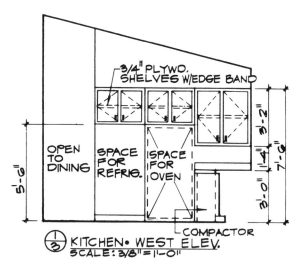

Figure 13.21 Kitchen: West elevation. (Courtesy of William F. Smith—Builder.)

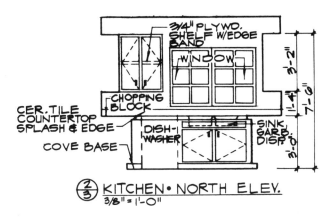

Figure 13.22 Kitchen: North elevation. (Courtesy of William F. Smith—Builder.)

ings, cabinets, appliances, partial walls, open shelves, and other features are given. Notice the dimensioning procedure and the noting method used.

A Lobby and Restroom

Figure 13.29 shows a partial floor plan for the lobby and restroom area of an office building. Figure 13.30 shows the North elevation of the men's toilet. Because this is a

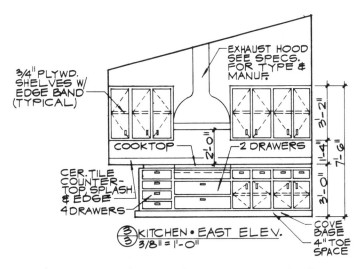

Figure 13.23 Kitchen: East elevation. (Courtesy of William F. Smith—Builder.)

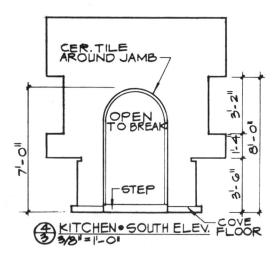

Figure 13.24 Kitchen: South elevation. (Courtesy of William F. Smith—Builder.)

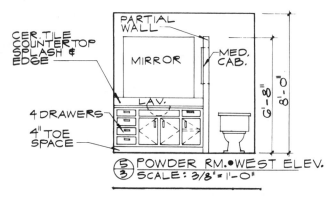

Figure 13.25 Powder room: West elevation. (Courtesy of William F. Smith—Builder.)

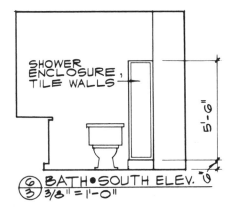

Figure 13.26 Bath: South elevation. (Courtesy of William F. Smith—Builder.)

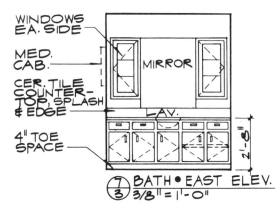

Figure 13.27 Bath: East elevation. (Courtesy of William F. Smith—Builder.)

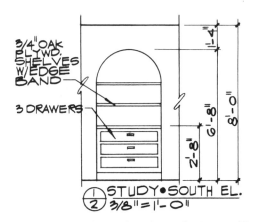

Figure 13.28 Study elevation. (Courtesy of William F. Smith—Builder.)

public facility, access for persons with disabilities is shown on both the partial floor plan and the interior elevation.

Additional interior elevations for a beach house and for a threatre are found in later chapters.

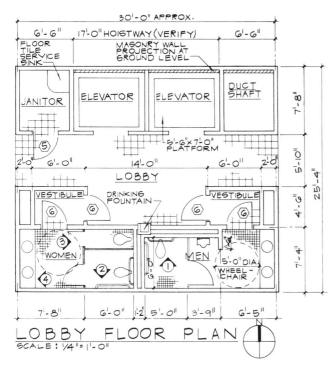

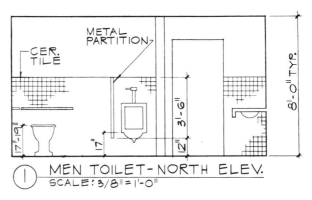

Figure 13.29 Partial floor plan of lobby and restroom. (Courtesy of Westmount, Inc., Real Estate Development, Torrance, CA.)

Figure 13.30 Men's toilet: North elevation. (Courtesy of Westmount, Inc., Real Estate Development, Torrance, CA.)

Templates

One of the best time-saving devices available for the drafting of interior elevations is a template, especially for plumbing fixtures. Plumbing fixtures have very difficult shapes to replicate with normal instruments, thus the use of a template similar to that shown on Figure 13.31 speeds up the drafting process.

If you need to draw ceramic tile, this template can provide you with ceramic tile spacing, as can be seen at the left. Shower heads and faucets are also positioned in relationship to a baseline at the bottom, which is the floor line.

Interior Elevation Drafting

The best way to transfer room sizes from a floor plan to an interior elevation is with the use of a pair of dividers. Dividers are most effective when the scale of the interior elevation is the same as or double the floor plan. See Figure 13.32. As seen in the building section, a proportional divider can be used if the scale is other than ¼" or ½". A scale of ⅜", a typical in-between scale used in drafting an interior elevation, can be accomplished by setting the proportional divider at ⅔.

Ryan Residence—Interior Elevation

Seven examples of interior elevations are provided to show the basic progression of the drafter through various stages: three elevations for the kitchen, three for a bathroom, and one for a utility room.

STAGE I (Figure 13.33). This is the block-out stage. Prior to this stage the drafter should consult the project book to become familiar with the shapes and sizes of

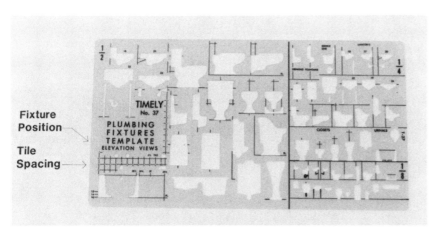

Figure 13.31 Plumbing fixture template. (Courtesy Timely Product Co.)

Figure 13.32 Drafting an interior elevation at ½″ scale from a ¼″-scale drawing.

the various kitchen appliances, plumbing fixtures, cabinets, and washer and dryer. The drafter starts by first laying out the ceiling line, the floor line, and the wall line. Next, changes are made in the ceiling level, owing to the presence of soffits or furred ceiling (lowered ceiling). With the use of a fade-away pencil, countertop levels and the underside of the upper cabinets are drafted.

STAGE II (Figure 13.34). Once the basic outline of the room is established, the doors and drawers are lightly outlined. If preconstructed cabinets are to be used, the distributor can usually help you size the doors and drawers based on the available sizes. A catalog listing basic sizes may be available in the project book. Basic available sizes are usually displayed on the back of these catalogs. If the cabinets are to be custom-built, then the designer of the firm should be consulted for the basic distribution of sizes to be used. In *The Professional Practice of Architectural Detailing*, a companion book to this one, a complete chapter is devoted to cabinets.

With the use of a template, plumbing appliances and the surrounding area are drawn. If the ceramic tile extends on the wall surface for only a couple of rows, this area is called a "splash." If it extends the entire height of the wall or at least to the height of a person, it is called a wainscot.

After placing the kitchen appliances, windows, and plumbing appliances, clearances are checked to see that they meet code requirements. For example, the water closet in one of the bathrooms is located between the tub and the cabinets. A 30″ minimum clearance is required by most municipalities. There are similar requirements for the space between the upper and base cabinets.

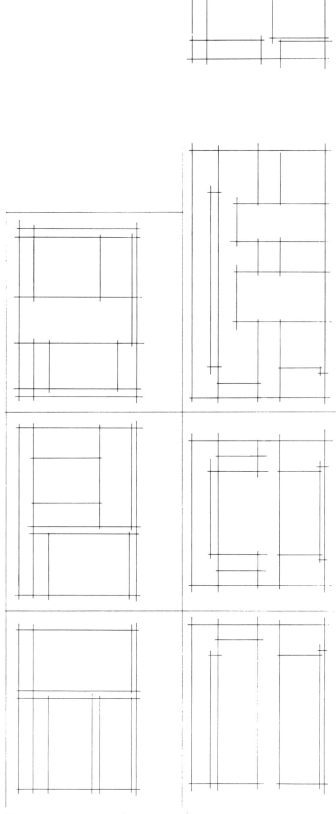

Figure 13.33 Interior elevations—Stage I.

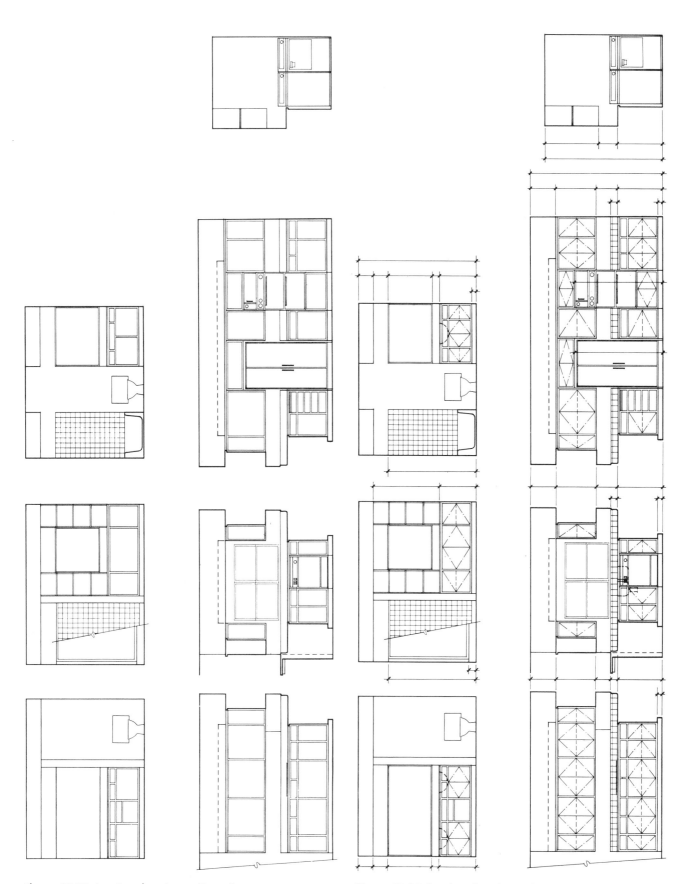

Figure 13.34 Interior elevations—Stage II.

Figure 13.35 Interior elevations—Stage III.

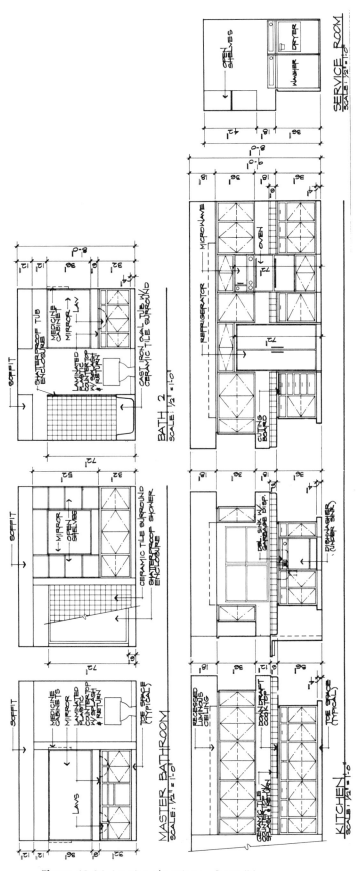

Figure 13.36 Interior elevations—Stage IV.

STAGE III (Figure 13.35). All information about cabinet sizes and configuration, door swings, and shelves, as well as all necessary vertical dimensions, are included at this stage. Note the location of the General Electric Space-Saver Dishwasher[1] as it is positioned in relation to the kitchen sink. Horizontal dimensions should not be included, as they are gotten from the floor plan. (An exception might be to size the width of a cabinet *not* bound on the ends with a wall and not dimensioned on the floor plan.)

STAGE IV (Figure 13.36). There are two ways to approach the final stage of a set of interior elevations. The first is to use a standardized office checklist. A second method is to develop one of your own, which should include the following:

A. Call-outs for all surface materials, other than that which exists on the finish schedule.

B. A description of all appliances, even those that are not on the surface facing the observer; for example, sinks, garbage disposals, recessed medicine cabinets.

C. A description of items that are not standard. The open shelves in the master bedroom is a classic example.

D. The use of standard conventions to denote shelves, cabinet door swings, drawers, and so forth.

E. Any clearances that need to be maintained. Refrigerator and oven/microwave are two good examples in this instance.

If a set of specifications are included in this set of drawings as a part of the construction documents, noting should be generic. For example, the note for tile should be stated simply as "ceramic tile"; the specific size, brand, color of grout, and so on would be covered in the specifications.

Profiling also plays an important part in the final stage. Notice how heavy the lines are around the perimeter so as to define the limits of the wall. Most other lines are drafted as a medium-dark line, except for objects that can be seen on the exterior elevation as well. This is why the window above the sink is drawn as a medium-light line.

Also note the appearance of dark objects that have been sectioned. The bath tub in Bath 2 is a good representation of this procedure.

Put yourself in the position of a contractor who must build this interior and ask yourself, "What will prevent me from building this kitchen or bathroom? What description, dimension, or clearance is missing?" Then note or dimension any missing elements.

[1]Courtesy General Electric.

SUMMARY

There are similarities and differences between exterior and interior elevations. Certain principles such as selecting, naming, and scaling are important to apply to both kinds of drawings. Generic terms are used to describe wall surfaces. Duplicate dimensions should be avoided. Disabled people and children need special consideration.

The ultimate goal of interior elevations is to convey information not found anywhere else about a specific wall.

IMPORTANT TERMS AND CONCEPTS

Interior elevations
Title references
N.I.C. (not in contract)
Cabinet doors: flush, flush overlay, lip
Face frame
Wall-to-floor intersection: topset, coving, base, shoe

REVIEW QUESTIONS

1. What is the main purpose of interior elevations?
2. How do interior elevations resemble exterior elevations? How do they differ from them?
3. Why are room widths not shown on interior elevations?
4. Give three examples of where horizontal dimensions are used in interior elevations.
5. What are some typical vertical heights you might find on an interior elevation of a kitchen? Give three examples.
6. What are some of the dimensions on an interior elevation that should be adapted to the needs of disabled persons?
7. What is the difference between a base and a shoe?
8. What does the abbreviation "N.I.C." stand for? Where and why is it used?
9. Name three uses of dotted (hidden) lines in drafting interior elevations.
10. What is generic noting?

LABORATORY PROBLEMS

1. Select a floor plan of a residence from a magazine. Make a list of the necessary interior elevations for such a structure.
2. Using the same floor plan, select a kitchen wall and freehand sketch the interior elevation.
3. Select a room other than the kitchen in your own residence and freehand sketch an interior elevation of the most unusual wall.
4. Refer to Chapter 8 ("Floor Plans"). Select a room that does not have an interior elevation included in this chapter and draft it using a ½" = 1'–0" scale.
5. Visit an office building. Sketch the floor plan of one of the floors. Draft an interior elevation of one of the major walls.

14

ARCHITECTURAL DETAILS

14

PREVIEW

There is much variety in the details than can be used in drafting. Sketched details for foundations, floor and wall framing, and window sections are of critical importance in resolving construction assemblies before drafting the final detail.

Communication with engineers and manufacturers is vital to help resolve details influenced by the structural members and by installation requirements.

OBJECTIVES

1. Understand how to design and solve construction assemblies using a scaled freehand sketch.
2. Be familiar with a wide range of architectural details you may face when you are preparing these details for a set of construction documents.

The Purpose of Architectural Details

Architectural **details** are enlarged drawings of specific architectural assemblies. These details are usually provided by the architect, and structural details are furnished by the structural engineer.

Architectural details are done for many different construction assemblies, including door and window details, fireplace details, stair details, and wall and roof assemblies. The number and kind of details needed for a given project depends entirely on the architect's or designer's estimate of what is needed to clarify the construction process. The contractor may request additional architectural details in the construction stage.

Architectural details often start with **freehand sketches** and an architectural scale in order to solve different construction assemblies in a structure. Once the details have been formulated in a scaled freehand sketch, they are then ready to be drafted in final form. Many details, such as standard foundation and wall assemblies, are relatively straightforward and do not require freehand sketches. The following sections provide examples of sketches and final forms of details for different residences to give you an understanding of what is required.

Using Details in Construction Documents

Freehand Detail Sketches: Mountain Residence

Architectural details encompass many construction assemblies, such as this mountain residence with its unique foundation details. This residence is treated in full in Chapter 17. Figure 14.1 shows a freehand sketch detail of an exterior bearing footing for this residence. There are some nonstandard conditions in this detail such as steel anchor clips for the connection of the floor joists to the mudsill (for lateral support), steel reinforcing placement in the wall for earth retention, and location of (and installation requirements for) a footing drain. Figures 14.2 and 14.3 show two other exterior footing conditions: Figure 14.2 shows a concrete floor condition below grade, and Figure 14.3 shows the wood deck connection to the exterior footing.

An interior foundation and masonry wall are also sketched in detail, showing steel reinforcing placement and floor joist assembly in Figure 14.4. Figures 14.5 and 14.6 show other interior footing conditions: Figure 14.5 shows a bearing footing with a concrete floor; Figure 14.6 shows a square concrete pier and reinforcing bars required to support a heavy concentrated load distributed by a 6 × 6 post. Study each of these carefully before proceeding further.

If you are asked to detail a wood beam and masonry wall connection, with the required assembly informa-

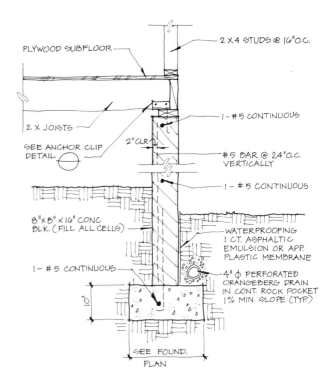

Figure 14.1 Detail of exterior bearing footing.

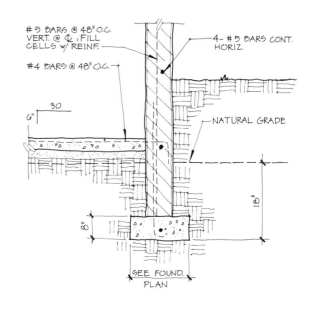

Figure 14.2 Detail of exterior footing.

tion, first draw a freehand sketch including the necessary information. Figure 14.7 shows such a sketch. The size of the steel plate dictates the masonry wall offset, and the embedment of the anchor bolts is 10″.

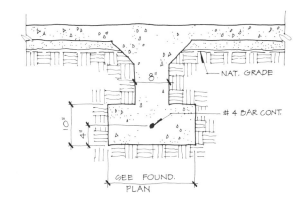

INTERIOR BEARING FOOTING

8"

NAT. GRADE

4 BAR CONT.

10"

4"

SEE FOUND.
PLAN

Figure 14.5 Detail of interior bearing footing.

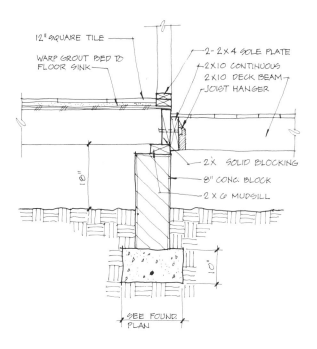

12" SQUARE TILE

WARP GROUT BED TO
FLOOR SINK

2-2 X 4 SOLE PLATE

2 X 10 CONTINUOUS

2 X 10 DECK BEAM

JOIST HANGER

2 X SOLID BLOCKING

8" CONC. BLOCK

2 X 6 MUDSILL

18"

10"

SEE FOUND.
PLAN

DECK @ EXTERIOR FOOTING

Figure 14.3 Detail of deck at exterior footing.

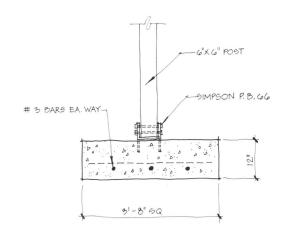

6" X 6" POST

SIMPSON P.B. 66

3 BARS EA. WAY

12"

3'-8" SQ

FOOTING @ WOOD POST

Figure 14.6 Detail of footing at wood post.

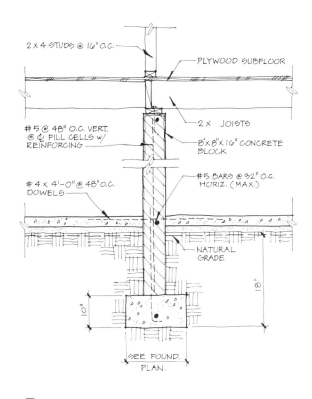

2 X 4 STUDS @ 16" O.C.

PLYWOOD SUBFLOOR

#5 @ 48" O.C. VERT.
@ ₵ FILL CELLS w/
REINFORCING

2 X JOISTS

8" X 8" X 16" CONCRETE
BLOCK

#4 X 4'-0" @ 48" O.C.
DOWELS

#5 BARS @ 32" O.C.
HORIZ. (MAX.)

NATURAL
GRADE

18"

10"

SEE FOUND.
PLAN.

INTERIOR CONC. BLOCK WALL

Figure 14.4 Detail of interior concrete block wall.

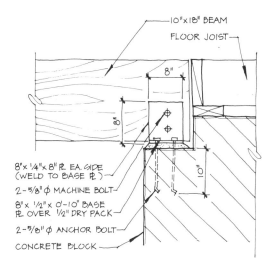

10" X 18" BEAM

FLOOR JOIST

8"

8"

8" X ¼" X 8" PL. EA. SIDE
(WELD TO BASE PL.)

2-⅝" ∅ MACHINE BOLT

8" X ½" X 0'-10" BASE
PL. OVER ½" DRY PACK

2-⅝" ∅ ANCHOR BOLT

10"

CONCRETE BLOCK

WOOD BEAM CONNECTION

Figure 14.7 Detail of wood beam connection.

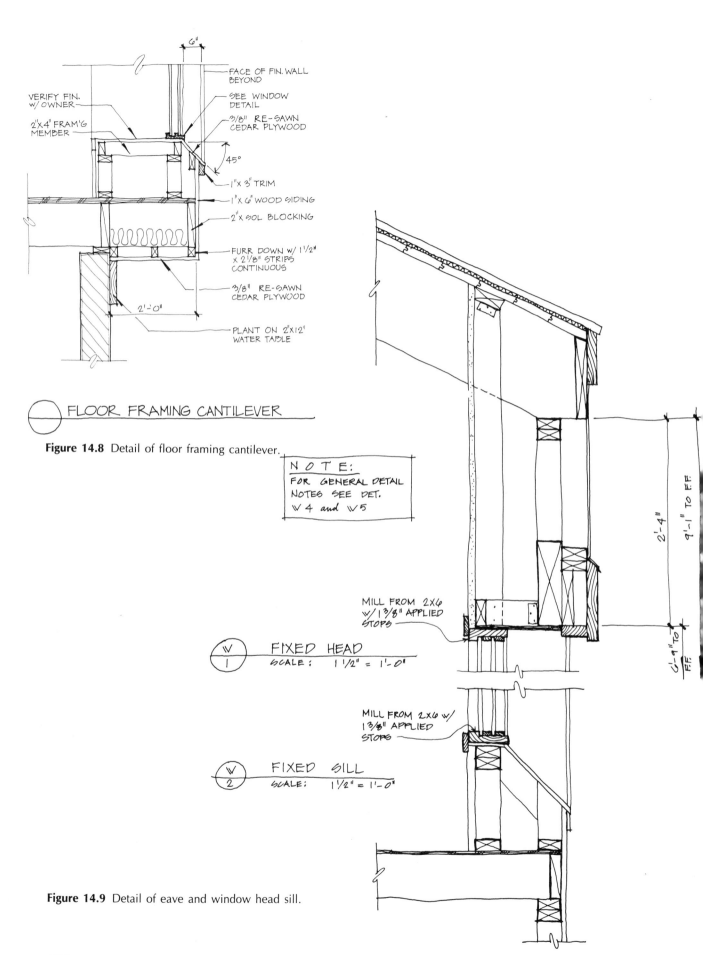

FACE OF FIN. WALL
BEYOND

SEE WINDOW
DETAIL

VERIFY FIN.
w/ OWNER

3/8" RE-SAWN
CEDAR PLYWOOD

2"x4" FRAM'G
MEMBER

45°

1"x 3" TRIM

1"x 6" WOOD SIDING

2"x SOL BLOCKING

FURR DOWN w/ 1 1/2"
x 2 1/8" STRIPS
CONTINUOUS

3/8" RE-SAWN
CEDAR PLYWOOD

2'-0"

PLANT ON 2"x12"
WATER TABLE

6"

FLOOR FRAMING CANTILEVER

Figure 14.8 Detail of floor framing cantilever.

N O T E :
FOR GENERAL DETAIL
NOTES SEE DET.
W 4 and W 5

MILL FROM 2x6
w/ 1 3/8" APPLIED
STOPS

W 1   FIXED HEAD
SCALE: 1 1/2" = 1'-0"

MILL FROM 2x6 w/
1 3/8" APPLIED
STOPS

W 2   FIXED SILL
SCALE: 1 1/2" = 1'-0"

2'-4"

9'-1" TO F.F.

6'-9" TO F.F.

Figure 14.9 Detail of eave and window head sill.

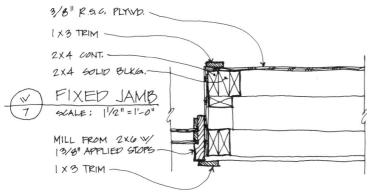

3/8" R.S.C. PLYWD.

1 X 3 TRIM

2 X 4 CONT.

2 X 4 SOLID BLKG.

FIXED JAMB
SCALE: 1 1/2" = 1'-0"

MILL FROM 2X6 W/
1 3/8" APPLIED STOPS

1 X 3 TRIM

Figure 14.10 Detail of window jamb.

An important factor in architectural detailing is providing details that are an integral part of the architectural design of the building. For example, if floor cantilevers and wood soffits are an integral part of the design, first design and solve these assemblies in sketch form, as shown in Figure 14.8, before completing the final detail. As this figure shows, creativity and craftsmanship in architectural detailing are as important as any other factors in designing a structure.

In this particular residence, we thought that the top of the head section of the windows and doors should have a direct relationship with the eave assembly. So we detailed the eave assembly with the various wood members forming a wood soffit directly above the head section of the window. See Figure 14.9. We sketched in detail the window sill and exterior wall assembly projecting down from the head section. From both these figures, 14.8 and 14.9, it was possible to design and detail the **jamb** section for this particular opening, using the established head and sill section as a guide for the detailed assembly. Figure 14.10 shows a freehand sketch of the jamb details. We used two wood stud walls at the window area to provide a deep architectural relief at the openings. See Figure 14.9.

Details: Beach Residence
(For additional details, see Chapter 7).

Foundation Details. The architectural details for this project were fairly conventional but were still worth investigating with freehand drawings. For example, we detailed the foundation details for this two-story residence to satisfy the sandy soil requirements. Figure 14.11 shows a detail for the exterior bearing wall. Because this soil did not provide good bearing qualities, we used horizontal reinforcing rods at the top and bottom of the foundation wall. Nonbearing walls still required a minimal footing to support the weight of the wall and a depth of concrete to receive the anchor bolts. See Figure 14.12. Because this residence has a change of floor levels, we provided a detail through the floor transitions. Figure 14.13 shows a detail at a location that

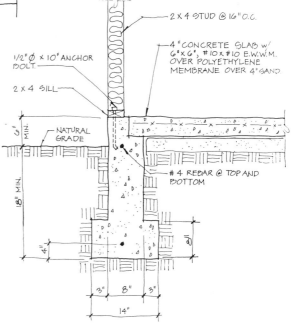

EXTERIOR BEARING

Figure 14.11 Detail of exterior bearing footing.

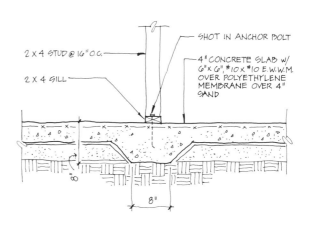

INTERIOR NON-BEARING

A

Figure 14.12 Detail of interior nonbearing footing.

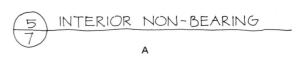

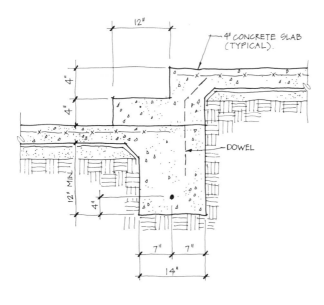

Figure 14.13 Detail of change of level with step.

has incorporated the **risers** and **tread.** (A riser is the vertical dimension of a stair step and the tread is the horizontal dimension.) The risers and tread are dimensioned, as are rebar ties for the connection of the upper concrete floor. (Rebar ties act as dowels to join two concrete elements.)

A large storage area and a mechanical room were located in the basement. A detail was needed to show the assembly for the basement and floor level changes. See Figure 14.14. The wood stud wall has been offset in front of the upper level concrete floor to provide a nailing surface for the wall finishes at both levels.

Details for Framing Assemblies. Architectural details for framing assemblies were also provided in these construction documents. One example is the eave detail. First, the project designer did a freehand drawing. Then this freehand drawing was given to a draftsperson for final drawing. Figure 14.15 shows the freehand sketch.

Figure 14.16 shows a study of a deck and handrail detail located directly above a recessed garage door. The deck assembly at the building wall is also detailed, because proper flashing and drainage are needed to prevent water leaks. Figures 14.17 and 14.18 resemble each other but show different floor framing conditions. Other deck and handrail conditions are also detailed. Figure 14.19 shows the flashing and handrail assemblies and a continuous wood soffit to be used at the wall cantilever.

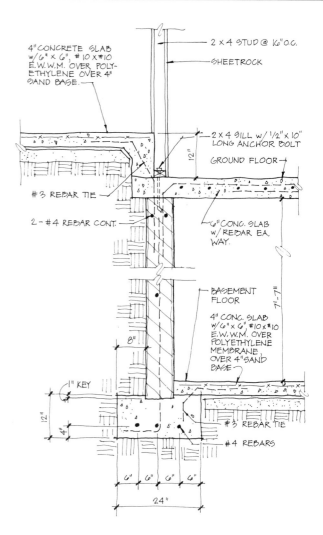

Figure 14.14 Detail of concrete block wall at basement—slab floor.

Details: Theatre

In some projects, structural complexities may dictate various construction assemblies. For example, a masonry and steel structure has many architectural details that are governed by structural engineering requirements. The detailer must coordinate these details with the structural engineer. Figure 14.20 shows a detail for a steel beam connection where the beam, steel decking, and concrete floor thickness have been designed by the structural engineer. From these required members, the architectural detail is developed showing wall materials, ceiling attachment, and underfloor space for mechanical and electrical runs. Figure 14.20 has a note to "SEE STRUCTURAL." This refers the reader to the structural engineer's drawings, which provide such information as

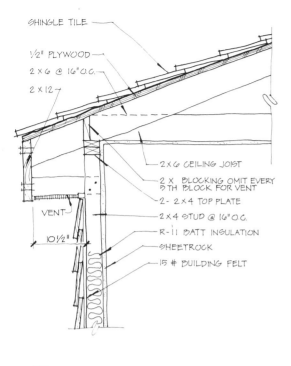

EAVE DETAIL

Figure 14.15 Eave detail.

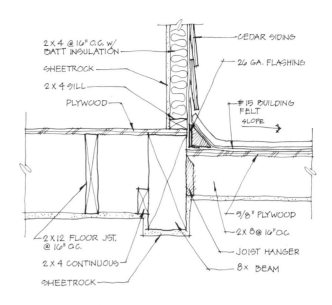

BEAM AND DECK @ GARAGE

Figure 14.17 Detail of beam and deck at garage.

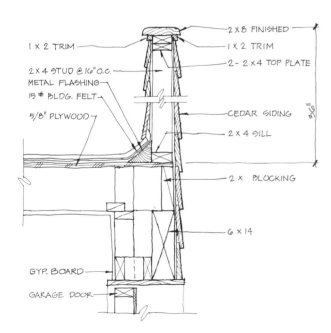

DECK RAILING & HDR. @ GARAGE

Figure 14.16 Detail of deck railing and header at garage.

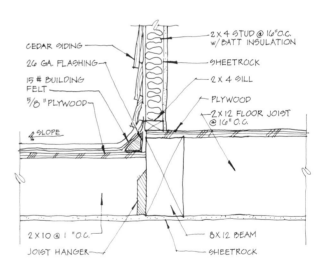

BEAM & DECK @ LIVING ROOM

Figure 14.18 Detail of beam and deck at living room.

type and length of welds for steel connections, and size and weight of steel members. Note the call-out on the steel beam of "W 8 × 10." The "W" refers to the shape of the beam (here a wide **flange**), the "8" refers to the depth of the beam (here 8 inches), and the "10" refers to the weight of the beam per lineal foot (here 10 lb per linear foot).

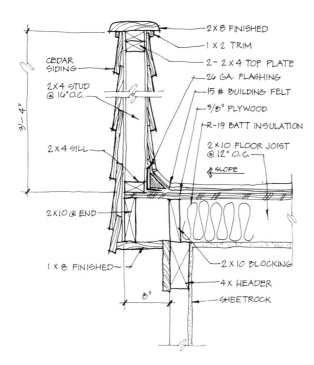

DECK RAILING ABOVE LIVING RM.

Figure 14.19 Detail of deck railing above living room.

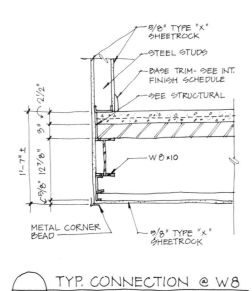

TYP. CONNECTION @ W8

Figure 14.20 Detail of typical connection at a steel beam.

A second example is shown in Figure 14.21. The steel stud framing is terminated at the bottom of the steel beam and extensive galvanized iron flashing has been used to cover and protect the intersection of the various members at the ridge.

Some architectural details become complex and require much study before the finished detail is drafted. See Figure 14.22. This eave and column detail is in-

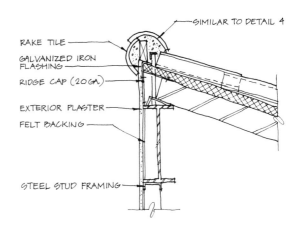

RIDGE @ MECHANICAL WELL

Figure 14.21 Detail of ridge at mechanical well.

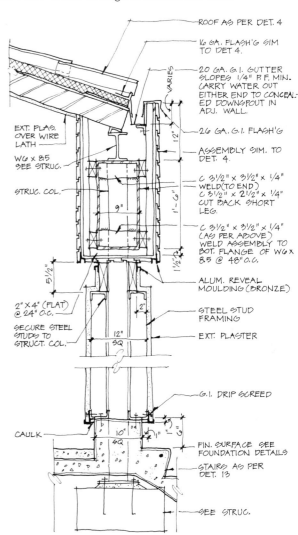

EAVE AND COLUMN DETAIL

Figure 14.22 Eave and column detail.

tricate and shows the entire column assembly from the foundation to the roof, including the eave detail. Notes refer the viewer to other details for more information. Usually, it is unnecessary and unadvisable to repeat all the information from one detail to another; changes made on one detail must be made on any other affected.

Many projects require a specific architectural detail to show conditions that will satisfy a governing building code requirement. Figure 14.23, for example, shows exactly where a fire protection coating is required under a steel roof decking that covers the structural steel angle on a masonry wall. This information is combined with a roof parapet detail. Figure 14.24 shows another detail for areas requiring fire protection.

Figure 14.25 shows a third example of this kind of detail. This detail of a handicapped ramp shows the required number of handrails, the height of the handrails

above the ramp, and the clear space required between the handrail and the wall. This information has also been combined with the structural requirements for the support of a low wall on the outside of the ramp.

Footing details may also be sketched for various conditions as an aid to the finished drawings. Figure 14.26 shows a footing detail supporting a steel stud wall and Figure 14.27 a footing detail supporting the masonry wall that separates the auditoriums.

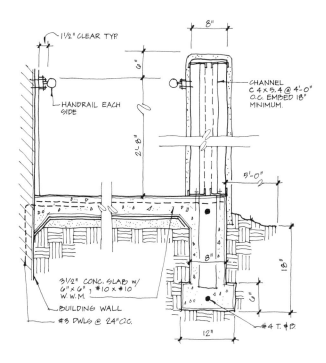

Figure 14.25 Ramp detail.

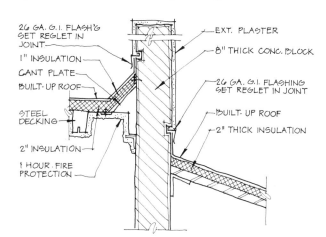

Figure 14.23 Parapet detail.

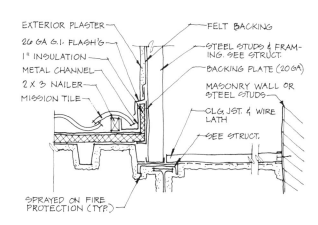

Figure 14.24 Base flashing detail.

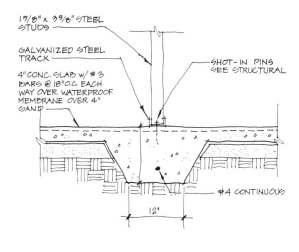

Figure 14.26 Steel stud footing detail.

eoften。

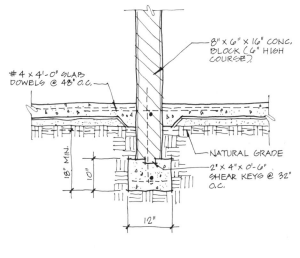

Figure 14.27 Block wall footing detail.

Hardline

Actually, this chapter should begin here, with hardlining of details, because that is what the final appearance of details should be. We hope we have not led you to believe that most detailing is done freehand—quite the contrary. Detailing is done freehand only at the conceptual level and confirmation stage to check whether, in fact, what was seen in the mind's eye really works. Freehand details are also used as a means of communication from the mind of the designer to the real world of the drafter. We hope you will view the first few pages of this chapter as just that, a visual communication with the reader, analyzing assembly ideas and confirming them practically with sketches.

Henceforth we will explore three details, from sketch to final hardline, to convey the proper method of translating freehand details into usable hardline details.

Finally, we will display a set of hardlined details from the Ryan Residence for a window, footing, and a fireplace.

Approach to Detailing

Before you hardline draft a detail, you must understand its primary and secondary functions. Although functions vary, they may be categorized within a few divisions.

A. Structural—The intent of a detail may be to reveal the method of connection between two structural members or to show the transition between wood and steel members and the connective device between them.

B. Architectural—The purpose of a detail may be to ensure that a particular architectural feature is ex-

plained, to maintain a certain aesthetic quality to a part of the building.

C. Environmental—A detail may reveal how to deal with environmental and natural forces such as sun, rain, wind, snow, and light, as well as man-made problems of noise, pollution, and so on.

D. Human Needs—A detail may ensure that a particular human need is meet. Stairs are a good example of this type of need, configured so as to allow a person to safely ascend or descend with the least amount of energy expended so as to avoid fatigue. This is done by formatting the proper angle of tread and riser. Special needs are explained in Chapter 3 (ADA), such as those of elderly or physical impaired persons.

E. Connection—It is critical to detail a transition of one plane into another; for example, the connection between the wall and the floor, or between the wall and the roof or ceiling.

F. Material Limits—A detail may reveal the limits of the material with which you are dealing. You can drill a hole into a 2 × 6 floor joist, but how large a hole before you weaken the member too much? The limits can be dimensioned or noted right in the detail.

G. Facilitation—In a tenant improvement drawing, a floor may be elevated to allow housing of computer cables. A detail can be drafted through this floor, showing the floor system support and the minimum clearances needed to accommodate the cables for maintenance.

Detailing Based on a Proper Sequence

STEP 1—The drafter can accomplish the crucial *block-out* stage by blindly copying the freehand sketch provided. Although this approach may be the most expedient, it misses two very important points: the drafter will never catch errors in the sketch, and the drafter becomes a tracer rather than a significant and valuable employee of the firm. Quickly outline the functional constraints of the detail and check to see that the sketch complies.

STEP 2—Once you have laid out the most significant form, its adjacent parts can now be drawn. For example, in drafting an exterior bearing footing for a wood floor system, do not draft the floor first and then add the footing; rather, draft the footing first as it is built.

STEP 3—Critical dimensioning is added.

STEP 4—Now notes should be strategically placed so they easily convey the message.

STEP 5—Designation of materials for the various pieces (wood, steel, earth, etc.) can be added at this point or at any of the previous stages.

STEP 6—Profiling and outlining are almost synonymous. Darken the perimeter of the most important shape or shapes in the detail.

STEP 7—Using the proper method described earlier in this book, add reference symbols, a title, and a scale so that each detail has a "name" and scale.

Shortcut

As details are drafted, their originals are often kept on file and adhesive labels applied to the working drawings. Very rarely will you ever have an opportunity to use a detail again in its entirety. However, it can be used as a tracer or altered easily. As a tracer, the original detail is placed under the vellum and the needed similar units traced.

Some offices have tracers prepared with minimal redundant information so the drafter can add information to the tracer. See Figure 14.28. For example, the context of a door might be drawn showing header, exterior skin, and interior wall covering, into which a particular brand of window might be fitted with special finishes around the perimeter.

If only a simple change is needed, such as changing the gravel under a slab to sand, a plain paper copier is used most effectively. First you make a plain paper copy. Next, void the undesirable information, textures, or dimensions with white-out chemicals (white acrylic paint will do), or simply cut out the unwanted information. Make another copy, using vellum in the paper cartridge. Draft the new information onto the vellum and make a new adhesive. File this second-generation drawing as a new original. In this way, countertops can be changed in base cabinet details without redrafting the entire detail and the overhang of an eave detail can be altered rapidly.

With a simple adjustment to your triangle, the cumbersome process of drawing guidelines for lettering or hatching for masonry can be easily accomplished. Two or three lines, spaced at ⅛" apart, are drawn on your triangle. Depending on the ink, these will be temporary or permanent. Lines can also be etched into a triangle with a modeling knife. See Figure 14.29. This triangle is etched, and the slot of the etching is filled with ink. Because the etching is on the angular portion of the triangle, you can combine two triangles, as shown in Figure 14.30, and draw horizontal lines. Flip the etched triangle while holding the lower triangle in place, and you automatically have vertical lines. This provides a rapid way of drawing floor tile on a plan or ceramic tile on an interior elevation. The possibilities are endless—for example, horizontal or vertical siding on an exterior elevation or an indication for a chain-link fence.

By skipping a etched line or two, you can duplicate distances of ⅛, ¼, or even ⅜.

Sizing Hardline Details

If you are working with a 24 × 36 sheet of vellum as formatted on Figure 5.39 and you extend the tick marks to form a matrix for detail placement, you will discover that the spaces measure 4 ⅝" high by 6½" wide. Outline a few of these spaces, as shown in Figure 14.31, on an 8½ × 11 sheet of paper as the size limits of the detail. Two spaces have been drawn so as to accommodate

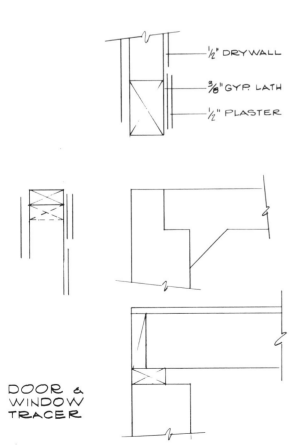

Figure 14.28 Window and door tracer.

Figure 14.29 Instrument for hatching.

Figure 14.30 Instrument for hatching.

details whose sizes exceed one space. This allows the drafter to stay within the limits of designated areas and not encroach on the drawing space allocated for another drawing or detail.

Most of the details were sized this way to fit onto individual sheets so that they can easily be stored in a file and transferred onto the large sheets in a predetermined position. See the portfolio of the Ryan Residence details at the end of this chapter.

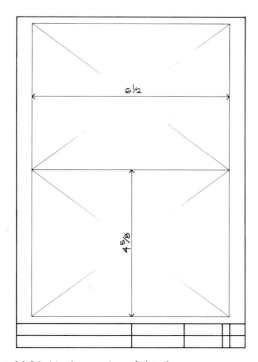

Figure 14.31 Maximum size of detail.

With the availability of word processing and CAD, the drawing zone has been further subdivided into the drawing area and the note or keynote area. See Figure 14.32. The detail placed on one side allows the noting (done by CAD, word processor, etc.) to be done with ease. The drafter finishes the detail by drawing the leaders, thus connecting the notes with the drawing. See Figure 14.33. A further refinement is the use of keynoting. This refers to the practice of giving each note a number or a

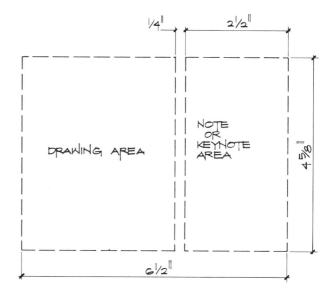

Figure 14.32 Detail format with noting area.

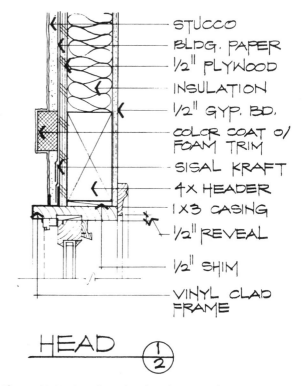

Figure 14.33 Window detail with noting format.

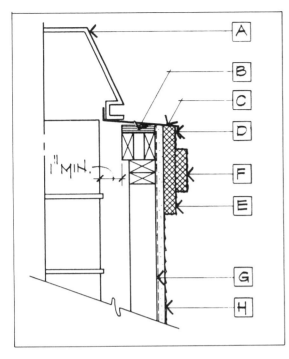

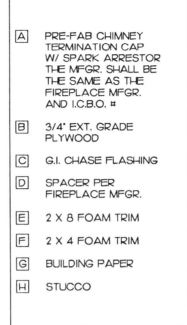

A	PRE-FAB CHIMNEY TERMINATION CAP W/ SPARK ARRESTOR THE MFGR. SHALL BE THE SAME AS THE FIREPLACE MFGR. AND I.C.B.O. #
B	3/4" EXT. GRADE PLYWOOD
C	G.I. CHASE FLASHING
D	SPACER PER FIREPLACE MFGR.
E	2 X 8 FOAM TRIM
F	2 X 4 FOAM TRIM
G	BUILDING PAPER
H	STUCCO

Figure 14.34 Chimney detail with keynoting format.

letter. When the detail is drafted, the leaders will have the corresponding number or letter pertaining to the note. See Figure 14.34. This method can be used by a manual drafter or by CAD, expediting the drawing procedure.

Footing Detail

The exterior bearing footing for the Ryan Residence is not unlike the freehand sketch found in Figure 14.11 and hardlined in Figure 14.36. The difference between one footing and another can be so subtle that it takes a trained eye to distinguish them. As you compare the freehand detail with the hardline detail mentioned in these two figures, note the size difference at the bottom, the thickness of the foundation wall, the number of rebars, backfill, and sand versus gravel under the slab. These are two details that look alike but are really totally different in how they react to the various forces acting on them.

Before we hardline the exterior bearing footing for the Ryan Residence, let's look at four considerations for this type of footing:

A. *Configuration.* Most typically used is a two-pour inverted "T" shape. Through the years the industry has found this to be the best distributor of weight while using the least amount of material. Much like snowshoes distributing concentrated loads through the legs onto a wide platform, the inverted T dis-

tributes weight over a vast area as long as it does not break. Notice how the weight from above is distributed on the soil in Figure 14.35(A). Surrounding the example are dimensions; "X" is based on the weight of the structure and the ability of the soil to hold up this weight by virtue of its quality.

As a rule of thumb, the thickness should be, as the example shows, ½ X. The depth of the footing, marked "A," is again a matter of the stability of the soil or the frost line, or even a requirement of building officials, as a minimum. The prevailing attitude is, however, that rather than use established maximums, soundness of construction should prevail. The amount the stem (of the inverted "T") that extends above the soil might be a matter of how high it should be to keep moisture from the first piece of wood to come in contact with the concrete or to prevent termite infestation.

B. *Soil.* The cost of a piece of property might be a matter of the view it provides, its convenience to various major streets, its slope, and so on, but many clients overlook the condition and quality of the soil. If a property has loosely filled soil (not permitted in many areas), the depth of the footing may have to extend far beyond the fill to firm soil, making the foundation very expensive. Moreover, in a marshy area where the bearing pressure of the earth (weight that can be put onto the soil measured in pounds per square foot) is minimal, the type of and shape of the foundation may dictate a prohibitively expensive system, making the property impractical if not unbuildable. See Figure 14.35(B).

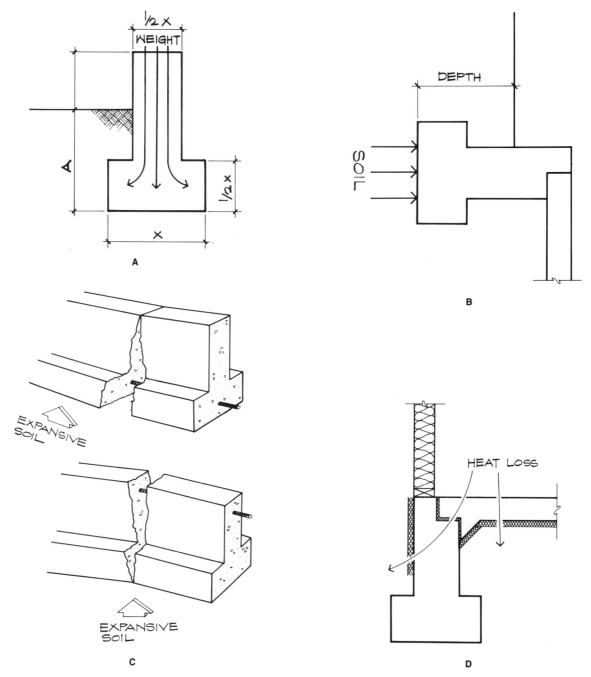

Figure 14.35 Footing concerns.

C. *Strength.* Concrete, an excellent material in compression, is very brittle in tension. The load imposed from above puts the concrete in compression, which is its strength. However, the footing travels the length of a wall, and with expansive soil or irregular loading, forms a beam that is in tension. This beam will break or shatter along the top or bottom, depending on the forces at work—thus the introduction of reinforcing bars, which are strong in tension, like a rope or chain, but rather weak in compression. By combining the two materials, we

have strength in both tension and compression. See Figure 14.35(C).

D. *Energy.* In this era of energy-efficient buildings, architects are paying extra attention to areas through which heat is lost. The movement of heat, as any physics major will tell you, is from hot to cold. In colder weather, we must heat structures such as the Ryan Residence using whatever natural resources are available: natural gas, petroleum products, or, in some cases, electricity. To keep it from leaving the structure, heat is contained by means of insulating floors, walls, and ceilings. Notice the various locations for insulation on the footing in Figure 14.35(D).

There are numerous other factors to consider in designing a footing. Where should the plastic membrane be put (if one is to be used)? Between the slab and the sand? Below the sand? How is the thickness of the slab determined? Does it require reinforcing? Backfill is still another factor—how much?—and so on. The answers to these questions relate to strength, energy conservation as a reaction to soil, and/or to the selected shape as mentioned before.

Ryan Residence—Exterior Bearing Footing

STAGE I (Figure 14.36). The grade line should be drawn first. This becomes the datum from which you can establish all of the necessary vertical dimensions, such as the distance to be placed between the floor and the grade. The width of the footing (bearing surface) is the next item to be measured. Half this width is centered for the stem wall. Footing thickness and slab thickness are positioned, and finally the beginning of the stud above the stem wall is drawn to create the slot for the slab.

STAGE II (Figure 14.37). After checking the accuracy of the first stage, proceed to the inclusion of the adjacent parts: insulation, sand or gravel, sill, the stud with its sheathing, and the termination points of the detail, which will be turned into break lines at a later stage.

STAGE III (Figure 14.38). This stage is actually a combination of Steps 3 and 5, dimensioning and material designation. Be sure to use the correct designation of material for each of the seven or so differing materials used here: plywood, batt insulation, rigid insulation, concrete, rebars, and so on.

STAGE IV (Figure 14.39). This is the final stage, which includes additional profiling and noting. To keep the noting consistent from detail to detail, many offices have a standard set of notes. The project manager may select the proper notes from this standard list and make them available to the drafter. In other offices, especially small offices, this practice may not be used at all; rather, the drafter is presumed to have the necessary training and ability to note a detail properly. Detailing on a CAD system is merely a matter of recalling the proper notes, which have been stored in the computer, and positioning them.

If the notes are word processed, the drafter merely prints the necessary notes onto an adhesive and applies

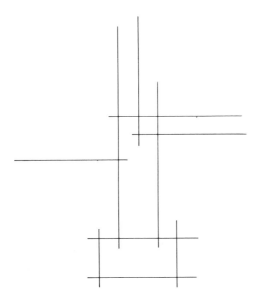

Figure 14.36 Exterior bearing footing—Stage I.

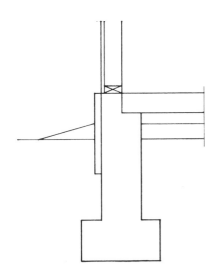

Figure 14.37 Exterior bearing footing—Stage II.

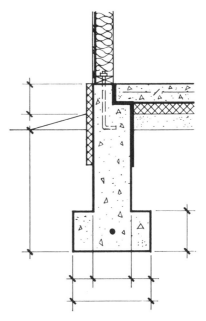

Figure 14.38 Exterior bearing footing—Stage III.

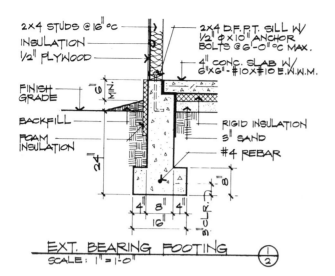

Figure 14.39 Exterior bearing footing—Stage IV.

them to the drawing in the form of a chart called "keynotes." See Figure 14.34. This procedure can easily be adapted to the computer as well.

Window Detail

Before drafting a window detail, the drafter should understand the action of the window's moving parts, its attributes, the installation procedure, and how to prepare the surrounding area before and after installation.

The window selected for the Ryan Residence is an Atrium double-tilt window. See Figure 14.40. It was selected because it is not the typical double-hung, casement, or sliding window, and because of its special features.

Figure 14.40 Atrium double-tilt window. (Courtesy The Atrium Door & Window Company, a Division of Fojtasek Companies, Inc.)

Action and Features

As seen in the diagram in Figure 14.41, the window tilts inward, creating a wind scoop as diagrammed in Figure 14.41(A). This makes the window ideal for placement adjacent to a bed or a desk, positioned on the windward side of the site, or, for that matter, anywhere you do not want direct wind. The windows pivot at the base, and the mechanism allows for ease of cleaning and removal. The insulated high-performance glass comprises two

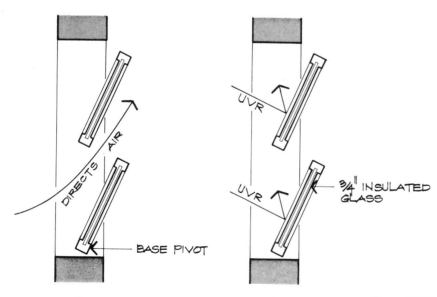

A   B   **Figure 14.41** Diagram of atrium double-tilt window.

sheets of glass with air space between them, making this a ¾" thick glazing. See Figure 14.40. The glass blocks ultraviolet rays to prevent damage to drapery, carpets, furniture, and humans. See Figure 14.41(B).

The exterior is vinyl clad with full bulb weatherstripping around its perimeter, and the interior is pine, which can be stained or painted to match the interior decor. Finally, removable wood grilles can be ordered to create a matrix pattern for a divided look. These divisions in a window are called lites. As with the main frame, these grilles are finished on the exterior and unfinished on the inside face. The grilles are clipped into place and are easily removed for window cleaning.

Insulation

By studying the installation method, the detailer can better emphasize certain features of the detail. As seen in the original photograph, there are fins around the perimeter that will be used to nail the window in place. Therefore, the rough opening (the rough framed opening) must have enough clearance to accommodate the preconstructed window. In this case the clearance will be ½" both vertically and horizontally, compensating for any irregularity in the framing members and allowing the window to be placed into the rough opening perfectly level. See Figure 14.42. The wood shim under the windowsill in this sketch functions as a leveling device while sealing the space between the rough sill and the finished sill of the window. See Figure 14.43.

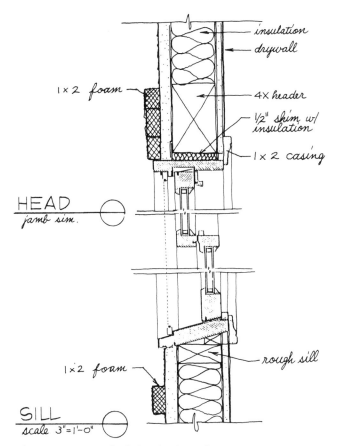

Figure 14.43 Finished sketch of window context.

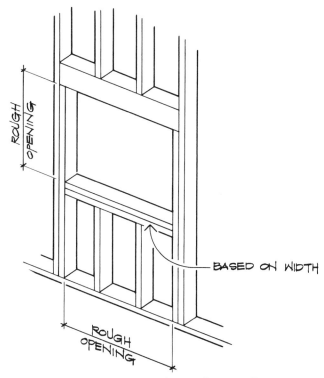

Figure 14.42 Rough opening for window installation.

Before and after the fin of the window is nailed to the wall, a moisture/vapor barrier is placed around the frame. The "Weatherproofing" section in Chapter 11 can acquaint you with the various materials used to waterproof windows and the reasons for the positioning of particular pieces of waterproofing material.

For the installation of this window, we use an asphalt-saturated kraft paper to cover the building and a secondary strip (a band of about 6"–8") of heavily saturated heavy weight kraft-type paper called sisal-kraft.

In Figure 14.44, note the positioning of the building paper and its secondary member, the sisal-kraft. Both sheets are placed under the fin on the sill, one half of the set placed under the fin on the jamb and both sheets over the fin on the head. This strategic placement acts to shed water and prevent its penetration. This method is unique to zone C (see the map in Figure 11.50).

Raised Frame

There will be raised plaster frames around the windows. Such frames, affectionately called "stucco bumps," can be produced in a number of ways. Two possible solutions are described as follows. The first is to use one or more pieces of wood to raise the surface, as seen in Figure 14.45. Notice how the building paper is carried

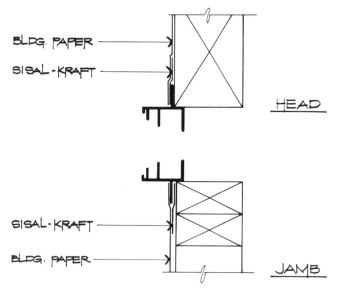

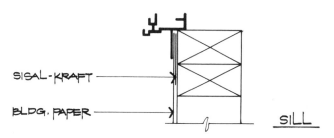

Figure 14.44 Placement of building paper around window.

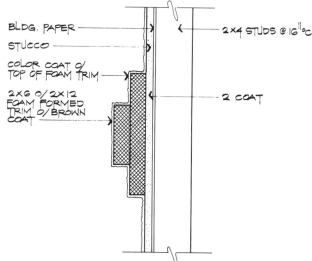

Figure 14.46 Raising a surface with foam.

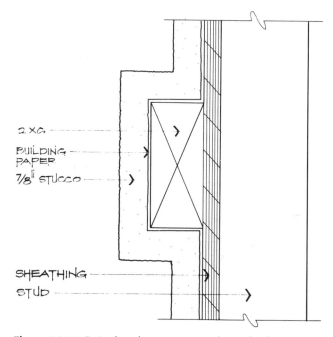

Figure 14.45 Raised surface using wood as a backing.

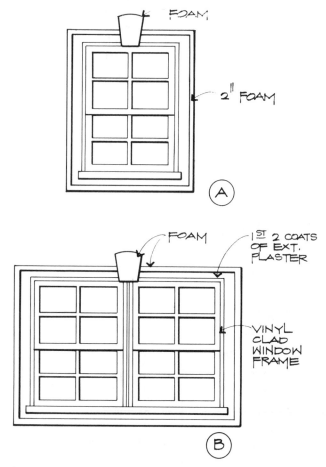

Figure 14.47 Raised frame of foam.

completely around the wood (including the metal mesh, which is not shown). The exterior plaster (stucco) follows the contour of the complete unit.

A second possible solution is the use of Styrofoam. See Figure 14.46. In this example two pieces of foam have been placed over the first two coats of stucco, which are called the scratch coat and the brown coat. The final coat (called the color coat) is placed over the

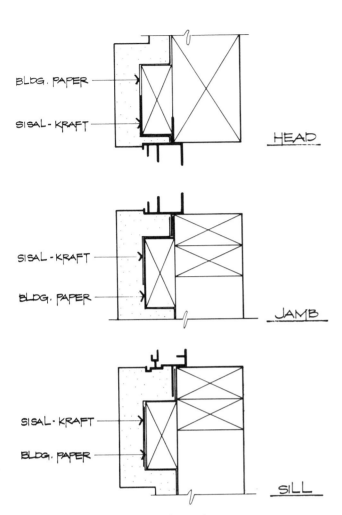

Figure 14.48 Raised frame of wood.

entire unit, completing the image as a whole. Notice the position of the building paper.

For the Ryan Residence, the second method is used and a keystone is placed at the top of this raised frame, as can be seen in elevation in Figure 14.47. Figure 14.48 shows the placement of the building paper and the sisal-kraft (called counterflashing).

Rough Opening Size

Most brochures provided by manufacturers contain written descriptions of a window itself and its various features, the available stock sizes, suggested details depending on the context, and a drawing of the window at $3'' = 1'-0''$ scale, which can be used as tracer or scissor-drafted into the detail. Figure 14.49 shows a drafter checking typical installation details and identifying the different features. This sheet is replicated on Figure 14.50. Figure 14.51 shows the drafter checking on the rough opening sizes. Many manufacturers list the available sizes in terms of rough opening so that the actual size of a window is ½″ smaller than the call-out size. For example, a DW2030 is really 19½″ × 29½″. Notice the drawing above the left hand on this photograph. It is drawn at $3'' = 1'-0''$ scale and can be used as a tracer or scissor-drafted, as is the case in the Ryan Residence project.

Ryan Residence—Window Detail

STAGE I (Figure 14.52). Actually, this is not a drawing stage but, rather, a preparation stage. The $3'' = 1'-0''$ vertical section provided by the manufacturer's literature is reproduced on a plain paper copier. See Figure

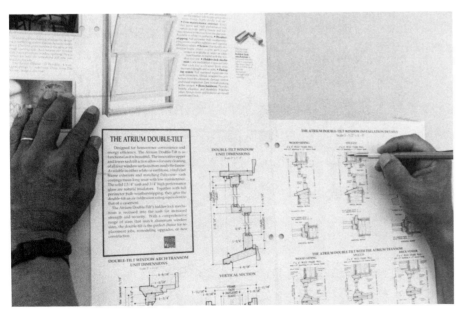

Figure 14.49 Suggested detailing by manufacturer. (Courtesy The Atrium Door & Window Company, a Division of Fojtasek Companies, Inc.)

THE ATRIUM DOUBLE-TILT WINDOW INSTALLATION DETAILS
Scale 1 - 1/2" = 1' - 0"

WOOD SIDING
2" x 4" WOOD FRAME WALL
with 1/2" sheathing & 1/2" interior finish

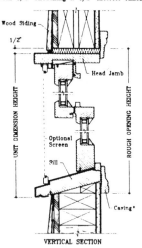

VERTICAL SECTION

* Furnished by others

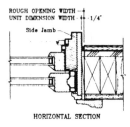

HORIZONTAL SECTION

STUCCO
2" x 6" WOOD FRAME WALL
with 1/2" sheathing & 1/2" interior finish

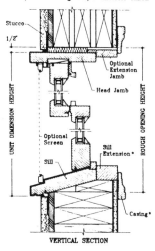

VERTICAL SECTION

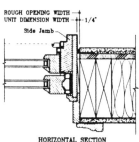

HORIZONTAL SECTION

BRICK VENEER
2" x 4" WOOD FRAME WALL
with 1/2" sheathing & 1/2" interior finish

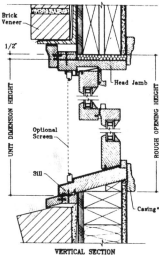

VERTICAL SECTION

* Furnished by others

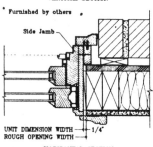

HORIZONTAL SECTION

THE ATRIUM DOUBLE-TILT WITH THE ATRIUM TRANSOM

WOOD SIDING
2" x 4" WOOD FRAME WALL
with 1/2" sheathing & 1/2" interior finish

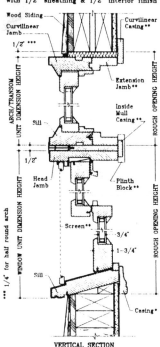

VERTICAL SECTION

STUCCO
2" x 6" WOOD FRAME WALL
with 1/2" sheathing & 1/2" interior finish

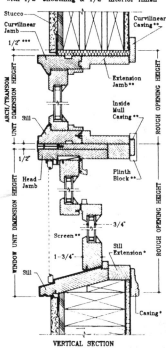

VERTICAL SECTION

BRICK VENEER
2" x 4" WOOD FRAME WALL
with 1/2" sheathing & 1/2" interior finish

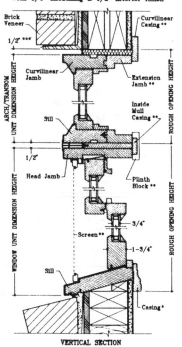

VERTICAL SECTION

Figure 14.50 Installation examples. (Courtesy The Atrium Door & Window Company, a Division of Fojtasek Companies, Inc.)

14.52(A). Unwanted information is removed with white-out correction fluid or white acrylic artist paint or is cut out with scissors. The remaining detail might look like Figure 14.52(B). This drawing is positioned on a piece of white bond paper and reproduced xerographically onto vellum. The first time you do this, it will take you longer than outright tracing, but if this Atrium Double-Tilt window is used again, you have a head start in the drawing process. Also note that we are using a double module.

STAGE II (Figure 14. 53). The rough framing is drawn on the drawing of the window. If you were tracing the outline of the window, this process would be reversed: rough framing would be drawn first, then the window would be traced within this context. Care must be taken in redrawing any important line that was invertantly eliminated or has faded away. The fin is especially important. Finally, the rough opening is established.

STAGE III (Figure 14.54). As we look at this detail, we should be able to see the lines of the jamb. To save time and for the sake of clarity, some offices do not put these lines into the detail. A true detail should include such lines, thus our choice to include them here. The interior and exterior wall coverings (skin) were drafted at this stage. Note the lining of the building felt over the fin for moisture control and the inclusion of insulation below the header. Finally, the raised window frame is drafted.

STAGE IV (Figure 14.55). Noting and referencing complete the detail. The positioning of notes is critical for

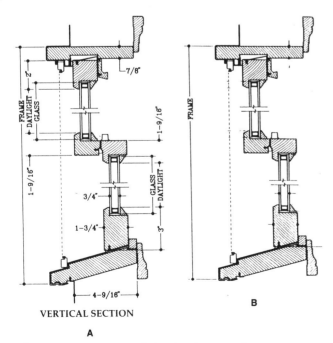

Figure 14.51 Rough opening sizes.

VERTICAL SECTION

A

Figure 14.52 3″ = 1′–0″ drawing by manufacturer.

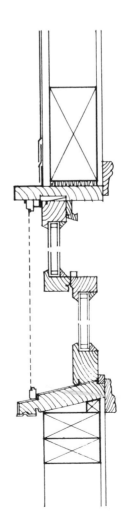

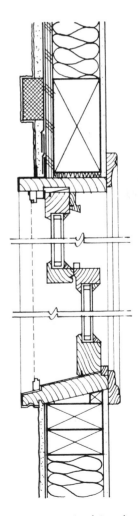

Figure 14.53 Laying out the rough frame.

Figure 14.54 Applying the interior and exterior skin onto the wall surface.

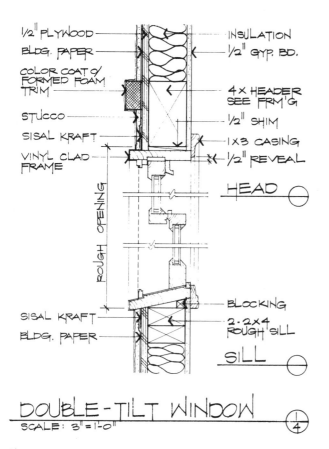

Figure 14.55 Noting and finishing the window detail.

ease of reading. Don't crowd the detail, but also avoid long leaders. Be sure to create a margin for uniformity of appearance.

Fireplace

Fireplaces have gone through quite an evolution over the past century: from masonry fireplaces, which are still built, to metal; from fully vented fireplaces using chimneys to those that do not. Some varieties burn wood as fuel, and others burn natural gas or, more recently, gelled alcohol.

Fireplaces can be built with remote control starters much like those used for television and VCRs. They can also be constructed to recirculate warm air. Fireplaces can be made to look like fireplaces or designed to look like furniture. And, much to the surprise of many clients, portable fireplaces are now manufactured, which burn gelled alcohol and can be moved from room to room, much the way furniture is rearranged. When you move, you take the fireplace with you.

Many of the metal fireplaces are fitted with recirculating air pockets. The air around the fire chamber is heated and redirected back into the room. You can even have a thermostat-controlled blower installed, which

increases the movement of the warm air, thus achieving greater efficiency in heat circulation. This means that 20,000 to 75,000 Btu/hr of heat can be recaptured. See Figure 14.56.

For the sake of this discussion, fireplaces are categorized as follows: •

Standard fireplace. The normal masonry units that are usually job-built and require the detailer to draft the fireplace from the throat. Often built of concrete block, brick, or stone.

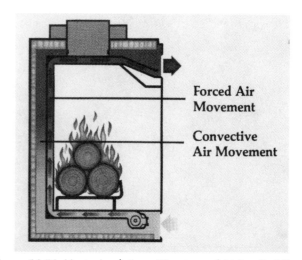

Figure 14.56 Heat circulation. (Courtesy of Majco Building Specialties, L.P.)

Figure 14.57 Majestic heat-circulating fireplace. (Courtesy of Majco Building Specialties, L.P.)

Prefabricated fireplaces. Built of steel, with the chimney built of double or triple wall units that snap together. A typical unit can be seen in Figure 14.57.

Direct vented fireplaces. Built of steel and similar to the prefabricated fireplaces previously described, except that they are vented directly out an adjacent wall. See Figures 14.58 and 14.59. Note the uninterrupted windows surrounding the fireplace in the photograph.

Portable fireplaces. Made of metal and built much like an oven, so that the outer surface gets warm but not hot to the touch. Can be housed in a cabinet like a television set and uses a clean-burning gelled alcohol.

Figure 14.58 Majestic wall-vented fireplace. (Courtesy of Majco Building Specialties, L.P.)

Ryan Residence Fireplace

For the Ryan Residence, the Majestic 42 unit was selected for its heat-circulating features. See Figure 14.57.

Much like the Atrium window discussed earlier, this fireplace has a metal fin (tab) around the perimeter of the front face that can be nailed to the surrounding framing. The metal fireplace must not come into contact with the framing around it. The manufacturer suggests a minimum clearance of about ½," but the local codes should be checked.

The chimney is a triple wall unit and does not necessarily go straight up through the ceiling and/or roof. Bends of 30° can be incorporated as the chimney goes through the space provided. This space, called the chimney chase, allows the chimney to pierce the ceiling or roof at a convenient point, so as not to interrupt the plane of the roof at an intersection (such as a valley) or bypass a beam or any other structural member. See Figure 14.60. Straps are then used to stabilize the chimney to the adjacent framing members. See Figure 14.61. Note the inclusion of a recommended 2" clearance space.

A fire-stop spacer should be used on top of the ceiling joist if there is an attic, or on the underside of the roof joist when there is an attic space. See Figure 14.62.

The total area around the opening (chase) should be insulated even if the wall is an inside wall. If the fireplace is on a second floor or on a first floor constructed of wood, the space under the fireplace should also be insulated. In fact, it is always best to read the installation manual before detailing the framework around the structure. The detailer should not worry about how the smoke is drafted out of the fire chamber or the inner workings of the fireplace, because the fireplace engineering has already been done by the Majestic company designers.

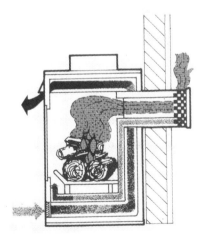

Figure 14.59 Wall-vented schematic. (Courtesy of Majco Building Specialties, L.P.)

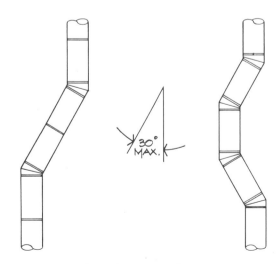

Figure 14.60 Bends in chimney section.

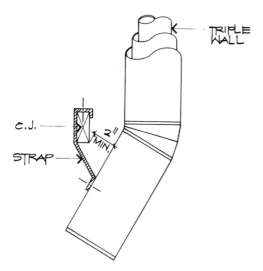

Figure 14.61 Attachment to adjacent members.

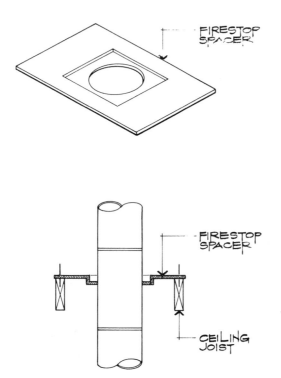

Figure 14.62 Chimney position.

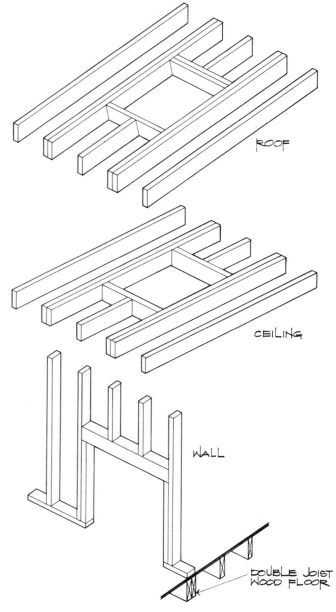

Figure 14.63 Framing an opening.

Framing. The walls around the prefabricated fireplace are framed in the same way as all other walls. Even the openings are framed in the same manner as other openings such as doors, skylights, windows, and so on. See Figure 14.63.

The framing on the Ryan Residence is rather unique because:

A. The fireplace is backed against a bearing wall.
B. The rafters of the main part of the roof will come down to the bearing wall.

C. The ceiling joists are running perpendicular to the main rafters.
D. The California framed roof also needs to be reframed with an opening.
E. The chimney will be contained inside a wood chase and capped with metal.

See Figure 14.64 for a model simulation of this area, Figure 14.65 for a sectional view of the fireplace, and Figure 14.66 for a good look at the total framing around the fireplace.

Putting the last two drawings together becomes the next task of the detailer. To see if this approach works, a freehand sketch might be made, such as that in Figure 14.67.

Figure 14.64 Model simulation of the framing through the roof.

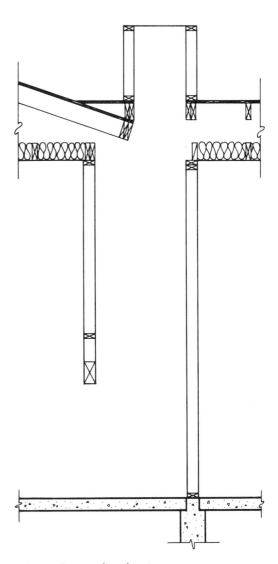

Figure 14.66 Surrounding framing.

Figure 14.65 Outline of the fireplace.

Chimney Above Roof. In most cases, a chimney must rise two feet higher than the highest part of the roof within a ten-foot radius. See Figure 14.68.

Chimney Chase. There are a number of ways of terminating the chimney above the roof. A round top termination, as seen in Figure 14.69, can be used to "top it off," and the finish will be left in this state. A second possibility is to purchase a constructed metal chase to cover this metal termination. A third suggestion is to use a wood chase with a constructed or custom-made cap. As you will note, this is the method used for the Ryan's fireplace (wood chase), and a form trim will be used on the detail to show variation, as seen in Figure 14.70.

Development of the Ryan Residence Fireplace

A full section of the Ryan Residence fireplace is developed in three stages.

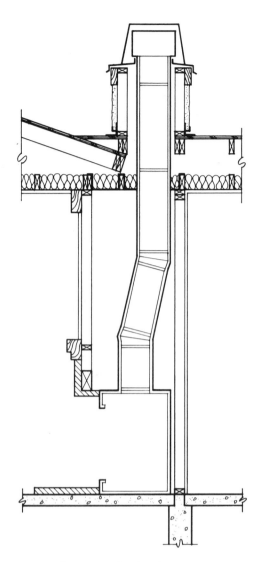

Figure 14.67 Full section of a fireplace.

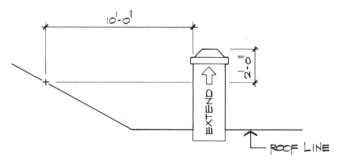

Figure 14.68 Chimney above roof.

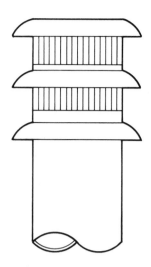

Figure 14.69 Round top termination.

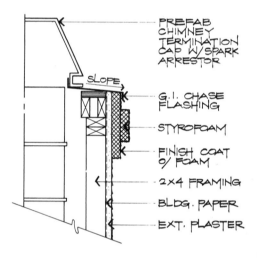

PREFAB
CHIMNEY
TERMINATION
CAP W/SPARK
ARRESTOR

SLOPE

G.I. CHASE
FLASHING

STYROFOAM

FINISH COAT
O/ FOAM

2×4 FRAMING

BLDG. PAPER

EXT. PLASTER

½ SECTION OF CHIMNEY   Ⓜ
SCALE: 1½" = 1'-0"

Figure 14.70 Half-section of chimney.

STAGE I (Figure 14.71). Fade-away pencil is used to detail the plate line, floor line, wall, and roof outline as this location is laid out. These lines establish the parameters within which the detailer can explore the framing members and place the prefabricated fireplace.

STAGE II (Figure 14.72). The ceiling joists and rafters are sized and positioned according to the framing plan. Because this is not a masonry fireplace, the drafter need not be concerned with a foundation. (For drafting full masonry fireplaces, read the chapter on fireplaces in the companion book, *The Professional Practice of Architectural Detailing.*)

Next, the fireplace is positioned in this cavity, wtih the minimum clearances required by code. At this stage the drafter must be conversant with code restrictions as well as the method of installation. For example, it is important to detail how the flue is stabilized within the cavity, what kinds of fire-stops are required, and where they are positioned. Manufacturers' literature includes installation instructions and

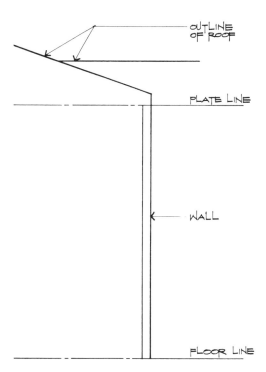

Figure 14.71 Establishing the parameters of the fireplace location—Stage I.

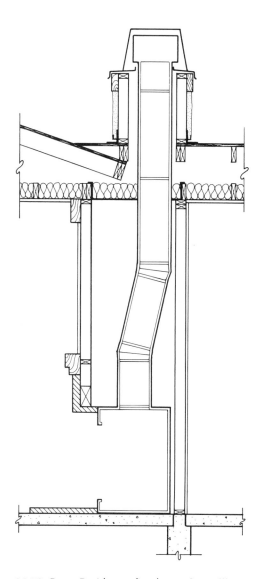

Figure 14.73 Ryan Residence fireplace—Stage III.

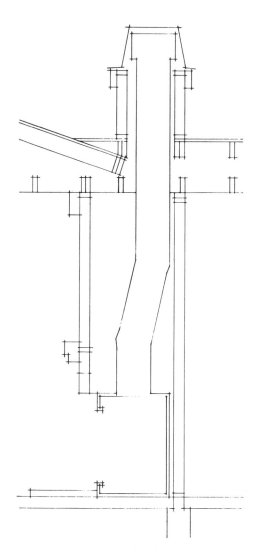

Figure 14.72 Ryan Residence fireplace—Stage II.

standard manufactured pieces that are available to make such installation possible. The drafter should also check with the project book to verify finish materials for the face of the fireplace and the hearth.

STAGE III (Figure 14.73). Once the materials have been checked, material designation is included in the detail. Wood, insulation, concrete, and even the outside wall of the metal fireplace are shown. At this stage sheet metal, such as for the cap, is drafted with a single heavy line.

STAGE IV (Figure 14.74). There are a number of items of which the detailer must be aware on all details, as well as those that are unique to specific details, as is the case with a fireplace. Unlike the footing detail, which describes a structural part of a building, the fireplace detail is one for which there already exists a context. The second factor that the detailer must identify and describe accurately is the prefabricated unit itself. Thus, the final stage must be dealt with much in the same fashion as the detail was developed.

First, within the final sequence, is the identification of the context: the rafters, the ceiling joist, the floor,

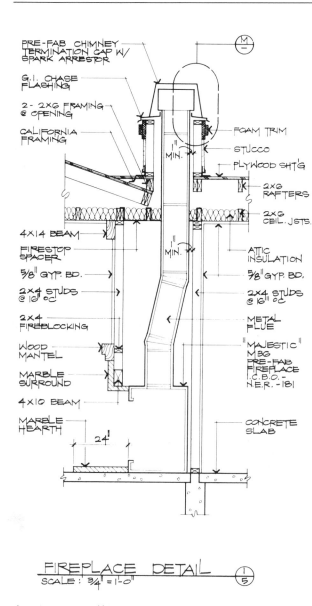

PRE-FAB CHIMNEY
TERMINATION CAP W/
SPARK ARRESTOR

G.I. CHASE
FLASHING

2 - 2X6 FRAMING
@ OPENING

CALIFORNIA
FRAMING

FOAM TRIM

STUCCO

PLYWOOD SHT'G

1" MIN.

2X6 RAFTERS

2X6 CEIL. JSTS.

4X14 BEAM

FIRESTOP
SPACER

5/8" GYP. BD.

2X4 STUDS
@ 16" OC

2X4
FIREBLOCKING

WOOD
MANTEL

MARBLE
SURROUND

4X10 BEAM

MARBLE
HEARTH

1" MIN.

ATTIC
INSULATION

5/8" GYP. BD.

2X4 STUDS
@ 16" OC

METAL
FLUE

"MAJESTIC"
M 36
PRE-FAB
FIREPLACE
I.C.B.O.-
N.E.R. -181

CONCRETE
SLAB

24"

FIREPLACE DETAIL   ①/5
SCALE : 3/4" = 1'-0"

Figure 14.74 Half-section of fireplace—Stage IV.

and the cell (surrounded with studs) within which the fireplace will be placed, including the housing for the chimney.

Next in this sequence is the identification of the fireplace and the flue, in such a way that the outline of the fireplace is clear in relationship to the surrounding structure.

The building code and the manufacturer's installation directions will reveal certain clearances that must be maintained and dimensioned, and attachments and fire-stop spacers which need to be identified. Positioning them is not alone sufficient.

Next, the decorative (noncombustible) portions that surround the opening, the chimney, the floor (hearth) and the wall plane of the fireplace, and the ceiling should be described and dimensioned.

Finally, if there are portions within this drawing that need to be enlarged and explored, reference bubbles or notes should be included to direct the reader to these details. Although it may seem that this is referring a detail to a detail, it is really not. (See the chimney portion of Figure 14.70). This drawing, as the title indicates, is a half-section—a hybrid between a building section and a full-blown detail.

PORTFOLIO OF ARCHITECTURAL DETAILS FOR THE RYAN RESIDENCE

A sampling of the architectural details that are used for the Ryan Residence are shown on Figures 14.75–14.92. They are shown at a larger scale than they would be if the details were incorporated into the working drawings in Chapter 15.

1. Exterior bearing footing	Figure 14.75
2. Interior bearing footing	Figure 14.76
3. Porch connection	Figure 14.77
4. Change of level	Figure 14.78
5. Depressed slab	Figure 14.79
6. Window	Figure 14.80
7. Door	Figure 14.81
8. Fireplace	Figure 14.82
9. Wood column to beam	Figure 14.83
10. Skylight	Figure 14.84
11. Eave	Figure 14.85
12. Trellis	Figure 14.86
13. Upper cabinet	Figure 14.87
14. Base cabinet	Figure 14.88
15. Exterior bearing footing—garage	Figure 14.89
16. Apron detail	Figure 14.90
17. Eave at garage	Figure 14.91
18. Half-section of chimney	Figure 14.92

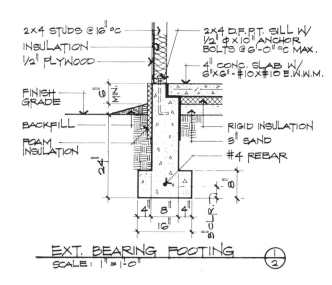

2X4 STUDS @ 16" OC

INSULATION

1/2" PLYWOOD

FINISH GRADE

BACKFILL

FOAM INSULATION

2X4 D.F. P.T. SILL W/
1/2" Φ X10" ANCHOR
BOLTS @ 6'-0" OC MAX.

4" CONC. SLAB W/
6"X6"- #10X#10 E.W.W.M.

RIGID INSULATION

3" SAND

#4 REBAR

24"

3" CLR.

8"

4" 8" 4"
16"

EXT. BEARING FOOTING   ①/2
SCALE : 1" = 1'-0"

Figure 14.75 Exterior bearing footing.

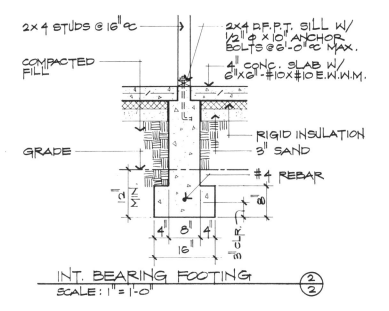

Figure 14.76 Interior bearing footing.

2×4 STUDS @ 16" OC

COMPACTED FILL

GRADE

2×4 D.F.P.T. SILL W/ 1/2"φ × 10" ANCHOR BOLTS @ 6'-0" OC MAX.

4" CONC. SLAB W/ 6"×6"-#10×#10 E.W.W.M.

RIGID INSULATION

3" SAND

#4 REBAR

d MIN.

8"

4" 8" 4"
16"

3" CLR.

INT. BEARING FOOTING
SCALE: 1" = 1'-0"
2/2

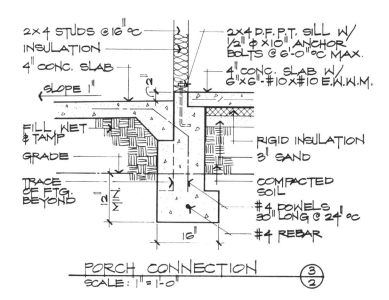

Figure 14.77 Porch connection.

2×4 STUDS @ 16" OC

INSULATION

4" CONC. SLAB

SLOPE 1"

FILL, WET & TAMP

GRADE

TRACE OF FTG. BEYOND

2×4 D.F.P.T. SILL W/ 1/2"φ × 10" ANCHOR BOLTS @ 6'-0" OC MAX.

4" CONC. SLAB W/ 6"×6"-#10×#10 E.W.W.M.

RIGID INSULATION

3" SAND

COMPACTED SOIL

#4 DOWELS 30" LONG @ 24" OC

#4 REBAR

d MIN.

16"

PORCH CONNECTION
SCALE: 1" = 1'-0"
3/2

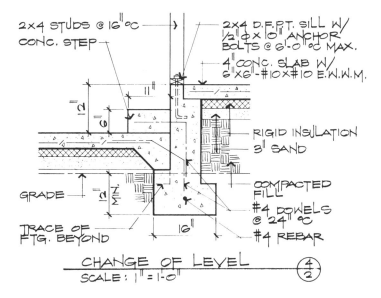

Figure 14.78 Change of level.

2×4 STUDS @ 16" OC

CONC. STEP

GRADE

TRACE OF FTG. BEYOND

2×4 D.F.P.T. SILL W/ 1/2"φ × 10" ANCHOR BOLTS @ 6'-0" OC MAX.

4" CONC. SLAB W/ 6"×6"-#10×#10 E.W.W.M.

RIGID INSULATION

3" SAND

COMPACTED FILL

#4 DOWELS @ 24" OC

#4 REBAR

d

6"

d MIN.

16"

CHANGE OF LEVEL
SCALE: 1" = 1'-0"
4/2

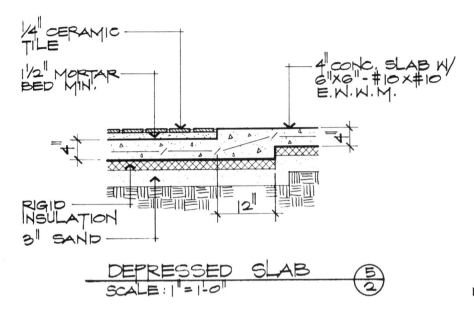

1/4" CERAMIC TILE

1 1/2" MORTAR BED MIN.

4" CONC. SLAB W/ 6"x6"-#10x#10 E.W.W.M.

4"

4"

RIGID INSULATION

3" SAND

12"

DEPRESSED SLAB
SCALE: 1"=1'-0"

(5/2)

Figure 14.79 Depressed slab.

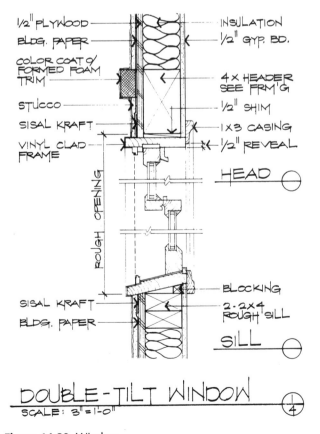

1/2" PLYWOOD

BLDG. PAPER

COLOR COAT o/ FORMED FOAM TRIM

STUCCO

SISAL KRAFT

VINYL CLAD FRAME

INSULATION

1/2" GYP. BD.

4X HEADER SEE FRM'G

1/2" SHIM

1X3 CASING

1/2" REVEAL

HEAD

ROUGH OPENING

SISAL KRAFT

BLDG. PAPER

BLOCKING

2-2x4 ROUGH SILL

SILL

DOUBLE-TILT WINDOW
SCALE: 3"=1'-0"

(1/4)

Figure 14.80 Window.

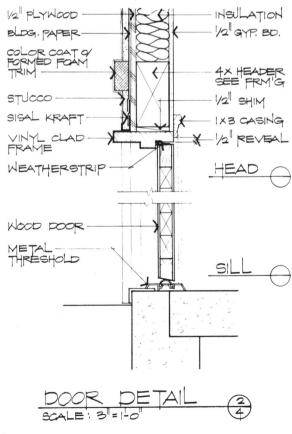

1/2" PLYWOOD

BLDG. PAPER

COLOR COAT o/ FORMED FOAM TRIM

STUCCO

SISAL KRAFT

VINYL CLAD FRAME

WEATHERSTRIP

INSULATION

1/2" GYP. BD.

4X HEADER SEE FRM'G

1/2" SHIM

1X3 CASING

1/2" REVEAL

HEAD

WOOD DOOR

METAL THRESHOLD

SILL

DOOR DETAIL
SCALE: 3"=1'-0"

(2/4)

Figure 14.81 Door.

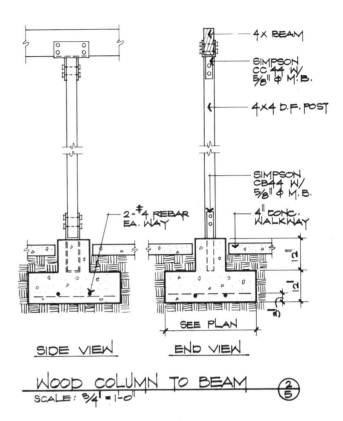

SIDE VIEW   END VIEW

WOOD COLUMN TO BEAM   (2/5)
SCALE: 3/4" = 1'-0"

4X BEAM

SIMPSON CC 44 W/ 5/8" Ø M.B.

4X4 D.F. POST

SIMPSON CB44 W/ 5/8" Ø M.B.

4" CONC. WALKWAY

2-#4 REBAR EA. WAY

SEE PLAN

Figure 14.83 Wood column to beam.

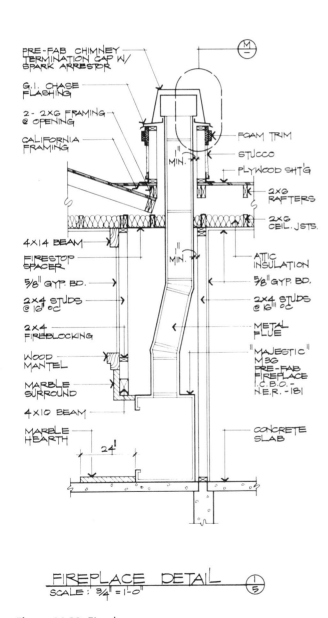

PRE-FAB CHIMNEY TERMINATION CAP W/ SPARK ARRESTOR

G.I. CHASE FLASHING

2-2X6 FRAMING @ OPENING

CALIFORNIA FRAMING

FOAM TRIM

STUCCO

1" MIN.

PLYWOOD SHT'G

2X6 RAFTERS

2X6 CEIL. JSTS.

4X14 BEAM

FIRESTOP SPACER

5/8" GYP. BD.

2X4 STUDS @ 16" OC

2X4 FIREBLOCKING

WOOD MANTEL

MARBLE SURROUND

4X10 BEAM

MARBLE HEARTH

ATTIC INSULATION

5/8" GYP. BD.

2X4 STUDS @ 16" OC

METAL FLUE

"MAJESTIC" M36 PRE-FAB FIREPLACE I.C.B.O.- N.E.R.-181

CONCRETE SLAB

1" MIN.

24"

FIREPLACE DETAIL   (1/5)
SCALE: 3/4" = 1'-0"

Figure 14.82 Fireplace.

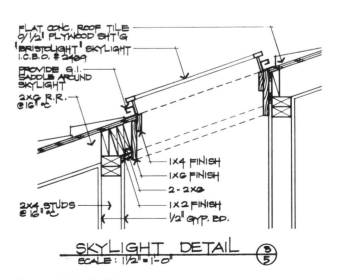

FLAT CONC. ROOF TILE O/ 1/2" PLYWOOD SHT'G

"BRISTOLIGHT" SKYLIGHT I.C.B.O. # 2489

PROVIDE G.I. SADDLE AROUND SKYLIGHT

2X6 R.R. @ 16" OC

2X4 STUDS @ 16" OC

1X4 FINISH

1X6 FINISH

2-2X6

1X2 FINISH

1/2" GYP. BD.

SKYLIGHT DETAIL   (3/5)
SCALE: 1 1/2" = 1'-0"

Figure 14.84 Skylight.

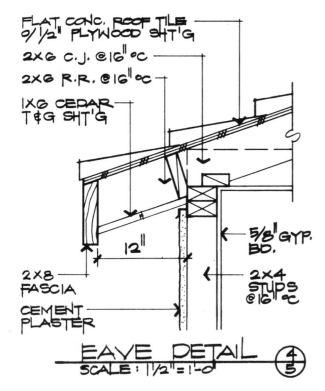

FLAT CONC. ROOF TILE
0/½" PLYWOOD SHT'G

2×6 C.J. @16" OC

2×6 R.R. @16" OC

1×6 CEDAR T&G SHT'G

12"

2×8 FASCIA

CEMENT PLASTER

5/8" GYP. BD.

2×4 STUDS @16" OC

EAVE DETAIL $\frac{4}{5}$
SCALE : 1½"=1'-0"

Figure 14.85 Eave.

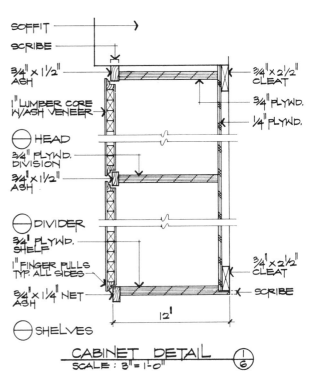

SOFFIT

SCRIBE

¾" × 1½" ASH

1" LUMBER CORE W/ASH VENEER

○ HEAD

¾" PLYWD. DIVISION

¾" × 1½" ASH

○ DIVIDER

¾" PLYWD. SHELF

1" FINGER PULLS TYP. ALL SIDES

¾" × 1¼" NET ASH

○ SHELVES

¾" × 2½" CLEAT

¾" PLYWD.

¼" PLYWD.

¾" × 2½" CLEAT

SCRIBE

12"

CABINET DETAIL $\frac{1}{6}$
SCALE : 3" = 1'-0"

Figure 14.87 Upper cabinet.

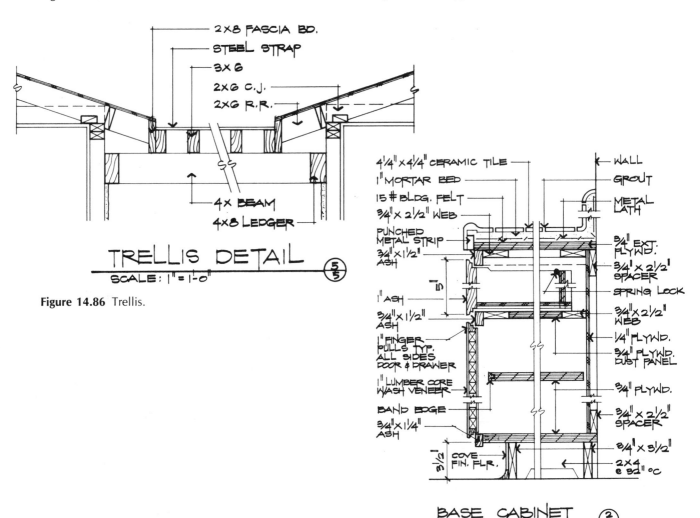

2×8 FASCIA BD.

STEEL STRAP

3×6

2×6 C.J.

2×6 R.R.

4× BEAM

4×8 LEDGER

TRELLIS DETAIL $\frac{5}{5}$
SCALE : 1" = 1'-0"

Figure 14.86 Trellis.

4¼" × 4¼" CERAMIC TILE

1" MORTAR BED

15 # BLDG. FELT

¾" × 2½" WEB

PUNCHED METAL STRIP

¾" × 1½" ASH

1" ASH

¾" × 1½" ASH

1" FINGER PULLS TYP. ALL SIDES DOOR & DRAWER

1" LUMBER CORE W/ASH VENEER

BAND EDGE

¾" × 1¼" ASH

COVE FIN. FLR.

3½"

WALL

GROUT

METAL LATH

¾" EXT. PLYWD.

¾" × 2½" SPACER

SPRING LOCK

¾" × 2½" WEB

¼" PLYWD.

¾" PLYWD. DUST PANEL

¾" PLYWD.

¾" × 2½" SPACER

¾" × 5½"

2×4 @ 32" OC

BASE CABINET $\frac{2}{6}$
SCALE : 3" = 1'-0"

Figure 14.88 Base cabinet.

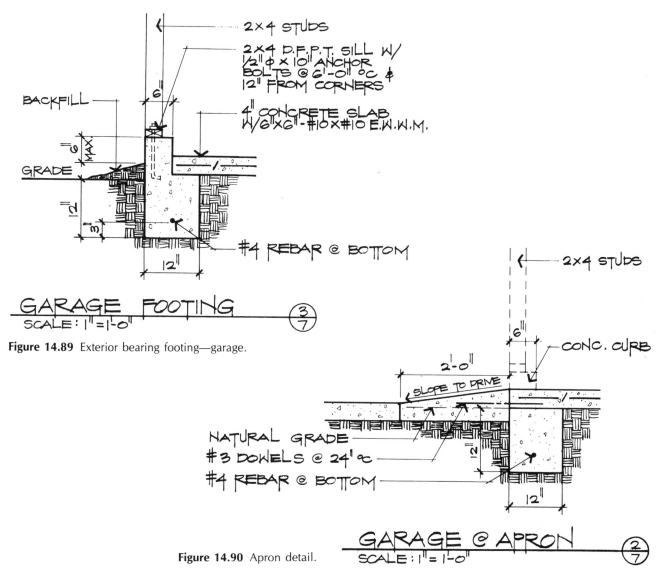

2×4 STUDS

2×4 D.F.P.T. SILL W/
1/2"Φ × 10" ANCHOR
BOLTS @ 6'-0" OC &
12" FROM CORNERS

4" CONCRETE SLAB
W/6"×6"-#10×#10 E.W.W.M.

BACKFILL

6"

6" MAX.

GRADE

12"

3"

12"

#4 REBAR @ BOTTOM

GARAGE FOOTING
SCALE: 1" = 1'-0" ③/⑦

Figure 14.89 Exterior bearing footing—garage.

2×4 STUDS

6"

CONC. CURB

2'-0"

SLOPE TO DRIVE

NATURAL GRADE
#3 DOWELS @ 24" OC
#4 REBAR @ BOTTOM

12"

12"

GARAGE @ APRON
SCALE: 1" = 1'-0" ②/⑦

Figure 14.90 Apron detail.

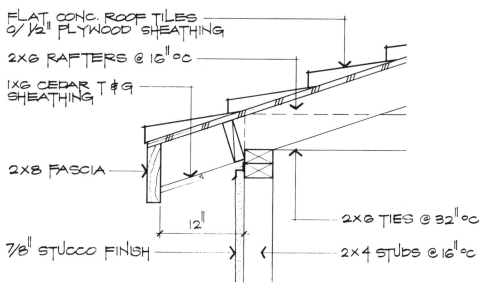

FLAT CONC. ROOF TILES
O/ 1/2" PLYWOOD SHEATHING

2×6 RAFTERS @ 16" OC

1×6 CEDAR T & G
SHEATHING

2×8 FASCIA

12"

2×6 TIES @ 32" OC

7/8" STUCCO FINISH

2×4 STUDS @ 16" OC

EAVE DETAIL
SCALE: 1 1/2" = 1'-0" ①/⑦

Figure 14.91 Eave at garage.

365

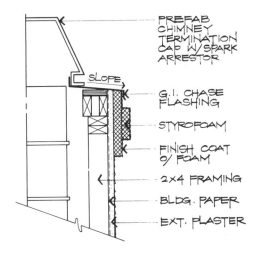

PREFAB
CHIMNEY
TERMINATION
CAP W/SPARK
ARRESTOR

SLOPE

G.I. CHASE
FLASHING

STYROFOAM

FINISH COAT
O/ FOAM

2×4 FRAMING

BLDG. PAPER

EXT. PLASTER

½ SECTION OF CHIMNEY ⓜ
SCALE: 1½" = 1'-0"

Figure 14.92 Half-section of chimney.

SUMMARY

A wide range of details are needed to provide solutions for construction assemblies. These details are first drawn in freehand form to solve a construction assembly before the final detail is drafted.

Details are the clearest way of showing how the plans for a particular structure meet architectural design requirements, building code requirements, and manufacturer's requirements for the installation of equipment. Details also provide essential guidance for the contractor and the construction process.

IMPORTANT TERMS AND CONCEPTS

Detailing
Freehand sketches
Jamb
Riser and tread

Flange
Pipe column and tube brace
Fireblocking
Waterproofing

REVIEW QUESTIONS

1. Why is it important to use freehand drawings for initial solutions of construction assemblies?
2. Architectural details include many parts of the structure. Name four.
3. Name two locations where reinforcing steel is used.
4. Where is the jamb section located for a window detail?
5. What is the main purpose of a nonbearing foundation?
6. Why is reinforcing steel used in a foundation design?

LABORATORY PROBLEMS

1. Using an architectural scale of ¾" = 1'-0", draw a freehand sketch of an exterior foundation detail incorporating the following:
   a. 12" wide and 6" thick footing

   b. 6″ wide foundation wall

   c. 24″ footing depth

   d. 2 × 4 D.F.P.T. mudsill

   e. 2 × 8 floor joist 16″ o/c

   f. ⅝″ thick plywood subfloor

   g. 2 × 4 stud exterior wall

2. Provide a freehand drawing of an eave detail with the following requirements:

   a. Scale: 1″ × 1′–0″

   b. Roof pitch: 2 in 12

   c. Roof material: composition and gravel

   d. Roof insulation: 1″ rigid board

   e. Roof sheathing: ⅝″ thick plywood

   f. 2 × 8 rafters

   g. 1′–0″ overhang

   h. 2 × 4 stud wall with 2 × 6 ceiling joist

3. Draw a freehand detail section of a 12″-wide flange steel beam with a bolted 2 × 4 nailer at the top flange. Show 2 × 10 joist hangers connected at the hanger. Indicate ⅝″ plywood subfloor above the joist. Use a scale of 1½″ = 1′–0″.

4. Provide a foundation detail in final drafted form using the requirements of Laboratory Problem 1.

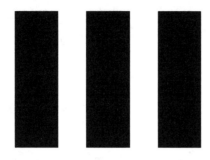

CASE STUDIES

15

CONCEPTUAL DESIGN AND CONSTRUCTION DOCUMENTS FOR A CONVENTIONAL WOOD RESIDENCE

NORTH ELEVATION

15

Conceptual Design

This chapter presents a hypothetical project, generated to provide a model for the student. The initial design and its subsequent changes are incorporated to illustrate the natural evolution of a design into a set of working drawings. Most of the changes are not based on design concepts or approaches, but rather create typical uncomplicated problems that might confront the beginning drafter. The rest of this book discusses a number of actually built projects.

Site Requirements

The design purpose is to create a three-bedroom, two-bath home that has room for growth. The site is a typical, yet irregular, city lot in Anytown, U.S.A. Because the zoning is R-1 (residential), the setbacks are the typical 20'–0" in the front, 5'–0" on the sides, and 15'–0" at the rear. Water flows to the rear in the direction of the lot's slope, which is greater beyond the rear property line. This slope creates a city view to the rear of the lot.

With the neighbors' play area to the East, there is normal play-activity noise in the late afternoon and early evening. See Figure 15.1.

Client Requirements

Along with three bedrooms and two baths, the clients request a family room, a kitchen, a living room oriented toward the view, and a formal dining room.

For security's sake, a security gate and entry were also requested. Most important, the structure had to be able to expand by 100 to 150 square feet to accommodate a den, study, or guest room.

Initial Schematic Studies

Using what is commonly called bubble diagramming, room relationships were quickly established. Most of the rooms were oriented, as seen in Figure 15.2, to the rear of the lot to take advantage of the view and avoid the street noise. With the prevailing wind coming from the northeast, each of these rooms will be well ventilated, which is especially needed for the kitchen. The garage is positioned at an angle to produce an entry court. Circulation is through the center of the structure, which serves as a spline or connector to all rooms, and visual relief from the hall/tunnel effect is achieved with the space between the front bedroom and the laundry. This space is made private by incorporating a visual barrier (to be determined by client) of bushes or a sculptural wall. While the children are young, this space can be used as a play area, and, as they grow into their teens, a reading space or private patio. It is this space that can later house the final guest room, computer room, or den with minimal cost.

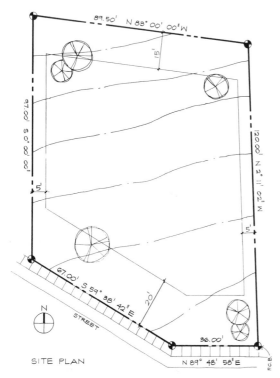

Figure 15.1 Ryan Residence site.

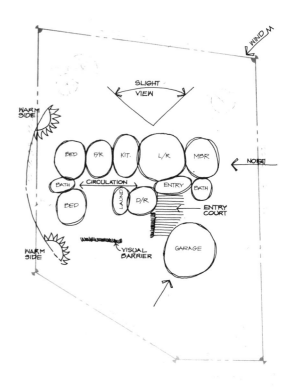

Figure 15.2 Bubble diagramming the Ryan Residence.

Preliminary Floor Plan

A preliminary floor plan is drawn as an overlay to the bubble diagram. This floor plan, as seen in Figure 15.3, was drawn freehand with suggested window and door placement and furniture layout. Furniture is often shown on a preliminary drawing to help the client better understand scale, but never on a drafted working drawing plan unless the items are built-in, such as closets, cabinets, or some appliances.

Client Changes

The preliminary floor plan plays a very important part in the development of a final configuration or shape of a

structure. It gives the client time to look at and discuss some of the important family needs or to make major changes before the project progresses too far.

Figure 15.4 shows the changes generated by the client—the slight enlargement of all bedrooms and the master bath. This was an attempt reduce the jogs in perimeter and to achieve cost reduction. The family room is to be expanded to about 15+ feet as the lot permits. The kitchen was redesigned so as to increase counter space, and the entry reworked to prevent the door from opening into the circulation pattern through the hall. Finally, and most significant, the possibility of the clients' purchasing a boat or recreational vehicle mandated consideration of a storage and maintenance area. (The clients were leaning heavily toward the purchase of a boat.)

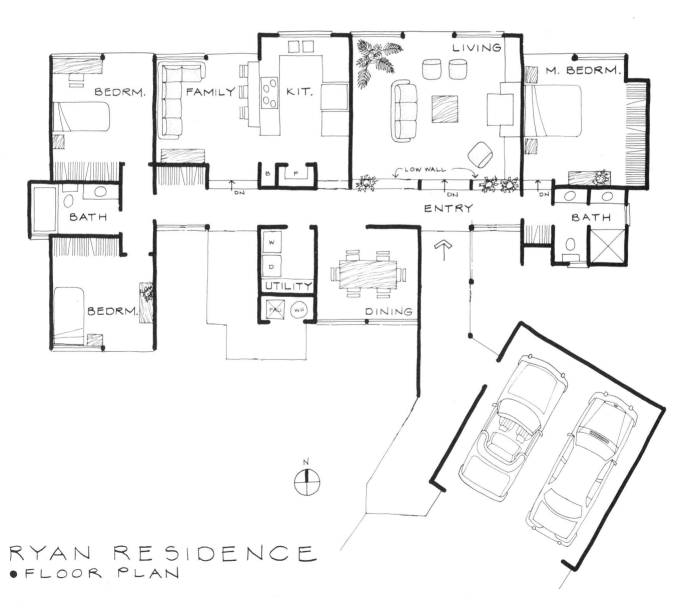

Figure 15.3 Preliminary floor plan—Ryan Residence.

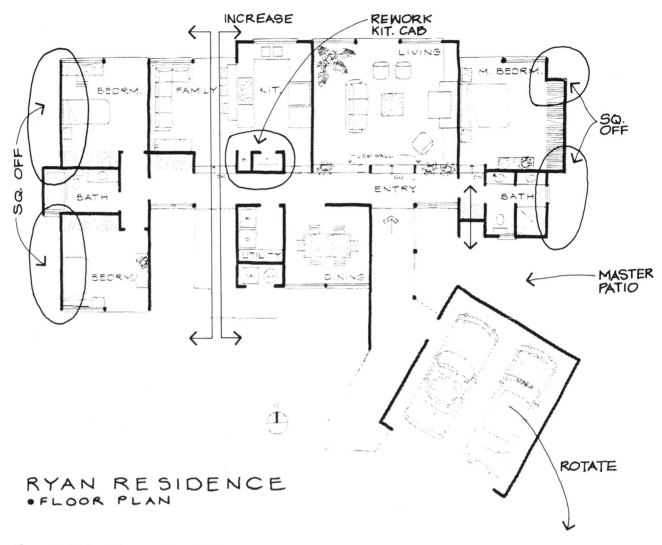

Figure 15.4 Client changes—Ryan Residence.

Adjusted Floor Plan

The adjusted floor plan is shown in Figure 15.5. Compare this with the original floor plan and note the changes. As indicated in Chapter 5, exterior and interior finishes are discussed with the client, along with the selection of appliances, roofing materials, shapes of the roof, positioning of skylight, window quality and types, among other features.

Model

For the sake of visualization, a model was constructed over a diazo copy of the preliminary floor plan. Because of the cost of model making, finished finite models are not always made, but simple massing models like those shown in Figure 15.6(A) and (B) can be. Figure 15.6(A) shows walls and door openings plus the change in level of one foot. The model was built of foam core board with black chart tape positioned to cover the top edge. Such a model allows the client to see the relationship of rooms three-dimensionally and the positioning of furniture in relation to the walls.

Figure 15.6(B) shows the roof and how it is structurally engineered. Additional information on this roof can be found at the end of Chapter 12.

Development of Elevations

The model helps the clients to visualize how the structure will look and to comprehend the preliminary exterior elevations, as seen in Figure 15.7.

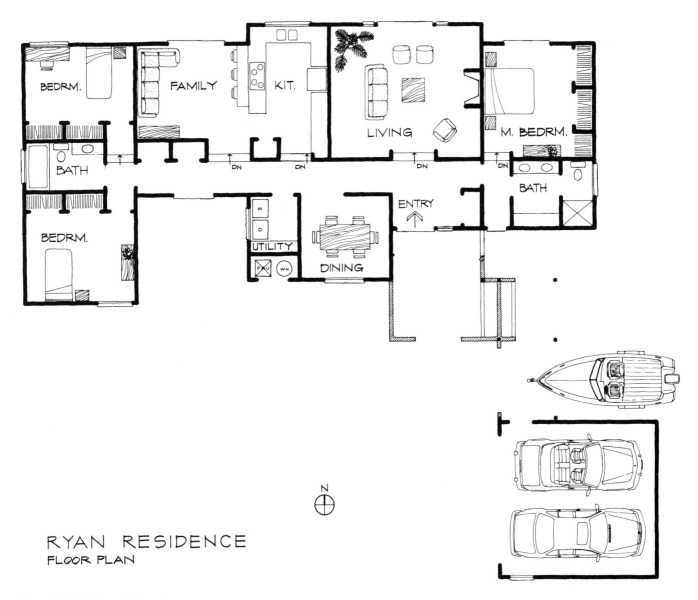

RYAN RESIDENCE
FLOOR PLAN

Figure 15.5 Adjusted floor plan.

Evolution of Ryan Residence Working Drawings

In each of the subsequent chapters, the case studies will be evolved stage by stage within the confines of the specific topic. For example, for the beach house (Chapter 16), the site plan is evolved over a four-stage sequence with descriptive commentary at each stage as to what was done, in what order, and why. For the foundation, again four stages are encountered, with explanations given at each stage, and so on through the floor plan, exterior elevations, and so forth.

The Ryan Residence is presented differently. The Ryan design and working drawings became the "thread" that ties this book together, starting with an explanation of how the transition is accomplished between design and working drawings in Chapter 5 and continuing through Chapter 14 with the evolution of specific drawings.

The different stages of development of the site plan are presented at the end of Chapter 6, the foundation plan in Chapter 7, the floor plan in Chapter 8 and so on, until Chapter 14, in which three of the major details are discussed as they are being hardlined.

It is for this reason that the stages of evolution in this chapter are abbreviated and more time will be spent discussing other facts of assembly, such as techniques of

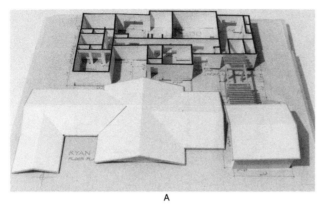

A   B

Figure 15.6 Floor plan and massing model of Ryan Residence.

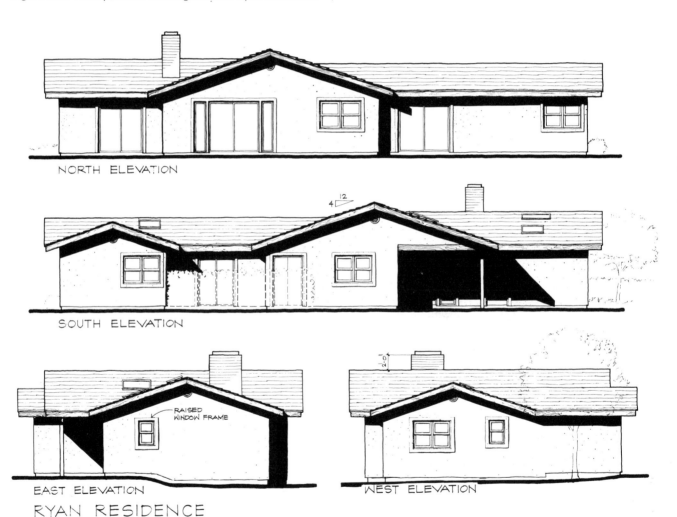

NORTH ELEVATION

SOUTH ELEVATION

4 [12]

EAST ELEVATION

RAISED
WINDOW FRAME

WEST ELEVATION

RYAN RESIDENCE

Figure 15.7 Preliminary exterior elevation—Ryan Residence.

drafting, roof strategy and topics other than those discussed in Chapters 6 through 15.

Cartoons

Complete sets of two types of cartoons are included in this chapter. First, there is the set in which simple rectangles are used to represent the various drawings (see Figures 15.8 through 15.13 and the cartoon of the garage in the *Study Guide*). Each of the more definitive cartoons, which use photocopy reductions of the preliminary design studies, is shown at the beginning of each sheet before it is evolved into the various stages.

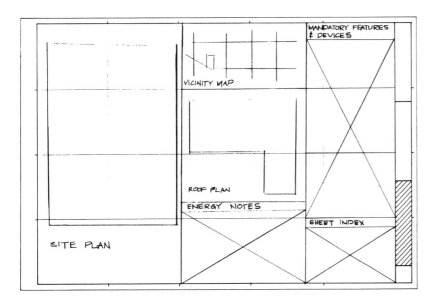

Figure 15.8 Cartoon of Sheet A-1
—Ryan Residence.

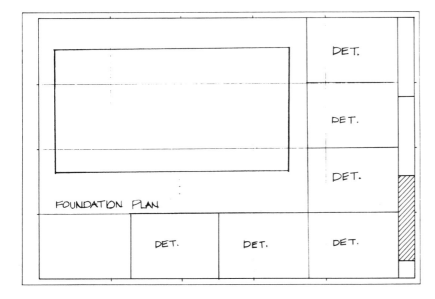

Figure 15.9 Cartoon of Sheet A-2
—Ryan Residence.

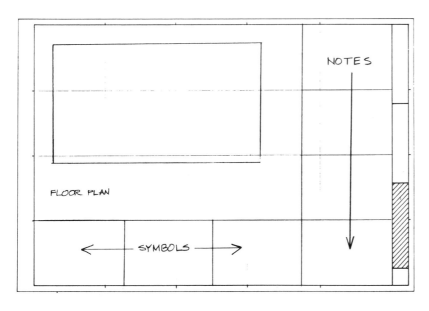

Figure 15.10 Cartoon of Sheet A-3
—Ryan Residence.

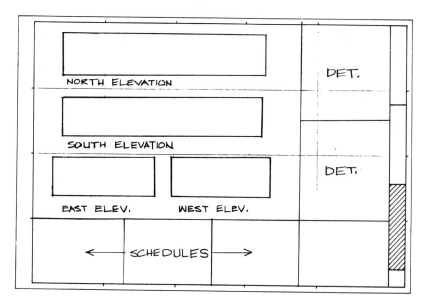

Figure 15.11 Cartoon of Sheet A-4
—Ryan Residence.

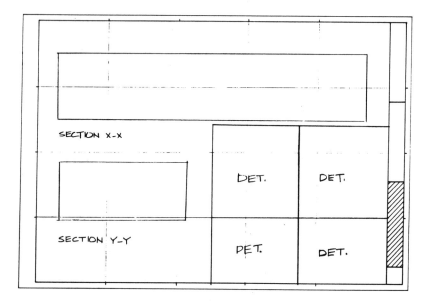

Figure 15.12 Cartoon of Sheet A-5
—Ryan Residence.

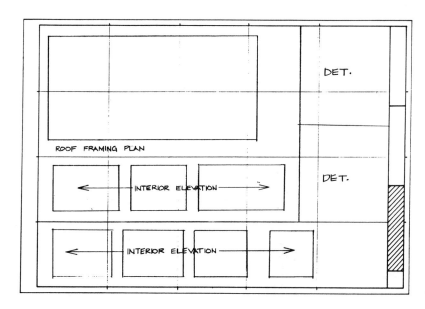

Figure 15.13 Cartoon of Sheet A-6
—Ryan Residence.

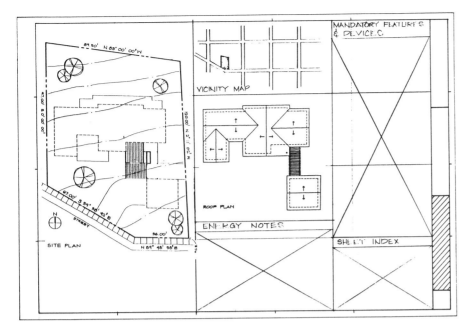

Figure 15.14 Cartoon of Ryan Residence site plan.

Single or Multiple Working Drawing Sheets Procedure

After looking at the cartoon of each sheet, the project architect must determine how these working drawing sheets will be evolved. Will a single drafter take on the responsibility of a single sheet, or will there be a number of drafters working on it? Can parts of a single sheet be delegated to two or three individuals, drawn on separate sheets, and assembled photographically? Once this decision is made by the project architect, the drafters are selected and delegated the drawings for which they are responsible. The multiple-drafter, multiple-drawing approach is used throughout this chapter in dealing with the Ryan Residence, whereas subsequent chapters will have a single drafter responsible for each sheet in the set.

Sheet A-1—Site Plan, Vicinity Map, Roof Plan, Notes

Check the cartoon of this sheet, in Figure 15.14, for the basic layout, and you will be able to see the pieces come together.

As stated earlier, the drawings can be done by a single individual or by two drafters. If two drafters are used simultaneously, there must be a clear-cut delegation of responsibilities, a format that will allow such a procedure to work, and an understanding by the project manager as to skills of the drafters.

As can be seen in the cartoon, Sheet A-1 will include the following:

1. Site plan
2. Vicinity map
3. Roof plan
4. Energy notes
5. Mandatory features and devices
6. Sheet index

The first three components will be done by one drafter, and the remaining three by a second drafter. In fact, in some offices, the clerical employee who is familiar with typing and/or word processing receives additional training in scissor drafting and might do the various notes.

If a third drafter becomes available, from time to time this person might be delegated the Vicinity Map and attach it to the first sheet via scissoring, by an adhesive made xerographically, by copier, or simply by using clear tape.

Whatever the procedure and delegation of responsibility, the two or three parts are assembled in a number of possible ways. The easiest is to use the site plan sheet as the master, paste or tape the other parts to this master, and then copy it onto a new master xerographically. This should be done with a plain paper copier, because as you paste or tape the various parts to the master you are building layers of paper and tape, making light penetration difficult. Thus the diazo method is not a desirable choice.

Photography can also be used. The pasted or taped master can be photographed and positives made. Be sure that the reproduction service you send your work to does not use a camera that produces the normal negatives and positives (which is expensive), but rather one that is not sensitive to shades of grey, which is not as

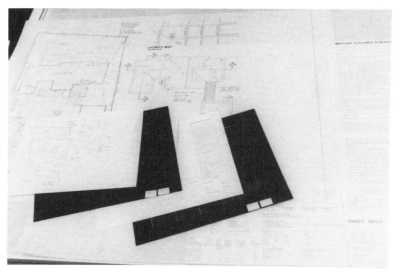

Figure 15.15 Original artwork negatives and positives.

expensive and will produce pencil drawings as if they were drawn in ink. The majority of the drawings in this book use this type of negatives and positives.

If the drawings have been done on two or three sheets of paper, and perhaps at different times, negatives can be made of each part and the camera department of the reprographic service can assemble them into one composite. Obviously, the negatives are smaller than the originals (for instance, 24 × 36 sheets with 9 × 12 negatives), which makes filing, handling, and storage easier. See Figure 15.15. Whatever the procedure, it must be determined ahead of time, and the advantages and disadvantages for the particular office must be discussed so as to make better use of the talent and skills available.

Note that with the photographic method the negatives can be used as masters and copies can be made on a

MANDATORY FEATURES & DEVICES

All openings marked * are security openings and the following notes shall apply:

A. Wood flush-type doors shall be 1 3/8" thick minimum with solid core construction.
B. Hollow core doors or doors less than 1 3/8" in thickness covered on the inside face with 16 gauge sheet metal attached with screws at 6" on centers around the perimeter or equivalent or
C. Wood panel type doors with panels fabricated of lumber not less than 9/16 inch thickness, provided shaped portions of the panels are not less than 1/4 inch thick. Individual panels shall not exceed 300 sq. ft. in area. Stiles and rails shall be of solid lumber in thickness with overall dimensions of not less than 1 3/8 inches and 3 inches in width. Mullions shall be considered a part of adjacent panels unless sized as required herein for stiles and rails except mullions not over 18 inches long may have an overall width of not less than 2 inches. Carved areas shall have a thickness of not less than 3/8 inches.
D. Glazed openings within 40 inches of the door lock when the door is in the closed position, shall be fully tempered glass or approved burglary resistant material, or shall be protected by metal bars, screens or grills having a maximum opening of 2 inches. The provisions of this section shall not apply to view ports or windows which do not exceed 2 inches in their greatest dimensions.
E. Door stops of in-swinging doors shall be of one piece construction with the jamb or joined by rabbet to the jamb.
F. All pin-type hinges which are accessible from outside the secured area when the door is closed shall have non-removable hinge pins. In addition, they shall have minimum 1/4 inch diameter steel jamb stud with 1/4 inch minimum protection unless the hinges are shaped to prevent removal of the door if the hinge pins are removed.
G. The strike plate for latches and the holding device for projecting deadbolts in wood construction shall be secured to the jamb and the wall framing with screws not less than 2 1/2 inches in length.
H. Specify deadbolts with hardened inserts; deadlocking latch key-operated locks on exterior; locks openable without key, special knowledge or special effort on interior; and type throw, and embedment of deadbolts for single swinging door, active leaf or pairs of doors.
I. Straight deadbolts shall have a minimum throw of 1 inch and an embedment of not less than 5/8 inch.
J. A hook-shaped or an expanding-lug deadbolt shall have a minimum throw of 3/4 inch.
K. Cylinder guards shall be installed on all cylinder locks whenever the cylinder projects beyond the face of the door or is otherwise accessible to gripping tools.
L. Sliding glass doors and sliding glass windows shall be capable of withstanding resistant tests and shall bear Force-Entry-Resistant labels.
M. Door hinge pins accessible from the outside shall be non- removable.

A. All equipment and materials to be certified by the manufacturer as complying with the governing Quality Standards established by the regulatory agency. Including HVAC equipment, water heaters, shower heads, faucets, thermostats and lamp ballasts.
B. Ceiling insulation - The weighted average U-value shall not exceed that which would result from using R-19 batt insulation.
C. Wall insulation - The weighted average U-value shall not exceed that which would result from using R-11 batt insulation.
D. Slab edge insulation - Slab edge insulation shall have water absorbtion and water vapor-transmission rates of no greater than 0.3% and 2 perm/inch respectively.
E. Masonry and factory built fireplaces shall be installed with tight fitting, closeable metal or glass doors, outside air intake with damper and flue damper. Continuous burning gas pilots are prohibited.
F. Backdraft dampers for all exhaust and fan systems shall be provided.
G. Heating system shall have a automatic thermostat with a clock mechanism which can program automatically to set back the thermostat set points for at least 2 periods within 24 hours.
H. Storage type water heater and backup tanks for solar heating systems shall be externally wrapped with insulation having a thermal resistance of R-12 or greater.
I. All return piping and recirculating hot water piping in unheated areas shall be insulated with a thermal resistance of R-3 or greater.
J. Seal and caulk all plumbing, electrical and other openings that penetrate the building envelope.
K. Ducts shall be constructed, installed and insulated as per Chapter 10 of the State Mechanical Code.
L. Provide R-11 insulation in raised wood floor area.
M. Post insulation compliance card in a conspicuous location in dwelling prior to final inspection.

SHEET INDEX

ENERGY NOTES

CERTIFICATE OF COMPLIANCE: Residential (Example)

Project Title --------------------
Project Address ---------------

Documentation Author ------
Compliance Method ---------
Climate Zone ---------------

General Information
Conditioned Floor Area ------ 1500 S.F.
Building Type ---------------- Single Family
Number of Story -------------- One
Floor Construction Type ---- Raised Wood
Infiltration Control ----------- Standard

Building Shell Insulation

Component Type	Insulation R-Value	Location Comments
Roof	R-19	Vaulted Ceiling
Walls	R-11	
Floor	R-11	Floor over Crawl Space
Door	R-0	

Glazing

Glazing Orientation	Area (S.F.)	Glass Type	Interior Shading	Exterior Shading	Roof Projection
Window 1 (SW)	24 S.F.	Double Pane	Shade	50% Screen	Yes
Window 2 (SW)	-	"	"	"	Yes
Window 3 (SW)	-	"	"	"	Yes
Window 4 (NW)	-	"	"	"	Yes
Door A (SE)	-	"	None	None	Yes
Door B (SE)	-	"	None	None	Yes

HVAC Systems

Heating			Cooling		
Make	Model	Capacity	Make	Model	Capacity
AJAX	C12345	65,800 B.T.u.	N/A	N/A	N/A

Heating Installed -------------------- 65,800 B.T.U.
Heating Allowed -------------------- 71,000 B.T.U.

Water Heating System

System Type	Tank Capacity	Make & Model	Energy Credit
Storage, Gas	40 Gal.	AJAX Rm 678	None

Special Features and Remarks
Compliance is based on performance method.

Compliance Statement
Provide performance specifications as is needed to comply with the governing State and/or Federal Regulatory Agency.

Designer
Name --------------
Company -------
Address ----------
Phone ------------
Signed -----------

Owner
Name -------
Company --
Address ----
Phone ------
Signed ------

Documentation Author
Name -------------
Company -------
Address ---------
Signed ----------

Enforcement agency
Name -------
Company --
Address ---
Signed ------

Figure 15.16 Notes for Sheet A-1.

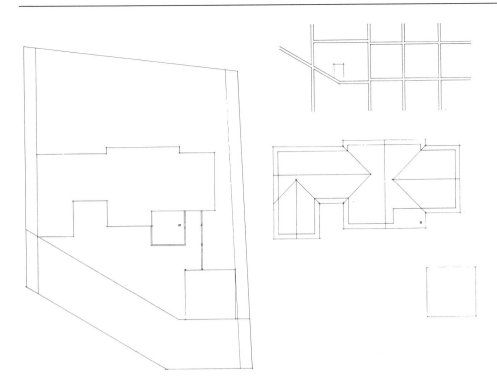

Figure 15.17 Site plan, roof plan, vicinity map—Stage I.

diazo machine. Because the negative is the reverse of the normal originals (black background and transparent lines), the result will be a copy similar to the old and seldom-used blueprint—the diazo reproduction will have white lines on a basically blue background.

If a computer is used by a CAD drafter, the entire drawing can be assembled, theoretically, in the computer by scaling and positioning the various components prior to printing (plotting, as it called).

STAGE I (Figure 15.17). Look at Figures 15.16 and 15.17. Compare them to the cartoon in Figure 15.8 and see their relative position on the 24 × 36 sheet.

STAGE II (Figure 15.18). Because the required setback lines were drawn with fade-away blue, they do not appear at this stage on the site plan. Hardlining has taken place as well as some detail work, such as the trellis between the house and the garage, the roof slope direction on the roof plan, the entry compound gates, the stamp-crete pattern at the entry, and the positioning of the house, garage, and driveway via dimension lines.

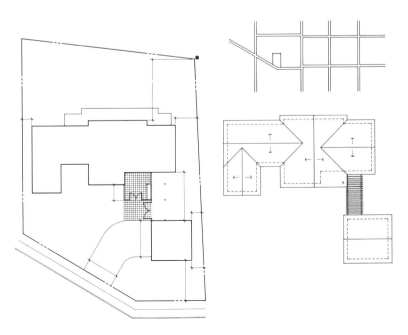

Figure 15.18 Site plan, roof plan, vicinity map —Stage II.

STAGE III (Figure 15.19). This is the final stage of the site plan, roof plan, and vicinity map. Once this is accomplished, the sheet is sent to a reproduction company and an 8½ × 11 negative of this sheet shot. This new negative and the notes (as seen in Figure 15.16) are printed together to form the complete Sheet A-1 and can be seen together in Figure 15.20.

Sheet A-2—Foundation Plan and Details

As seen in the cartoon in Figure 15.21, this sheet will contain the foundation plan and a few of the typical footing details. This sheet, like the first sheet, will be done by two drafters. One drafter will draw the foundation plan, and the other will execute the footing detail. Both drafters must be aware of the formatting and positions of their drawings relative to the sheet.

The two completed drawings will be merged photographically or, if CAD is used, merged in the computer and plotted as a single sheet.

Footing Details

The details, as shown in Figures 15.22, 15.23, and 15.24, are drawn in three stages. Each of these stages represents two of the normal six stages described in Chapter 14.

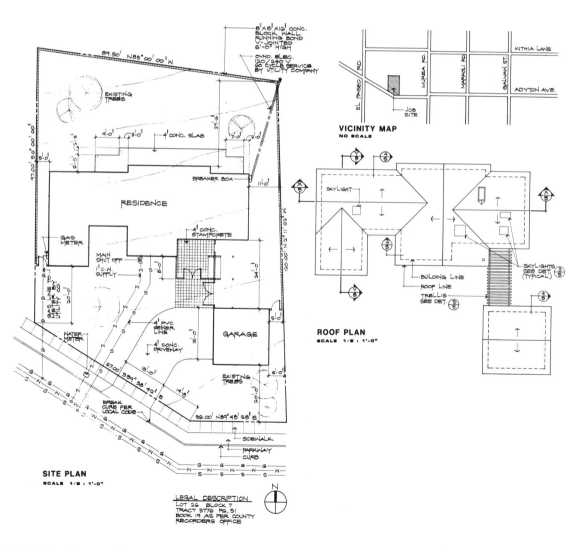

Figure 15.19 Site plan, roof plan, vicinity map—Stage III.

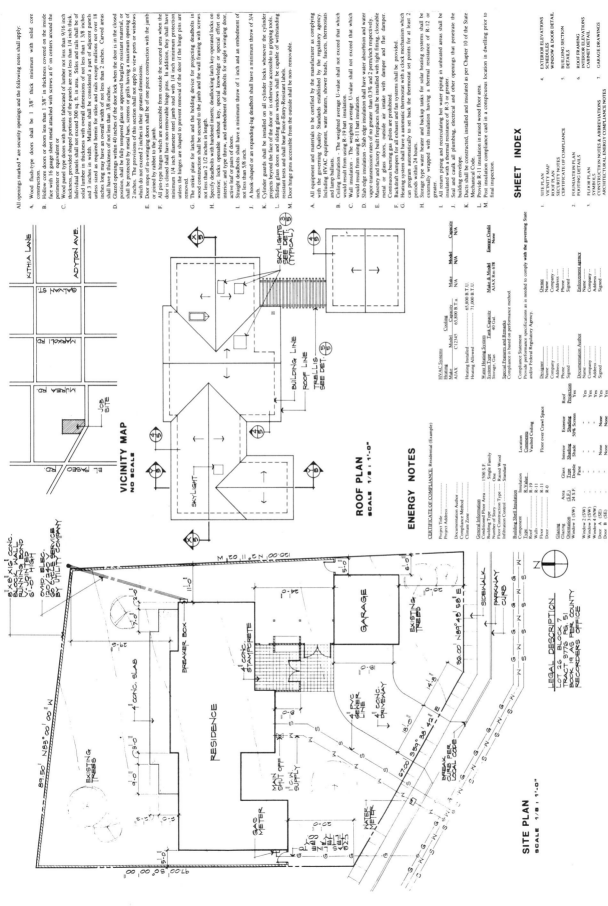

MANDATORY FEATURES & DEVICES

All openings marked * are security openings and the following notes shall apply:

A. Wood flush-type doors shall be 1 3/8" thick minimum with solid core construction.

B. Hollow core doors or doors less than 1 3/8" in thickness shall be covered on the inside face with 16 gauge sheet metal attached with screws at 6" on centers around the perimeter or equivalent or the

C. Wood panel type doors with panels fabricated of lumber not less than 9/16 inch thickness, provided shaped portions of the panels are not less than 1/4 inch thick. Individual panels shall not exceed 300 sq. ft. in area. Stiles and rails shall be of solid lumber in thickness with overall dimensions of not less than 1 3/8 inches and 3 inches in width. Mullions shall be considered as a part of adjacent panels unless sized as required herein for stiles and rails except mullions not over 18 inches long may have an overall width of not less than 2 inches. Carved areas shall have a thickness of not less than 3/8 inches.

D. Glazed openings within 40 inches of the door lock when the door is in the closed position, shall be fully tempered glass or approved burglary resistant material, or shall be protected by metal bars, screens or grills having a maximum opening of 2 inches. The provisions of this section shall not apply to view ports or windows which do not exceed 2 inches in their greatest dimensions.

E. Door stops of in-swinging doors shall be of one piece construction with the jamb or joined by rabbet to the jamb.

F. All pin-type hinges which are accessible from outside the secured area when the door is in the closed shall have non-removable hinge pins. In addition, they shall have a minimum 1/4 inch diameter steel jamb stud with 1/4 inch minimum protection unless the hinges are shaped to prevent removal of the door if the hinge pins are removed.

G. The strike plate for latches and the holding device for projecting deadbolts in wood construction shall be secured to the jamb and the wall framing with screws not less than 2 1/2 inches in length.

H. Specify deadbolts with hardened inserts; deadlocking latch key-operated locks on exterior; locks operable without key, special knowledge or special effort on interior; and type throw, and embedment of deadbolts for single swinging door, active leaf or pairs of doors.

I. Straight deadbolts shall have a minimum throw of 1 inch and an embedment of not less than 5/8 inch.

J. A hook-shaped or an expanding-lug deadbolt shall have a minimum throw of 3/4 inch.

K. Cylinder guards shall be installed on all cylinder locks whenever the cylinder projects beyond the face of the door or is otherwise accessible to gripping tools.

L. Sliding glass doors and sliding glass windows shall be capable of withstanding resistant tests and shall bear Force-Entry-Resistant labels.

M. Door hinge pins accessible from the outside shall be non-removable.

A. All equipment and materials to be certified by the manufacturer as complying with the governing Quality Standards established by the regulatory agency. Including HVAC equipment, water heaters, shower heads, faucets, thermostats and lamp ballasts.

B. Ceiling insulation - The weighted average U-value shall not exceed that which would result from using R-19 batt insulation.

C. Wall insulation - The weighted average U-value shall not exceed that which would result from using R-11 batt insulation.

D. Slab edge insulation - Slab edge insulation shall have water absorbtion and water vapor-transmission rates of no greater than 0.3% and 2 perm/inch respectively.

E. Masonry and factory-built fireplaces shall be installed with tight fitting, closeable metal or glass doors, outside air intake with damper and flue damper. Continuous burning gas pilots are prohibited.

F. Backdraft dampers for all exhaust and fan systems shall be provided.

G. Heating system shall have a automatic thermostat with a clock mechanism which can program automatically to set back the thermostat set points for at least 2 periods within 24 hours.

H. Storage type water heater and backup locks for solar heating systems shall be externally wrapped with insulation having a thermal resistance of R-12 or greater.

I. All return piping and recirculating hot water piping in unheated areas shall be insulated with a thermal resistance of R-3 or greater.

J. Seal and caulk all plumbing, electrical and other openings that penetrate the building envelope.

K. Ducts shall be constructed, installed and insulated as per Chapter 10 of the State Mechanical Code.

L. Provide R-11 insulation in raised wood floor area.

M. Post insulation compliance card in a conspicuous location in dwelling prior to final inspection.

SHEET INDEX

1. SITE PLAN
   VICINITY MAP
   ROOF PLAN
   SECURITY NOTES
   CERTIFICATE OF COMPLIANCE

2. FDN INSULATION PLAN
   FOOTING DETAILS

3. FLOOR PLAN
   SYMBOLS
   CONSTRUCTION NOTES & ABBREVIATIONS
   ARCHITECTURAL ENERGY COMPLIANCE NOTES

4. EXTERIOR ELEVATIONS
   SCHEDULES
   WINDOW & DOOR DETAIL

5. BUILDING SECTION
   DETAILS

6. ROOF FRAMING
   INTERIOR ELEVATIONS
   CABINET DETAIL

7. GARAGE DRAWINGS

VICINITY MAP
NO SCALE

ROOF PLAN
SCALE 1/8 : 1'-0"

ENERGY NOTES

CERTIFICATE OF COMPLIANCE: Residential (Example)

Project Title
Project Address

Documentation Author

Compliance Method
Climate Zone

General Information
Conditioned Floor Area — 1500 S.F.
Building Type — Single Family
Number of Story — One
Floor Construction Type — Raised Wood
Infiltration Control — Standard

SITE PLAN
SCALE 1/8 : 1'-0"

LEGAL DESCRIPTION
LOT 26 BLOCK 7
TRACT 3776 PG. 51
BOOK 19 AG PER COUNTY
RECORDERS OFFICE

Figure 15.20 Two drawings merged to form Sheet A-1.

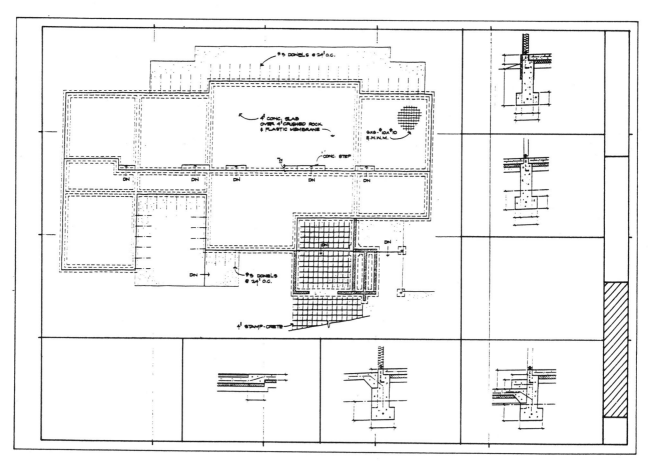

Figure 15.21 Cartoon of Ryan Residence foundation plan.

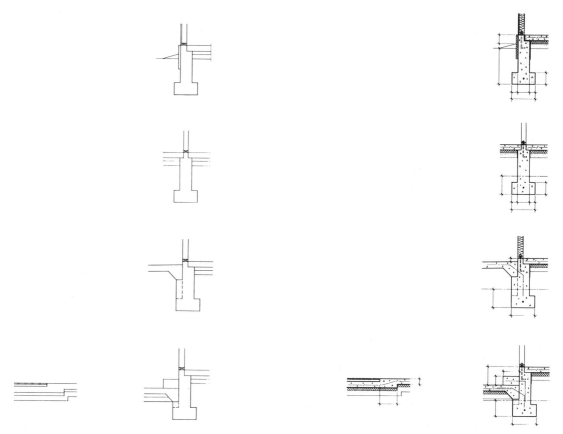

Figure 15.22 Footing details—Stage I.

Figure 15.23 Footing details—Stage II.

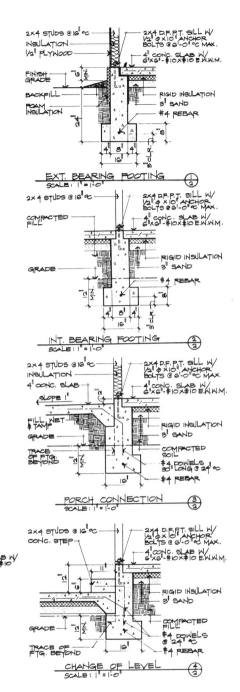

Figure 15.24 Footing details—Stage III.

Both the Foundation Plan and these details are based on preliminary freehand detail sketches similar to those presented at the beginning of Chapter 14.

For a close-up look at these footing details, refer to "Portfolio of Architectural Details for the Ryan Residence" on page 260.

Foundation Plan

The foundation plan was evolved in three stages (Figures 15.25, 15.26, and 15.28), with an intermediate stage after Stage II, which can be seen on Figure 15.27. The project manager asked for a check print after Stage II and, noticing the absence of three necessary interior bearing footings, used this opportunity to incorporate the planter change at the entry. Two of the interior bearing footings are a result of the struts, and the third a result of California frame at the front bedroom. At the conclusion of Stage III (the final stage), the detail sheet and foundation plan sheet were merged in the same manner as the site plan and became Sheet A-2. See Figure 15.29.

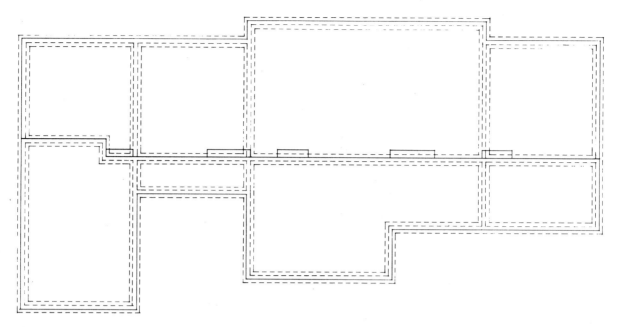

Figure 15.25 Foundation plan—Stage I.

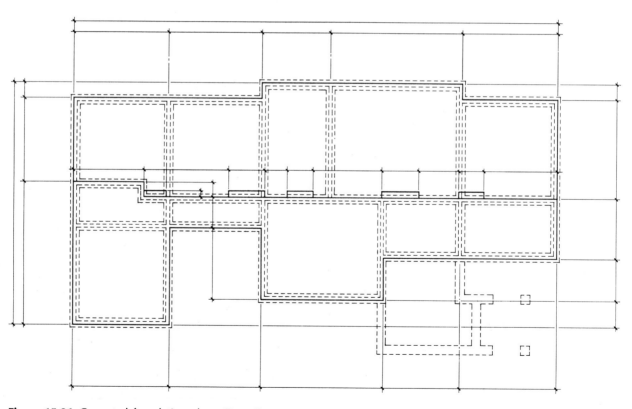

Figure 15.26 Corrected foundation plan—Stage II.

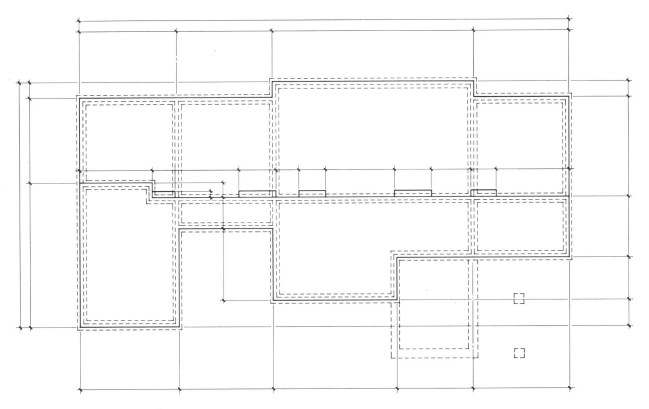

Figure 15.27 Foundation plan—Stage II.

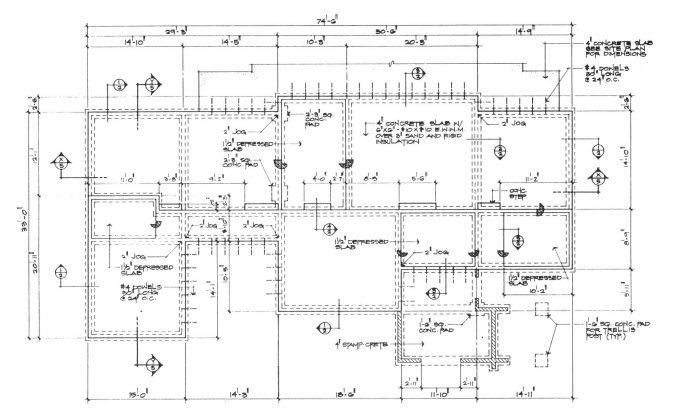

Figure 15.28 Foundation plan—Stage III.

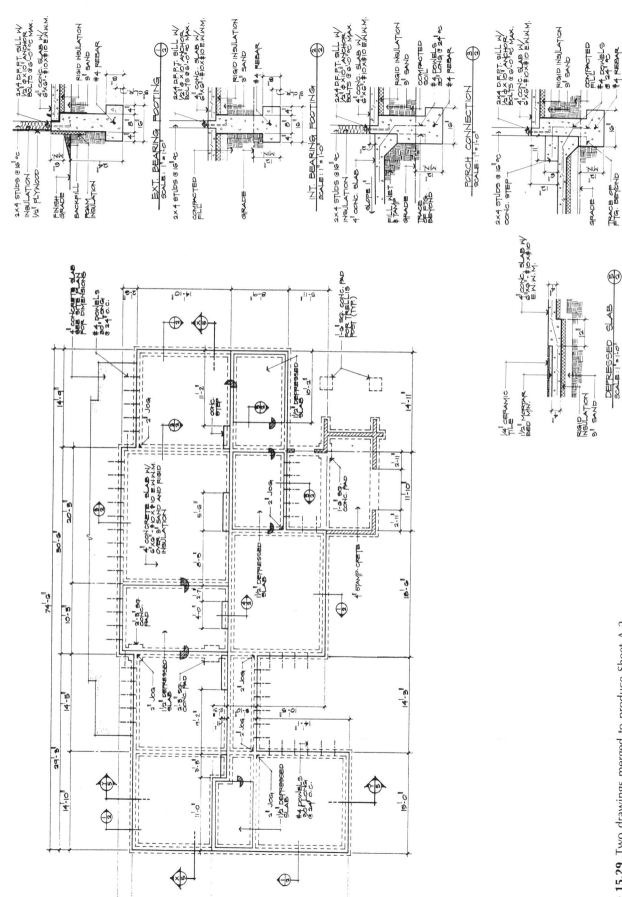

Figure 15.29 Two drawings merged to produce Sheet A-2.

Sheet A-3—Floor Plan, Construction Notes, and Electrical and Utility Symbols

Sheet A-3, like Sheets A-1 and A-2, will be done by two individuals. While one evolves the floor plan, the other will position the construction notes, electrical and utility symbols, and abbreviations. Electrical and utility symbols and abbreviations, standard items in most offices, can be transferred to an adhesive sheet and then mounted directly onto the floor plan sheet. Construction notes can be typed or word processed, printed onto an adhesive sheet, and mounted onto the floor plan sheet. See Figure 15.30.

The position of the floor plan, electrical and utility symbols, and the construction notes can be found in the cartoon of Sheet A-3 (Figure 15.31).

To allow the drafter of the floor plan to work at his or her own speed without interruptions, two separate drawings will be made and merged photographically.

The positioning of the abbreviations, notes, and symbols can be done in one stage, as in Figure 15.32.

Figure 15.30 Placement of construction notes onto the floor plan sheet.

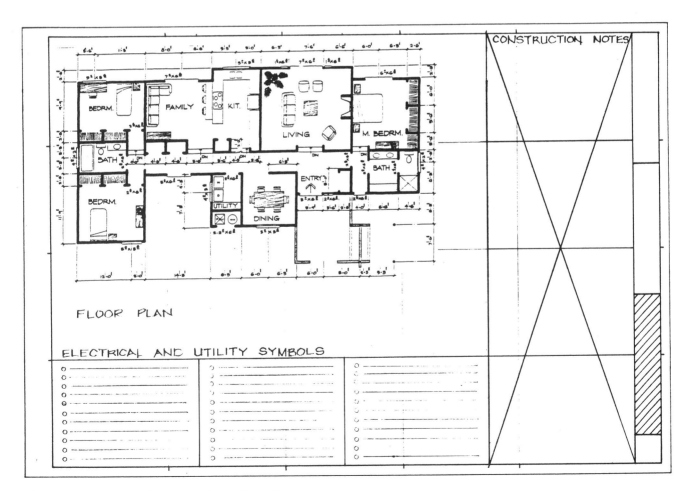

Figure 15.31 Cartoon of Ryan Residence floor plan.

CONSTRUCTION NOTES

1. The contractor and all sub-contractors shall verify all dimensions and conditions at the site, and shall notify the Engineer of any discrepancy. Cross-check details and dimensions shown on the structural drawings with related requirements on the architectural, mechanical, civil and electrical drawings.

2. Floor and wall openings, sleeves, variation in the structural slab elevations, depressed areas and all other architectural, mechanical, electrical and civil requirements must be coordinated before the contractor proceeds with construction.

3. In all cases where a conflict may occur such as between items covered by specifications and notes on the drawings, or between general notes and specific details, the Architect and/or the Engineer shall be notified and he will interpret the intent of the contract documents.

4. Details noted as typical shall apply in all cases unless specifically shown or noted otherwise.

5. Where no specific detail is shown, the framing or construction shall be identical similar to that indicated for like cases of construction on this project.

6. Workmanship and materials shall conform to the requirements of the 1991 edition of the Uniform Building Code.

7. In no case shall working dimensions be scaled from plans, section or details on structural drawings.

8. The precise dimensions and locations of all doors and window openings shall be determined from architectural plans and details. Other wall and floor openings as required by mechanical, electrical or similar requirements shall be verified from shop drawings, equipment data, dimensions, etc., as required.

WOOD

1. Plywood roof sheathing shall be 1/2 inch thick, APA Rated Sheathing, Exposure 1. Plywood floor sheathing shall be 3/4" inch thick, APA Rated "STURD-I-FLOOR," Exposure I, T & G. All plywood shall conform to U.S. Product Standard PS 1-83.

2. Plywood sheets shall be laid with the long dimension and face grain perpendicular to the rafters and the sheets shall be staggered as shown on the plans. Each sheet shall contain a minimum of 8 sq. ft. and shall extend to three bearing.

3. Plywood diaphragm shall be inspected and approved before the roofing is applied.

4. All horizontal framing members shall be Douglas Fir No. 2 grade or better for 2 x members and Douglas Fir No. 1 grade or better for 4 x members or larger (or as noted).

5. Minimum nailing shall be per Table 25-Q of the Uniform Building Code.

6. All bolt heads and nuts bearing on wood shall have washers.

7. Rafters, purlins or beams shall not be notched or dapped in any manner unless detailed.

8. All hangers and standard framing hardware unless otherwise noted shall be as manufactured by AJAX Company and are identified by numbers as shown in the latest catalog.

CONCRETE

1. All concrete shall be of 150 lb. per cu. ft. density and shall attain an ultimate compressive strength at 28 days of 2000 psi.

2. Cement shall be Type I or II Portland cement per ASTM C-150.

3. No pipes or ducts shall be placed in structural concrete nless specifically detailed.

4. Refer to architectural drawings for all molds, grooves, clips, ornaments, grounds, and other inserts to be cast in concrete.

5. All reinforcing, dowels, anchor bolts and other inserts shall be secured in proper position prior to placing concrete.

REINFORCING STEEL

1. All reinforcing bars shall be new billet steel conforming to ASTM A-615-81, Grade 60.

2. All bars shall be free from bends or kinks except as detailed and shall be free from any material which would tend to reduce the bond. Except for slabs on grade, concrete block shall not be used to support or space reinforcement.

3. Reinforcement marked "CONTINUOUS" spliced with a lap of 24 bar diameters (1'-3" minimum) in concrete (unless noted otherwise and 40 bar diameters (2'-0" minimum) in masonry. Stagger adjacent splices 10'-0" minimum.

4. All welding in conjunction with reinforcing steel shall be done with properly selected electrodes. Adequate preheat, interpass temperatures and controlled cooling shall be utilized to provide sound crack-free welds.

5. All reinforcing shall be supported in conformance with the latest edition of "Reinforcing Concrete – A Manual of Standard Practice."

6. Reinforcing shall have the following minimum cover (or as noted on drawings)
   a. Formed surfaces in contact with earth — 2"
   b. Surfaces deposited directed against earth — 3"

7. Mesh reinforcement shall conform to ASTM A-185.

ELECTRICAL AND UTILITY SYMBOLS

1. WALL SWITCH SINGLE POLE
2. WEATHERPROOF SWITCH SINGLE POLE
3. WALL SWITCH 3-WAY
4. CONVENIENCE OUTLET-DUPLEX
5. WEATHERPROOF DUPLEX
6. TRIPLEX
7. FOURPLEX
8. CONVENIENCE OUTLET 1/2 SWITCH
9. CONVENIENCE OUTLET (WITH HEIGHT)
10. GROUND FAULT INTERRUPTER
11. 220V DUPLEX OUTLET
12. SPECIAL PURPOSE
13. SINGLE FLOOR OUTLET W/ COVER PLATE
14. WALL FIXTURE
15. CEILING OUTLET DUPLEX
16. CEILING FIXTURE
17. LIGHT & FAN/SEPARATE SWITCHING
18. HEAT, LIGHT, FAN/SEPARATE SWITCHING
19. EXHAUST FAN
20. PULL CHAIN
21. RECESSED CEILING FIXTURE
22. FLOOD LIGHT
23. FLUORESCENT LIGHT
24. UNDERGROUND STUB-OUT W.P. BOX
25. "J" BOX
26. TELEVISION ANTENNA
27. TELEPHONE JACK
28. PUSH BUTTON
29. DOOR BELL
30. SMOKE DETECTOR
31. POWER PANEL
32. CIRCUIT BREAKER
33. THERMOSTAT
34. FUEL GAS
35. KEY
36. HOSE BIBB

ABBREVIATIONS

A.B.	- anchor bolt
M.B.	- machine bolt
BLK	- block
BLKG	- blocking
BOT.	- bottom
C.M.U.	- concrete masonry unit
CL	- clear
CLG	- ceiling
CONC.	- concrete
CONT.	- continuous
E.S.	- each side
E.W.	- each way
F.A.	- framing anchor
E.N.	- edge nail
I.N.	- intermediate nailing
B.N.	- boundary nailing
T.N.	- toe nailing
P.T.	- pressure treated
N.S.	- near side
F.S.	- far side
I.S.F.	- inside face
O.S.F.	- outside face
OPG	- opening
V.	- vertical
H.	- horizontal
O.C.	- on center
NLR	- nailer
NLG	- nailing
R.	- rafter
STL.	- steel
WL	- wall
TYP.	- typical
MIN.	- minimum
EX.	- existing
E.G.	- exterior grade
F.G.	- finish grade

Figure 15.32 Format of symbols, abbreviations, and notes.

Floor Plan

The floor plan is positioned on the sheet. As can be seen on the cartoon, the floor plan will occupy 12 of the 20 available modules on the sheet. As explained at the end of Chapter 8, the floor plan will be evolved in five stages, as replicated in Figures 15.33, 15.34, 15.35, 15.36 and 15.37.

Sheet A-3 is complete when the drawing in Figure 15.32 is merged photographically with Figure 15.37. See Figure 15.38.

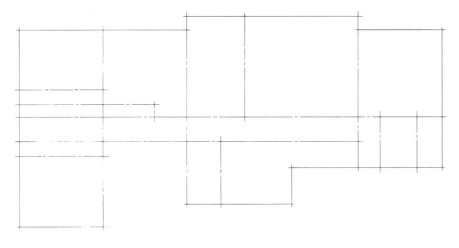

Figure 15.33 Floor plan—Stage I.

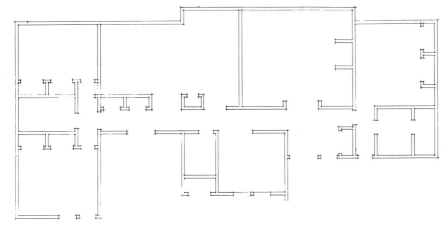

Figure 15.34 Floor plan—Stage II.

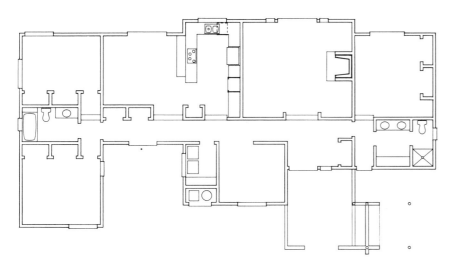

Figure 15.35 Floor plan —Stage III.

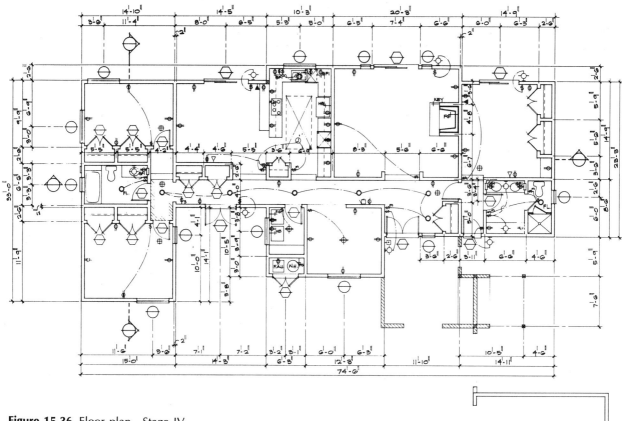

Figure 15.36 Floor plan—Stage IV.

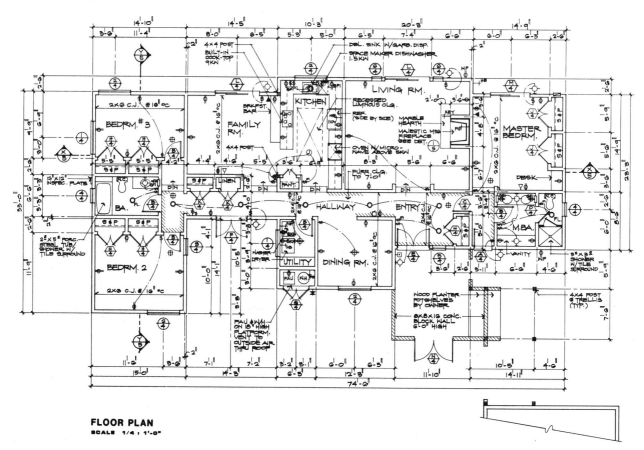

FLOOR PLAN
SCALE 1/4 : 1'-0"

Figure 15.37 Ryan Residence floor plan—Stage V.

CONSTRUCTION NOTES

1. The contractor and all sub-contractors shall verify all dimensions and conditions at the site, and shall notify the Engineer of any discrepancy. Cross-check details and dimensions shown on the structural drawings with related requirements on the architectural, mechanical, civil and electrical drawings.

2. Floor and wall openings, sleeves, variation in the structural slab elevations, depressed areas and all other architectural, mechanical, electrical and civil requirements must be coordinated before the contractor proceeds with construction.

3. In all cases, where a conflict may occur such as between items covered by specifications or notes on the drawings, or between general notes and specific details, the Architect and/or the Engineer shall be notified and he will interpret the intent of the contract documents.

4. Details as noted as typical shall apply in all cases of construction on this project.

5. Where no specific detail is shown, the framing or construction shall be identical or similar to that indicated for like cases of construction to the requirements of the 1991 edition of the Uniform Building Code.

6. Workmanship and materials shall conform to the requirements of the Uniform Building Code.

7. In no case shall working dimensions be scaled from plans, section or details on structural drawings.

8. The precise dimensions and locations of all doors and window openings shall be determined from architectural plans and details. Other wall and floor openings as required by mechanical, electrical or similar requirements shall be verified from shop drawings, equipment data, dimensions, etc., as required.

WOOD

1. Plywood roof sheathing shall be 1/2 inch thick, APA Rated Sheathing, Exposure 1. Plywood floor sheathing shall be 3/4" inch thick, APA Rated "STURD-I-FLOOR," Exposure I, T & G. All plywood shall conform to U.S. Product Standard PS I-83.

2. Plywood sheets shall be laid with the long dimension and face grain perpendicular to the rafters and the sheets shall be staggered as shown on the plans. Each sheet shall contain a minimum of 8 sq. ft. and shall extend to three bearing.

3. Plywood diaphragm shall be inspected and approved before the roofing is applied.

4. All horizontal framing members shall be Douglas Fir No. 2 grade or better for 2 x members and Douglas Fir No. 1 grade or better for 4 x members or larger (or as noted).

5. Minimum nailing shall be per Table 25-Q of the Uniform Building Code.

6. All bolt heads and nuts bearing on wood shall have washers.

7. Rafters, purlins or beams shall not be notched or dapped in any manner unless detailed.

8. All hangers and standard framing hardware unless otherwise noted shall be as manufactured by AJAX Company and are identified by numbers as shown in the latest catalog.

CONCRETE

1. All concrete shall be of 150 lb. per cu. ft. density and shall attain an ultimate compressive strength at 28 days of 2000 psi.

2. Cement shall be Type I or II Portland cement per ASTM C-150.

3. No pipes or ducts shall be placed in structural concrete unless specifically detailed.

4. Refer to architectural drawings for all molds, grooves, clips, ornaments, grounds, and other inserts to be cast in concrete.

5. All reinforcing, dowels, anchor bolts and other inserts shall be secured in proper position prior to placing concrete.

REINFORCING STEEL

1. All reinforcing bars shall be new billet steel conforming to ASTM A-615-81, Grade 60.

2. All bars shall be free from bends or kinks except as detailed and shall be free from any material which would tend to reduce the bond. Except for slabs on grade, concrete block shall not be used to support or space reinforcement.

3. All reinforcing marked "CONTINUOUS" spliced with a lap of 24 bar diameters (1'-3" minimum) in concrete (unless noted otherwise and 40 bar diameters (2'-0" minimum) in masonry. Stagger adjacent splices 10'-0" minimum.

4. All welding in conjunction with reinforcing steel shall be done with properly selected electrodes. Adequate preheat, interpass temperatures and controlled cooling shall be utilized to provide sound crack-free welds.

5. All reinforcing shall be supported in conformance with the latest edition of "Reinforcing Concrete – A Manual of Standard Practice."

6. Reinforcing shall have the following minimum cover (or as noted on drawings)
    a. Formed surfaces in contact with earth .... 2"
    b. Surfaces deposited directed against earth ...... 3"

7. Mesh reinforcement shall conform to ASTM A-185.

FLOOR PLAN
SCALE 1/4 : 1'-0"

ABBREVIATIONS

N.S.	- near side
F.S.	- far side
I.S.F.	- inside face
O.S.F.	- outside face
OPG.	- opening
C.M.U.	- concrete masonry unit
V.	- vertical
H.	- horizontal
CLG	- ceiling
O.C.	- on center
CONC.	- concrete
NLR	- nailer
CONT.	- continuous
NLG	- nailing
E.S.	- each side
R.	- rafter
E.W.	- each way
STL	- steel
F.A.	- framing anchor
WL	- wall
E.N.	- edge nail
TYP.	- typical
I.N.	- intermediate nailing
MIN.	- minimum
B.N.	- boundary nailing
EX.	- existing
T.N.	- toe nailing
E.G.	- exterior grade
P.T.	- pressure treated
F.G.	- finish grade

ELECTRICAL AND UTILITY SYMBOLS

1.	WALL SWITCH SINGLE POLE		13.	SINGLE FLOOR OUTLET W/ COVER PLATE
2.	WEATHERPROOF SWITCH SINGLE POLE		14.	WALL FIXTURE
3.	WALL SWITCH 3-WAY		15.	CEILING OUTLET DUPLEX
4.	CONVENIENCE OUTLET-DUPLEX		16.	CEILING FIXTURE
5.	WEATHERPROOF DUPLEX		17.	LIGHT & FAN/SEPARATE SWITCHING
6.	TRIPLEX		18.	HEAT, LIGHT, FAN/SEPARATE SWITCHING
7.	FOURPLEX		19.	EXHAUST FAN
8.	CONVENIENCE OUTLET 1/2 SWITCH		20.	PULL CHAIN
9.	CONVENIENCE OUTLET (WITH HEIGHT)		21.	RECESSED CEILING FIXTURE
10.	GROUND FAULT INTERRUPTER		22.	FLOOD LIGHT
11.	220V DUPLEX OUTLET		23.	FLUORESCENT LIGHT
12.	SPECIAL PURPOSE		24.	UNDERGROUND STUB-OUT W.P. BOX
			25.	"J" BOX
			26.	TELEVISION ANTENNA
			27.	TELEPHONE JACK
			28.	PUSH BUTTON
			29.	DOOR BELL
			30.	SMOKE DETECTOR
			31.	POWER PANEL
			32.	CIRCUIT BREAKER
			33.	THERMOSTAT
			34.	FUEL GAS
			35.	KEY
			36.	HOSE BIBB

Figure 15.38 Two drawings merged to form Sheet A-3.

Sheet A-4—Exterior Elevations, Schedules, and Window and Door Details

As can be seen in the cartoon (Figure 15.39), there are three components to this sheet. The exterior elevation, the details, and the schedules. Three drafters will be used to bring this sheet to its conclusion—one for each of the components.

The exterior elevation will occupy 3 of the 4 vertical modules in the sheet, and 3¾ of the horizontal modules. This will leave a wider band at the right for the details and a full vertical module at the bottom for the schedules.

Stages

The exterior elevations were evolved in four stages, as shown in Figures 15.40, 15.41, 15.42 and 15.44, with Figure 15.43 used as a check print. Schedules will be evolved in two stages, as shown in Figures 15.44 and 15.45. Window and door details will be evolved in three stages, with their final stages merged together to form a single sheet.

Descriptions of these stages are presented at the end of Chapter 11 and are repeated here.

The drafter selected to draft the exterior elevation should be the same person who drafted the building section, because both drawings reveal vertical dimensions and both use the same pitch development and ceiling heights.

Check Print—Figure 15.43

The check print reveals a couple of small omissions and a rather large error, which will be corrected in the final stage.

The small omissions are the skylights. Looking at the South elevation, you will notice that two of the skylights extend above the top of the ridge. Both of these skylights should be seen on the North elevation.

The large error is the overhang on the roof. It is drawn as a 2'–0" overhang, but it should be 12 inches. This makes a difference in the visual appearance of the elevations and in the height of the fascia. It will also place the trellis over the master bedroom door in a different location, but position the planter below it correctly.

Compare this check print with Figure 15.44, the final

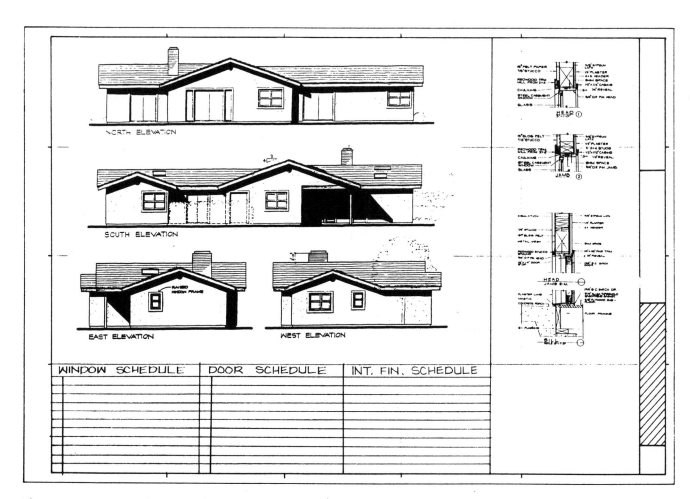

Figure 15.39 Cartoon of Ryan Residence exterior elevation.

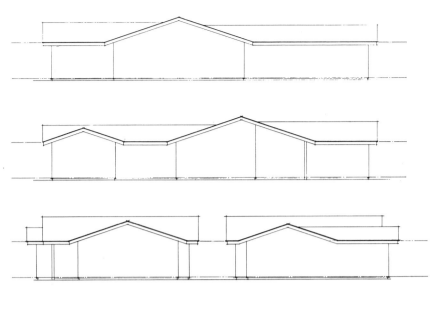

Figure 15.40 Exterior elevations
—Stage I.

Figure 15.41 Exterior elevations
—Stage II.

Figure 15.42 Exterior elevations
—Stage III.

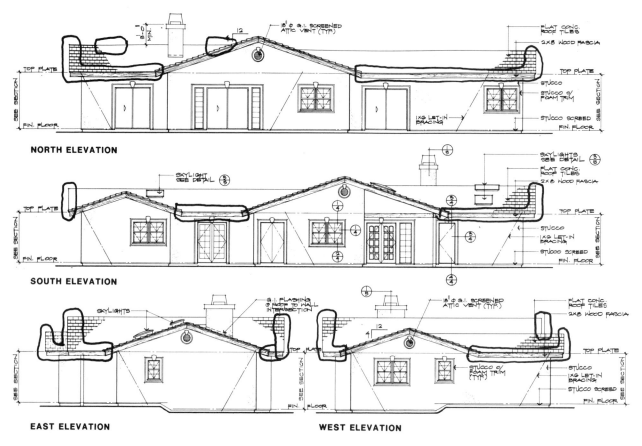

Figure 15.43 Exterior elevation check print.

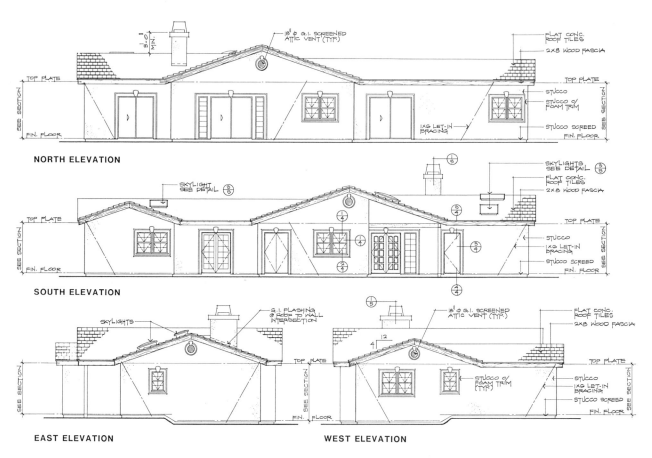

Figure 15.44 Ryan Residence exterior elevations—Stage IV.

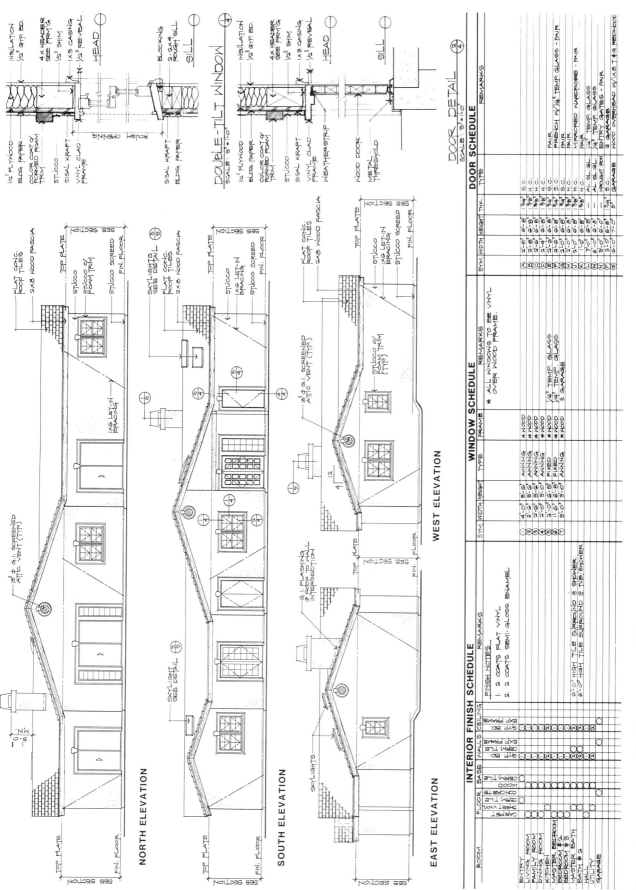

Figure 15.45 Merging of the three segments of Sheet A-4.

397

stage. Because the exterior elevations have been hard-lined, it would be difficult to erase the ends of the roof and raise the fascia. To redraft the entire sheet would take too much time, even if you were able to trace the elevations, because all elevations are affected.

The decision by the project manager was to make a xerographic copy at the same size, cut out the affected areas, and reprint (xerographically) cut-out copy onto an erasable vellum.

The final stage is not the original sheet corrected but, rather, a xerographic image corrected. Compare Figure 15.42 with Figures 15.43 and 15.44.

STAGE V (Figure 15.45). This drawing is the result of merging the three components to form Sheet A-5.

Sheet A-5—Building Section and Details

There are two major divisions to this sheet, the building section and the details. The two divisions can readily be

seen in the cartoon in Figure 15.46 and will be delegated to two drafters. As in previous steps, the drawings will be merged in the final stage into one drawing.

The drafter who drafted the foundation plan and/or the roof framing plan is an ideal candidate to draft the building section because of his or her familiarity with the framing system involved.

Likewise, the drafter who developed the footing details and the window and door details is a logical choice to draft the detail portion of the sheet. Because of that person's familiarity with detail procedures as well as the finishes used in the decor of this house, he or she can ensure a degree of consistency and uniformity to the structure. Both building sections will remain in their original positions (as proposed by the cartoon), but the positions of the details will change. The change is caused by the increase of scale in the fireplace detail and the addition of the trellis detail.

The fireplace detail will occupy the position originally held by the wood column-to-beam and skylight detail.

The wood column-to-beam detail will now occupy the original position of the fireplace, and the skylight detail will move beneath the wood column-to-beam

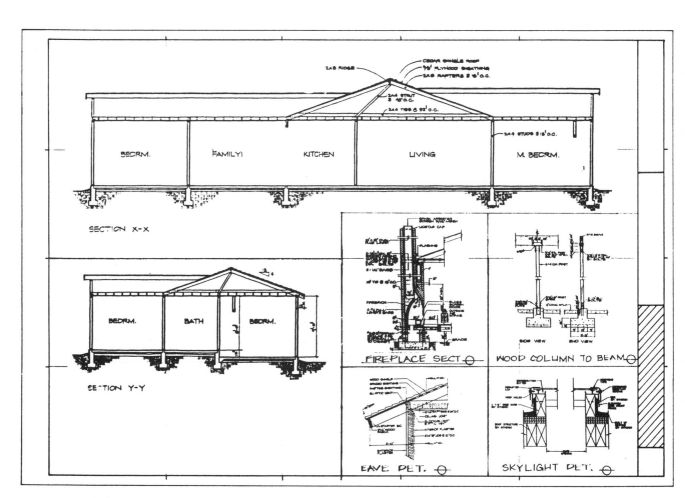

Figure 15.46 Cartoon of Ryan Residence building section.

detail and replace the eave detail. The eave and newly added trellis detail will both occupy the space below building section Y-Y. See Figures 15.47 and 15.48 for evolution of the details as well as the new formatting.

Each drawing will be reproduced many times during the course of the project. Many copies will go to contractors for estimates of cost, and the various municipali-

ties will require sets of drawings. An art jury for a particular community might require as many as 15 sets for review. As a single contractor is selected, the subcontractors will also require sets (carpenters, plumbers, electricians, etc.). It is for this reason that formatting and a conservative use of space are essential; reformatting was done on this sheet.

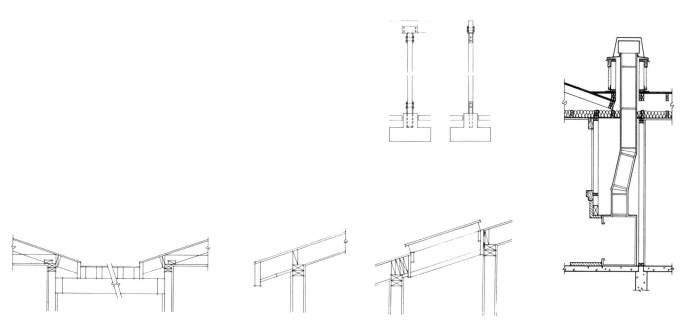

Figure 15.47 Ryan Residence: Special condition details—Stage I.

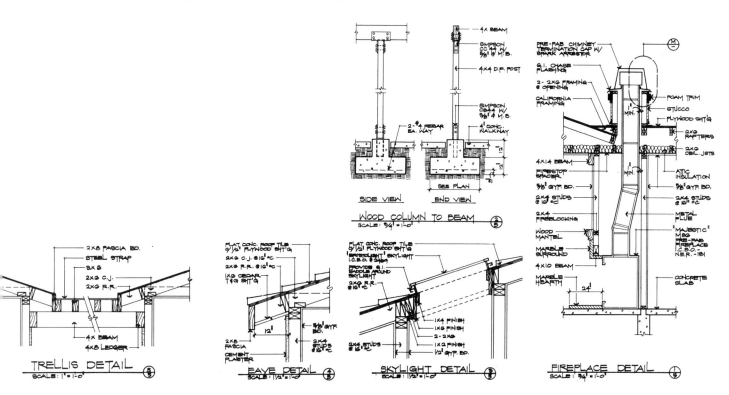

Figure 15.48 Ryan Residence: Special condition details—Stage II.

Building Section and Details

The building section was evolved in four stages. See Figures 15.49, 15.50, 15.51, 15.52. In the descriptions of the various stages, which are found at the end of Chapter 10, an interim figure was included to show the correction of a major error in the preliminary stage in the development. The explanation will clarify the sudden change that occurs in building section Y-Y.

Merging—Figure 15.53

The final stages of the details and the building section, Figures 15.48 and 15.52, were merged to form the final image of Sheet A-5.

Sheet A-6—Roof Framing Plan, Interior Elevations, and Cabinet Details

As can be seen in the cartoon for Sheet A-6, Figure 15.54, there are three components to this sheet: the roof framing plan, the interior elevations, and the cabinet details. Again we will utilize the skills of three drafters. The cabinet details will be done in three stages, as seen in Figures 15.55, 15.56 and 15.57. The interior elevations will be developed in four stages, as seen in Figures 15.58, 15.59, 15.60, and 15.61. A description of the evolution of these interior elevations can be found at the end of Chapter 13.

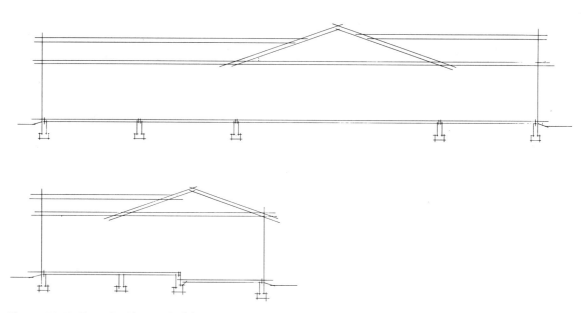

Figure 15.49 Ryan Residence: Building section—Stage I.

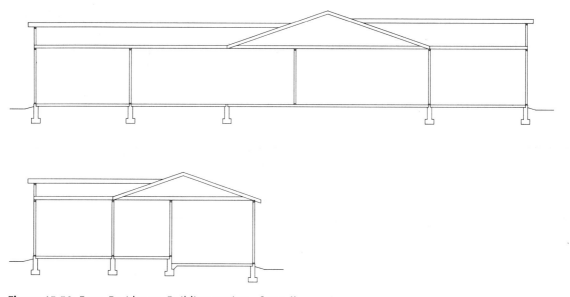

Figure 15.50 Ryan Residence: Building section—Stage II.

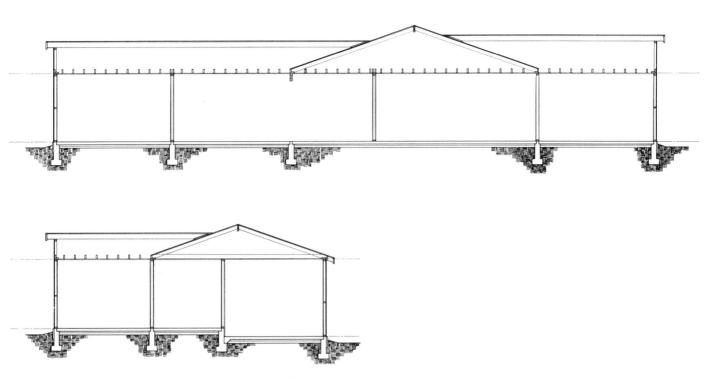

Figure 15.51 Ryan Residence: Building section—Stage III.

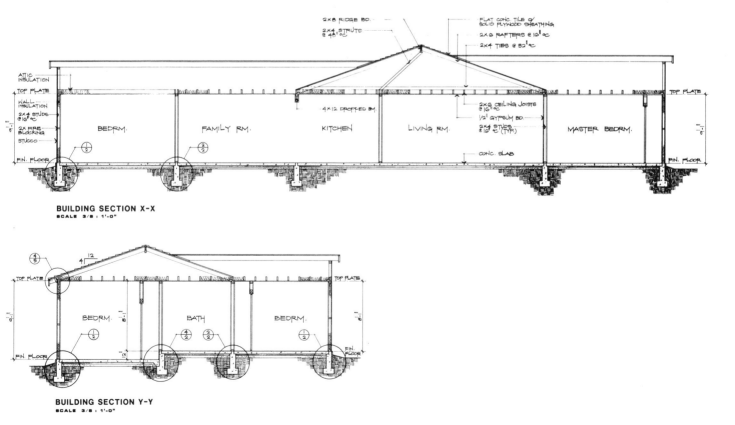

2×8 RIDGE BD.

2×4 STRUTS @ 48" OC

FLAT CONC. TILE O/ SOLID PLYWOOD SHEATHING

2×6 RAFTERS @ 16" OC

2×4 TIES @ 32" OC

ATTIC INSULATION

TOP PLATE

WALL INSULATION

2×4 STUDS @ 16" OC

2×6 CEILING JOISTS @ 16" OC

½" GYPSUM BD.

2×4 STUDS @ 16" OC (TYP.)

TOP PLATE

2×6 FIRE BLOCKING

STUCCO

BEDRM.

FAMILY RM.

4×12 DROPPED BM.

KITCHEN

LIVING RM.

MASTER BEDRM.

FIN. FLOOR

CONC. SLAB

FIN. FLOOR

BUILDING SECTION X-X
SCALE 3/8 : 1'-0"

4 │ 12

TOP PLATE

BEDRM.

BATH

BEDRM.

TOP PLATE

FIN. FLOOR

FIN. FLOOR

BUILDING SECTION Y-Y
SCALE 3/8 : 1'-0"

Figure 15.52 Ryan Residence: Building section—Stage IV.

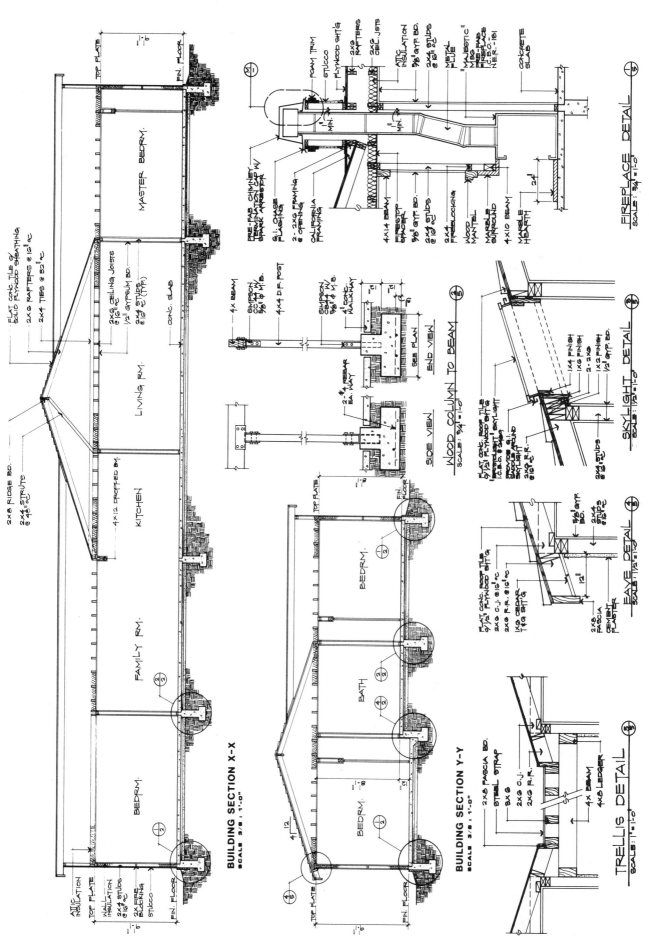

Figure 15.53 Sections and details merged to form Sheet A-5.

The roof framing plan will be done in three stages, as seen in Figures 15.62, 15.63, and 15.64. A description of its evolution can be found at the end of Chapter 12 with an explanation of the stages.

Cabinet Details

The typical upper and base cabinets are drafted for the Ryan Residence. For a look at these details in their final form, see Figures 14.87 and 14.88 of Chapter 14 in the section called "Portfolio of Architectural Details for the Ryan Residence."

STAGE I (Figure 15.55). This is the decision-making stage, which includes the selection of the type of cabinet door, the quality of the cabinets, and the countertop material.

As seen in this figure, the cabinets will have finger-pull, lumber-core doors. Of the three qualities of cabinets available and described definitively in the companion book, *The Professional Practice of Architectural Detailing,* the Ryan Residence will use a custom-type cabinet. The countertop will be $4\frac{1}{4} \times 4\frac{1}{4}$ ceramic tile over a mortar bed.

STAGE II (Figure 15.56). The material designation is done at this stage, as well as kick space and drawer size dimensioning.

Normally, custom cabinets come with a flush door that requires a door stop as well as a drawer stop. Because a finger-pull door was selected, this eliminates the need for the door stop. The door stop was also eliminated on the jamb portion of the upper cabinet, but on the bottom of the upper cabinet and base cabinets the face frame was lowered to create the door stop. This was not changed, and the edge of the plywood was banded. This oversight will be corrected in Stage III.

STAGE III (Figure 15.57). Because the errors were corrected between Stages II and III, this would be a good time to compare the drawings and note the changes. Look behind the drawers and at the two lower shelves of the upper cabinet and of the base cabinet.

Finally, all of the parts are identified and labeled, and the finishing touches are put onto the detail.

Merging

The three components were merged photographically, as described earlier, to produce Sheet A-6. See Figure 15.65.

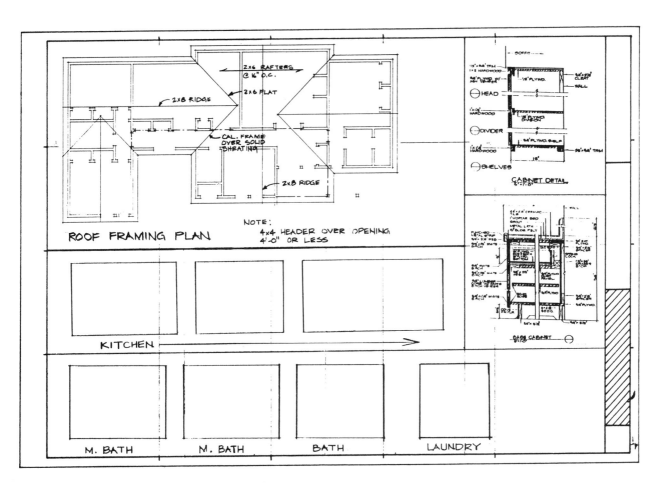

Figure 15.54 Cartoon of Ryan Residence roof framing.

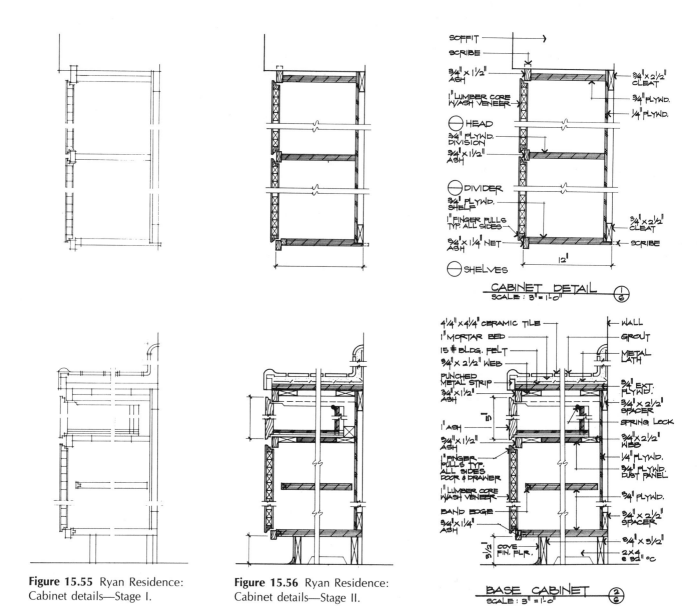

SOFFIT
SCRIBE
3/4" x 1/2" ASH
1" LUMBER CORE W/ASH VENEER
HEAD
3/4" PLYWD. DIVISION
3/4" x 1/2" ASH
DIVIDER
3/4" PLYWD. SHELF
1" FINGER PULLS TYP. ALL SIDES
3/4" x 1/4" NET ASH
SHELVES

3/4" x 2 1/2" CLEAT
3/4" PLYWD.
1/4" PLYWD.

3/4" x 2 1/2" CLEAT
SCRIBE

12"

CABINET DETAIL ①/6
SCALE : 3" = 1'-0"

4 1/4" x 4 1/4" CERAMIC TILE
1" MORTAR BED
15 # BLDG. FELT
3/4" x 2 1/2" WEB
PUNCHED METAL STRIP
3/4" x 1/2" ASH
1" ASH
3/4" x 1/2" ASH
1" FINGER PULLS TYP. ALL SIDES DOOR & DRAWER
1" LUMBER CORE W/ASH VENEER
BAND EDGE
3/4" x 1/4" ASH
COVE
FIN. FLR.

WALL
GROUT
METAL LATH
3/4" EXT. PLYWD.
3/4" x 2 1/2" SPACER
SPRING LOCK
3/4" x 2 1/2" WEB
1/4" PLYWD.
3/4" PLYWD. DUST PANEL
3/4" PLYWD.
3/4" x 2 1/2" SPACER
3/4" x 3 1/2"
2 x 4 @ 32" OC

BASE CABINET ②/6
SCALE : 3" = 1'-0"

Figure 15.55 Ryan Residence: Cabinet details—Stage I.

Figure 15.56 Ryan Residence: Cabinet details—Stage II.

Figure 15.57 Ryan Residence: Cabinet details —Stage III.

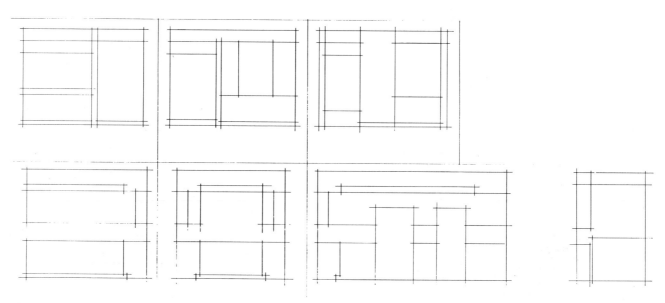

Figure 15.58 Ryan Residence: Interior elevations—Stage I.

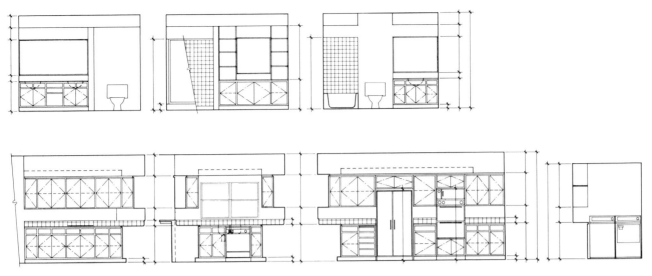

Figure 15.59 Ryan Residence: Interior elevations—Stage II.

Figure 15.60 Ryan Residence: Interior elevations—Stage III.

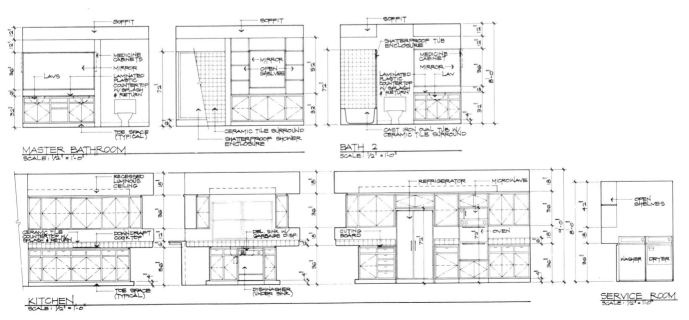

MASTER BATHROOM
SCALE: 1/2" = 1'-0"

BATH 2
SCALE: 1/2" = 1'-0"

KITCHEN
SCALE: 1/2" = 1'-0"

SERVICE ROOM
SCALE: 1/2" = 1'-0"

Figure 15.61 Ryan Residence: Interior elevations—Stage IV.

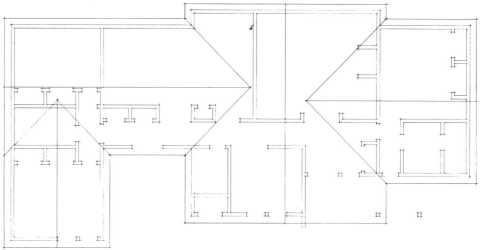

Figure 15.62 Ryan Residence: Roof framing plan—Stage I.

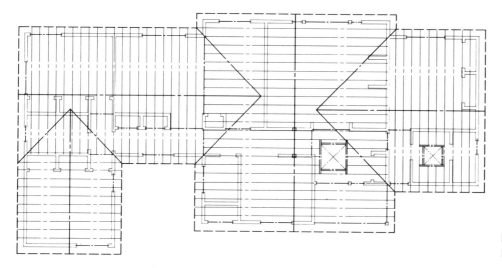

Figure 15.63 Ryan Residence: Roof framing plan—Stage II.

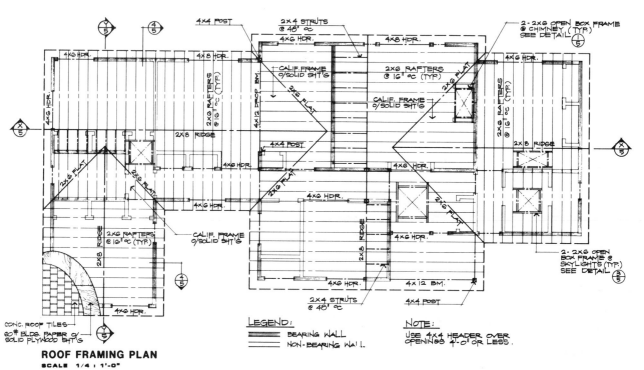

Figure 15.64 Ryan Residence: Roof framing plan—Stage III.

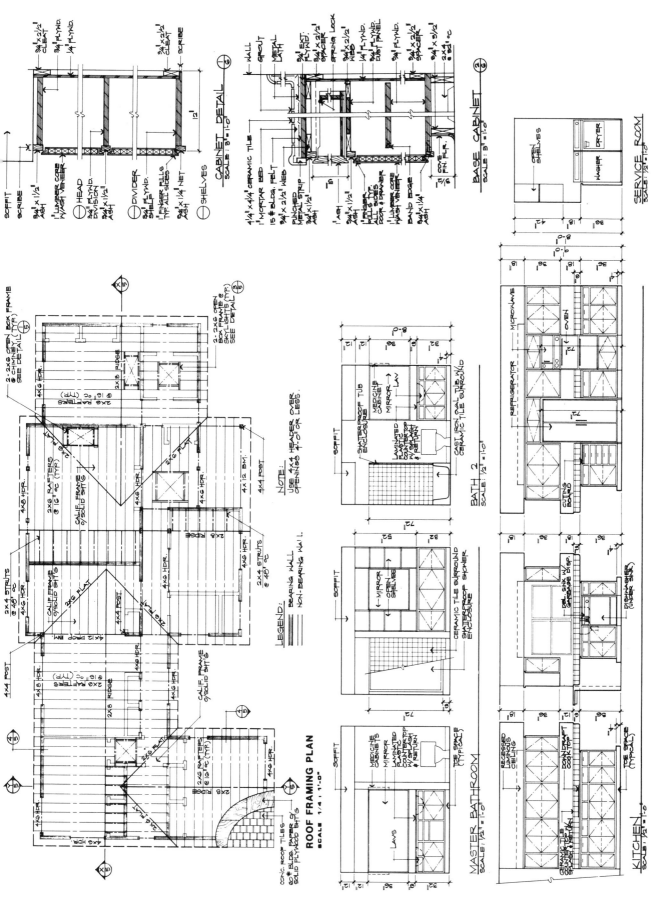

Figure 15.65 Three drawings merged to form Sheet A-6.

407

Sheet A-7—Ryan Residence Garage

The garage of the Ryan Residence was evolved entirely on a separate sheet. At a single glance, the reader can see the evolution of a complete set of drawings for the simplest of all structures, a garage.

Sheet A-7 contains the following:

A. Floor plan
B. Foundation plan
C. Roof framing plan
D. Building section
E. Exterior elevations
F. Three typical details

Compare the garage with the evolution of the Ryan Residence and you will find that the typical titles used in both sets will be alike.

In some offices that specialize in residential work, a sheet such as this might exist as a standard for a typical detached two-car garage. A xerographic master can be made of this master onto vellum and adjusted to meet the needs of each new project.

Let's say that the master was drafted as a hip roof for use with the Ryan Residence, but needed to be changed to a gable roof. The procedure is rather simple. The areas that have to be changed can be covered with white bond paper; for example, the entire roof framing plan, the tops of the exterior elevations, or any other areas.

The drawing is then xerographically reproduced as a vellum original, and the new information hand drafted and incorporated into the system.

If the garage was developed by a computer and CAD drafted, it becomes a simple matter for the CAD drafter to recall the garage sheet, and delete, correct or change the drawing to suit the new requirements.

Sheet-size limits suggested that the garage be placed on a separate sheet for the Ryan Residence. Because we were using a rather small sheet to evolve this set of drawings (24 × 36), the format did not allow the floor plan of the garage to be included, for example, with the floor plan of the residence itself. The same was true of the roof framing plan, foundation plan, and so on.

The garage will be evolved in three stages. The cartoon of the garage can be found in the Student Manual, and the plan will be hand-drafted by one drafter.

STAGE I (Figure 15.66). Prior to starting sheet A-7, the plan of this garage was drafted onto an 8½ × 11 sheet of paper. This will be traced three times onto the original. Its position, based on the cartoon of the garage, can be drawn with a fade-away pencil. Slide the 8½ × 11 under the vellum and trace the outline once for the floor plan; then slide the 8½ × 11 to its new position and trace it again for the foundation plan. Finally, the 8½ × 11 drawing is moved again and traced as a basis for the roof framing plan.

Rather than measuring the width and depth on a scale (which might be faster), the 8½ × 11 can be positioned and used as a measuring device for the exterior elevations. It can also be used to measure the width of the building section when the required distance is measured off twice (you may find use of a divider to be much faster). What this does for the beginning drafter is to maintain accuracy of measurement throughout the complete sheet.

Details can be gotten from a standard file of details, (which is often available in the office), traced, scissored, or reproduced onto an adhesive and mounted in the proper position. For this drawing, we will use details from the companion book *The Professional Practice of Architectural Detailing.*

STAGE II (Figure 15.67). The first thing the drafter did at this stage was to block out the details for the eave and the footing. These were then checked against the building section, the various plans, and the elevations.

Next, the floor plan and foundation plan were dimensioned. This included the diagonal dotted lines on the floor plan that represent the diaphragm bearing. These two 1 × 4 members stretch from one corner to the opposite corner. Because they are laid flatwise above the ties, they can be slightly bowed to miss each other as they cross. Much like reinforcing the open end of a cardboard box, the diaphragm bracing keeps the top end of the garage from becoming deformed.

The rafters, the ridge, and the look-outs are next to be drawn on the roof framing plan. These members were drawn in their entirety. However, this is not the way an office would have you draft. Instead, the ridge and rafters would be drawn as center lines, or the roof would be drawn diagrammatically, as shown in Chapter 12.

The roof structure was drafted in this manner so that you can actually see, on a drawing, how it would appear.

Notice, next, how the material designations have been placed in the building section, details, and elevations.

Finally, the window and door are positioned and drawn onto the exterior elevations along with the let-in brace and the two required vents (one per car). These are placed between the studs and above the bottom plate. Look at the exterior bearing footing and note that the bottom plate is above the floor level. This factor should be taken into consideration when positioning the vents on the elevations.

STAGE III (Figure 15.68). This is the noting and referencing stage and will be the final stage for this sheet. Because there is no checklist for the garage, the garage plan should be checked against the items listed in "Set Check," the following section of this chapter.

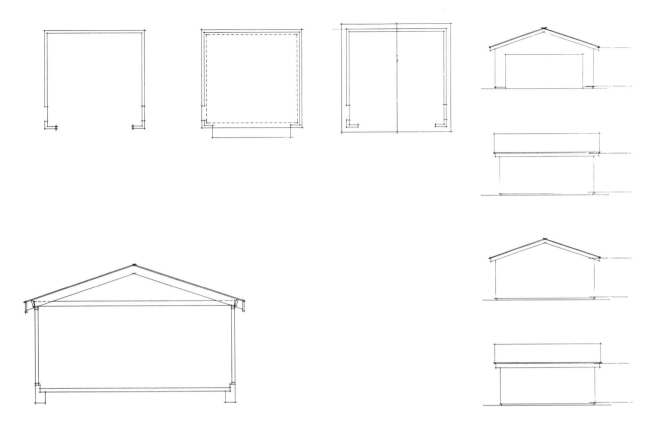

Figure 15.66 Ryan Residence: Garage—Stage I.

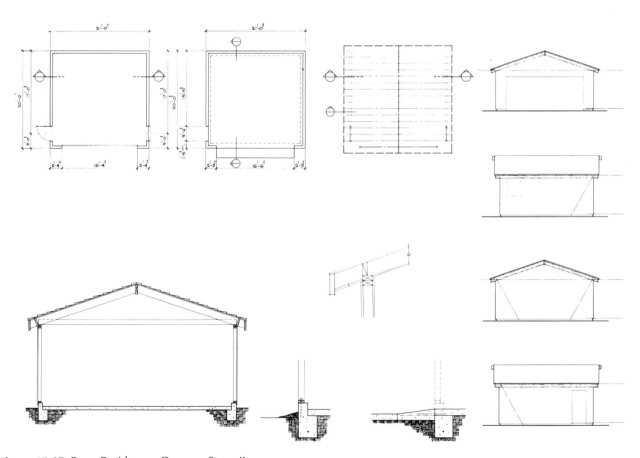

Figure 15.67 Ryan Residence: Garage—Stage II.

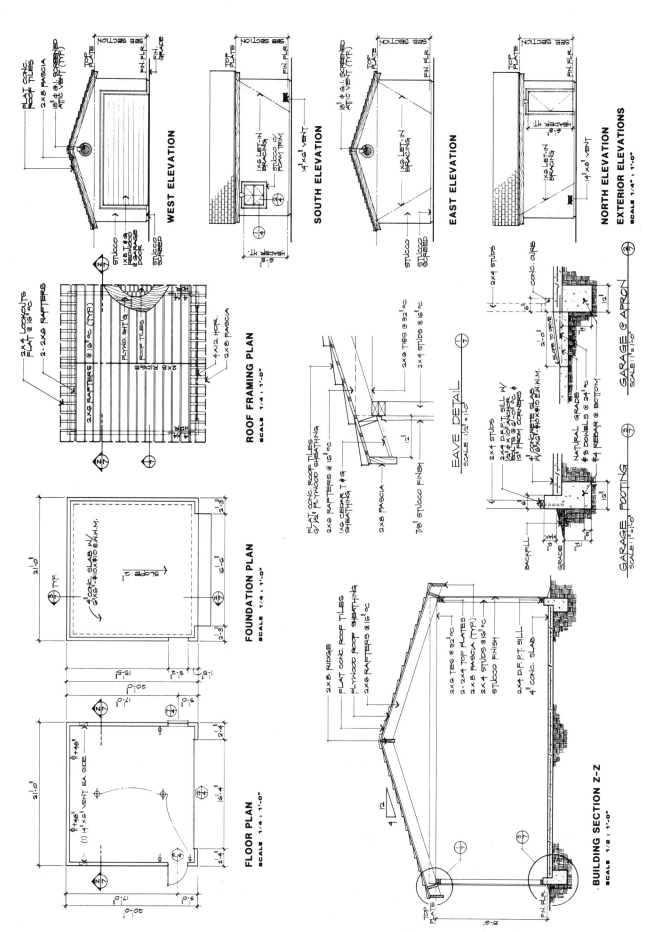

Figure 15.68 Ryan Residence: Garage—Stage III.

Set Check

In-House Plan Checker

Every office has a plan checker. It may be the architect, the project manager, or the job captain. Along with checking the plans for the same type of items that a Department of Building and Safety might check for, he or she will check to see that the sheets coordinate with each other and have correctly included all of the client's needs and changes.

Dimensions (Horizontal)

Even if the dimensions have been checked for errors in addition, the dimensions of one sheet are again checked against another. The floor plan measurements are checked with the dimensions posted on the foundation plan to validate, in fact, that this foundation will set properly under the walls shown and dimensioned on the floor plan.

The side yards on the site plan are added to the overall width of the building, as expressed on the foundation plan or floor plan; two inches are added for the thickness of the skin of the building (stucco, in the case of the Ryan Residence) and this total checked against the size of the lot as expressed around the perimeter of the site in the form of metes and bounds. This check validates that, in fact, the structure will, with its measurements and setbacks, fit and situate itself correctly onto the property.

If the plan check was done properly at the various stages, this final check becomes nothing more than a pro forma check.

Remember, just because a dimension is given does not automatically mean that the component has been dimensioned properly. As expressed in Chapter 7, it is important to think in terms of size and location.

To merely size an object is of little value if the craftsperson does not know where to position it (location). The opposite is also true. A pier or a beam may be positioned (located), but if the craftsperson does not know its size, the information is of little use.

Dimensions (Vertical)

Because most of the main drawings included in this set are plans, it might appear that the horizontal distances are the main dimensions to check. Nothing could be further from the truth. Vertical dimensions should be checked throughout the set. With the floor plan as the main sheet for horizontal dimensions, the building section becomes the basis for most vertical dimensions. For example, anytime you extend a roof over an area, such

as the entry, you should check the framing to see if there is enough space for a door and the header above the door. Head clearance above a stairwell should always be checked, as well as the space through which a beam might travel.

Anytime you pierce a horizontal plane or an angular plane—such as a roof, floor, or ceiling—with a skylight, stairwell, chimney, or some such object, a section should be drawn to check for clearances.

Cross-Referencing

A critical step is to check any cross-referencing. Especially if there is more than one drafter on a job, it is essential to see that all references to details actually refer to details that do in fact exist, and that the proper letter or number is included in each reference bubble. For example, the eave area of a building section may refer to an eave detail. The checker must be sure the name given to the detail, such "D," is the same that exists in the detail. Remember, reference bubbles are divided in two. The upper half houses the name and the lower half indicates the number of the sheet on which you can find this detail.

The most common error made by a beginning drafter is in the section lines and section references. The section line is most often drawn across plans. For example, when a section is taken through the center of a floor plan, there is a reference bubble on each end. Each bubble is split in two, with the top containing the letter name for the section and the bottom of the showing the page number of the building section.

Let us say the title to a particular section is X-X. Under the section, the title should read "Building Section X-X." On each of the bubbles on the floor plan there should be only one X. Therefore, the reader will look at one X and search for the other to complete the section (slice) through the building. Beginners often put an X-X in each of the reference bubbles, thinking that this is its name.

Plan Check and Correction

For the beginning drafter, it would be good practice to visit the local Department of Building and Safety to find out how it checks plans, or to obtain a set of simple plans that has gone through this process and study the list of corrections required by that particular municipality.

Over the years many offices have developed a checklist, often referred to as a punch list. Familiarity with these forms and lists cannot help but make you a more conscientious and effective drafter.

16

CONCEPTUAL DESIGN AND CONSTRUCTION DOCUMENTS FOR A WOOD BUILDING— BEACH HOUSE

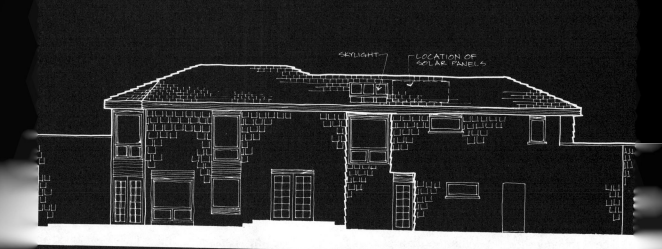

SKYLIGHT

LOCATION OF SOLAR PANELS

SOUTH ELEVATION

Residence of Mr. and Mrs. Ted E

16

Conceptual Design

The site for this project was a small beach lot fronting the ocean in a southern California community. The site dimensions are 35 feet in width and 110 feet in depth, with the 35-foot dimension adjacent to a private road. The site ownership also included an additional 35 feet on the opposite side of the private road easement. Figure 16.1 graphically illustrates the site plan, showing its relationship to the ocean, access road, and compass direction.

Site Development Regulations

Site development regulations, enforced by the community's planning commission, covered building setback requirements, building height limit, parking requirements, and the allowable building coverage of the site. These are considered together with the site and floor plan development.

Other regulatory agencies included a design review board and a State coastal commission. The design review board primarily dealt with the architectural design of the building and the landscaping plan. The coastal commission is concerned with the protection of historical landmarks, access to the public beach, and energy conservation through, for example, the use of solar collectors to augment domestic water heating.

After researching all the site development regulations and gathering the design data for our clients' needs, we started the conceptual design process.

Clients' Requirements

The clients, a middle-aged husband and wife whose children no longer live at home, wanted to develop the site to its maximum potential. The site allowed a two-story residence with a maximum floor area of 2,900 square feet measured from the inside wall dimensions. Given these two factors, they wanted the following rooms: living room, dining room, kitchen, study or family room, guest bath, mud room and laundry, and three bedrooms with two full bathrooms. They also wanted a two-car garage and shop area. Because this was a beach site, they also wanted to have sun decks wherever possible, as well as a sheltered outdoor area for winter.

Initial Schematic Studies

Our initial schematic studies worked around relationships among the rooms as well as room orientation on the site. Room orientation required that we locate the major rooms, such as the living room, dining room, and master bedroom, so that they would face the ocean and capture a coastline view. The garage and entry court needed to be adjacent to the private road for accessibility.

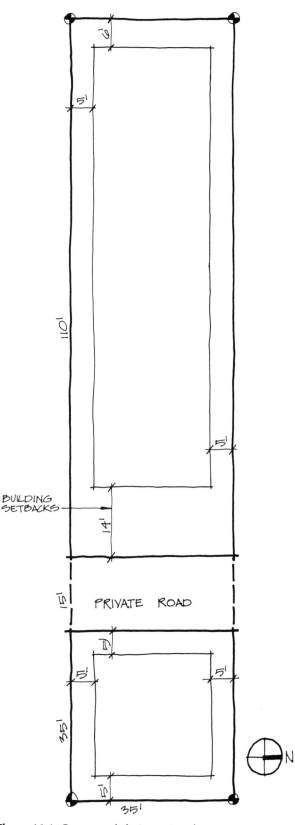

Figure 16.1 Conceptual design—site plan.

Because the site is small and because the setback regulations further reduced the buildable area, we obviously needed to design a two-story building to meet the clients' requested number of rooms.

First Floor. Figure 16.2 shows a schematic study of the first floor level. This figure also illustrates some early decisions we made: locating the entry court on the leeward side of the building; providing a view and access to the beach from the living, dining, and family rooms; locating the mud room and laundry in an area that would afford accessibility from the outside and to the beach; and providing a basement area for the mechanical system for space heating as well as a boiler for the solar collectors.

Second Floor. We developed a schematic study for the second floor level to show the desired location and relationships among the rooms as well as possible sun deck locations. We wanted all bedrooms to have direct access to a sun deck. See Figure 16.3.

Preliminary Floor Plans

Using the schematic studies as a basis for the various room locations, we developed scaled preliminary floor plan drawings.

First Floor. The first floor level, as Figure 16.4 shows, was planned to follow the site contour, which sloped to the beach. So we included floor transitions from the living room, dining room, and family room levels. Our choice of forty-five degree angles on the exterior window wall areas was influenced by a coastline view in the Southwest direction. As you can see, these angles in turn influenced other areas of the floor plan. At this stage, the scaled plan adhered to all the setback requirements and was within the allowable floor area established by the design review board.

Second Floor. The second floor preliminary plan, as Figure 16.5 shows, was basically an extension of the first floor level. It provided a master bedroom with an ocean view and had sun decks adjacent to the bedroom areas. A portion of the hall, which provided the circulation to the various rooms, was opened to the entry below. This gave the entry a high ceiling and allowed both areas to have natural light from a skylight.

Roof and Exterior Elevation Studies

From these preliminary floor plans, we developed roof and exterior elevation studies to investigate any design problems that might require some minor floor plan adjustments. We made these adjustments as we drew the floor plans for the construction documents.

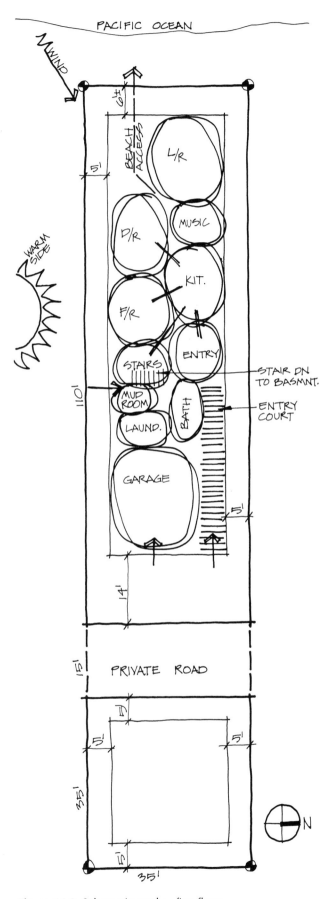

Figure 16.2 Schematic study—first floor.

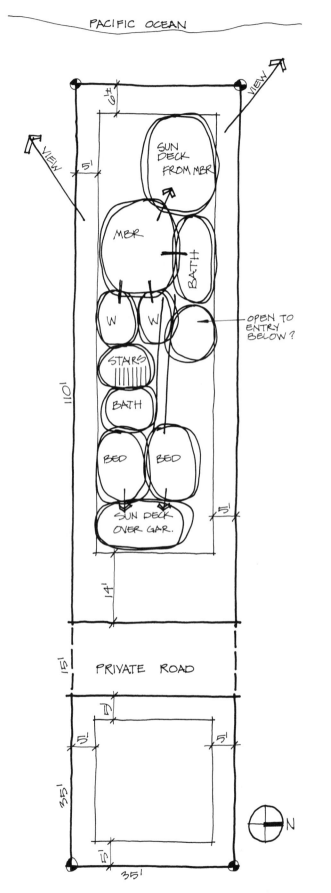

PACIFIC OCEAN

VIEW

VIEW

SUN DECK FROM MBR

MBR

BATH

W   W

OPEN TO ENTRY BELOW ?

STAIRS

BATH

BED   BED

SUN DECK OVER GAR.

PRIVATE ROAD

N

Figure 16.3 Schematic study—second floor.

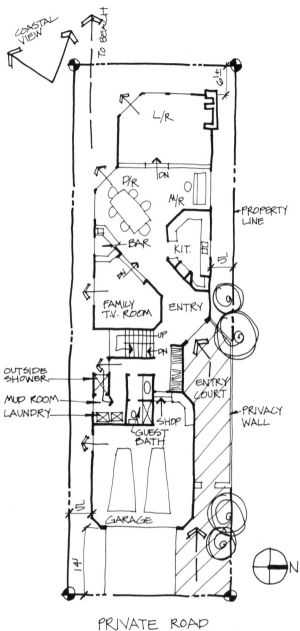

COASTAL VIEW

TO BEACH

L/R

D/R

M/R

BAR

KIT.

PROPERTY LINE

DN

FAMILY T.V. ROOM

ENTRY

UP

DN

OUTSIDE SHOWER

MUD ROOM LAUNDRY

SHOP

GUEST BATH

ENTRY COURT

PRIVACY WALL

GARAGE

N

PRIVATE ROAD

Figure 16.4 First floor preliminary plan.

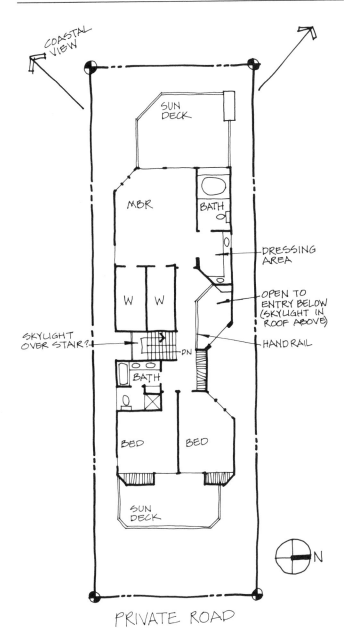

Figure 16.5 Second floor preliminary plan.

Roof Design. The development of the exterior elevations started with the roof design. We decided to use a roof pitch of 4½ in 12 to achieve an angle conducive to using solar collectors. We planned to locate these collectors on the recommended South side of the plane of the roof. This roof pitch provided the maximum height allowed by the design review board; it also determined the roof material. We selected shingle tile for the roof and cedar shingles for the exterior walls. Because salt air causes metal corrosion, we used wood windows and doors with a creosote stain finish. The glass was double glazing throughout to provide greater insulation during both the winter and summer months.

Exterior Elevations. The window designs combined fixed glass and operable sections as well as separate operable sections. Using the previously mentioned design criteria, we developed sketches of the exterior elevations. Figure 16.6 shows the four sides of this residence using these exterior materials and window elements. Because the material on the exterior was wood, we also exposed the wood lintel over the windows and doors.

After we completed these studies, we submitted them to the clients and to the various regulatory agencies. We incorporated their adjustments and refinements into the final drawing of the construction documents.

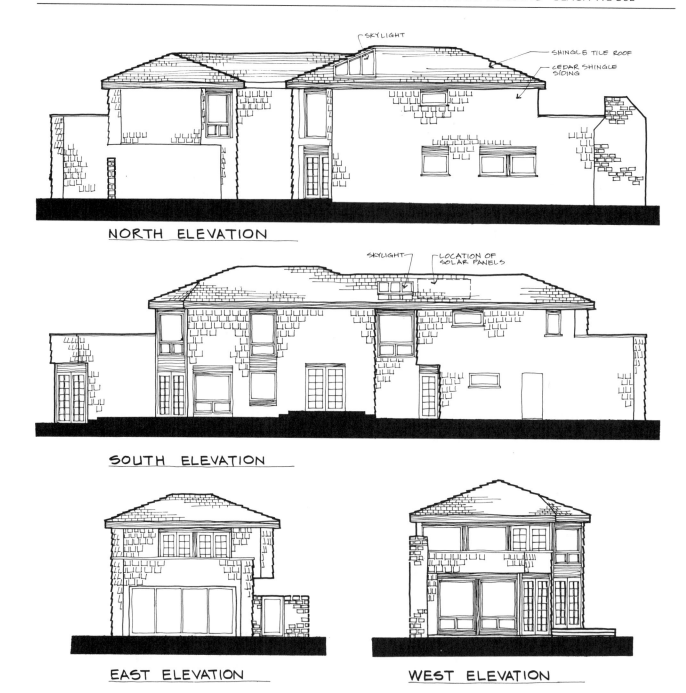

Figure 16.6 Conceptual design–exterior elevations.

Site Plan

Stage 1

The first stage of the site plan (see Figure 16.7) eventually results in a combination site plan and roof plan. After planning the sheet layout, we traced the site layout from the civil engineer's drawing. We established the perimeter of the structure from both the ground floor and upper floor plan. We also did a light layout of the vicinity map at this stage. The set of double lines at each end of the structure are second floor decks. Note the entry patio on one of the sides.

The roof is what is called a hip roof. The horizontal and perpendicular lines represent the top or peak of the roof (called the ridge), while the angular lines (always drawn at 45° to maintain a constant slope of the roof) represent what are called the hip and the valley. The hip and the valley mark the transition from one plane to another. See Figure 16.8.

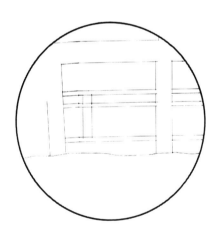

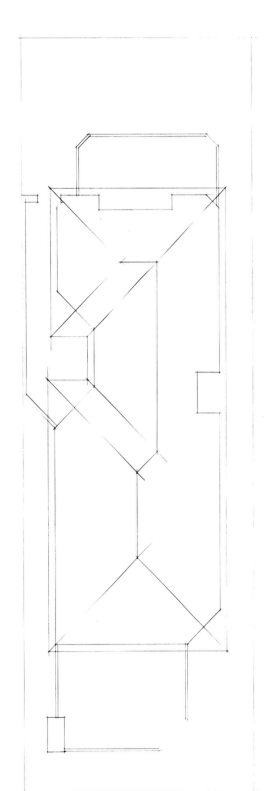

Figure 16.7 Site plan—Stage I.

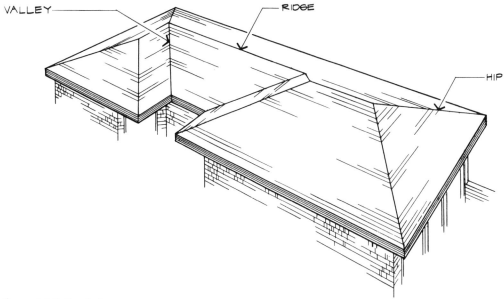

Figure 16.8 Roof view.

Stage II

After confirming the correct setbacks and the size of the structure in relationship to the site, we began the line darkening process. See Figure 16.9. On the vicinity map, we cut the plastic lid from a coffee can as a template for darkening the outline of the beach at the left. This is good practice for irregular lines for a beginner. An experienced drafter performs this freehand.

All lines on the site plan were darkened. Notice the change in the roof outline at the rear of the structure. Figure 16.10 shows the geometry to perform this cutting of the roof.

The outline of the structure was changed to a hidden line. Had the roof plan been separate from the site plan, the building would have been solid and the roof outline would have been dotted. The lines representing the shape of the roof would also have been eliminated. Skylights were put in two locations, at the entry and on the opposite side of the roof.

The round shapes found around the perimeter are planters. We next included the material designation for brick pavers as well as the wood benches at the back of the lot. We also made a correction in the size of the fireplace at this stage.

The series of close parallel lines at the front and the rear of the building indicated the guardrail around the deck created by a smaller second floor. The very small rectangular pieces attached to these parallel guardrail lines represent scuppers. Scuppers are used for draining water that accumulates on the deck and are usually made of sheet metal. In this case, they project through an opening in the guardrail and allow the water to drip to the ground. They protrude beyond the surface of the guardrail to stop water from flowing onto the surface of the guardrail.

There are various levels on the ground surface. A look at the final stage of the building section (Figure 16.34) shows the different heights. The area adjacent to the family room is the highest; the property slopes downward to the rear and to the front from here. The lot slopes up again on the other side of the private road.

Stage III

Relocating the Vicinity Map. A check at this point showed that the vicinity map was in an inconvenient location. (See Figure 16.7). The general notes and sheet index still had to be located on this sheet. It was better to have the index on the right hand side opposite the binding edge where it is more accesible. So the vicinity map was moved, but not redrawn. (See Figure 16.11). We did this as follows:

1. A new sheet of vellum was placed over the original sheet.
2. Using a mat knife and a straightedge, both sheets were cut in half lengthwise at the same time.

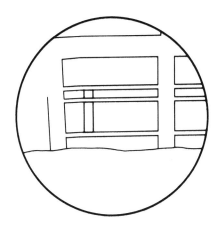

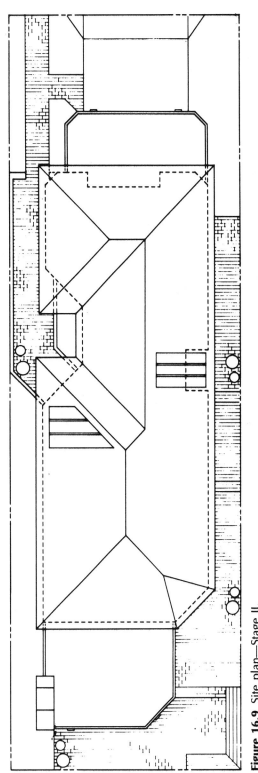

Figure 16.9 Site plan—Stage II.

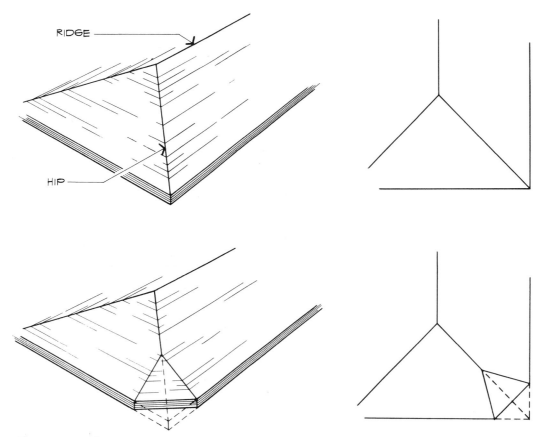

Figure 16.10 Change of a normal hip roof.

3. The upper half of the original sheet was replaced with the newly cut vellum and taped on the reverse side using transparent tape.
4. The original ½ sheet containing the vicinity map was placed over this newly assembled drawing in the now desired position.
5. Another cut around the vicinity map and through the 2 sheets of vellum was then made.
6. The cut out of the vicinity map was then taped in the new location with transparent tape on the reverse side.

The vicinity map was then finished by shading the subject property and identifying adjoining streets and the Pacific Ocean.

Setbacks, Improvements, and Notes.   The setbacks—that is, the dimensions needed to locate the structure—were then added to the site plan. All improvements were dimensioned next. These improvements were located from the property line or the building itself. The direction of the slope of the roof, the decks, and even such areas as the driveway we indicated by arrows and/or notes.

Notes were next to be added and we used broad general terms. Utility lines were shown. Notice the abbreviation "P.O.C." (point-of-connection) to the various utility lines. The sewer line is marked with an "S",

the gas line with a "G", and the water main with a "W". We showed hose bibb locations (garden hose connections) as well as the various steps around the lot.

Reference bubbles for the skylight areas were drawn to refer to a specific detail. Finally, we added the legal description at the extreme right.

Stage IV

The final stage for the site plan sheet is shown in Figure 16.12. In the previous stage we nearly finished the site and roof plan. All that remained was to add roof texture, which we did to show a variety of techniques. Some architectural offices prefer not to invest a drafter's time in this type of activity and leave the roof as it was in the previous stage.

We made a correction to one of the skylights because we found that the exterior wall below forced a separation. Finally, we added the title, North arrow, construction notes, and sheet index. As you can see, the construction notes are not hand lettered, but they could have been. In this case, the notes were typed onto a piece of vellum cut from the larger sheet, then spliced back in when the typing was completed. Other methods already discussed in earlier chapters could have been used to apply the notes to the larger vellum.

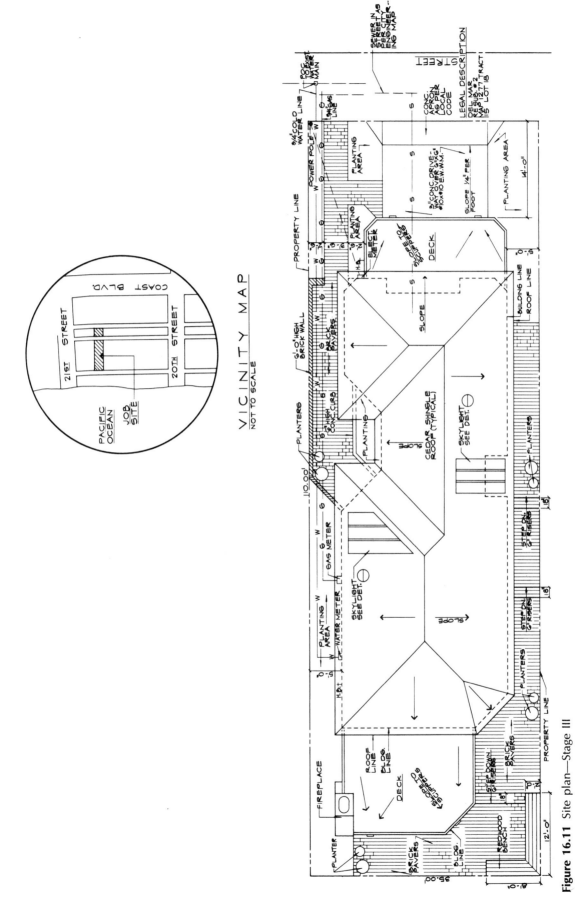

Figure 16.11 Site plan—Stage III

423

GENERAL NOTES

CONSTRUCTION NOTES

GENERAL NOTES

1. The contractor and all subcontractors shall verify all dimensions and conditions at the site, and notify the Architect of any discrepancy.

2. All workmanship and materials shall conform to the Uniform Building Code (15 edition).

3. All covering to be cement plaster, tile or approved equal. 6 ft. above floor at showers or tubs with showers. Water glass other enclosure doors and panels must be 3/16" fully tempered, 1/4" enclosure doors and panels must be 3/16" fully tempered, 1/4" and structural elements to be water resistant. Glass within foundation plate line.

4. Provide corrosion resistant deep screwed between stucco at the foundation plate line.

5. All interior door opening headers to be 4" x 4" unless otherwise noted.

WOOD

1. All horizontal framing members shall be Douglas Fir No. 2 grade or better for 2 x members and No. 1 grade or better for 4 x.

2. All vertical framing members to be stud grade or better.

3. Plywood decking at floor and roof shall be as indicated on plans.

4. Provide double joists under all parallel partitions.

5. Joists greater than 4" in depth and rafters greater than 8" shall be solid blocked at all bearing points and to have 2 x solid blocking or cross bridging at 8' maximum for rafters.

6. Fireblock stud walls and partitions at floor, ceiling, soffit and at midheight of all walls over 8' high. Bridging required if over 10' high.

7. Provide clearance for wood members above grade as follows: 6" for mudsills, 12" for girders, 18" for joists.

8. Where retaining walls or concrete walls at g.c level lower than the adjacent grade shall be placed in metal wall boxes or the area within 12" from wood shall be treated for any contact with metal.

9. Provide rafter ties 2 x 4 o.c. immediately above ceiling joists or ceiling joists shall not be smaller than the rafters they support. Provide strut supports for purlins to bearing walls not smaller than 2 x 4 with an unbraced length not over and not flatter than 45° from horizontal.

10.

11. Provide 15 lb. felt paper under wood siding.

12. Minimum nailing shall be as per structural notes. Provide diagonal bracing at corners and every 25 lineal feet of wall.

LATH, PLASTER AND WALLBOARD

1. Lath, plaster, and wallboard shall conform the Chapter 47 of the Uniform Building Code. Inspection is required for all interior or exterior in-place lath or wallboard after all plastering materials are delivered on site and after all lathing joints, or before any joints and fasteners have been taped or finished.

CONCRETE AND REINFORCING

1. All concrete shall be 150 lb. per cubic foot density and shall attain a minimum compressive strength of 2,000 psi at 28 days.

2. House, parge and slabs to have 1/2" thick concrete slab with 6 x 6/10 wire mesh over 4" of sand or gravel, each way over 4" minimum of sand or gravel. See Foundation Details for placement of reinforcing to limit infiltration.

3. Saturate the soil 18" deep before pouring concrete slab. Fill and loose subsoil shall be consolidated by puddling or tamping. Extend 1/2" x 12" anchor bolts minimum into footing 2.6" o.c.

4. All rebars shall be free of kinks and shall be free of concrete reinforcing bars and lapped bars as shown. All splices in masonry or 24" min. standard reinforcing in concrete, 40 diameters in masonry or 24" min. 30 diameters in concrete, lap footings and splices in placed cover over reinforcing shall be as follows:

   A. Concrete against earth (formed) = 3"
   B. Concrete against earth (formed) = 3/4"

6. Size and spacing of reinforcing steel shall be as indicated in foundation plan and details.

MASONRY

1. All masonry shall conform to Chapter 24 of the Uniform Building Code.

2. Mortar other than gypsum mortar used in masonry construction shall be classified in accordance with a) the material and proportions set forth in Table 24-A, or b) properties as established by laboratory tests as set forth in U.B.C.

3. Grout shall be proportioned by volume and shall have sufficient water to produce consistency for pouring without segregation of the constituents and shall be as indicated in Foundation Plan and Details.

4. Masonry veneer shall comply with Chapter 30 of the U.B.C.

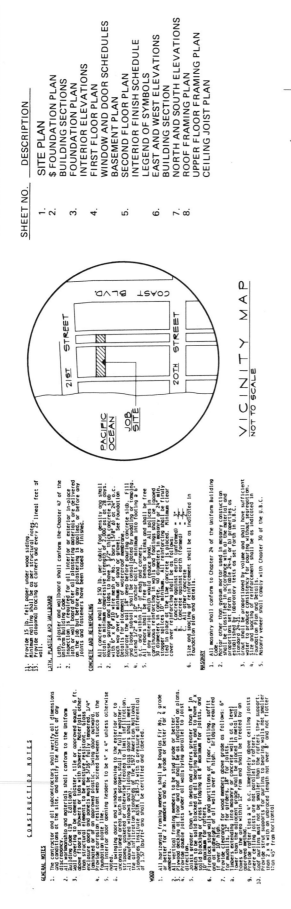

VICINITY MAP
NOT TO SCALE

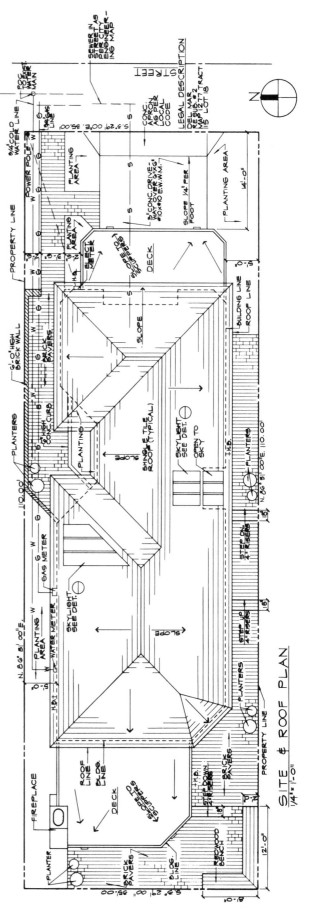

SITE & ROOF PLAN
1/4" = 1'-0"

Figure 16.12 Site plan—Stage IV.

Foundation Plan: Slab

There are two foundation plans shown here, concrete slab and wood floor. These are shown to illustrate their differences and how they are drafted.

Stage I

Figure 16.13 shows the layout stage for both the foundation plan and two building sections. The basement retaining wall footing size has been dictated by the fact that the top of the retaining wall is restrained by the concrete floor slab.

The dotted and solid lines of the foundation plan show the shape of the footing and foundation walls. The double solid line around the perimeter of the garage represents a 6″ curb that extends above the grade far enough to keep the sill away from termites.

All walls are bearing walls except the two in the laundry room, represented by a pair of dotted lines. The rectangle between the family room and the dining room, drawn with a solid line, represents a step down.

The foundation plan and details are used to figure the shape of the building sections. The horizontal lines between floors in the sections represent the thickness of the slab floor. The three horizontal lines between the lower floor and the upper floor are the header (support beam at openings) line for windows and doors, the plate line, and the floor line.

The two lines between the upper floor and the roof are the header line and the plate line. The angular lines represent the rafters. The building section on the left was taken through the dining room and between the kitchen and living room. The other building section was taken through the family room and entry to show the basement and how the entry extends through both floors (this will become visible in the next stages of the drawing).

Stage II

Figure 16.14 shows the beginning of the dimensioning stage for the foundation and the refinement stage for the building sections. These cross-sections could appear on the same sheet as the longitudinal section in order to group similar drawings. However, for learning purposes, the building sections are shown here with the foundation plan.

The sizes for the various members in the building section were obtained from the structural engineer's framing plan. However, with this type of structure, this framing plan could have been done "in house."

Freehand sketches of details help greatly at this stage. See the illustrations in Chapter 14 for architectural details.

The dimensions at the corners of the structure for the angles are not really necessary but they are included to help the contractor. The rectangle at the left top corner is the foundation for the fireplace. Local codes should be checked for fireplace requirements. The dots represent the vertical steel included in earthquake areas. Check the sheets to make sure that every exterior and interior wall (and the foundation under them) can be located from either side. Check for size and location.

Stage III

Building Sections. At this stage the building sections are being refined. See Figure 16.15. The quality of lines is improved, and the material designations for such items as concrete, masonry, and insulation is the delineation of the structural components such as joists, studs, beams, and rafters. Here we tried to show what the roof would look like based on the precise location of the cutting plane. Rather than seeing the ridge at the top of the building section, the cutting plane exposes this end view of the rafters. We could have taken, instead, an offset section by moving the cutting plane running through the building to expose the most comprehensible structure. If we had done this, we would have exposed the ridge at the top rather than the rafters.

Notice the location of the beam on the left building section and the furred (lowered) ceiling. On the right building section, notice too how the stud goes from almost the ground level to the roof, two stories tall. These are 2 × 6 studs rather than the normal 2 × 4 studs because of the increased vertical span. The eaves (intersection of the roof and wall) are closed off by a horizontal member.

Structurally, the building section shows the retaining wall in the basement. Because the slab is pinned (attached) to the outer walls, it stops the walls of the basement from caving inward.

Foundation Plan. This is the stage during which the numerical values are added. The dimensions must coincide with the floor plan. Both *must* be to the stud line. The edge of the concrete foundation wall is also the stud line. Detail reference bubbles are located and the material designation for the masonry in the fireplace is drafted. See Figure 16.15.

Stage IV

This is the noting stage—the final stage for both the building sections and the foundation plan. See Figure 16.16.

Sections. We first established vertical distances which were taken from floor line to plate line. Each room that the building sections cut through is labeled to make its cutting location clear. We next labeled parts of the building: floor, ceilings, and roof coverings, plus special beams, and so forth. Detail reference bubbles, scale, and titles completed this portion of the sheet.

Foundation Plan. After double checking the dimensions, we put in the building section reference bubbles and their symbols. Notes were added next. These

notes take the form of descriptions of the slab, sizes of spread footings, or notes describing the drafter lined, as in the case of the steps. Omission of the waterproof (W.P.) membrane in the garage area was also noted, as was the slope of the slab. The title, scale, and North arrow finished this sheet.

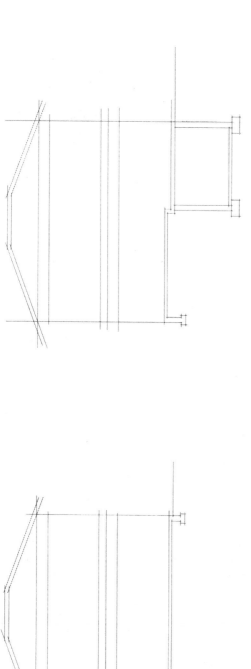

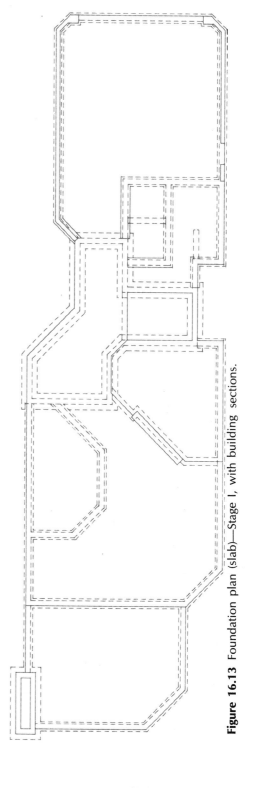

Figure 16.13 Foundation plan (slab)—Stage I, with building sections.

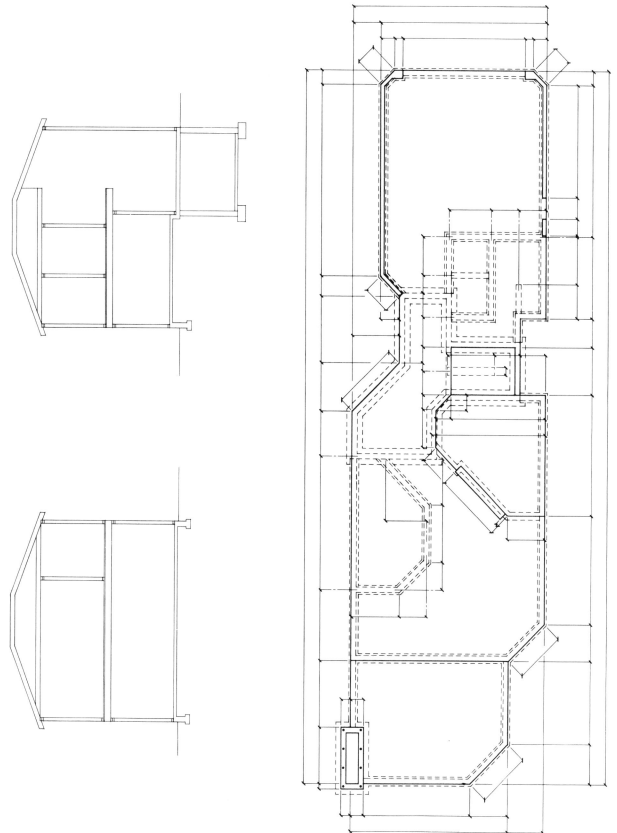

Figure 16.14 Foundation plan (slab)—Stage II, with building sections.

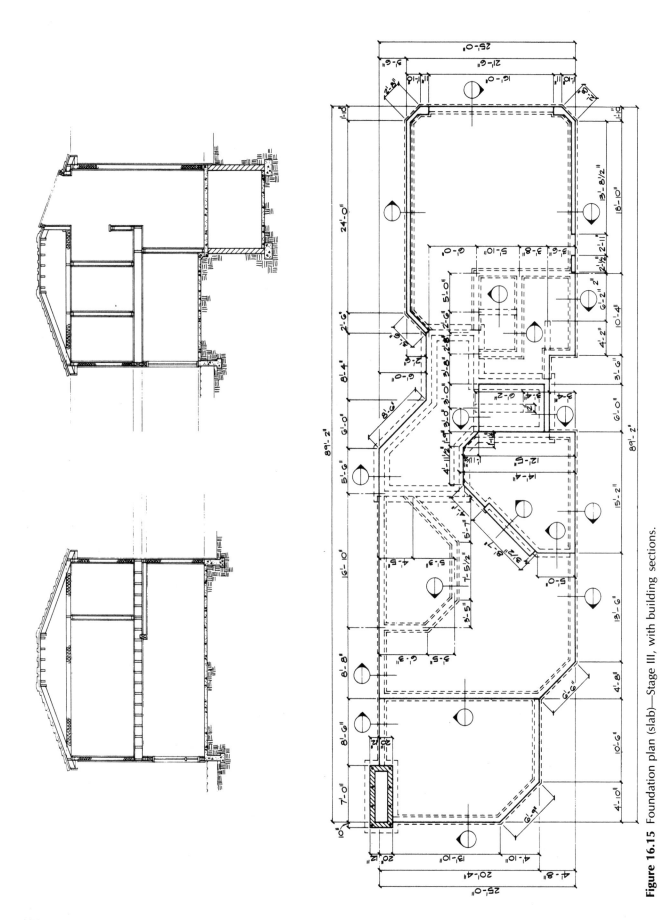

Figure 16.15 Foundation plan (slab)—Stage III, with building sections.

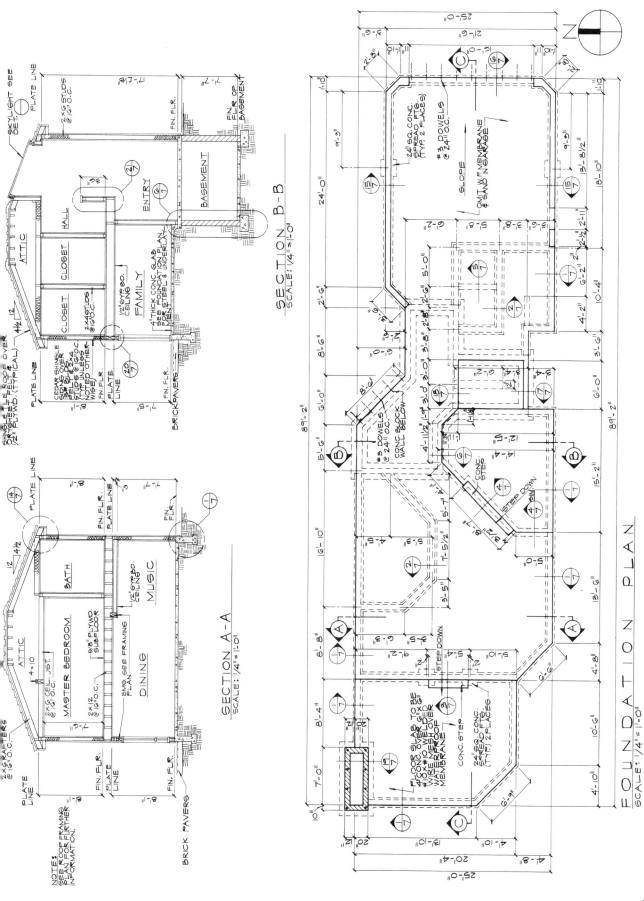

Figure 16.16 Foundation plan (slab)—Stage IV, with building sections.

Foundation Plan: Wood

Both a wood floor and concrete slab floor system were developed for this beach house. While preparing two foundation plans for a single project is not customary, it was done here for comparison so that the reader can see the difference of appearance between a wood and concrete floor. The slab foundation will be used throughout the remainder of this set of drawings.

Stage I

The layout of the foundation plan (Figure 16.17) was done after the floor plan had been finalized to the point where all exterior and interior walls were established.

The structural considerations should always be analyzed so that the design of the foundation can take those considerations into account. Basically, there were three levels in this structure. On the first floor the rooms are on one level with the exception of the living room near the fireplace and the triangular family room. However, the foundation plan shows four levels: the three mentioned above plus the basement located directly below the entry.

The footing for the basement retaining wall is large because it is not restrained at the top and acts as a full cantilever. The dotted lines in the basement area represent footing shape. The dotted lines do not extend into the area below the hall between the garage and entry; because the leg of the footing is so large that the garage and entry overlap each other, they are treated as a solid mass. The garage is the only area that is a slab on the ground. The double lines around the edge represent the width of the 6″ wall. This extends above the ground to keep the wood sill away from the ground level, protecting it from termites.

The square forms represent the piers. One form, adjacent to the kitchen, is not square but rectangular. Because of the design of this structure, two girders were going to land on this pier, so the pier size was increased.

The rectangular shape at the corner of the living room represents the fireplace and the dots represent the reinforcing bars to be placed vertically. The series of center lines between the laundry room and the garage represents dowels that hold the slab of the garage to the foundation wall of the house.

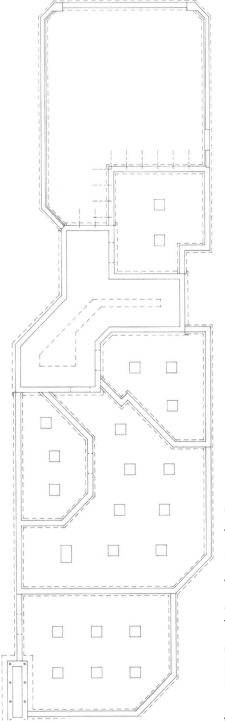

Figure 16.17 Foundation plan (wood)—Stage I.

Note the solid and dotted lines around the perimeter of the foundation walls. The solid line, like the one in the garage, represents a break in the portion that extends above the slab level and is for a door. The dotted lines represent an opening for access from one underfloor area to another. From the basement there is access to any of three underfloor areas. There is also access to the area below the kitchen from the area below the dining room. This access is located where there is no supporting wall or partition. There is also underfloor access near the fireplace.

The basement wall is concrete block and does not follow the block module. We decided to forego the block module measurement because it was costly and unnecessary for this small a use.

Stage II

We made a check print on which freehand dimension lines, actual dimensions, notes, and missing items like girders and so on were drawn. See Figure 16.18. This information was then transferred onto the final drawing. The following stages illustrate the placement of the information from the check print.

The space above the foundation plan on this sheet was allocated to the interior elevations. Stage II of the foundation plan also became Stage I of the interior elevations. The elevation on the top left is the downstairs bathroom; the one directly to the right is the bathroom on the upper floor; the last two on the right of the top row are the master bath. The three directly below are interior elevations of the kitchen.

The outline of the foundation plan was now confirmed and checked for size. Dimension lines were introduced. Because of the various angles throughout the structure, dimension lines were often crossed by extension lines and other dimension lines. The extension lines on the bottom left corner were broken for the dimension lines. We did this because dimension lines take precedence over extension lines.

Girders were overlooked and were added at a later stage. A final correction that might be made later using this stage for comparison is a wall that separates the two sets of stairs. The dotted lines representing the end of the retaining wall disappear, because the space between the dotted lines is filled with a footing for the new wall. A look at the building sections will explain this better.

Stage III

Compare Stage II and III drawings (Figures 16.18 and 16.19) at the stair and notice the change in the pattern of the hidden lines. Because the walls of the basement and the fireplace were masonry units, the material designation for masonry (diagonal lines) was drafted.

We next added the numbers for the dimensions. See Figure 16.19. These dimensions must always coincide with the floor plan's. We also included reference bubbles for details at this stage. We drew vertical dimension lines on the interior elevations, cleaned up all lines, and drafted additional details such as door swing designations, shelves, and handles on doors and drawers.

Stage IV

Interior Elevations. Here we added material designations such as ceramic tile on interior elevation #1 and kick space material. See Figure 16.20. We deleted the solid line for the refrigerator by using the erasing shield method. The numerical values for the vertical dimension lines were next to be included. We eliminated small corrections such as the lines above and below the oven. Finally, we put the notes in. Remember that a set of written specifications is included as part of these construction documents. Our notes, therefore, were general in nature, and descriptive but not specific. Reference bubble numbers and titles completed this step.

Foundation Plan. The main difference between this stage and the previous stage was the inclusion of girders (floor beams to support floor joists). They are shown by a very dark center line. Joists are shown by a dark line and arrows (half arrowheads); these show the size, spacing, and direction of the floor joists. See Figure 16.20.

The floor joists were running parallel to the garage door in the area of the bathroom, stairs, and entry. The rest of the house—family room, dining room, kitchen, music room, and living room—had floor joists running perpendicular to the garage door.

A rectangle with a single diagonal line indicates the break in the foundation wall between one area and the next. A note on the bottom left explains the drafting system being used. Additional notes about venting were added in the garage area. This would show up in drafted form on the exterior elevation if an exterior elevation of a wood floor system were drafted. Reference bubble numbers, title, scale, and North arrow complete this drawing.

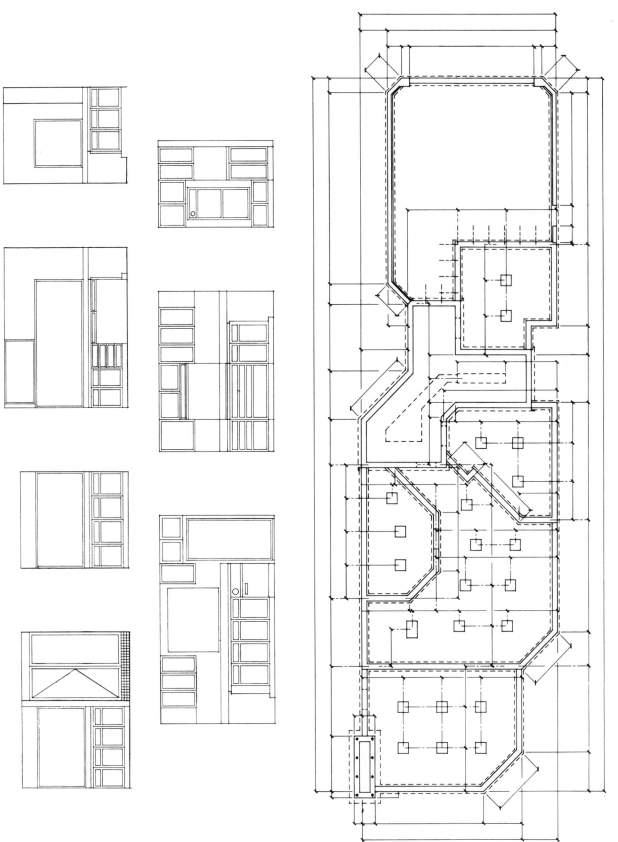

Figure 16.18 Foundation plan (wood)—Stage II, with interior elevations.

432

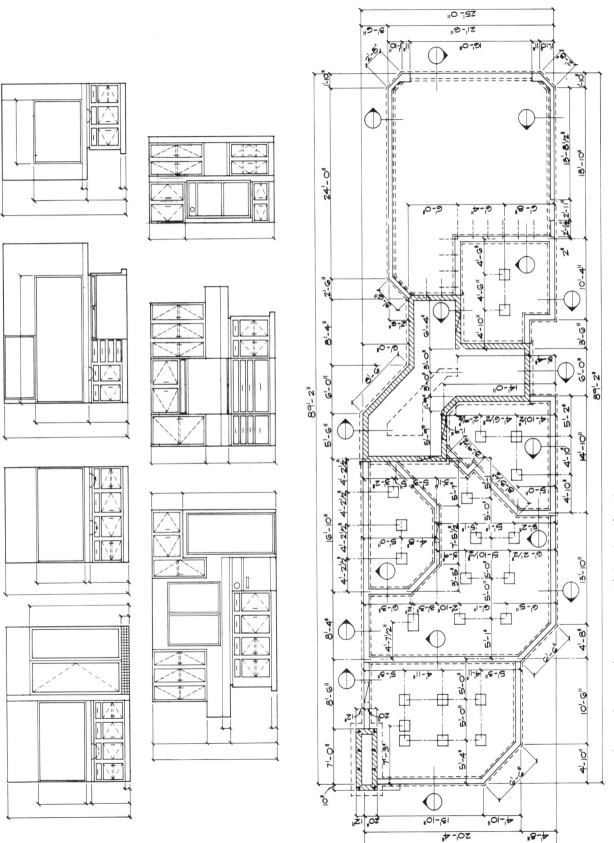

Figure 16.19 Foundation plan (wood)—Stage III, with interior elevations.

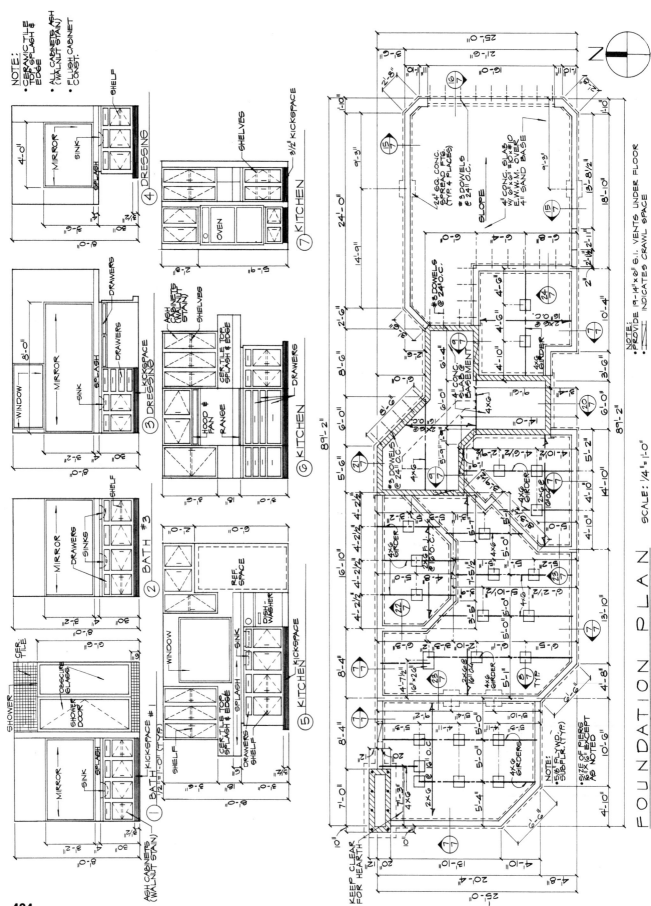

Figure 16.20 Foundation plan (wood)—Stage IV, with interior elevations.

First Floor Plan

Stage I

While the lines in Figure 16.21 appear dark because of the photographic method used in textbook reproduction, this is actually the light block-out stage. Measurements are carefully taken from the preliminary floor plan, verified, and checked against the site plan.

The door jambs of the garage and entry are enlarged to give the illusion of a thicker wall construction. The "U" shaped area in the kitchen was designed to eventually house a built-in oven. The area with the shower adjacent to the laundry room functions as the mud room. Here those coming in from the beach can wash off sand and change out of bathing suits before entering the main portion of the house.

Stage II

At this stage, all equipment was placed in the kitchen and the bathrooms. See Figure 16.22. Note the wet bar between the dining room and the family room. The stairs to the basement and to the upper level are shown. Most important are the level changes that are beginning to show between the living room and dining room and the dining room and family room, and the slight change between the garage and the house. Windows and doors around the perimeter were also located. The wall lines were darkened. Sepia copies were made for the structural, mechanical, and electrical consultants.

Stage III

Figure 16.23 shows the preliminary layout stage for the window and door schedules. The format is normally established by office standards. This format follows the AIA standard with allowances for specific structures. This information usually comes from the designer and/or architect.

This is also the preliminary stage for the basement plan. The basement is made of concrete block but is so small it will not follow the block module. Had the area been larger, a standard block module would have been used. The basement area was designed to house the boiler for the solar collectors and the mechanical equipment for space heating.

This is a critical step in the plan because it is the dimension line stage. This step also includes variations of line quality because while the dimension lines must be precise, they must not take away from the main body of the drawing. Every wall and partition must be located and every door and window must be sized. See Chapter 8, on floor plans, for a method for wood structures.

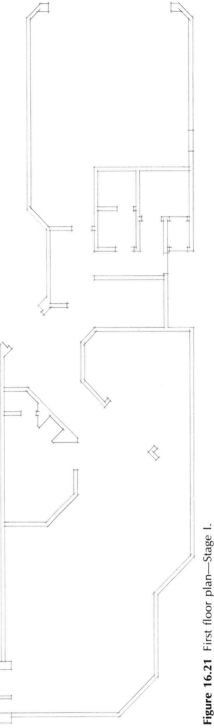

Figure 16.21 First floor plan—Stage I.

The measurements on the angular walls were included to help the contractor check accuracy. These dimensions must not only be graphically correct but trigonometrically correct as well. Because of the many angles, many dimension lines may cross each other. This crossing should be kept to a minimum.

Electrical fixtures are also shown. This floor plan eventually incorporated a complete electrical plan. Larger buildings, however, often have a separate electrical plan.

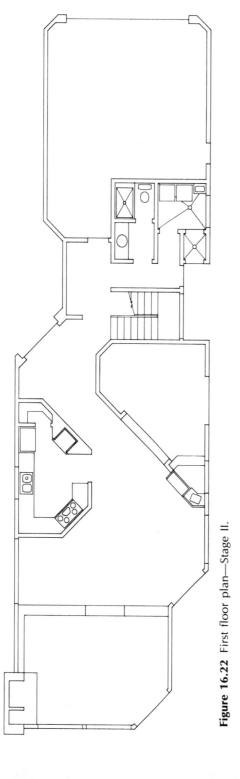

Figure 16.22 First floor plan—Stage II.

At this stage, dimensioning could be established by indicating the dimensions directly on a check print of the floor plan. Door and window designations were also added at this stage.

Stage IV

The window and door schedules were now due to be finished. See Figure 16.24. Remember that each door and window described is different. The schedules do not list every single door and window, just each different *type* of door or window. For example, the #2 window is used frequently in the plan, but is only listed once in the schedule.

Fixed windows are also listed here because they are manufactured and brought to the job. If fixed windows are built on the job site, the size is dimensioned on the exterior elevation and not listed on the schedule. The identification numbers for windows and doors found in the "SYM" (symbol) column of the schedule were put into reference bubbles on the plan. Since both the plan and the schedules were on the same sheet, the reference bubbles did not need to be divided into halves to show the sheet number.

Manufacturers' numbers and brand names are not on this sheet. These will be included on the specifications. However, switches to electrical outlet lines were included at this stage.

On the door schedule, the abbreviation "S.C." is for solid core, "H.C." for hollow core, and "P.P.T." for polished plate tempered. Some schedules also use numbers for doors and letters for windows.

Stage V

Corrections were made on the schedules after checking with the senior drafter. Room titles were now included on the floor plan. See Figure 16.25. Various pieces of equipment such as the range, oven, and sink were described, as were other parts of the structure such as closets, garage doors, lift counter for the bar, and so on. The titles are general and do not include the construction method, finish, or function. Naturally, the dimensions were checked again and corrections made where necessary. Titles, scale, and North arrow completed this sheet.

Second Floor Plan

Stage I

The upper floor plan has many walls that align themselves with the walls below on the ground floor. Therefore, the light blockout of the upper floor plan (Figure 16.26) was done by first overlaying the vellum on top of the ground floor plan and using the information from the preliminary floor plan.

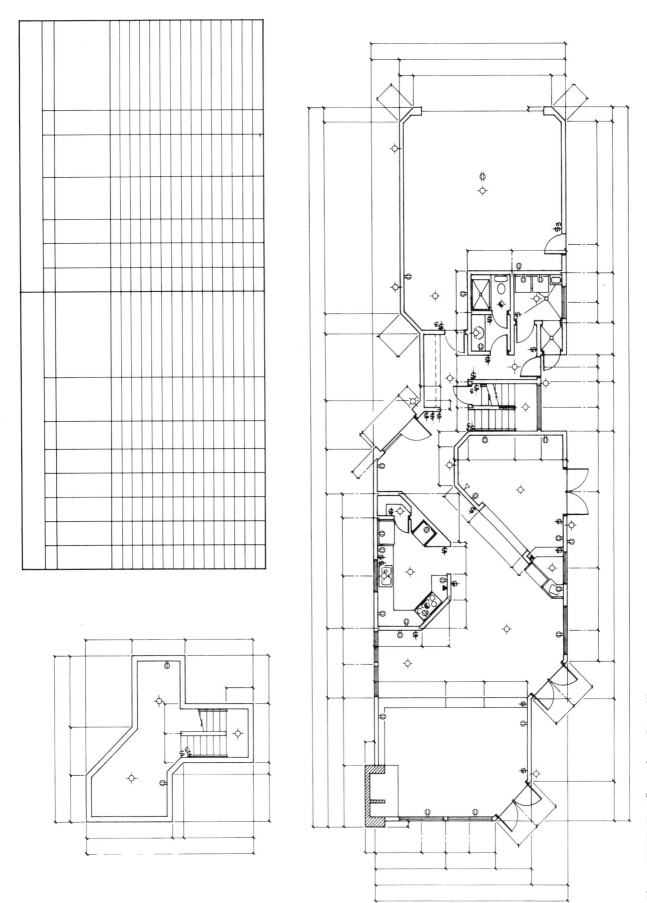

Figure 16.23 First floor plan—Stage III.

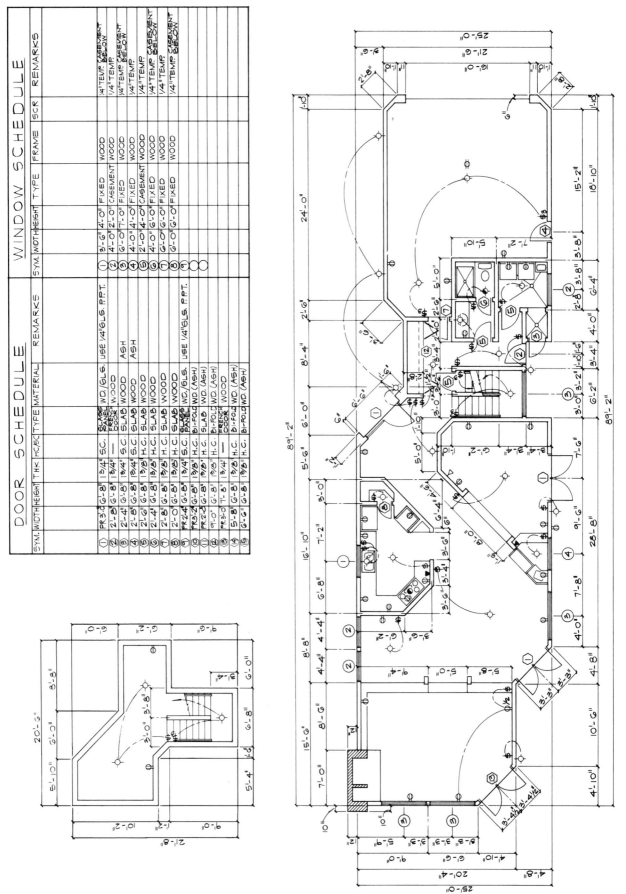

Figure 16.24 First floor plan—Stage IV.

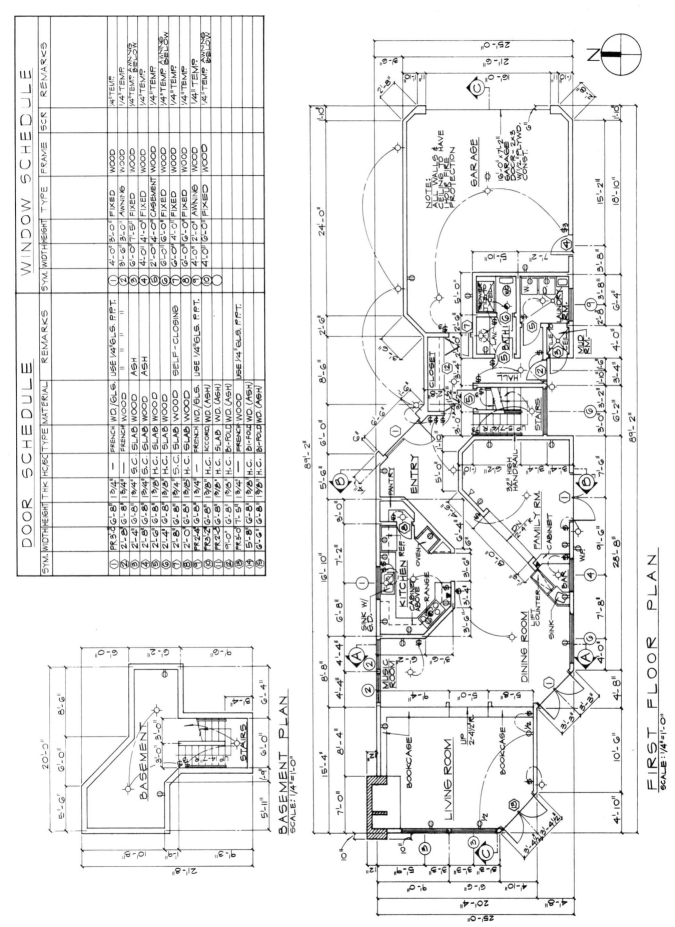

Figure 16.25 First floor plan—Stage V.

439

The exterior walls, stairs, entry, and fireplace were good locations to register one drawing with another. Check the preliminary upper floor plan (Figure 16.5) for various room names. Note the deck areas, the upper entry area (the entry is two stories high), the cantilever (overhang without support) of one of the bedrooms near the entry, and the two walk-in wardrobe closets in the master bedroom.

Stage II

Figure 16.27 shows the stage at which bathroom equipment, closet poles, stairs, and several windows were located and the handrail around the opening at the upper entry was drawn. Hard lines were drawn for the walls and the intersecting corners were cleaned up with an eraser. The rectangle adjacent to the sunken tub is a planter. A planter over the entry would be added later.

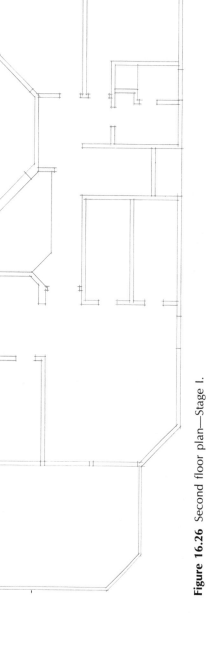

Figure 16.26 Second floor plan—Stage I.

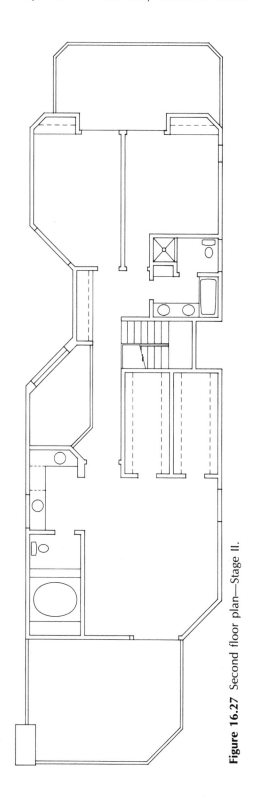

Figure 16.27 Second floor plan—Stage II.

Stage III

A chart, called the finish schedule, for the description of the finish on the various wall and floor surfaces was begun in the top left corner. To the right of the finish schedule is the legend for the various symbols used, such as electrical outlets, switches, and telephone jacks. See Figure 16.28.

We added dimension lines to the floor plan. As with the foundation plan, the dimension lines were not done initially on this plan but rather were done freehand on a check print, checked for accuracy, and transferred to this sheet.

We decided to incorporate the electrical plan into the floor plan. So we included switches, outlets, duplex convenience outlets, and so on here. Doors and windows were also completed. Compare this drawing with the final stage (Figure 16.30) and determine whether any dimensions were changed or corrected.

Stage IV

The symbol legend, showing various symbols used on the floor plan, was now finished. See Figure 16.29. The interior finish schedule was partly finished. Window and door numbers were included on the floor plan. We also placed two smoke detectors in the hall.

After discussion with the clients, we decided to use bi-fold doors rather than sliding doors into the master bath. We changed the wall that separates the stairs. This change then affected the foundation plan. See Stage II of the foundation plan, Figure 16.14. The electrical switch to outlet lines were also included at this stage.

Finally, we added dimensions. These dimensions had to be checked against those on the lower floor plan. It is always important to check walls that line up under one another.

Stage V

We then filled in the interior finish schedule on a check print based on consultation with the clients. The information was then transferred to this sheet. See Figure 16.30.

We added notes at this stage which included titles and necessary area descriptions. As with the ground floor plan, the notes are general in nature and do not describe construction methods, workmanship, or installation requirements that are described in the specifications. Addition of the main title completed this sheet.

Building Section/Elevations

Because of the available space, the longitudinal section and two of the narrow elevations were combined. Many

of the lines drawn on the first stages should be lightly identified in pencil and later erased.

Stage I

Elevations. At this preliminary stage (Figure 16.31), floor lines, header lines, plate lines, and ridge lines were lightly blocked out. All of these measurements were taken from the sections.

Building Section. This drawing coordinates the foundation plan, basement plan, first floor plan, second floor plan, and roof plan with preliminary details or structural decisions already made. The stairs were drawn in first, since their horizontal and vertical dimensions are critical.

Stage II

Building Section. Compare the stair footing area in Figure 16.32 with the foundation plan (slab) in Figure 16.16. A basement wall between the stairs was now included. All interior and exterior walls were also outlined using Western frame construction, and the location of walls and guardrails was taken from the floor plan.

The upper floor level was definitely established as were the various horizontal members. Specific sizes of these members were obtained from the structural engineer, architect, or another supervisor. All of the lines were cleaned up and darkened.

Elevations. The previous stage had established all of the horizontal lines. This stage now produced all the vertical and angular roof lines. The vertical lines were obtained from the floor plans. The elevation on the left side now begins to show a cantilever. The elevation on the right begins to show the exterior form of the fireplace. Both elevations also begin to show the outline of the balcony and the roof forms.

A drawing of a roof can be constructed from scratch, like a building section, or the shape can be obtained from the building section itself. Still another way is to orthographically project it from the roof plan, if such a drawing is available. Note that all of the horizontal lines that were drafted in the first stage do not appear here. They are there, but drafted so lightly that the reproduction process did not print them.

Stage III

Building Section. All of the individual members were drafted in at this stage. Of particular interest is the top of the roof. See Figure 16.33. Examine the second floor plan (Figure 16.30) or the roof framing plan (Figure 16.40). These show where this actual section slice was taken.

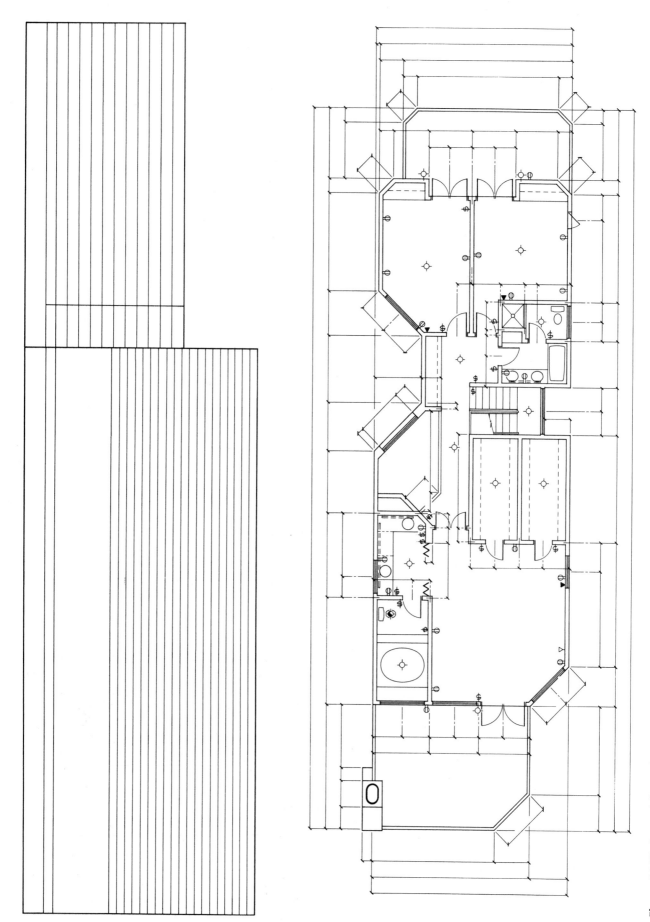

Figure 16.28 Second floor plan—Stage III.

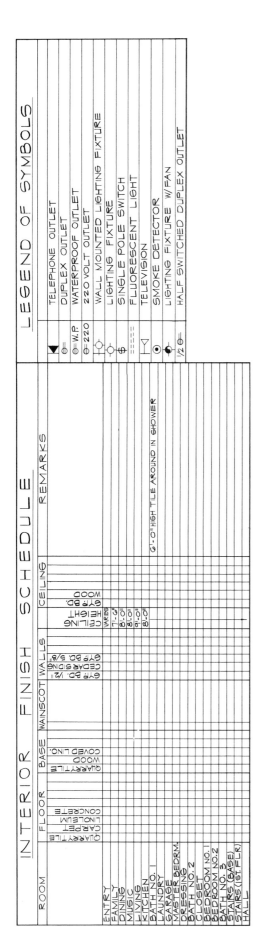

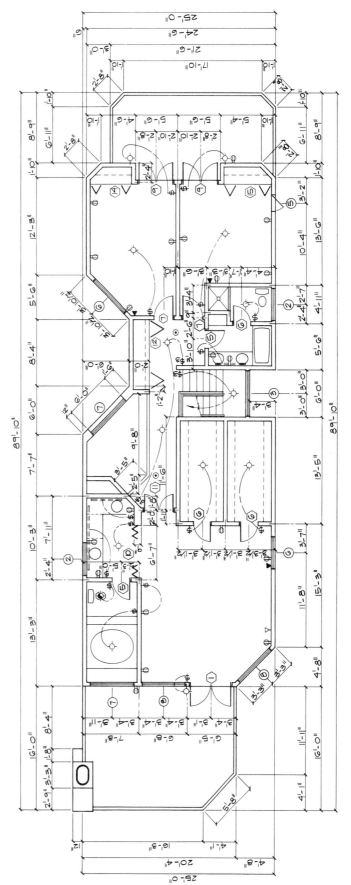

Figure 16.29 Second floor plan—Stage IV.

443

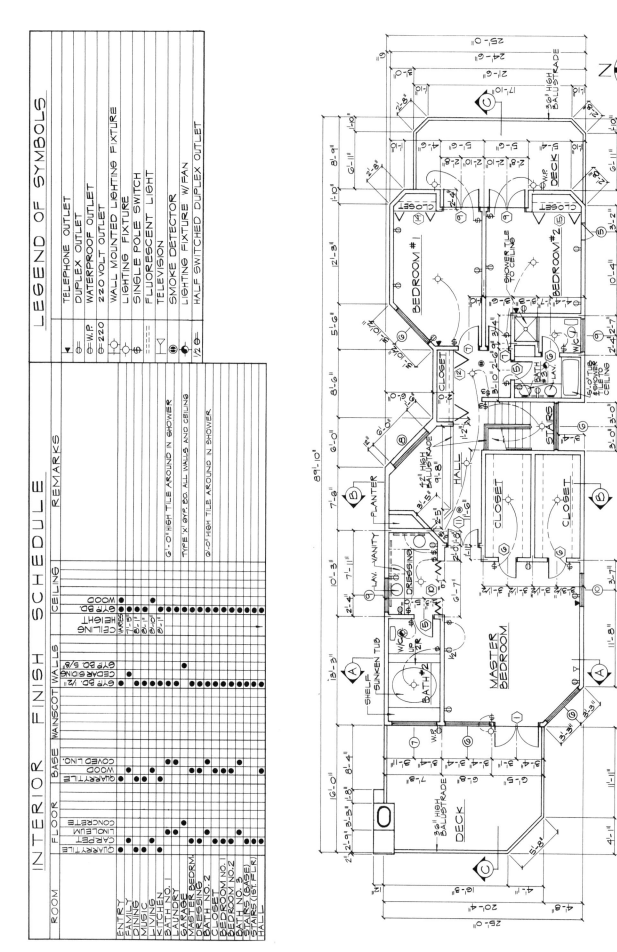

Figure 16.30 Second floor plan—Stage V.

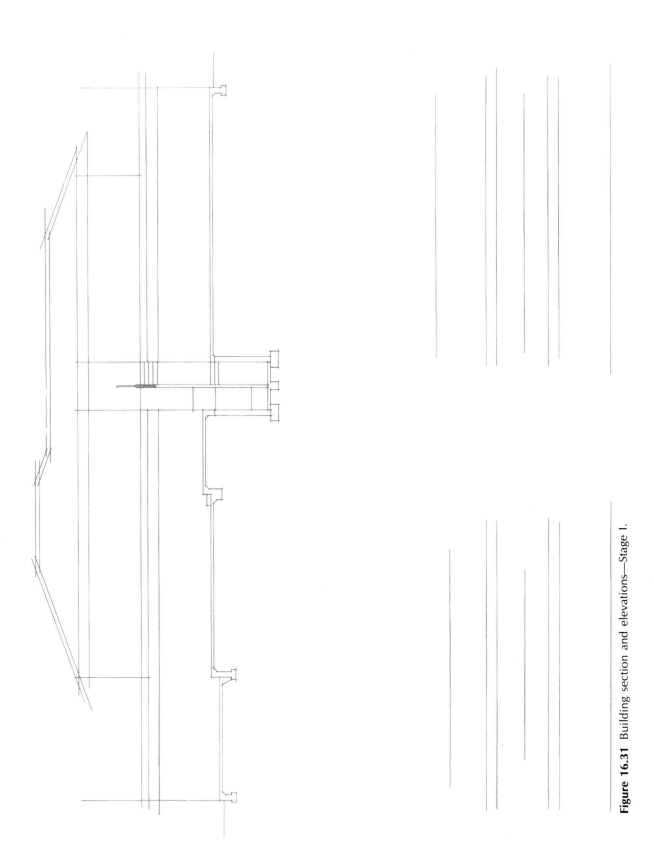

Figure 16.31 Building section and elevations—Stage I.

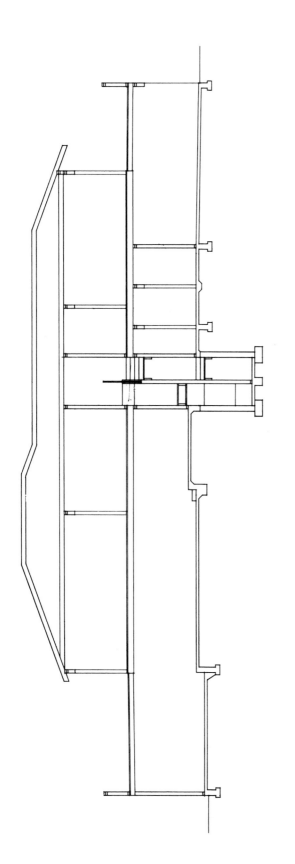

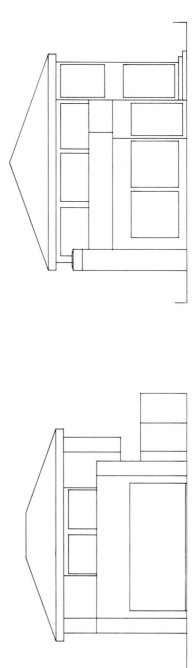

Figure 16.32 Building section and elevations—Stage II.

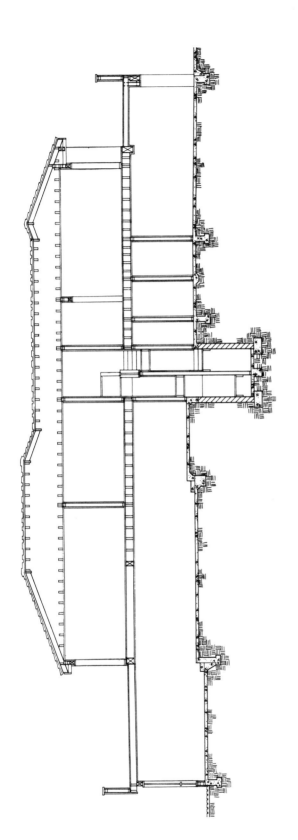

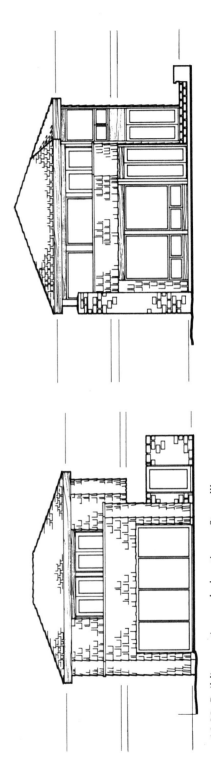

Figure 16.33 Building section and elevations—Stage III.

The ridge, especially at the left, is missed by the slice and therefore shows the rafters coming forward. An offset section would pick up the ridge but we decided to show a straight slice. Not shown is the ridge behind sloping up and back away. You should refer to the details relevant to this structure that are found in Chapter 14. These details, such as footing details, guardrails, and eave details, help explain, in an enlarged form, some of the critical areas in the structure.

Material designations—earth, concrete block, concrete, and shingle tile—were added at this stage.

Elevations. Material designations for the roof, the surface of the wall, and the masonry units were drafted. The total surface material is *not* shown. There is, however, enough shown to identify the material and to help the profiling, which was also completed at this stage. Windows and door shapes were confirmed from the manufacturer's literature and drawn accurately.

Stage IV

This was the final stage for both the building section and the exterior elevations.

Exterior Elevations. Vertical dimensions were referred to the building section for the sake of clarity and to avoid duplication. See Figure 16.34. The hidden lines designating the swing of doors and windows were drafted, together with the divisions (called lights) in the french doors. Various notes were placed on the elevations to identify such items as the fascia, shingles, gate, and garage door.

Building Section. Vertical heights were established based on the type of framing chosen and the head clearance required by local code. We obtained basic framing member sizes and noted them from the structural engineering drawings. You should look at this drawing (Section C-C in Figure 16.34) together with the foundation plan and roof framing plan. Together, they answer many questions. Detail references, room titles, drawing title, and scale finished this drawing.

Exterior Elevations

Stage I

Before starting the exterior elevations, you should always carefully study two drawings: the floor plans and building sections. The floor plans give the width and length of the structure. In this case, the upper floor is not the same size as the lower floor. The building section establishes all the heights.

In Figure 16.35, the heights were layed out lightly first and then identified lightly in pencil. The elevations to be drawn here were the North and South elevations. Looking at the upper (North) elevation, the first two lines at the bottom of the layout are floor lines. The next two lines above these are the header lines (tops of windows). And above these, two lines run the full width of the sheet. The lower is the plate line and the upper is the floor line for the second floor. The next short line is the top of the guardrail on the balcony.

The next two long lines above the guardrail line are the header line and plate line, respectively. Finally, the two top lines are the ridge of the roof. These should usually be lightly drawn in.

The lower (South) elevation resembles the upper, but the lines are reversed (left becomes right and right becomes left) because the elevation being drafted is a view in the opposite direction. Another difference is the variation in the floor lines and header lines for the first floor in the South elevation.

Stage II

Study Figure 16.36. This is the stage that gave the exterior elevation shape. The floor plan was used to locate exterior wall lines and windows, and the roof plan was used to help define the outline of the roof.

Stage III

At this stage, shown in Figure 16.37, lines were polished. Notice the extremely dark line at the bottom of the exterior elevations and the dark lines around the perimeter of the structure as well as those defining the changes of plane. Texture was added to the roof as well as to the walls. We did not waste time covering the entire surface of the wall or roof with the texture; we only did the perimeter to help the profile lines. The wall material shown is cedar shingles and the roof material, tile shingles. Wood graining of the exposed lintel was used above the doors and windows.

Stage IV

Vertical dimensions in Figure 16.38 refer to the building sections. A special note is also included to direct the reader to the building sections for dimensions. All callouts are generic in nature and depend on the specifications for specific material, quality, size, and workmanship. Roof material and wall surface material are called out with such identifying notes as "chimney," "wall," and "fixed glass." Finally, the title and scale were drawn. Note location for future solar panels.

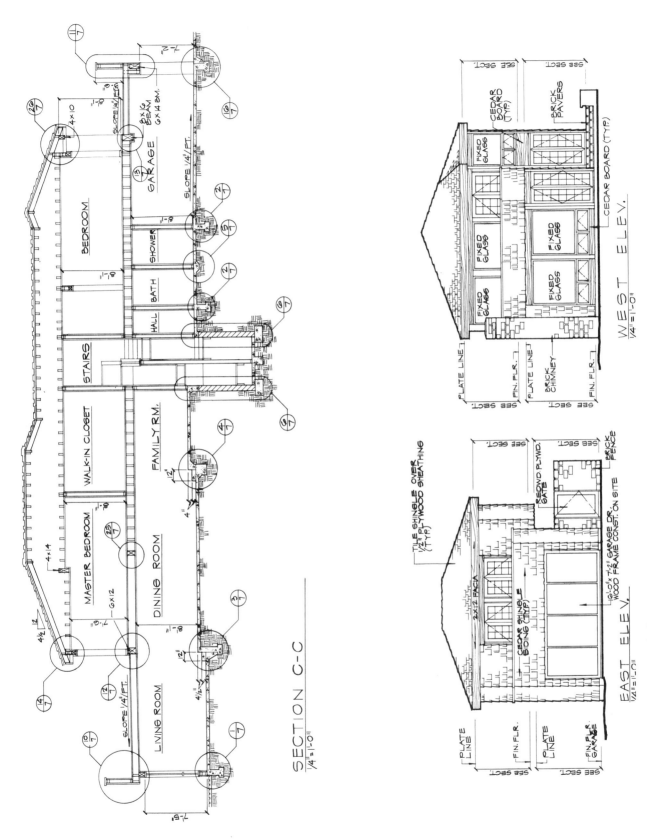

Figure 16.34 Building section and elevations—Stage IV.

449

Figure 16.35 Exterior elevations—Stage I.

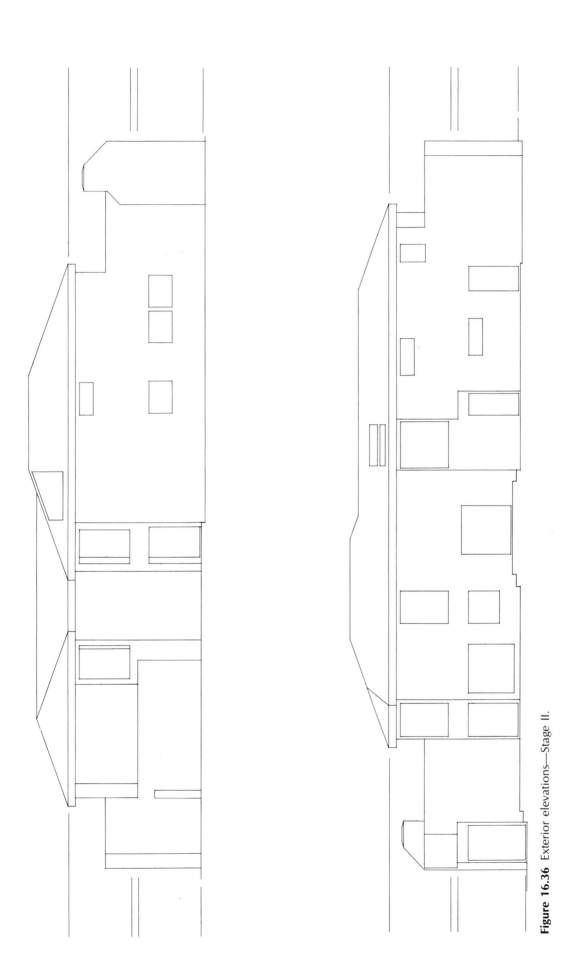

Figure 16.36 Exterior elevations—Stage II.

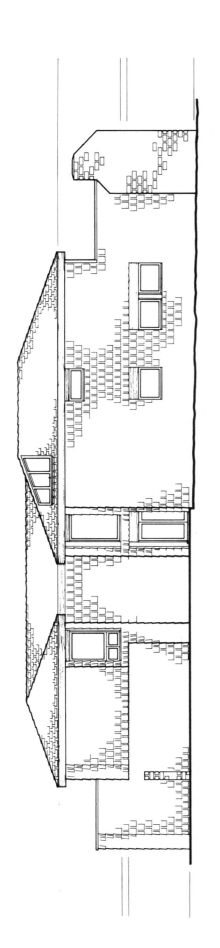

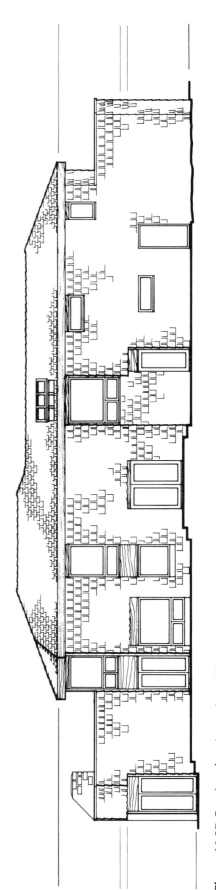

Figure 16.37 Exterior elevations—Stage III.

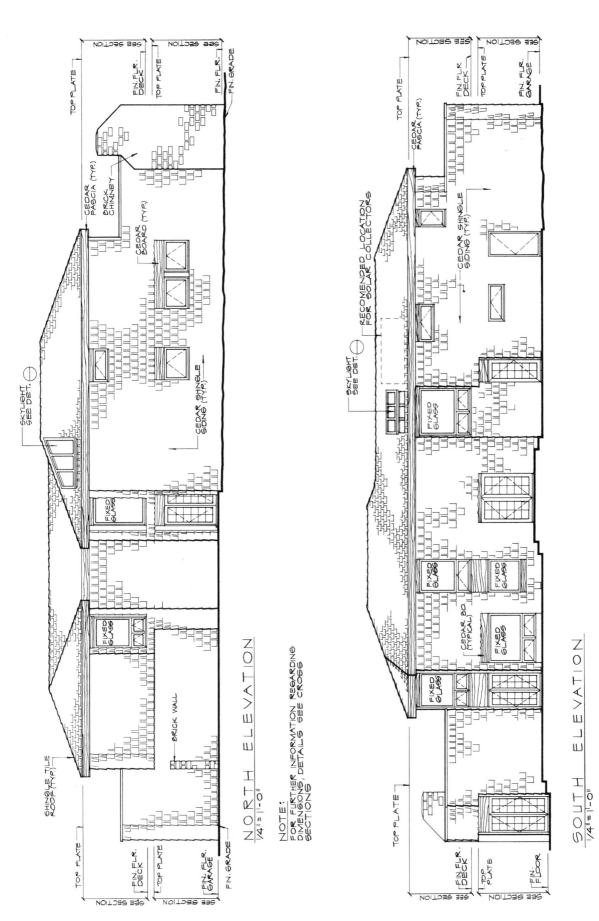

Figure 16.38 Exterior elevations—Stage IV.

453

Framing Plan

Stage I

Prior to drafting a framing plan we needed to make a number of decisions. These included approach, size, and method. First, we need to decide on our approach —that is, whether to use directional arrowheads or actually draft each framing member. Both approaches are shown in Figure 16.39. Scale (size) was the second major decision. Available sheet size and clarity were the deciding factors here. Third, we had to decide on method. We needed to draft a framing plan over a sepia copy of the specific plan involved.

First Floor and Second Floor Plans.   There are three plans here. The top left is the first floor plan showing the floor framing for the second floor. The drawing adjacent to it is a floor plan for the second floor which indicates the ceiling joists for the second floor. The largest of the three plans shows the second floor plan with the roof framing plan.

In our office, the two smaller plans could have been drafted from scratch or the specific floor plan involved could have been reduced photographically or by a plain paper copier onto vellum.

On the small framing plans, we decided to demonstrate the abbreviated method of showing the members, that is, drafting of all beams and headers but not all joists. The floor and ceiling joists are shown by a dimension-type line using a ½ arrowhead on each end. Beams are drafted showing the actual thickness of the members while headers are shown over windows and doors as a center-line type line.

Second Floor with Roof Framing Plan.   On the roof framing plan, headers are shown as center lines, beams are drafted to actual size, and the ridge, hip rafters, and valley members are drafted showing their full size. A hip rafter rests on the corner of the structure and is held in place by the forces from the rafters coming against it from either side. Rafters themselves are drafted with a center-line type line.

All exterior walls and interior bearing walls are drafted solid (i.e., using solid lines). All nonbearing walls are drafted using dotted lines.

Three things make this roof unique. First, the framing around the skylights. The skylight above the entry area (see the floor plan for roof description) is a single opening while the one over the stair area is two skylights. The framing around the skylights is not too unlike the opening for a roof access or an opening for an interior chimney.

Most corners of structures have 90° corners. One conventional framing for such a corner is to bisect the 90° corner with a hip rafter. A good example of such

framing can be found at the corner where the master bathroom tub is found.

A variation can be found on the opposite corner where the wall angles at 45°. Here, we actually have two corners with a hip rafter near the ridge. This hip rafter joins other members, which in turn bisect the 45° corners. This creates a weak spot in the roof. To strengthen it, 4 × 4 posts are added to the wall and a beam is installed parallel to the 45° wall. Two additional 4 × 4 posts are placed on top of this beam to support the members that bisect the 45° bend in the wall.

If you look carefully, you can tell when a beam sits on a post or a post on a beam. If the beam sits on a post, you will see the two parallel lines that simulate the beam drafted over the post. If the post sits on top of the beam, the lines of the beam stop short of the post.

The use of a roof with a normal 90° angle over walls at 45° angles is also unique. This condition called for cantilevered beams that protrude from the wall parallel to the roof to form a 90° intersection which supports the roof. These beams enter deeply into the wall of the structure. This construction was used in a number of places, as you can see on the framing plan for the roof.

Stage II

To better understand the three drawings in Figure 16.40, look at the final stage of the building section and elevations shown in Figure 16.34. The top left drawing, the second floor framing plan, uses half-arrows to indicate the direction of the various members. A close look at this drawing shows many interesting features. The deck on the left side has 2 × 10 members while the area adjacent has 2 × 12 members. The two-inch difference allows for the difference between the floors of the deck and the inside of the house. The direction of the floor joists changes from one area to another and their spacing also changes. Open areas are crossed out ("X") as in the entry area. Headers (beams over windows and doors) are also noted throughout the drawing as are certain beams to hold up posts which in turn will hold up the roof. Extremely large sizes were selected for the framing plan because the structure is in an earthquake area, and the roof material is heavy.

Above the garage, the members were again placed perpendicular to the floor joists under the floor of the house. Two things result from this change of direction. First, the floor of the deck can be sloped away from the house for water drainage. Second, the reduced size of the floor joists allows for a larger beam over the garage door without sacrificing head clearance.

The ceiling in the garage is therefore *not* flush as in the living room at the rear. The long building section (Figure 16.34) shows this clearly. The change of spacing of the floor joists above the garage was produced by the dis-

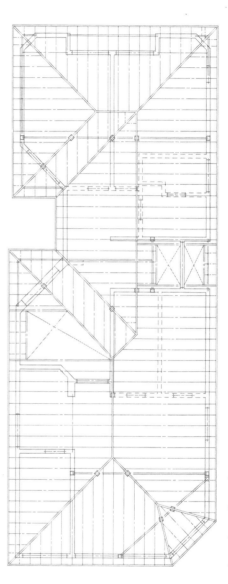

Figure 16.39 Framing plan—Stage I.

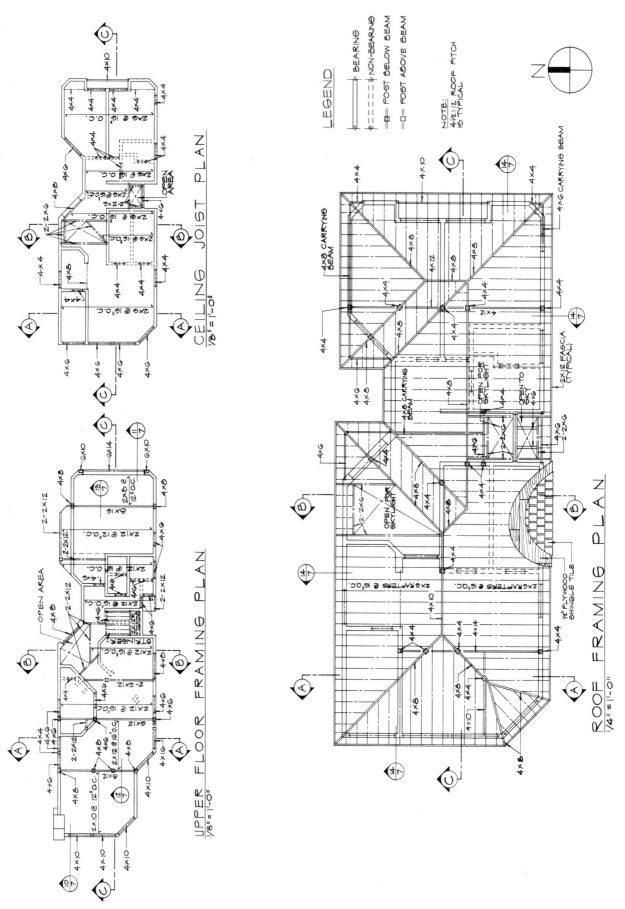

Figure 16.40 Framing plan—Stage II.

tance the joist had to travel: 2 × 12 at 12″ o.c. (on centers) to start and eventually 16″ o.c. A hidden line between these shows where the change of spacing took place.

The posts (square forms) drawn throughout must be looked for very carefully. Some are under the floor plan while others are above and often located inside walls of the second floor. Compare the floor plans here with the roof framing plan and you will find many post locations.

We also used the same method the structural engineer used in the roof framing plan to show the location of these posts. If the post is drawn solid with no lines interrupting the perimeter of the post, the post is above. If the lines of the joist or beam are drawn through it, the post is below. See the legend in Figure 16.40. All sizes and locations were obtained from the structural engineer.

The floor joists of the second floor become the ceiling joists of the lower floor. The ceiling joist plan of the upper floor is shown on the top right. We chose to show all of the headers for the second floor on this drawing rather than on the roof framing plan. Of special interest is the framing around openings like the skylights.

On the roof framing plan, the dotted walls are non-bearing and the solid wall lines are load bearing walls. An explanation is given on the legend on the far right.

The framing of the Northwest corner (top left corner of the roof framing plan) is the most typical framing for a hip roof with no special beams needed to carry the weight of the roof. However, such is not the case with the other corners. A careful look at the various corners reveals how the structural engineer designed the beams and posts to carry the weight of this unique roof.

The rafters are all 2 × 6 @ 16″ o.c. Title, scale, and North orientation completed this drawing.

REVIEW QUESTIONS

1. What type of regulatory agencies govern this structure and what were their concerns?
2. State the reason for the following decisions:
   a. Five in twelve roof slope
   b. Wood windows
3. What are the scuppers used for in this structure?
4. What are the main differences in visual appearance between the wood floor plans and the on-the-ground slab foundation plans?
5. On what two drawings could solar collectors appear?

17

CONCEPTUAL DESIGN AND CONSTRUCTION DOCUMENTS FOR A WOOD BUILDING— MOUNTAIN CABIN

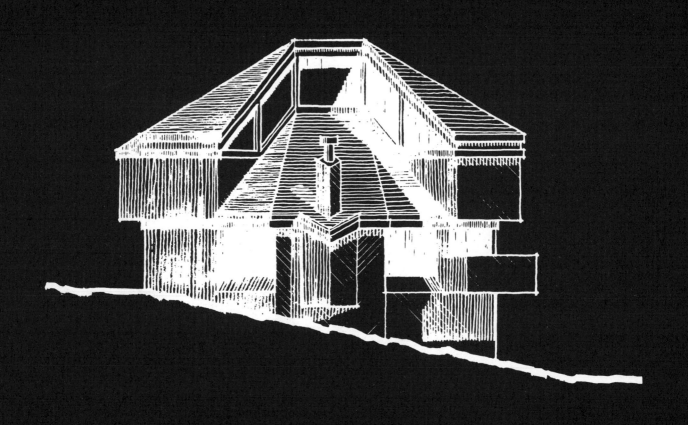

17

Conceptual Design

Site Requirements

The design purpose for this project was to provide a three-bedroom residence for a young family. The site is located in a mountainous area of Northern California noted for skiing. The area receives as much as 144 inches of snow during the winter. The site is on a cul-de-sac and is irregular in shape with an approximate area of 7,200 square feet. This site has many pine trees, two of which are over 150 feet tall. The clients wished to preserve as many as possible. The topography of the site slopes from North to South with a cross fall of 10 feet.

Clients' Requirements

As well as wanting three bedrooms, the clients requested a formal dining room, kitchen, den, living room, powder room, and two bathrooms. The man, whose hobby is cabinet making, wanted a shop area, and the woman, whose profession is photography, re-

quested a studio. Both were preferably to be located in the garage or basement area. A single car garage would be adequate for the clients' needs.

Initial Schematic Studies

The conceptual approach was to place the main entrance at the high side of the site, so that the low side of the site would accommodate a basement and garage area. This approach would use the topography to its best advantage. The initial plan was also influenced by the two giant pine trees located on the upper slope.

Near the main entrance, a gallery provided circulation for the living room, dining room, powder room, and kitchen. A circular staircase provided access to the basement and upper floor. Because of the topography, we decided to lower the living room floor, which in turn gave it a higher ceiling.

Schematic drawings—loose freehand sketches—provided us with a visual tool for defining areas and their interrelationships. Figure 17.1 shows the schematic

Figure 17.1 Schematic studies.

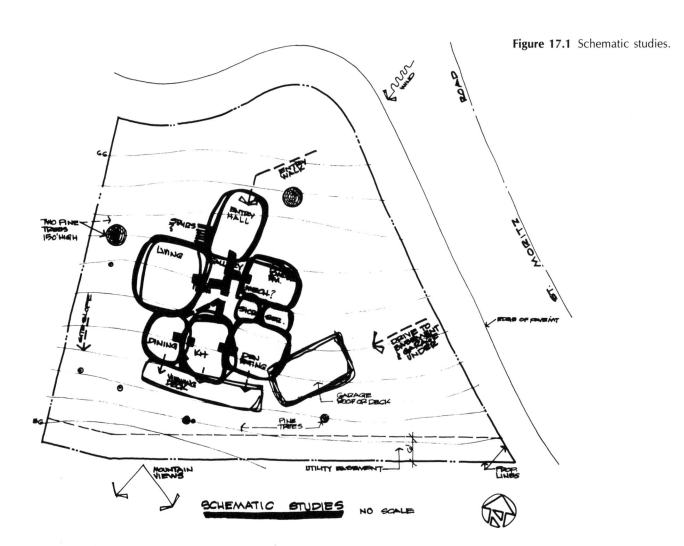

study for the first level. Similar schematic studies defined the upper and basement floor areas.

Scaled freehand floor plans that evolved from these schematic studies established the basic format for the finished drawings. Figures 17.2, 17.3, and 17.4 show these preliminary floor plans.

Roof and Exterior Elevation Sketches

As the first and second floor plans were refined, the initial concept and solutions for the roof plan evolved. The geometry of the plan and the need for steep roof pitches became an important design concern. Figure 17.5 shows a freehand sketch of the initial roof plan.

After we completed the floor and roof plan studies, we developed the exterior elevations. We drew scaled freehand elevations incorporating suggested exterior materials and architectural details. With the clients' approval, these drawings became our basic design for the finalized exterior elevations. Figures 17.6 and 17.7 show drawings of the initial exterior conceptual designs.

In addition to these initial conceptual designs, further studies including framing and construction methods and architectural details were analyzed in preparation for the final construction documents.

Figure 17.2 Preliminary—first floor plan.

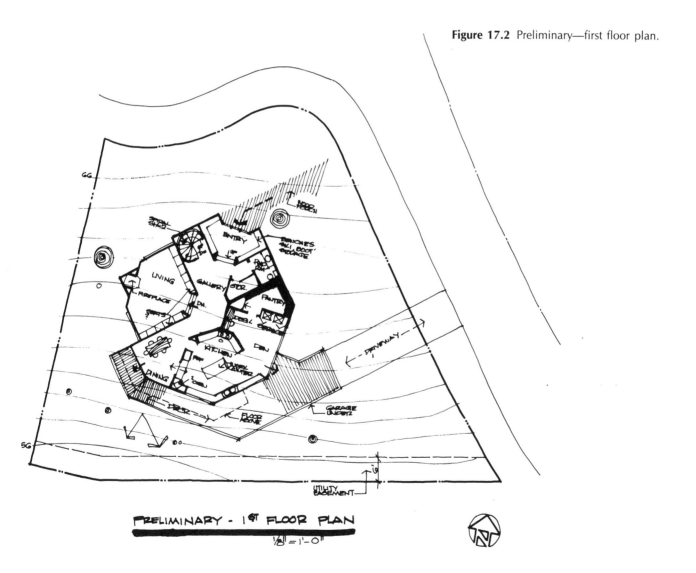

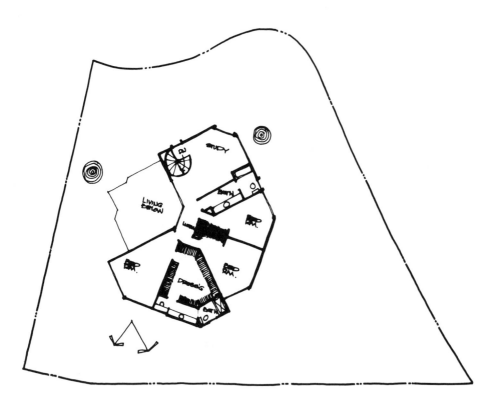

PRELIMINARY · 2ND FLOOR PLAN

⅛"=1'-0"

Figure 17.3 Preliminary
—second floor plan.

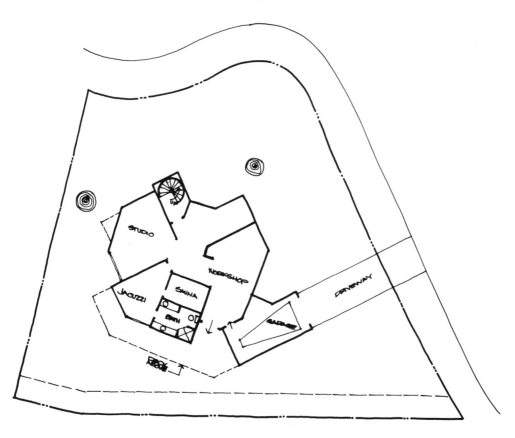

PRELIMINARY · BASEMENT FLOOR PLAN

⅛"=1'-0"

Figure 17.4 Preliminary
—basement floor plan.

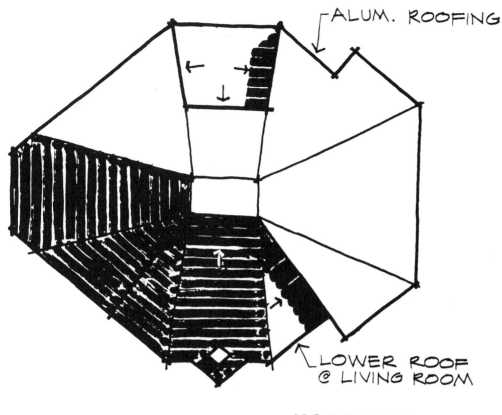

ROOF PLAN

Figure 17.5 Roof plan—conceptual design.

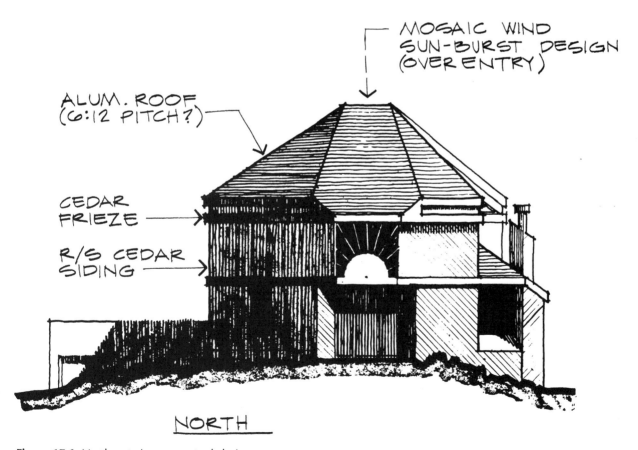

NORTH

Figure 17.6 North exterior conceptual design.

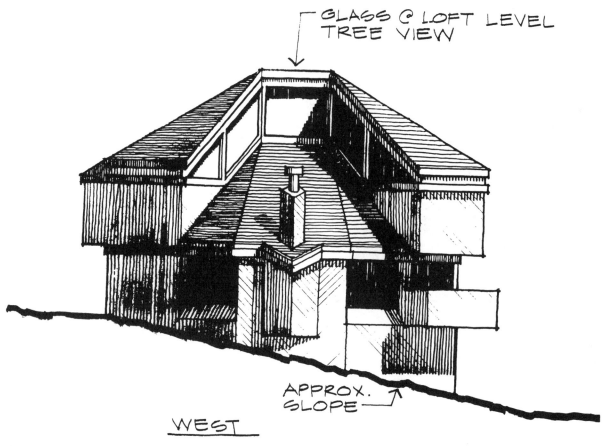

GLASS @ LOFT LEVEL
TREE VIEW

APPROX.
SLOPE

WEST

Figure 17.7 West exterior conceptual design.

Site Plan

Stage I

Before beginning to draw the site plan, you must obtain an accurate plat map and/or topography map and description of the site. Usually this information is provided by a civil engineer. See Chapter 6, on site plans.

We first lightly drew the property lines or "perimeter lines" of the site. See Figure 17.8. Next the existing contours were drawn to show the present condition of the site. (Finished contour lines are added at a later stage.)

Any streets, curbs, parkways, and so on are added at this stage. Trees on the site that are to remain are shown as small circles, but new landscaping is not shown. The dotted lines toward the bottom of the page indicate sewer lines.

Stage II

The location of the structure on the site is critical. Many factors govern the placement on the site, including

orientation to the sun, prevailing winds, code requirements, setbacks, and easements.

The solid lines on the site plan indicate the outline of the structure, and the dotted lines indicate the walls below. See Figure 17.9. The roof plan was drawn at the top right corner so that the draftsperson could locate and dimension the structure to a solid line. The complex shape of the roof made the accurate drafting of the roof plan difficult.

Stage III

At this stage, the immediately visible items around the perimeter of the structure were added. This included drives, a patio slab on the left side, and the deck and steps at the top. See Figure 17.10. The rectangular object at the right represents a slab for a gas tank to be added later and the small square at the top left represents the water meter. The deck and the trees were textured as was the roof plan. Note how the center portion of the roof was left without texture. This untextured portion represents flat metal as opposed to the corrugated metal used on the rest. We also darkened many of the major lines at this point.

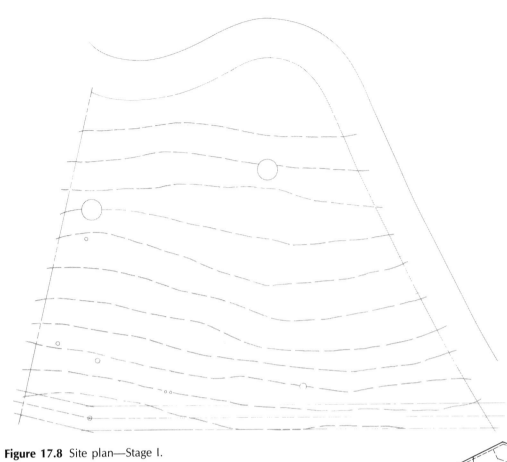

Figure 17.8 Site plan—Stage I.

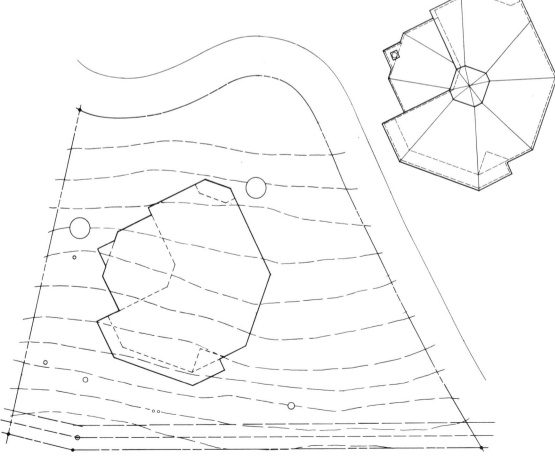

Figure 17.9 Site plan—Stage II.

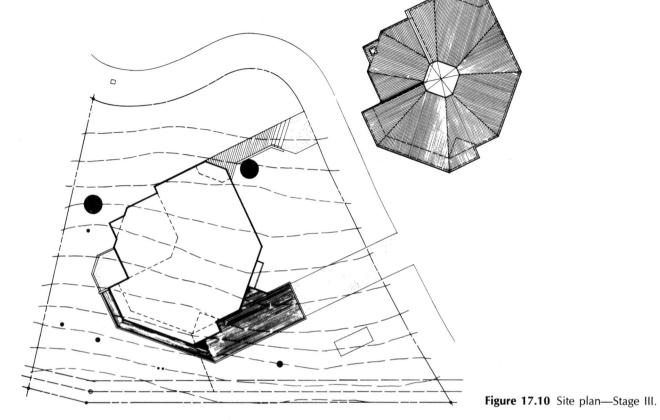

Figure 17.10 Site plan—Stage III.

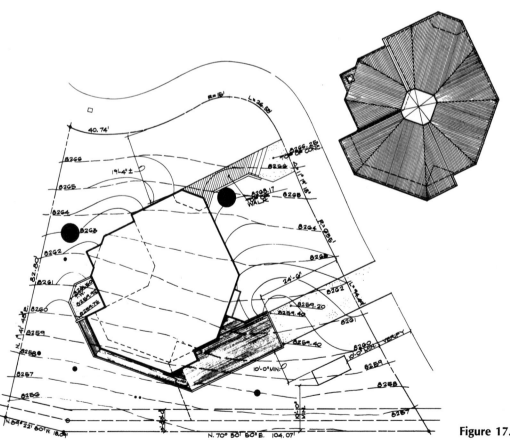

Figure 17.11 Site plan—Stage IV.

466

Stage IV

Next we drew the new contour of the ground. Because we drew the original contour using a standard dotted line, we drew the new contour with solid lines. Compare Figure 17.11 with Figure 17.10. Some existing contour lines blend into a new solid line; this shows that part of the earth remained as it was originally and portions of it changed. (The 8265 contour line at the top left corner of the site on Figure 16.11 is a good example of this combination.) Numerical elevation values were then added to each contour line, each number representing a change of one foot. We next added dimensions for the location of the structure on the lot.

Examine how the top of the concrete walk and the driveway height in relationship to the finished grade (contour) are shown. The top of the wood walk adjacent

to the concrete is designated first, followed by the concrete elevation at the patio. ("T.W." means top of wall.) This designation accomplishes two things: it shows the elevation (height), and it insures good water drainage.

The directions and lengths (including radius in the case of an arc) of the lines describing the exterior perimeter of the lot were added next.

Stage V

The final stage involved the noting. See Figure 17.12. The notes described material such as roofing, driveway surface, and porch, and utilities such as water and sewer were called out along with the easement (a right-of-way). We also noted special equipment or special construction procedures such as the propane tank on the site plan and the flashing on the roof plan.

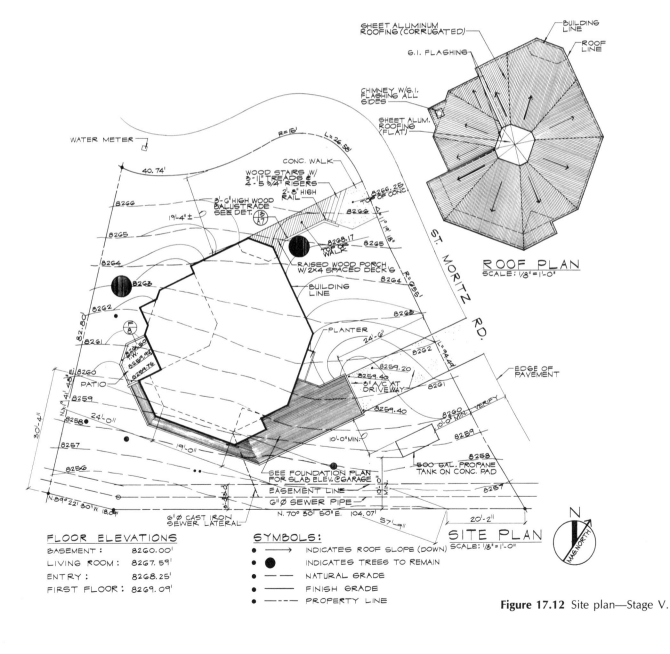

Figure 17.12 Site plan—Stage V.

We called out the building line and roof lines to avoid any confusion of lines. We designated the slope of the roof by arrows to indicate the direction of water flow.

We labeled the final elevations of the various rooms in chart form, below the site plan itself. These elevations should always correspond with the foundation plan. We also prepared a chart of the various symbols used, to avoid confusion or misinterpretation.

Finally, we added the title, scale, and North orientation symbol. The orientation arrow is carried on every plan, including the floor plans and foundation plans.

Foundation Plan

Stage 1

The basic shape of the foundation plan is based on the floor plan and the location of the loads the foundation must carry and distribute to the ground. Here, the floor plan of the basement was traced. See Figure 17.13.

The walls in the foundation plan were drawn with solid lines because the walls are concrete block and act as part of the footing, going above the grade. The spread footings were drawn with hidden lines because they are below the grade.

Normally, sizes of the footings are obtained from structural engineering drawings or from a preliminary detail sketched by the architect. Some walls take heavier loads than others, so the width of the footing varies throughout structures. If structural engineering drawings are not available at this stage, the structural engineer is asked specific questions. A floor plan, a preliminary foundation plan, and rough elevations and sections are also sent to the structural engineer who determines the loads and the necessary sizes of the footings to support the walls. For a simple structure, loads and footing sizes can be determined in the office and a structural engineer need not be consulted.

This particular project required a structural engineer because of its location and unique shape. Heavy snow loads were computed for the structure, and what appear on the plan to be excessive sizes of members are actually necessitated by earthquake precautions and snow loads.

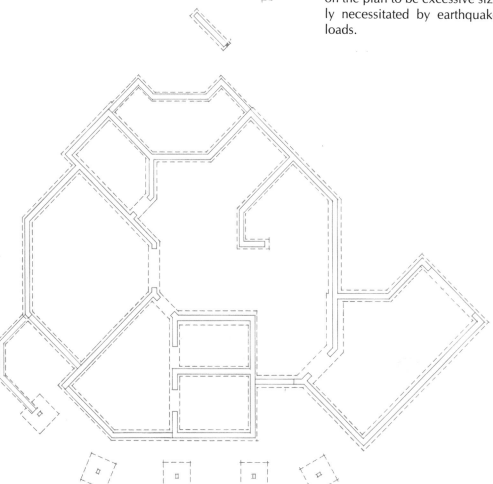

Figure 17.13 Foundation plan—Stage I.

The five column pads at the bottom of the structure, as the dotted lines indicate, were realigned in subsequent drawings because these changes took place after additional computations were made.

During the evolution of a set of drawings, there are constant changes. As each drawing progresses, additional information and understanding of the structure produces change.

Stage II

Outlining the decks was the next step, together with the addition of the structural members at the top of the plan.

See Figure 17.14. The edge of the patio slab at the bottom was then added, and the structural members for the wood deck were drawn at the top of the plan.

Dimension lines were added next—at the *end* of walls and wall openings because of the use of concrete block modular units. Normally, exterior dimension lines are put in first, followed by interior dimension lines. In this example, the first dimension line is spaced away from the objects ½″, and each subsequent dimension line is spaced ½″ away from the preceding one.

If a dimension line crosses an extension line, the extension line is broken; if a dimension line crosses another dimension line, decide which of the two is the

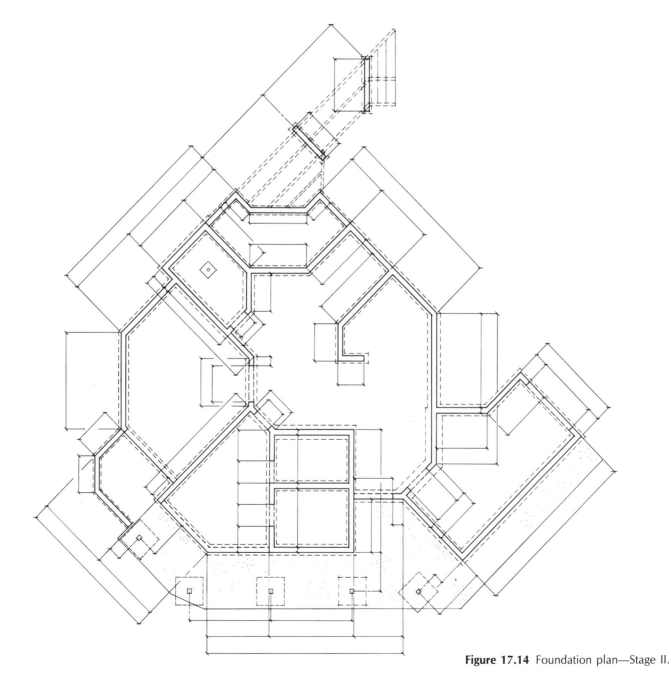

Figure 17.14 Foundation plan—Stage II.

major or more critical and break the other; if a dimension line crosses an object line, allow clarity to dictate which is to be broken.

Stippling (dots) helped to define the concrete patio area. The pad for the column on the right was repositioned at this time, as was the second from the left. Compare its position now with its position in the previous stage, shown in Figure 17.13. We made this change after the structural engineer finished the structural drawings.

Stage III

At the stage shown in Figure 17.15, the dimensioning was added. If you want to know the number of blocks in

a given wall in Figure 17.15, divide that dimension by 16″ or 1.3′, which is the size of the block and mortar.

Masonry opening (M.O.) sizes were carefully selected in conjunction with the door sizes and jamb details. There are basically two ways to dimension widths of footings. One is on the foundation plan as indicated on Figure 17.15; the other is by dimensioning the footing on the foundation detail. One reason for dimensioning on the foundation plan is that footings vary in widths.

As you look closely at these various dimensions, you will notice that the dimension lines occasionally cross. An example of this is found toward the lower center of the plan. A 5′–4″ M.O. horizontal dimension crosses a 15′–4″ vertical dimension. Had the 5′–4″ dimension been raised higher, the crossing dimension could have

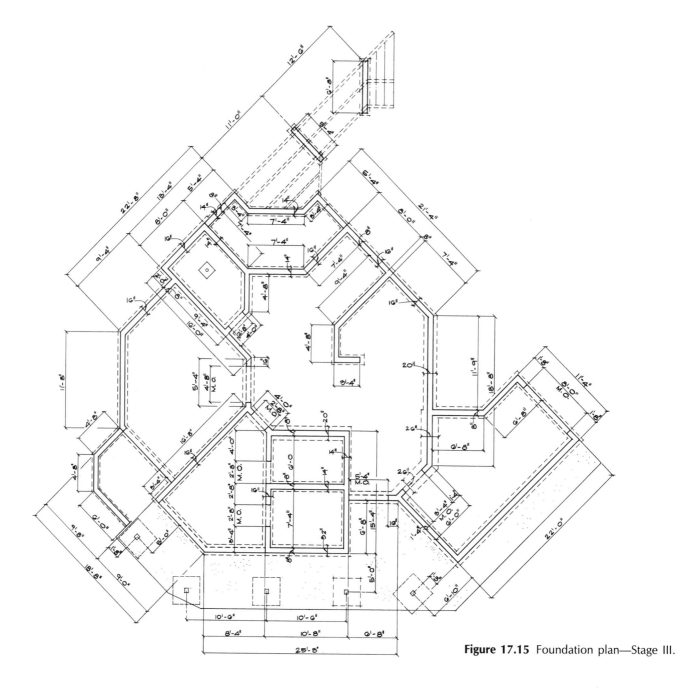

Figure 17.15 Foundation plan—Stage III.

been avoided. Proximity was the determining factor here.

The column locations at the bottom have two 10'–6" dimensions. The dimension line to the right of the 10'–6" dimension and above the 6'–8" dimension is missing. We did this to help the contractor locate the columns from the most accessible point.

At this stage of a project, you should make a diazo copy before you put any dimensions on the sheet. All dimensions should be put on the proof copy, checked, then lettered on the original drawing.

Stage IV

Based on decisions made in conference with the head draftsperson or job captain, detail reference bubbles and cross-section indications were now included. See Figure 17.16. The bubbles with the large triangles are for the cross-section and the others are for the details. The small point on the detail bubbles indicates viewing direction. Detailing should almost always put the inside of the structure on the right and outside on the left.

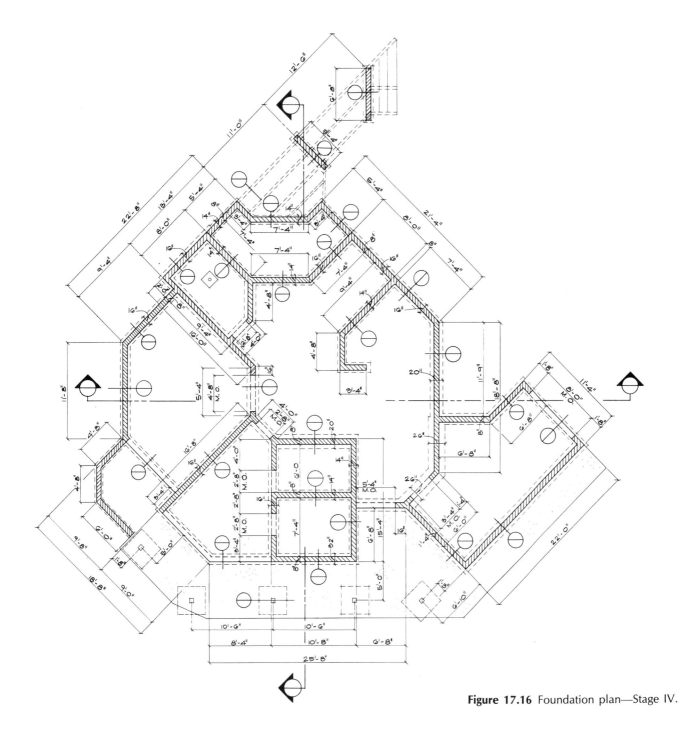

Figure 17.16 Foundation plan—Stage IV.

Stage V

Figure 17.17 shows the final step in the evolution of the foundation plan. Our task here was mainly to note and reference. We added a simplified point to the detail reference bubble. We also included a note in the garage to indicate the elevation of the finish floor (FF) and made a reference notation for the slab at left. Finally, we added the title, scale, and North orientation.

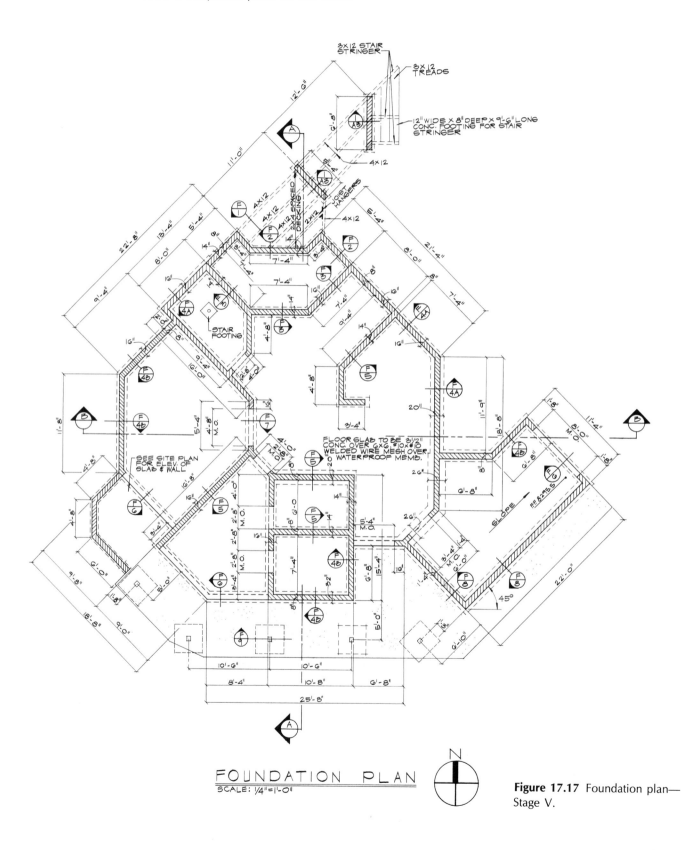

Figure 17.17 Foundation plan—Stage V.

Basement Floor Plan

Stage I

There are three levels in this structure. We started with the lowest floor, that is, the basement. See Figure 17.18. This was called the basement rather than the first floor because the entry is on the floor above. To do a preliminary layout of this level, we took measurements from the preliminary floor plan. The walls of the basement are made of concrete block so it was important to check and stay with the multiples of this block module size. (Block module dimensions must also be checked against the foundation plan and all subsequent floors above it.) Note the appearance of the concrete block units in Figure 17.19.

At this stage, the layout was done lightly so that it did not matter if lines overlapped. (Use a 2H lead or harder.) Door swings and windows would be added in Stage II. Portions of the first floor were cantilevered beyond the edges of the basement floor plan and were shown with dotted lines.

The five columns shown at the bottom near the dotted lines support the beam for the floor above. At this stage these supports were tentative and awaited confirmation by the structural engineer, who could increase the size or number of the columns or change their position.

You should always check the preliminary section before drawing this sheet as it gives important information such as critical connections, concrete block size, and possible guidance as to the position of the walls in relation to the first floor walls. In this case, the walls were located at 45° and the columns at 45° and 22½°.

Stage II

Wall locations were checked, verified, and relocated where necessary at this stage. See Figure 17.20. The walls were then darkened and items such as stairs, bathroom fixtures, and a dumbwaiter (the square with an "X" inside, near the top right) were included. The round circle at the right is a water heater.

If interior elevations have been sketched, you should view these before locating equipment or fixtures.

Stage III

The first change that was made in Stage III came from the structural and foundation plans and is shown in Figure 17.21. The extreme right column was lined up with the wall to the right (garage wall), and the column second from the left was lined up with the others in the center.

All the door swings and windows were now drafted in. We noticed a conflict of the door swings at the

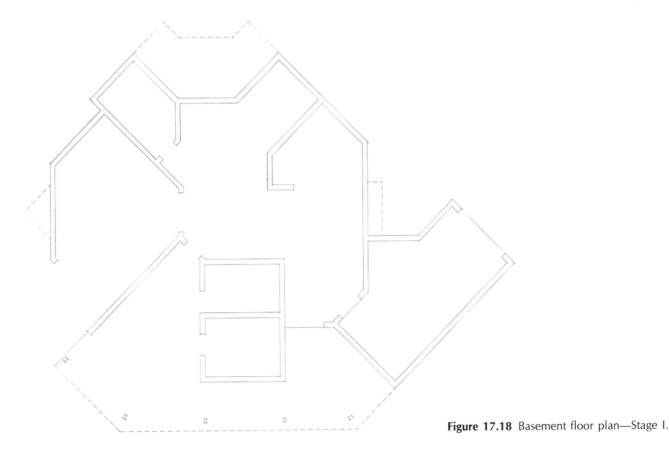

Figure 17.18 Basement floor plan—Stage I.

Figure 17.19 Basement wall.

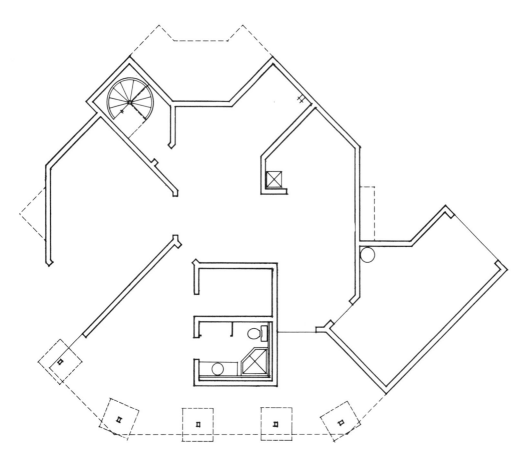

Figure 17.20 Basement floor plan—Stage II.

474

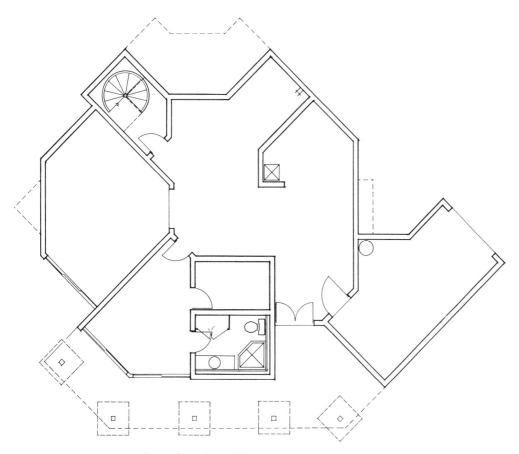

Figure 17.21 Basement floor plan—Stage III.

bathrooms. Correction could have been done at a later stage but we chose to do it here.

Stage IV

Hidden lines at the top of the floor plan shown in Figure 17.22 and those extending beyond the rear of the garage indicate the floor above. These dotted lines were dimensioned from known locations such as existing columns and existing parts of the building. We did this because the relationship of one dotted line to the other (columns) could be seen best on this plan. Notice that this decision would mean that the deck did not need to be dimensioned on the first-floor plan.

The extension lines for the columns use center-line type lines as they were dimensioned to the center. Extension lines for all others are solid.

As you study this stage, check the cross-section to see the relationship of the columns to the main body of the structure. Remember that the walls are masonry.

Because of the very nature of the unusual shape of the building and the presence of both dimension and exten-

sion lines, the extension and dimension lines were broken often.

Again, because the structure is masonry at this level, the dimensions are to the edges of the wall and the interior walls are treated differently from wood stud interior walls, which are dimensioned to the center. Openings, too, are dimensioned to the width of the opening.

Stage V

At this point you can make a check print so that you can put the numerical values on it, check the dimensions against the block module size, and check the overall dimensions against the sum of the individual parts. See Figure 17.23

In this case, as the dimensions were placed on the original drawing, openings could be called out. Masonry extensions are often labeled "F.O.M.," meaning face of masonry. Each dimension should be and was checked against the foundation plan.

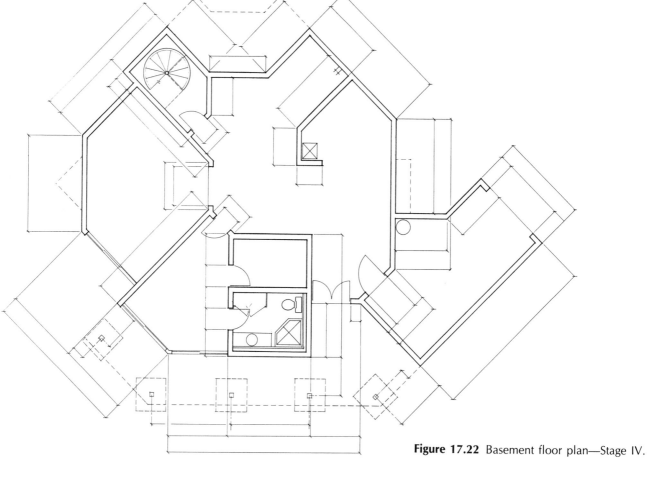

Figure 17.22 Basement floor plan—Stage IV.

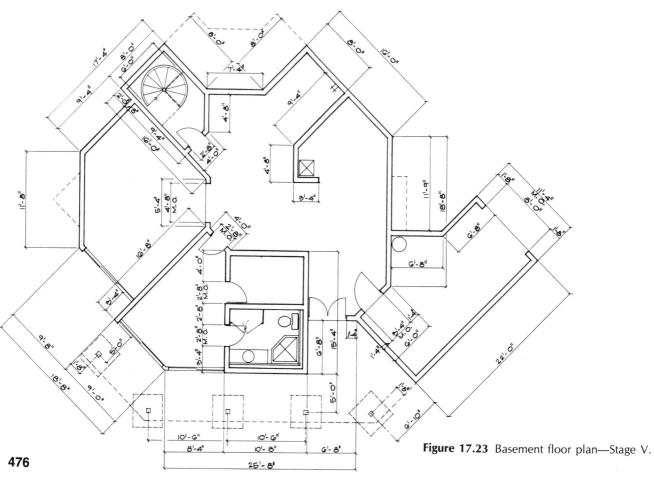

Figure 17.23 Basement floor plan—Stage V.

Stage VI

As the dimensions were located the material designations for the walls were included. These are the diagonal lines between the wall lines and represent concrete block. See Figure 17.24. Some architectural offices do not like this block designation because it is the same as brick's. There are actually at least five different ways of representing concrete block, ranging from drawings of the actual block to a crisscross pattern. We used a series of diagonal lines to represent the masonry walls because of the scale.

We left the material designations step until after the dimensions were located, in case we needed to change anything. We then added room titles and some noting and placed the door and window bubbles.

We also included here a cold water line (CW), a hot water line (HW), and a floor drain (FD) in the room adjacent to the workshop. This area was to be the photographic darkroom, added later and not shown here.

Many of the areas projecting beyond the outer limits of the basement floor above are shown dotted. Many of them are labeled. This helped others to orientate themselves and to visualize the structure. We also included the title and scale.

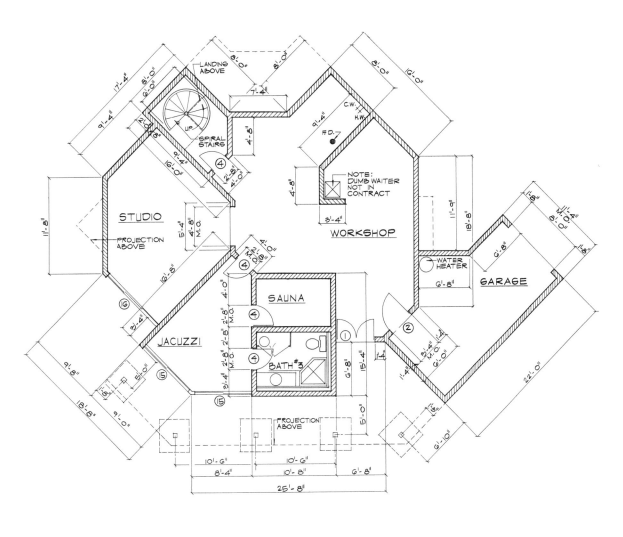

Figure 17.24 Basement floor plan—Stage VI.

Stage VII

During a discussion between the drafter and a senior person, it was decided that the dotted lines which represent the five concrete pads should be eliminated from the plan shown in Figure 17.25. They appear on the foundation plan and would be duplicated here.

Also, since the pads are below grade, it would be incorrect to show them on the basement floor plan.

The building section lines were now included, as were the interior elevation reference symbols (see Bath #3 for circles with arrows on them) and the reference bubbles for the plumbing fixtures that refer to the plumbing fixture schedule. Finally, the title and North orientation were located.

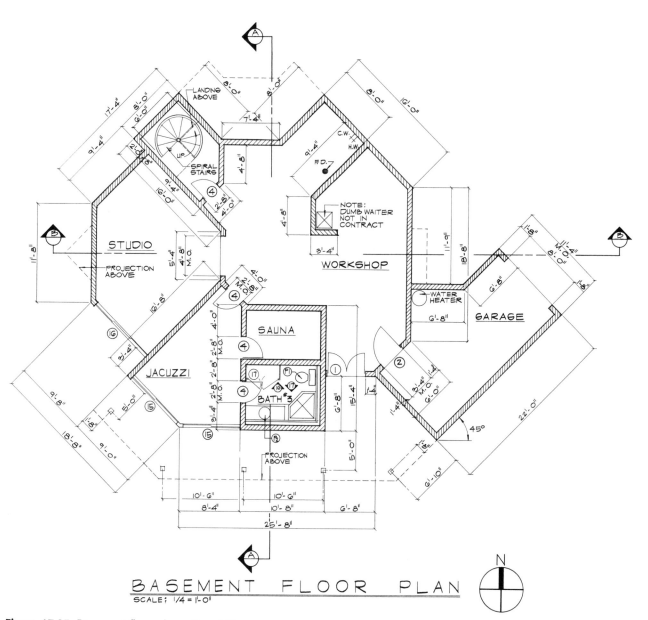

Figure 17.25 Basement floor plan—Stage VII.

First Floor Plan

Stage I

We lightly blocked out all the exterior and interior walls. The first floor plan differs from the basement floor plan in that it overlaps the basement floor plan. Look at the preliminary floor plans in Figure 17.26 and compare them with Figures 17.27 and 17.28. Figure 17.27 looks into the kitchen. The dining room is to the extreme right. Look carefully at the extreme right center of the photo-graph and see the pass-through between the dining room and the kitchen. Figure 17.28 is a view of the den. The drop in floor level marks the beginning of the sunken living room.

The first task was to identify the walls that line up with the basement walls and block those out. Because of the severe angles involved, many of the intersections of the walls were widened to maintain a rectangular shape. There are two levels with two steps between them; the lower portion at the left is the living room.

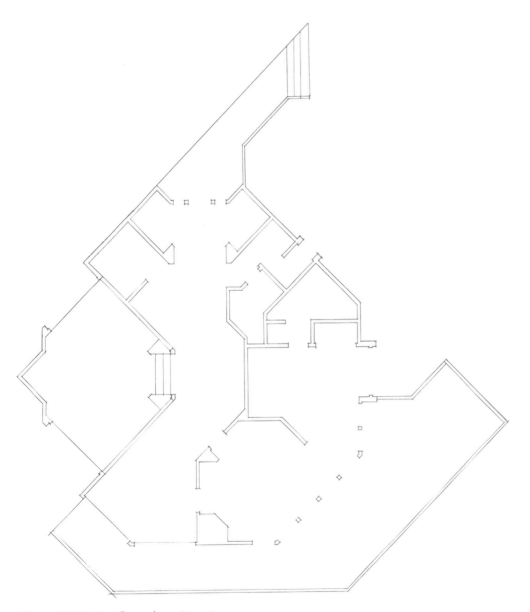

Figure 17.26 First floor plan—Stage I.

Figure 17.27 View looking into the kitchen.

Figure 17.28 View looking toward the den.

Stage II

To differentiate between the deck and the interior, we added wood texture to the deck area. See Figure 17.29. The fireplace is prefabricated, with masonry around the front face. The stairs and all equipment are now drawn. See Figure 17.30. Special hose bibbs are shown for the washer and refrigerator. There are built-in seats and window seats in the living room.

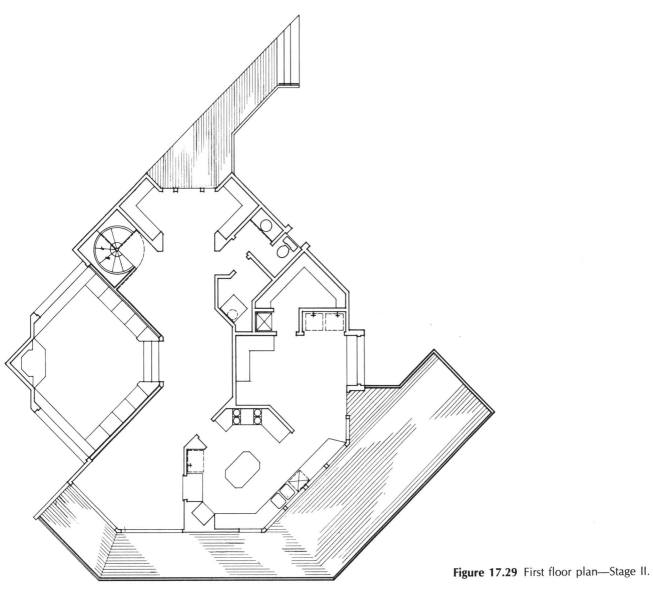

Figure 17.29 First floor plan—Stage II.

Figure 17.30 Top view of spiral staircase.

Stage III

Doors and their swing direction were now added. This includes the bifold door in front of the washer/dryer unit at the right of the drawing. See Figure 17.31. Windows were also added. The door at the right leading out to the deck is slightly lost in the lines that represent the deck material. This could change when the reference bubble is added. The designation for the wood texture could have been added after the doors were drawn.

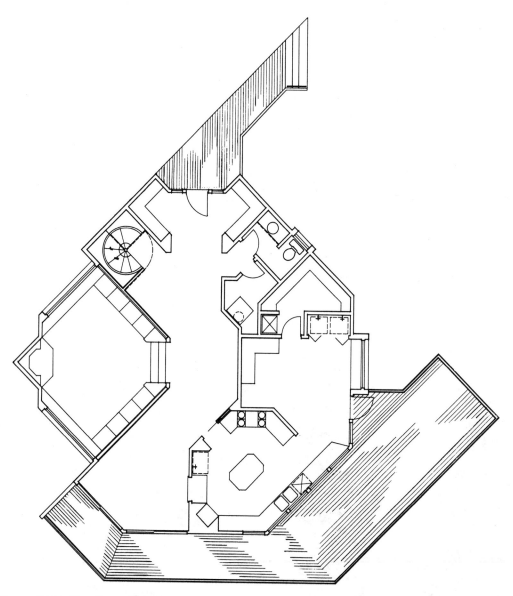

Figure 17.31 First floor plan—Stage III.

Stage IV

It was now time for the dimensioning. You should review the chapter on floor plans (Chapter 8) before reading further. An aid at this stage is to make a print and freehand draw all dimensions on it before proceeding on the original vellum sheet.

Because of the many angles on the floor plan, many dimension lines and extension lines will probably cross. To maximize clarity and avoid confusion, we drew extension lines to two locations: the edge of the stud (noted at a later stage) and the center of a wall. The centers have a center line, while the outside stud line

extension lines have solid medium-weight lines. See Figure 17.32.

We checked all walls that lined up with the basement wall (concrete block) for concrete block modules. In some instances, we located the windows by locating the columns in between; others that were close (within 6″ of an adjacent wall) we located by the window detail. The window behind the water closet in the bathroom was located but the size was not dimensioned. The window schedule would determine the size.

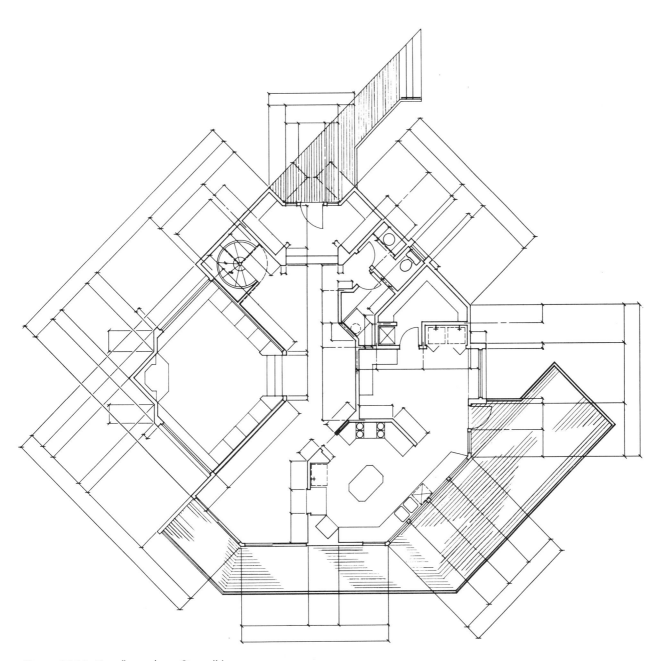

Figure 17.32 First floor plan—Stage IV.

Stage V

To understand the floor plan dimensions compare Figure 17.33 with the plan for the floor below. In both the basement and the foundation plans, sizes are dictated by the concrete block module. Many of the walls here line up with the walls below. Study the garage dimensions, the location of the columns, and the location and size of the stairs. By overlaying the original drawing of this plan on the basement plan, we could check for wall alignment.

Once again, a print was made of the sheet and the numerical values were placed and checked before they were added to the original. We again made certain the

overall dimensions totaled the sum of their parts and corresponded with the block modules.

The deck at the bottom, adjacent to the kitchen, was not dimensioned here. The basement floor plan had already dictated its size and shape. While it could have been dimensioned here, it would have been a duplication.

If any dimension is critical, the term "hold" can be placed after it. This was not the case here. Plus and minus (±) notations, indicating minimum and maximum dimensions, could also be shown at this stage, if required.

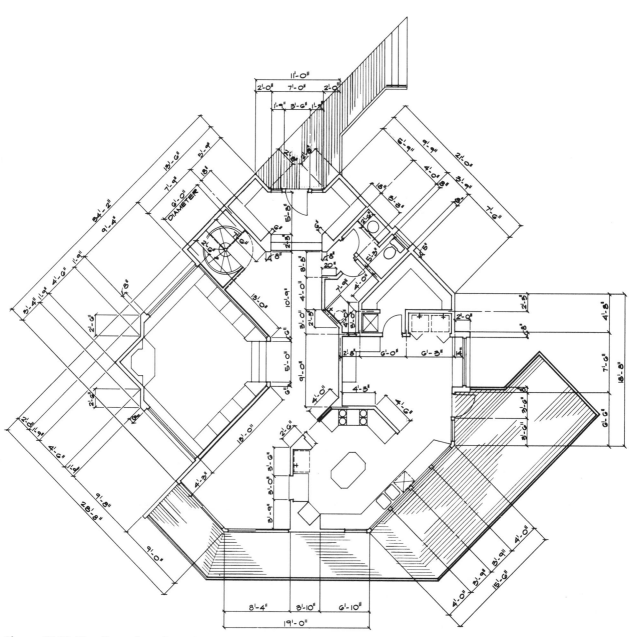

Figure 17.33 First floor plan—Stage V.

Stage VI

The cross-section reference symbol was now included, as well as the reference bubbles for the windows and doors and much of the noting. See Figure 17.34. Many of the items noted are not typical items: window seats, balustrades, and the end of the built-up roofing on the deck, for example. The call-out for the dryer vent on the right side was not spelled correctly and was corrected in the next stage.

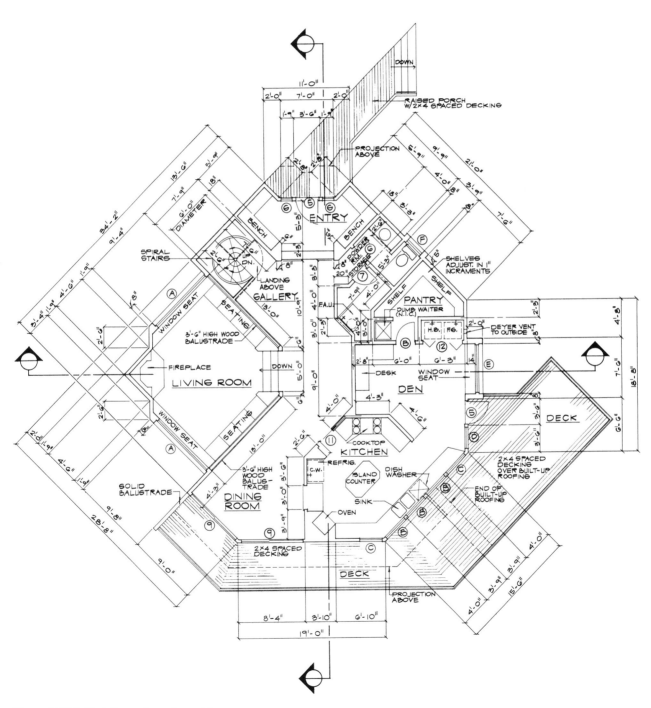

Figure 17.34 First floor plan—Stage VI.

Stage VII

Figure 17.35 shows the final step in the evolution of the first floor plan. Spelling and numerical values are usually checked at this stage by use of a check print. The bulk of the interior elevation reference symbols are in the kitchen; these are circles with arrows on them similar to the cross-section reference symbol. The appliance and plumbing fixtures have a circle and leader pointing to them. These refer to the appliance schedule and plumbing fixture schedule. See Figure 17.70. Finally, the title, scale, and North orientation were added.

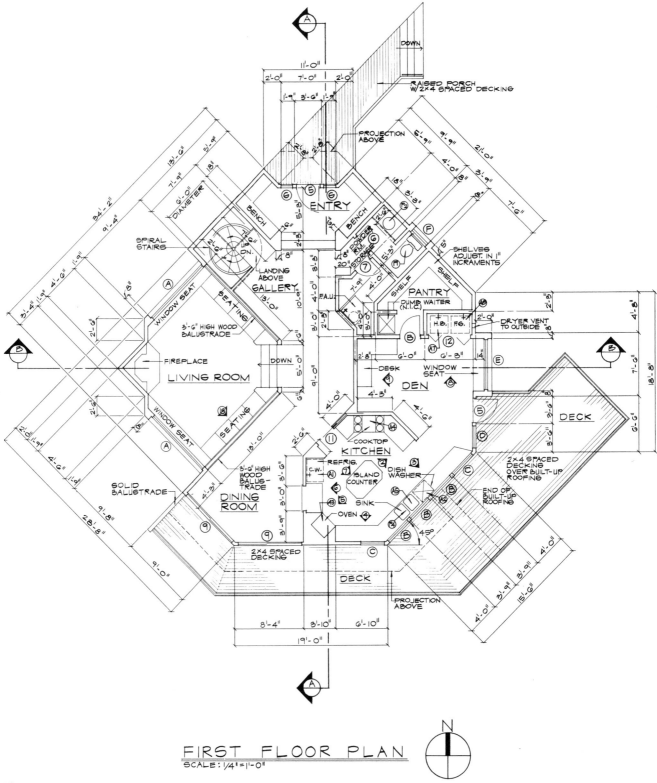

Figure 17.35 First floor plan—Stage VII.

Second Floor Plan

Stage I

The first step for the second floor plan, shown in Figure 17.36, was to identify the walls that lined up with the floor below because these dimensions were set. Any change would affect not only the first floor plan but the basement floor plan and foundation plan as well. Figure 17.37 shows the relationship between the various floors. Figure 17.38 shows the cantilever of the second floor over the first floor and the basement below. The opening

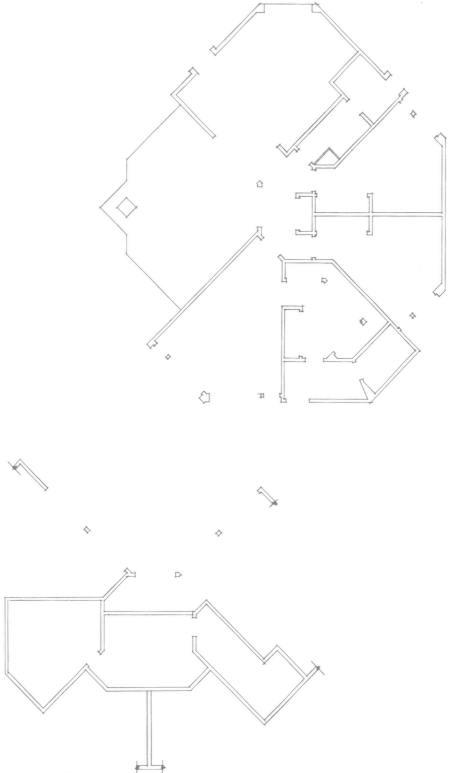

Figure 17.36 Second floor plan—Stage I.

is actually the garage door space, and this is helpful in orienting the photo to the drawing. Because a heavy timber floor was used, it did not matter that the other walls did not line up.

The single line area to the left on Figure 17.36 represents the living room, which can be seen from the hall in the center of the second floor plan.

The atttic plans at the bottom of the sheet were turned to fit in this drawing area. Normally, they would have been drawn as if they could be placed on top of the second-floor plan. In this example, the T-shaped wall of the attic plan lines up with the large T-shaped wall on the right side of the second-floor plan.

Stage II

As on the previous floor plans, the next step was to add items such as stairs, bathroom fixtures, and clothes poles in the wardrobes. See Figure 17.39. The rectangular area with an "X" in it toward the center of the plan represents the disappearing stair to the attic. The dotted lines to the right of the disappearing stair represent the attic balcony. These two features will help you orient the attic to the second-floor plan.

Figure 17.37 Relationship of the various floors.

Figure 17.38 Cantilever of second floor over first floor.

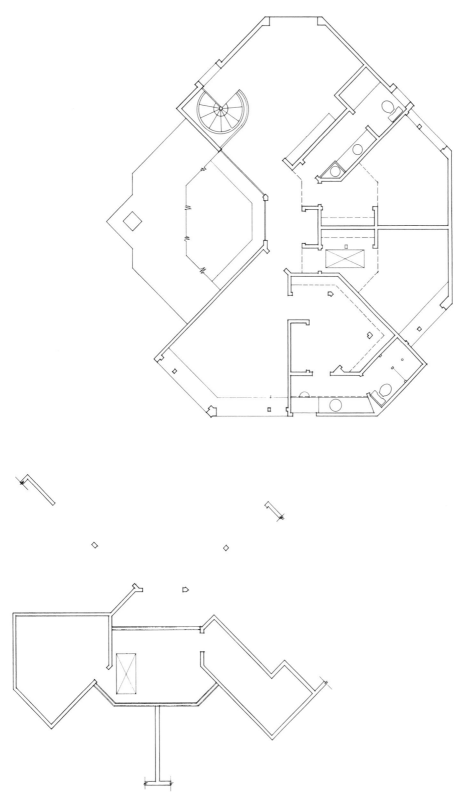

Figure 17.39 Second floor plan—Stage II.

The living room area was dealt with in an unusual way. We used a partial break to expose the interior of the living room. The extreme left area is still the roof of

the living room. The line between the edge of the hall and the break line represents the edge of the second floor. The decision to extend the floor beyond the guardrail in the hall was based on aesthetic reasons as well as safety. Look at the section (Figure 17.63) for a better visual picture of this area.

A double line was used around the spiral stair to indicate the handrail. The single line area indicates the place where people actually descend the stair.

Stage III

In Stage II, the disappearing stair was shown as a solid line. Stage III changed this to a hidden line because this section is above eye level. See Figure 17.40. We changed this line simply with an erasing shield and eraser.

Doors, direction of swing, and windows were then added, including bifold doors on the wardrobe closets. The chimney flue was added and the windows on the attic plan, located at the bottom. Refer to the sections to understand the relationship between these windows and the second-floor plan. These were the windows that extended above the second floor.

Stage IV

At the dimensioning stage, shown in Figure 17.41, all exterior and interior walls were located. Once again, all walls lining up on the two floors had to have the same dimensions (in this case, concrete block dimensions) if they lined up with the basement.

The windows were then dimensioned. If the windows were within 6" of an adjacent wall, the jamb detail located the window. The same was true with doors. The attic plan was not dimensioned. We wanted the second-floor plan to dictate the size and shape of the attic, because the walls of the second floor and the attic were aligned.

To understand the vertical relationship of the floors, imagine the disappearing stair to the attic; there are

handrails on both sides of the hall. As you stand in front of the shorter of the two handrails, you can look down into the hall below as well as through a high window to the exterior. This gives this area a special open quality.

Stage V

Compare this stage, shown in Figure 17.42, with the previous stage, shown in Figure 17.41. The attic floor plan has a new location at the bottom of the drawing. At first we thought the two plans would not fit on the same sheet unless we isolated the attic plan. Now, having drawn the attic plan, we found that the plan would fit into the upper plan. The drawing was so simple that we just drafted it again. If this had been a complex drawing needing hours to draft over, we could have moved it by splicing the vellum into place with tape or by the photographic method. Review this method if you have forgotten it (see Chapter 2).

The numerical values of the various dimensions were then added.

Stage VI

This was the final step. See Figure 17.43. Reference bubbles were located for the interior elevations. This symbol is a circle with an arrow similar to the one used as a cross-section reference with a number in it. Note Number 14 and Number 15 at the bottom of the floor plan.

Plumbing fixtures were also called out by a circle with a leader pointing to the specific plumbing fixture. The numbers such as P-1, P-2, and P-3 refer to the plumbing fixture schedule. See Figure 17.70

Door and window reference bubbles were located. Then we added section lines. Examine sections A-A and B-B carefully. Finally, we added the various notes and the main title, scale, and North orientation.

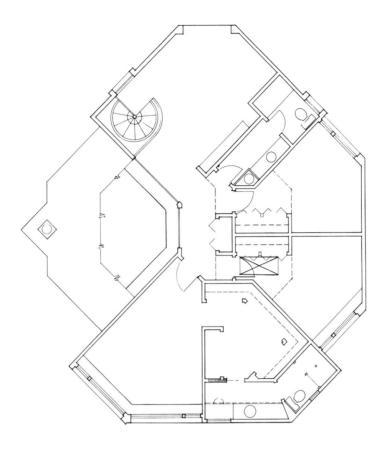

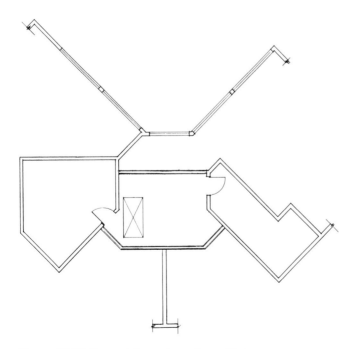

Figure 17.40 Second floor plan—Stage III.

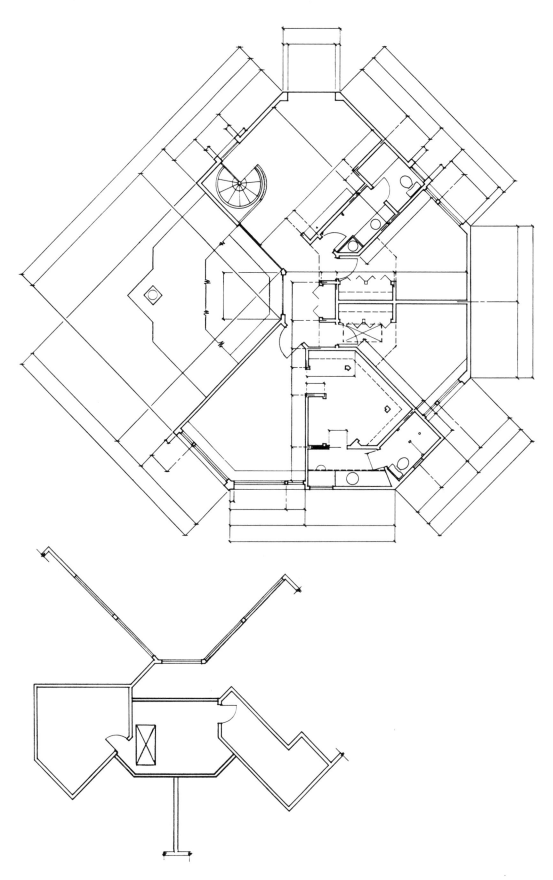

Figure 17.41 Second floor plan—Stage IV.

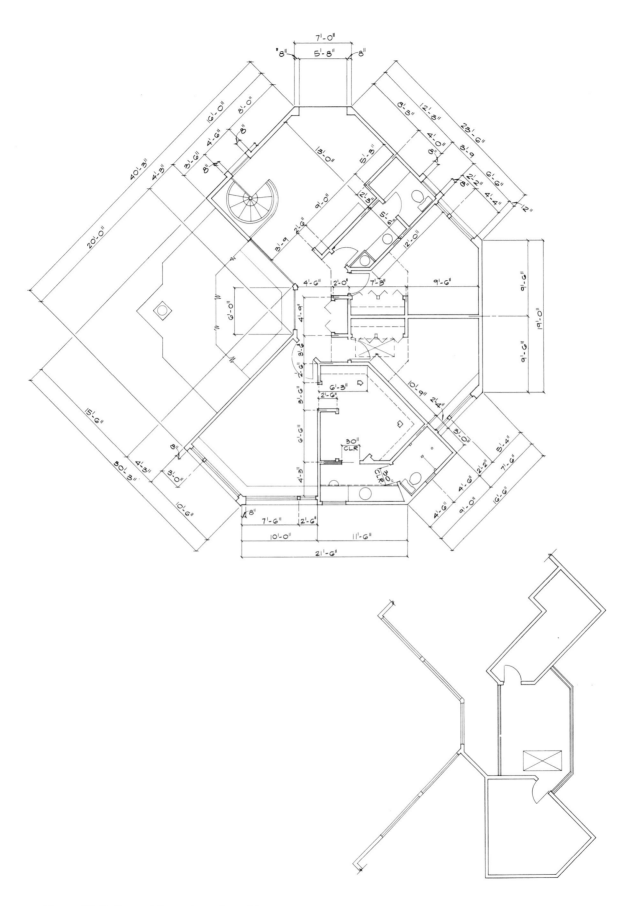

Figure 17.42 Second floor plan—Stage V.

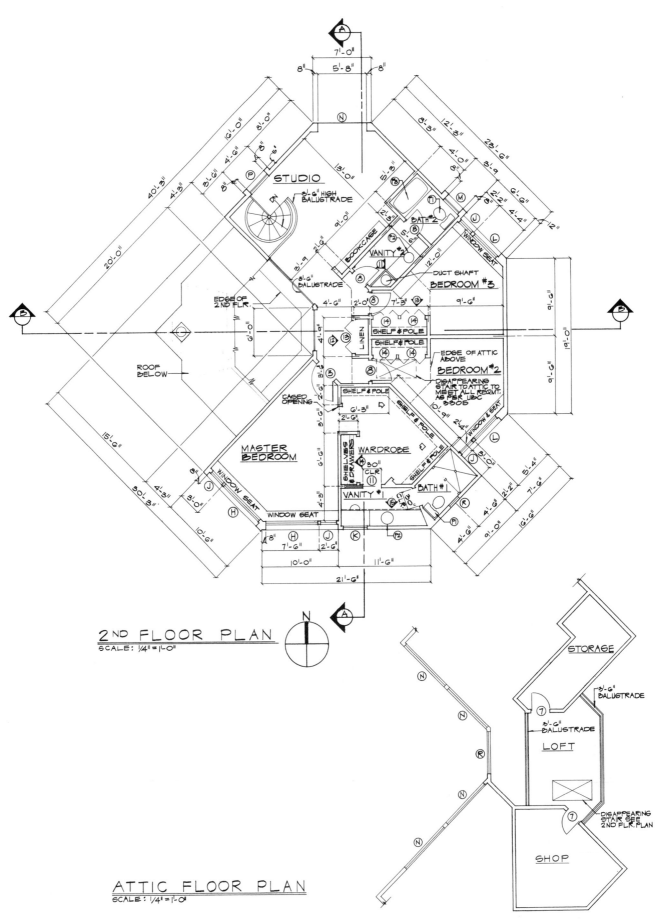

2ND FLOOR PLAN
SCALE: 1/4" = 1'-0"

ATTIC FLOOR PLAN
SCALE: 1/4" = 1'-0"

Figure 17.43 Second floor plan—Stage VI.

494

Elevations

Stage 1

The elevations are among the last drawings to be done because they depend on the sections and floor plans. See Figures 17.44 and 17.45.

From the cross-section we obtained the plate lines and the floor lines. As with the cross-section, we put some of the heights on the right side and others, such as the living room, on the left. We checked the bottom floor line with both the cross sections and verified it with the site plan. Most of the finished grade levels were arrived at during this procedure.

Plate lines had to be constantly checked because this structure does not have the customary eight-foot plate heights throughout the building. The plate line in this instance varies from 8'–2" to 9'–2" in height.

The light vertical lines on this drawing are taken from the exterior wall of the floor plans.

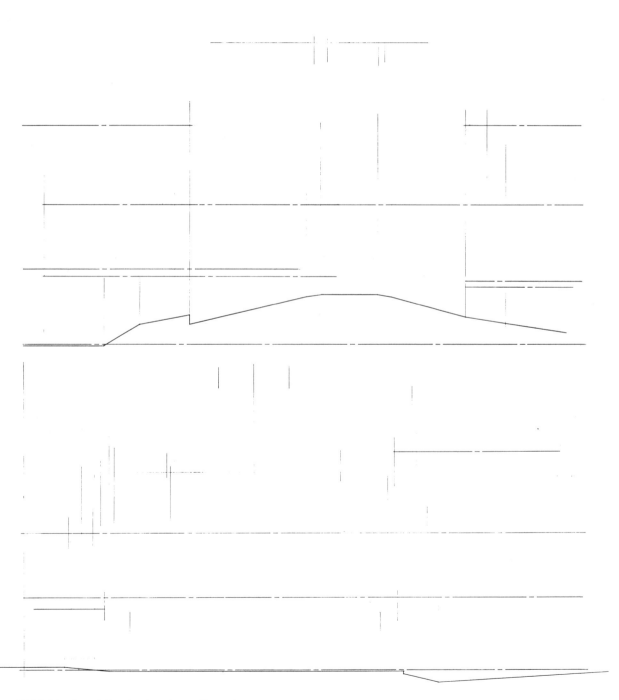

Figure 17.44 North and South elevations—Stage I.

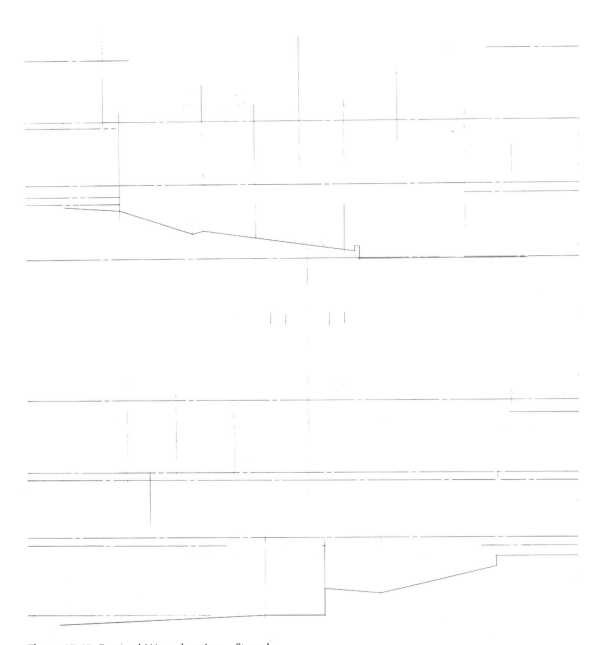

Figure 17.45 East and West elevations—Stage I.

Stage II

Our next step was to determine the basic outline and shape of the building. We checked preliminary elevations with the cross-section and any available detail sketches, such as eave and balcony details. We could not draw the elevations until these detail decisions were made. It is not uncommon to draw the structural members lightly to produce accurate elevations.

From the roof plan we developed the roof configuration as shown in Figures 17.46 and 17.47. Direct projection is the desired method for drawing this complicated roof in elevation form.

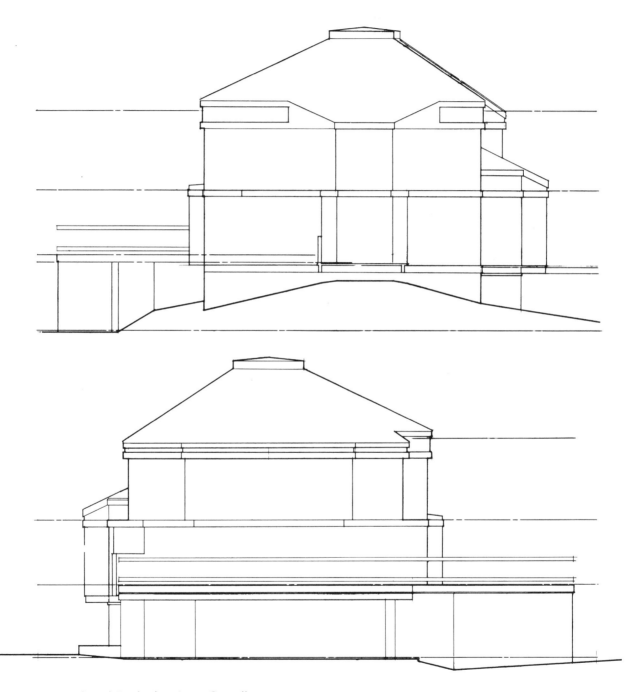

Figure 17.46 North and South elevations—Stage II.

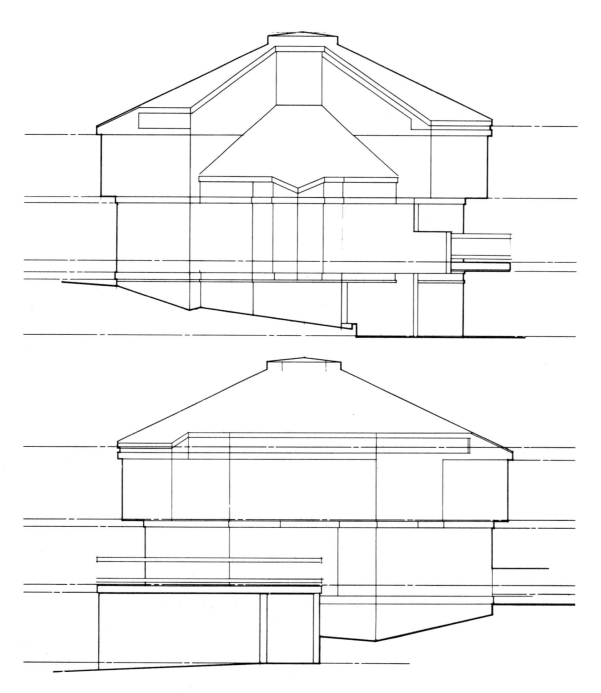

Figure 17.47 East and West elevations—Stage II.

498

Stage III

All of the doors and windows were now located on the elevation. See Figures 17.48 and 17.49. Many of the windows and doors appear out of scale because the elevations are drawn as direct orthographic projections from the floor plan and because the plan has unusual angles. We also indicated the swing of the doors with a dotted line. The "X" in some of the sliding doors indicates that the door can be opened. An arrowhead would also indicate the direction in which the door opens.

The surface (face of the wall) of the structure and the surface of the roof were given a texture, and proper symbols for the various material indications were given to ensure correct selection. The roof was to be made of corrugated sheet aluminum over rigid insulation.

Guardrails and vertical rails around the balcony were also included, as Figures 17.50 and 17.51 show. We also finished the chimney. The client requested a stained glass window above the front door, which we included at this stage.

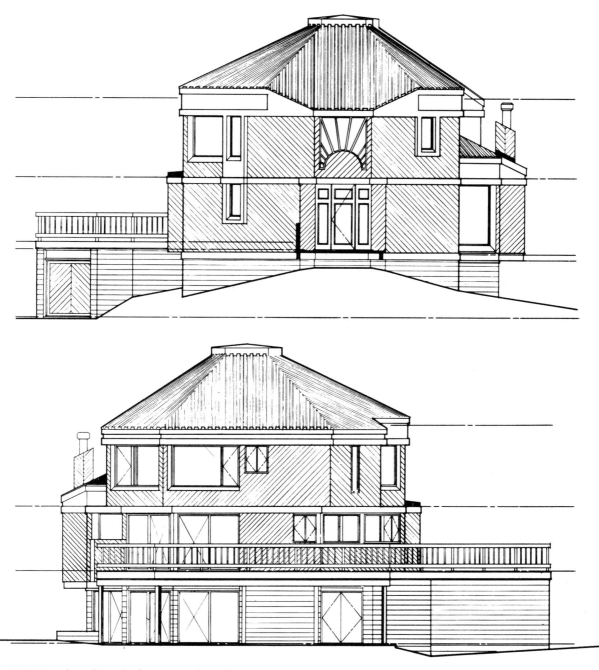

Figure 17.48 North and South elevations—Stage III.

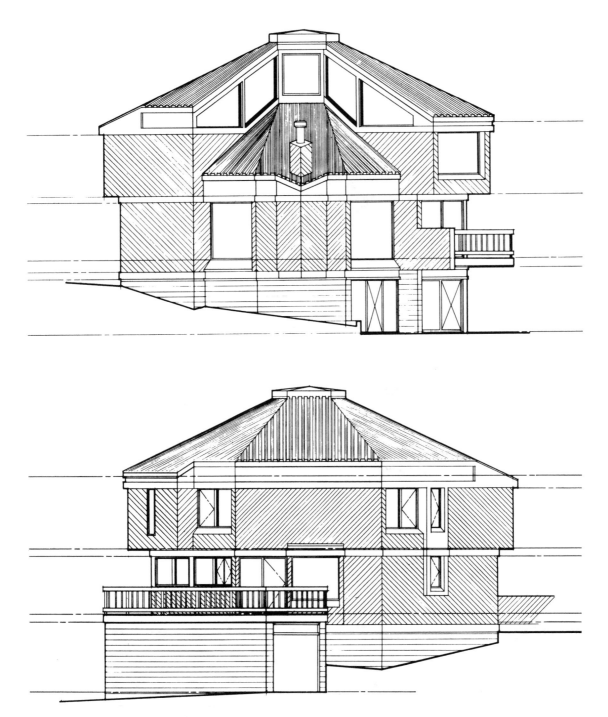

Figure 17.49 East and West elevations—Stage III.

Figure 17.51 Guardrail over garage.

Figure 17.50 Guardrail.

Stage IV

All of the elevations received dimensions at this stage. See Figures 17.52 and 17.53. Because all the vertical heights were based on the sections, the dimensions on the sections had to be verified before we placed them on the elevations. Because of the height variations, many of the floor lines and plate lines were further described by extensive notes. See an example at the top left of the top elevation: "Typical Plate Line, at exterior walls (2nd Floor Only)."

The lowered living room resulted in many different dimensions from one side of the elevation to the other. Because the plate line and floor line notations were placed on the left side of the top elevation (North elevation), the leader then crossed the dimension line. This was later changed in Figure 17.57.

Keep abbreviations to a minimum. When using them, follow a list that is widely subscribed to, like the list of the American Institute of Architects. For example, one

abbreviation used here was "R.S.C.", rough sawn cedar. (See Figure 17.54 for a photograph of this exterior finish.)

After we made a diazo copy of Stage III, we saw that the material texture was drawn too lightly, so we redrew much of the material designation in Stage IV.

The next detail to be drawn was now chosen (see Figure 17.55). Often, the details are already sketched at this stage. Sometimes even the finish details are already drafted, because the elevations are often the last drawing to be prepared. The detail shown in Figure 17.55 is the window on the right side of the North elevation. Since the sketch was taken below the window to expose additional portions of the structure, the reference bubble line had to extend far below the window to simulate this detail section.

At this point, the direction the structure faced was noted and titles were given. Figure 17.56 shows a

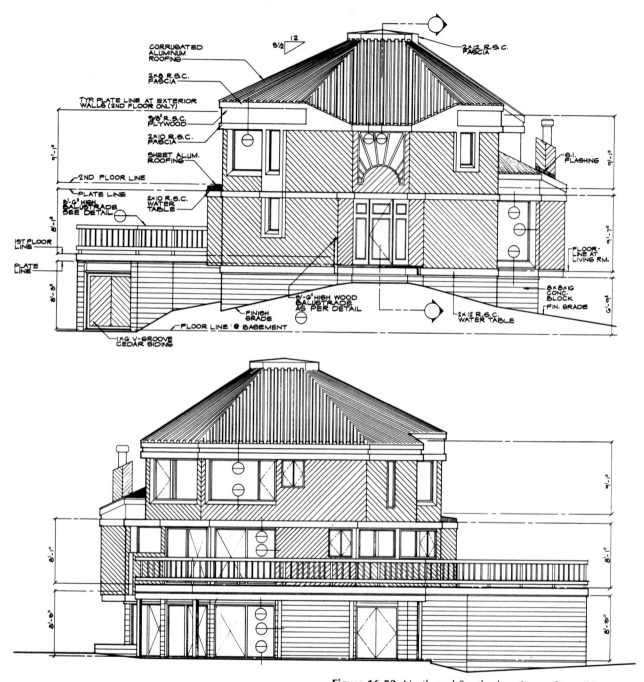

Figure 17.52 North and South elevations—Stage IV.

Figure 16.52 North and South elevations—Stage IV.

Northwest view of the structure. This drawing helps viewers understand the complicated geometry of the building and reasons for the unusual shape, such as tree location. West and East elevation titles were located.

Material descriptions are not always repeated on all elevations. Here, a note was simply added on the bottom left corner of the East elevation to direct attention to another source for missing information. This note could have been added to the South elevation as well.

Stage V

Since the East and West elevations were now basically finished, we moved on to the North and South elevations. See Figure 17.57. We took three significant steps here. First, we corrected the dimensioning on the North elevation. Because the dimension lines crossed the leaders of some of the notes on the left side, we relocated the notes and dimensions to improve the drawing.

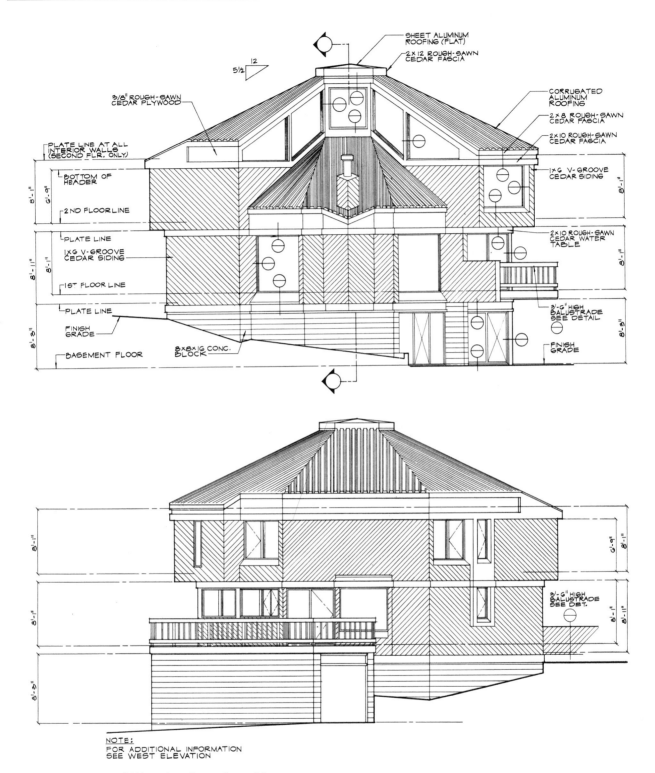

Figure 17.53 East and West elevations—Stage IV.

Second, we included a key plan (as described in Chapter 11) at the bottom of the sheet. We then decided that because the structure was such an unusual shape, we should include both titles and numbers on the elevations.

Finally, we placed titles in the proper location for all the elevations, and put the numbers from the key plan in circles after each title. See Figures 17.57 and 17.58.

Figure 17.54 Rough sawn cedar exterior.

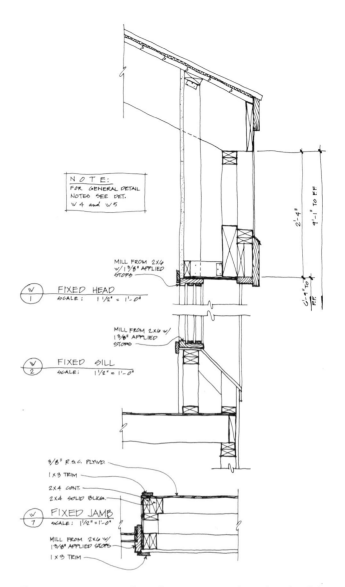

NOTE:
FOR GENERAL DETAIL
NOTES SEE DET.
W 4 and W 5

MILL FROM 2X6
w/ 1 3/8" APPLIED
STOPS

W 1 FIXED HEAD
SCALE: 1 1/2" = 1'-0"

MILL FROM 2X6 w/
1 3/8" APPLIED
STOPS

W 2 FIXED SILL
SCALE: 1 1/2" = 1'-0"

2'-4"

9'-1" TO EF

6'-4" TO FF

3/8" R.S.C. PLYWD.
1 X 3 TRIM
2X4 CONT.
2X4 SOLID BLKG.

W 7 FIXED JAMB
SCALE: 1 1/2" = 1'-0"

MILL FROM 2X6 w/
1 3/8" APPLIED STOPS
1 X 3 TRIM

Figure 17.55 Eave and window section on the right side of the North elevation—detail.

Figure 17.56 Northwest view of structure.

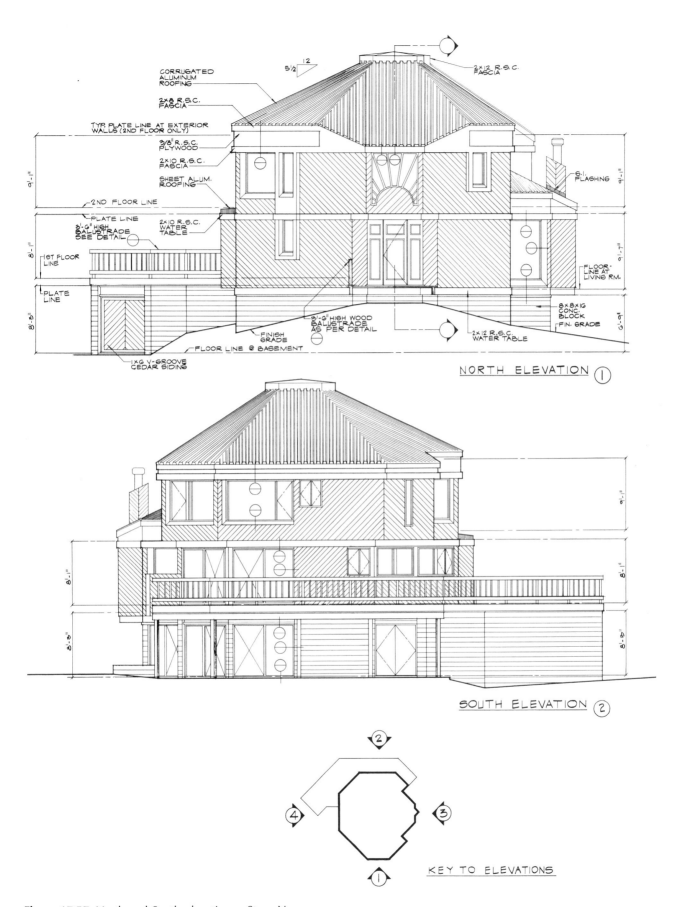

Labels on North Elevation (top drawing):

CORRUGATED ALUMINUM ROOFING
2×8 R.S.C. FASCIA
TYP. PLATE LINE AT EXTERIOR WALLS (2ND FLOOR ONLY)
3/8" R.S.C. PLYWOOD
2×10 R.S.C. FASCIA
SHEET ALUM. ROOFING
2ND FLOOR LINE
PLATE LINE
3'-6" HIGH BALUSTRADE SEE DETAIL
2×10 R.S.C. WATER TABLE
1ST FLOOR LINE
PLATE LINE
FINISH GRADE
3'-6" HIGH WOOD BALUSTRADE AS PER DETAIL
FLOOR LINE @ BASEMENT
1×6 V-GROOVE CEDAR SIDING

5½ | 12
2×12 R.S.C. FASCIA
G.I. FLASHING
FLOOR LINE AT LIVING RM.
8×8×16 CONC. BLOCK
FIN. GRADE
2×12 R.S.C. WATER TABLE

9'-1"   8'-1"   8'-5"
9'-1"   9'-7"   6'-9"

NORTH ELEVATION ①

SOUTH ELEVATION ②

9'-1"   8'-1"   8'-5"

②
④   ③
①

KEY TO ELEVATIONS

Figure 17.57 North and South elevations—Stage V.

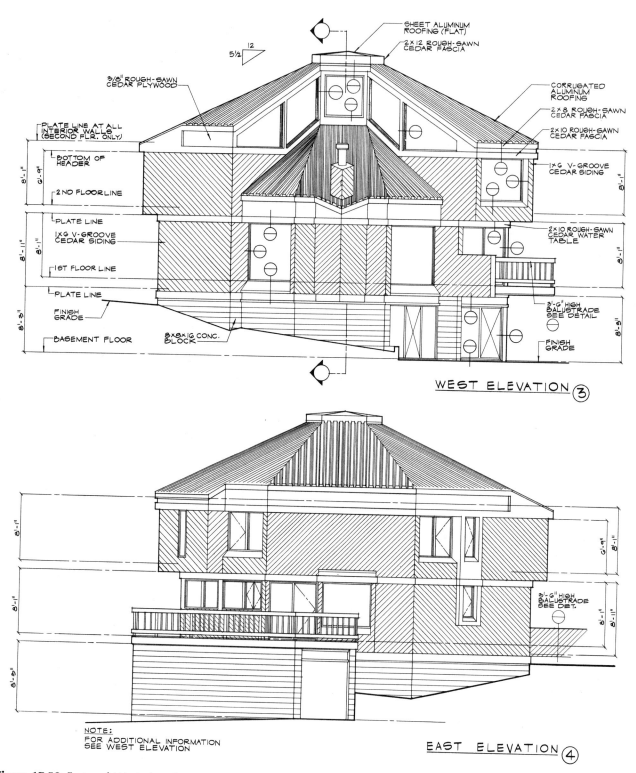

SHEET ALUMINUM
ROOFING (FLAT)

2×12 ROUGH-SAWN
CEDAR FASCIA

CORRUGATED
ALUMINUM
ROOFING

2×8 ROUGH-SAWN
CEDAR FASCIA

2×10 ROUGH-SAWN
CEDAR FASCIA

1×6 V-GROOVE
CEDAR SIDING

3/8" ROUGH-SAWN
CEDAR PLYWOOD

5½ | 12

PLATE LINE AT ALL
INTERIOR WALLS
(SECOND FLR. ONLY)

BOTTOM OF
HEADER

2 ND FLOOR LINE

PLATE LINE

1×6 V-GROOVE
CEDAR SIDING

1ST FLOOR LINE

2×10 ROUGH-SAWN
CEDAR WATER
TABLE

PLATE LINE

FINISH
GRADE

3'-6" HIGH
BALUSTRADE
SEE DETAIL

8×8×16 CONC.
BLOCK

FINISH
GRADE

BASEMENT FLOOR

WEST ELEVATION ③

NOTE:
FOR ADDITIONAL INFORMATION
SEE WEST ELEVATION

3'-6" HIGH
BALUSTRADE
SEE DET.

EAST ELEVATION ④

Figure 17.58 East and West elevations—Stage V.

506

Building Sections

Stage I

Cross-sections should be among the first drawings attempted. If a preliminary section was not drawn, it should be drawn at this stage.

Based on the contour of the property, the roof slope decisions were made with regard to ceiling heights at each level. These heights, translated into precise floor and plate heights, were the first to be drawn.

There were two sections to be drafted. See Figure 17.59. The section at the bottom of the page would have a change of level at the living room, so we decided to put the regular plate lines and floor lines on the right and the living room floor and plate lines on the left. We again checked the basement floor line against the site plan.

Figure 17.59 Building sections—Stage I.

The light vertical lines represent the width of the structure taken from the floor plans.

Most offices construct quick sketches of various details before and during the development of the section drawings. Even pictorial sketches are developed to clarify the architect's intentions and avoid problems.

Stage II

Based on the quick sketches and detail sketches, interior and exterior walls were located from the various plans and thickness was added to the members. See Figure 17.60. The intersection of the various horizontal and vertical planes took much thought, because the aesthetic ideas and structural assembly concepts were largely explained through this drawing.

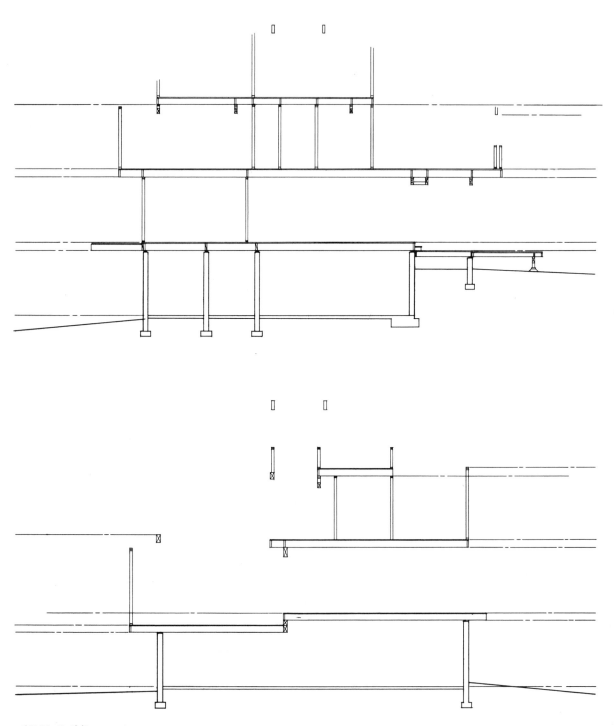

Figure 17.60 Building sections—Stage II.

Stage III

After studying the various detail sketches and framing plans from the structural engineer, we could now accurately draft the roof, ceilings, and floors. See Figure 17.61. We also added special features such as lowered ceilings, steps for the lowered living room, and the prefabricated fireplace. We obtained sizes for items like the prefabricated fireplace from the manufacturer's literature.

The proper material symbols for the materials could now be included, along with symbols for masonry, soil, and insulation. Because of the size of this reproduction, we eliminated items like the gravel or sand under the slab and the plastic membrane. If the scale had been larger than $1/8'' = 1'-0''$, we could have included these.

Now we could lightly lay out the exterior elevations.

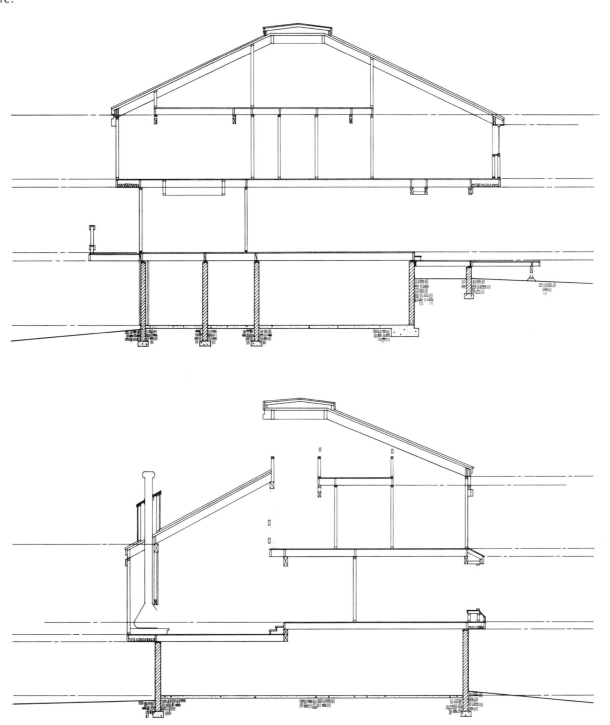

Figure 17.61 Building sections—Stage III.

Stage IV

All items requiring a call-out were next to be added—all the materials and sizes of members and all of the floor and plate lines, including their dimensions. See Figure 17.62. This is such a complicated building, structurally, that our dimensions included unusual dimensions like locations of tops of beams, plate lines for interior walls, and even bottoms of headers. We also added the height of the chimney in relation to the roof. Notice the location of the notes and the attempt of the drafter to align the notes so as to produce a margin.

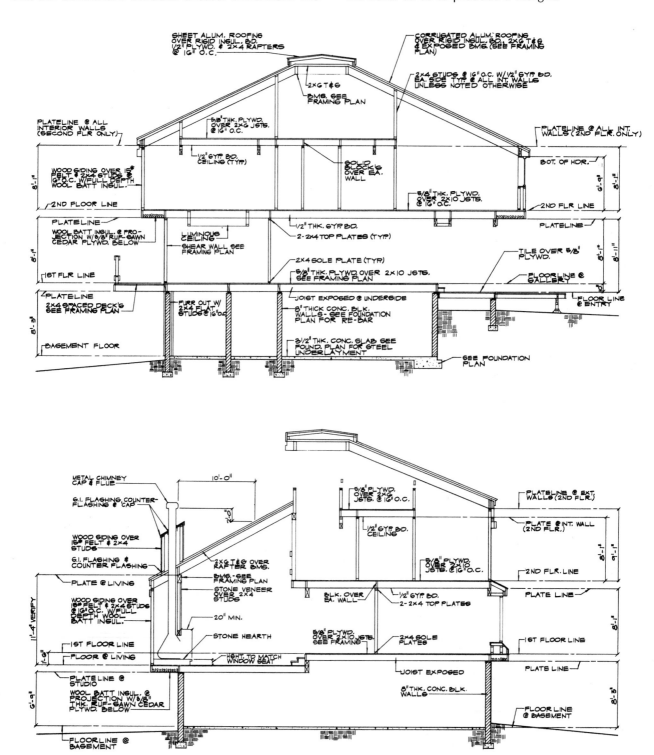

Figure 17.62 Building sections—Stage IV.

Stage V

All of the areas requiring a detail for clarification were now referenced. While we had already drawn most of the details freehand, and had solved many of the problems at the design stage, the need for additional details became apparent as the drawing of the formal architectural section was done. See Figure 17.63. Note how all of the detailed areas are circled and referenced.

Missing notes such as the 3½″ concrete slab on Section B-B were now added, as well as room titles, main sheet title, and scale.

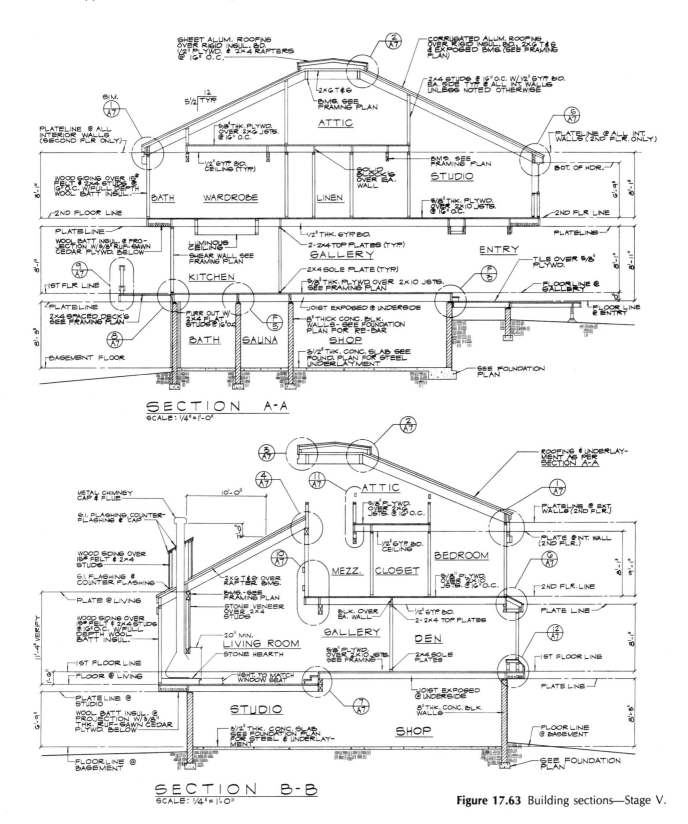

Figure 17.63 Building sections—Stage V.

First Floor Framing Plan

There were various ways the drawing shown in Figure 17.64 could have been done. The easiest was to have a structural engineer (or engineer) compute and draft the plan. The second was to ask the structural engineer to indicate the engineered beams freehand. This information could then be transcribed into drafted form.

To transcribe this information into a finished drafted form, a floor plan is drawn or traced onto a new vellum, and the engineering information is added. Or a reproducible can be made of the floor plan at an early stage and the engineering materials then added. Reproducibles can be made either photographically (the method used in Figure 17.64) or by a diazo process. The sepia process is a common diazo method of obtaining a reproducible.

In anticipation of using the photographic method, we made an early-stage copy of the original floor plan. We placed a piece of vellum over this copy and drafted the structural engineer's drawings. We then sent the two drawings to a blueprint service and combined them photographically. For simplicity, we deleted many connection notes and detail reference bubbles. See Figures 17.65 and 17.66. Figure 17.65 shows the staggered blocking, the joist hangers, and the built-up beam. Figure 17.66 shows clearly on the left the transition and method of construction between wood, steel, and concrete masonry units.

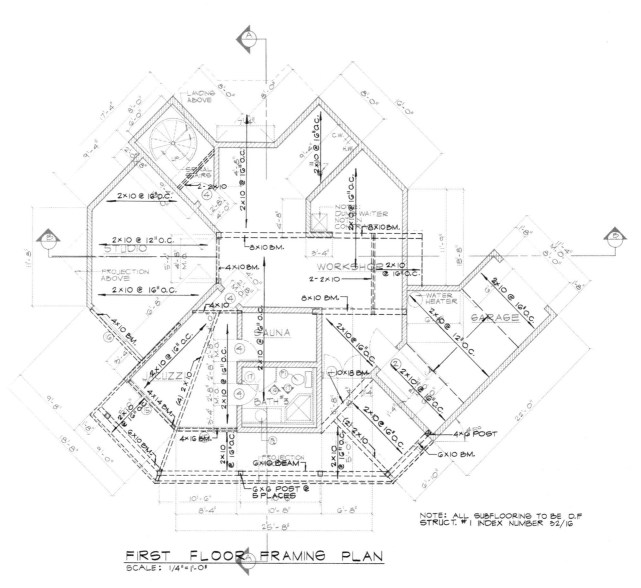

Figure 17.64 First floor framing plan.

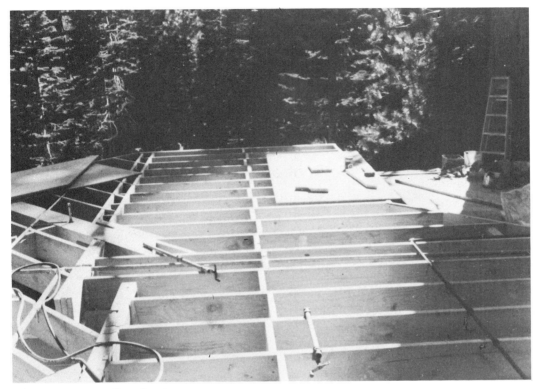
Figure 17.65 First floor framing.

Figure 17.66 Transition between masonry, steel, and wood.

Second Floor Framing Plan

Like the drawing for the first floor framing plan, the drawing shown in Figure 17.67 applies the principles of composite drafting discussed in Chapter 2. The main members, as usual, were drawn in first—the 10 × 10 beams and the 8¾″ × 9¾″ glue laminated beams. The smaller beams and headers were drawn next. "HDR DOWN" indicates a header below the level represented. The single dimension-type lines with arrows at each end represent repeated members such as 2 × 10 @ 16″ o.c. The single lines represent plywood on the walls chosen to resist seismic or wind problems. Even the nailing is specific (8d or 16d). Placing a vellum over a copy of an early-stage drawing of the second floor plan and carefully aligning the sheets, the structural engineer made a drawing similar to Figure 17.64. A drawing such as this can be roughly done on a print of the floor plan and then transferred to the vellum sheet.

Because this building is constructed of heavy timber, the main members were drawn first: the 10 × 10 beams

and 2 × 10 members were indicated by arrows because of spacing and quantity.

Look at the floor above and see what wall loads are placed on the framing members. Note again that because the structure must withstand heavy snow loads, the framing members are larger than normal. (Figure 17.68.)

Also note the glue laminated beams on the right of the framing plan. Glue laminated beams are many layers of wood glued together for strength. Plywood nailed on the wall below the second floor framing is shown by a single solid line, or by dotted lines (indicating a beam) with a solid line between. This plywood helps offset wind and seismic problems.

Roof and Attic Floor Framing Plans

Figure 17.68 used the same procedure as Figure 17.64, the first floor framing plan, and Figure 17.67, the second floor framing plan. Two interesting features of this plan are the dotted line indicating the roof line (perimeter of the roof) and the note sizing those beams now labeled.

Figure 17.67 Second floor framing plan (composite).

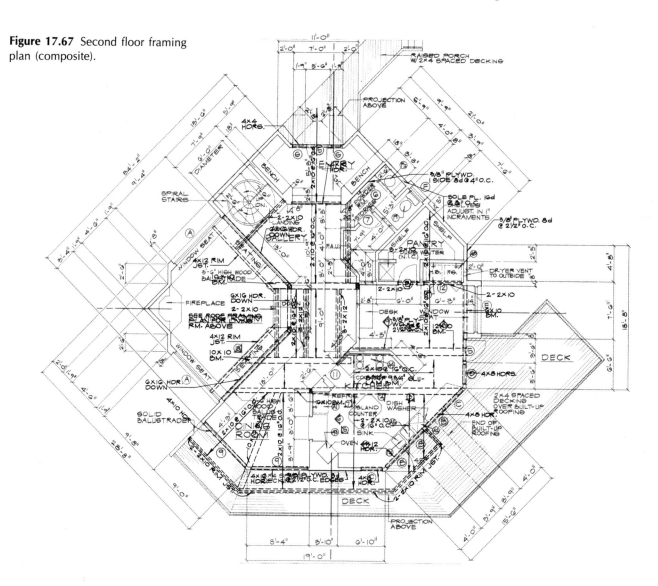

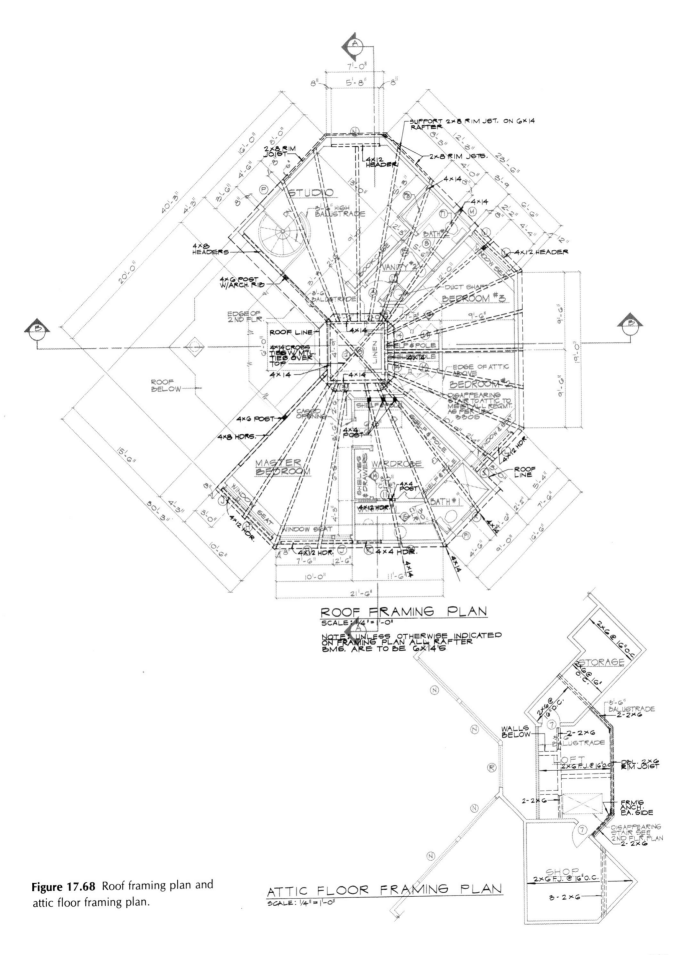

Figure 17.68 Roof framing plan and attic floor framing plan.

ROOF FRAMING PLAN
SCALE: 1/4" = 1'-0"

NOTE: UNLESS OTHERWISE INDICATED ON FRAMING PLAN ALL RAFTER BMS. ARE TO BE 6×14'S

ATTIC FLOOR FRAMING PLAN
SCALE: 1/4" = 1'-0"

Schedules

Five schedules were to be included in this particular set of construction documents: the door, window, finish, plumbing fixture, and appliance schedules.

Stage I

A preliminary form, shown in Figure 17.69, was made to ensure that all schedules would fit on one sheet and that the space distribution would be sufficient to contain the required information. Using the scheduling procedure described in Chapter 9, the vellum was inked.

Many finish schedules use angular lines at the top for material descriptions. The form used here has all lines perpendicular for easy reading.

The first stage included gathering the necessary information from the client and then from manufacturers' literature and putting it in order on a preliminary form.

Stage II

Figure 17.70 shows the schedule with information filled in. Because of the complexity of this project, the written specifications would be comprehensive. As a result, we only gave general descriptions for such items as "Wood."

On the window schedule below the remarks area in Figure 17.70 there is a reference to double-pane insulated glass. This was used to protect against the cold climate conditions and to prevent heat loss. Head, jamb, and sill spaces were left for future details.

When items were repeated, as on the door schedule under "Slab," and "Wood," either a line or a line with an arrowhead was drawn to show repetition.

Because the space we had allocated for the interior finish schedule was limited, we deleted various columns. This gave us space for another finish material. We needed space for a "wainscot" column, leaving two spaces for additional wainscot information. One space under the letter "W" was deleted, which allowed for other notations.

The slot titled "ceiling height" on the interior finish schedule, could be left blank or noted as "varies" with an arrow below indicating the lack of a standard height. Check the final drawing on the cross-section and note the great variation in ceiling heights.

The schedules were not completed sufficiently to give a clear idea of the choices and their functions.

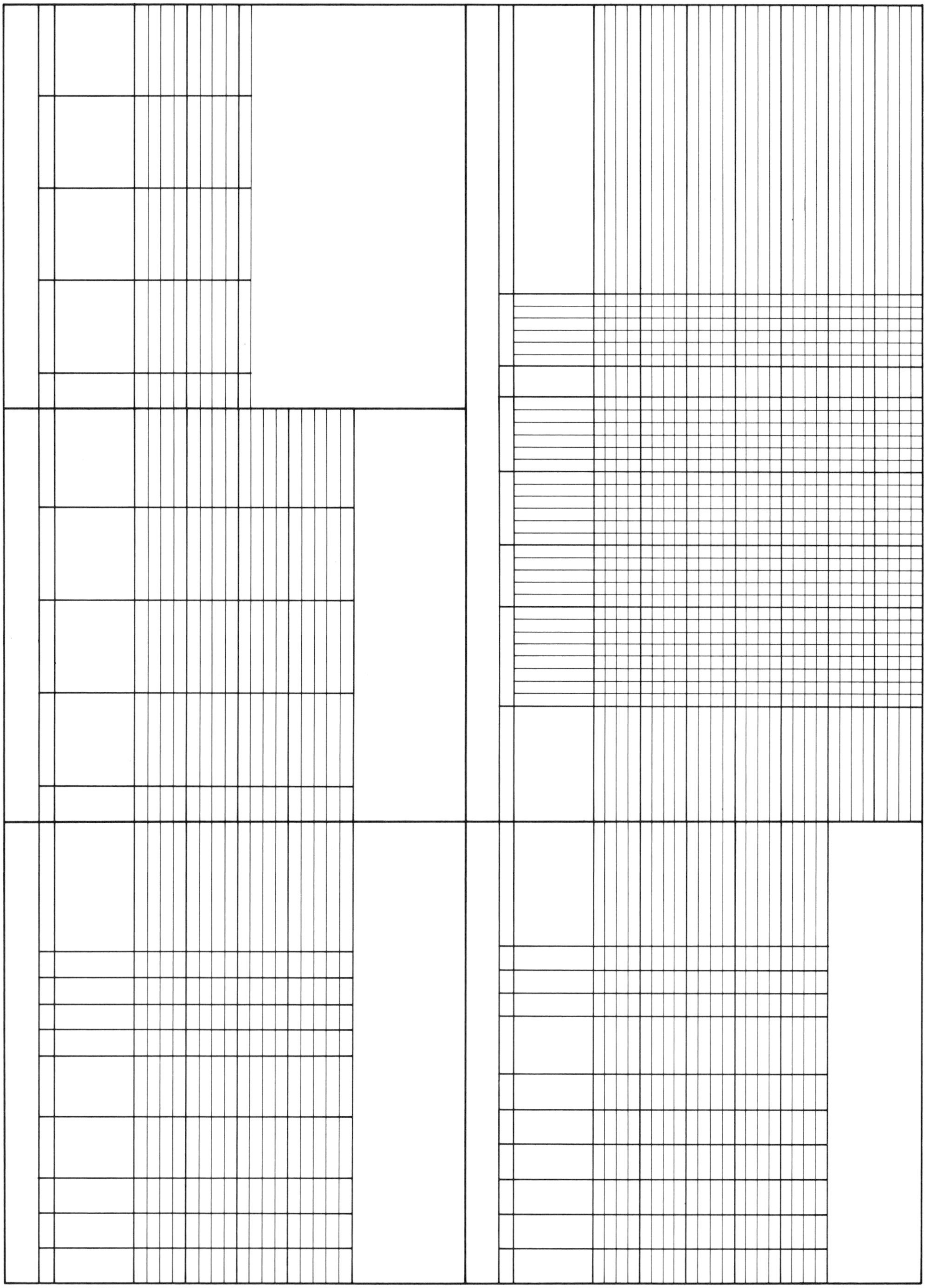

Figure 17.69 Schedules—Stage I.

WINDOW SCHEDULE

SYM.	WIDTH	HGT.	TYPE	FRAME MATERIAL	SCR	HEAD	JAMB	SILL	REMARKS
A	9'-0"	7'-0"	FIXED	WOOD					
B	8'-0"	4'-0"	FIXED	WOOD					
C	8'-0"	6'-0"	CSMT.	WOOD					
D	8'-0"	7'-0"	FIXED	WOOD					
E	6'-0"	7'-0"	FIXED	WOOD					
F	2'-6"	6'-0"	CSMT.	WOOD					
G	1'-6"	1'-6"	FIXED	WOOD					
H	6'-6"	5'-0"	FIXED	WOOD					
J	2'-0"	5'-0"	CSMT.	WOOD					
K	8'-0"	8'-6"	CSMT.	WOOD					
L	6'-0"	5'-0"	FIXED	WOOD					
M	2'-6"	5'-0"	CSMT.	WOOD					NOTE: ALL GLAZING TO BE DOUBLE-PANE INSULATED GLASS UNLESS NOTED OTHERWISE
N	VERIFY GLASS SIZES W/FRAME OPENING			WOOD					
P	8'-0"	4'-0"	CSMT.	WOOD					
Q	5'-0"	5'-0"	FIXED	WOOD					

APPLIANCE SCHEDULE

SYM.	ITEM	MANUFACTURER	CATALOG NO.	REMARKS
A1	REFRIGERATOR	SEARS	W46HG406GN	TAWNY GOLD
A2	DISHWASHER	KITCHEN AID	KDC-17	HARVEST GOLD
A3	DBL OVEN	GENERAL ELECT.	JK25 & PT	GOLD
A4	COOK TOP	THERMADOR	TMH45	GOLDEN TONE
A5	GARB. DISPOSAL	IN-SINK-ERATOR	77	STAINLESS
A6	RANGE HOOD	TRADEWIDE	MASTERPIECE	FAN VC 500
A7	WASHER	MAYTAG	A606	HARVEST GOLD
A8	DRYER	MAYTAG	D606	HARVEST GOLD
A9	FOOD WARMER	CORY	FW 324	GOLD
A10	WATER HEATER			
A11	FORCED AIR UNIT			
A12	SAUNA HEATER			
A13	JACUZZI	RIVEARA	7x7 GIBRALTER	WHITE W/BLUE

PLUMBING FIXTURE SCHEDULE

SYM.	ITEM	MANUFACTURER	CATALOG NO.	REMARKS
P1	WATER CLOSET	AMERICAN STD.	CADET	WHITE
P2	LAVATORY	AMERICAN STD.	OVALYN	WHITE
P3	TUB	AMERICAN STD.	DILDOR	WHITE
P4	KITCHEN SINK	COMMERCIAL	790-4 (42x21)	HARVEST-GOLD

DOOR SCHEDULE

SYM.	WIDTH	HGT.	THK.	HC/SC	TYPE	MATERIAL	HEAD	JAMB	SILL	REMARKS
1	FR 2'-6"	6'-8"	1-3/4"	S.C.	SLAB	WOOD				DOUBLE HINGED
2	3'-4"	6'-8"	1-3/4"	H.C.						
3	3'-0"	6'-8"	1-3/8"	H.C.						
4	2'-8"	6'-8"	1-3/8"	H.C.						
5	3'-0"	8'-0"	1-3/4"	S.C.						
6	2'-4"	6'-8"	1-3/8"	H.C.						
7	2'-4"	6'-8"	1-3/8"	H.C.	SLAB	WOOD (ASH)				
8	2'-6"	6'-8"	1-3/8"	H.C.	SL.GL.	ALUM.				
9	8'-0"	7'-0"	1/4"PT		SL.GL.	ALUM.				
10	2'-0"	7'-0"	1/4"PT		POCKET	WOOD (ASH)				
11	2'-6"	6'-8"	1-3/8"	H.C.	BI-FOLD	WOOD (ASH)				
12	FR 2'-6"	6'-8"	1-3/8"	H.C.	BI-FOLD	WOOD (ASH)				
13	FR 1'-6"	6'-8"	1-3/8"	H.C.	BI-FOLD	WOOD (ASH)				
14	3'-0"	6'-8"	1-3/8"	H.C.	SL.GL.	ALUM.				
15	8'-0"	6'-8"	1/4"PT		SL.GL.	ALUM.				
16	9'-0"	6'-8"		H.C.	SLAB	WOOD				
17	FR 2'-6"	6'-8"								18"x12" LOUV. TOP & BOT.

INTERIOR FINISH SCHEDULE

ROOM	FLOOR	BASE	WAINSCOT	WALLS	CEILING	CEILING HEIGHT	REMARKS
ENTRY							
GALLERY							
LIVING ROOM							
DINING ROOM							
DEN							
KITCHEN							
PANTRY							
POWDER RM.							
STORAGE							
MASTER BEDRM.							
WARDROBE							
VANITY NO. 1							
BATH NO. 1							USE WATER PROOF DRYWALL
BEDROOM NO. 2							
BEDROOM NO. 3							
VANITY NO. 2							
BATH NO. 2							USE WATER PROOF DRYWALL
STUDIO NO. 1							
HALL							
STUDIO NO. 2							
WORKSHOP							
SAUNA							
JACUZZI							
BATH NO. 3							USE WATER PROOF DRYWALL
SHOP							
STAIR (BASEMENT)							
STAIR (1ST FLR.)							
STAIR (2ND FLR.)							

Floor sub-columns: RESILIENT FLR., CARPET, EXP. CONC., LINOLEUM, VINYL ASBES., HARDWOOD, CER. TILE, TERRAZZO
Base sub-columns: TOPSET, WOOD, CER. TILE, COVED, PAINT
Wainscot sub-columns: TERRAZZO, CER. TILE, PAINT
Walls sub-columns: PLASTER, EXT. MASONRY, EXT. WOOD, 5/8" DRYWALL, WALLPAPER, PAINT
Ceiling sub-columns: PLASTER, AC PLASTER, EXP. WOOD, 5/8" DRYWALL, ILLUM., EXP. JST. & SUB FLR.

Figure 17.70 Schedules—Stage II.

Basement, First Floor, and Second Floor Electrical Plans

Like the framing plans, the electrical plans (Figures 17.71, 17.72, and 17.73) were drawn on separate sheets placed over the drawings of the respective floor plans. The electrical plans and the floor plans were later combined photographically.

As Figure 17.72 shows, these are not exclusively electrical plans. There are items such as "FG" (fuel gas) and "HB" (hose bibb) located along with the electrical items.

A notation at the top left indicates additional switching on other floors, 220 volt outlets, "WP" (waterproof) outlets, dimmer switches, and references to outlet location information the owner would supply.

Figure 17.73 shows a fire warning system. Many municipalities now require smoke alarms or smoke detectors.

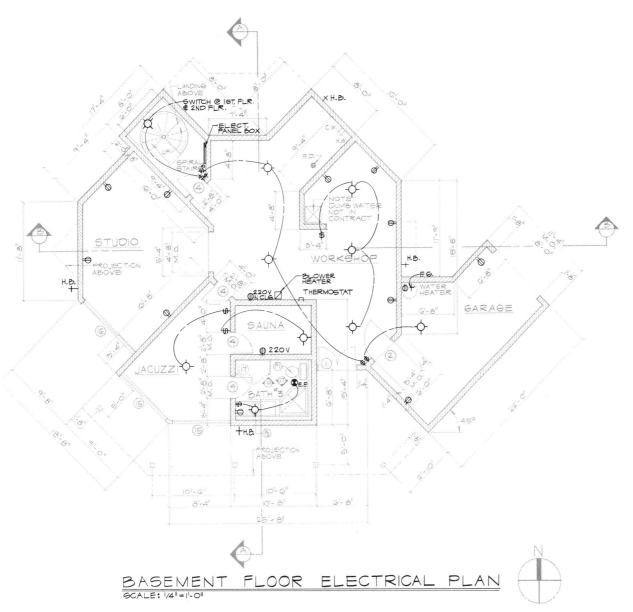

BASEMENT FLOOR ELECTRICAL PLAN
SCALE: 1/4"=1'-0"

Figure 17.71 Basement floor electrical plan.

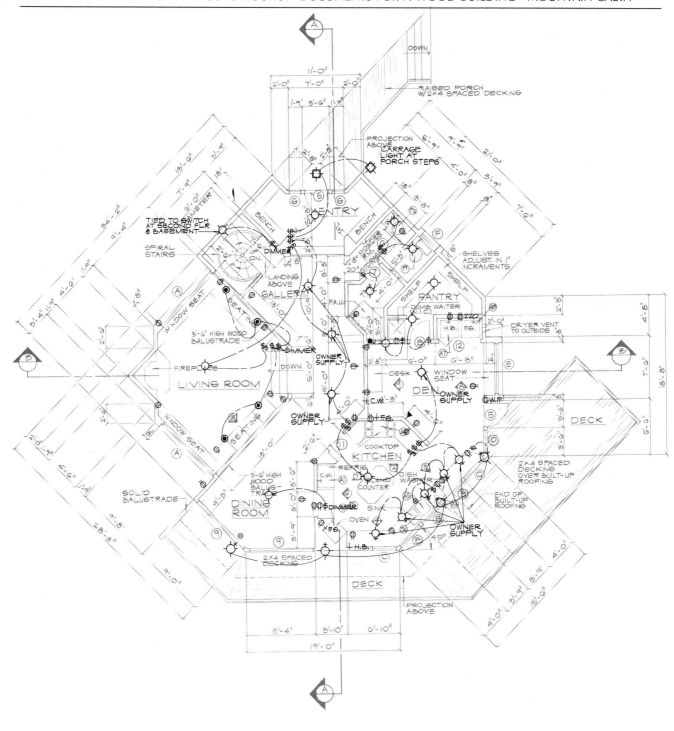

Figure 17.72 First floor electrical plan.

REVIEW QUESTIONS

1. Name four factors that influence the conceptual design process.
2. On the site plan, what types of lines are used for the natural and finished grades?
3. What procedure is recommended prior to the lettering of dimensions on the original drawing?
4. Name an important consideration when concrete blocks are used.
5. Give five factors used to finalize the first floor plan.

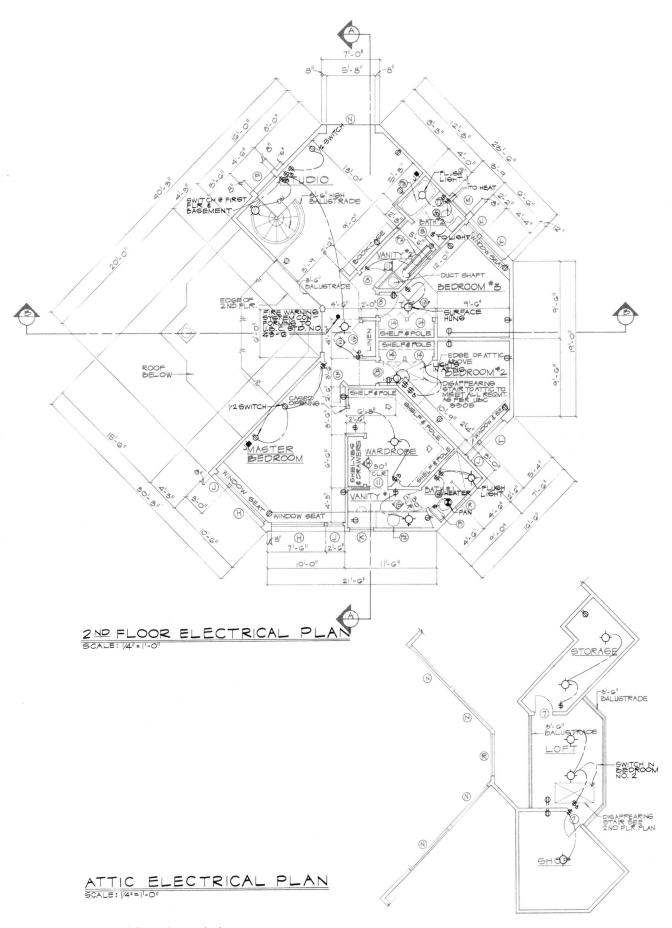

2ND FLOOR ELECTRICAL PLAN
SCALE: 1/4" = 1'-0"

ATTIC ELECTRICAL PLAN
SCALE: 1/4" = 1'-0"

Figure 17.73 Second floor electrical plan.

18

CONCEPTUAL DESIGN AND CONSTRUCTION DOCUMENTS FOR A STEEL AND MASONRY BUILDING—THEATRE

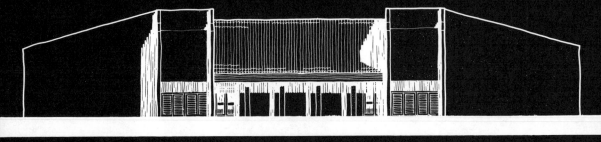

WEST ELEVATION

18

Conceptual Design

Site and Client Requirements

The client required a theatre building with six separate auditoriums of 200 seats each. The sloping site of approximately three acres also had stringent architectural restrictions.

The proposed structure, with six auditoriums, office, restrooms, storage and food areas, required approximately 26,000 square feet of area. The seating area dictated the required on-site parking of 400 automobiles.

To satisfy fire requirements, the primary building materials selected were structural steel and concrete block. The concrete block also would provide an excellent sound barrier between the auditoriums and the lobby.

The initial concept provided for three auditoriums on each side of a central service core. This core would contain the lobby, toilet facilities, food bar, and storage areas. The core would provide controlled circulation and access to the auditoriums, facilities, and required fire exits. Efficient arrangements for the 200 seats and fire code requirements governed the auditorium di-

mensions. The wall dimension also had to be compatible with the concrete block module. The upper floor level would contain the projection rooms, manager's office, employee toilet, and additional storage rooms. Stair location for this upper area was also governed by fire department and building code design criteria.

Initial Schematic Studies

After programming the basic physical requirements for this proposed project, we began schematic site development.

Stage I

The irregularly shaped site had a West to East cross fall averaging 22 feet from the lowest to the highest grade. See Figure 18.1. Complicating the site further was a 25-foot-wide utility easement located near the center of the site. We could not build any of the structure in this easement.

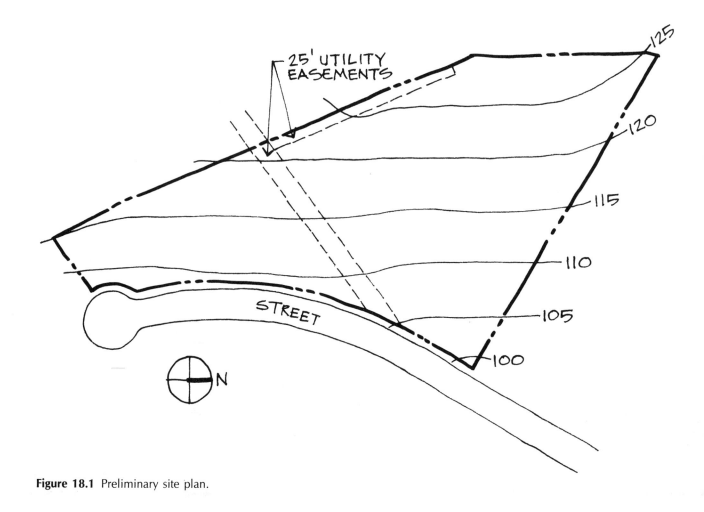

Figure 18.1 Preliminary site plan.

Stage II

In the intial schematic site study, shown in Figure 18.2, the structure is located north of the utility easement on the upper portion of the site. We thought this location would provide the most suitable parking layout for access to the theatre as well as a higher floor elevation for site drainage. The site entrance for automobiles is from the East property line only.

Stage III

After the schematic site development was completed, we designed the scaled preliminary first floor plan (Figure 18.3) and preliminary parking layouts. Client requirements determined the first level floor plan. Parking layouts and automobile circulation were designed to be compatible with the natural topography of the site; we paralleled the parking stalls and driveways with the existing grades. We also terraced the parking levels. This reduced the amount of rough and finish grading to be done. Stairs, as well as ramps for the handicapped, were provided at the front of the theatre.

Stage IV

From the scaled preliminary first floor plan, we made overlay studies of the second floor. Correct projector port locations for each auditorium, and required exit locations, determined the second floor design. Other spaces and their locations were more flexible. See Figure 18.4.

Stage V

Buildings in the area where this theatre is located are subject to the jurisdiction of an architectural review committee, with written criteria being given for exterior appearances and materials. One of these restrictions stated that the roof must be of mission tile with a minimum pitch of 4 in 12. Another requirement was that all roof-mounted mechanical equipment must be shielded from view. By providing the required sloping roof planes over the auditoriums and the rear and front lobby access, we created a well that would screen the roof-mounted heating and ventilating equipment.

For aesthetic reasons, we decided to soften the facade of the building by breaking up the long exterior blank walls at the rear of the auditoriums. We added a heavy timber arbor to provide shadows on the blank walls. See Figure 18.5A. The arbor stain and general design were chosen to be compatible with mission tile. To provide an acceptable finish, we covered the concrete block with a plaster finish. To enhance the exterior and further define the design elements, as well as to fulfill building department requirements, we added concrete columns in the colonnade. Instead of using three-dimensional drawings for presentation, a conceptual model was constructed defining the general massing of the building as well as major architectural features. This model is shown in Figure 18.5B.

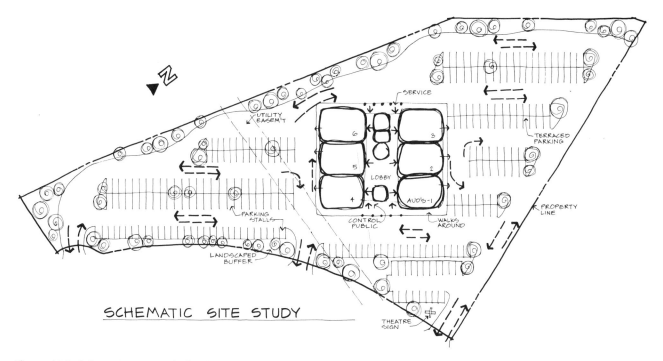

Figure 18.2 Schematic site study for theatre.

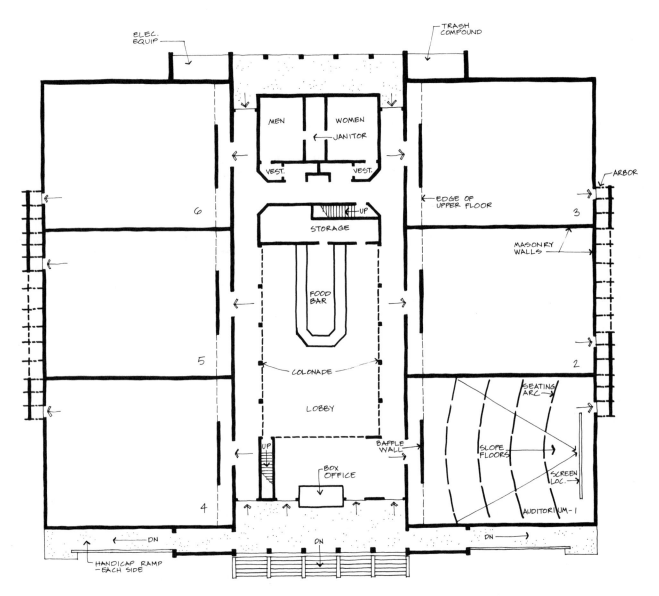

Figure 18.3 Preliminary ground floor plan.

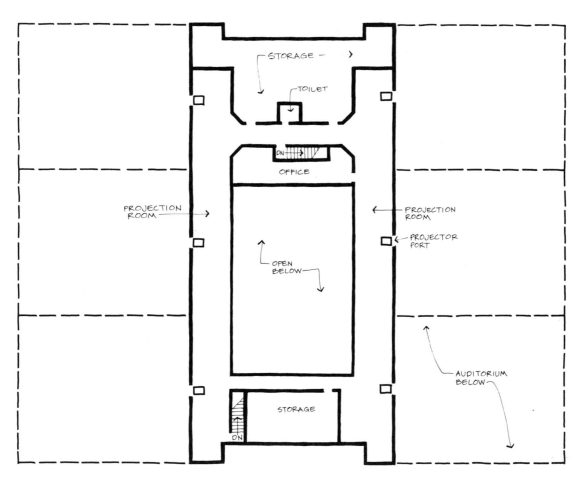

Figure 18.4 Preliminary upper floor plan.

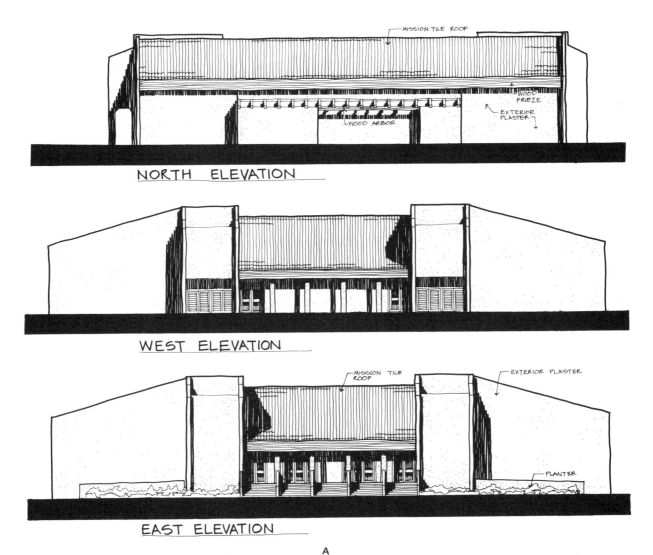

NORTH ELEVATION

WEST ELEVATION

EAST ELEVATION

A

Figure 18.5A Preliminary exterior elevations.

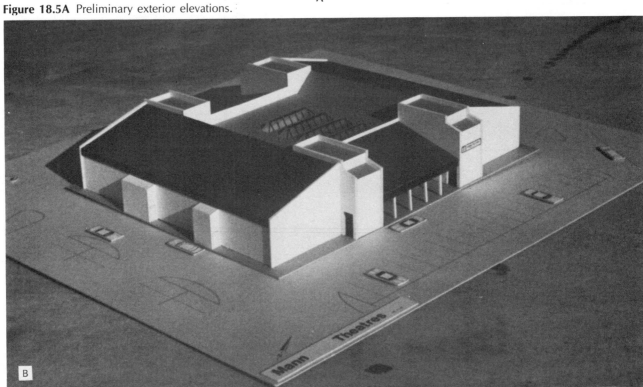

Figure 18.5B Conceptual model.

Site Plan

The primary purpose of the site plan was to locate the structure on the lot and indicate the proposed parking plan. Depending on its complexity, site plan may or may not be combined with the grading plan. For this project, the grading plan, the site plan, and the paving plan were done separately. Figure 18.6 is an aerial photo of the completed project.

Stage I

Our first step was to describe with lines the perimeter of the lot. See Figure 18.7. A formal description of the site is obtained from the client or civil engineer. The civil engineering survey shows and locates easements (right-of-access). In this case, the easement was a sewer easement, shown by dotted lines through the center and at the top of the lot.

The property contour is shown with a center-line type line to contrast it with the dotted lines of the easement. Property contours are shown with dotted lines or central-line type lines.

The center line of the road is shown here as a solid line, as are the road itself and the sidewalk. The circle at the left indicates a **cul-de-sac** (the end of the road with an area for turning around).

Stage II

Our main task at this stage was to locate the structure. See Figure 18.8. Location must always be done very carefully, using the preliminary site plan and the civil engineer's site plan. In this case, the easement through the center of the lot was a key factor in locating the structure.

Figure 18.6 Aerial photo of finished site. (William Boggs Aerial Photography. Reprinted with permission.)

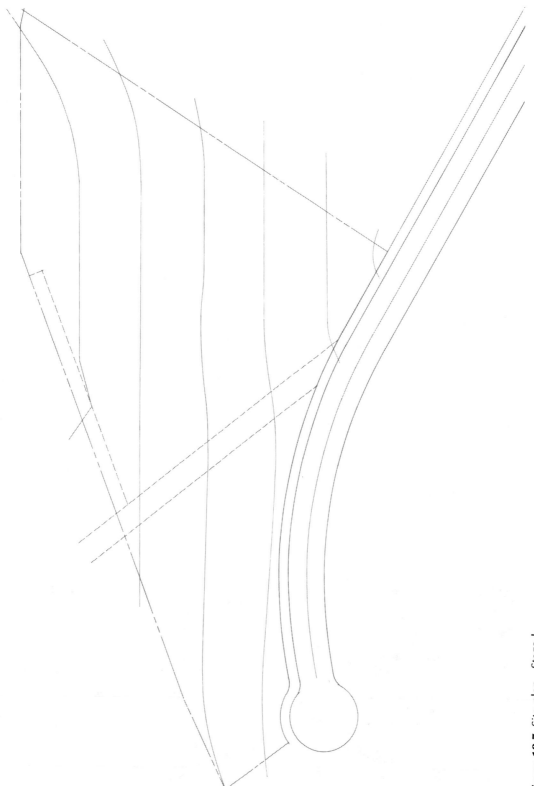

Figure 18.7 Site plan—Stage I.

530

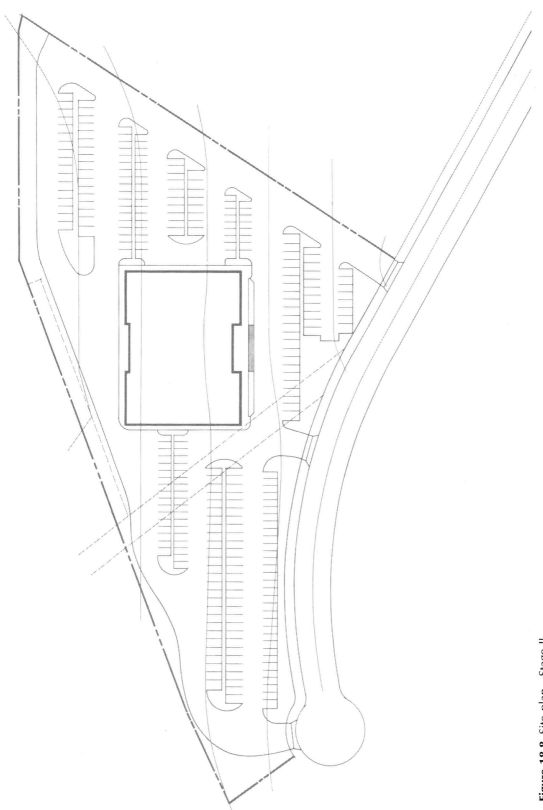

Figure 18.8 Site plan—Stage II.

The 400 parking stalls were next located. We needed to take into account such regulations as:

1. Turning radius of a standard car
2. Parking stall requirements
3. Permissible ratio of compact stalls to regular stalls
4. Aisles required between rows of parking
5. Dedicated green space requirement, if any
6. Ratio of parking spaces for persons with disabilities; their required distance to the point of entry, etc.

At this stage, also, the property line was darkened.

Stage III

Look carefully around the perimeter of the structure in Figure 18.9 and notice the dimension lines locating the building from the property lines.

Stage IV

Here, we added the property lines with their North orientations and respective lengths. See Figure 18.10. The dimensions that located this structure were added next.

Parking stalls and islands were dimensioned and located next. Notice again that the parking layout follows the contour lines. Streets were labeled, and the drawing titled. The scale and North arrow were added.

The shape of the site was complicated and we had many parking stalls to show, so we drew a separate partial grading plan. Figure 18.11A shows the overall site with a shaded area that is enlarged in Figure 18.11B. The letters "T.C." means "top of curb." The number on the top indicates the height (elevation) to the top, while the bottom number indicates the elevation to the bottom of the curb. These numbers are expressed in decimals; a difference of 0.5 is equal to 6 inches. By following the numbers around the curb, the direction of water flow can be determined. A 1% and a 2% slope are also shown periodically.

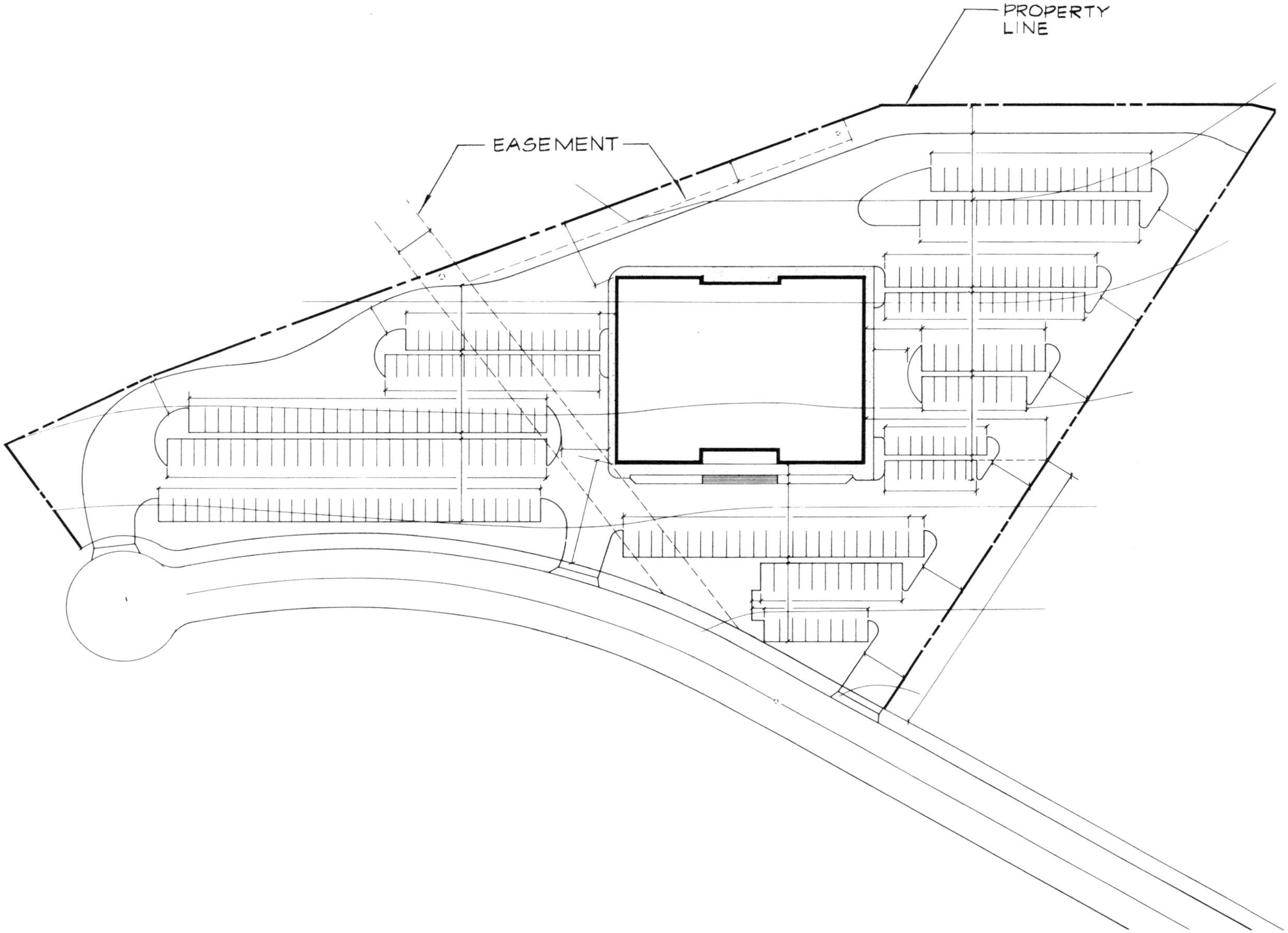

PROPERTY LINE

EASEMENT

Figure 18.9 Site plan—Stage III.

533

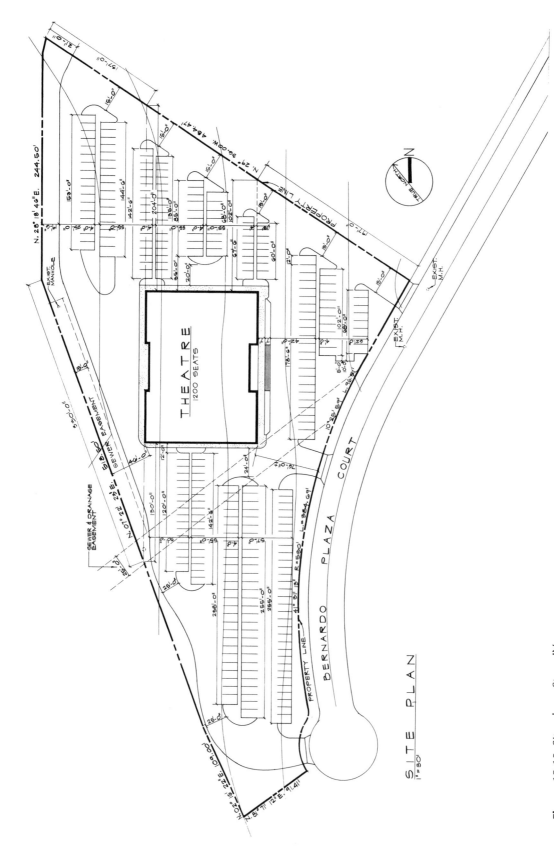

Figure 18.10 Site plan—Stage IV.

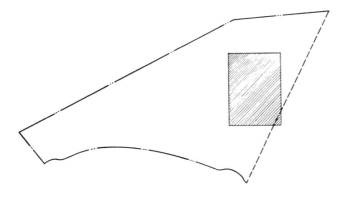

Figure 18.11A Portion of grading plan to be enlarged.

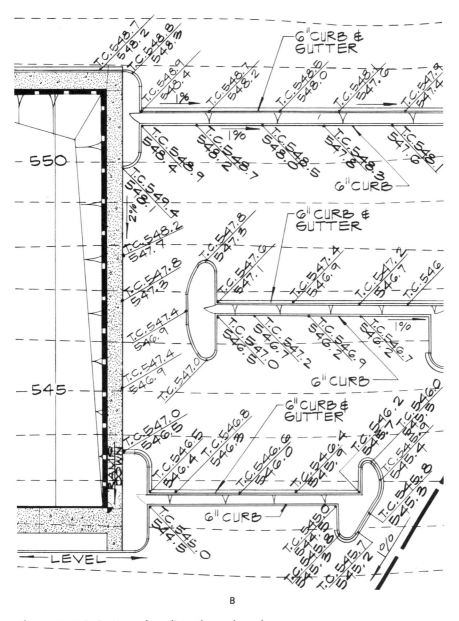

B

Figure 18.11B Portion of grading plan enlarged.

Foundation Plan

Stage I

The foundation plan was traced directly from the floor plan. See Figure 18.26. Sizes and location had to conform to the concrete block module.

To better understand the evolution of this plan, see Figures 18.12 and 18.13. Both the aerial photograph and the ground level view show how the property is graded. Stakes were used to guide the large earth-moving equipment, as you can see in Figure 18.14. Figures 18.15 and 18.16 show the chalk lines indicating the position of the wall columns, and Figure 18.17 shows trenched footings. A **back hoe** (trenching machine) was then used to dig the required trenches.

Pilasters (periodic widenings of a wall) act as columns to support members above. On interior walls, pilasters are seen from either room, while exterior pilasters can be seen only from the inside, so that the face of the exterior wall can remain flat. Pilaster sizes are obtained from the structural drawing; a few typical sizes are used. If you start a foundation drawing before you have these required sizes, you can still trace the walls and indicate the tentative location of the columns and pilasters with light cross lines to show the center.

Figure 18.18 shows the first stage in the preparation of the foundation plan. In this drawing, lines are dotted lines, but often, at this initial stage, the outline is drawn with light solid lines.

Four lines are needed to represent the walls of concrete block and the footing below the grade. At some locations, where the footing is continuous but the wall is

Figure 18.12 Graded site without structure. (William Boggs Aerial Photography. Reprinted with permission.)

Figure 18.13 Grading the property.

Figure 18.14 Stakes placed by surveyor.

Figure 18.15 Chalk lines for foundation.

Figure 18.16 Chalked lines ready for trenching. (William Boggs Aerial Photography. Reprinted with permission.)

not, there are only two lines. The squares drawn with dotted lines represent concrete pads for steel pipe columns.

The exit doors at the rear of each auditorium are interesting features of this project. Each exit was designed to be sheltered by a wall with a trellis above.

The rectangular areas adjacent to the easterly side are ramps for the handicapped. (Every feature of this theatre had to accommodate persons with disabilities. These features include restroom facilities, widths of openings and halls, and ramps for wheelchairs.)

The columns toward the center of the structure would hold up the upper floor. Figure 18.19 shows these columns and also the forms placed for the entry stairs adjacent to the ramps for the disabled. The columns were carefully aligned with the upper floor walls and first floor walls.

Figure 18.17 Trenched footings.

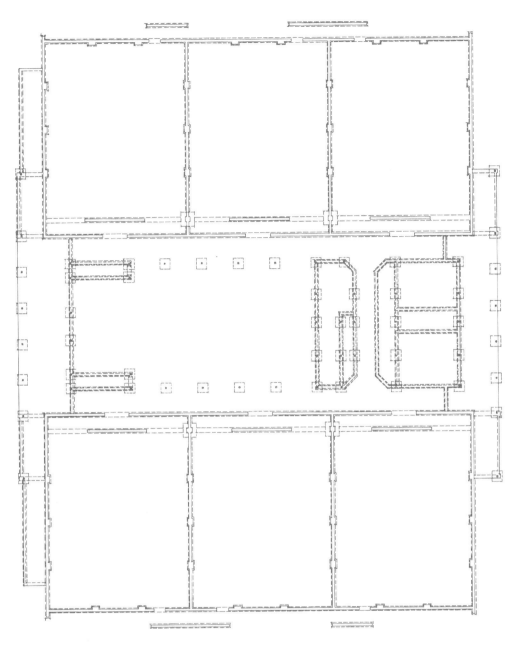

Figure 18.19 Columns to support upper floor and forms for the stairs adjacent to the handicap ramps.

Stage II

The inclusion of the stairs in Figure 18.20 clearly identifies the entry to the theatre. The two lines extending from each column with several perpendicular lines in them represent **brick pavers** (patterned brick on ground level).

The arc lines within one of the auditoriums represent the subtle changes of levels. This was done only once because the floors in all six auditoriums are the same.

All exterior and interior dimension lines were added next, taking care to ensure a proper block module.

The reference bubbles on the outside of the overall dimension lines are called, collectively, a matrix of the dimensional reference plane. This matrix is used to locate columns, walls, and structural members above (not seen in this drawing).

Stage III

Major section lines were added at this stage, as were detail reference bubbles. See Figure 18.21. Some of the section symbols break the overall dimension lines. This is not desirable but we had to do it because of space limitations.

At the top right auditorium (looking at the building from the side where the entry is) notice two reference bubbles piggy-backed. This indicates that two details of these columns are available elsewhere, one architectural and the other a structural detail. The section bubbles with a flag-like symbol on the opposite side indicate wall sections.

In the lobby, next to the columns, are hexagonal symbols. These are concrete pad symbols and will have numbers or letters in them corresponding with the chart introduced at the bottom right. Each concrete pad for the various columns varied enough to necessitate a chart rather than individual dimensions.

We finally added the material designation for the walls (the hatching lines within the wall lines).

Stage IV

Noting, referencing, and actual numerical values of dimensions were now added. See Figure 18.22. Noting included describing the floor material, such as the ceramic tile in the restrooms and brick pavers at the front of the theatre. We indicated slopes on the ramps for the disabled. We noted special widening instructions along the perimeter of the foundation wall as well as sizing of pilasters. At the center of the structure around the concession stand, a note reads "3" ⬚ × ³⁄₁₆" tube typ. unless noted otherwise." Many of the columns at the rear of the concession stand and around the restroom area have a diagonal line indicating a different size.

Numerical values were placed, each being checked to ensure that the overall dimensions fell within the block module. Some of the values are missing near the schedule at the bottom. These dimensions are picked up later.

All of the detail and section reference bubbles were noted and the axial reference planes (the numbers across the top and the letters along the right side) were finished.

Stage V

The dimensions overlooked in the previous stage were picked up here. See Figure 18.23. A set of dimensions describes the slope of the floor in the auditorium nearest the **column pad** schedule.

The hexagon-shaped symbols next to the column pads were now sized, using the column pad schedule. Size, depth, and reinforcing are now indicated. If this structure had had only a few pads, we would have dimensioned them at their location.

The center of the arc that established the slope of the auditoriums was located on the outside of the building. Notice the broken 29'–4" dimension line on Figure 18.23. Since the arcs were symmetrical, we used a center-line type line to designate the middle of the auditorium. From this point we placed a series of numbers on a dimension line with arrowheads on it. Each arrowhead points to a specific arc and each arc was dimensioned with a note indicating two measurements. The first gives the distance traveled versus the change in the height; the second gives a ratio. For example, the first note closest to the center of the building reads, "up 16.15" in 12'–11" and 1.25" per ft," meaning the vertical distance traveled. In 12'–11" means the horizontal distance the 16.15" vertical distance is measured in. In other words, for every horizontal foot traveled, there is 1.25" vertical distance achieved. This ratio is based on the seating arrangement, viewing requirements, and the most comfortable walking slope for the audience.

Since all the auditoriums were to be the same, only one dimension was necessary, with a note to that effect placed in the center. Section references were labeled and the main sheet title and scale were added. This was the final stage.

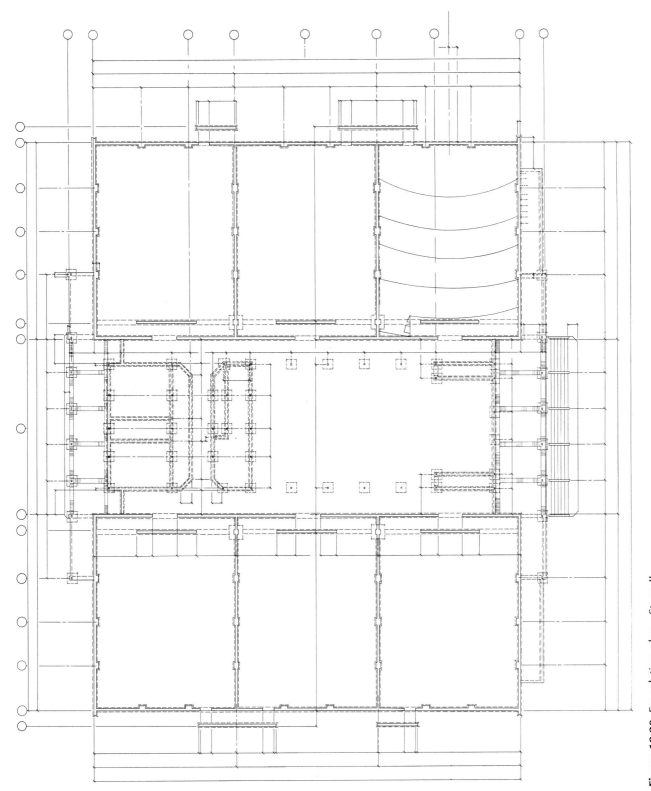

Figure 18.20 Foundation plan—Stage II.

541

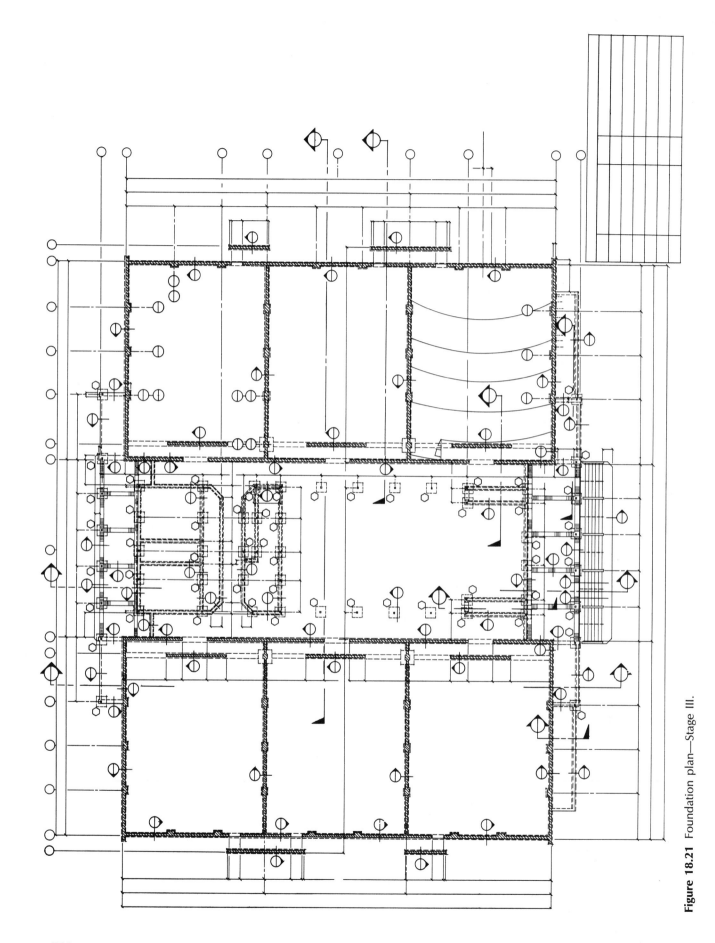

Figure 18.21 Foundation plan—Stage III.

542

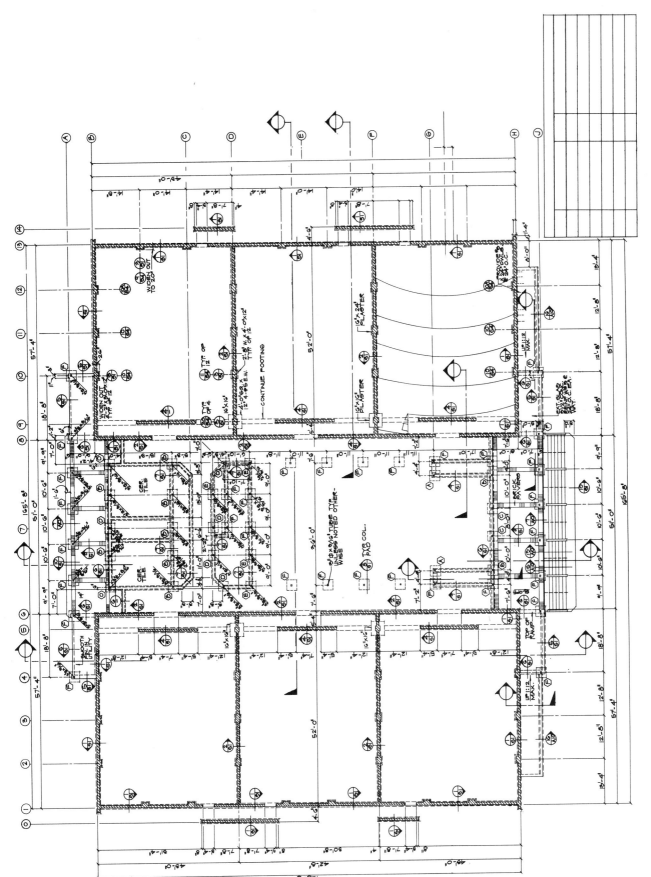

Figure 18.22 Foundation plan—Stage IV.

543

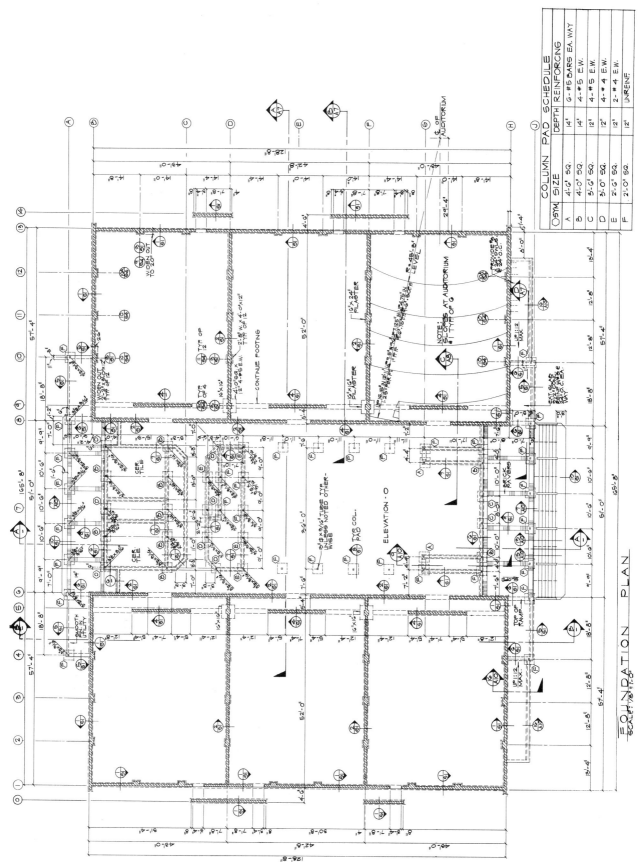

Figure 18.23 Foundation plan—Stage V.

Ground Floor Plan

Stage I

The floor plan is taken from the preliminary floor plan. Because this was the first drawing to be laid out, we had to take care to conform to the block module.

Clients may supply prototype plans based on their experience in a particular business. This particular client had determined that this would be a six-theatre structure with 200 seats in each theatre. Seating, the level for each row of seats, and fire restrictions were all design factors affecting the structure. We researched all of these factors prior to drawing the preliminary floor plan.

Compare the aerial photograph, Figure 18.24, with Figure 18.25 to see what was actually being constructed. Figures 18.24 and 18.25 show the construction sequence in relationship to the floor plan found on Figure 18.26.

In Figure 18.26, the columns toward the center of the theatre support the upper floor. (The upper floor accommodates the projectors and allows projectionists to move from one projector to another.) Near the rear of the building are the restrooms and snack bar storage. The two partial rectangles near the front of the theatre are stairwells.

Stage II

At the bottom of the left and right sides of the plan, we added a planter and a ramp for disabled people. See Figure 18.27. Stairs were added throughout the plan, and we added a set of dotted lines in each auditorium to represent the motion picture screens. The size of the screen was determined by the seating capacity and client needs. Dividing walls were drawn within the stairs at the front. Notice at the front and rear of the building the brick pavers as described in the foundation plan. These pavers were drawn with textured concrete within them.

At the center of the structure is the concession stand. The textured area represents a tile floor and the blank space, the counter. We added toilet partitions and lavatories to the restrooms, leaving larger stalls for persons with disabilities. Toilets can be added here or later.

At the center of each restroom entry, the small area for telephones also accommodates handicapped people. The small circles with a darkened cross indicate fire extinguishers. We added fire sprinkler symbols in the trash area in the rear of the building. Line quality becomes important here to differentiate between walls, floor patterns, and fixtures.

Stage III

Interior and exterior dimension lines were now added. See Figure 18.28. These dimensions *must* always be double-checked with the foundation plan to insure proper alignment of the walls with the foundation. As the floor plan was dimensioned first, the concrete block module was followed.

The axial reference plane bubbles across the top and to the right correspond with walls, columns, and any structural members above, and form the reference plane matrix. We also indicated door swings.

Stage IV

All of the reference bubbles were now located. See Figure 18.29. Full architectural section references, wall sections, door reference bubbles, and interior elevation reference symbols were included. Each room would later receive a number as well as a title, so we drew in underlines for the names and rectangular boxes for the numbers.

At the entry, we drew plants in the planters to clearly differentiate the planter areas from the ramps. The planters and plants were later included in the elevation (Figure 18.49) for clarity and consistency.

The material designation for the walls, indicated by hatching lines in the wall lines, was drafted next.

Stage V

Numerical values for the dimension lines were now included. See Figure 18.30. Each dimension had to be checked with the foundation plan. Accuracy at this stage is critical. Compare the radial dimension line added in Auditorium #2 with Auditorium #1 on the foundation plan (Figure 18.23).

We noted typical items such as pilaster sizes and the location of the screens, and unique items such as the location of fire extinguishers. Area titles and room titles were the next items to be noted.

We labeled the reference plane bubbles next. The stair notations refer to the finish schedule in the same way that the door letters refer to the door schedule. Finally, the drawing title, scale, and North arrow were added.

Figure 18.24 Aerial view of completed wall. (William Boggs Aerial Photography. Reprinted with permission.)

Figure 18.25 View of entry, lobby, and back of theatres.

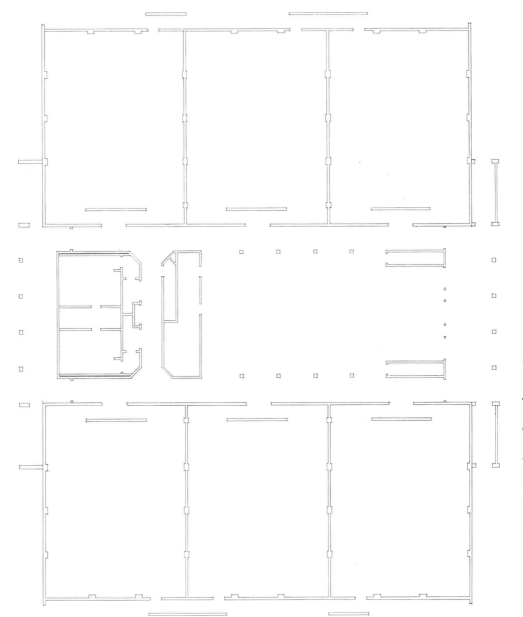

Figure 18.26 Ground floor plan—Stage I.

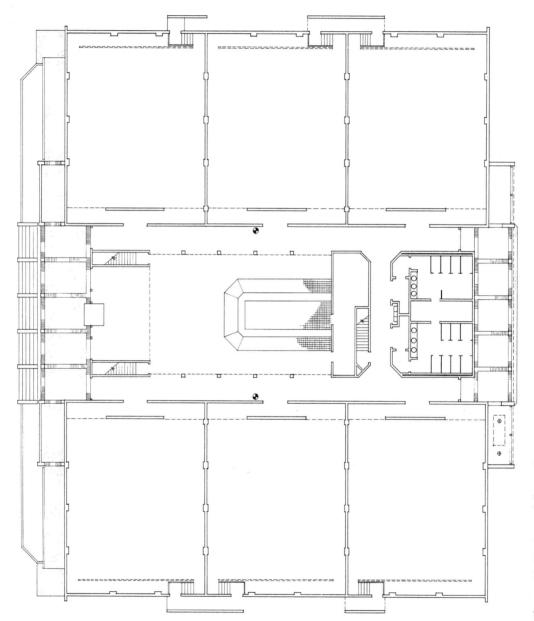

Figure 18.27 Ground floor plan—Stage II.

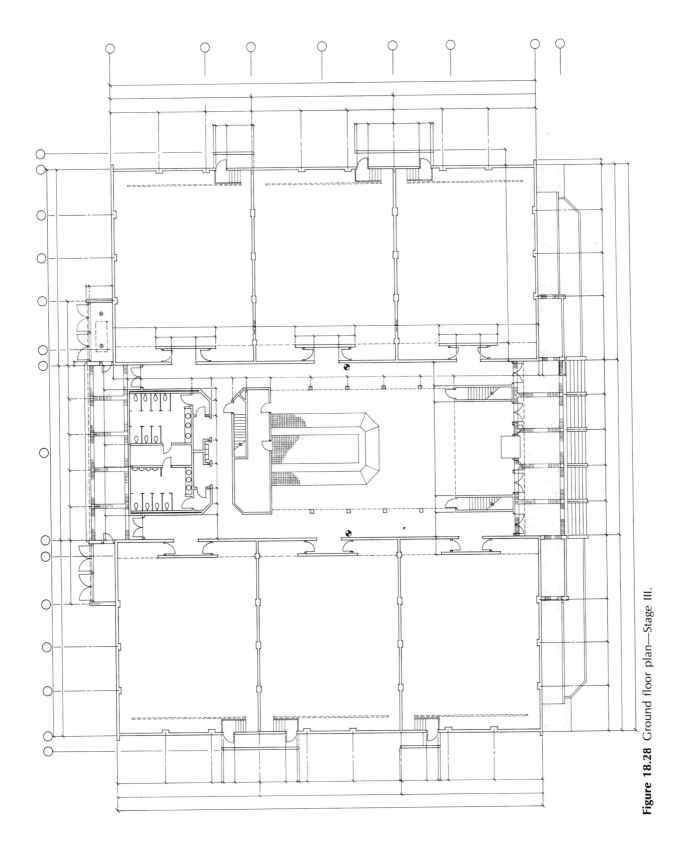

Figure 18.28 Ground floor plan—Stage III.

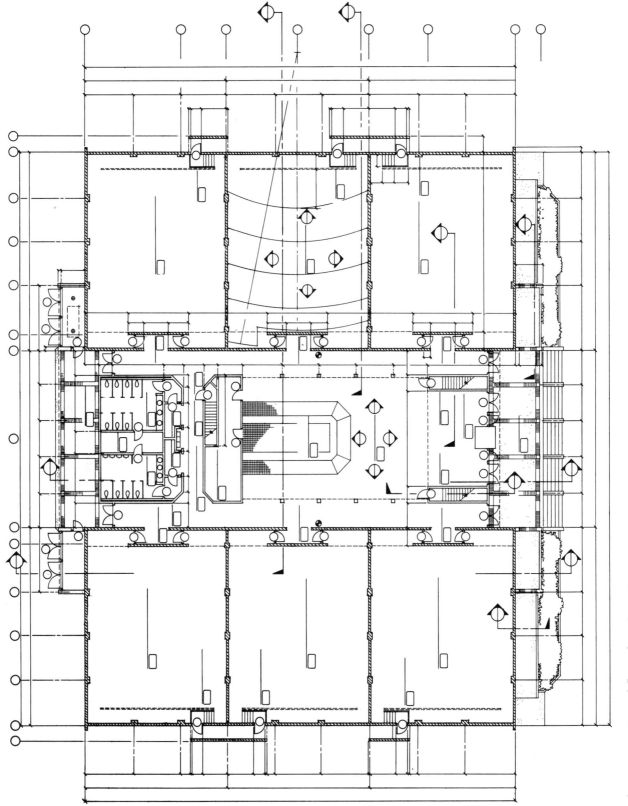

Figure 18.29 Ground floor plan—Stage IV.

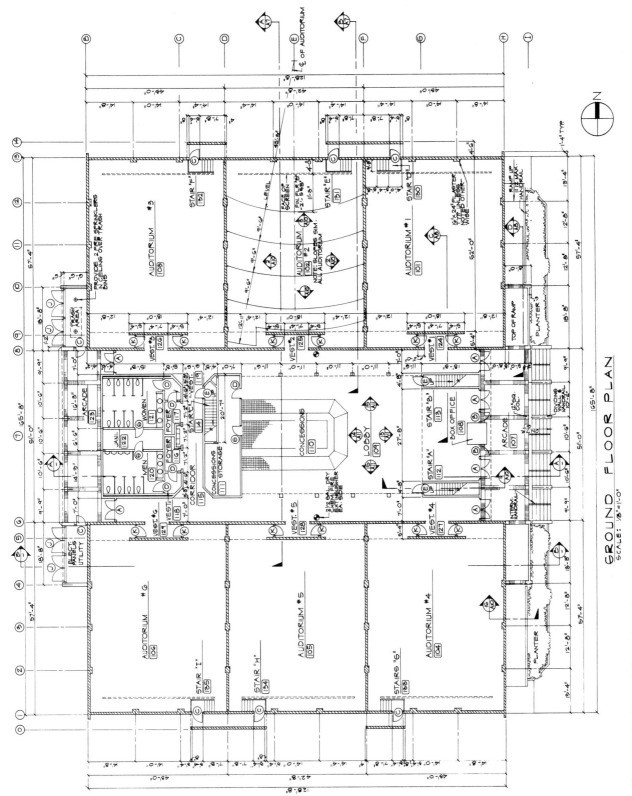

Figure 18.30 Ground floor plan—Stage V.

551

Upper Floor Plan

Stage I

We included the six auditoriums in the upper floor plan (see Figure 18.31) because the upper portions of the auditoriums were adjacent to the upper floor. The center of the structure is the lobby, which extends to the roof.

We located the projection windows according to their required angle. Figure 18.32 shows the interior of the structure. Note the projection windows and the connectors below to attach the upper floor. We took care to align the walls of the upper floor with the walls below.

Another view of this relationship is seen in the structural sections (for instance, in Section B-B in Figure 18.53).

Stage II

This stage (Figure 18.33) shows the stairs, restroom facilities, two fire extinguishers (one circle on each side) and, most important, the projectors and the space they occupy. A rectangle with a line through it next to a circle was the symbol we selected to represent the projectors.

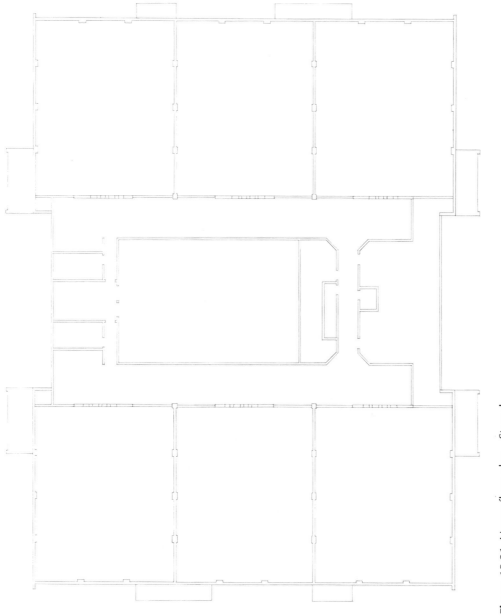

Figure 18.31 Upper floor plan—Stage I.

Figure 18.32 View looking toward lobby.

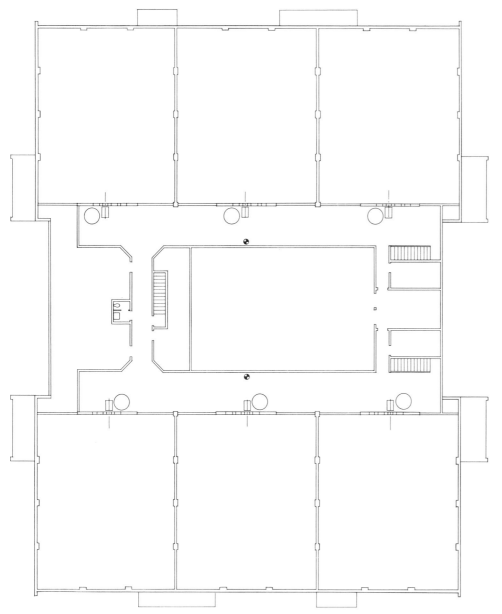

Figure 18.33 Upper floor plan—Stage II.

Stage III

The upper floor plan affects only the central part of the building, but the dimensions shown on it relate to the overall structure. So our first step was to add the necessary dimension line. See Figure 18.34.

The foundation plan and the first floor plan were consulted to maintain consistency in dimensioning. This correspondence would be checked again when numerical values were added to the drawing. Finally, we drafted the material designation for the concrete block and located the door symbols.

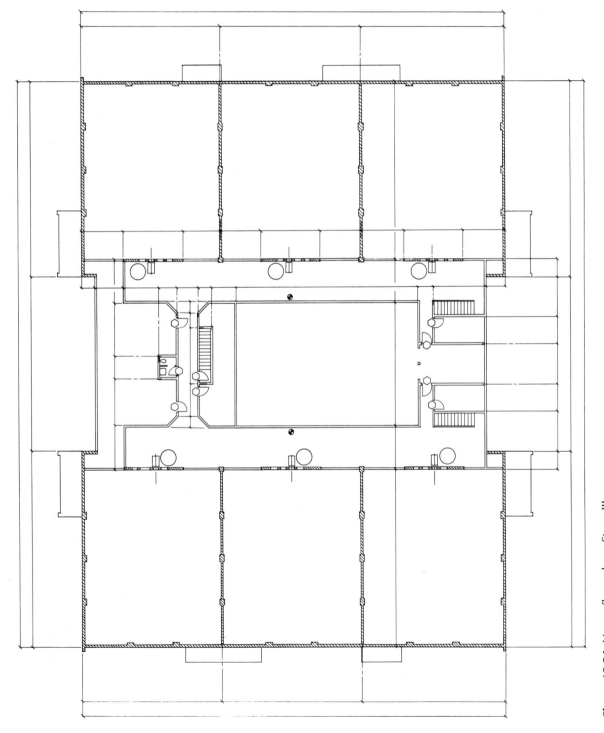

Figure 18.34 Upper floor plan—Stage III.

Stage IV

The main difference between this stage and the previous one is the addition of most of the dimension numbers. See Figure 18.35. The dimensions had to be checked against the floor plan of the floor below, and both had to be checked to ensure correct concrete block module dimensions.

Stage V

In this final stage, Figure 18.36, interior elevation reference bubbles were added, together with all necessary lettering. Some dimensions that were missing in Figure 18.35 now appear.

Doors and windows were checked with the schedule and filled in. Stair A and Stair B do not indicate the size

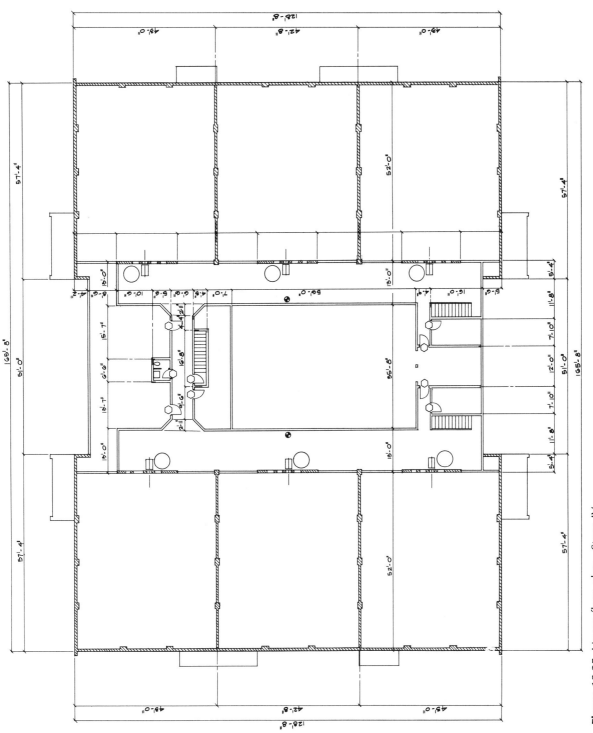

Figure 18.35 Upper floor plan—Stage IV.

or number of treads and risers. Details or sections provide their size, shape, and proportion. Look at the first floor plan (Figure 18.30) at the stair area and note the cutting plane line for a detail section.

The rooms in Figure 18.36 are numbered with three digits beginning with a "2", for the floor reference. The auditoriums were previously numbered on the first floor plan; the upper floor plan shows the upper portion of the auditoriums (without room numbers).

The central portion of the plan is open to the area below as indicated. Using this scale, it was difficult to show the small toilet at the rear. Therefore, we made an enlarged floor plan and elevation of Room 208 on the partial floor plan and the interior elevation sheet.

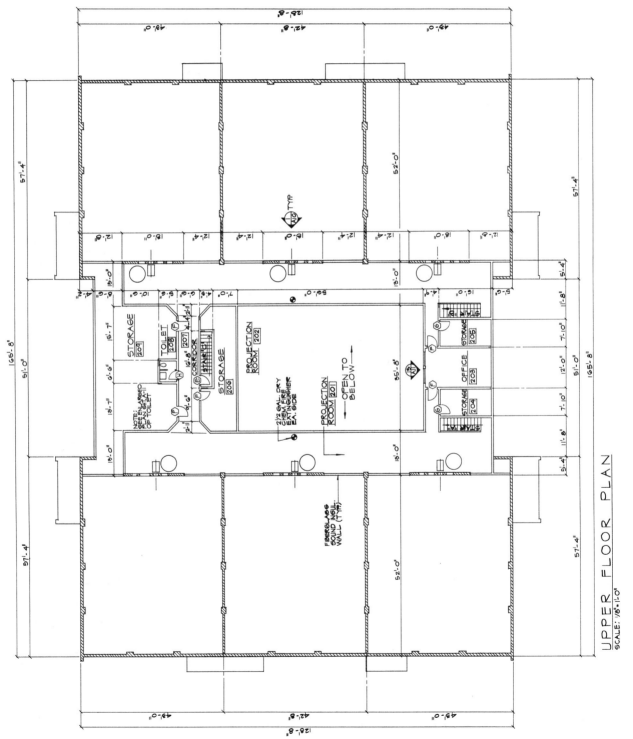

Figure 18.36 Upper floor plan—Stage V.

Partial Floor Plan and Interior Elevations

Stage I

The partial floor plan shown in Figure 18.37 was drawn at a larger scale than the other plans. It includes the concession areas and restrooms. Only a few interior elevations are drafted here.

Here, the partial floor plan is drawn twice the size of the first floor plan. We took the measurements from the first floor plan. At this scale, we could also show the double wall for the plumbing. (See the wall with toilets.)

The four rectangles at the bottom of the drawing represent columns. Two more columns appear to be located next to the walls but are actually inside the walls. They were included for visual continuity and have no structural implications.

The left half of the drawing was blocked out to receive the interior elevations, with one exception: the floor plan of the toilet on the upper floor level located slightly left of center on the drawing. The rectangle to the right of the upper floor toilet would become the interior elevation for that toilet, while the long rectangle at the bottom would become the interior elevation of the entry to the restrooms and telephone area.

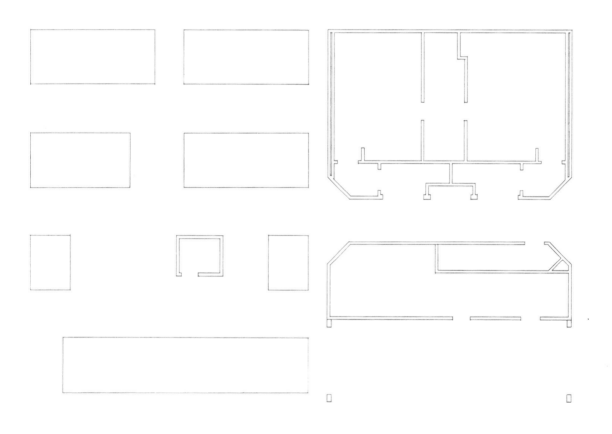

Figure 18.37 Partial floor plan and interior elevations—Stage I.

Stage II

The partial floor plan now shows the plumbing fixtures and the floor material in the restrooms. See Figure 18.38. The rectangles at the center near the entry to the restrooms are drinking fountains. Across the hall are the stairs to the upper level.

The wall material was now added to the interior elevations. Various fixtures such as urinals, paper towel dispensers, grab bars for the disabled, and drinking fountains were also added.

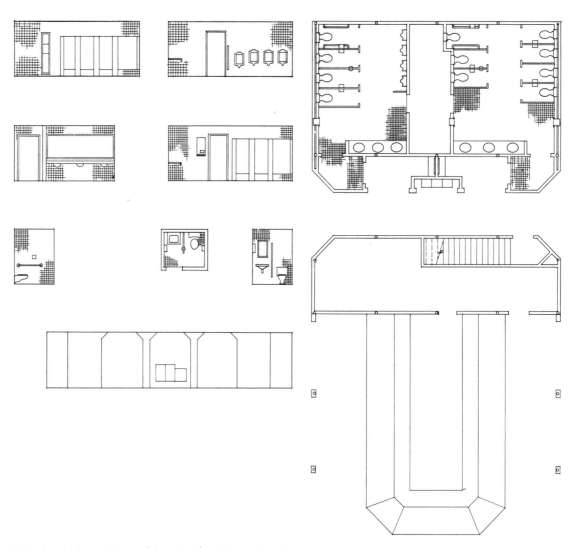

Figure 18.38 Partial floor plan and interior elevations—Stage II.

Stage III

All of the necessary dimension lines not included on the ground floor plan were not located on this sheet (see Figure 18.39), as well as some of the critical dimensions on the interior elevations. Door swings were shown by dotted lines. We added the designation of floor material in the concession area.

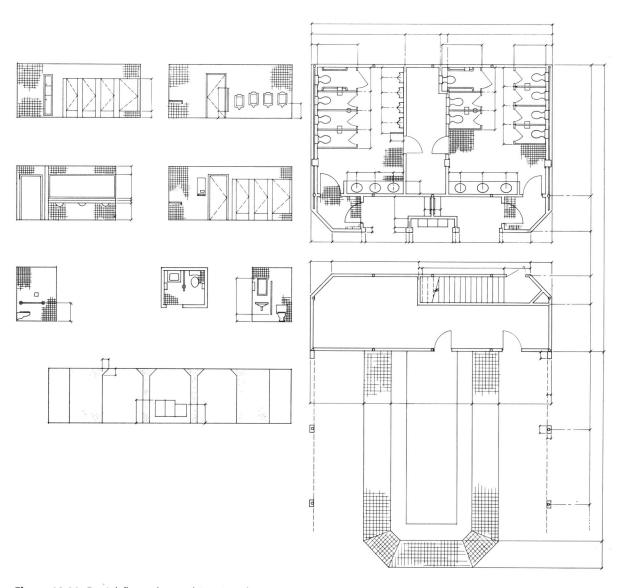

Figure 18.39 Partial floor plan and interior elevations—Stage III.

Stage IV

We established the numerical values for the dimensions shown in Figure 18.40 by checking the upper floor plan, foundation plan, and first floor plan. The dimension to the right side of the concession counter ends in a series of dots, indicating that the structure continues; break lines were not used.

The reference bubbles with arrows on them refer to the interior elevations. Only a few typical examples are shown here; in reality, there should be an interior elevation for every symbol shown.

Among the interior elevations, there is a plan and interior elevation for the upper floor toilet. This is unusual but the available paper space determined place-

ment. Pay attention to the structural columns and the double stud wall behind the water closet designed for the plumbing.

Next, dimensions of the heights of the interior elevations were added. Various typical items such as mirrors were located and given sizes. Handicap requirements were again checked and items such as grab bars were properly located.

Material indications for walls and floors were called out. This was done broadly (generically) because the written specifications would be used for a more definitive explanation. Last, additional notes, main titles, and scale were added.

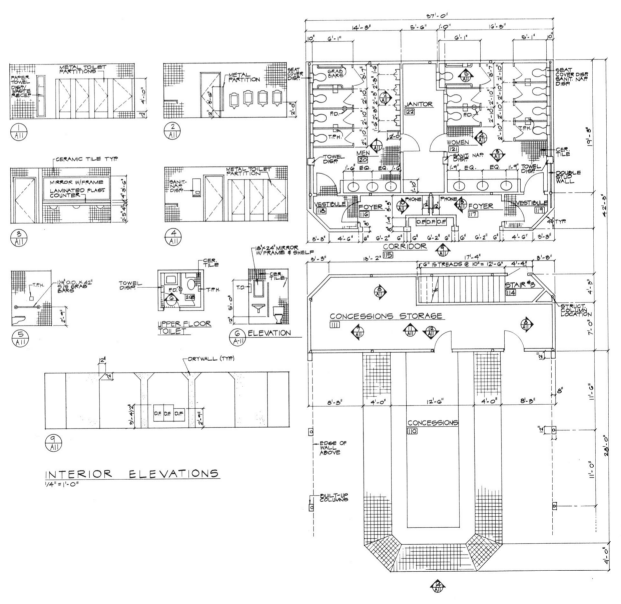

Figure 18.40 Partial floor plan and interior elevations—Stage IV.

Exterior Elevations

Elevations are developed from scratch, and are not traced from any other drawings unless extremely accurate preliminary drawings have been prepared. In most sets of drawings, the elevations are among the last to be completed because they are dependent on the floor plan, sections, roof plan, and so on. To better see how exterior elevations evolve, first read the chapter on building sections (Chapter 10). Figures 18.41 and 18.42 show how the exterior of the project actually appears as the construction proceeds, and Figures 18.43 and 18.44 show front and rear views of the construction when completed.

Figure 18.41 Front of theatre. (William Boggs Aerial Photography. Reprinted with permission.)

Figure 18.42 Front of theatre showing ramp for the disabled. (William Boggs Aerial Photography. Reprinted with permission.)

Figure 18.43 Front view of finished structure. (Photography: Kent Oppenheimer.)

Figure 18.44 Rear view of finished structure.

Stage I

We decided to draft only three exterior elevations rather than the normal four because the structure is symmetrical and the North and South elevations are similar. The horizontal lines in Figure 18.45 represent several items; the two floor levels, the top of the parapet, the tops of the beams, and the top of the beam at the canopy over the door. (The sloped, dotted line on the bottom elevation is the angle of the ramp for persons with disabilities.)

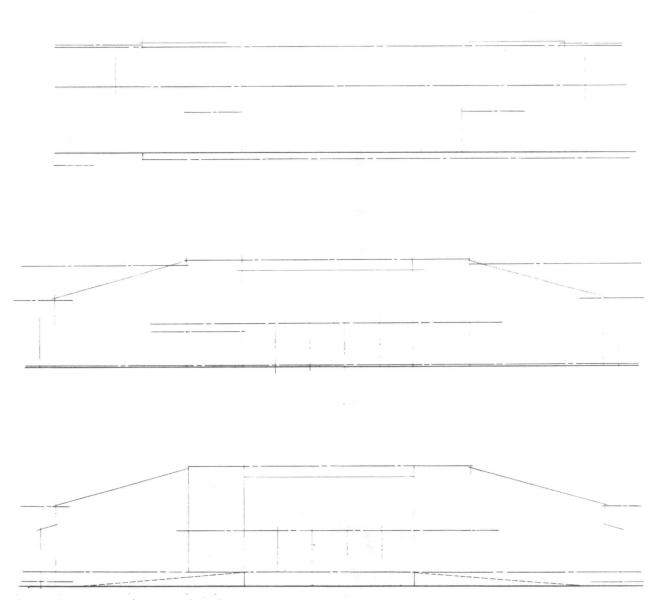

Figure 18.45 Exterior elevations—Stage I.

Stage II

The small, light vertical lines shown in Figure 18.46 locate the various beams and columns. These locations were taken from the reference bubbles on the floor plan. The complete structure would later be referenced by the column locations.

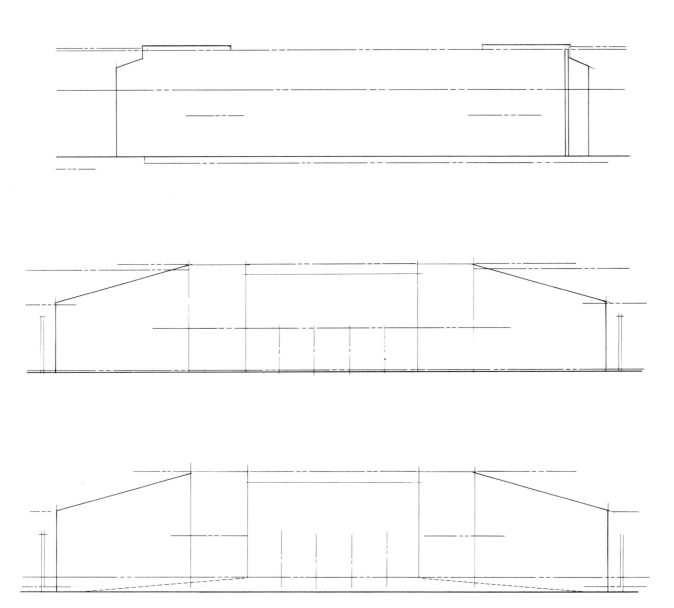

Figure 18.46 Exterior elevations—Stage II.

Stage III

Where Stage II indicated the vertical heights, Stage III established the outline of the building itself. See Figure 18.47. Column locations, wall thicknesses, independent walls at the exit were all established at this point. These measurements were obtained from the various plans, such as the floor plan, foundation plan, and the architectural sections. Each of these drawings used a dimensional system. This was helpful in the development of this structure because it gave specific points of reference. Heights, width, and depth of the structure were all referenced to this system.

For orientation purposes, the top elevation is the North elevation; the center is the West elevation; and the bottom is the East elevation and entry to the theatre. The two rectangular shapes toward the center of the North elevation repesent the walls protecting the patrons at the exit.

The top center line on the West elevation is a point of reference. It is the top of the parapet wall extending above the roof plan. The series of vertical lines toward the center represent columns and the two horizontal lines above the columns represent the fascia.

The ramp on either side of the entry is indicated wih dotted lines. See the East elevation, Figure 18.47. At the

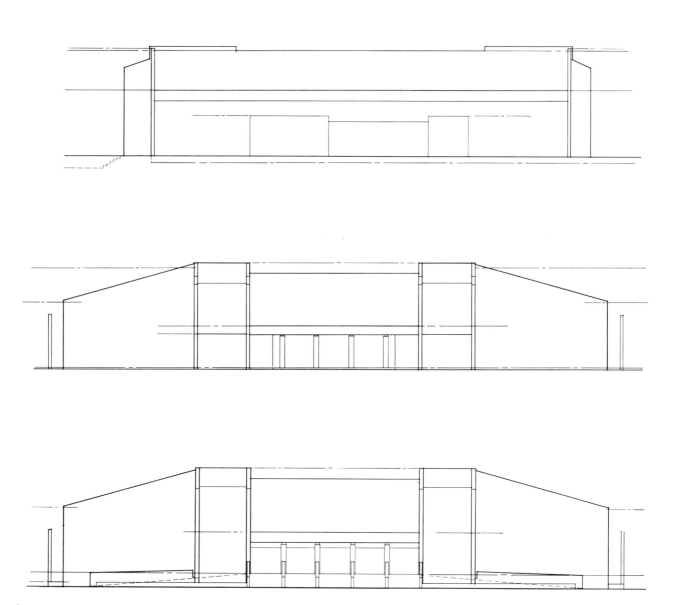

Figure 18.47 Exterior elevations—Stage III.

center are columns with handrails drawn in front of them. Stairs would be added later.

Stage IV

Now that we had a basic configuration we could describe some of the smaller shapes. See Figure 18.48. We added the arbor, or shaded walk, to the North elevation. Refer back to Figure 18.46. The line above the wood arbor is the wood frieze (band of wood). The opening is located at the left.

To the West elevation, we added rear doors, the doors for the storage area, and the arbor at each end. We positioned steps and doors on the East elevation.

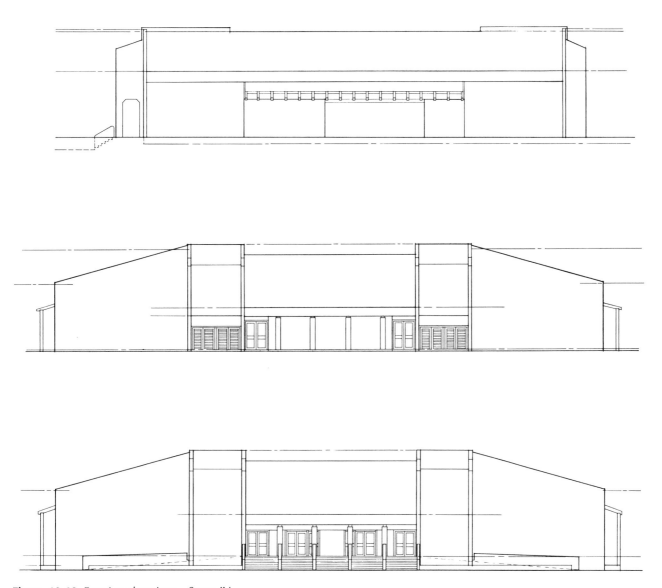

Figure 18.48 Exterior elevations—Stage IV.

Stage V

This was the final stage and included a multitude of items. See Figure 18.49.

Texture. Roof material was designated. We also stippled the cement plaster that was to cover the concrete masonry units. We added plants in the planter on the East elevation to be consistent with the plants we showed on the floor plan.

Dimensions. Dimensions of the two floor levels were added. Some dimensions were referenced to the building sections (Figure 18.53) for clarity.

Notes. The surface material was called out. We also added title and scale.

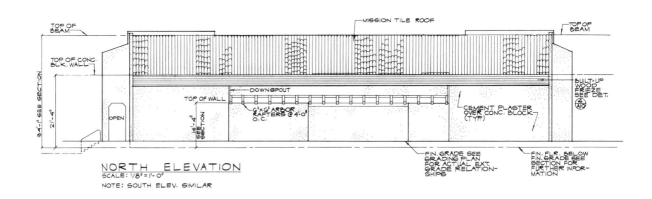

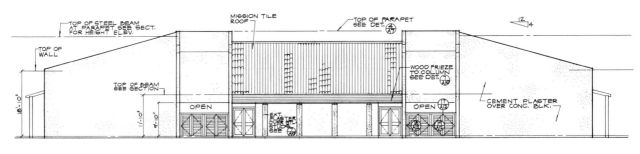

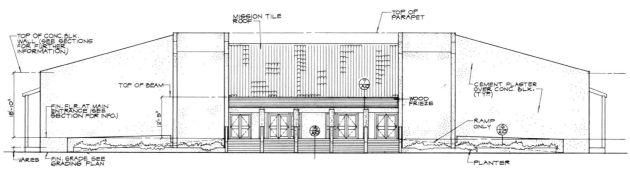

Figure 18.49 Exterior elevations—Stage V.

Building Sections

Stage I

The drawings developed in Figures 18.50 through 18.53 are architectural building sections, not structural sections. This sheet is a classic example of how the available drawing area and number of sections to be drawn dictate the approach.

For example, the top section in Figure 18.50 has six break lines representing the removal of three areas. At this point, we could have changed scales or kept the same scale while eliminating the least important or the most redundant area. (We use the term redundant to mean an area that remains the same for long lengths.) We could either have two areas broken out and lose one major steel girder (see Figure 18.53) or have three areas broken out and save the girder. Because the location of the beams showed so much about heights and the structural assembly method, we decided to have three areas broken away and save the beam.

Another approach we could have taken would have been to use match lines and then slice the structure into two pieces, aligning one above the other. Because of the size of the structure, this would have left a lot of unused space on one side of the sheet and would have required our adding another sheet for the other section. This additional sheet would also have had extra space on it.

We approached the lower section by using a break line and eliminating a large portion of the theatre. The structure is symmetrical and the auditorium to the right would have been duplicated on the left. There would be no break in the center portion of the theatre (the lobby) or the auditorium on the right.

First, we located all of the steel beams as well as their corresponding foundation below. Using the framing and foundation plans together with structural details helped greatly in developing this drawing.

Since the floor of the auditorium sloped, we used two floor levels to describe the structure: Level "A" and Level "B." Level "A" is the top of the auditorium slope and "B" the bottom.

The vertical lines above some of the beams in Figure 18.50 would have reference bubbles added to them in the next stage, so they could be keyed to other drawings.

Stage II

We added reference bubbles for the beams at this stage (Figure 18.51), but only above continuous beams, so some beams on the upper section and many on the lower sections have no reference bubbles.

We also studied available details at this time. When details are not available, freehand details should be sketched to solve many of the intersections of wall and floors or roofs. Based on this information, we drafted the interior walls and upper floor.

Stage III

As drawings become more complicated, the floor plan should always be reviewed to clarify the various parts of the section.

The sections now began to show the wall material designations, the soil under the foundation, the corrugated steel decking at the upper floor level, and the mission tile roof. See Figure 18.52. The steel decking under the mission tile is in side view in the lower section, so the corrugation does not show. The view of the floor decking in the upper section is an end view and shows the corrugation.

The suspended ceiling at various locations was now indicated. Because of the intended use of the structure and the materials chosen, we used many fireproofing techniques. For example, many of the steel beams have a freehand line drawn around them. These represent a sprayed-on fire protection material. A specific description of this spray material would be included later in the specifications.

Stage IV

At this stage, we completed the noting and dimensioning. See Figure 18.53.

Dimensioning. First we had to keep the dimensions consistent with the other drawings. Each letter of the matrix and each number had to align with the proper column, beam, or footing pad. After checking, they were vertically located. The term "T.B." means "top of beam." These beams were dimensioned by notation and were measured from one of the two floor levels. The abbreviation "T.S.G." means tapered steel girder.

Dimension lines were now added to the floors and ceilings, and the top of walls. Because the space between the upper floor and the ceiling below it had been determined by details, it too was included.

Reference. We drew many reference bubbles showing locations of details or special wall sections. These were carefully selected.

Noting. Most of the noting explained a material or a method of erection or the dimensions themselves. The section titles, scales, and room names were added. There is also a special note about fire protection below the title "Section A-A."

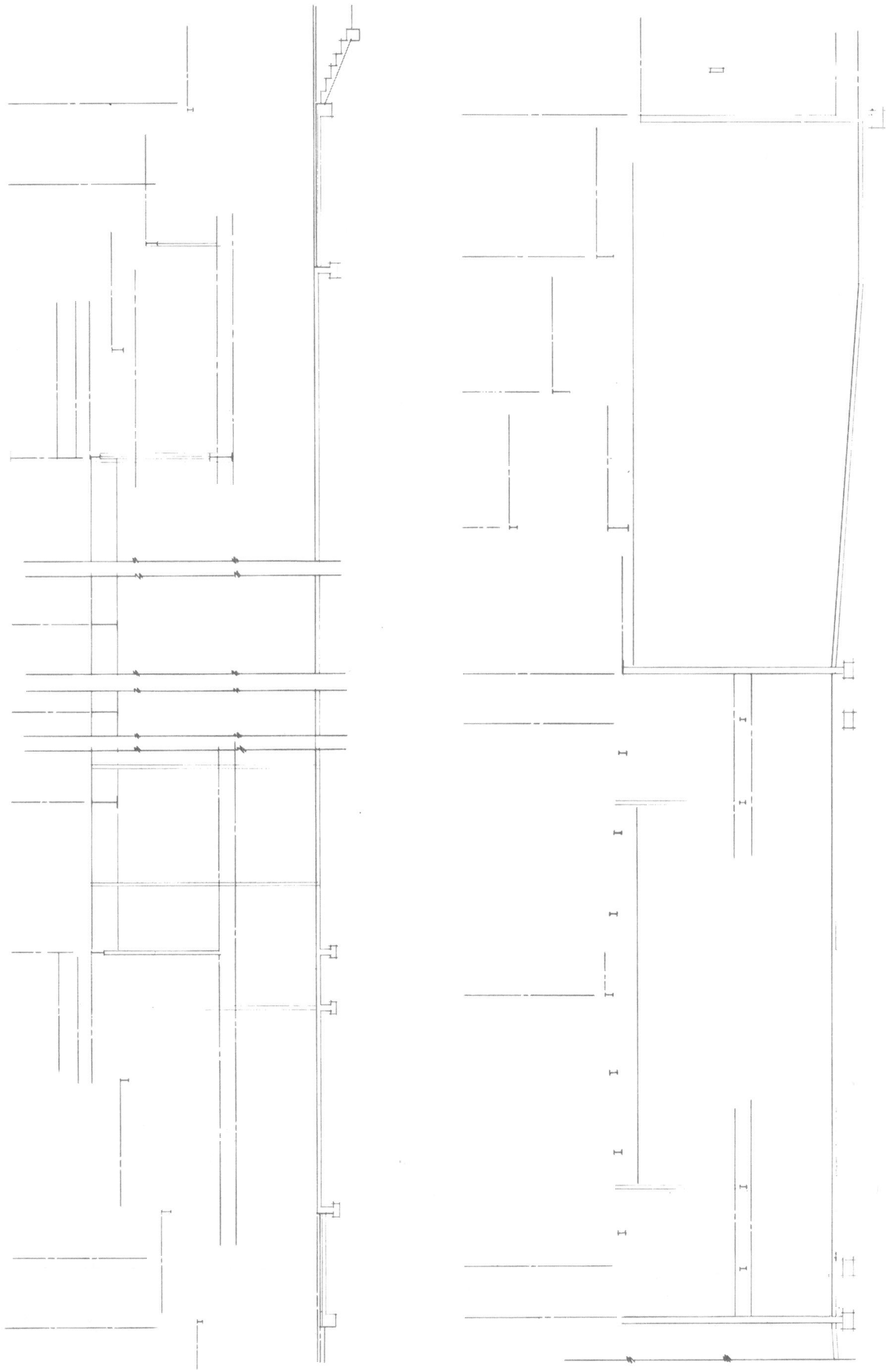

Figure 18.50 Building sections—Stage I.

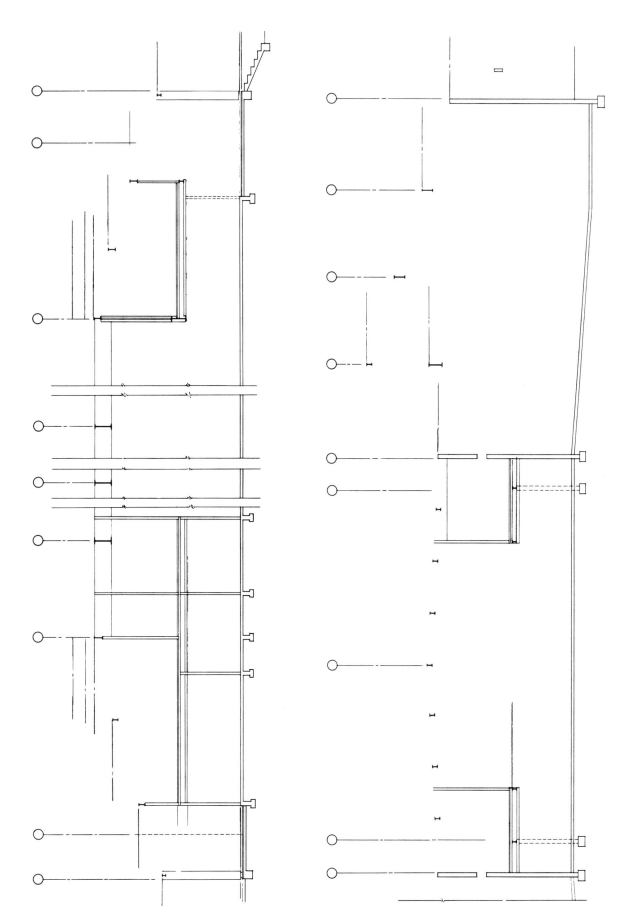

Figure 18.51 Building sections—Stage II.

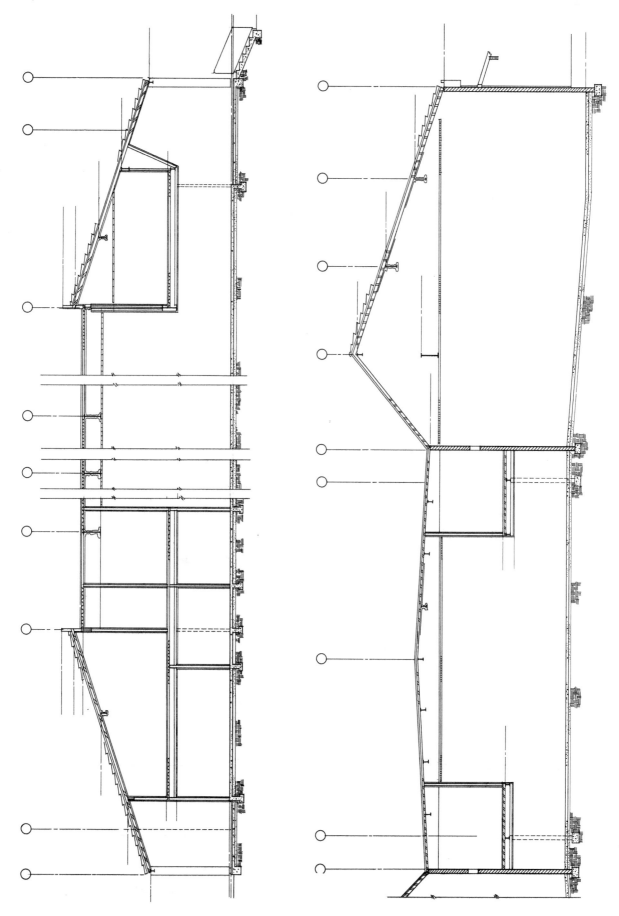

Figure 18.52 Building sections—Stage III.

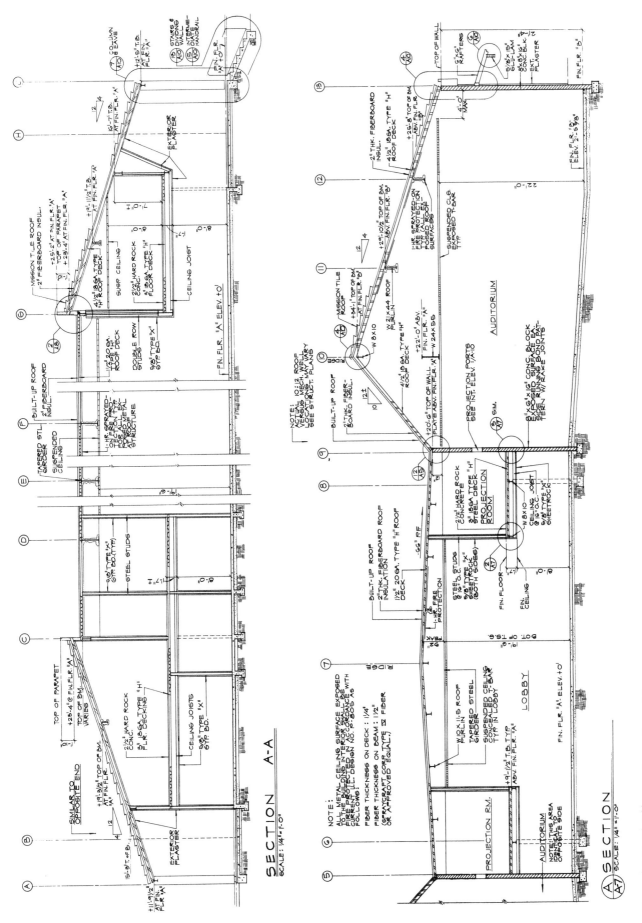

Figure 18.53 Building sections—Stage IV.

Roof Plan

Review the first floor plan, the upper floor plan, the sections, and the preliminary elevations before starting to study this roof plan.

Stage I

First we traced the roof plan from the first floor plan. See Figure 18.54. The dotted lines located the major interior walls. Note that the design called for the exterior walls to extend above and beyond the tops of the roof.

The five major divisions of the roof are the top, bottom, left, right, and center. The top, bottom, left, and right portions all slope away from the structure. The center portion slopes in two directions with a ridge at the center. Because the four major portions around the center rose higher than the center, roof drains were required. See Figure 18.55. These drains and the surrounding areas will be mentioned later.

The exterior walls on Figure 18.54 were drawn slightly wider than the interior walls because they represented exterior plaster over concrete block. Note the configuration of the arbor over the exterior exits from each auditorium.

Stage II

To better understand this roof, as shown in Figure 18.56, look at the sketch of its central portion in Figure 18.55. The line at the very center is the ridge. This ridge produces a gable type roof at the central portions. The surrounding portions are higher and so the slope of this gable roof needs to be drained at its edges. Roof drains, commonly called scuppers, were added at strategic points.

As you can see by comparing the sketch with the plan, portions of the low point of the gable roof remained flat to accept air-conditioning equipment. Other portions sloped down from the vertical plane like a shed roof. Sheet metal saddles, called crickets, were positioned to control the flow of water on the roof and to direct it toward the roof drains. The small circles near the roof drains represent the overflow drains provided in case the regular scuppers clog.

On two sides of the structure, we added reference bubbles to correspond with those on the plans and sections. Skylights (still visible in Figure 18.61) were not shown because they were deleted earlier at the request of the client.

Stage III

At this stage, the reference bubbles were numbered and lettered. See Figure 18.57. Numerical values for all the dimension lines were added next. The slope of the roofs were designated by arrows. Arrows at the edges of the roof show the slope of the gutters toward the downspout.

All dimensions were verified with the building section in this chapter, and the engineering drawings were checked for correct column and beam locations. Finally, detail reference bubbles were drawn. The details were selected at an earlier stage.

Stage IV

The final roof construction, described by the plan in Figure 18.58, actually differs from the drawing in Figure 18.57. This happens quite often as better solutions, the pressure of economic considerations, or construction restrictions change the final plans. Figure 18.59, the aerial photograph of the finished structure, shows how we departed from the original design.

All descriptive notes were included at this stage. In many of the notes, measurements, pitches, and ratios are indicated. Detail numbers, titles, and scale were the final items added. At each step, the water drainage system and the location of potential leakage areas were considered.

Figure 18.54 Roof plan—Stage I.

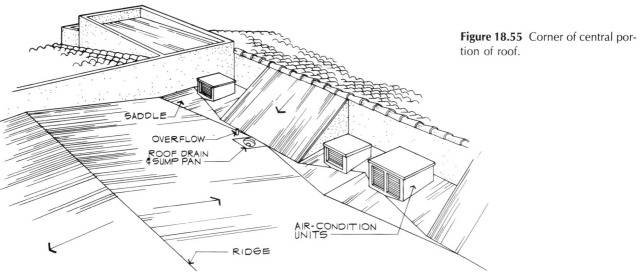

SADDLE

OVERFLOW

ROOF DRAIN
& SUMP PAN

AIR-CONDITION
UNITS

RIDGE

Figure 18.55 Corner of central portion of roof.

575

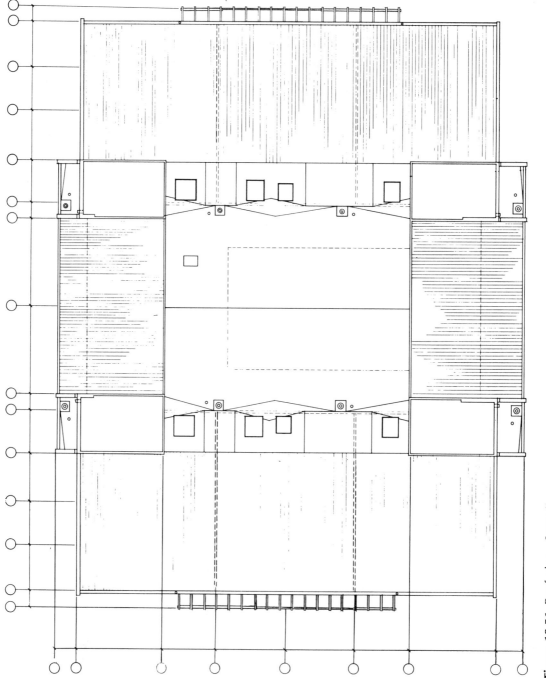

Figure 18.56 Roof plan—Stage II.

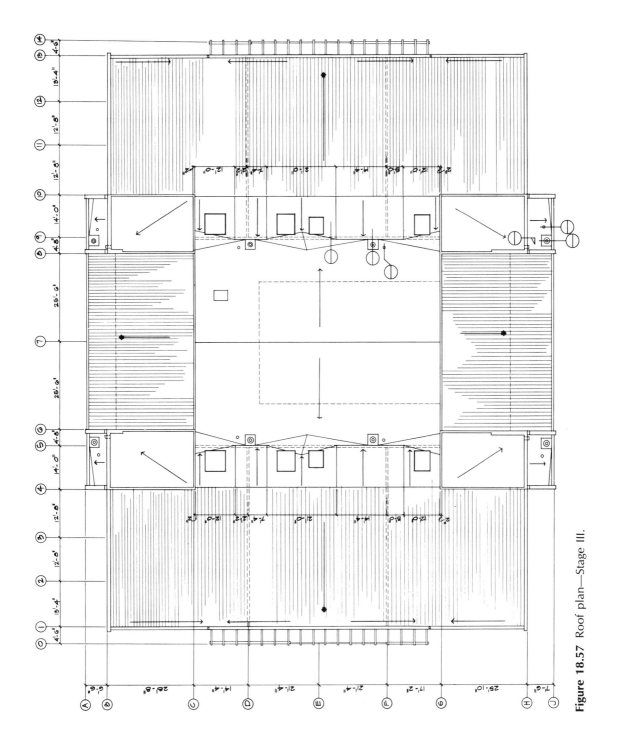

Figure 18.57 Roof plan—Stage III.

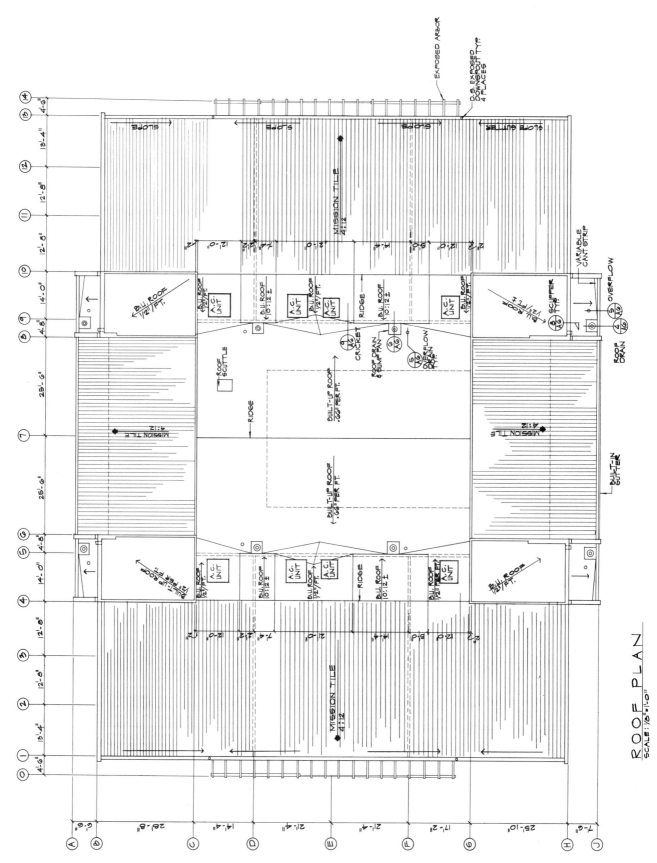

Figure 18.58 Roof plan—Stage IV.

Figure 18.59 Aerial photo of finished roof. (William Boggs Aerial Photography. Reprinted with permission.)

Roof Framing Plan

For a description of the parts of the roof framing plan, refer to the roof and ceiling framing chapter (Chapter 12). Here, we will describe the approach and method used to obtain the necessary information for this plan, and how the plan was drafted.

Stage I

First, a reproducible and a diazo print were made of the floor plan at an early stage without dimensions or notes. See Figure 18.60. The diazo print was then sent to the structural engineer for structural information (column and beam locations, etc.).

Stage II

The engineer returned the diazo print with his sketches, and the refined sketches were then drafted onto the reproducible. See Figure 18.61. Notice the skylights and recall that they were deleted at a later stage, at the client's request.

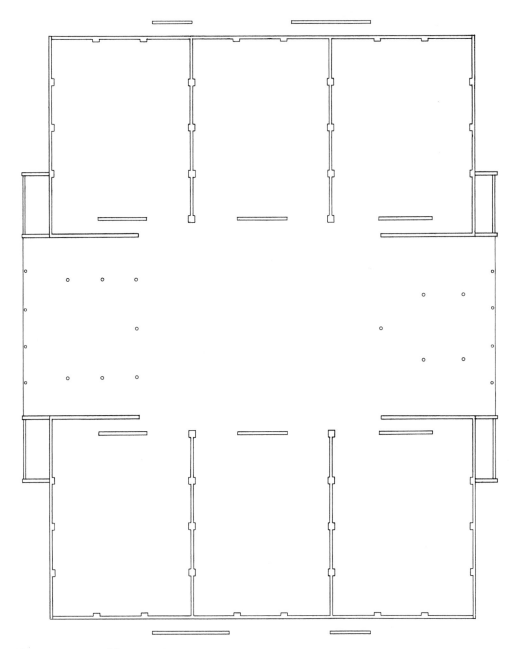

Figure 18.60 Roof framing plan—Stage I.

REVIEW QUESTIONS

1. What was the basic building material used? Why was this material used?
2. What type of restrictions were established by the architectural review committee?
3. Research your geographical area and indicate the requirements for your particular region.
   a. Parking stall requirements
   b. Ratio of stalls for compact cars to regular stalls
   c. Dedicated green space requirement
   d. Ratio of parking spaces for disabled people to the total number of parking spaces, maximum distance to entry
4. On which side of the lot is the sewer easement located?
5. Explain where and how the floor slope for the auditoriums is located.
6. What provisions are there for disabled persons in this theatre?

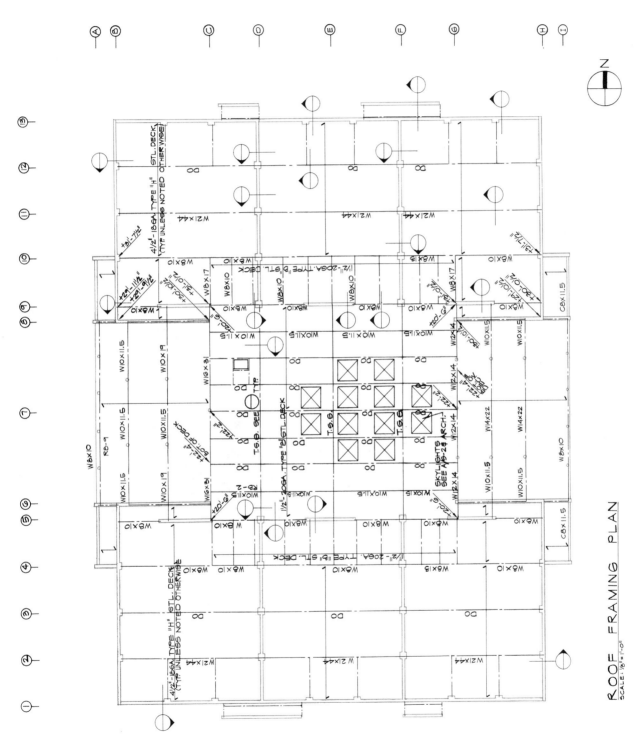

ROOF FRAMING PLAN

SCALE: 1/8" = 1'-0"

Figure 18.61 Roof framing plan—Stage II.

19

TENANT IMPROVEMENTS

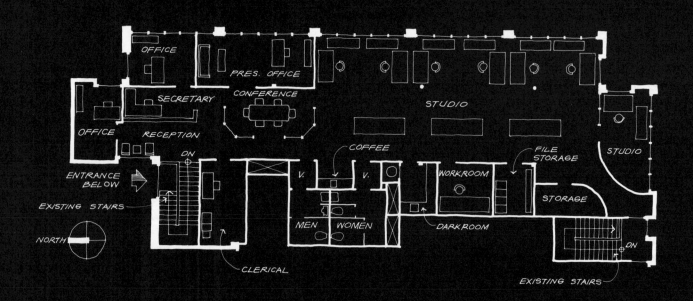

19

Introduction

The purpose of this chapter is to illustrate the procedures for the development of tenant improvements for specific spaces in two existing office buildings.

Building A, which has a large undeveloped open space with nonrequired travel and exit corridors yet to be constructed, will illustrate the necessary design procedures to satisfy corridor and exit travel to an existing lobby and two stairwells. Construction assemblies for exit corridor walls will be detailed to satisfy specific building code requirements.

Three tenant suite spaces will be illustrated as an example of the partial development for a large floor area. Exit requirements for these three spaces will be discussed with an example of a tenant separation-wall assembly that will be constructed between the various suites. Building A and its illustrations provide an example of open space planning for tenant suites, required exiting, and wall construction requirements. Working drawings for the tenant suites are not illustrated.

Building B will demonstrate the entire procedure for developing an undeveloped floor area into a suite for a specific tenant. This procedure will include drawings for the assigned floor area reflecting the requirements of the tenant for the function of his or her business. At the end of this chapter, these drawings will be finalized into working drawings, with explanations of the various stages necessary to complete the drawings for construction and bidding purposes.

The term "tenant improvement," also referred to as "space planning," primarily deals with the internal planning of nonresidential buildings. Such buildings may be used for offices, industrial parks, medical facilities, manufacturing plants, and similar entities.

A "tenant" is defined as the user who will occupy a space, within one of the aforementioned types of buildings, for his or her type of business of professional use.

The "improvement" of a space, in most cases, is defined as the construction of the interior walls, doors, windows, ceilings, movable partitions, and specialty items that may be required for the function of the tenant's daily tasks. Improvements also include cabinetry, hardware, plumbing fixtures, finished floors, carpeting, and finished painting. Such improvement usually includes supplementary heating, ventilating, and air-conditioning systems, sized and installed for a designated space or area.

The internal planning deals with task areas enclosed within walls with various construction assemblies. The tenant, that is, the user, will provide the necessary design criteria for the designer to plan the various task areas. Design criteria may include such information as room use, room sizes, and toilet facilities; electrical, telephone and equipment locations; special lighting requirements and desired floor, wall, and ceiling finishes.

In most cases, the designer or draftsperson will plan within a designated area of an existing structure or may plan an entire floor area. Generally, designated areas are found in multitenant buildings and vary in square footage. It should be noted that tenant improvement may also entail redeveloping an existing constructed space. This condition requires that the room dimensions, lighting fixtures, structural components, equipment locations, and existing electrical and mechanical locations are verified prior to the preliminary design process.

Existing Floor Level—Building A

With a given floor plan for an existing three-story undeveloped structure, we can explore potential floor areas for tenant use. Figure 19.1 illustrates the second floor level of this building. As illustrated, the existing stairwells, men's and women's toilet facilities, elevator shaft, telephone room, and janitor's room have been constructed according to building code requirements. The first prerequisite is to establish a corridor that satisfies all exit requirements of the governing building and fire codes.

Exit Corridors

Figure 19.2A shows a corridor that satisfies code requirements relative to width and location. A three-dimensional drawing illustrates the corridor in Figure 19.2B. The walls and ceiling construction of the corridor must meet the code requirements for a one-hour fire-rated assembly. A detailed construction section of this assembly is depicted in Figure 19.3. Metal studs are illustrated; however, wood studs may be used if they meet the governing fire code requirements. It should be noted that most building codes require exit doors into the corridor to have a 20-minute fire-rated assembly, as designated in the corridor section in Figure 19.3.

Tenant Areas

After establishing an exit corridor that will be used by various tenants on this floor, designated areas or floor areas required to satisfy the particular users' space requirements may now be formulated. In dealing with a tenant's area requirements, the designer must adhere to building code criteria relative to the number of exits required for a specific area.

An example of required exiting is depicted in Figure 19.4A showing that Suite A has a floor area of 3,200

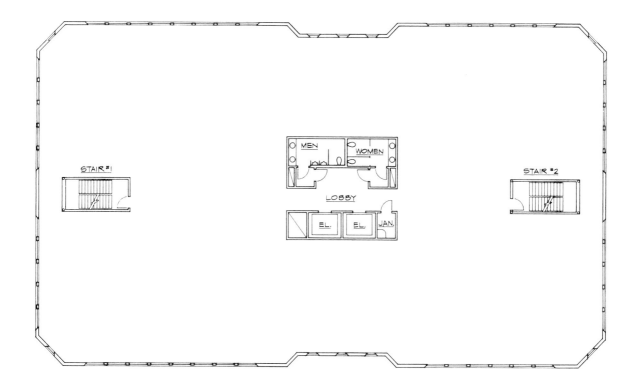

SECOND FLOOR PLAN
SCALE: 1/8"=1'-0"

Figure 19.1 Existing undeveloped floor.

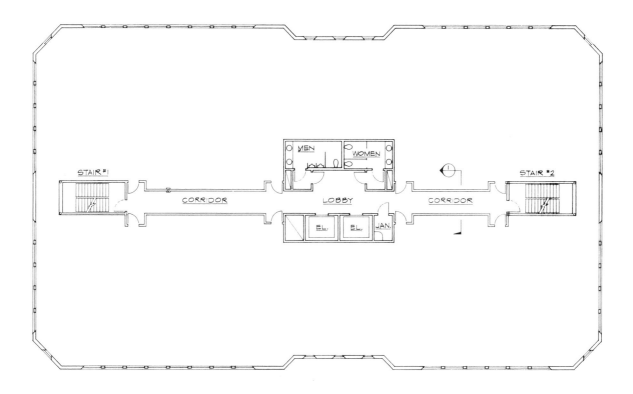

SECOND FLOOR PLAN
SCALE: 1/8"=1'-0"

Figure 19.2A Exit corridor location.

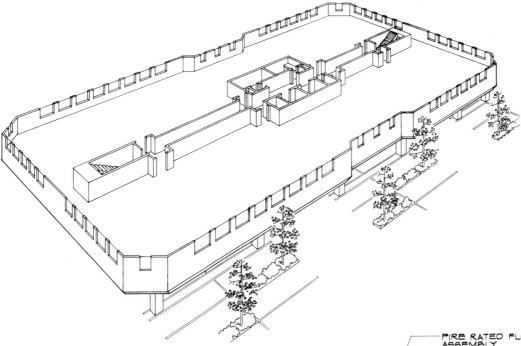

Figure 19.2B Pictorial view of corridor.

square feet. Because of this suite's area and occupant load, the building code requires two exit doors to the corridor. According to the code, these two doors must be separated by a distance of one-half the length of the diagonal dimension of this area. See Figure 19.4A. Figure 19.4B illustrates this condition pictorially. This code requirement will be a primary factor in the internal planning of this suite. As shown in Figure 19.5A, the floor area of Suite C is less than 1,600 square feet; according to the building code this suite requires only one exit to the common corridor. It should be noted that additional toilet facilities may be required by the building code authorities, predicated on the number of employees occupying the particular suites. This would be a planning factor for the tenant improvement design. Figure 19.5B illustrates this suite pictorially.

Tenant Separation Wall

When there are numerous tenants on a given floor level, local building department authorities and building codes may require a one-hour fire-rated wall assembly between each tenant area. Figure 19.6 illustrates a nonload-bearing, one-hour fire-rated wall assembly incorporating metal studs and gypsum board. A nonloading-bearing wall is one that does not support ceiling or floor weight from above or any other weight factors distributed to this wall. Wall insulation is shown as a means to decrease noise transmission between the various tenants.

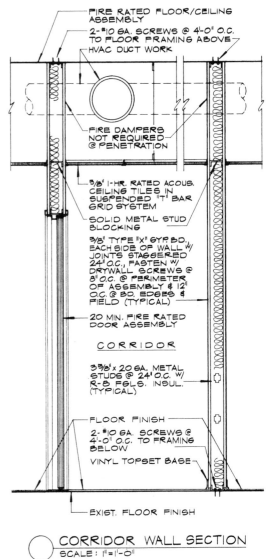

FIRE RATED FLOOR/CEILING ASSEMBLY

2-#10 GA. SCREWS @ 4'-0" O.C. TO FLOOR FRAMING ABOVE

HVAC DUCT WORK

FIRE DAMPERS NOT REQUIRED @ PENETRATION

5/8" 1-HR. RATED ACOUS. CEILING TILES IN SUSPENDED "T" BAR GRID SYSTEM

SOLID METAL STUD BLOCKING

5/8" TYPE "X" GYP. BD. EACH SIDE OF WALL W/ JOINTS STAGGERED 24" O.C., FASTEN W/ DRYWALL SCREWS @ 8" O.C. @ PERIMETER OF ASSEMBLY & 12" O.C. @ BD. EDGES & FIELD (TYPICAL)

20 MIN. FIRE RATED DOOR ASSEMBLY

CORRIDOR

3 5/8" x 20 GA. METAL STUDS @ 24" O.C. W/ R-8 FGLS. INSUL. (TYPICAL)

FLOOR FINISH

2-#10 GA. SCREWS @ 4'-0" O.C. TO FRAMING BELOW

VINYL TOPSET BASE

EXIST. FLOOR FINISH

CORRIDOR WALL SECTION
SCALE: 1"=1'-0"

Figure 19.3 Fire-rated corridor construction.

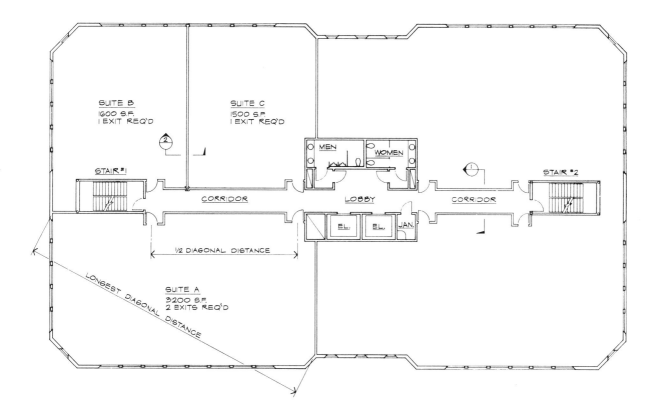

SECOND FLOOR PLAN
SCALE: 1/8" = 1'-0"

Figure 19.4A Suites A, B, and C.

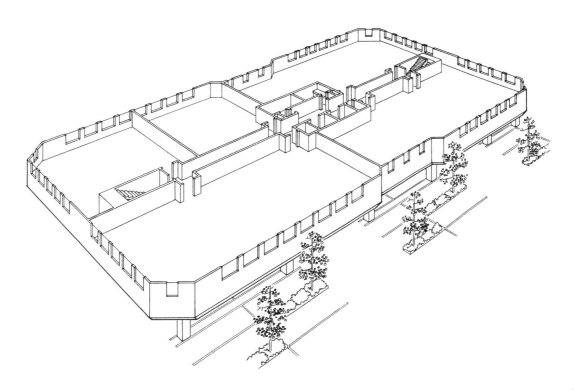

Figure 19.4B Pictorial view of tenant separation walls.

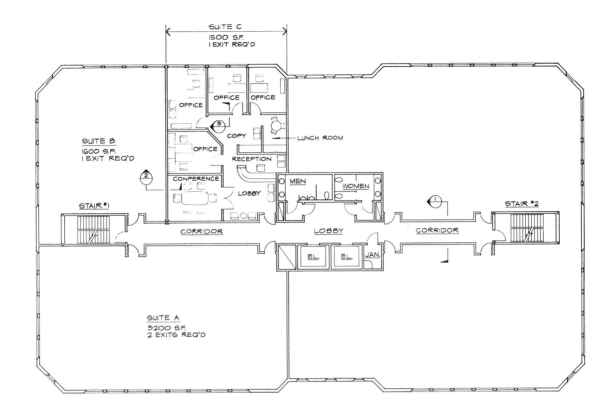

SUITE C
1500 S.F.
1 EXIT REQ'D

OFFICE

OFFICE OFFICE

SUITE B
1600 S.F.
1 EXIT REQ'D

COPY

LUNCH ROOM

OFFICE

RECEPTION

CONFERENCE

LOBBY

MEN

WOMEN

STAIR #1

STAIR #2

CORRIDOR

LOBBY

CORRIDOR

EL. EL. JAN.

SUITE A
3200 S.F.
2 EXITS REQ'D

SECOND FLOOR PLAN
SCALE: 1/8"=1'-0"

Figure 19.5A Floor plan—Suite C.

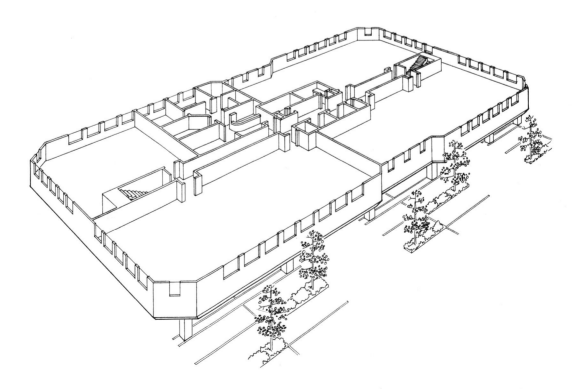

Figure 19.5B Pictorial view—Suite C.

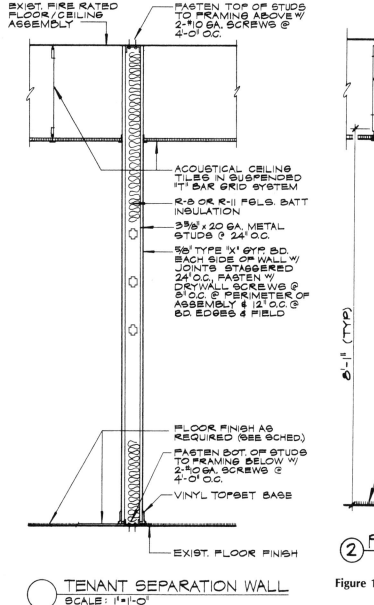

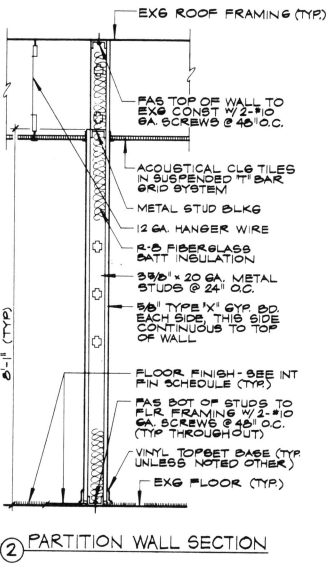

TENANT SEPARATION WALL
SCALE : 1" = 1'-0"

Figure 19.6 Tenant separation wall.

PARTITION WALL SECTION

Figure 19.7 Partition wall section 3.

Development of Working Drawings—Building B

The construction technique for a wall assembly used within a specific suite may vary. Figure 19.7 illustrates an example of a wall partition section used in offices for tenant improvements. Note that this wall partition extends to the roof framing in order to reduce the sound transmission between the various rooms and halls.

Building A has been used to illustrate the basic procedures and requirements for potential suite developments within a large, existing, undeveloped floor space. Building B, however, will illustrate the procedures implemented in an architect's office for the tenant improvement design and the completion of working drawings.

As discussed earlier, internal suite planning is developed from the tenant's criteria that satisfy the needs for his or her business function.

In planning a given undeveloped space on the second floor of an existing office building, the designer will visit the space and verify the structural components such as columns and beam heights. The designer and staff will take measurements to verify existing inside area dimensions, column locations, window sizes, and the spacing of window mullions. In some cases, mechanical and/or plumbing components such as exhaust ducts, roof drainage pipes, and water lines for domestic and mechanical use may be located in this undeveloped space. If so, they should be plotted on the initial plan layout.

Figure 19.8A shows the undeveloped floor plan of an existing second floor level of a two-story office building. The working drawing process for the improvement of Suite 201, as shown in Figure 19.8B, will start with the tenant requirements and the verification of the existing space and conditions. Note in Figure 19.8B the existing steel columns, stairs, mechanical shafts, roof drain lines, windows, and window mullion locations.

Planning of Task Areas

The tenant for this designated space deals with graphic communications and has provided the designer with a list of the various rooms needed, their preferred sizes, their use, and their relationships to each other.

Schematic Study

The rooms specified by the tenant include a reception area, three offices, a conference room, a large studio accommodating numerous drawing boards, a small stu-

dio for air brush media, a copy room, and a storage room. The tenant also desired a coffee area with cabinets and sink and a service area for cleanup of art implements. The location of walls and rough plumbing for the restrooms are existing; therefore, these rooms would require only finishing.

Given the preceding information dealing with specific task areas, schematic studies can now begin in order to show tentative room locations and their relationship to one another. Figure 19.9 illustrates a conceptual floor plan in schematic form, which will be used in discussing the various areas and their locations with the tenant.

Following this procedure, a preliminary floor plan will be developed to scale, including suggested locations for the required furniture. This drawing may be done in freehand, as is shown in Figure 19.10.

Upon the tenant's acceptance of the preliminary plan, Figure 19.11 now shows the required room locations and sizes. Note that the division walls between the offices, adjacent to the exterior wall with windows and mullions, are located to intersect at the window mullions and concrete column locations. This eliminates the problem of a division wall abutting into a glass area, which obviously would be undesirable.

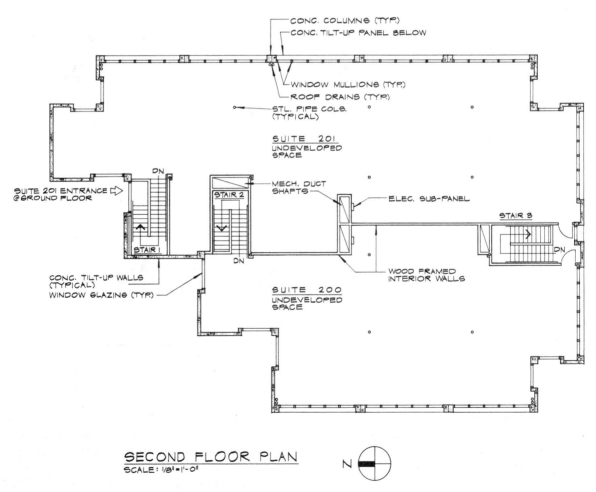

Figure 19.8A Undeveloped floor area plan—Building B.

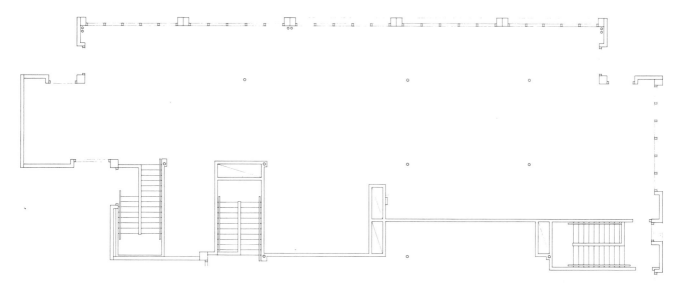

Figure 19.8B Existing undeveloped floor area—Suite 201.

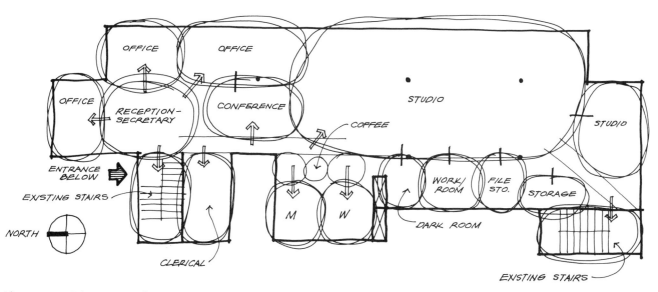

Figure 19.9 Schematic study.

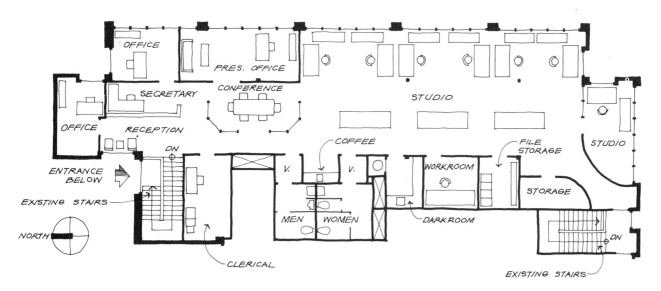

Figure 19.10 Preliminary floor plan.

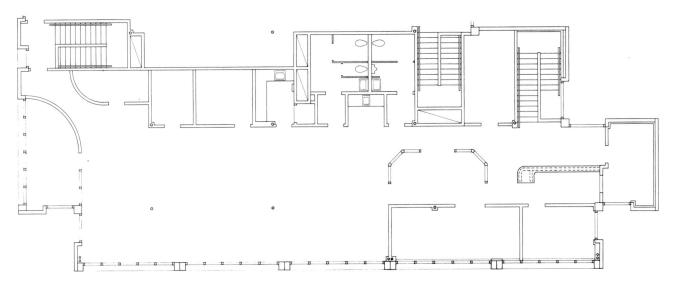

Figure 19.11 Wall development plan.

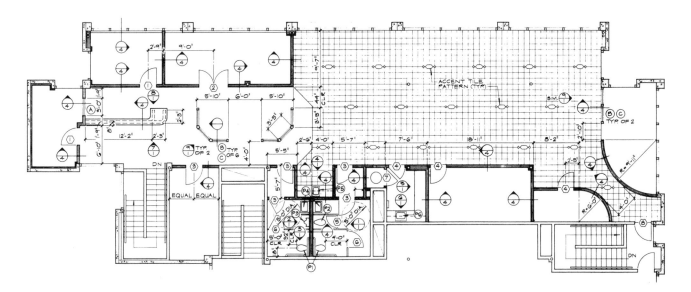

Figure 19.12 Wall shading and wall symbols.

The location of existing structural columns presents planning obstacles as they relate to various spaces. It would be desirable to conceal a column within a division wall wherever possible. Note in Figure 19.11 that some of the existing steel pipe columns have been incorporated into various wall locations.

Interior Partition Wall Construction

Now that the locations of walls, doors, and windows have been established, details for the construction of these components will be designed as a part of the working drawings for this tenant improvement project.

For the sake of clarity, it is recommended that the existing walls and new walls be delineated differently.

For example, the existing walls can be drawn with two separate lines, and new walls with two lines pouchéd or shaded in order to distinguish between them. Wall symbols can be used for reference. Note the wall shading and wall symbols in Figure 19.12. The main structural consideration in detailing nonbearing interior walls is to provide lateral stability. Figure 19.13 illustrates a partition wall section that is terminated a few inches above the ceiling finish material. For this assembly, the wall will be braced with metal struts in compression from the top of the wall to the existing structural members above, as shown on Figure 19.13. A photograph of a metal strut used for lateral wall support is illustrated in Figure 19.14. This wall assembly uses steel studs for the wall structure; however, wood studs are also used for parti-

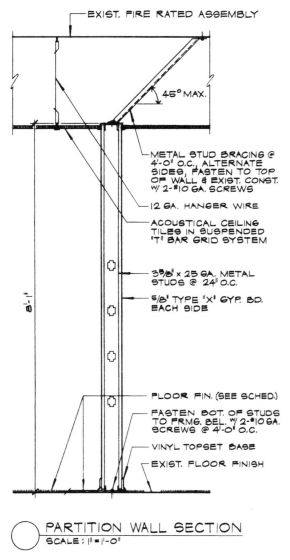

EXIST. FIRE RATED ASSEMBLY

45° MAX.

METAL STUD BRACING @ 4'-0" O.C., ALTERNATE SIDES, FASTEN TO TOP OF WALL & EXIST. CONST. W/ 2-#10 GA. SCREWS

12 GA. HANGER WIRE

ACOUSTICAL CEILING TILES IN SUSPENDED "T" BAR GRID SYSTEM

3⅝" x 25 GA. METAL STUDS @ 24" O.C.

⅝" TYPE "X" GYP. BD. EACH SIDE

FLOOR FIN. (SEE SCHED.)

FASTEN BOT. OF STUDS TO FRMG. BEL. W/ 2-#10 GA. SCREWS @ 4'-0" O.C.

VINYL TOPSET BASE

EXIST. FLOOR FINISH

8'-1"

PARTITION WALL SECTION
SCALE: 1" = 1'-0"

Figure 19.13 Nonbearing partition wall.

tion wall assemblies. A photograph of steel stud framing members is shown in Figure 19.15. As shown in Figure 19.13, the finish ceiling members will terminate at each wall partition, because the use of this wall assembly will dictate that walls be constructed prior to the finished ceiling. This method provides more design flexibility for the ceiling and lighting layout, which is illustrated and discussed later in regard to the design and layout of the ceiling plan. Figure 19.13 illustrates a suspended ceiling, which is assembled with 12-gauge hanger wires and metal runners supporting the finish ceiling material. In regions of the country where there is earthquake activity, the suspended ceiling areas are braced to minimize lateral movement. One method is shown in Figure 19.13, where 12-gauge wire at a 45° angle is assembled in a grid pattern, providing lateral stability for the suspended ceiling.

In cases where the ceiling is installed prior to the construction of the wall partitions, a similar method for stabilizing the wall, as shown in Figure 19.16, will be incorporated into the wall assembly. For the working drawings of this tenant improvement project, the wall section illustrated in Figure 19.13 will be used.

It often happens that in tenant improvement projects, the tenant or user will require additional soundproofing methods for the wall construction that separates specific areas. Figure 19.17 illustrates a separation wall terminating at the roof or floor system of an existing structure. This method helps to reduce the transmission of sound from one area to another through the ceiling and plenum areas. A plenum area, a space used primarily for the location of mechanical ducts and equipment, is usually located above the finished ceiling. Figure 19.18 is a photograph of a small mechanical unit in the plenum area, which will distribute warm and cold air to the various tenant areas. It was decided that the studio

Figure 19.14 Stabilizing strut.

Figure 19.15 Wall framing—steel studs.

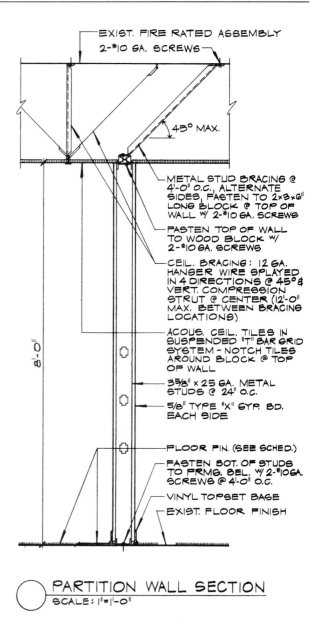

EXIST. FIRE RATED ASSEMBLY
2-#10 GA. SCREWS
45° MAX.

METAL STUD BRACING @ 4'-0" O.C., ALTERNATE SIDES, FASTEN TO 2×3×6" LONG BLOCK @ TOP OF WALL W/ 2-#10 GA. SCREWS

FASTEN TOP OF WALL TO WOOD BLOCK W/ 2-#10 GA. SCREWS

CEIL. BRACING: 12 GA. HANGER WIRE SPLAYED IN 4 DIRECTIONS @ 45° & VERT. COMPRESSION STRUT @ CENTER (12'-0" MAX. BETWEEN BRACING LOCATIONS)

ACOUS. CEIL. TILES IN SUSPENDED "T" BAR GRID SYSTEM - NOTCH TILES AROUND BLOCK @ TOP OF WALL

3⅝" × 25 GA. METAL STUDS @ 24" O.C.

⅝" TYPE "X" GYP. BD. EACH SIDE

FLOOR PIN. (SEE SCHED.)

FASTEN BOT. OF STUDS TO FRMG. BEL. W/ 2-#10GA. SCREWS @ 4'-0" O.C.

VINYL TOPSET BASE

EXIST. FLOOR FINISH

8'-0"

PARTITION WALL SECTION
SCALE: 1"=1'-0"

Figure 19.16 Nonbearing partition wall.

would not have a finished ceiling so that the mechanical ducting for the heating, cooling, and ventilation could be exposed (shown later in the ceiling plan). In this case, the wall partitions will be detailed to extend to, and be secured at, the roof rafters (illustrated in Figure 19.19). Note that where the walls and rafters are not adjacent to each other, 2 × 4 blocking at 4'–0" o.c. is installed to stabilize the wall laterally.

Often, as in this project, a mechanical equipment room is required to enclose a mechanical unit that will provide cooling, heating, and ventilating for a particular suite only. However, because of the noise produced by certain mechanical units, it is good practice to detail the walls of the mechanical room in such a way that the noise of the motors is minimized. A detail of one of the walls is shown in Figure 19.20. Note that sound-absorbing board is installed on the inside of the mechanical room.

Existing Wall Furring

In projects where there are existing unfinished concrete or masonry walls, it will be desirable to furr out these

walls in order to provide for electrical and telephone service and to develop a finished wall surface. Furring is adding a new inner wall to the main wall behind. Figure 19.21 illustrates a wall section where 1⅝-inch metal furring studs are attached to the existing unfinished concrete wall surface. In this detail, ⅝-inch thick gypsum wall board has been selected for the interior wall finish.

Interior Glass Wall Partition

The tenant requested the use of glass wall partitioning to partially enclose the conference room area. The use of glass and metal frames for wall partitions still requires horizontal stability, as is necessary for other types of wall partitions. A section through this glass wall partition

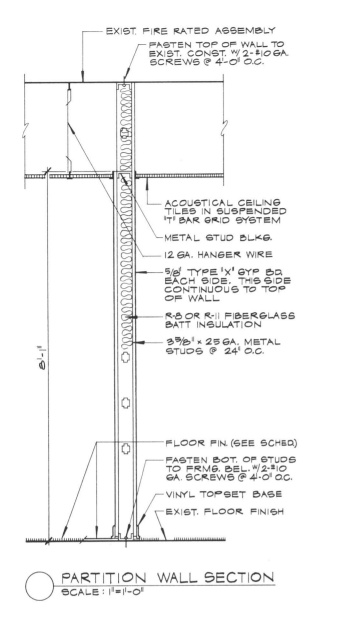

EXIST. FIRE RATED ASSEMBLY

FASTEN TOP OF WALL TO
EXIST. CONST. W/ 2-#10 GA.
SCREWS @ 4'-0" O.C.

ACOUSTICAL CEILING
TILES IN SUSPENDED
"T" BAR GRID SYSTEM

METAL STUD BLKG.

12 GA. HANGER WIRE

5/8" TYPE "X" GYP BD.
EACH SIDE. THIS SIDE
CONTINUOUS TO TOP
OF WALL

R-8 OR R-11 FIBERGLASS
BATT INSULATION

3 5/8" × 25 GA. METAL
STUDS @ 24" O.C.

FLOOR FIN. (SEE SCHED.)

FASTEN BOT. OF STUDS
TO FRMG. BEL. W/ 2-#10
GA. SCREWS @ 4'-0" O.C.

VINYL TOPSET BASE

EXIST. FLOOR FINISH

8'-1"

PARTITION WALL SECTION
SCALE : 1"=1'-0"

Figure 19.17 Sound deterrent partition wall.

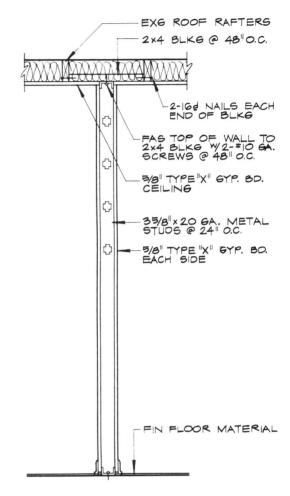

EXG ROOF RAFTERS

2x4 BLKG @ 48" O.C.

2-16d NAILS EACH
END OF BLKG

FAS TOP OF WALL TO
2x4 BLKG W/ 2-#10 GA.
SCREWS @ 48" O.C.

5/8" TYPE "X" GYP. BD.
CEILING

3 5/8" × 20 GA. METAL
STUDS @ 24" O.C.

5/8" TYPE "X" GYP. BD.
EACH SIDE

FIN FLOOR MATERIAL

Figure 19.19 Wall section.

Figure 19.18 Mechanical unit.

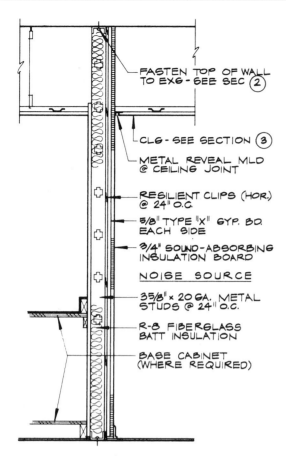

Figure 19.20 Sound wall section.

FASTEN TOP OF WALL TO EXG - SEE SEC ②

CLG - SEE SECTION ③

METAL REVEAL MLD @ CEILING JOINT

RESILIENT CLIPS (HOR.) @ 24" O.C.

5/8" TYPE "X" GYP. BD. EACH SIDE

3/4" SOUND-ABSORBING INSULATION BOARD

<u>NOISE SOURCE</u>

3 5/8" × 20 GA. METAL STUDS @ 24" O.C.

R-8 FIBERGLASS BATT INSULATION

BASE CABINET (WHERE REQUIRED)

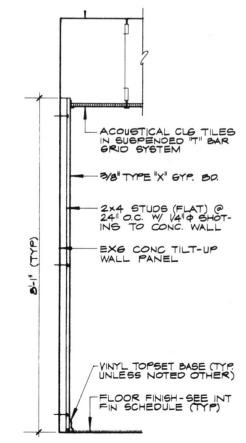

Figure 19.21 Existing wall furring.

ACOUSTICAL CLG TILES IN SUSPENDED "T" BAR GRID SYSTEM

5/8" TYPE "X" GYP. BD.

2×4 STUDS (FLAT) @ 24" O.C. W/ 1/4"∅ SHOT-INS TO CONC. WALL

EXG CONC TILT-UP WALL PANEL

VINYL TOPSET BASE (TYP. UNLESS NOTED OTHER)

FLOOR FINISH-SEE INT FIN SCHEDULE (TYP)

8'-1" (TYP)

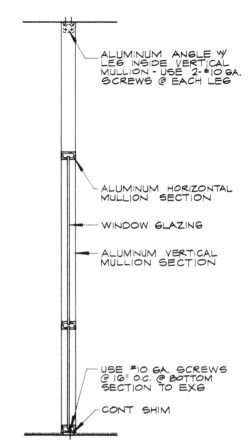

Figure 19.22 Glass wall partition.

ALUMINUM ANGLE W/ LEG INSIDE VERTICAL MULLION - USE 2-#10 GA. SCREWS @ EACH LEG

ALUMINUM HORIZONTAL MULLION SECTION

WINDOW GLAZING

ALUMINUM VERTICAL MULLION SECTION

USE #10 GA. SCREWS @ 16" O.C. @ BOTTOM SECTION TO EXG

CONT SHIM

is shown in Figure 19.22. Note that all glazing will be tempered glass, as required by building codes and for the safety of the user.

Low Wall Partition

A low wall and countertop are provided to separate the reception area from the secretarial area. This 42-inch high wall will be attached to the adjacent wall and anchored at the base, as indicated in Figure 19.23. The stability of a low wall is most critical at the base; therefore, the method of assembly will be determined by the structural components of the existing structure.

Interior Door and Window Assemblies

The door and window assemblies will be detailed to illustrate to the contractor the type of headers over the openings and the types of door and window frames that have been selected. The stabilization at the top of these assemblies will be identical or similar to the stabilization for the wall partitions. Figure 19.24 depicts the use of a metal header over the door opening, incorporating the use of a hollow metal door frame. The manufacturer and type of metal door frame will be called out on the door schedule.

Wall partitions that incorporate windows will be detailed to delineate the type of header, window frame

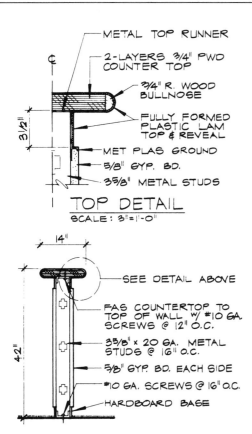

TOP DETAIL
SCALE: 3"=1'-0"

- METAL TOP RUNNER
- 2-LAYERS 3/4" PWD COUNTER TOP
- 3/4" R. WOOD BULLNOSE
- FULLY FORMED PLASTIC LAM TOP & REVEAL
- MET PLAS GROUND
- 5/8" GYP. BD.
- 3⅝" METAL STUDS

14"

- SEE DETAIL ABOVE
- FAS COUNTERTOP TO TOP OF WALL W/ #10 GA. SCREWS @ 12" O.C.
- 3⅝" x 20 GA. METAL STUDS @ 16" O.C.
- 5/8" GYP. BD. EACH SIDE
- #10 GA. SCREWS @ 16" O.C.
- HARDBOARD BASE

4'-2"

Figure 19.23 Low wall partition.

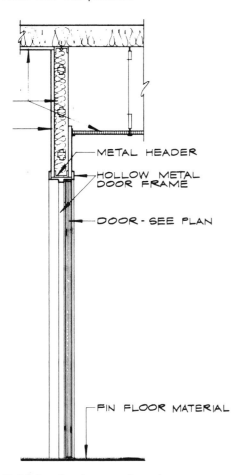

- METAL HEADER
- HOLLOW METAL DOOR FRAME
- DOOR - SEE PLAN
- FIN FLOOR MATERIAL

Figure 19.24 Interior door—wall section.

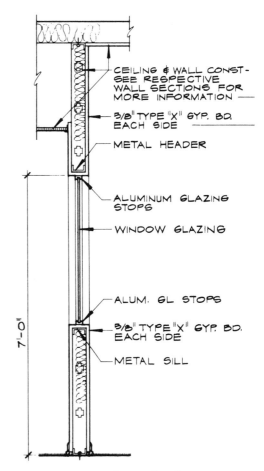

- CEILING & WALL CONST- SEE RESPECTIVE WALL SECTIONS FOR MORE INFORMATION
- 5/8" TYPE "X" GYP. BD. EACH SIDE
- METAL HEADER
- ALUMINUM GLAZING STOPS
- WINDOW GLAZING
- ALUM. GL STOPS
- 5/8" TYPE "X" GYP. BD. EACH SIDE
- METAL SILL

7'-0"

Figure 19.25 Interior window and wall section.

material, and the construction of the wall portion in the assembly. The interior window located between office 3 and the secretarial area is detailed in a wall section illustrated in Figure 19.25.

The sizes, thickness, and types of doors and windows will be stipulated on the door and window schedules (illustrated later in this chapter). It should be noted that upon completion of the detailing for the various partition walls and door and window assemblies, these details will be referenced on the floor plan, using circles and numbers as a means of identification.

Electrical and Communication Plan

After the locations of partition walls, doors, windows, and furniture have been established, the architect or space planner, consulting with the tenant, may now proceed to develop an electrical and communication plan. The electrical portion of this plan will consist of the location of convenient electrical outlets installed approximately 12 inches above the floor, unless noted otherwise by a dimension at the outlet. The communication installation will comprise telephone jacks, a connection for the facsimile (fax) equipment, and a rough-in electrical service for the tenant's computer hardware. An electrical and communication plan prepared for this tenant of Building B is illustrated in Figure 19.26. It should be noted that on some projects the electrical and communication design may be so complex that separate plans must be provided and delineated for clarity.

Ceiling Plan

A ceiling plan will be drawn to delineate the following: location of ceiling lighting fixtures, symbolized for reference to the lighting fixture schedule; suspended ceiling design; the type of system to be specified; and other types of ceiling finishes. Switch locations for the various lighting fixtures will also be shown on this plan.

For this project, it was decided that a suspended ceiling system with recessed lighting fixtures would be specified for offices 1, 2, and 3. As mentioned earlier and detailed in Figure 19.13, the walls will be installed

first, thus providing the designer with greater design flexibility for the layout of the suspended ceiling grid system and the location of lighting fixtures. To illustrate the design flexibility of this wall installation method, the ceiling plan shown in Figure 19.27 shows the suspended ceiling and lighting fixtures to be symmetrical within the offices, thereby creating a more pleasing ceiling design and lighting fixture location. Mechanical ducts for heating and cooling these offices will be installed and concealed above the suspended ceiling system. Note that the walls are drawn with two lines only, inasmuch as there are no wall openings at the ceiling level.

At the request of the tenant, the remaining rooms and task areas will not have a suspended ceiling system; rather, gypsum wallboard will be attached directly to the existing structural roof members, with the gypsum board being finished and painted. For wall reference, see Figure 19.19.

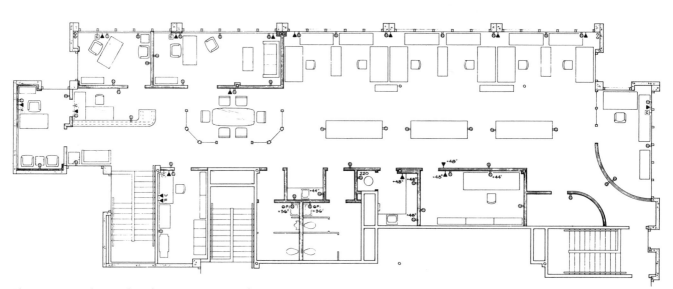

Figure 19.26 Electrical and communication plan.

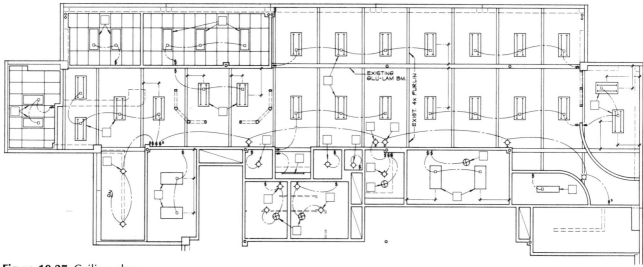

Figure 19.27 Ceiling plan.

The selection of the ceiling finish and location was to allow the mechanical ducts to be exposed and painted. These round mechanical ducts, exposed and painted, will provide a decor compatible with the artwork and graphic design produced by this tenant. A photograph of the exposed mechanical ducts and lighting fixtures is shown in Figure 19.28. On the ceiling plan, as depicted in Figure 19.27, the designer has shown the desired location of the mechanical ducts and supply registers. The consulting mechanical engineer will specify the sizes of the ducts, type of supply registers, and type of equipment to be used, in the mechanical drawings.

As previously mentioned, the lighting fixtures will be given a reference symbol that will also be on the electrical fixture schedule. The schedule will provide a description of the fixtures, including the manufacturer and model numbers. Designation of the finished ceiling material may be shown on the ceiling plan for convenience; in any case, these finishes will be designated on the interior finish schedule. Electrical and interior finish schedules, as well as other schedules, are discussed and illustrated later in the chapter.

Interior Elevations

Interior elevations will be provided to illustrate cabinets, counter heights, plumbing fixture locations, and location of hardware accessories. Restroom elevations will illustrate the clearances and hardware locations for compliance with the American with Disabilities Act (ADA) requirements. There are only two restrooms, one for women and one for men, and each will be designed to satisfy the requirements set forth in the current ADA recommendations.

Figure 19.29 depicts one wall of a restroom, showing the required water closet seat heights, the length of grab bars, and their heights above the floor. In the final working drawings a reference symbol will be shown on

Figure 19.28 Exposed ducts and supply register.

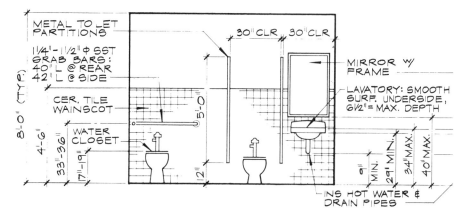

Figure 19.29 Restroom wall elevation.

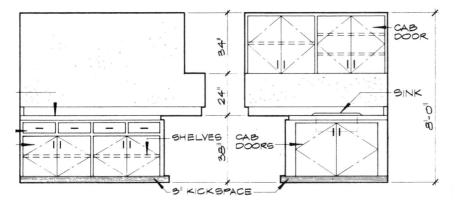

Figure 19.30 Cabinet elevations.

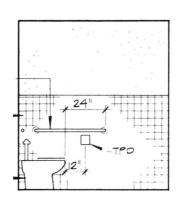

Figure 19.31 Hardware location.

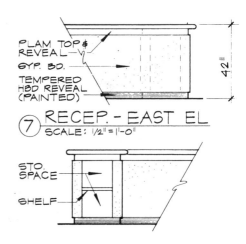

Figure 19.33 Low wall elevation.

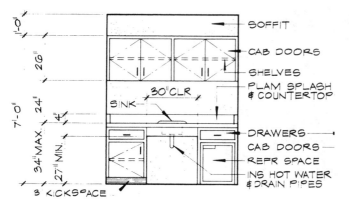

Figure 19.32 Coffee bar cabinets.

the floor plan and included on the corresponding interior elevation. These corresponding symbols will provide clarity for those reviewing the working drawings. The cabinet dimensions and clearances delineated on the interior elevations are shown in Figure 19.30. In most cases, restroom walls will be delineated to show the location of toilet accessories and other types of hardware. Figure 19.31 is drawn to indicate the locations, as dimensioned, for the toilet paper and towel dispensers.

As requested by the tenant, cabinets have been provided in the coffee bar area for storage of dishes, utensils, coffee, and other necessities for the employees. See Figure 19.32. Low division walls will be drawn to illustrate the height, finish, and method of construction. Figure 19.33 depicts the low division wall between the reception and secretarial areas. Note that the wall construction method is referenced on the elevation. See Figure 19.23, which illustrates a section through the wall.

Schedules

Schedules are incorporated into the working drawings for most tenant improvement projects. The schedules for this project include the door schedule, window schedule, plumbing fixture schedule, interior finish schedule, electrical fixture schedule, and furnishing schedule. The door schedule, shown in Figure 19.34, provides the door symbol, door size and thickness, door material, frame material, and selected door finish. Even though few windows are incorporated, a window schedule is provided. See Figure 19.35.

DOOR SCHEDULE

SYM	WIDTH	HEIGHT	THK	HC/SC	TYPE	MATERIAL	REMARKS
①	3'-0"	7'-0"	13/4"	SC	SLAB	WOOD	PLAM FIN (COFFEE)
②	PR.2'-8"	"	"	"	"	"	" "
③	3'-0"	"	"	"	"	"	" " (BLACK)
④	2'-10"	"	"	"	"	"	" " "
⑤	2'-2"	5'-0"	1"	"	"	MET FACE	BLACK
⑥	2'-10"	"	"	"	"	"	"
⑦	"	"	13/8"	HC	"	PNT GD WD	WATER HEATER DR
⑧	3'-0"	7'-0"	13/4"	SC	"	WOOD	3/4 HR./SELF-CLSG.

Figure 19.34 Door schedule.

WINDOW SCHEDULE

SYM	WIDTH	HEIGHT	GL.THK	TYPE	FRAME MTL	REMARKS
Ⓐ	3'-0"	4'-0"	1/4"	FIXED	AL/DARK BRZ	CLEAR GL
Ⓑ	3'-2"	2'-6"	"	"	"	TINTED GL
Ⓒ	"	4'-2"	"	"	"	CLR GL, ABV Ⓑ

Figure 19.35 Window schedule.

PLUMBING FIXTURE SCHEDULE

SYM	ITEM / MODEL NO.	MANUFACTURER	REMARKS
Ⓟ1	WC, ELONG. RIM, 18" RIM HT	FIXTURES INC.	WHITE
Ⓟ2	WATER CLOSET	"	"
Ⓟ3	WALL HUNG URINAL	"	"
Ⓟ4	" " LAV	"	"
Ⓟ5	BAR SINK	"	SST, 5" DEEP
Ⓟ6	SINK	"	" , 9" "

Figure 19.36 Plumbing fixture schedule.

Figure 19.36 depicts the plumbing fixture schedule, which lists the type of fixture, manufacturer, and model designation. Note on the floor plan the designated plumbing fixture symbols, which are referenced to the plumbing schedule shown on Figure 19.36. The interior finish schedule designates the various rooms and their respective floor, wall, and ceiling finishes. See Figure 19.37.

The electrical fixture schedule, shown on Figure 19.38, identifies the type of electrical fixture, the manufacture, and the corresponding model number. Note that the electrical fixture symbols are designated only on the ceiling plan, shown in Figure 19.27. Other schedules are discussed and illustrated in Chapter 9.

Finally, to complete the necessary schedules, a furnishing schedule is provided. This schedule will depict furniture sizes, manufacturers, and the desired finish materials. See Figure 19.39

Working Drawings

The following paragraphs desribe the working drawings at various stages of their development for this tenant improvement project.

Floor Plan

STAGE I (Figure 19.40). At a larger scale, the draftsperson lightly blocked out all the existing exterior and interior walls for the area identified as Suite 201. This drawing included existing windows, structural col-

INTERIOR FINISH SCHEDULE

ROOM/AREA	FLOOR			BASE			WALLS		CEILING			REMARKS
	CARPET & PAD	VINYL TILE	SHEET VINYL	VINYL TOPSET	COVED FLR	"J" MOLDING	5/8" TYPE "X" G.B.		5/8"-2'×4' SUS CLG	5/8" TYPE "X" G.B.	EXP. FRAMING	
RECEPT./SEC.	●			●			●				●	
OFFICE - 1	●			●			●		●			
OFFICE - 2	●			●			●		●			
OFFICE - 3	●			●			●		●			
CONFERENCE	●			●							●	STOREFRONT GL WALLS (SEE EL)
CLERICAL WRKRM	●			●			●		●			
RESTROOMS		●			●		●		●			CT WSCT, ENAMEL PNT (SEE INT ELS)
VESTIBULES		●			●		●		●			
COFFEE BAR		●		●			●		●			
STUDIO - 1		●		●			●				●	SEE PLAN FOR FLR TILE PATTERN
DARKROOM		●		●			●		●			
PAINT/WORKROOM		●		●			●		●			
STORAGE		●				●	●		●			
STUDIO-2	●					●	●				●	
STAIRS						●	●		●			
DNSTRS LOBBY	●					●	●		●			

Figure 19.37 Interior finish schedule.

ELECTRICAL FIXTURE SCHEDULE

SYM	ITEM/MODEL NO.	MANUFACTURER	LAMP	
E1	2'x4' RECESSED W/ PRISMATIC LENS	LIGHTDESIGN INC.	4-40W	FLUR. TUBES
E2	2'x4' SURF. MT W/ PRISMATIC LENS	"	"	"
E3	1'x4' DO	"	2-40W	"
E4	2'x4' OPEN TUBE INDUS. W/"ICE-TONG" HANGERS	"	4-40W	"
E5	4' STRIP/UNDER CAB	"	1-40W	"
E6	12"φ SURF. MT W/ OP ACRYLIC LENS	"	2-60W	A19 BULBS
E7	4"φ DO	"	1-75W	"
E8	SURF. MT/PORCELAIN	"PROPRIETARY"	1-60W	"

Figure 19.38 Electrical fixture schedule.

FURNISHING SCHEDULE

SYM.	WIDTH	DEPTH	HEIGHT	ITEM / MODEL NO.	MANUFACTURER	REMARKS
F1	60"	30"	29"	EXECUTIVE DESK	FURNITURE INC.	ROSEWOOD
F2	"	"	"	SECRETARIAL DESK	"	TEAK
F3	"	24'	26"	FREESTANDING TYPING TABLE	"	"
F4	90"	35"	28"	CONFERENCE TABLE	"	ROSEWOOD
F5	48"	24'	29"	WORKTABLE	"	BLACK PLAM TOP
F6	23"	26"	40'	HI-BACK DESK CHAIR	"	ROSEWOOD TRIM
F7	22"	24"	32"	ARMCHAIR	"	" "
F8	18"	20"	30"	SECRETARIAL CHAIR	"	BLACK
F9	22"	24"	31"	SIDECHAIR	"	ROSEWOOD
F10	80"	32"	26"	3-SEAT SOFA	"	COFFEE
F11	62"	"	"	2- "	"	"
F12	48"	21"	17"	COFFEE TABLE	"	ROSEWOOD
F13	18"	18"	19"	SQUARE TABLE	"	"
F14	24"	24"	"	" " "	"	TEAK
F15	48"	13"	72'	BOOKCASE	"	ROSEWOOD
F16	36'	"	"	" "	"	"
F17	72"	37½"	37"	DRAFTING/WORK TABLE	ARCHSTATION INC.	BLACK
F18	72"	24"	29"	FOLDING TABLE	FURNITURE INC.	BLACK PLAM TOP
F19	60"	21"	29"	3-DRAWER REF DESK	N/A	CUSTOM-SEE DRAWING
F20	96'	24'	29"	FOLDING TABLE	FURNITURE INC.	BLACK PLAM TOP
F21	72"	13"	60"	BOOKCASE	"	WHITE MELAMINE
F22	48"	"	"	" " "	"	"
F23	19"	21"	44½"	VARIABLE HT DRAFTING CHAIR	ARCHSTATION INC.	BLACK
F24	23"	26"	"	" " " ARMCHAIR	"	"

Figure 19.39 Furnishing schedule.

umns, roof drain leaders, stairwells, and mechanical shafts. Also included in this first-stage drawing was the initial site plan layout.

STAGE II (Figure 19.41). After the required room locations and their sizes were determined from the schematic drawings in Figure 19.10, wall locations were established with their accompanying dimension lines only. All the existing and new walls were darkened for future clarity. Doors and their swing directions were now added, along with wheelchair clearances in the men's and women's restrooms. The various interior elevations were lightly blocked out and the site plan—illustrating the exact location of Suite 201 in this existing structure—was finalized.

STAGE III (Figure 19.42). At this stage of the floor plan, all the wall partitions were dimensioned, and the new walls darkened solid to distinguish them from the existing walls. Note that in the reference room, next to the darkroom, a wall was eliminated to provide more

space for equipment. See Stage II. Door symbols and their numbers were now incorporated, along with plumbing fixture symbols and their accompanying designations. Also included are reference bubbles for the various wall sections with their designated numbers and locations. Interior elevation reference symbols have been added and will later be located on their respective wall elevations. Symbols for glass sizes are shown at the various glass partition locations. At this stage of the floor plan, the specified tile floor and accent pattern locations are delineated in the studio area. The lines on the interior elevations are darkened and profiled for clarity with material designations, cabinet door swings, incorporating the various dimension lines.

STAGE IV (Figure 19.43). This is the final stage for the floor plan, interior elevations, and site plan. On the floor plan a wall legend is included, illustrating the various wall conditions. All final notes and room

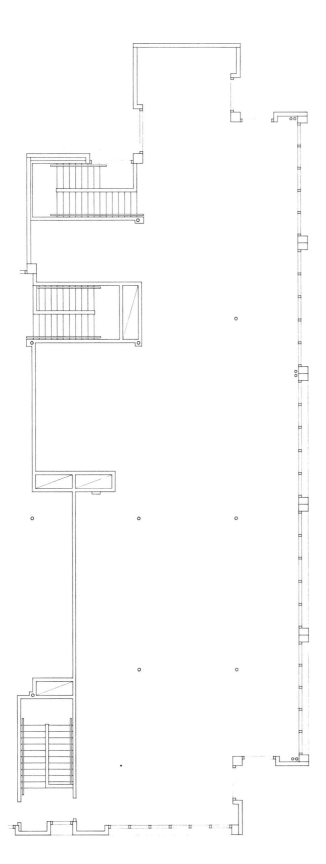

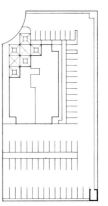

Figure 19.40 Floor plan—Stage I.

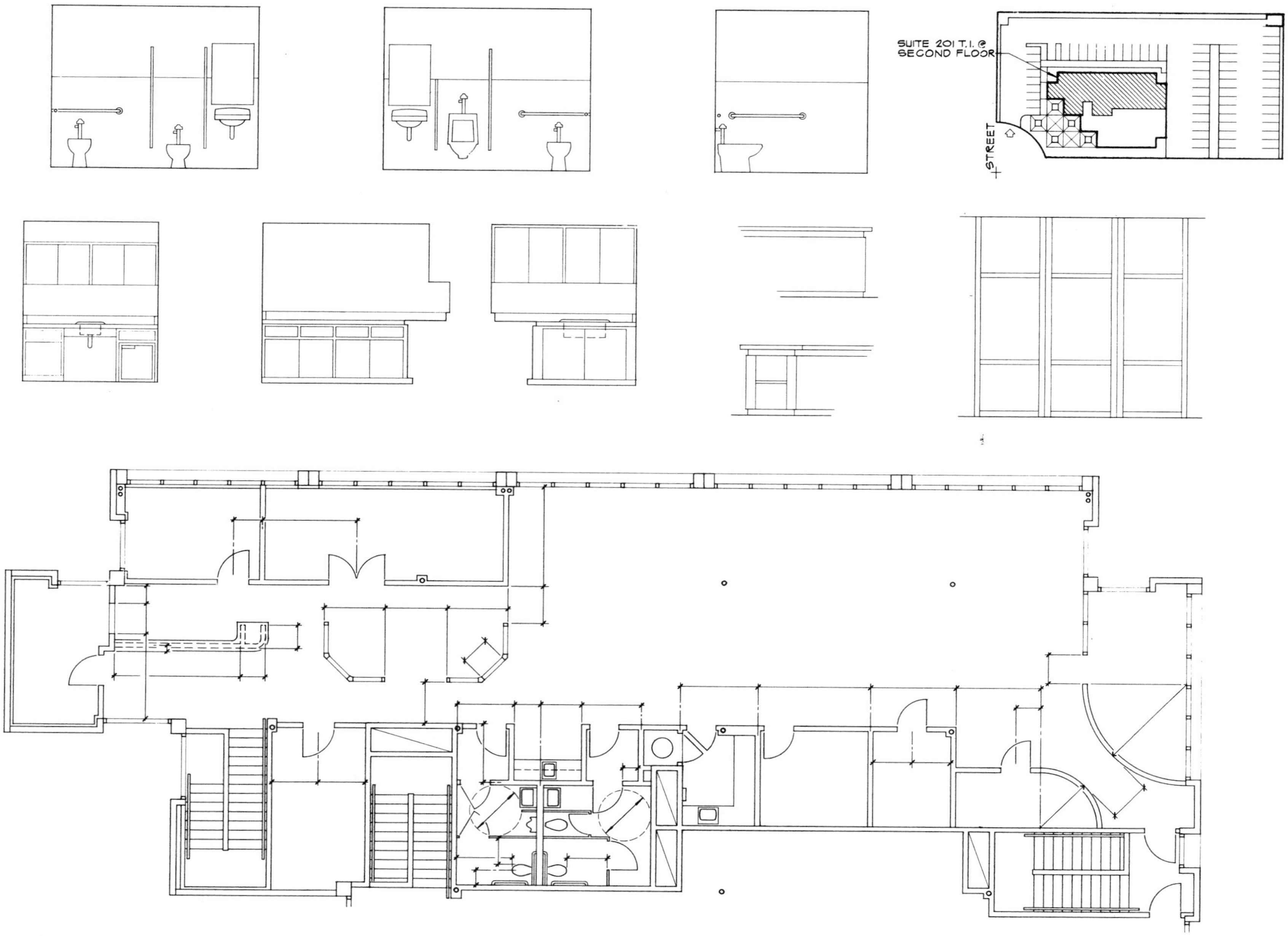

Figure 19.41 Floor plan—Stage II.

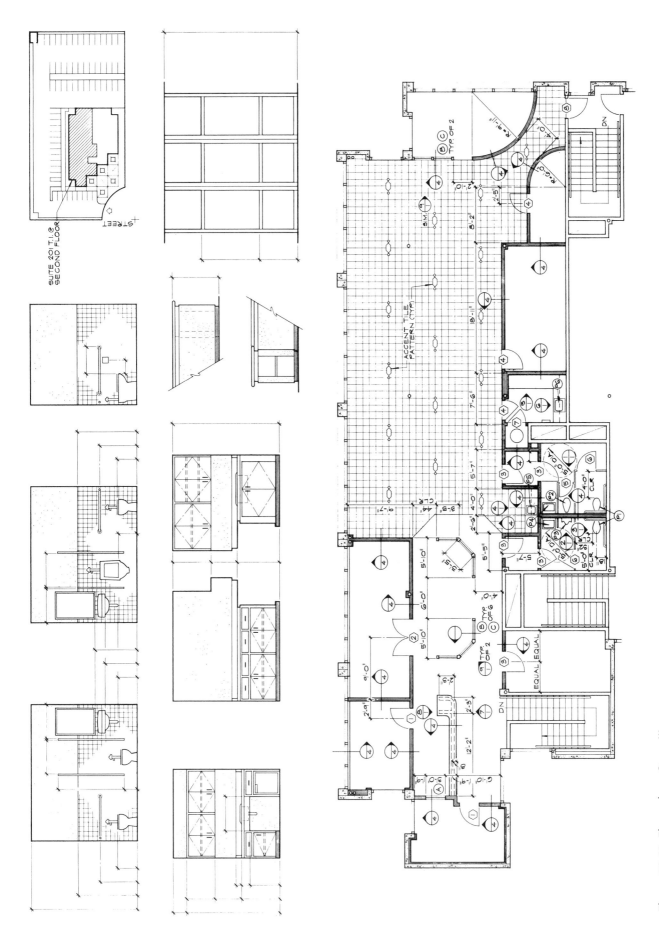

Figure 19.42 Floor plan—Stage III.

605

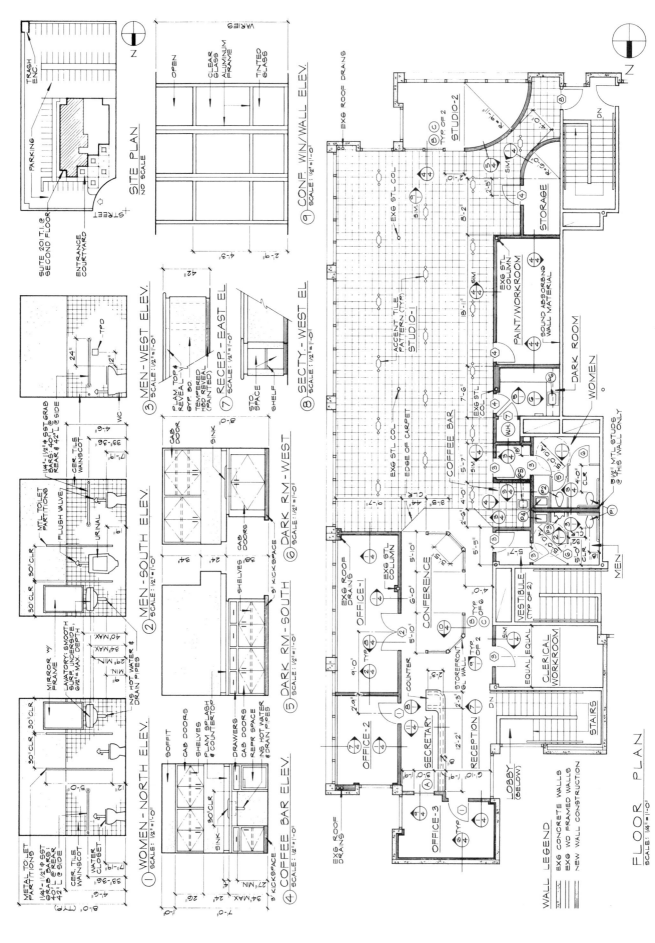

Figure 19.43 Floor plan—Stage IV.

designations have been lettered, and the designated wall detail numbers placed in the various reference bubbles. Lettering and dimensioning on the interior elevations are now finalized, along with the titling and reference numbering for various wall elevations as they relate to the floor plan. Final notes are lettered on the site plan and titles provided for the site plan and floor plan. The scales used for various drawings are now lettered and located below the drawing titles.

Furnishing, Electrical, and Communication Plan

STAGE I (Figure 19.44). The initial step for this stage was to draft a floor plan incorporating the exterior walls, interior partitions, plumbing fixtures, and cabinet locations. Note that door swings and their directions are not delineated. In many offices this stage may be a reproduction of an earlier floor plan stage.

STAGE II (Figure 19.45). The first concern at this stage was to lay out all the required furniture necessary for the function of the tenant's business. With the furniture location established, electrical, telephone, and facsimile outlets can now be located as required by the tenant. Also included at this stage is a furnishing schedule, which will be completed at a later stage.

STAGE III (Figure 19.46). For the completion of the electrical plan and furnishing layout, symbols for furniture identification are located accordingly and lettered for reference on the furnishing schedule. Final notes are provided for electrical outlet locations, as well as for the various furnishing items that will be supplied by the tenant. The furnishing schedule is now completed, providing symbol designation, sizes, and manufacturers' equipment designations. A legend is drawn and completed for the identification of electrical symbols, such as for the types of outlets and switches. General construction notes covering the various construction phases are now included with this drawing.

Ceiling Plan

STAGE I (Figure 19.47). At this stage the exterior and interior walls are lightly blocked out, illustrating the walls as they appear at the ceiling level.

STAGE II (Figure 19.48). The exterior and interior walls are darkened to provide greater clarity at this stage. The three office areas that will have a suspended ceiling system have been delineated to illustrate the grid pattern, lighting fixture location, and their symbols for identifications. Also shown are the light switches for the various lighting fixtures. All the surface-mounted lighting fixtures, exhaust fans, and accompanying switches for the various fixtures are completed in this stage. Fixture symbols are now located for the identification of the various electrical

fixtures. The symbols will be completed at a later stage. Finally, schedules for the doors, electrical fixtures, plumbing fixtures, and room finishes are drawn

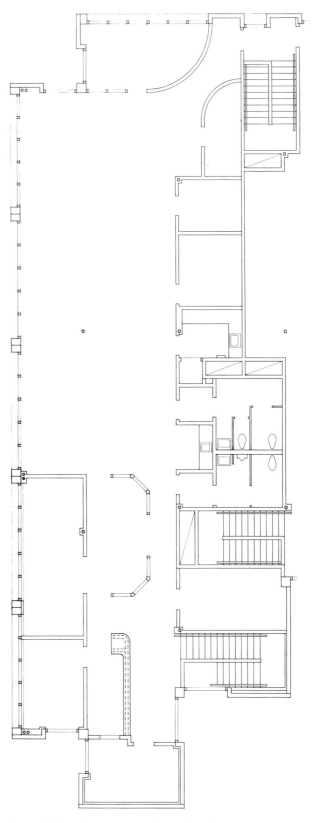

Figure 19.44 Electrical plan–furnishing layout—Stage I.

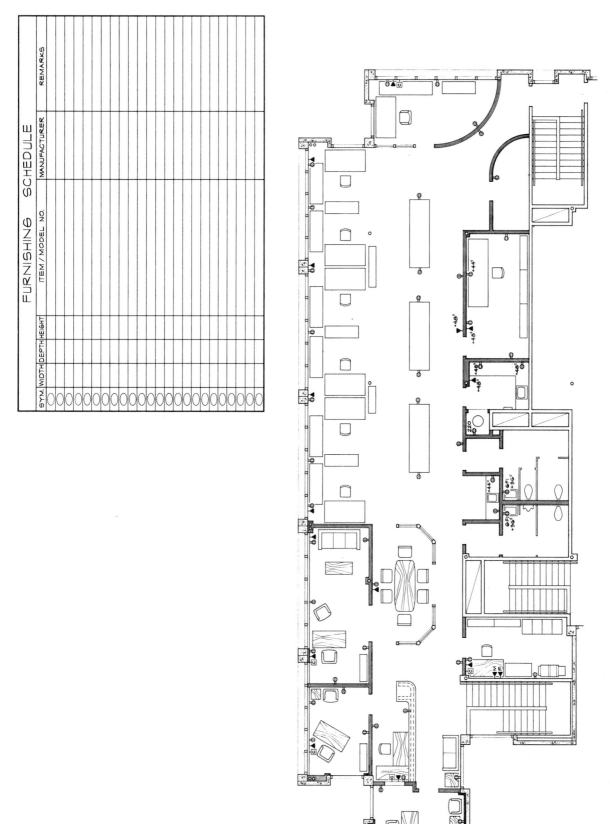

Figure 19.45 Electrical plan—furnishing layout—Stage II.

SYMBOL LEGEND

SYM.	DESCRIPTION
◢	TELEPHONE OUTLET, F=FAX M=MODEM
⊞	COMPUTER NETWORK JUNCTION
◐	DUPLEX OUTLET
◐GFI	w/ GROUND FAULT INTERRUPTER
◐220	220 VOLT OUTLET
$	SINGLE POLE TOGGLE SWITCH
$3	3-WAY SWITCH
EXIT	EXIT SIGN (BATTERY)

GENERAL CONSTRUCTION NOTES

1. The contractor and all sub-contractors shall verify all dimensions and conditions at the site, and shall notify the Architect of any discrepancy

2. All architectural, mechanical, plumbing and electrical requirements must be coordinated before the contractor proceeds with construction.

3. In all cases where a conflict may occur such as between items covered by specifications and notes on the drawings, or between general notes and specific details, the Architect shall be notified and he will interpret the intent of the contract documents.

4. Details noted as typical shall apply in all cases unless specifically shown or noted otherwise.

5. Where no specific detail is shown, the framing or construction shall be identical or similar to that indicated for like cases of construction on this project.

6. In no case shall working dimensions be scaled from plans, sections or details on the drawings.

7. Workmanship and materials shall conform to the requirements of the current edition of the Uniform Building Code.

8. All fire rated walls shall use fire rated gypsum board and be fire-taped.

9. All Plumbing, Electrical, and Mechanical installations shall comply with their respective/ governing codes.

10. All legal exits shall be openable from inside without the use of a key, special knowledge or effort.

11. Metal studs by "Metal Studs Inc." (or approved equivalent), ICBO #0000. See details and sections for more information.

12. Suspended Ceiling System by "Gypsum Ceilings Inc." (or approved equivalent), ICBO #0000. Installation shall be per Ch. 47 of the UBC & the following requirements:

    A. Lateral support provided by 4- #12ga wires splayed in 4 directions at 90° apart. Connect wires to the main runner within 2" of the crossrunner & to the structure above at an angle not exceeding 45° from the plane of the ceiling. These lateral support points shall be at 12'-0" o.c. (max) in each direction, with the first point within 4' of the wall.

    B. Provide vertical compression struts at the center of the lateral support points described above in item "A". Compression struts may be of metal stud material

    C. Discontinuous ends of main runners and crossrunners shall be vertically supported within 8" of the discontinuous end.

    D. Lighting fixtures and air diffusers shall be supported directly by wires to the structure above.

FURNISHING SCHEDULE

SYM.	ITEM / MODEL NO.	WIDTH	DEPTH	HEIGHT	MANUFACTURER	REMARKS
F1	EXECUTIVE DESK	60"	30"	29"	FURNITURE INC.	ROSEWOOD
F2	SECRETARIAL DESK	"	24"	26"	"	TEAK
F3	FREESTANDING TYPING TABLE	"	24"	28"	"	
F4	CONFERENCE TABLE	90"	35"	29"	"	ROSEWOOD
F5	WORKTABLE	48"	24"	29"	"	BLACK PLAM TOP
F6	HI-BACK DESK CHAIR	23"	26"	40"	"	ROSEWOOD TRIM
F7	ARMCHAIR	22"	24"	32"	"	BLACK
F8	SECRETARIAL CHAIR	18"	20"	30"	"	ROSEWOOD
F9	SIDECHAIR	22"	24"	31"	"	COFFEE
F10	3-SEAT SOFA	80"	32"	29"	"	ROSEWOOD
F11	2- "	G2"	32"	29"	"	
F12	COFFEE TABLE	48"	21"	17"	"	
F13	SQUARE TABLE	18"	18"	19"	"	TEAK
F14	BOOKCASE	24"	13"	72"	"	ROSEWOOD
F15	"	48"	13"	72"		
F16	"	36"				
F17	DRAFTING/WORK TABLE	72"	37 1/2"	57"	ARCHSTATION INC.	BLACK
F18	FOLDING TABLE	72"	24"	29"	FURNITURE INC.	BLACK PLAM TOP
F19	3-DRAWER REF DESK	60"	2'1"	29"	N/A	CUSTOM-SEE DRAWING
F20	FOLDING TABLE	72"	24"	29"	FURNITURE INC.	BLACK-PLAM TOP
F21	BOOKCASE	72"	13"	60"	"	WHITE MELAMINE
F22	"	48"	13"			
F23	VARIABLE HT DRAFTING CHAIR	19"	2'1"	44 1/2"	ARCHSTATION INC.	BLACK
F24	ARMCHAIR	23"	26"			

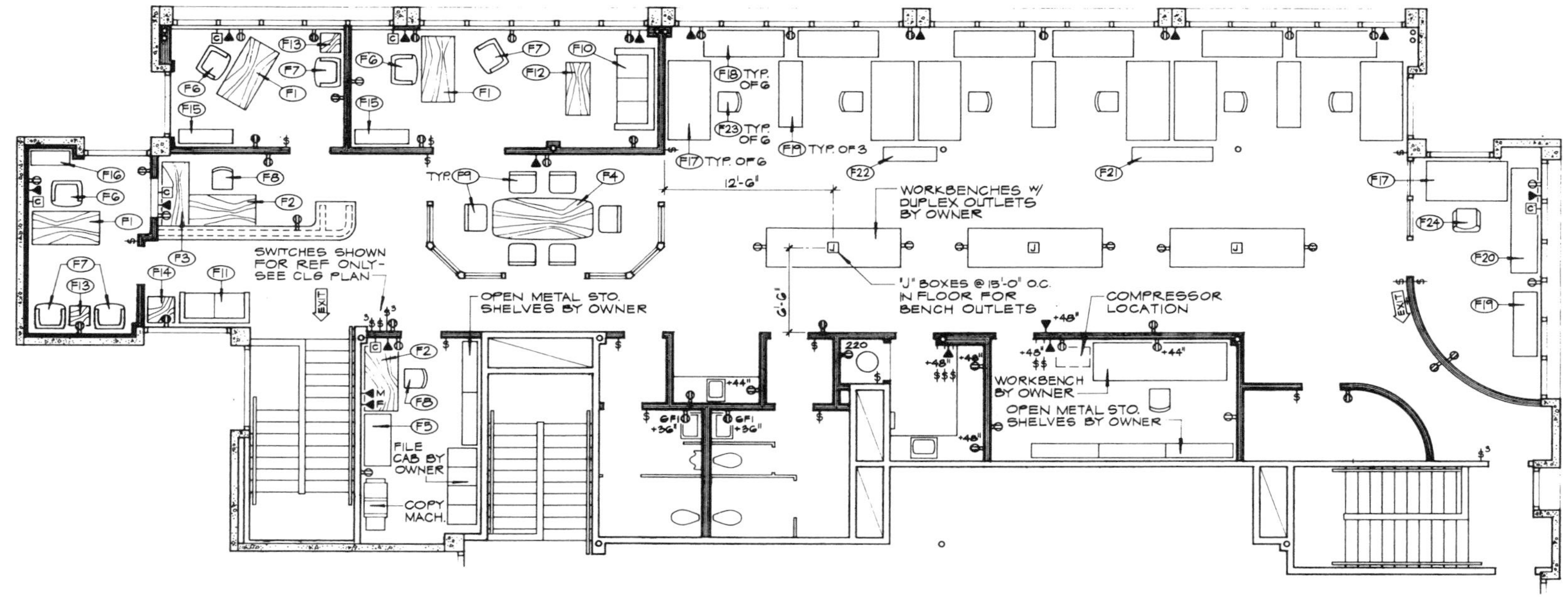

ELECTRICAL PLAN / FURNISHING LAYOUT
SCALE: 1/4" = 1'-0"

Figure 19.46 Electrical plan-furnishing layout—Stage III.

in preparation for listing the various sizes, materials, and manufacturers' identification numbers.

STAGE III (Figure 19.49). The final stage of the ceiling plan is to letter all the lighting fixture symbols and locate the heating supply air ducts and diffusers. Dimensioning of some of the various lighting fixtures has now been completed, as have the final notes, the title of the drawing, and the scale designation.

The various schedules, which were blocked out in Stage II, are now completed, providing all necessary information and symbol identification.

Partition Walls and Sections

The final step in the development of the working drawings for this project is to provide sections for the various partition walls and other related wall assemblies. Initially, the drawing process for these partition walls is to lightly block out the partition wall section and progressively delineate the various members required for the completion of the detail. The completed detail is now profiled with line quality that will provide clarity to the drawing. Finally, lettering, leader lines, and arrows are incorporated in the detail. The progression of these partition wall sections is depicted in Figures 19.50 through 19.54.

Figures 19.55 and 19.56 illustrate additional partition wall sections as they progress toward completion of their respective details. Figure 19.57 depicts the completed drawings for all the partition wall sections.

The purpose and function of the various partition wall sections, as illustrated in Figure 19.57, are as follows: Partition wall section ① illustrates the wall assembly between the studio and office 1, defining the size and gauge of the metal studs and their spacing. Wall insulation and the wall finish are defined, as well as the attachment to the floor and ceiling. Ceiling heights are also noted.

Partition wall section ② indicates that the wall is to extend all the way to the roof framing in order to provide additional soundproofing between offices 1 and 2.

The assembly of partition wall section ③ illustrates the condition where the wall terminates just above the suspended ceiling members. To stabilize this wall for lateral support, metal wall braces are attached to the top of the wall and the roof framing. This partition wall assembly occurs in the coffee bar and restroom areas.

Partition wall section ④, which is to be erected between the darkroom and the paint/workroom, is detailed for the wall to continue up to the roof framing with sound-absorbing insulation board applied on the paint/workroom side. Note that resilient clips are called for to provide greater soundproofing capability.

The partition wall assembly that divides studios 1 and 2 is illustrated on partition wall section ⑤. This assem-

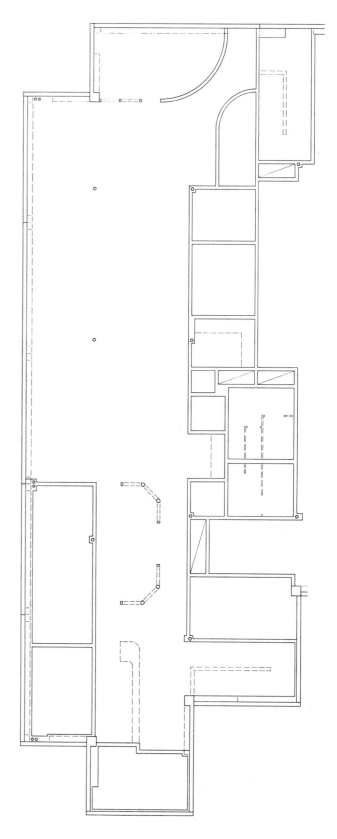

Figure 19.47 Ceiling plan—Stage I.

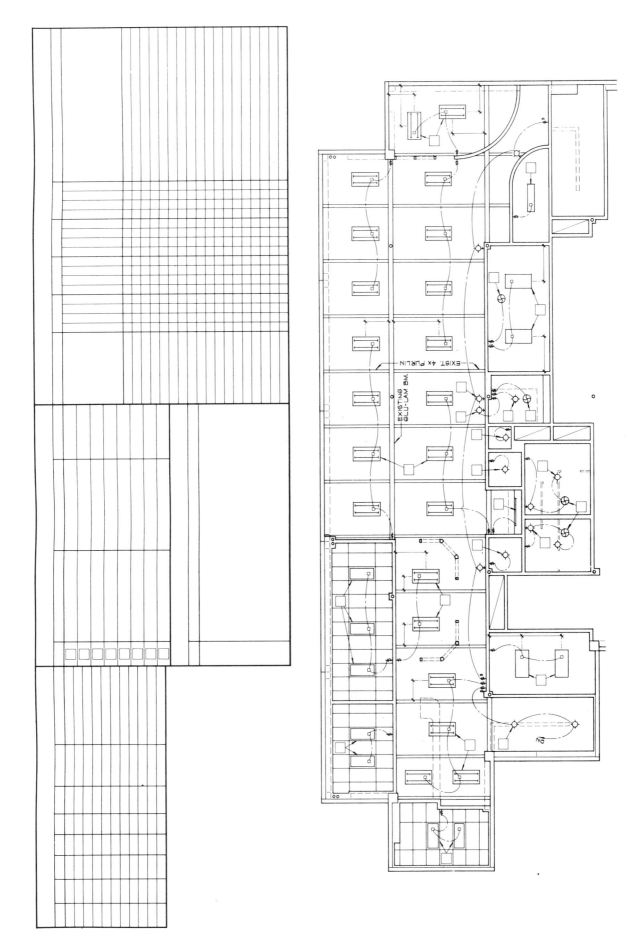

EXISTING GLU-LAM BM.

EXIST. 4x PURLIN

ON

Figure 19.48 Ceiling plan—Stage II.

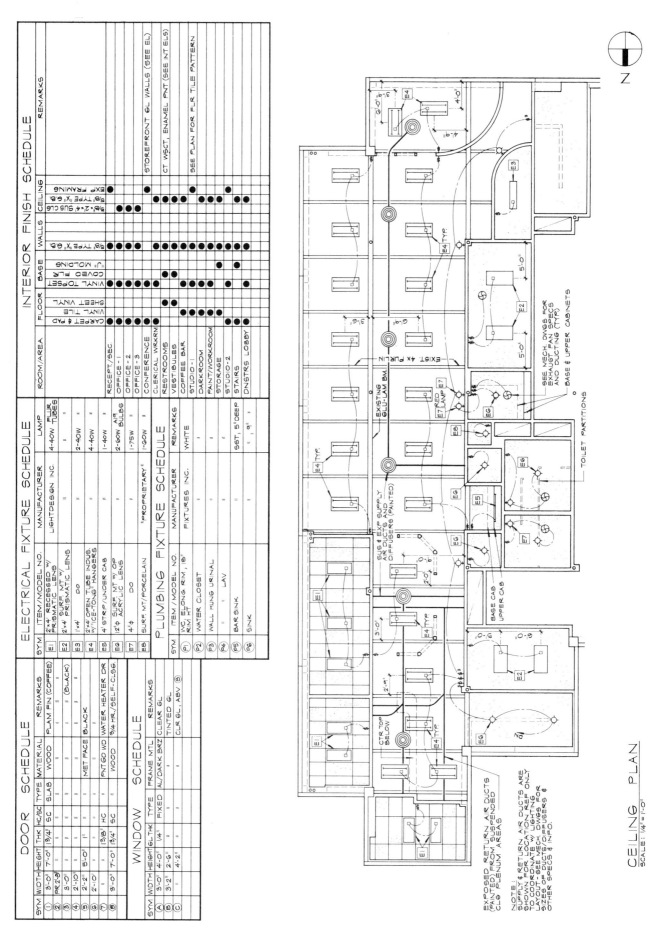

CEILING PLAN
SCALE: 1/4" = 1'-0"

Figure 19.49 Ceiling plan—Stage III.

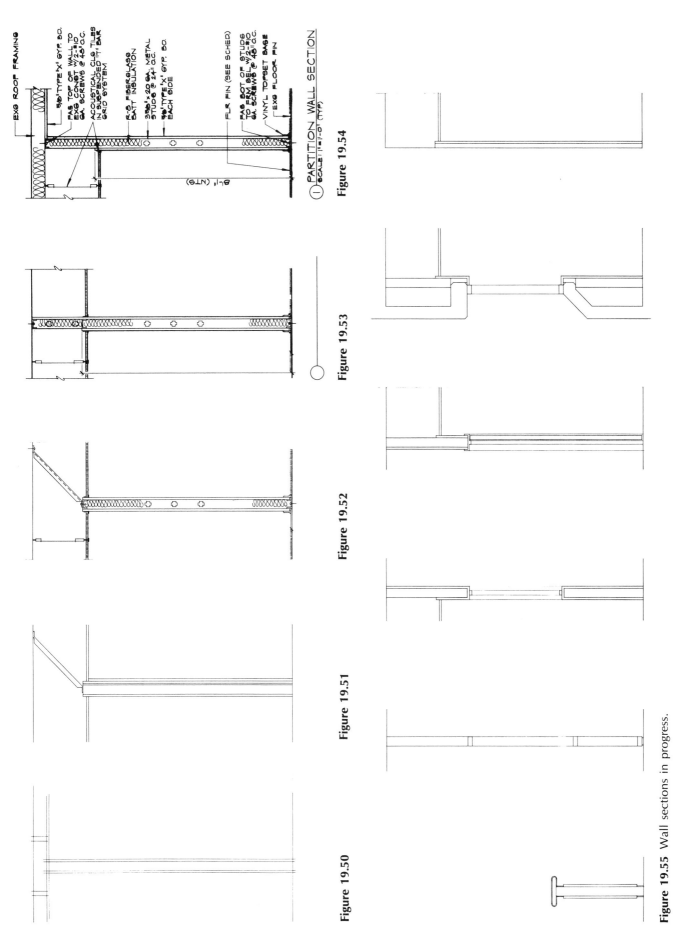

Figure 19.54

PARTITION WALL SECTION
SCALE: 1"=1'-0" (TYP)

EXG ROOF FRAMING

5/8" TYPE 'X' GYP. BD.

FAS TOP OF WALL TO
EXG CONST W/1/2-#10
GA. SCREWS @ 48" O.C.

ACOUSTICAL CLG TILES
IN SUSPENDED 1"x1" BAR
GRID SYSTEM

R-9 FIBERGLASS
BATT INSULATION

3 5/8" x 20 GA. METAL
STUDS @ 24" O.C.

5/8" TYPE 'X' GYP. BD.
EACH SIDE

FLR FIN (SEE SCHED)

FAS BOT OF STUDS
TO FRM BEL W/1/2-#10
GA. SCREWS @ 48" O.C.

VINYL TOPSET BASE

EXG FLOOR FIN

8'-11" (NTS)

Figure 19.53

Figure 19.52

Figure 19.51

Figure 19.50

Figure 19.55 Wall sections in progress.

613

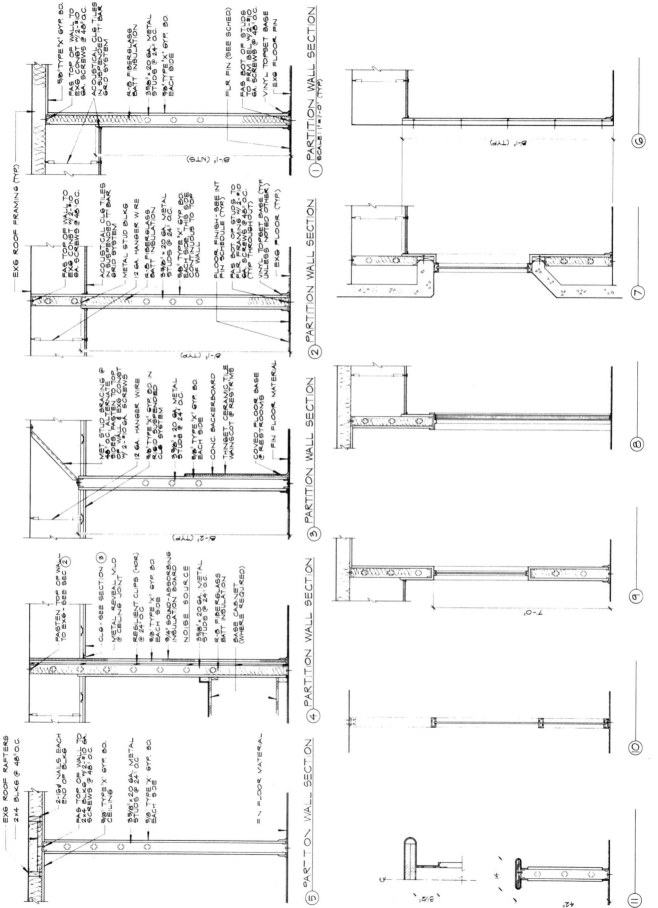

Figure 19.56 Wall sections in progress.

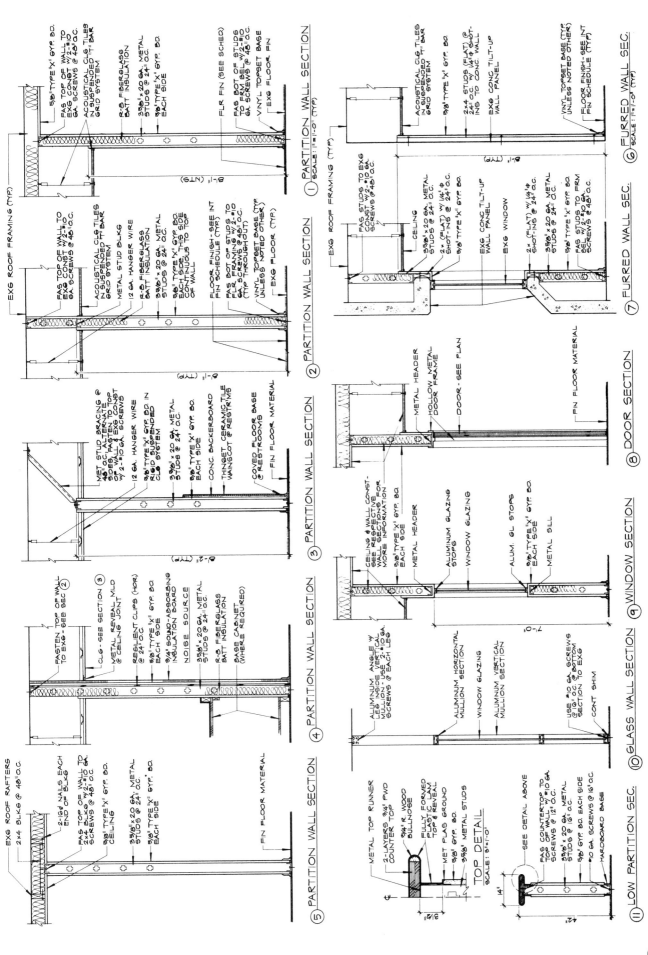

Figure 19.57 Completed partition wall sections.

615

bly provides for the partition wall to terminate at the roof framing, with no wall insulation. Note that there are no suspended ceilings in these areas, and that it will be necessary to provide 2 × 4 blocking between the existing roof rafters in order to attach the wall at that level when the roof rafters do not coincide with the wall locations.

Existing unfinished concrete walls, which are located in office 3, will be finished with ⅝"-thick gypsum board. To attach the gypsum board and provide a space for electrical and telephone conduits, the wall will be furred out with 2 × 4 flat studs attached to the concrete wall. This detail is illustrated on furred wall section ⑥.

Another furred wall condition that will be detailed occurs at the exterior walls that include unfinished concrete and window areas. Because of the wall configuration at the window locations, short sections of steel studs and gypsum board are detailed below and above the glass areas with various attachment methods. See furred wall section ⑦.

Interior passage door assemblies are detailed as shown on door section ⑧. This detail illustrates the type of door frame, door header, and wall construction and finish above the door.

As indicated on the floor plan, a window is located between office 3 and the secretarial area. This wall and window assembly will be detailed to illustrate the window height, type of glazing, glass stops, and wall construction and finishes above and below the window area. Note the change of ceiling heights and finishes between these areas. This detail is depicted on window section ⑨.

The conference area is to be partially screened with glass and aluminum wall partition. The design and location of the various aluminum members are illustrated on glass wall section ⑩. For lateral stabilization of this partition, the attachment of the vertical aluminum mullions at the floor and roof framing is most important.

The final partition section for this project is the low partition section ⑪. First, this detail illustrates the height and width of the low partition and the various members that are required for this assembly. Because the low partition acts as a space divider, it also serves as a countertop. A portion of this countertop is detailed at a larger scale, illustrating the countertop finish and shape, and showing the wall finishes directly below the countertop.

APPENDIX A

A SURVEY OF REGIONAL DIFFERENCES

This appendix presents the results of a nationwide survey that collected information about regional differences in code requirements, materials used, climatic and geological concerns, and recommended construction techniques.

Figure A.1 Distribution of cities in survey.

Table A.1 Cities Responding to Survey

Alabama	Tallahassee	*Maryland*	*New Jersey*	*South Dakota*
Mobile	Tampa	Annapolis	Camden	Aberdeen
Montgomery		Hagerstown	Newark	Rapid City
Tuscaloosa	*Georgia*		Patterson	
	Atlanta	*Massachusetts*		*Tennessee*
Alaska	Columbus	Cambridge	*New Mexico*	Jackson
Anchorage	Macon	Leominster	Albuquerque	Knoxville
Fairbanks	Rome	New Bedford	Carlsbad	Nashville
Kodiak	Savannah	Springfield	Las Cruces	
			Santa Fe	*Texas*
Arizona	*Hawaii*	*Michigan*		Austin
Page	Hilo	Kalamazoo	*New York*	Dallas
Phoenix	Honolulu	Lansing	Buffalo	Fort Worth
Scottsdale		Midland	Ogdensburg	San Antonio
Tucson	*Idaho*	Mt. Pleasant	Syracuse	
Yuma	Boise	Saginaw		*Utah*
	Coeur D'Alene		*North Carolina*	Coalville
Arkansas	Moscow	*Minnesota*	Charlotte	Logan
Fort Smith	Nampa	Albert Lea	Greensboro	Ogden
Little Rock		Anoka		Provo City
N. Little Rock	*Illinois*	Fairmont	*North Dakota*	Salt Lake City
	Decatur	Grand Rapids	Bismarck	
California	Rock Island	Plymouth	Fargo	*Virginia*
Anaheim	Springfield	St. Paul	Grand Forks	Danville
Eureka		Two Harbors	Jamestown	Roanoke
Glendale	*Indiana*			
Los Angeles	Evansville	*Mississippi*	*Ohio*	*Vermont*
Sacramento	Fort Wayne	Gulfport	Akron	Burlington
San Diego	South Bend	Jackson	Cincinnati	Rutland
		Natchez	Dayton	
Colorado	*Iowa*			*Washington*
Boulder	Altoona	*Missouri*	*Oklahoma*	Aberdeen
Brighton	Cedar Rapids	Columbia	Bartlesville	Bellevue
Brush	Des Moines	Jefferson City	Lawton	Des Moines
Colorado Springs	Fort Madison	Kansas City	Oklahoma City	East Wenatchee
Craig	Indianola	Springfield		Ephrata
Denver	Mason City		*Oregon*	Seattle
Durango	Sioux City	*Montana*	Astoria	Spokane
Englewood	Waterloo	Billings	Corvallis	Tacoma
Fort Collins		Bozeman	Grants Pass	Walla Walla
Golden	*Kansas*	Great Falls	Portland	
Littleton	Abilene	Helena	Salem	*West Virginia*
Louisville	El Dorado	Missoula	Sweet Home	Bluefield
Salida	Garden City			Charleston
Woodland Park	Wichita	*Nebraska*	*Pennsylvania*	Morgantown
		Holdridge	Philadelphia	Parkersburg
Connecticut	*Kentucky*	Lincoln	Pittsburgh	
Hartford	Ashland	Seward	York	*Wisconsin*
New Britain	Frankfort			Eau Claire
Wethersfield	Paducah	*Nevada*	*Rhode Island*	Green Bay
		Carson City	Providence	Madison
Delaware	*Louisiana*	Henderson		Milwaukee
Laurel	Monroe	Las Vegas	*South Carolina*	Woodland
Newark	New Orleans	Reno	Charleston	
			Columbia	*Wyoming*
Florida	*Maine*	*New Hampshire*		Casper
Daytona Beach	Auburn	Claremont		Cheyenne
Miami	Portland	Manchester		Cody
Pensacola	Waterville	Rochester		

Figure A.2 States using uniform building codes.

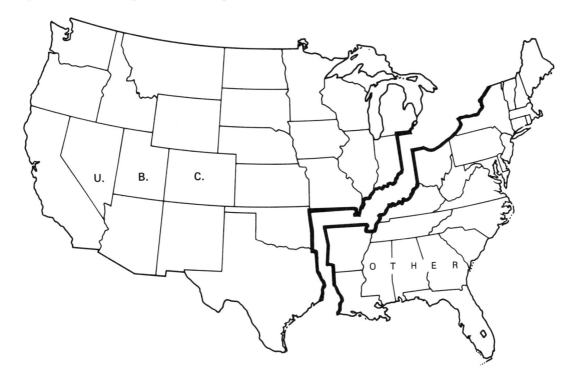

Figure A.3 Use of wood in residential structures based on questionnaire.

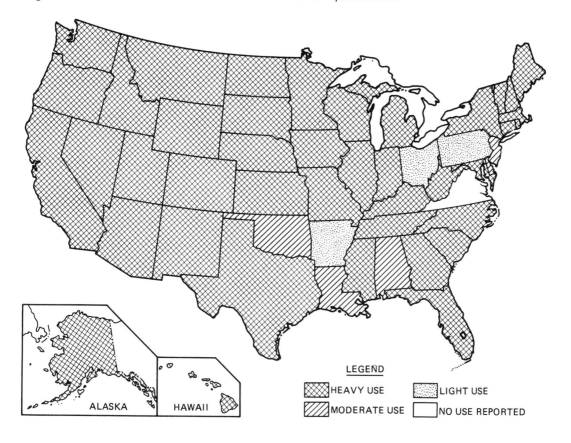

Figure A.4 Use of masonry in residential structures based on questionnaire.

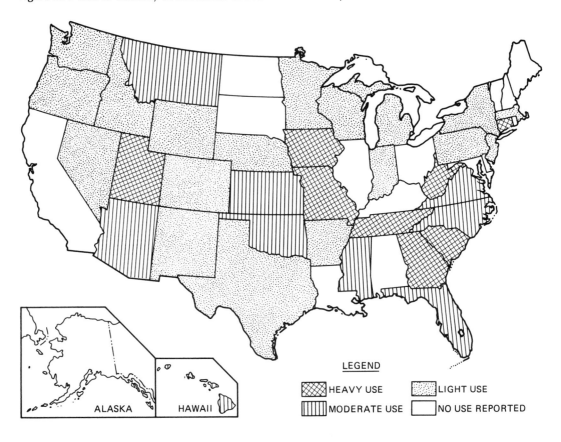

Figure A.5 Use of masonry in commercial structures based on questionnaire.

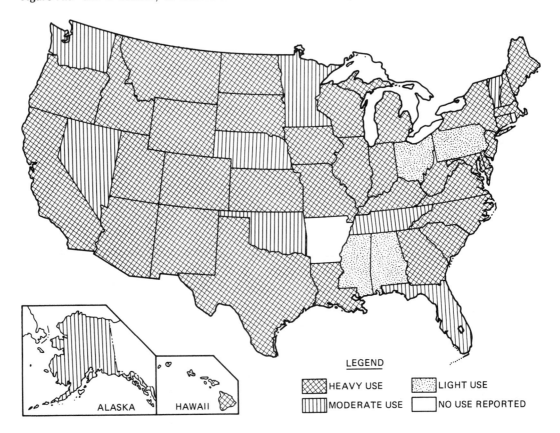

Figure A.6 Use of steel in commercial structures based on questionnaire.

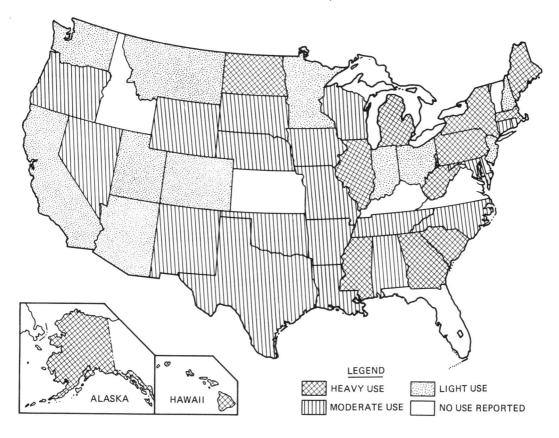

Figure A.7 Use of wood in commercial structures based on questionnaire.

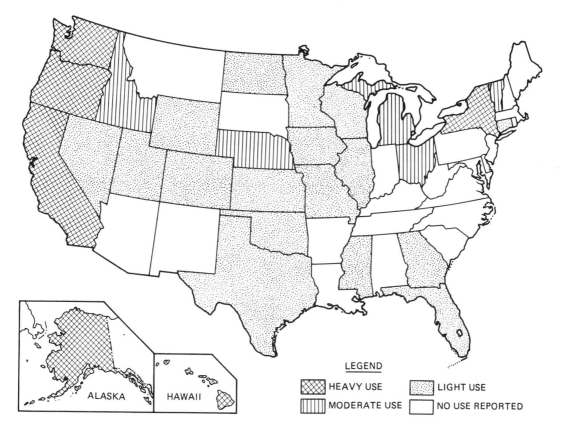

Figure A.8 Use of concrete in commercial structures based on questionnaire.

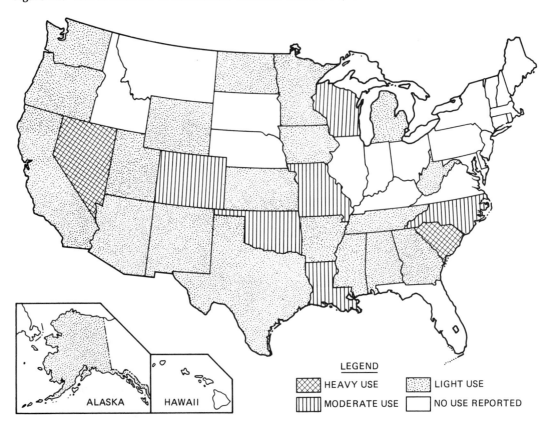

Figure A.9 Use of steel in industrial structures based on questionnaire.

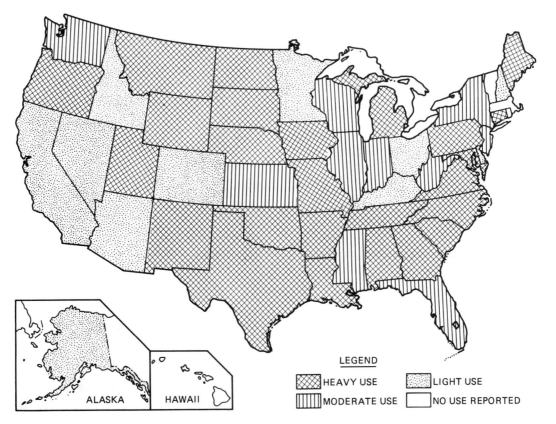

Figure A.10 Use of masonry in industrial structures based on questionnaire.

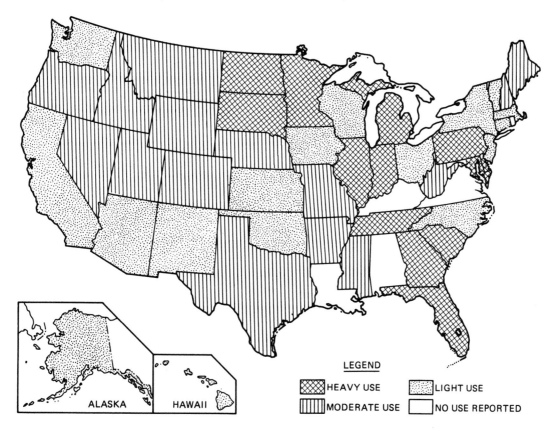

LEGEND

HEAVY USE   LIGHT USE

MODERATE USE   NO USE REPORTED

Figure A.11 Use of concrete in industrial structures based on questionnaire.

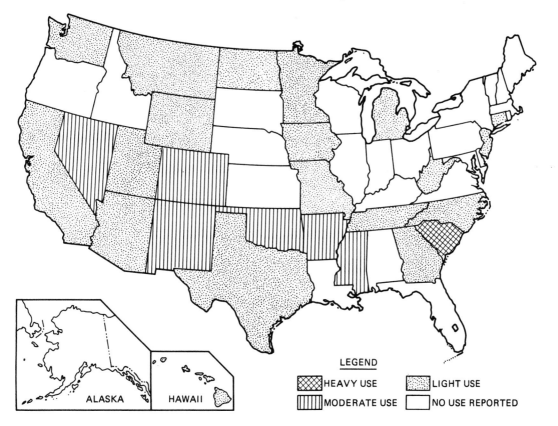

LEGEND

HEAVY USE   LIGHT USE

MODERATE USE   NO USE REPORTED

Table A.2 Special Concerns of the States by Building Departments

	Wind	Snow	Seismic	Fire	Energy	Found. Desi	Flooding	Live/Dead Loads	Struc. Desi.	Frost Depth	Hurricane	Insulation	Handicapped	Water Table	Flr/Roof Loads	Temperature	Rain	Frost	Ext. Fin.	Drainage	Vert. Load
Alabama	●				●		●	●			●										
Alaska	90 ● 100	40 ●	●		●	●															
Arizona	●	●	●	●								●					●				
Arkansas					●																
California	●		●	●	●	●														●	
Colorado	●	25 ● 175	●		●			●		●		●		●							
Connecticut	●	●								●											
Delaware	●			●																	
Florida	●		●								●										
Georgia	●				●	●					●										
Hawaii	●		●								●										
Idaho	●	25 ● 40	●			●				●											
Illinois	25 ●	30 ●		●		●															
Indiana	●	●						●		●	●			●							
Iowa	●	30 ● 40		●	●					●			●		●						
Louisiana	●					●		●													
Kansas	●	●	●						●												
Kentucky	●		●			●	●													●	
Maine		●																			●
Maryland																					
Massachussetts		●	●		●		●	●	●				●	●							
Michigan	●	●		●	●					●			●	●					●		
Minnesota	●	●			●	●		●	●	●			●		●					●	
Mississippi	●						●				●									●	
Missouri	●	●		●			●	●		●		●									

Table A.2 (*continued*)

	Wind	Snow	Seismic	Fire	Energy	Found. Des.	Flooding	Live/Dead Loads	Struct. Des.	Frost Depth	Hurricane	Insulation	Handicapped	Water Table	Flr/Roof Loads	Temperature	Rain	Frost	Ext. Fin.	Drainage	Vert. Load
Montana	●	●	●			●			●	●				●							
Nebraska	●	30 ●	●													●					
Nevada	●	●	●				●									●					
New Hampshire		●	●	●	●																
New Jersey							●														
New Mexico	30 ●	●	●						●							●		●			
New York		●		●	●				●												
No. Carolina	●	●		●				●													
No. Dakota	●	30 ●				●															
Ohio		●		●	●	●															
Oklahoma	15 ●	25 ●	●					●													
Oregon	15 ● 20	25 ●	●	●	●	●	●		●			●	●				●				
Pennsylvania							●														
Rhode Island				●				●							●						
South Carolina	●		●				●														
South Dakota	●	●							●												
Tennessee	●	20 ●						●	●						●						
Texas	●	●			●	●	●	●			●										
Utah		20 ● 100	●																		
Vermont		●																	●		
Virginia						●	●														
Washington	●	30 ●	●	●		●						●	●			●	●	●			
W. Virginia	●	●		●		●															
Wisconsin		●		●																	
Wyoming	●	●		●																	

APPENDIX B

Table B.1 Fraction to Metric Conversion

Fractions of Inch	64ths of Inch	Decimals	Millimeters	Fractions of Inch	64ths of Inch	Decimals	Millimeters
—	1	.015625	0.397	—	33	.515625	13.097
1/32	2	.031250	0.794	17/32	34	.531250	13.494
—	3	.046875	1.191	—	35	.546875	13.891
1/16	4	.062500	1.588	9/16	36	.562500	14.288
—	5	.078125	1.984	—	37	.578125	14.684
3/32	6	.093750	2.381	19/32	38	.593750	15.081
—	7	.109375	2.778	—	39	.609375	15.478
1/8	8	.125000	3.175	5/8	40	.625000	15.875
—	9	.140625	3.572	—	41	.640625	16.272
5/32	10	.156260	3.969	21/32	42	.656250	16.669
—	11	.171875	4.366	—	43	.671875	17.066
3/16	12	.187500	4.763	11/16	44	.687500	17.463
—	13	.203125	5.159	—	45	.703125	17.859
7/32	14	.218750	5.556	23/32	46	.718750	18.256
—	15	.234375	5.953	—	47	.734375	18.653
1/4	16	.250000	6.350	3/4	48	.750000	19.050
—	17	.265625	6.747	—	49	.765625	19.447
9/32	18	.281250	7.144	25/32	50	.781250	19.844
—	19	.296875	7.541	—	51	.796875	20.241
5/16	20	.312500	7.938	13/16	52	.812500	20.638
—	21	.328125	8.334	—	53	.828125	21.034
11/32	22	.343750	8.731	27/32	54	.843750	21.431
—	23	.359375	9.128	—	55	.859375	21.828
3/8	24	.375000	9.525	7/8	56	.875000	22.225
—	25	.390625	9.922	—	57	.890625	22.622
13/32	26	.406250	10.319	29/32	58	.906250	23.019
—	27	.421875	10.716	—	59	.921875	23.416
7/16	28	.437500	11.113	15/16	60	.937500	23.813
—	29	.453125	11.509	—	61	.953125	24.209
15/32	30	.468750	11.906	31/32	62	.968750	24.606
—	31	.484375	12.303	—	63	.984375	25.003
1/2	32	.500000	12.700	1	64	1.000000	25.400

Table B.2 Feet to Meter Conversion

Feet	Meters	Feet	Meters	Feet	Meters	Feet	Meters	Feet	Meters
0	0.00000	50	15.24003	100	30.48006	150	45.72009	200	60.96012
1	.30480	1	15.54483	1	30.78486	1	46.02489	1	61.26492
2	.60960	2	15.84963	2	31.08966	2	46.32969	2	61.56972
3	.91440	3	16.15443	3	31.39446	3	46.63449	3	61.87452
4	1.21920	4	16.45923	4	31.69926	4	46.93929	4	62.17932
5	1.52400	5	16.76403	5	32.00406	5	47.24409	5	62.48412
6	1.82880	6	17.06883	6	32.30886	6	47.54890	6	62.78893
7	2.13360	7	17.37363	7	32.61367	7	47.85370	7	63.09373
8	2.43840	8	17.67844	8	32.91847	8	48.15850	8	63.39853
9	2.74321	9	17.98324	9	33.22327	9	48.46330	9	63.70333
10	3.04801	60	18.28804	110	33.52807	160	48.76810	210	64.00813
1	3.35281	1	18.59284	1	33.83287	1	49.07290	1	64.31293
2	3.65761	2	18.89764	2	34.13767	2	49.37770	2	64.61773
3	3.96241	3	19.20244	3	34.44247	3	49.68250	3	64.92253
4	4.26721	4	19.50724	4	34.74727	4	49.98730	4	65.22733
5	4.57201	5	19.81204	5	35.05207	5	50.29210	5	65.53213
6	4.87681	6	20.11684	6	35.35687	6	50.59690	6	65.83693
7	5.18161	7	20.42164	7	35.66167	7	50.90170	7	66.14173
8	5.48641	8	20.72644	8	35.96647	8	51.20650	8	66.44653
9	5.79121	9	21.03124	9	36.27127	9	51.51130	9	66.75133
20	6.09601	70	21.33604	120	36.57607	170	51.81610	220	67.05613
1	6.40081	1	21.64084	1	36.88087	1	52.12090	1	67.36093
2	6.70561	2	21.94564	2	37.18567	2	52.42570	2	67.66574
3	7.01041	3	22.25044	3	37.49047	3	52.73051	3	67.97054
4	7.31521	4	22.55525	4	37.79528	4	53.03531	4	68.27534
5	7.62002	5	22.86005	5	38.10008	5	53.34011	5	68.58014
6	7.92482	6	23.16485	6	38.40488	6	53.64491	6	68.88494
7	8.22962	7	23.46965	7	38.70968	7	53.94971	7	69.18974
8	8.53442	8	23.77445	8	39.01448	8	54.25451	8	69.49454
9	8.83922	9	24.07925	9	39.31928	9	54.55931	9	69.79934
30	9.14402	80	24.38405	130	39.62408	180	54.86411	230	70.10414
1	9.44882	1	24.68885	1	39.92888	1	55.16891	1	70.40894
2	9.75362	2	24.99365	2	40.23368	2	55.47371	2	70.71374
3	10.05842	3	25.29845	3	40.53848	3	55.77851	3	71.01854
4	10.36322	4	25.60325	4	40.84328	4	56.08331	4	71.32334
5	10.66802	5	25.90805	5	41.14808	5	56.38811	5	71.62814
6	10.97282	6	26.21285	6	41.45288	6	56.69291	6	71.93294
7	11.27762	7	26.51765	7	41.75768	7	56.99771	7	72.23774
8	11.58242	8	26.82245	8	42.06248	8	57.30251	8	72.54255
9	11.88722	9	27.12725	9	42.36728	9	57.60732	9	72.84735
40	12.19202	90	27.43205	140	42.67209	190	57.91212	240	73.15215
1	12.49682	1	27.73686	1	42.97689	1	58.21692	1	73.45695
2	12.80163	2	28.04166	2	43.28169	2	58.52172	2	73.76175
3	13.10643	3	28.34646	3	43.58649	3	58.82652	3	74.06655
4	13.41123	4	28.65126	4	43.89129	4	59.13132	4	74.37135
5	13.71603	5	28.95606	5	44.19609	5	59.43612	5	74.67615
6	14.02083	6	29.26086	6	44.50089	6	59.74092	6	74.98095
7	14.32563	7	29.56566	7	44.80569	7	60.04572	7	75.28575
8	14.63043	8	29.87046	8	45.11049	8	60.35052	8	75.59055
9	14.93523	9	30.17526	9	45.41529	9	60.65532	9	75.89535

1 inch	= 0.02549 meter	4 inches = 0.10160 meter	7 inches = 0.17780 meter	10 inches = 0.25400 meter
2 inches	= 0.05080 meter	5 inches = 0.12700 meter	8 inches = 0.20320 meter	11 inches = 0.27940 meter
3 inches	= 0.07620 meter	6 inches = 0.15240 meter	9 inches = 0.22860 meter	12 inches = 0.30480 meter

Table B.2 *(continued)*

Feet	Meters	Feet	Meters	Feet	Meters	Feet	Meters	Feet	Meters
250	76.20015	300	91.44018	350	106.68021	400	121.92024	450	137.16027
1	76.50495	1	91.74498	1	106.98501	1	122.22504	1	137.46507
2	76.80975	2	92.04978	2	107.28981	2	122.52985	2	137.76988
3	77.11455	3	92.35458	3	107.59462	3	122.83465	3	138.07468
4	77.41935	4	92.65939	4	107.89942	4	123.13945	4	138.37948
5	77.72416	5	92.96419	5	108.20422	5	123.44425	5	138.68428
6	78.02896	6	93.26899	6	108.50902	6	123.74905	6	138.98908
7	78.33376	7	93.57379	7	108.81382	7	124.05385	7	139.29388
8	78.63856	8	93.87859	8	109.11862	8	124.35865	8	139.59868
9	78.94336	9	94.18339	9	109.42342	9	124.66345	9	139.90348
260	79.24816	310	94.48819	360	109.72822	410	124.96825	460	140.20828
1	79.55296	1	94.79299	1	110.03302	1	125.27305	1	140.51308
2	79.85776	2	95.09779	2	110.33782	2	125.57785	2	140.81788
3	80.16256	3	95.40259	3	110.64262	3	125.88265	3	141.12268
4	80.46736	4	95.70739	4	110.94742	4	126.18745	4	141.42748
5	80.77216	5	96.01219	5	111.25222	5	126.49225	5	141.73228
6	81.07696	6	96.31699	6	111.55702	6	126.79705	6	142.03708
7	81.38176	7	96.62179	7	111.86182	7	127.10185	7	142.34188
8	81.68656	8	96.92659	8	112.16662	8	127.40665	8	142.64669
9	81.99136	9	97.23139	9	112.47142	9	127.71146	9	142.95149
270	82.29616	320	97.53620	370	112.77623	420	128.01626	470	143.25629
1	82.60097	1	97.84100	1	113.08103	1	128.32106	1	143.56109
2	82.90577	2	98.14580	2	113.38583	2	128.62586	2	143.86589
3	83.21057	3	98.45060	3	113.69063	3	128.93066	3	144.17069
4	83.51537	4	98.75540	4	113.99543	4	129.23546	4	144.47549
5	83.82017	5	99.06020	5	114.30023	5	129.54026	5	144.78029
6	84.12497	6	99.36500	6	114.60503	6	129.84506	6	145.08509
7	84.42977	7	99.66980	7	114.90983	7	130.14986	7	145.38989
8	84.73457	8	99.97460	8	115.21463	8	130.45466	8	145.69469
9	85.03937	9	100.27940	9	115.51943	9	130.75946	9	145.99949
280	85.34417	330	100.58420	380	115.82423	430	131.06426	480	146.30429
1	85.64897	1	100.88900	1	116.12903	1	131.36906	1	146.60909
2	85.95377	2	101.19380	2	116.43383	2	131.67386	2	146.91389
3	86.25857	3	101.49860	3	116.73863	3	131.97866	3	147.21869
4	86.56337	4	101.80340	4	117.04343	4	132.28346	4	147.52350
5	86.86817	5	102.10820	5	117.34823	5	132.58827	5	147.82830
6	87.17297	6	102.41300	6	117.65304	6	132.89307	6	148.13310
7	87.47777	7	102.71781	7	117.95784	7	133.19787	7	148.43790
8	87.78258	8	103.02261	8	118.26264	8	133.50267	8	148.74270
9	88.08738	9	103.32741	9	118.56744	9	133.80747	9	149.04750
290	88.39218	340	103.63221	390	118.87224	440	134.11227	490	149.35230
1	88.69698	1	103.93701	1	119.17704	1	134.41707	1	149.65710
2	89.00178	2	104.24181	2	119.48184	2	134.72187	2	149.96190
3	89.30658	3	104.54661	3	119.78664	3	135.02667	3	150.26670
4	89.61138	4	104.85141	4	120.09144	4	135.33147	4	150.57150
5	89.91618	5	105.15621	5	120.39624	5	135.63627	5	150.87630
6	90.22098	6	105.46101	6	120.70104	6	135.94107	6	151.18110
7	90.52578	7	105.76581	7	121.00584	7	136.24587	7	151.48590
8	90.83058	8	106.07061	8	121.31064	8	136.55067	8	151.79070
9	91.13538	9	106.37541	9	121.61544	9	136.85547	9	152.09550
								500	152.40030

1 inch	= 0.02540 meter	4 inches = 0.10160 meter	7 inches = 0.17780 meter	10 inches = 0.25400 meter
2 inches	= 0.05080 meter	5 inches = 0.12700 meter	8 inches = 0.20320 meter	11 inches = 0.27940 meter
3 inches	= 0.07620 meter	6 inches = 0.15240 meter	9 inches = 0.22860 meter	12 inches = 0.30480 meter

Table B.3

Feet	Meters	Feet	Meters	Feet	Meters	Feet	Meters	Feet	Meters
0	0.00000	50	164.04167	100	328.08333	150	492.12500	200	656.16667
1	3.28083	1	167.32250	1	331.36417	1	495.40583	1	659.44750
2	6.56167	2	170.60333	2	334.64500	2	498.68667	2	662.72833
3	9.84250	3	173.88417	3	337.92583	3	501.96750	3	666.00917
4	13.12333	4	177.16500	4	341.20667	4	505.24833	4	669.29000
5	16.40417	5	180.44583	5	344.48750	5	508.52917	5	672.57083
6	19.68500	6	183.72667	6	347.76833	6	511.81000	6	675.85167
7	22.96583	7	187.00750	7	351.04917	7	515.09083	7	679.13250
8	26.24667	8	190.28833	8	354.33000	8	518.37167	8	682.41333
9	29.52750	9	193.56917	9	357.61083	9	521.65250	9	685.69417
10	32.80833	60	196.85000	110	360.89167	160	524.93333	210	688.97500
1	36.08917	1	200.13083	1	364.17250	1	528.21417	1	692.25583
2	39.37000	2	203.41167	2	367.45333	2	531.49500	2	695.53667
3	42.65083	3	206.69250	3	370.73417	3	534.77583	3	698.81750
4	45.93167	4	209.97333	4	374.01500	4	538.05667	4	702.09833
5	49.21250	5	213.25417	5	377.29583	5	541.33750	5	705.37917
6	52.49333	6	216.53500	6	380.57667	6	544.61833	6	708.66000
7	55.77417	7	219.81583	7	383.85750	7	547.89917	7	711.94083
8	59.05500	8	223.09667	8	387.13833	8	551.18000	8	715.22167
9	62.33583	9	226.37750	9	390.41917	9	554.46083	9	718.50250
20	65.61667	70	229.65833	120	393.70000	170	557.74167	220	721.78333
1	68.89750	1	232.93917	1	396.90083	1	561.02250	1	725.06417
2	72.17833	2	236.22000	2	400.26167	2	564.30333	2	728.34500
3	75.45917	3	239.50083	3	403.54250	3	567.58417	3	731.62583
4	78.74000	4	242.78167	4	406.82333	4	570.86500	4	734.90667
5	82.02083	5	246.06250	5	410.10417	5	574.14583	5	738.18750
6	85.30167	6	249.34333	6	413.38500	6	577.42667	6	741.46833
7	88.58250	7	252.62417	7	416.66583	7	580.70750	7	744.74917
8	91.86333	8	255.90500	8	419.94667	8	583.98833	8	748.03000
9	95.14417	9	259.18583	9	423.22750	9	587.26917	9	751.31083
30	98.42500	80	262.46667	130	426.50833	180	590.55000	230	754.59167
1	101.70583	1	265.74750	1	429.78917	1	593.83083	1	757.87250
2	104.98667	2	269.02833	2	433.07000	2	597.11167	2	761.15333
3	108.26750	3	272.30917	3	436.35083	3	600.39250	3	764.43417
4	111.54833	4	275.59000	4	439.63167	4	603.67333	4	767.71500
5	114.82917	5	278.87083	5	442.91250	5	606.95417	5	770.99583
6	118.11000	6	282.15167	6	446.19333	6	610.23500	6	774.27667
7	121.39083	7	285.43250	7	449.47417	7	613.51583	7	777.55750
8	124.67167	8	288.71333	8	452.75500	8	616.79667	8	780.83833
9	127.95250	9	291.99417	9	456.03583	9	620.07750	9	784.11917
40	131.23333	90	295.27500	140	459.31667	190	623.35833	240	787.40000
1	134.51417	1	298.55583	1	462.59750	1	626.63917	1	790.68083
2	137.79500	2	301.83667	2	465.87833	2	629.92000	2	793.96167
3	141.07583	3	305.11750	3	469.15917	3	633.20083	3	797.24250
4	144.35667	4	308.39833	4	472.44000	4	636.48167	4	800.52333
5	147.63750	5	311.67917	5	475.72083	5	639.76250	5	803.80417
6	150.91833	6	314.96000	6	479.00167	6	643.04333	6	807.08500
7	154.19917	7	318.24083	7	482.28250	7	646.32417	7	810.36583
8	157.48000	8	321.52167	8	485.56333	8	649.60500	8	813.64667
9	160.76083	9	324.80250	9	488.84417	9	652.88583	9	816.92750

Table B.3 *(continued)*

Feet	Meters	Feet	Meters	Feet	Meters	Feet	Meters	Feet	Meters
250	820.20833	300	984.25000	350	1,148.29167	400	1,312.33333	450	1,476.37500
1	823.48917	1	987.53083	1	1,151.57250	1	1,315.61417	1	1,479.65583
2	826.77000	2	990.81167	2	1,154.85333	2	1,318.89500	2	1,482.93667
3	830.05083	3	994.09250	3	1,158.13417	3	1,322.17583	3	1,486.21750
4	833.33167	4	997.37333	4	1,161.41500	4	1,325.45667	4	1,489.49833
5	836.61250	5	1,000.65417	5	1,164.69583	5	1,328.73750	5	1,492.77917
6	839.89333	6	1,003.93500	6	1,167.97667	6	1,332.01833	6	1,496.06000
7	843.17417	7	1,007.21583	7	1,171.25750	7	1,335.29917	7	1,499.34083
8	846.45500	8	1,010.49667	8	1,174.53833	8	1,338.58000	8	1,502.62167
9	849.73583	9	1,013.77750	9	1,177.81917	9	1,341.86083	9	1,505.90250
260	853.01667	310	1,017.05833	360	1,181.10000	410	1,345.14167	460	1,509.18333
1	856.29750	1	1,020.33917	1	1,184.38083	1	1,348.42250	1	1,512.46417
2	859.57833	2	1,023.62000	2	1,187.66167	2	1,351.70333	2	1,515.74500
3	862.85917	3	1,026.90083	3	1,190.94250	3	1,354.98417	3	1,519.02583
4	866.14000	4	1,030.18167	4	1,194.22333	4	1,358.26500	4	1,522.30667
5	869.42083	5	1,033.46250	5	1,197.50417	5	1,361.54583	5	1,525.58750
6	872.70167	6	1,036.74333	6	1,200.78500	6	1,364.82667	6	1,528.86833
7	875.98250	7	1,040.02417	7	1,204.06583	7	1,368.10750	7	1,532.14917
8	879.26333	8	1,043.30500	8	1,207.34667	8	1,371.38833	8	1,535.48000
9	882.54417	9	1,046.58583	9	1,210.62750	9	1,374.66917	9	1,538.71083
270	885.82500	320	1,049.86667	370	1,213.90833	420	1,377.95000	470	1,541.99167
1	889.10583	1	1,053.14750	1	1,217.18917	1	1,381.23083	1	1,545.27250
2	892.38667	2	1,056.42833	2	1,220.47000	2	1,384.51167	2	1,548.55333
3	895.66750	3	1,059.70917	3	1,223.75083	3	1,387.79250	3	1,551.83417
4	898.94833	4	1,062.99000	4	1,227.03167	4	1,391.07333	4	1,555.11500
5	902.22917	5	1,066.27083	5	1,230.31250	5	1,394.35417	5	1,558.39583
6	905.51000	6	1,069.55167	6	1,233.59333	6	1,397.63500	6	1,561.67667
7	908.79083	7	1,072.83250	7	1,236.87417	7	1,400.91583	7	1,564.95750
8	912.07167	8	1,076.11333	8	1,240.15500	8	1,404.19667	8	1,568.23833
9	915.35250	9	1,079.39417	9	1,243.43583	9	1,407.47750	9	1,571.51917
280	918.63333	330	1,082.67500	380	1,246.71667	430	1,410.75833	480	1,574.80000
1	921.91417	1	1,085.95583	1	1,249.99750	1	1,414.03917	1	1,578.08083
2	925.19500	2	1,089.23667	2	1,253.27833	2	1,417.32000	2	1,581.36167
3	928.47583	3	1,092.51750	3	1,256.55917	3	1,420.60083	3	1,584.64250
4	931.75667	4	1,095.79833	4	1,259.84000	4	1,423.88167	4	1,587.92333
5	935.03750	5	1,099.07917	5	1,263.12083	5	1,427.16250	5	1,591.20417
6	938.31833	6	1,102.36000	6	1,266.40167	6	1,430.44333	6	1,594.48500
7	941.59917	7	1,105.64083	7	1,269.68250	7	1,433.72417	7	1,597.76583
8	944.88000	8	1,108.92167	8	1,272.96333	8	1,437.00500	8	1,601.04667
9	948.16083	9	1,112.20250	9	1,276.24417	9	1,440.28583	9	1,604.32750
290	951.44167	340	1,115.48333	390	1,279.52500	440	1,443.56667	490	1,607.60833
1	954.72250	1	1,118.76417	1	1,282.80583	1	1,446.84750	1	1,610.88917
2	958.00333	2	1,122.04500	2	1,286.08667	2	1,450.40927	2	1,614.17000
3	961.28417	3	1,125.32583	3	1,289.36750	3	1,453.12833	3	1,617.45083
4	964.56500	4	1,128.60667	4	1,292.64833	4	1,456.69000	4	1,620.73167
5	967.84583	5	1,131.88750	5	1,295.92917	5	1,459.97083	5	1,624.01250
6	971.12667	6	1,135.16833	6	1,299.21000	6	1,463.25167	6	1,627.29333
7	974.40750	7	1,138.44917	7	1,302.49083	7	1,466.53250	7	1,630.57417
8	977.68833	8	1,141.73000	8	1,305.77167	8	1,469.81333	8	1,633.85500
9	980.96917	9	1,145.01083	9	1,309.05250	9	1,473.09417	9	1,637.13583
								500	1,640.41667

Table B.4 Concrete Block Dimensional Chart

TABLE A (MODULAR) — 3/8" HORIZ. AND VERTICAL MORTAR JOINTS

LENGTH	NO. 16" LONG BLOCKS	HEIGHT	NO. 4" HIGH BLOCKS	NO. 8" HIGH BLOCKS
0'-8"	1/2	0'-4"	1	
1'-4"	1	0'-8"	2	1
2'-0"	1 1/2	1'-0"	3	
2'-8"	2	1'-4"	4	2
3'-4"	2 1/2	1'-8"	5	
4'-0"	3	2'-0"	6	3
4'-8"	3 1/2	2'-4"	7	
5'-4"	4	2'-8"	8	4
6'-0"	4 1/2	3'-0"	9	
6'-8"	5	3'-4"	10	5
7'-4"	5 1/2	3'-8"	11	
8'-0"	6	4'-0"	12	6
8'-8"	6 1/2	4'-4"	13	
9'-4"	7	4'-8"	14	7
10'-0"	7 1/2	5'-0"	15	
10'-8"	8	5'-4"	16	8
11'-4"	8 1/2	5'-8"	17	
12'-0"	9	6'-0"	18	9
12'-8"	9 1/2	6'-4"	19	
13'-4"	10	6'-8"	20	10
14'-0"	10 1/2	7'-0"	21	
14'-8"	11	7'-4"	22	11
15'-4"	11 1/2	7'-8"	23	
16'-0"	12	8'-0"	24	12
16'-8"	12 1/2	8'-4"	25	
17'-4"	13	8'-8"	26	13
18'-0"	13 1/2	9'-0"	27	
18'-8"	14	9'-4"	28	14
19'-4"	14 1/2	9'-8"	29	
20'-0"	15	10'-0"	30	15
20'-8"	15 1/2	10'-4"	31	
21'-4"	16	10'-8"	32	16
22'-0"	16 1/2	11'-0"	33	
22'-8"	17	11'-4"	34	17
23'-4"	17 1/2	11'-8"	35	
24'-0"	18	12'-0"	36	18
24'-8"	18 1/2	12'-4"	37	
25'-4"	19	12'-8"	38	19
26'-0"	19 1/2	13'-0"	39	
26'-8"	20	13'-4"	40	20
27'-4"	20 1/2	13'-8"	41	
28'-0"	21	14'-0"	42	21
28'-8"	21 1/2	14'-4"	43	
29'-4"	22	14'-8"	44	22
30'-0"	22 1/2	15'-0"	45	
30'-8"	23	15'-4"	46	23
31'-4"	23 1/2	15'-8"	47	
32'-0"	24	16'-0"	48	24
32'-8"	24 1/2	16'-4"	49	
40'-0"	30	16'-8"	50	25
50'-0"	37 1/2	17'-0"	51	
60'-0"	45	17'-4"	52	26
70'-0"	52 1/2	17'-8"	53	
80'-0"	60	18'-0"	54	27
90'-0"	67 1/2	18'-4"	55	
100'-0"	75	18'-8"	56	28
200'-0"	150	19'-0"	57	
300'-0"	225	19'-4"	58	29
400'-0"	300	19'-8"	59	
500'-0"	375	20'-0"	60	30

TABLE B (NON-MODULAR) — 7/16" HORIZONTAL MORTAR JOINT

HEIGHT	NO. 4" HIGH BLOCKS	HEIGHT	NO. 8" HIGH BLOCKS
0'-4 1/16"	1		
0'-8 1/8"	2	0'-8 1/16"	1
1'-0 3/16"	3		
1'-4 1/4"	4	1'-4 1/8"	2
1'-8 5/16"	5		
2'-0 3/8"	6	2'-0 3/16"	3
2'-4 7/16"	7		
2'-8 1/2"	8	2'-8 1/4"	4
3'-0 9/16"	9		
3'-4 5/8"	10	3'-4 5/16"	5
3'-8 11/16"	11		
4'-0 3/4"	12	4'-0 3/8"	6
4'-4 13/16"	13		
4'-8 7/8"	14	4'-8 7/16"	7
5'-0 15/16"	15		
5'-5"	16	5'-4 1/2"	8
5'-9 1/16"	17		
6'-1 1/8"	18	6'-0 9/16"	9
6'-5 3/16"	19		
6'-9 1/4"	20	6'-8 5/8"	10
7'-1 5/16"	21		
7'-5 3/8"	22	7'-4 11/16"	11
7'-9 7/16"	23		
8'-1 1/2"	24	8'-0 3/4"	12
8'-5 9/16"	25		
8'-9 5/8"	26	8'-8 13/16"	13
9'-1 11/16"	27		
9'-5 3/4"	28	9'-4 7/8"	14
9'-9 13/16"	29		
10'-1 7/8"	30	10'-0 15/16"	15
10'-5 15/16"	31		
10'-10"	32	10'-9"	16
11'-2 1/16"	33		
11'-6 1/8"	34	11'-5 1/16"	17
11'-10 3/16"	35		
12'-2 1/4"	36	12'-1 1/8"	18
12'-6 5/16"	37		
12'-10 3/8"	38	12'-9 3/16"	19
13'-2 7/16"	39		
13'-6 1/2"	40	13'-5 1/4"	20

TABLE C (NON-MODULAR) — 1/2" HORIZONTAL MORTAR JOINT

HEIGHT	NO. 4" HIGH BLOCKS	HEIGHT	NO. 8" HIGH BLOCKS
0'-4 1/8"	1		
0'-8 1/4"	2	0'-8 1/8"	1
1'-0 3/8"	3		
1'-4 1/2"	4	1'-4 1/4"	2
1'-8 5/8"	5		
2'-0 3/4"	6	2'-0 3/8"	3
2'-4 7/8"	7		
2'-9"	8	2'-8 1/2"	4
3'-1 1/8"	9		
3'-5 1/4"	10	3'-4 5/8"	5
3'-9 3/8"	11		
4'-1 1/2"	12	4'-0 3/4"	6
4'-5 5/8"	13		
4'-9 3/4"	14	4'-8 7/8"	7
5'-1 7/8"	15		
5'-6"	16	5'-5"	8
5'-10 1/8"	17		
6'-2 1/4"	18	6'-1 1/8"	9
6'-6 3/8"	19		
6'-10 1/2"	20	6'-9 1/4"	10
7'-2 5/8"	21		
7'-6 3/4"	22	7'-5 3/8"	11
7'-10 7/8"	23		
8'-3"	24	8'-1 1/2"	12
8'-7 1/8"	25		
8'-11 1/4"	26	8'-9 5/8"	13
9'-3 3/8"	27		
9'-7 1/2"	28	9'-5 3/4"	14
9'-11 5/8"	29		
10'-3 3/4"	30	10'-1 7/8"	15
10'-7 7/8"	31		
11'-0"	32	10'-10"	16
11'-4 1/8"	33		
11'-8 1/4"	34	11'-6 1/8"	17
12'-0 3/8"	35		
12'-4 1/2"	36	12'-2 1/4"	18
12'-8 5/8"	37		
13'-0 3/4"	38	12'-10 3/8"	19
13'-4 7/8"	39		
13'-9"	40	13'-6 1/2"	20

Notes:

1—For exact wall length or height dimensions subtract thickness of one mortar joint.
2—For exact opening dimensions add thickness of one mortar joint to height and width.
3—For design simplicity and economy of construction plan dimensions should be determined from table A (modular).
4—When using combinations of 8" high and 4" high blocks a detailed wall section should be made to establish height dimensions.

Table B.5 Brick Dimensional Chart

VERTICAL BRICK COURSES

NUMBER OF BRICKS AND JOINTS	HEIGHT	
	3/8" JOINTS	1/2" JOINTS
1 brk. & 1 jt.	2 5/8"	2 3/4"
2 brks. & 2 jts.	5 1/4"	5 1/2"
3 brks. & 3 jts.	7 7/8"	8 1/4"
4 brks. & 4 jts.	10 1/2"	11"
5 brks. & 5 jts.	1'- 1 1/8"	1'- 1 3/4"
6 brks. & 6 jts.	1'- 3 3/4"	1'- 4 1/2"
7 brks. & 7 jts.	1'- 6 3/8"	1'- 7 1/4"
8 brks. & 8 jts.	1'- 9"	1'-10"
9 brks. & 9 jts.	1'-11 5/8"	2'- 0 3/4"
10 brks. & 10 jts.	2'- 2 1/4"	2'- 3 1/2"
11 brks. & 11 jts.	2'- 4 7/8"	2'- 6 1/4"
12 brks. & 12 jts.	2'- 7 1/2"	2'- 9"
13 brks. & 13 jts.	2'-10 1/8"	2'-11 3/4"
14 brks. & 14 jts.	3'- 0 3/4"	3'- 2 1/2"
15 brks. & 15 jts.	3'- 3 3/8"	3'- 5 1/4"
16 brks. & 16 jts.	3'- 6"	3'- 8"
17 brks. & 17 jts.	3'- 8 5/8"	3'-10 3/4"
18 brks. & 18 jts.	3'-11 1/4"	4'- 1 1/2"
19 brks. & 19 jts.	4'- 1 7/8"	4'- 4 1/4"
20 brks. & 20 jts.	4'- 4 1/2"	4'- 7"
21 brks. & 21 jts.	4'- 7 1/8"	4'- 9 3/4"
22 brks. & 22 jts.	4'- 9 3/4"	5'- 0 1/2"
23 brks. & 23 jt.	5'- 0 3/8"	5'- 3 1/4"
24 brks. & 24 jts.	5'- 3"	5'- 6"
25 brks. & 25 jts.	5'- 5 5/8"	5'- 8 3/4"
26 brks. & 26 jts.	5'- 8 1/4"	5'-11 1/2"
27 brks. & 27 jts.	5'-10 7/8"	6'- 2 1/4"
28 brks. & 28 jts.	6'- 1 1/2"	6'- 5"
29 brks. & 29 jts.	6'- 4 1/8"	6'- 7 3/4"
30 brks. & 30 jts.	6'- 6 3/4"	6'-10 1/2"
31 brks. & 31 jts.	6'- 9 3/8"	7'- 1 1/4"
32 brks. & 32 jts.	7'- 0"	7'- 4"
33 brks. & 33 jts.	7'- 2 5/8"	7'- 6 3/4"
34 brks. & 34 jts.	7'- 5 1/4"	7'- 9 1/2"
35 brks. & 35 jts.	7'- 7 7/8"	8'- 0 1/4"
36 brks. & 36 jts.	7'-10 1/2"	8'- 3"
37 brks. & 37 jts.	8'- 1 1/8"	8'- 5 3/4"
38 brks. & 38 jts.	8'- 3 3/4"	8'- 8 1/2"
39 brks. & 39 jts.	8'- 6 3/8"	8'-11 1/4"
40 brks. & 40 jts.	8'- 9"	9'- 2"
41 brks. & 41 jts.	8'-11 5/8"	9'- 4 3/4"
42 brks. & 42 jts.	9'- 2 1/4"	9'- 7 1/2"
43 brks. & 43 jts.	9'- 4 7/8"	9'-10 1/4"
44 brks. & 44 jts.	9'- 7 1/2"	10'- 1"
45 brks. & 45 jts.	9'-10 1/8"	10'- 3 3/4"
46 brks. & 46 jts.	10'- 0 3/4"	10'- 6 1/2"
47 brks. & 47 jts.	10'- 3 3/8"	10'- 9 1/4"
48 brks. & 48 jts.	10'- 6"	11'- 0"
49 brks. & 49 jts.	10'- 8 5/8"	11'- 2 3/4"
50 brks. & 50 jts.	10'-11 1/4"	11'- 5 1/2"
51 brks. & 51 jts.	11'- 1 7/8"	11'- 8 1/4"
52 brks. & 52 jts.	11'- 4 1/2"	11'-11"
53 brks. & 53 jts.	11'- 7 1/8"	12'- 1 3/4"
54 brks. & 54 jts.	11'- 9 3/4"	12'- 4 1/2"
55 brks. & 55 jts.	12'- 0 3/8"	12'- 7 1/4"
56 brks. & 56 jts.	12'- 3"	12'-10"
57 brks. & 57 jts.	12'- 5 5/8"	13'- 0 3/4"
58 brks. & 58 jts.	12'- 8 1/4"	13'- 3 1/2"
59 brks. & 59 jts.	12'-10 7/8"	13'- 6 1/4"
60 brks. & 60 jts.	13'- 1 1/2"	13'- 9"
61 brks. & 61 jts.	13'- 4 1/8"	13'-11 3/4"
62 brks. & 62 jts.	13'- 6 3/4"	14'- 2 1/2"
63 brks. & 63 jts.	13'- 9 3/8"	14'- 5 1/4"
64 brks. & 64 jts.	14'- 0"	14'- 8"
65 brks. & 65 jts.	14'- 2 5/8"	14'-10 3/4"
66 brks. & 66 jts.	14'- 5 1/4"	15'- 1 1/2"
67 brks. & 67 jts.	14'- 7 7/8"	15'- 4 1/4"
68 brks. & 68 jts.	14'-10 1/2"	15'- 7"
69 brks. & 69 jts.	15'- 1 1/8"	15'- 9 3/4"
70 brks. & 70 jts.	15'- 3 3/4"	16'- 0 1/2"
71 brks. & 71 jts.	15'- 6 3/8"	16'- 3 1/4"
72 brks. & 72 jts.	15'- 9"	16'- 6"
73 brks. & 73 jts.	15'-11 5/8"	16'- 8 3/4"
74 brks. & 74 jts.	16'- 2 1/4"	16'-11 1/2"
75 brks. & 75 jts.	16'- 4 7/8"	17'- 2 1/4"
76 brks. & 76 jts.	16'- 7 1/2"	17'- 5"

HORIZONTAL BRICK COURSES

NUMBER OF BRICKS AND JOINTS	LENGTH OF COURSE	
	3/8" JOINTS	1/2" JOINTS
1 brk. & 0 jt.	0'- 8"	0'- 8"
1 1/2 brks. & 1 jt.	1'- 0 3/8"	1'- 0 1/2"
2 brks. & 1 jt.	1'- 4 3/8"	1'- 4 1/2"
2 1/2 brks. & 2 jts.	1'- 8 3/4"	1'- 9"
3 brks. & 2 jts.	2'- 0 3/4"	2'- 1"
3 1/2 brks. & 3 jts.	2'- 5 1/8"	2'- 5 1/2"
4 brks. & 3 jts.	2'- 9 1/8"	2'- 9 1/2"
4 1/2 brks. & 4 jts.	3'- 1 1/2"	3'- 2"
5 brks. & 4 jts.	3'- 5 1/2"	3'- 6"
5 1/2 brks. & 5 jts.	3'- 9 7/8"	3'-10 1/2"
6 brks. & 5 jts.	4'- 1 7/8"	4'- 2 1/2"
6 1/2 brks. & 6 jts.	4'- 6 1/4"	4'- 7"
7 brks. & 6 jts	4'-10 1/4"	4'-11"
7 1/2 brks. & 7 jts.	5'- 2 5/8"	5'- 3 1/2"
8 brks. & 7 jts.	5'- 6 5/8"	5'- 7 1/2"
8 1/2 brks. & 8 jts.	5'-11"	6'- 0"
9 brks. & 8 jts.	6'- 3"	6'- 4"
9 1/2 brks. & 9 jts.	6'- 7 3/8"	6'- 8 1/2"
10 brks. & 9 jts.	6'-11 3/8"	7'- 0 1/2"
10 1/2 brks. & 10 jts.	7'- 3 3/4"	7'- 5"
11 brks. & 10 jts.	7'- 7 3/4"	7'- 9"
11 1/2 brks. & 11 jts.	8'- 0 1/8"	8'- 1 1/2"
12 brks. & 11 jts.	8'- 4 1/8"	8'- 5 1/2"
12 1/2 brks. & 12 jts.	8'- 8 1/2"	8'-10"
13 brks. & 12 jts.	9'- 0 1/2"	9'- 2"
13 1/2 brks. & 13 jts.	9'- 4 7/8"	9'- 6 1/2"
14 brks. & 13 jts.	9'- 8 7/8"	9'-10 1/2"
14 1/2 brks. & 14 jts.	10'- 1 1/4"	10'- 3"
15 brks. & 14 jts.	10'- 5 1/4"	10'- 7"
15 1/2 brks. & 15 jts.	10'- 9 5/8"	10'-11 1/2"
16 brks. & 15 jts.	11'- 1 5/8"	11'- 3 1/2"
16 1/2 brks. & 16 jts.	11'- 6"	11'- 8"
17 brks. & 16 jts.	11'-10"	12'- 0"
17 1/2 brks. & 17 jts.	12'- 2 3/8"	12'- 4 1/2"
18 brks. & 17 jts.	12'- 6 3/8"	12'- 8 1/2"
18 1/2 brks. & 18 jts.	12'-10 3/4"	13'- 1"
19 brks. & 18 jts.	13'- 2 3/4"	13'- 5"
19 1/2 brks. & 19 jts.	13'- 7 1/8"	13'- 9 1/2"
20 brks. & 19 jts.	13'-11 1/8"	14'- 1 1/2"
20 1/2 brks. & 20 jts.	14'- 3 1/2"	14'- 6"
21 brks. & 20 jts.	14'- 7 1/2"	14'-10"
21 1/2 brks. & 21 jts.	14'-11 7/8"	15'- 2 1/2"
22 brks. & 21 jts.	15'- 3 7/8"	15'- 6 1/2"
22 1/2 brks. & 22 jts.	15'- 8 1/4"	15'-11"
23 brks. & 22 jts.	16'- 0 1/4"	16'- 3"
23 1/2 brks. & 23 jts.	16'- 4 5/8"	16'- 7 1/2"
24 brks. & 23 jts.	16'- 8 5/8"	16'-11 1/2"
24 1/2 brks. & 24 jts.	17'- 1"	17'- 4"
25 brks. & 24 jts.	17'- 5"	17'- 8"
25 1/2 brks. & 25 jts.	17'- 9 3/8"	18'- 0 1/2"
26 brks. & 25 jts.	18'- 1 3/8"	18'- 4 1/2"
26 1/2 brks. & 26 jts.	18'- 5 3/4"	18'- 9"
27 brks. & 26 jts.	18'- 9 3/4"	19'- 1"
27 1/2 brks. & 27 jts.	19'- 2 1/8"	19'- 5 1/2"
28 brks. & 27 jts.	19'- 6 1/8"	19'- 9 1/2"
28 1/2 brks. & 28 jts.	19'-10 1/2"	20'- 2"
29 brks. & 28 jts.	20'- 2 1/2"	20'- 6"
29 1/2 brks. & 29 jts.	20'- 6 7/8"	20'-10 1/2"
30 brks. & 29 jts.	20'-10 7/8"	21'- 2 1/2"
30 1/2 brks. & 30 jts.	21'- 3 1/4"	21'- 7"
31 brks. & 30 jts.	21'- 7 1/4"	21'-11"
31 1/2 brks. & 31 jts.	21'-11 5/8"	22'- 3 1/2"
32 brks. & 31 jts.	22'- 3 5/8"	22'- 7 1/2"
32 1/2 brks. & 32 jts.	22'- 8"	23'- 0"
33 brks. & 32 jts.	23'- 0"	23'- 4"
33 1/2 brks. & 33 jts.	23'- 4 3/8"	23'- 8 1/2"
34 brks. & 33 jts.	23'- 8 3/8"	24'- 0 1/2"
34 1/2 brks. & 34 jts.	24'- 0 3/4"	24'- 5"
35 brks. & 34 jts.	24'- 4 3/4"	24'- 9"
35 1/2 brks. & 35 jts.	24'- 9 1/8"	25'- 1 1/2"
36 brks. & 35 jts.	25'- 1 1/8"	25'- 5 1/2"
36 1/2 brks. & 36 jts.	25'- 5 1/2"	25'-10"
37 brks. & 36 jts.	25'- 9 1/2"	26'- 2"
37 1/2 brks. & 37 jts.	26'- 1 7/8"	26'- 6 1/2"
38 brks. & 37 jts.	26'- 5 7/8"	26'-10 1/2"
38 1/2 brks. & 38 jts.	26'-10 1/4"	27'- 3"

NUMBER OF BRICKS AND JOINTS	LENGTH OF COURSE	
	3/8" JOINTS	1/2" JOINTS
39 brks. & 38 jts.	27'- 2 1/4"	27'- 7"
39 1/2 brks. & 39 jts.	27'- 6 5/8"	27'-11 1/2"
40 brks. & 39 jts.	27'-10 5/8"	28'- 3 1/2"
40 1/2 brks. & 40 jts.	28'- 3"	28'- 8"
41 brks. & 40 jts.	28'- 7"	29'- 0"
41 1/2 brks. & 41 jts.	28'-11 3/8"	29'- 4 1/2"
42 brks. & 41 jts.	29'- 3 3/8"	29'- 8 1/2"
42 1/2 brks. & 42 jts.	29'- 7 3/4"	30'- 1"
43 brks. & 42 jts.	29'-11 3/4"	30'- 5"
43 1/2 brks. & 43 jts.	30'- 4 1/8"	30'- 9 1/2"
44 brks. & 43 jts.	30'- 8 1/8"	31'- 1 1/2"
44 1/2 brks. & 44 jts.	31'- 0 1/2"	31'- 6"
45 brks. & 44 jts.	31'- 4 1/2"	31'-10"
45 1/2 brks. & 45 jts.	31'- 8 7/8"	32'- 2 1/2"
46 brks. & 45 jts.	32'- 0 7/8"	32'- 6 1/2"
46 1/2 brks. & 46 jts.	32'- 5 1/4"	32'-11"
47 brks. & 46 jts.	32'- 9 1/4"	33'- 3"
47 1/2 brks. & 47 jts.	33'- 1 5/8"	33'- 7 1/2"
48 brks. & 47 jts.	33'- 5 5/8"	33'-11 1/2"
48 1/2 brks. & 48 jts.	33'-10"	34'- 4"
49 brks. & 48 jts.	34'- 2"	34'- 8"
49 1/2 brks. & 49 jts.	34'- 6 3/8"	35'- 0 1/2"
50 brks. & 49 jts.	34'-10 3/8"	35'- 4 1/2"
50 1/2 brks. & 50 jts.	35'- 2 3/4"	35'- 9"
51 brks. & 50 jts.	35'- 6 3/4"	36'- 1"
51 1/2 brks. & 51 jts.	35'-11 1/8"	36'- 5 1/2"
52 brks. & 51 jts.	36'- 3 1/8"	36'- 9 1/2"
52 1/2 brks. & 52 jts.	36'- 7 1/2"	37'- 2"
53 brks. & 52 jts.	36'-11 1/2"	37'- 6"
53 1/2 brks. & 53 jts.	37'- 3 7/8"	37'-10 1/2"
54 brks. & 53 jts.	37'- 7 7/8"	38'- 2 1/2"
54 1/2 brks. & 54 jts.	38'- 0 1/4"	38'- 7"
55 brks. & 54 jts.	38'- 4 1/4"	38'-11"
55 1/2 brks. & 55 jts.	38'- 8 5/8"	39'- 3 1/2"
56 brks. & 55 jts.	39'- 0 5/8"	39'- 7 1/2"
56 1/2 brks. & 56 jts.	39'- 5"	40'- 0"
57 brks. & 56 jts.	39'- 9"	40'- 4"
57 1/2 brks. & 57 jts.	40'- 1 3/8"	40'- 8 1/2"
58 brks. & 57 jts.	40'- 5 3/8"	41'- 0 1/2"
58 1/2 brks. & 58 jts.	40'- 9 3/4"	41'- 5"
59 brks. & 58 jts.	41'- 6 1/8"	42'- 1 1/2"
59 brks. & 58 jts.	41'- 1 3/4"	41'- 9"
59 1/2 brks. & 59 jts.	41'- 6 1/8"	42'- 1 1/2"
60 brks. & 59 jts.	41'-10 1/8"	42'- 5 1/2"

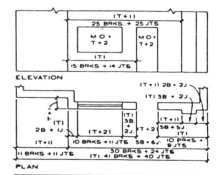

ELEVATION

PLAN

EXAMPLE SHOWING USE OF TABLE

T: Dimensions and number of joints as given in the table, that is, one joint less than the number of bricks.

T + 1: One brick joint added to figure given in the table, that is, the number of bricks is equal to the number of joints.

T + 2: Two brick joints added to figure given in the table, that is, one joint more than the number of bricks.

APPENDIX C

SYMBOLS USED AS ABBREVIATIONS:

$\angle$	angle
$\mathₑ$	centerline
C	channel
d	penny
$\perp$	perpendicular
PL	plate
ϕ	round or diameter
$\square$	square

ABBREVIATIONS:

ABV	above
AFF	above finished floor
ASC	above suspended ceiling
ACC	access
ACFL	access floor
AP	Access panel
AC	acoustical
ACPL	acoustical plaster
ACT	acoustical tile
ACR	acrylic plaster
ADD	addendum
ADH	adhesive
ADJ	adjacent
ADJT	adjustable
AGG	aggregate
A/C	air conditioning
ALT	alternate
AL	aluminum
ANC	anchor, anchorage
AB	anchor bolt
ANOD	anodized
APX	approximate
Arch	architect (ural)
AD	area drain
ASB	asbestos
ASPH	asphalt
AT	asphalt tile
AUTO	automatic
BP	back plaster (ed)
BSMT	basement

BRG	bearing
BPL	bearing plate
BJT	bed joint
BM	bench mark
BEL	below
BET	between
BVL	beveled
BIT	bituminous
BLK	block
BLKG	blocking
BD	board
BS	both sides
BW	both ways
BOT	bottom
BRK	brick
BRZ	bronze
BLDG	building
BUR	built up roofing
BBD	bulletin board
CAB	cabinet
CAD	cadmium
CPT	carpet (ed)
CSMT	casement
CI	cast iron
CIPC	cast-in-place concrete
CST	cast stone
CB	catch basin
CK	calk (ing) caulk (ing)
CLG	ceiling
CHT	ceiling height
CEM	cement
PCPL	cement plaster (portland)
CM	centimeter(s)
CER	ceramic
CT	ceramic tile
CMT	ceramic mosaic (tile)
CHBD	chalkboard
CHAM	chamfer
CR	chromium (plated)
CIR	circle
CIRC	circumference

CLR	clear (ance)
CLS	closure
COL	column
COMB	combination
COMPT	compartment
COMPO	composition (composite)
COMP	compress (ed), (ion), (ible)
CONC	concrete
CMU	concrete masonry unit
CX	connection
CONST	construction
CONT	continuous or continue
CONTR	contract (or)
CLL	contract limit line
CJT	control joint
CPR	copper
CG	corner guard
CORR	corrugated
CTR	counter
CFL	counterflashing
CS	countersink
CTSK	countersunk screw
CRS	course (s)
CRG	cross grain
CFT	cubic foot
CYD	cubic yard
DPR	damper
DP	dampproofing
DL	dead load
DEM	demolish, demolition
DMT	demountable
DEP	depressed
DTL	detail
DIAG	diagonal
DIAM	diameter
DIM	dimension
DPR	dispenser
DIV	division
DR	door
DA	doubleacting
DH	double hung

DTA	dovetail anchor	FLR	floor (ing)	INCIN	incinerator
DTS	dovetail anchor slot	FLCO	floor cleanout	INCL	include (d), (ing)
DS	downspout	FD	floor drain	ID	inside diameter
D	drain	FPL	floor plate	INS	insulate (d), (ion)
DRB	drainboard	FLUR	fluorescent	INSC	insulating concrete
DT	drain tile	FJT	flush joint	INSF	insulating fill
DWR	drawer	FTG	footing	INT	interior
DWG	drawing	FRG	forged	ILK	interlock
DF	drinking fountain	FND	foundation	INTM	intermediate
DW	dumbwaiter	FR	frame (d), (ing)	INV	invert
		FRA	fresh air	IPS	iron pipe size
EF	each face	FS	full size		
E	east	FBO	furnished by others	JC	janitor's closet
ELEC	electric (al)	FUR	furred (ing)	JT	joint
EP	electrical panelboard	FUT	future	JF	joint filler
EWC	electrical water cooler			J	joist
EL	elevation	GA	gage, gauge		
ELEV	elevator	GV	galvanized	KCPL	Keene's cement plaster
EMER	emergency	GI	galvanized iron	KPL	kickplate
ENC	enclose (ure)	GP	galvanized pipe	KIT	kitchen
EQ	equal	GSS	galvanized steel plate	KO	knockout
EQP	equipment	GKT	gasket (ed)		
ESC	escalator	GC	general contract (or)	LBL	label
EST	estimate	GL	glass, glazing	LAB	laboratory
EXCA	excavate	GLB	glass block	LAD	ladder
EXH	exhaust	GLF	glass fiber	LB	lag bolt
EXG	existing	GCMU	glazed concrete masonry	LAM	laminate (d)
EXMP	expanded metal plate		units	LAV	lavatory
EB	expansion bolt	GST	glazed structural tile	LH	left hand
EXP	exposed	GB	grab bar	L	length
EXT	exterior	GD	grade, grading	LT	light
EXS	extra strength	GRN	granite	LC	light control
		GVL	gravel	LP	lightproof
FB	face brick	GF	ground face	LW	lightweight
FOC	face of concrete	GT	grout	LWC	lightweight concrete
FOF	face of finish	GPDW	gypsum dry wall	LMS	limestone
FOM	face of masonry	GPL	gypsum lath	LTL	lintel
FOS	face of studs	GPPL	gypsum plaster	LL	live load
FF	factory finish	GPT	gypsum tile	LVR	louver
FAS	fasten, fastener			LPT	low point
FN	fence	HH	handhole		
FBD	fiberboard	HBD	hardboard	MB	machine bolt
FGL	fiberglass	HDW	hardware	MI	malleable iron
FIN	finish (ed)	HWD	hardwood	MH	manhole
FFE	finished floor elevation	HJT	head joint	MFR	manufacture (er)
FFL	finished floor line	HDR	header	MRB	marble
FA	fire alarm	HTG	heating	MAS	masonry
FBRK	fire brick	HVAC	heating/ventilation/air con-	MO	masonry opening
FE	fire extinguisher		ditioning	MTL	material (s)
FEC	fire extinguisher cabinet	HD	heavy duty	MAX	maximum
FHS	fire hose station	HT	height	MECH	mechanic (al)
FPL	fireplace	HX	hexagonal	MC	medicine cabinet
FP	fireproof	HES	high early-strength cement	MED	medium
FRC	fire-resistant coating	HC	hollow core	MBR	member
FRT	fire-retardant	HM	hollow metal	MMB	membrane
FLG	flashing	HK	hook (s)	MET	metal
FHMS	flathead machine screw	HOR	horizontal	MFD	metal floor decking
FHWS	flathead wood screw	HB	hose bibb	MTFR	metal furring
FLX	flexible	HWH	hot water heater		

MRD	metal roof decking	**PVC**	polyvinyl chloride	**SC**	solid core
MEHR	metal threshold	**PE**	porcelain enamel	**SP**	soundproof
M	meter (s)	**PTC**	post-tensioned concrete	**S**	south
MM	millimeter (s)	**PCF**	pounds per cubic foot	**SPC**	spacer
MWK	millwork	**PFL**	pounds per lineal foot	**SPK**	speaker
MIN	minimum	**PSF**	pounds per square foot	**SPL**	special
MIR	mirror	**PSI**	pounds per square inch	**SPEC**	specification (s)
MISC	miscellaneous	**PCC**	precast concrete	**SQ**	square
MOD	modular	**PFB**	prefabricate (d)	**SST**	stainless steel
MLD	molding, moulding	**PFN**	prefinished	**STD**	standard
MR	mop receptor	**PRF**	preformed	**STA**	station
MT	mount (ed), (ing)	**PSC**	prestressed concrete	**ST**	steel
MOV	movable	**PL**	property line	**STO**	storage
MULL	mullion			**SD**	storm drain
		QT	quarry tile	**STR**	structural
NL	nailable			**SCT**	structural clay tile
NAT	natural	**RBT**	rabbet, rebate	**SUS**	suspended
NI	nickel	**RAD**	radius	**SYM**	symmetry (ical)
NR	noise reduction	**RL**	rail (ing)	**SYN**	synthetic
NRC	noise reduction coefficient	**RWC**	rainwater conductor	**SYS**	system
NOM	nominal	**REF**	reference		
NMT	nonmetallic	**RFL**	reflect (ed), (ive), (or)	**TKBD**	tackboard
N	north	**REFR**	refrigerator	**TKS**	tackstrip
NIC	not in contract	**REG**	register	**TEL**	telephone
NTS	not to scale	**RE**	reinforce (d), (ing)	**TV**	television
		RCP	reinforced concrete pipe	**TC**	terra cotta
OBS	obscure	**REM**	remove	**TZ**	terrazzo
OC	on center (s)	**RES**	resilient	**THK**	thick (ness)
OP	opaque	**RET**	return	**THR**	threshold
OPG	opening	**RA**	return air	**TPTN**	toilet partition
OJ	open-web joist	**RVS**	reverse (side)	**TPD**	toilet paper dispenser
OPP	opposite	**REV**	revision (s), revised	**TOL**	tolerance
OPH	opposite hand	**RH**	right hand	**T&G**	tongue and groove
OPS	opposite surface	**ROW**	right of way	**TSL**	top of slab
OD	outside diameter	**R**	riser	**TST**	top of steel
OHMS	ovalhead machine screw	**RVT**	rivet	**TW**	top of wall
OHWS	ovalhead wood screw	**RD**	roof drain	**TB**	towel bar
OA	overall	**RFH**	roof hatch	**TR**	transom
OH	overhead	**RFG**	roofing	**T**	tread
		RM	room	**TYP**	typical
PNT	paint (ed)	**RO**	rough opening		
PNL	panel	**RB**	rubber base	**UC**	undercut
PB	panic bar	**RBT**	rubber tile	**UNF**	unfinished
PTD	paper towel dispenser	**RBL**	rubble stone	**UR**	urinal
PTR	paper towel receptor				
PAR	parallel	**SFGL**	safety glass	**VJ**	v-joint (ed)
PK	parking	**SCH**	schedule	**VB**	vapor barrier
PBD	particle board	**SCN**	screen	**VAR**	varnish
PTN	partition	**SNT**	sealant	**VNR**	veneer
PV	pave (d), (ing)	**STG**	seating	**VRM**	vermiculite
PVMT	pavement	**SEC**	section	**VERT**	vertical
PED	pedestal	**SSK**	service sink	**VG**	vertical grain
PERF	perforate (d)	**SHTH**	sheathing	**VIN**	vinyl
PERI	perimeter	**SHT**	sheet	**VAT**	vinyl asbestos tile
PLAS	plaster	**SG**	sheet glass	**VB**	vinyl base
PLAM	plastic laminate	**SH**	shelf, shelving	**VF**	vinyl fabric
PL	plate	**SHO**	shore (d), (ing)	**VT**	vinyl tile
PG	plate glass	**SIM**	similar		
PWD	plywood	**SKL**	skylight	**WSCT**	wainscot
PT	point	**SL**	sleeve	**WTW**	wall to wall

WH	wall hung	**WHB**	wheel bumper	**WB**	wood base
WC	water closet	**W**	width, wide	**WI**	wrought iron
WP	waterproofing	**WIN**	window		
WR	water repellent	**WG**	wired glass		
WS	waterstop	**WM**	wire mesh		
WWF	welded wire fabric	**WO**	without		
W	west	**WD**	wood		

Source: Task Force #1, National Committee on Office Practice, American Institute of Architects, published in AIA Journal, January 1974.

GLOSSARY

ADA The Americans with Disabilities Act, which is a civil rights law that was enacted in 1992.

Adjustable Triangle A triangle made with a movable portion that is calibrated to produce a variety of angular lines.

Anchor Bolts Metal rods, varying in diameter, to join and secure one material to another.

Appliques A transparent or translucent adhesive film used primarily for notes and details.

Axial Load A weight that is distributed symmetrically to a supporting member, such as a column.

Axial Reference Plane The dimensional reference system produces a series of planes. The planes are collectively called the axial reference plane.

Back Hoe A mechanical device used to dig a trench of a specific width and for any length. Used primarily in foundation work or in trenching for underground service such as utility lines, etc.

Balloon Framing A system in wood framing in which the studs are continuous without an intermediate plate for the support of second-floor joists.

Baluster A vertical member that supports handrails or guardrails.

Balustrades A horizontal rail held up by a series of balusters.

Bar Chart A calendar that graphically illustrates a projected time allotment to achieve a specific function.

Base A trim or moulding piece found at the interior intersection of the floor and the wall.

Beam A weight-supporting horizontal member.

Blocking The use of internal members to provide rigidity in floor and wall systems. Also used for fire draft stops.

Blueprint A print with white lines and a blue background.

Break Line A line used to indicate that an object has been foreshortened. Two break lines are used to indicate a portion of an object has been removed.

Brick Pavers A term used to describe special brick to be used on the floor surface.

Buck A frame found around doors.

Building Code Divisions Those sections and chapters that pertain to the various types of buildings, construction materials, and engineering criteria for various materials and construction methods.

Building Envelope The components of a building that enclose spaces that are subject to the transferring of thermal energy from or to the exterior of the building.

Building Section A cross-section through any portion of a building that illustrates a system and structural members for the erection of that portion.

Caisson A below-grade concrete column for the support of beams or columns.

Cantilever A structural condition wherein a member extends beyond a support, such as a roof overhang.

Cement Plaster Plaster that is comprised of cement rather than gypsum.

Checklist List of items used to check drawings.

Check Print A copy used to review for corrections, errors, or changes.

Column A vertical weight-supporting member.

Column Pad An area of concrete in the foundation for the support of weight distributed into a column.

Composite Drafting The process of making a single drawing by combining a variety of drawings. Usually done by photography.

Computer-Aided Drafting (CAD) The process of programming a computer to draft.

Concrete Block A rectangular concrete form with cells in them.

Construction Documents A set of legal contract documents of drawings and specifications that graphically and verbally describe what is required for a specific construction project.

Contour Line A line that represents the change in level from a given datum point.

Coving The curving of the floor material against the wall to eliminate the open seam between floor and wall.

Cross-Section A slice through a portion of a building or member that depicts the various internal conditions of that area.

Cul-de-Sac A curved turnaround with the radius determined by the traffic load, located at the end of a street.

Datum Point Reference point.

Detail An enlarged drawing to show a structural aspect, an aesthetic consideration, a solution to an environmental condition, or to express the relationship between materials or building components.

637

Diazo   The process of producing a print using light-sensitive chemicals on bond paper and an ammonia developer.

Dimensions   Numerical values used to indicate size and distance.

Dimensional Reference System   A system based on a three-dimensional axis. This system produces a three-dimensional matrix to which the plan, section, or elevation can be drafted.

Direct Projection   A drafting term used to describe the process of transferring measurements from a source directly—for example, projecting the width of an elevation directly from the floor plan.

Dowel   A metal or wood cylindrical member used for the joining and strengthening of structural elements.

Drafting Machine   Drafting instrument constructed very much like a human arm on which scales are mounted to draft horizontal, vertical, and angular lines.

Duct   Usually sheet metal forms used for the distribution of cool or warm air throughout a structure.

Easement   The right or privilege to have access to or through another piece of property, such as a utility easement.

Eave   That portion of the roof that extends beyond the outside wall.

Egress   A place to exit. The act of exiting a building.

Elevation   The front, side, or back view of a structure.

Energy Design Computations   Computations that deal with energy design factors and formulas for determining whether or not a building is in compliance with the governing energy standards.

Eraser Drafting   See **Reproduction Drafting.**

Face of Stud (F.O.S.)   Outside surface of the stud. Term used most often in dimensioning or as a point of reference.

Fascia   A horizontal member located at the edge of a roof overhang.

Finish Grade   The soil elevation in its final state upon completion of construction.

Fire Draft Stop   A member of varying materials placed in walls, floors, and ceilings to prevent a rapid spread of fire.

Flashing   Sheet metal to make a construction joint weathertight.

Floor Joist   Structural member for the support of floor loads.

Floor Plan   A horizontal section taken at approximately eye level.

Flush   Even, level, or aligned.

Flush Overlay   Term frequently found in cabinet making to denote a door that covers the frame of the cabinet itself.

Footing   The concrete base of a building foundation that distributes the weight of the structure on a required area of earth.

Foundation Plan   A drawing that graphically illustrates the location of various foundation members and conditions that are required for the support of a specific structure.

Framing Connectors   Metal devices, varying in size and shape, for the purpose of joining wood framing members together.

Frieze   A decoration or ornament shaped to form a band around a structure.

Frost Line   The depth at which frost penetrates the soil.

Furred Ceiling   The construction for a separate surface beyond the main ceiling or wall that provides a desired air space and modifies interior dimensional conditions.

Generic   Grouping or class. In drafting, used to denote items without using brand names.

Girder   A horizontal structural beam for the support of secondary members such as floor joists.

Glue-Laminated Beam   A beam comprised of a series of wood members glued together.

Guidelines   Light lines used for preliminary layout of a series of drafted lines. Also used for lettering.

Head   The top of a window or door frame.

Header   A horizontal structural member spanning openings, such as doors and windows, for the support of weight above the openings.

Header Line   Line used to which the typical underside of the header is measured.

Hidden Lines   Dotted lines drafted with long dashes with spaces between them. Used to represent lines that exist but cannot be seen.

Hip Rafter   A rafter that bisects a corner and extends from the top plate to the ridge.

Industrial Park   A development of buildings that is primarily used for manufacturing and warehousing.

Interior Elevation   A straight-on view of the surface of the interior walls of a structure.

Isometric Drawing   A form of a pictorial drawing in which main lines are equal in dimension. Normally drawn using 30°, 90° angle.

Jamb   The side portion of a door, window, or any opening.

Jog   Offset.

Joist Hanger   A metal connector for the end support of floor and ceiling joists.

Key Plan   A plan reduced in scale used for orientation purposes.

Lateral Supports   Individual members or constructed assemblies that support elements of a building that are subject to horizontal forces.

Leader Line   Line used from the beginning or end of phrases to point out objects.

Masonry   The construction term for materials such as brick, concrete block, or stone.

Masonry Opening   The actual distance between masonry units where an opening occurs. Does not include the wood or steel framing around the opening.

Masonry Veneer   A layer of masonry units that are bonded to a frame or masonry wall.

Material Designation Lines   Lines used to represent different types of material.

Metal Strut   A metal member used for the purpose of stabilizing the top of nonbearing interior partitions.

Metal Studs   Metal wall-framing members made of galvanized iron and aluminum that vary in size and gauge.

Modules   A system based on a single unit of measure.

Monolithic One-Pour System   A method of poured-in-place concrete construction that is without joints.

Mortar   The mixture of cement, sand, lime, and water that provides a bond for the joining of masonry units.

Mullion   A horizontal or vertical member used for supporting glass.

Nailer   A wood member attached to a steel, concrete, or masonry element for the purpose of connecting other materials with the use of nails.

Nailing Schedule A schedule found in building codes that determines minimum nailing for various wood-framing assemblies.

Net Size The actual size of an item.

Nominal Size The call-out size. May not be the actual size of the item.

Occupancy The type of use for a specific building.

Office Standards Standards subscribed to by a single office.

Offset A jog in a wall.

One-Hour Fire Resistive Construction The time period in which a through-penetration fire stops the spread of fire.

Overlay Drafting The process of overlaying a series of drawings on others to produce a finished product. See also **Reprodrafting.**

Pad Term used for isolated concrete pier.

Parapet A low wall extending above the roof level.

Paste-up Drafting See **Reprodrafting.**

Photo-Drafting The use of photography to produce a base onto which drafting can be done.

Pier A concrete or masonry pillar for the purpose of structural support.

Pilaster A rectangular pier integral with a wall for the purpose of strengthening the wall and supporting axial loads.

Pin Drafting See **Reprodrafting.**

Pivot Point The point at which the end of one plane adjoins another.

Plane Any two-dimensional surface.

Planking A term for wood members having a minimum rectangular section of 1½" to 3½" in thickness. Used for floor and roof systems.

Plan Template Plastic sheet with various forms in plan view punched out to aid in drafting.

Plan View A top view.

Plate Height The distance between the floor and the top of the two top plates above the studs.

Plat Map A drawing of a surveyed piece of land illustrating boundaries, bearings, dimensions, and location.

Plenum A predetermined air space for the use of mechanical systems such as heating and air conditioning.

Post-Hold-Down A metal connector partially embedded in concrete for the purpose of anchoring down a wood post.

Pouché To darken areas between lines on a drawing to make them stand out.

Profiling Darkening the outline of an object to emphasize a specific shape.

Proportional Divider Device used to transfer measurements from one scale to another.

Purlin A horizontal beam spanning between trusses or columns for the purpose of supporting roof-framing members.

Rafter The uppermost structural member found in a roof.

Reference Bubble Symbol used to coordinate details to their origin.

Reprodrafting Using reproduction methods as a means to produce drafted documents. Also called eraser drafting, paste-up drafting, photo-drafting, overlay drafting, system drafting, pin drafting, and scissors drafting.

Reproduction Drafting The process of using any form of reproduction (such as photography) to aid in the drafting process.

Ridge The topmost point at which two sloping roof planes meet.

Riser The vertical portion of a stair.

Roof The top portion of a structure.

Rough Opening An unfinished opening in preparation for finished frames of doors, windows, and other assemblies.

Schedule A chart with reference symbols and related information such as that used for windows and door schedules.

Schematic Drawings Initial drawings usually drawn freehand for relationship studies.

Scissors Drafting A method in which existing drawings are spliced together to form another drawing, or a procedure in which existing drawings are pasted together and photographed. See also **Reprodrafting.**

Screen Drafting A method of producing a secondary original that has different shades of gray on which new information can be drafted. The new information will stand out because of the contrast.

Scupper An opening to allow the flow of water from a roof or deck on a structure.

Section A drawing representing a splice through part of a structure depicting the internal conditions at that location.

Seismic Pertaining to earthquake forces.

Seismic Forces Those forces that are developed from earthquakes.

Sepia Process of producing a print on tracing paper that is coated with light-sensitive chemicals and developed with the use of ammonia.

Setback The dimensional factor for clearances to property lines.

Shear Wall A wall designed to resist lateral forces such as wind or earthquakes.

Sheathing Individual boards covering interior or exterior framing members, such as roof rafters or wall studs.

Shoe Usually a small piece of wood found at the intersection of the wall and the floor.

Sight Line Direction in which one views an object.

Sill The horizontal member located at the lower portion of a window or a door.

Single Glaze One sheet of glass varying in thickness and size for use in window assemblies.

Site Plan A drawing that graphically illustrates a plot of ground, dimensioned building location, and other construction information required for the site development.

Soffit The finished underside of a horizontal surface such as a boxed-in eave or floor overhang.

Specifications That part of the construction documents that verbally identifies the materials and equipment to be installed in a structure.

Stair Tread The horizontal surfaces of a stair run.

Steel-Reinforcing Bars Round, deformed steel rods, varying in diameter sizes, for the purpose of strengthening concrete.

Stud Vertical wood members in a wall.

Stud Line Surface of the stud, usually the outside surface.

Subfloor A flooring of unfinished boards or plywood on which a finished floor is to be applied.

Supply Registers A metal grille used for directing the flow of warm and cold air to conditioned spaces.

System Drafting See **Reprodrafting.**

Tenant Improvement The space that deals with the internal planning of a nonresidential building for specific users. Also referred to as space planning.

Tongue and Groove Continuous edge of a board that has been milled with a groove on one edge and a tongue on the other for a tight joining.

Topography A detailed description or a graphic representation of the physical characteristics of a piece of land.

Top Plate The uppermost horizontal piece in a stud wall.

Topset A decorative member found on the interior of a structure at the intersection of the floor and the wall.

Tract Drafter Instrument mounted on a horizontal and vertical track used to draft horizontal, vertical, and angular lines. A pencil is pressed against the instrument and moved with it. This is called tracking.

Transparent and Translucent Film Film created with light-sensitive chemicals. Can be purchased with an adhesive backing.

Tread The horizontal portion of a stair.

Tributary Area An accumulated area directed to a specific point, such as the weight of a floor area directed to a specific supporting column.

Trimmers Members found around windows, doors, or any openings parallel to the studs, joists, or rafters.

Truss A framework of members used to support vertical loads over large spans.

Two-Pour System Term used in concrete construction in which concrete is poured in two extended time periods.

Uniform Building Code A code of building laws developed to provide better building construction for the safety of the general public.

Vellum Special grade of paper on which working drawings are drafted.

Wainscot A lining placed over interior walls for protection of the vertical surface and normally less than the full height of the wall.

Western (Platform) Framing A method of wood framing in which the studs are terminated at each level by two horizontal plates for the support of floor framing at the next level.

Word Processing The process of typing information into a computer for ease of correction, storage, and recall.

Brief portions of the text in this book appeared earlier in *The Professional Practice of Architectural Detailing* by Osamu A. Wakita and Richard M. Linde, © 1977 by John Wiley & Sons, Inc. The following illustrations also appeared in that book: Figures 2.32, 2.33, 2.34, 2.35, 2.36, 4.19, 4.10, 4.12, 4.13, 4.14, 4.20, 4.21, 4.22, 4.24, 4.25, 8.34, 8.35, 10.11. Tables 2, 3, 4.

INDEX